EN

FOREST

ROUTE 109—
PRENZLAU—
WANDLITZ—
BASDORF

SCHÖNWALDE

S-BAHN

BIESENTHAL

BERNAU

S-BAHN

NIEDER-
SCHÖN-
HAUSEN
SCHLOSS
(ULBRICHT'S
OFFICIAL H.Q.)

SKI
MPOUND
OMM.
GS)

NIEDER
SCHÖN-
HAUSEN

PANKOW

BAHNHOLNER
STR.

HOHEN
SCHON-
HAUSEN

STRAUSBERG

STRAUSBERG

EL
AIR-
FIELD (FR.)

BAHN

FRIEDRICH-
STR. STATION

ARY

SSD PRISON
IN HOHEN
SCHONHAUSEN

ANHALTER STR.

OSTBAHN-
HOF

KARLS-
HOR-ST

SOVIET
BERLIN
COMMAND
H.Q.

NG
N

TEMPELHOF
AIRFIELD (U.S.)

SPREE

ADLERSHOF

S-BAHN

GR. MÜGGEL—

STEGLITZ

BRITZ

JOHANNISTHAL
TETLOW CANAL

SEE
MÜGGEL HILLS
AND FOREST

FÜRSTENWALDE

MARIEN—
FELDE

SPREE

MILI-
Y AND
MATIC
ON
ALLEE

SCHÖNEFELD
AIRFIELD
(SOV.)

MAKLOW

S-BAHN

RING

S-BAHN

ERKNER
FOREST

FRANKFURT—
ON-ODER

ÜNSDORF
Q. OF SOVIET
CCUPYING
RCES)

ROUTE 90

COTTBUS—
DRESDEN
AUTOBAHN →

KÖNIGS
WUSTER-
HAUSEN

RAILWAY
DETOUR TO
THURINGIA →

COTTBUS

THE IDES OF AUGUST

By the same author

Antoine de Saint-Exupery: His Life and Times
George Sand: A Biography

THE IDES

OF

AUGUST

The Berlin Wall
Crisis • 1961

CURTIS CATE

M. EVANS AND COMPANY, INC.
NEW YORK

Library of Congress Cataloging in Publication Data

Cate, Curtis, 1924-
   The ides of August

   Bibliography: p.
   Includes index.
    1.   Berlin wall (1961-   ) I. Title
DD881.C37   943′.155′087   78-3552
ISBN 0-87131-255-7

M. Evans and Company, Inc.
216 East 49 Street
New York, New York 10017

Manufactured in the United States of America
9 8 7 6 5 4 3 2 1

Niemand hat die Absicht, eine Mauer zu errichten.
(Nobody intends to erect a wall.)

—Walter Ulbricht, June 15, 1961

To
the scores who have been killed while trying to scale it,
the thousands who have been wounded and dragged away before
they could reach it, the millions who have been spiritually
maimed by its erection in August 1961.

CONTENTS

KEY TO MAPS

PART ONE
THE EXODUS

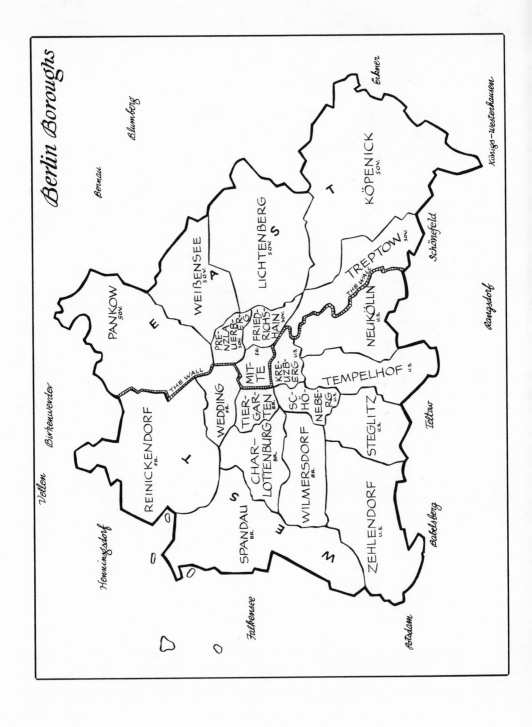

Berlin Boroughs

1

Early August

For weeks they had been coming over to the West, and in
ever increasing numbers—the young and the old, the lean and
the fat, the bearded and the balding, the luckier ones with a
suitcase or two, the less fortunate with little more than the
clothes they were wearing. Not since 1953 had Berlin seen such
an exodus—an exodus that was beginning to assume the proportions of a stampede. Able to accommodate three thousand refugees, the twenty-five three-story apartment blocks in the
Marienfelde emergency camp, on the southern fringe of the
U.S. sector, were now choked to overflowing, as were the
twenty-nine other temporary camps that had been set up to
absorb the flood. The processing procedures employed to sift
genuine from bogus refugees—East German spies infiltrated in
their midst—had all but broken down, and new interrogation
teams had been hurriedly formed at other refugee camps in the
Federal Republic. Airplanes flying out of West Berlin were
packed—as on the East-West corridor to Hanover, where there
were now twenty-one daily flights instead of the customary thirteen.

In the Red Cross shack at one end of Hanover's Langenhagen
Airport, soup was being ladled out to the latest group of refugees. Barbara Groneweg, who had fled from the East herself
some sixteen years before, sat interviewing these newcomers for
her newspaper, the *Frankfurter Rundschau*, a daily generally
favorable to West Germany's Social Democrats.

"Still," she objected to a young locksmith who had been complaining about the "near starvation over there"—in the Soviet
zone—"you seem on the whole better fed and clothed than five
or six years ago."

"All right," he conceded, lowering his spoon. "I'll grant you
it's been a bit better in recent years—until this one anyway. But
this one's been a disaster. They've even run out of potatoes over

3

there. And they won't import anything, even when the harvest's been completely washed out."

No, he went on in answer to her next question, it wasn't because of low wages that he'd decided to pick up and leave; five hundred marks wasn't all that bad, after all. But—and this was a phrase she was to hear repeated over and over—"if they seal off Berlin, we'll be left sitting in the trap. And then they can do with us as they please."

From the northwest came intermittent gusts of wind, driving raindrops against the windowpanes and low clouds over the tent-dotted beach. This gray, drizzly Friday came after a soaking Thursday; there seemed to be no letup in the foul weather that for days now had plagued this particular bit of Baltic coast, in what had once been known as the province of Pomerania. Like the thousands of other holiday-makers who had flocked to this crowded shore, Klemens Krüger almost felt like heading home, so inhospitable was the weather. Unlike them, however, he was free to return to his home in West Germany. Indeed, he could have chosen to spend his August vacation near one of several, more sun-blessed stretches of sand—the Côte d'Azur, the Costa Brava, or mountainous Dalmatia—all beyond the reach of the luckless inhabitants of the German Democratic Republic (DDR). But he had preferred to share their lot out of sympathy for his less fortunate compatriots and for Kollow, the fisherman in whose simple village house he was staying.

To the east beyond Ahlbeck lay the Polish–East German border, a frontier separating the two Communist states that was almost as impermeable as that dividing the two Germanies. Why? It made no sense. But the Russians had turned Swine-münde into a Russo-Polish naval base, and the entire area had been decreed off-limits to the inhabitants of East Germany. Probably they were afraid that what had once been German territory might again be reclaimed as their own if the inhabitants of the DDR were ever allowed over in droves. So the seaside resort of Misdroy was now 100 percent Polish, and the ferry and steamboat traffic that had once linked it to Ahlbeck, Rügen, and Stralsund had been stopped and the wooden wharfs allowed to rot. Even the fish had been nationalized; some had been made

Polish, others German by virtue of an arbitrary decree, an invisible demarcation line which no fisherman on either side could oversail with impunity.

Wherever Krüger looked there were tents—thousands, indeed tens of thousands, of them covering the beaches, pitched atop the sand dunes, scattered among the fir trees farther back. They were inhabited by drillers, welders, factory hands, Comrade Doctors, Comrade Teachers, and kids of varying ages who had come here with their automobiles, motorbikes, camp and kitchen gear, cameras, volleyballs, and rubber animals. The hygienic facilities were primitive, and many of the campers had apparently come down with dysentery. To make matters worse, food was in short supply. Green vegetables and meat were scarce, and there were no potatoes or fish. Krüger, who was no newcomer to this region, found it hard to believe. What, no potatoes? No fish? In this corner of Mecklenburg-Pomerania, where they had once abounded all year round? When he sought an explanation, he was greeted with a helpless shrugging of shoulders or a resigned shaking of the head, followed by some vague remark to the effect that somewhere, unspecified, there was a "bottleneck," or that "the plan went haywire," or more concretely, that it was because agriculture had been collectivized. "The peasants don't work any more and are engaged in passive resistance."

Someone had turned on the radio for the morning news. In East Berlin the Volkskammer was due to meet at ten o'clock in an emergency session. "Something's going to happen," remarked Kollow the fisherman. "They're up to some kind of mischief. For the last two days they've been pulling policemen out of here and sending them to Berlin. They're concentrating all the men they have."

Over the Sender Freies Berlin wavelength came the news that the number of refugees fleeing to the West had risen to over two thousand. But from East Berlin's Deutschlandsender there was not one word about it. For hours the station had been playing lively march music interspersed with spot news flashes. Titov had just spent twenty-four hours circling the globe in a sputnik before returning safely to earth. The papers had splashed the story all over their front pages, hailing it as a great victory for socialism. But the readers Krüger talked to didn't seem impressed. "Military intimidation," they mumbled. "The Russians are up to something, that's for sure."

"Have you heard the latest?" Krüger heard a woman say. "There are no more buses leaving for Berlin. They've all been requisitioned by the police."

One could sense it everywhere—a general nervousness, an almost paralyzing anxiety. Anybody wishing to flee should clear out now, some said, before Ulbricht closes the hatch. No, that's something he can't do, argued others; the West will then intervene. But in truth no one knew exactly what was going to happen. Was the West ready to risk a war over the Berlin sector boundaries? Look at what happened in Hungary, said some, skeptically shaking their heads. Krüger listened while someone told of a young woman who had had a delirious fit during the night. Her sons were in the West. Now, she too wanted to get out; she was afraid she would never see her sons again. But her husband held her back: "We'll leave in the autumn. There will still be time in the fall."

2

It would have been difficult to find a more central place to live than the Karl-Liebknecht-Strasse, where Kurt Kasischke occupied a modest one-room flat. In better times this might not have been the administrative heart of the Prussian capital, but it was about as close as one could comfortably get to the nerve center of Walter Ulbricht's DDR. Not that this much mattered to Kasischke, a Wehrmacht veteran who cared little for the new regime and who had known another, far more glamorous Berlin. What really counted was the rent, and the rent here was dirt cheap.

To the west, flanked by two river branches—like Paris's Nôtre Dame—was the war-scarred cathedral, with its roofless, burned-out dome. It had once faced the Hohenzollern Stadtschloss, the ruined shell of which the Communists had finally dismantled in order to make room for a parade ground, now known as the Marx-Engels-Platz, where Ulbricht could celebrate his birthday (June 30) and other memorable anniversaries by solemnly reviewing the boot-stamping battalions of his Nationale Volksarmee, East Germany's fledgling army. From the Platz it was but a step to the most important contemporary landmark of all: a long, many-windowed edifice, built in the functional style of the Third Reich, which served as headquarters for the Party's Central Committee.

The view up Unter den Linden had once been inspiring, but such it was no longer. The Zeughaus armory was still standing next to the Neue Wache war memorial, in front of which Kasischke had so often mounted guard in the late 1930s as a member of the crack "Wachbataillon Berlin." Farther up, near the ruins of the Kronprinz Palace, Frederick the Great was no longer stoop-shoulderedly seated on his sculptured horse, having been carted off to Potsdam years before as the detested embodiment of Prussian authoritarianism. To the right the buildings of the Humboldt University (previously the Friedrich Wilhelm University) were for the most part intact, but that was about all. The fashionable shops and restaurants had completely disappeared, replaced by shantylike kiosks and shabbily constructed edifices that had prematurely aged. On both sides there were vacant lots and desolate expanses next to which some solitary relic—like the surviving wing of the Adlon Hotel—remained defiantly erect. The white-marble elegance of the new Soviet embassy merely emphasized the drabness of the rest, a drabness extending up the kilometer-long avenue as far as the Brandenburg Gate, where the Soviet sector ended and the British one began.

The prewar elegance of Berlin seemed to have emigrated westward, like the Kranzler cafe, now flourishing once again in a double-decked rotunda on the Kurfürstendamm. Even for those, like Kurt Kasischke, who could do no more than window-shop, pausing to admire the Persian rugs and transistor radios, the abstract paintings and antique weapons exhibited in transparent showcases mounted in the middle of the sidewalk on pedestals of stone, the Kurfürstendamm was electric with excitement. Unter den Linden, on the other hand, seemed dead or depressingly suburban. The old-time chic was gone, and even the lindens that had given the famous avenue its name had vanished, uprooted by the Nazis to make way for flagpoles and imitation spires, from the tops of which the National Socialist regime could flaunt the banner-tokens of its triumphs. Gone too was the delicate scent of summer blossoms, replaced by the lingering smell of brick dust, horse manure, and gasoline fumes spouted from the rusting exhaust of some superannuated truck.

Yet, like so many others who had managed to land a better-paid job in one of the western sectors, fifty-year-old Kurt Kasischke had no intention of leaving East Berlin. Whether eastern or western, the four sectors were all part of the same great city, and as such were governed by Four-Power agreements that had successfully withstood Soviet intimidation and Stalin's 1948–49 blockage.

His was not a purely personal opinion. It was shared by tens of thousands of other Berliners who commuted regularly from their more or less humble abodes in the East, where the rent was rock bottom, to their workplaces in the West. Many traveled from places outside the city limits, such as Potsdam and Babelsberg, near the southwestern tip of the U.S. sector; and a few hardy souls were even known to come all the way from Jüterborg, more than sixty kilometers to the south.

For a *Grenzgänger* ("border crosser") like Karl Behrens, it meant an hour-long train ride from Bernau (twenty-five kilometers northeast of Berlin) to the vehicle repair shop where he worked in the French sector. For the young and pretty Ursula Heinemann, who had been hired as a waitress at the Plaza Hotel, near the Kurfürstendamm, it meant a forty-five-minute trip on the Stadtbahn from her home in the Schöneweide area of East Berlin to the Savignyplatz in the West. Others—like construction worker Emil Goltz, now helping to rebuild the bomb-flattened wastes of northern Kreuzberg, in the U.S. sector—could usually reach their places of work in less than half an hour. Some, like the window-washer Karl Gunkel, could even pedal into West Berlin and back, using one of the arches of the Brandenburg Gate or the equally important crossing point of the Potsdamer Platz, where the American, British, and Soviet sectors converged.

Nor was this human traffic all one way by any means. More than ten thousand West Berliners crossed over daily to work in East Berlin. Many were doctors or nurses employed by hospitals or clinics in the Soviet sector. Some were technicians, others Party members who preferred to work in the proletarian East rather than in the capitalistic West. Quite a few were actors or actresses—like Carola Kusch, the attractive brunette wife of a successful West Berlin dentist and under contract to the Deutsches Theater in East Berlin. So great was the prestige of this theater troupe, put together by Max Reinhardt in the late 1920s, that it played every night to a packed house. Their repertory being limited to classic German drama, stage managers and actors had suffered little interference from Ulbricht and his Party colleagues, who occasionally came to watch a play with an imposing retinue of bodyguards. Half the ensemble were West Berliners, as were half or more of the audiences. For actors and spectators, or at any rate for most of them, it was comforting to think that German culture, like the city of Berlin, was fundamentally one and indivisible.

Such too was the comforting illusion the casual traveler could entertain as his plane skimmed over the last chimney pots and slanted roofs to land at Tempelhof. Nowhere on the ground below was there anything to suggest that this was a divided, still less an isolated, city. Bordered on three sides by lakes and forests, it did not look fenced in or cut off from the surrounding countryside in any way. The dozen railway lines, radiating out in all directions like the multitude of roads, seemed to be functioning normally, even if the arterial bloodstream was thin and the heartbeat a trifle slow. The very abundance of greenery made Berlin look more like a suburb than a metropolis of 3.3 million souls; in a sense it was. A sprawling suburb 24 miles long from north to south and 28 miles wide from east to west, its 340 square miles included 30 lakes, 2 rivers, half a dozen canals, 6 forests, a score of parks and heaths, 3 major airfields, and thousands of cultivated garden plots, where everything from sunflowers to crab apples could be farmed.

Because the city's many lakes were linked by canals, affluent Berliners before the war could board their yachts and sail all the way up to the Baltic, some 180 kilometers to the north. Although no one dared to journey any longer through Ulbricht's proletarian republic, this wealth of waterways and woods had proved a vital factor in enabling the West Berliners to overcome the feeling of municipal cramp imposed on them by the 1948–49 blockade and by the travel restrictions that had later kept them from visiting the outlying communities and cities of the Soviet zone.

In the three western sectors of the city there were not less than twenty-three lakes, almost all offshoots of the Havel, where water lovers could take refuge from the summer heat by swimming or sailing. Four times larger than Paris's Bois de Boulogne, the Grunewald was so extensive that it could provide just about everything—except waterfalls and mountains—that a nature lover might wish. In all, 17 percent of the total surface of West Berlin was arable land. Some of it was even given over to grazing—for the cows that helped to supply precious dairy products to the inhabitants of the western sectors.

As for the garden plots, they numbered in the thousands. Most belonged to Berliners living in the more densely populated center. On weekends they would travel to the city's outlying areas to spend the day digging, hoeing, and pruning and the night inside a bungalow or hut, where there was usually electricity to see by, a stove to cook on, and a cot to sleep on.

The professionals, like truck gardener Harald Grabowski, actually lived on the plots they cultivated most of the year round. His own, situated on the very edge of the U.S. sector in the southeastern part of Neukölln, was separated from the Soviet sector by a ditch. The previous summer East German bulldozers had gone to work deepening and widening the ditch, but no further effort had been made to render it impassible. There was no need, however, to test his muscles on its slopes, since any time he wanted to, Grabowski could walk, bicycle, or motor down the Sonnenallee into the Soviet sector.

Although at certain points, like the Potsdamer Platz, the exact location of the boundary separating the Soviet sector from the western sectors was indicated by a white line painted on the asphalt, along most of its twenty-seven miles it was invisible. At its northern and southern extremities it traversed open fields, cut through stretches of woodland, threaded its way through vegetable plots and truck gardens. In some places—where it glided along a river or canal bank or followed the stone wall of a railway embankment—it formed a natural obstacle; elsewhere it was as porous as a membrane.

There was nothing along the eight-hundred-yard stretch of the Zimmerstrasse, separating the northern Kreuzberg from the Mitte borough, to indicate that it all belonged to the Soviet sector—nothing, that is, except the presence of Vopo[1] guards stationed by the corner of the north-south Friedrichstrasse. Virtually all the shops located immediately south of the Zimmerstrasse catered to inhabitants of the Soviet sector. Their craving for dependable footwear seemed virtually inexhaustible to Hans Dornberg, who ran a shoe shop in the U.S. sector while maintaining a mistress (now eight months pregnant) who lived in East Berlin. His neighbor, a jolly if somewhat balding sexagenarian named Otto Müller, did an equally brisk trade in wristwatches, gold chains, and cheap ornaments, as did Gerhard Buchow, whose photography shop was frequently visited by East Berliners. Some came over to buy ball-point pens, others to take in a western film at the City Kino movie house. Hans-Horst Brandt, who ran the tobacco shop next door, received an average of one hundred such visitors per day, many of them Communist officials who worked on the nearby Wilhelmstrasse at the House of Ministries, as Goering's former aviation headquarters was now called. While the hardier among them made furtive visits to his shop to buy Western cigarettes or pipe tobacco, the less courageous would arrange to have the coveted goods delivered to them at a pharmacy located on the northern edge of the Friedrichstrasse-Zimmerstrasse intersection.

Few areas of the battered city had been more savagely blitzed than this northern half of the Kreuzberg borough, once the newspaper center of old Berlin. The urban landscape in places had been so leveled that from the upper-floor windows of his

---

[1]East German contraction of *Volkspolizist*, a member of the People's Administrative Police (composed of Transport, Traffic, Criminal, and Administrative police departments, as well as a *Kasernierte Volkspolizei*, "Garrisoned Police," made up of paramilitary units). Similarly, Grepo is a contraction of *Grenzpolizist*, "Border Policeman."

apartment on the Leuschnerdamm, in the U.S. sector, the Catholic sacristan Hans Klar could clearly see the Archangel's verdigris-covered statue and the yellow brick façade of the Saint Michael Community Church. Most of his eight thousand parishioners were East Berliners, who did not need to cross from one sector to another, as he did, to reach the church, located on a lawn- and shrub-filled square well within the Soviet sector. His Lutheran colleague, the Reverend Heinz Paul, who lived on the curving Bethaniendamm, could reach Saint Thomas's—an equally ugly yellow brick church situated on the nearby Mariannenplatz—without leaving Kreuzberg and the U.S. sector. His parishioners, however, more than twice as numerous as Klar's in a city with strong Protestant traditions, were spread over two boroughs, for more than thirty-five hundred of them lived in East Berlin.

If the invisible boundary line separating East from West Berlin was more keenly felt at the Potsdamer Platz, it was because the aerial bombardments of World War II had reduced it to an almost featureless no man's land. The once car- and tram-cluttered Piccadilly of old Berlin was now but a ghost of its noisy, horn-honking and whistle-blowing self. Most of its landmarks had been blown to smithereens—like the venerable Potsdamer Bahnhof, the oldest of the imperial city's railway stations, and the Hotel Fürstenhof, where liveried doormen with white gloves used to stand ready to bow over the opened doors of gleaming Mercedes limousines. What was left of the square looked like a wasteland, watched over by two fire-blackened silhouettes: the ruins of the Columbia Haus, once the modernistic home of travel agencies and industrial concerns before becoming a Gestapo interrogation prison, and the ungainly brick mass of the Haus Vaterland, an entertainment center where Wehrmacht veterans and others had tried to forget the rigors of the front in the arms of waltzing Fräuleins.

The tense vicissitudes of peace, which had followed the cruel vicissitudes of war, had also left their mark. In 1952 the tram tracks had been torn up on orders from the Soviet occupation authorities, who had also put an end to intersector bus services and direct telephone communications, to emphasize the separate identity of the eastern sector of Berlin over and against the capitalistic West. A few months later both the Columbia Haus and the Haus Vaterland had been put to the torch by East Berlin rioters protesting the high-handed tyranny of a detested regime. Loudspeakers had been brought up to bombard the U.S. sector with a barrage of "Ami, go home!" exhortations to which the newspapers of West Berlin had replied by erecting a tall electric-bulb screen for the flashing of news bulletins toward the East.

Still, something of the city's battered unity had managed to survive the stresses of the Cold War. Traffic between the East and the West had not been totally interrupted. Motorists could still cross from one sector to another after a routine scrutiny of registration and identity papers, although the inhabitants of East Berlin were usually subjected to inspection by Customs officials on the return trip. The carless could travel back and forth on the U-Bahn or the various S-Bahn lines, including the north-south, partly underground line that Hermann Goering had completed shortly before the outbreak of World War II. Nor was there anything to keep pedestrians or cyclists from crossing from one sector to another.

At the Potsdamer Platz, as at other points along the intersector boundary, the commercial incentives were mostly to be found on the western side. Although there was little on the bomb-blasted Leipziger Strasse to tempt the purses of West Berliners, a whole colony of makeshift booths had mushroomed on the western fringe of the square, largely for the benefit of customers from the East who were offered American cigarettes, Coca-Cola and other soft drinks, elastic bands, safety pins, paper napkins, flashlights, light bulbs, batteries, and other items not available in the state-run stores of the Soviet sector. The People's Police of East Berlin made little effort to halt this intersector commerce, although there were recognized limits it was unwise to transgress. Thus the East Berliners who frequented Karl Fabian's leather-goods shop on the Potsdamer Strasse were careful to hide the secondhand West German magazines they had picked up, under their shirts, blouses, or raincoats before returning home. Otherwise they ran the risk of being forcibly divested of this literary contraband by the policemen or Customs officials posted on the other side of the square.

No such problems confronted the many East Berliners who frequented the Aladin and the Camera, two small movie theaters reached via a passageway in a partly bombed-out building of this same Potsdamer Strasse. Their owner, Friedrich-Wilhelm Foss, had had one of his movie theaters bombed out of existence and another expropriated by the Communists before he had decided to make a fresh start in the West. Now the movie houses, each with a 350-seat capacity, offered 6 consecutive showings, the first beginning punctually at 10:00 A.M. and the last ending shortly before midnight. Those who came over from the East could pay in East marks: 25 pfennigs for the morning and early afternoon performances, one mark from 4:00 P.M. on.

Although these two movie houses had occasionally been attacked in the East Berlin press for being "cesspools of American gangster culture," neither was ever short of clients from the East. Some, being Volkspolizei officials, came over in civilian clothes, but their secretaries usually wore military skirts, more or less concealed under raincoats, and an ordinary blouse. Reichsbahn employees made no attempt to hide their dark blue uniforms as they tramped over from the S-Bahn station exit on the Platz, nor did functionaries working at the nearby House of Ministries, on the Wilhelmstrasse, bother to remove the red badges from their buttonholes indicating that they were Party members.

On the Boyenstrasse, two kilometers to the north, the invisible boundary between the Soviet and French sectors ran along the northwestern side, so that the entire street surface was technically speaking in East Berlin. But it had never occurred to fifty-five-year-old Charlotte Hansen, who lived in one of the three remaining houses on the French-sector side, to consider it as such. Her twin sister, Irma, lived in a house just opposite. Their apartments, hardly more than thirty yards apart, were on the same third-floor level, so that they could wave or even call to each other from their windows.

The weekends, or part of them at any rate, were almost always spent together. Irma and her husband, Otto, who worked as a cabinetmaker in West Berlin while officially residing in the East, did not own a television set. So on Saturdays after an early supper, they would cross the street to enjoy a cup or two of coffee while watching the popular Dutch comedian Lou Van Burg perform on the Hansens' television set, and on Sundays they would come back for other, more varied programs.

Fifteen years had passed since the Hansens had been forced to abandon their home in Pomerania, now incorporated into Poland. Those years had not been easy—they had often been tense—but the storms of the outer world seemed to have raged above their heads, leaving their little backwater street largely undisturbed. When another of Charlotte's sisters, who lived out in the country at Strausberg (twenty-five kilometers east of Berlin), had recently said to her, "Lotte, watch out! The day may soon come when they will put up a wall to keep you from crossing over to see Irma," Charlotte had simply shrugged it off. Why after all these years would they undertake anything so mad, so senseless?

Half a mile farther on, the situation was almost exactly the reverse. Until 1938 the official demarcation line separating the borough of Wedding from that of Mitte had run down the middle of the cobbled Bernauer Strasse. But in that year the street cleaners of Wedding had put up such a fuss over this awkward arrangement that the authorities had finally agreed to advance the borough's administrative limits to the edge of the houses on the southern side. Thanks to this fluke decision, the paved surface of the Bernauer Strasse, including the second sidewalk, had ended up after the war under French jurisdiction, while the tenement houses on the southern side were incorporated into the Soviet sector of occupation.

The forcible eviction of landlord "exploiters" and the boarding up of many ground-level shops on this side of the street had done nothing to improve the run-down appearance of its houses, drab architectural products of the Wilhelmian Age. Pathetic too was the spectacle of East Berlin housewives queuing up on French-occupation territory to gain access to a Soviet sector butcher's shop, where cans of People's Own Enterprise (VEB) goulash made from Mecklenburg or Halberstadt sausages were prominently displayed to conceal the paucity of fresh meat. If they did so, it was simply because the cost of such foodstuffs in the East was far lower than in the West—that is, on the other side of the street, where grocery stores and makeshift booths exhibited tempting assortments of coffee, chocolate, cigarettes, shoes, paperback books, vegetables, bananas, oranges, pineapples, and other fruit unobtainable in the Soviet sector.

The reassuring proximity of these shops and stalls was one of the reasons why fifty-nine-year-old Bruno Hinz had felt no compelling need to abandon the tenement house where he, his wife, Erna, and their twelve-year-old son, Peterle, had lived for some time, along with twenty-nine other East Berlin families and a score of children. Each weekday morning he would walk out the front door and make his way on foot to the Wedding town hall, where as a veteran member of the Social Democratic party, he had found employment as a clerk. Any time he wished to he could walk down the Bernauer Strasse and call on his brother, Heinz, who lived three hundred yards away on the northern side of the street. To be sure, the Vopos would occasionally show up, entering the house from the back with the keys they previously had had made for this purpose. But so far they had limited their inspections to basement rooms and attics, which had yielded nothing particularly suspect.

Why then should he get needlessly worked up by the latest headlines in the *Telegraf* (his favorite newspaper due to its Socialist orientation), which spoke of thousands of refugees streaming into the Marienfelde refugee camp? Other border crossers might feel threatened by the measures the East Berlin authorities were planning to take against the "profiteers" and "parasites" who lived in the East while holding jobs in one of the western sectors. But Bruno Hinz had lived too long in the eye of the storm to yield to such panicky emotions. With freedom but a step from one's own front door, there was nothing to be afraid of.

Tomorrow, Saturday, would be the same as today, no matter what the headlines blared. At noon, as usual, he would leave his town-hall office, his week's work completed, and in the evening, after putting the young Peterle to bed, Erna and he would walk down to the Atlantic cinema on the Brunnen-strasse in time for the 8:30 showing. The film they were advertising was British. *Saturday Night, Sunday Morning* was the curious title—but reasonably appropriate for the quiet weekend ahead.

3

Late May

Eight weeks before, in May, Nikita Sergeyevich Khrushchev had set out from Moscow on the long train trip to Vienna, where he was to meet the new American president, John F. Kennedy. It had seemed at first more like a holiday than anything else—with stations along the line festooned with flags and streamers, and crowds of peasants from the nearby kolzhozes, sovzhozes, and tractor stations assembled to shout their deep-throated "Hoorah!" as the train passed. At the provincial terminus of Mukatchevo, he had been much amused by a crimson streamer—so long that it covered the entire station front—inscribed with the quaint Ukrainian words: *Dobro pozhalouvati, dorogoy Nikito Sergiivich!* (May you live well, dear Nikita Sergeyevich!).

At Čierna, the first stop beyond the border, the Czechoslovak flags had been as numerous as the Russian, while next to the Chairman's many portraits were others of Antonin Novotny, First Secretary of the Czechoslovak Communist party. There had been the usual embraces with local dignitaries; the Czech and Soviet national anthems had rung out amid flourishes of trumpets and clashes of cymbals; the young girls had tripped forward in their embroidered blouses and headbands to offer bread and salt to the distinguished visitor, while the Young Pioneers filled his arms with flowers.

But it was at Bratislava that his hosts had really outdone themselves, draping the public buildings with blood-red streamers that seemed to vie with each other in their lavishness of praise: "We are all with you, dear Nikita Sergeyevich!" "Glory to Khrushchev—the unshakable champion of peace!" "For N. S. Khrushchev—unlimited confidence!" And most succinctly of all: "Khrushchev equals peace!"

After they both had addressed the flag- and flower-waving multitude, promising to work for a relaxation of international tension and a final solution to the Berlin problem, Novotny had driven his distinguished guest up the tortuous road to the castle heights of Smolenice, from whose recently repaired casements Khrushchev was offered a dramatic view of the muddy-green Danube, flowing from Vienna (hidden just beyond the western horizon) on across the rich Hungarian plain toward Budapest. Napoleon too had once enjoyed this view after signing the Treaty of Pressburg with Emperor Franz II of Austria, whom he had recently humbled at Austerlitz. Six years later his French grenadiers had stormed back up these heights and put the once impregnable fortress to the torch in order to make clear to the restive inhabitants of the Danubian plain who was now master of Europe—a position that had not kept him from being exiled to Elba three years later.

It should for other reasons too have been a sobering panorama for the former Donbass miner and mechanic who had climbed to the pinnacle of Soviet power in the tumultuous aftermath of Stalin's death. Just five years before, hundreds of Russian tanks and artillery pieces had been ordered across this plain to drown a counterrevolutionary revolt in blood. Had the lesson sunk in sufficiently for everyone to know who now was master of Central Europe? Nikita Khrushchev was confident that it had.

There seemed little reason to doubt it as, later that same day, the special train took him on toward the quaint town of Trenčin, over whose dark roof tops bouquets of fireworks rose in his honor. What kind of welcome was waiting for him in Vienna he did not know. But here, on the confines of his proletarian empire, the auspices were excellent. Unlike John Kennedy, who had suffered a spectacular humiliation at the hands of Fidel Castro only six weeks earlier, he, Nikita Sergeyevich, already felt like a winner.

John F. Kennedy's approach to the summit meeting in Vienna had been more hurried but also more spectacular. During their two-day stopover in Paris, the young American president and his wife were treated to a state dinner and reception for fifteen hundred guests at the Elysée Palace, a gala banquet in Versailles' dazzling Galerie des Glaces, a special performance by the Paris Opera Ballet in the recently restored Royal Theater of Versailles, and a sparkling display of fireworks over the stately gardens of Le Nôtre. Nothing—not even the drenching rain that spoiled the wreath-laying ceremony at the tomb of the Unknown Soldier under the Arc de Triomphe—could dampen the enthusiasm of the sidewalk crowds for the presidential pair.

In Austria the welcome, though less exuberant than it had been in France, was nonetheless warm. Thousands of umbrella-waving Viennese were willing to brave the early-June showers in order to cheer the presidential limousine as it passed on its way to the Hofburg Palace—in marked contrast to the hundreds who had gathered in front of the Sud-Ost Bahnhof to welcome Khrushchev's train the previous evening. Any credit the Russian leader had acquired as a member of the ruling Kremlin group which had granted Austria its independence in 1955, had clearly not erased the bitter memories of the Soviet occupation, when the historic Schwarzenbergplatz had been forcibly renamed the Stalinplatz and made to accommodate an ungainly Red Army tank. Nor had the Viennese forgotten Khrushchev's patronizing reference to Austria's enforced neutrality during his state visit to their capital in June 1960, when he had attacked the United States and West Germany, two countries with which Austria maintained particularly cordial relations.

Once the two leaders found themselves face to face on June 3, however, there had been little cause for American rejoicing. A disappointing Saturday was followed by a dismal Sunday. Khrushchev's early-morning visit to the Schwarzenbergplatz, where he had laid a wreath of red roses on the Red Army soldiers monument, seemed to have made him more intransigent than ever. On the Berlin problem his mind was made up, he bluntly told Kennedy. It was an outrage that a peace settlement should not have been reached in Germany sixteen years after the end of World War II. If the United States and its Western Allies were not interested in a peace settlement, then the Soviet Union would go ahead on its own and sign a separate peace treaty with the German Democratic Republic. The treaty would establish a "free city" in West Berlin and automatically terminate all Western occupation rights. There would be no Soviet interference in the internal affairs of the West Berliners, but they would have to negotiate new road and railway transit rights for goods and people crossing the territory of the henceforth fully sovereign and independent East German state.

In effect, this statement amounted to an ultimatum: Either the United States and its allies agreed to enter into peace negotiations on the future of Germany and West Berlin, or the Soviet Union was going to act unilaterally. After that, any violation of East Germany's "sovereign" rights on land, sea, or in the air would be met by force.

"I want peace," Khrushchev concluded, "but if you want war, that is your problem."

"It is you, not I, who wants to force a change," Kennedy insisted. But this had cut no ice with the increasingly truculent Nikita, who finally declared that his decision was irrevocable. If necessary, he would sign a separate peace with East Germany not later than December.

"Then it will be a cold winter," was Kennedy's parting rejoinder.

"Is it always like this?" the young president had asked Llewellyn Thompson at the end of the first day. "About par for the course," his ambassador to Moscow had replied. Charles Bohlen had agreed. Khrushchev had been aggressive, as was his habit.

Could it be that Charles de Gaulle was right in thinking that negotiations with the Russians on the Berlin problem was a waste of time, since Khrushchev and the other Kremlin leaders were unwilling to make any significant concessions on the vital question of a plebiscite or free elections throughout Germany— that is, East as well as West—needed to establish an all-German government? But the general had been careful to add that the bellicose talk and the picturesque phraseology ("Berlin is a bone stuck in our throat . . . a splinter that must be removed from the heart of socialist Europe") did not mean that the canny Ukrainian actually wanted war. After all, he could have long since ordered his tanks to occupy West Berlin. Instead, for two and a half years Khrushchev had been issuing ultimatums ("If an international peace treaty settling the German problem is not signed within six months, we will sign a separate peace treaty with the German Democratic Republic"), but he had let each new deadline expire without making a move to implement the threat. The important thing, therefore, was not to be rattled and to stand one's ground. Since the Russians were not prepared to make any significant concessions, there was no point in the Allies entering into new negotiations. Their readiness to do so would be interpreted as a sign of weakness; and they could all too easily be placed on the defensive—accused of being un-reasonably "intransigent" — and finally pressured into making dangerous concessions on their rights of occupation in Berlin.

How admirably logical and coherent it all sounded. It even echoed Kennedy's feeling that Eisenhower and his then secre-tary of state, Christian Herter, had come close to making dangerous concessions in 1959 by agreeing to reduce the size of the U.S. garrison in Berlin and to limit the democratic prop-aganda and intelligence activities emanating from the city's western sectors. Still, De Gaulle's stand-pat attitude seemed to Kennedy too narrow and negative an approach. One had, after all, to give Khrushchev his due. He had boldly toppled Stalin from his pedestal and significantly altered Leninist ideology by declaring that a war between the socialist and capitalist systems was not necessarily inevitable. A man capable of formulating a new doctrine of "peaceful coexistence" was someone with whom it theoretically should be possible to deal. Slamming the door on him might only aggravate the crisis, undermine his position in the Kremlin, and help bring to power a more implacable and hostile leader.

After four crowded days, during much of which he had been forced to speak through interpreters, it was a relief for Kennedy to fly on to London, where he could converse with Harold Mac-millan and others in his own tongue. Having had his fill of formal conferences and state banquets—another dinner was scheduled for that evening (June 5) at Buckingham Palace—Kennedy asked Macmillan if they might not meet in private, so that each could feel perfectly free to say exactly what was on his mind without risk of damaging leaks or indiscretions. Macmillan readily assented. He was equally anxious not to be "reported verbally," as he later noted in his diary, "and then misrepresented by hearsay, so that the Americans would think that we were 'yellow' and the French and Germans (who *talk* 'tough' but who have no intention of doing *anything* about Berlin) could ride out on us." It had happened before, and he was determined not to let it happen again.

Despite the disparity in age—at sixty-seven the white-whiskered prime minister was as old as Khrushchev—Kennedy and Macmillan hit it off again, as they had ten weeks before during their first encounter at Key West, Florida. Macmillan too had been given a rough time by the unpredictable Nikita during the ten-day trip he had made to the Soviet Union in February of 1959. But the Russians' recent success in rocketing Yuri Gagarin into space seemed to have made them even cockier. They were beginning to assume the arrogance of conquerors, and Khrushchev was already boasting of the USSR's industrial might, saying that his country would soon be overtaking the most advanced of capitalist societies in the production of material wealth. Napoleon once said that God was on the side of the heaviest artillery, and Khrushchev now seemed out to prove that the god of diplomacy was on the side of the heaviest rocketry. In fact, during their two-day confrontation in Vienna, Kennedy had felt at times as though he were meeting Napoleon—a Napoleon at the very peak of his power. It had been a most disquieting experience.

Macmillan agreed that Khrushchev was a formidable and baffling personality, able to move from extreme cordiality to wrath and near hositility with disconcerting ease. He was extremely sensitive about his own and the Soviet Union's dignity, yet brutally insensitive to the feelings of others. He could be vulgar yet dignified, ruthless and at the same time sentimental. He was quick in argument, never missing or overlooking a point, and he had an extraordinary memory. He was a very odd mixture indeed, a strange combination of Peter the Great and Lord Beaverbrook. But the important thing was not to drive him into a corner, where he might feel trapped and react with violence.

For this reason, Macmillan felt it vital not to slam the door in his face—which was basically what De Gaulle and Adenauer had been proposing—by categorically refusing to enter into future negotiations on the German problem. Perhaps there was no way of stopping Khrushchev from signing a separate peace treaty with East Germany, in which case they would simply have to ride out the storm. The important thing was to decide exactly what constituted a valid *casus belli*. For all his apparent intransigence, even De Gaulle was of the opinion that neither the French nor the British nor the Americans were prepared to go to war over the question of who—a Russian or an East German sergeant—should have the right to examine the papers of Allied soldiers traveling overland between Berlin and the Federal Republic. Only another blockade would justify a resort to arms.

Kennedy shared this feeling. It was why he had agreed to a personal meeting with Khrushchev, remarking: "I would rather meet him for the first time at the summit, not the brink." But there was no disguising the melancholy fact that the summit meeting in Vienna had not been a success. Instead of gentle slopes leading to a Promised Land of peace, it had yielded a rugged panorama, scarred by chasms and abysses.

Not long after takeoff in the U.S. Air Force jet that was carrying him back across the Atlantic, the president asked Evelyn Lincoln, his secretary, to file the papers he had been examining; he would like to get some sleep, since he was going to have a busy day ahead of him in Washington. While clearing the table, she spied a slip of paper that had fallen to the ground. She picked it up, tucked it in with the rest, and carried the documents back to her seat.

As she was filing the classified material, she came upon the slip of paper she had retrieved. Now she understood why the president had looked so glum in Vienna. On the slip of paper were two lines, in Kennedy's own handwriting:

"I know there is a God—and I see a storm coming;
If He has a place for me, I believe I am ready."

4

June 7.

Late in the evening, as was his custom—for it was a rare day on which he spent less than twelve hours at his desk—Walter Ulbricht had himself driven back to his new home, located some twenty miles northeast of Berlin on the fringe of the Bernau forest. As the chauffeur drove northward, past the truck gardens and the stuccoed villas of the Pankow suburbs (where he and his Politburo colleagues had once lived), the first secretary of the Party could relax with the feeling of having completed a good day. For three successive nights and days, units of the Nationale Volksarmee had engaged in joint summer maneuvers with Soviet occupation troops—to the evident satisfaction of marshals Rodion Malinovsky, defense minister of the USSR, and Andrei Grechko, commander of the forces of the Warsaw Pact, who had been his guests at a midday banquet in the East German Defense Ministry. The years of training that many NVA officers had received in the military academies of the Soviet Union had obviously paid off. Regardless of what many of the rank and file might feel about maneuvering alongside their former conquerors, they had proved themselves disciplined soldiers in the field.

Even more significant for the first secretary of the Party was the confidential information he had been given about the Vienna summit meeting. It had been relayed to him by Mikhail Pervukhin, the Soviet ambassador to the DDR, and by members of the Soviet High Commission in Karlshorst, to whom he was in the habit of telephoning toward the end of each working day.[2] Nikita Sergeyevich Khrushchev had returned from Vienna with the feeling that he had triumphed in his dialectical fencing with

[2]DDR. *Deutsche Demokratishe Republik* ("German Democratic Republic.") The German abbreviation, now universally used east and west of the Elbe, will henceforth designate East Germany.

John Kennedy. He had found the young president weak and irresolute, and had so rattled him that in his televised "Report to the Nation," on June 6, Kennedy had spoken of "somber talks" and of a "very sober two days" spent in an exchange of views with the Soviet chairman.

The contents of the June 4 memoranda, which Khrushchev had given to Kennedy in Vienna, were also most encouraging. Pervukhin, who had brought Ulbricht an official copy, had told him of the Kremlin's decision to have the TASS news agency release the texts the next day, June 9, even though this was a breach of diplomatic protocol. A German translation was also to be released over the ticker tapes of ADN.[3]

Nor was this all. The Soviet Foreign Ministry had just issued three stiff notes to the British, French, and U.S. embassies in Moscow, protesting the Bonn government's decision to have the Bundesrat, the Federal Republic's upper legislative chamber, meet in plenary session in West Berlin on June 16. An equally stiff protest had been delivered to the West German embassy in Moscow, denouncing Bonn's decision as a "major new provocation" against the USSR, the German Democratic Republic, and other socialist states.

These were heartening developments. Although there was no telling what the unpredictable Nikita Sergeyevich might do next, this time it did look as if he had committed himself and the Soviet Union to the early conclusion of a peace treaty. Admittedly, Khrushchev had blown hot and cold on the subject for the past two years. He had been won over to the idea only because it seemed an appropriate answer to the Bonn government's decision to request atomic arms for the Bundeswehr. After *Neues Deutschland* had dramatically announced, in late October of 1958, that "all Berlin lies on the territory of the DDR" and that the Western powers had "undermined" their rights to a continued "sojourn" in the city, Khrushchev had delivered a major address at the Sports Palace in Moscow, in

[3]ADN *Allgemeiner Deutscher Nachrichtendienst* ("General German News Service"), East Germany's leading news agency. Not to be confused with DPA, the Deutsche Presse-Agentur, West Germany's leading news agency.

which he had proclaimed the Soviet government's intention of denouncing the Potsdam agreement and of transferring to a "sovereign DDR" the rights defined therein. Finally, on November 27, after one more abortive effort to entice the Bonn government into direct negotiations on Soviet terms, Andrei Gromyko, the Russian foreign minister, had delivered an official note to the ambassadors of the three Western powers informing them than the Potsdam agreement had been repudiated and that West Berlin had to be transformed within six months into a "free city"—or else!

But it was he, Walter Ulbricht, rather than the Western powers, who had been subsequently humiliated. Taking the ebullient Khrushchev at his word, he and his Party colleagues had gone around exulting, "You'll see, by the end of next spring at the latest, West Berlin will be ours!" The radio stations of East Berlin had even been instructed to play the sentimental hit tune *Wenn der weisse Flieder wieder blüht* ("When the White Lilac Blooms Again") over and over, almost nightly, as though to inform the West Berliners that the hour of "liberation" was at hand. But the deadline had expired, the masters of the Kremlin, as though overcome by amnesia, had made no effort to honor their pledges, and the disc jockeys had had to change their tune.

Periodically since then, one or another Soviet leader had taken up the cry for a German peace treaty and a free-city solution for West Berlin. But it was lip service, no more. A little over a year before, in May 1960, Khrushchev had even treated Ulbricht and several thousand Party activists to a numbing cold shower in East Berlin, declaring that patience was needed, that a German peace treaty would not necessarily be signed within the six- or eight-month time span he had previously laid down. "We are realists and will not pursue an adventurous policy." It had been a chilling experience and one that Walter Ulbricht was not ready to forget.

Yes, learning to live with Nikita Sergeyevich Khrushchev was not an easy business. Temperamentally they belonged to two different species—Khrushchev being as jolly and loquacious as Ulbricht was tense, self-conscious, and close-mouthed. Caution had served Ulbricht well in 1953 during the uncertain months after Stalin's death, when it had been so difficult to foresee just who was going to be the next top dog in the Kremlin. It had been a shock to be bluntly informed by a Politburo faction that included Malenkov and Beria, whom Ulbricht had always regarded as being as staunchly Stalinist as himself, that the general offensive against private property, launched with a lot of fanfare in July 1952, would have to be put into cold storage ten months later. The drive to force East German farmers and artisans into collectivized *Produktionsgenossenschaften* had encountered widespread resistance, led to thousands of arrests, and incited tens of thousands to seek refuge in West Berlin or the Federal Republic. The first and most obvious consequence of this collectivization through terror had been to precipitate a drastic shortage of potatoes, meat, coal, and other staples. But was this a valid reason for turning back? Stalin too had encountered desperate resistance when he had decided to collectivize agriculture and industry in the Soviet Union, but he had had the strength of will to carry on.

Determined to prove that he was made of the same stern stuff, Ulbricht had refused to relax the pressure. Instead, he had decreed that the existing norms for factory output, as established in the First Five-Year Plan, were to be raised by 10 percent. To merit the wages they were receiving, workers would have to toil that much harder, or face a reduction in their earnings. Since in all but rare cases factory output could not be increased overnight because the raw materials and other supplies were lacking, the workers of the Soviet zone of occupation had been quick to realize what this meant in practice: a 10-percent cut in their already meager earnings.

Fearing the worst, the Politburo in Moscow had sent its leading German expert, High Commissioner Vladimir Semyonov, back to Berlin to force Ulbricht to toe the new priority-for-consumer-goods line. But the last-minute repeal of the recently raised work norms came too late to head off the mass revolt of June 17, 1953, which spread like wildfire across East Germany, with workers in every major city and industrial center sacking Party offices and opening packed jails, in many cases with the connivance of the local police.

Es hat alles keinen Zweck
Der Spitzbart, der muss weg.
Spitzbart, Bauch und Brille
Sind nicht Volkes Wille.

("There are no two ways about it,
The Goatee, he must go.
Goatee, Paunch and spectacles
Are not the People's Will.")

The crowds assembled on the Alexanderplatz had chanted these words, mocking the detested *apparatchik*, who had cultivated a Lenin-like goatee without acquiring any of the latter's oratorical charisma.

Ironically, this June 17 uprising helped to save the man most responsible for it. Confronted with the wholesale collapse of a regime they had forcibly imposed on a subjugated people, the Russians called out their armored units and drowned the rebellion in blood. Ulbricht was spirited out of the beleaguered Central Committee building and driven to safety in a Soviet tank. But the concessions they had been prepared to grant when they felt relatively secure, the Russians no longer dared to make now that the weakness of their satellite had been exposed. Ulbricht had to be supported willy-nilly, no matter how unpopular he might be.

Criticism that might have been justified only a month or two before was now no longer opportune—as Ulbricht's leading adversary in the East German Politburo was soon to learn. This person was Wilhelm Zaisser, the notorious "General Gomez" of the Spanish civil war who had been appointed minister of state security and thus the boss of the dreaded *Staatssicherheitsdienst* ("State Security Service."), or SSD. Zaisser's opposite number in the Kremlin was Lavrenti Beria, boss of the even more dreaded Soviet secret police, whom his Politburo rivals were determined to cut down to size. For a skilled in-fighter like Ulbricht, it was a simple matter to link their two names, thereby making sure that the downfall of the second would lead to the disgrace of the first.

Thus, although neither of them had particularly wanted it,

Ulbricht and Khrushchev had found themselves allied in a joint struggle for survival. But this alliance of convenience between persons of such contrasting personalities more than once threatened to run aground.

The year 1956 had been particularly perilous. The trouble had started in February, at the Twentieth Congress of the Soviet Communist party, when first Mikoyan and then Khrushchev had begun demolishing the elaborate mythology built up around Stalin. For someone like Ulbricht, who had repeatedly praised Stalin's political and military genius and who had even hailed him as "the greatest living theoretician of scientific socialism," this was strong medicine indeed. Yet no leader of a Soviet satellite country had been quicker to trim his sails to the new anti-Stalin wind. Streets and factories that had been named after the Georgian dictator were hastily renamed. In Berlin the Stalinallee was officially rebaptized the Karl-Marx-Allee, while the Stalinist style of architecture, which had been imported from Moscow for one part of the war-blitzed avenue, was replaced by another, supposedly less stereotyped mode of construction for the balance.

Weathering the subsequent storm, however, had not been easy. In May, Ulbricht was publicly hooted down during a meeting of the agriculture faculty at Leipzig University. In June, Hungary's Stalinist dictator Rakosi was overthrown, while intellectuals of the Petöfi Circle began publicly clamoring for freedom of expression and an end to tyrannical constraints. In Poland thirty-six thousand political prisoners were released from jail, prominent Stalinists were booted out of office, and the Warsaw government was finally forced to bow to a Poznan workers' strike by promising reforms and accepting a new leader, Wladyslaw Gomulka, pledged to pursue a "national" socialistic line that was no longer to be dictated in the Kremlin. East Berlin's Humboldt University was in the grip of a similar ferment, encouraged by the DDR's leading poet and playwright, Bertolt Brecht.

The feeling of discontent had even spread to the Politburo, where it was shared by Karl Schirdewan, the Central Committee secretary generally considered the number two man in the Party, and Ernst Wollweber, a one-time sabotage expert

who had succeeded Wilhelm Zaisser as minister of state security. If communism was to survive in the German Democratic
Republic, they argued, it would have to become more popular,
less authoritarian and dogmatic in decreeing from above what
the regime's subjects needed and desired.

With opposition like this at the top as well as at the bottom, it
seemed only a matter of time before Ulbricht would join other
East European Stalinists in disgrace. But he was saved once
again by a popular revolt, this time in Budapest. For Khrushchev and the Kremlin leadership, there could be no more talk
of concessions in Berlin when Russian tanks and howitzers were
needed to restore order in Hungary. The twenty Soviet divisions
stationed in East Germany were placed on the alert as a warning
to potential trouble makers. For his part Ulbricht did everything
he could to keep news of the Budapest revolt from filtering into
the heavily censored newspapers and radio broadcasts—the East
German press, as he put it, not being "a seismograph for the
recording of mistaken conceptions or anti-Marxist theories."

Some of Ulbricht's Party colleagues had thought the moment
ripe to solve the still unsettled problem of Berlin through bold,
unilateral action. The proposal they submitted to the Soviet
ambassador, Georgi Puskin, was simple: Since the West Berliners were disturbed about events in Budapest and were planning a giant protest rally in front of the Schöneberg Rathaus,
why not send over several hundred Party activists, disguised as
Halbstarke ("hooligans"), to work the mob up to fever pitch?
The demonstrators would be encouraged to march through the
Brandenburg Gate and down Unter den Linden as far as the
Soviet embassy. Here, after a few windows had been conveniently smashed, Russian tanks would be waiting to rout the "aggressors." They would be driven back into the western sectors,
which Soviet and East German troops would then occupy to put
an end to the "chaos" and to the "provocations" of the warmongers. The Americans, so these Party activists argued, were too
paralyzed by the Suez crisis and their own election campaign to
be able to react, and the annexation would be a fait accompli
before Washington knew what had happened.

The Soviet ambassador's reaction was lukewarm, as was
Khrushchev's two months later to a watered-down variation of

this scheme which Ulbricht submitted to him in January 1957. The idea was that Moscow would announce that henceforth *all* Berlin would be regarded as the capital of the German Democratic Republic. The consequence of this action would be the abrogation of the various Four-Power agreements that had been worked out between 1945 and 1949 to regulate the movements of individuals and goods among the four sectors of the city. But unless it was backed by action, the announcement Ulbricht was suggesting would mean nothing; and now that Eisenhower had been overwhelmingly reelected to the White House, and the Suez crisis was behind him, Khrushchev was not prepared to risk a major confrontation.

Still he had to admit that Ulbricht had successfully insulated his country from the volcanic upheavals in the Danubian plain. He might not be liked, he might even be intensely unpopular with his own people, but he had proved his efficiency in cowing restless students and clapping critical intellectuals into jail. *Die Intellektuellen brauchen einen Schlag ins Genick* ("The intellectuals need a blow in the nape of the neck") was the no-nonsense language Ulbricht had used to justify the use of State Security agents who, disguised in workmen's overalls and dungarees, had invaded university lecture halls and even cafes and nightclubs, and beaten up all "negatively inclined" students. These were the methods Hilter had once employed, and they hadn't kept him from being immensely popular with his countrymen. So maybe Ulbricht was right in thinking that this was the only way to deal with his fellow Germans. It was probably wiser under the circumstances to live with a less than popular boss who had proved his toughness than to bring in a newcomer whose mere advent might be interpreted as a sign of weakness, and thus unleash the revolt it was meant to forestall.

The decisive factor, however, was not economic, or even inner-political, as Ulbricht had the quick-wittedness to realize before his opponents. It had to do with East Germany's international status. In September 1957, Khrushchev made a special trip to Berlin, where Ulbricht's DDR received official Soviet recognition as a sovereign state. The ambitious dream Stalin had once harbored in the first postwar years—that of a socialist-communist Germany—had long since been abandoned, as had the idea that West Germany could be kept neutral and disarmed in return for a vague promise of eventual reunification. West Germany had prospered, had been admitted to NATO, was developing its own army, and, in July 1957, had signed on as one of the founding members of the European Economic Community. There seemed no further point in trying to use the reunification issue as a means of increasing one's personal popularity. The issue, from the point of view of practical politics, was dead. The answer to the threat posed by the establishment of NATO and a West European Common Market was a similar process of integration in the East. Economically and militarily, East Germany must be more closely integrated into the Eastern block.

The drift of events in Europe thus gave Ulbricht a weapon with which to rout his enemies. Those who had been advocating a general relaxation of pressure at home were not simply utopians; they were "deviationists" bent on subordinating the vital "socialization" of East Germany to the mythical cause of national reunification. The correct Party line should be the very opposite: Help Moscow to forge the monolithic solidarity of the Soviet block.

To combat a man who was so ready to champion the Russian cause was a feat even Khrushchev was not prepared to try. In December 1957 Gerhard Ziller, the Central Committee secretary responsible for economic affairs, committed suicide in despair over a policy that, in breaking East Germany's traditional trade links with the West, was more likely to impoverish than enrich the country—as was already the case in neighboring Czechoslovakia. But who was going to waste tears over Ziller? Certainly not Ulbricht, still less the masters of the Kremlin.

But this policy had an inevitable corollary. If East Germany was to be developed into a self-sustaining and independent state, its sovereignty had to be extended to encompass the three sectors of West Berlin. These areas of "capitalist infection" had to be eliminated, lest they end up fatally contaminating the entire body politic of the German Democratic Republic.

Here too, Ulbricht was happy to discover, he and Comrade Khrushchev saw eye to eye—at any rate in words. For both, West Berlin was an artificial survival of World War II, an intolerable challenge to the dignity and sovereignty of the DDR.

It was the living symbol of the Cold War, a forward bastion, or *Frontstadt*, aggressively maintained one hundred miles into East German territory. It was a bone stuck in the throat of East European socialism, a festering tooth that had to be extracted, or at least neutralized.

The only question was, just how was this process of sterilization going to be performed?

The new residential compound which Walter Ulbricht's black Zis was now approaching was located just beyond the village of Wandlitz near a well-tarred country road that led through woodlands to the town of Bernau. Four square miles in area, this strictly off-limits settlement included a score of recently erected villas surrounded by lawns, ponds, and trees, and protected by a six-foot reinforced-concrete wall which at night was always floodlit. The forbidding concrete wall could easily have been taken for that of some country prison, so heavily was it guarded by jack-booted sentinels—some dressed in field-gray uniforms, others in workmen's overalls—who were equipped with Tommy guns, field glasses, and police dogs. All told, there were 160 of them, hand-picked members of the celebrated *Wachregiment*, a force of more than four thousand fanatically loyal volunteers placed under the direct control of the minister of state security.

Critics of the Ulbricht regime liked to scoff at this "red ghetto," artificially erected on the fringes of the Bernau forest. But it was a luxurious ghetto that boasted a House of Culture large enough to include a banquet hall, movie theater, restaurant, bar, and library; a swimming pool with movable glass panels to make it open-air in summer; a kindergarten, a clinic, several hairdresser and massage parlors, a gymnasium, half a dozen tennis courts, and even a rifle range. There were cottages, apartments, and barracks for chauffeurs, servants, and watch-guard personnel in a specially built extramural village, which also included an ultra-modern shopping center, service garages and mechanical workshops, a boiler house, an electricity-generating plant, and a water-pumping station. The compound could thus survive a general power failure, and it could call on the nearby Soviet garrison—an armored unit stationed a few kilometers up the road at Bernau—to defend it in the unlikely event that enemies of the regime staged an assault.

Less imaginative than Frederick the Great, when he laid out the fountained vistas and statued terraces of Sans Souci at Potsdam, the designers of the proletarian paradise at Wandlitz had aligned the score of central villas in six parallel rows, and with a sense of Prussian efficiency had reduced them to a single architectural pattern. Each villa had two upper floors, the topmost being for the servants. They all had three or four bedrooms, a dining room, a library-office complete with the most up-to-date telephone equipment, a picture-windowed living room spacious enough to contain a winter garden, and an ample basement. But for the rest, each occupant had been allowed to furnish his new home according to his individual taste.

Happy to forget his humble Brunswick origins, Otto Grotewohl, the aging Socialist who for years had served as figurehead cochairman of the *Sozialistische Einheitspartei,* had generously indulged his fancy for expensive carpets, old paintings, and Renaissance and baroque antiques. The bathrooms, at his wife's insistence, had been tiled in Italian marble; the library was panelled in African mahogany; and his movie room was adorned with a stage curtain composed of ancient and modern coins which a small corps of numismatic experts had collected from all over the globe.

The villa of Willi Stoph—the gaunt ex-artilleryman who had returned to Berlin in 1945 on Marshal Zhukov's staff and later been named minister of the interior, minister of defense, and deputy prime minister—bristled with an imposing array of halberds, broadswords, flintlocks, and cuirasses. Hilde Benjamin—"Red Hilde", as she was often called for the pitiless zeal with which, as minister of justice, she had prosecuted the "enemies of the state"—had had her music room panelled in ebony. Another Politburo member, Alfred Neumann, had given free rein to his passion for monumental armchairs and candelabra.

Ulbricht himself had displayed characteristic restraint. A person of simple tastes, he was content to live with his second wife, Lotte Kühn, and their adopted daughter, Beate, in a solidly middle-class décor of well-upholstered sofas and lace-covered tables. The only luxuries he had permitted himself, in keeping with his abstemious inclinations—for he neither drank nor smoked—were a dining-room floor made of Venetian glass mosaics and some Chinese silk hangings for his living-room walls.

Although few of his privileged neighbors were as athletically inclined as Walter Ulbricht, who liked to begin the day with ten minutes of calisthenics or a jog through the nearby wood, almost all had welcomed the move from the suburban compound in Pankow to the proletarian Petit Trianon at Wandlitz. Their loyalty to Popular Democracy and to the "socialist-progressive" cause was, of course, above question; but there had always been the danger that some family member might be tempted to go shopping in West Berlin, where the wealth of capitalist goods displayed was so much richer than in the Soviet sector. Now, with their own well-stocked shopping center offering imported luxury goods denied to the ordinary East German, the chances of such aberrations were correspondingly diminished.

For a veteran Politburo member like the burly Hermann Matern, who had contributed to the downfall of Ulbricht's enemies in the two major crises of 1953 and 1956–58, all this was a matter of course—as it was to Erich Honecker, the former Saarland roofer whom Ulbricht had first picked to develop the important *Freie Deutsche Jugend* ("Free German Youth"), or FDJ, and whom he had later made responsible for national security, a Politburo job that made him the Party's watchdog over the two key ministries of defense and state security. But for others whose fortunes had not been as closely linked to Ulbricht's star—like theorist Albert Norden, foreign trade specialist Bruno Leuschner (a kind of East German Mikoyan), or Friedrich Ebert, son of the Weimar Republic's first president and now mayor of East Berlin—being admitted to the Wandlitz "club" was the final consecration.

The most reluctant to leave the Pankow compound—with its chicken-wire fencing, glaring arc lamps, and *Schlagbaum* barriers—was, curiously enough, the man directly responsible for the protection of his fellow comrades: Erich Mielke, minister of state security. In Pankow he had installed himself in a large house once occupied by Hermann Goering. Although it was only a couple of miles from this house to his main office in the Ministry of State Security, Mielke had filled his Pankow home with sophisticated communications gadgetry designed to guarantee him against possible surprises at home or abroad. Telex machines could provide him with instant information, while the radio transmitting and receiving equipment made it possible for him to contact subordinates at the simple turn of a dial. He could thus maintain twenty-four-hour vigilance while watching movies in his private projection room, making film enlargements in his photographic laboratory, or outlaughing, outsinging, and out-drinking his beer- and schnapps-loving friends in his rustic bar-room.

Although all the Wandlitz villas were lavishly supplied with telephones directly connected with administrative or Party offices, Mielke sensed that things would never be quite the same again, since it would be difficult to lure his hard-drinking pals out for a boisterous evening—a thirty-kilometer trip in each direction. But his attempts to convince Ulbricht that he would be out of touch with the vital Ministry of State Security after office hours had fallen on deaf ears. Others—like Karl Maron, minister of the interior, or Otto Winzer, the power behind the throne at the Ministry of Foreign Affairs—had already made the move. There was no reason to make a special exception for the minister of state security. Besides, providing continued protection in his Pankow fortress for a man who had many enemies was an extravagance the East German Workers-and-Peasants-State could not afford. And so, after six months of wrangling, Mielke had finally moved himself and his belongings into Wandlitz villa number 8.

There was, however, one consolation. In his new abode there was a roomy basement that he had soundproofed so as not to disturb the evening pastimes or slumbers of his neighbors. Here, to the accompaniment of Prussian march music, Erich Mielke could go on indulging in his favorite sport: pistol target practice.

Being quick on the draw may not have been the quality that had first attracted the attention of his party superiors, but a cold-blooded readiness to gun down dangerous opponents had unquestionably contributed to his ascension. Like so many other sons of working-class families in the Communist Wedding district, the young Erich Mielke had joined the Party youth movement during the topsy-turvy months after the 1918 armistice, when Germany, having lost its Kaiser and been transformed into a more or less liberal republic, seemed about to follow Russia's Bolshevik example. For a while he had worked as a packer in a warehouse shipping department, before trying his hand at journalism for the Communist newspaper *Rote Fahne* ("*Red Flag*"). His fearlessness had much to commend it, but he was of too combative a disposition to make a really good reporter, and his physical appearance hardly invited confidences. With his short legs and oxlike shoulders, from which protruded an almost neckless head adorned by flabby cheeks and a pair of small, ratlike eyes, Erich Mielke had the look and the build of a barroom bouncer. And it was indeed as a two-fisted bruiser that he had first made his mark in the frequent clashes that had opposed him and his Party comrades to the pro-Weimar Socialists and the anti-Weimar Nazis.

Charged with willful homicide, after having two police captains shot down on the Bülowplatz, where the Communist party was holding an illegal rally, Mielke had been forced to go underground. But his readiness to obey the toughest orders impressed Komintern officials in Moscow. Providing him with false papers, they helped him escape to Belgium and, via freighter, on to Leningrad. In the Ukraine, to which he was sent as a member of a grain-collecting unit, he again demonstrated his toughness, helping to requisition the last grain reserves that desperate villagers had concealed from the authorities, so that Party officials and their guards would not go hungry even if the local peasants starved. His reward—admission to the Frunze Military Academy in Moscow—was not long in coming.

Already fairly well versed in Russian when the civil war broke out in Spain, Mielke again impressed his superiors by his callous indifference to humanitarian considerations. Many were the comrades who could not later recall ever having seen him at the front. The reason was simple: as an NKVD major and political commissar for front- and rear-line units, Mielke had his hands full purging the international brigades of anti-Stalinist "Fascists" (anarchists, Socialists, Trotskyists, and so forth).

At the conclusion of World War II, most of which he spent

working for the Red Army's espionage department, Mielke returned to Germany and was assigned to the buildup of a new, reliably Communist Ministry of the Interior in Saxony. This, the most industrialized province of East Germany, had experienced a brief period of occupation by U.S. troops in May 1945, before the Americans had withdrawn to the demarcation lines agreed upon at Yalta. The Red Army's subsequent arrival had been accompanied by so much looting and raping that veteran Communists who had survived the Nazi holocaust were reduced to despair. A strong hand was needed to deal with persons daring to express unflattering comparisons. Mielke did not spare the whip. Displaying the same ruthless disregard for amenities he had already demonstrated in the Ukraine and Catalonia, he helped Russian NKVD officers round up "Fascists" by the hundreds while Socialists reluctant to cooperate with the Communists were arrested by the thousands.

Mielke had then been summoned back to Berlin to help his former superior, Wilhelm Zaisser, organize the regime's "kommissariats"—embryonic forerunners of a full-fledged political police. In 1950, when the now ubiquitous SSD was raised to top-echelon status as the Ministry of State Security and allowed to move into the huge headquarters the Russian NKVD had just vacated, Mielke was promoted to state secretary and given the rank of lieutenant general.

Like Ulbricht, Wilhelm Zaisser, and most of the Party big shots in East Berlin, Mielke had been taken completely by surprise by the workers' revolt of June 1953. But his reaction, from Ulbricht's point of view, was commendably brutal. In a couple of weeks his leather-jacketed agents rounded up more than a thousand "ringleaders" who were jailed as "agents of the imperialist powers" (the same powers that had not lifted a finger to help them).

Three years later, when the Hungarian uprising threatened to touch off a second revolt in East Germany, the Party leaders were informed by Ernst Wollweber, the new minister of state security, that discipline had collapsed and all hell broken loose in the Leuna chemical works near Merseburg, in Saxony. Some prominent Party member must be sent there fast to pacify the restless workers. But who? There was a sudden dearth of volunteers for this ticklish assignment. The veteran Socialist, Otto Grotewohl, suggested that Fritz Selbmann, as minister of industry, was the best qualified to go. Selbmann immediately bowed out, saying he had no idea what he should say to the workers. He had recommended Bruno Leuschner, who ran the Economic Planning Board. "I've got nothing to do with individual plants," Leuschner had riposted, adding that it had to be Selbmann, or else Winkler, who ran the Department of Chemical Production. Someone else recommended Gerhard Ziller, the Central Committee secretary responsible for economic affairs.

The discussion continued in this buck-passing vein for several minutes. Ulbricht sat there saying nothing, his cheek muscles more than usually taut, his lips more than usually pursed; his cold eyes, behind the steel-rimmed glasses, stared off into space. But when he finally spoke, it was to the point. "I don't understand this discussion of yours. Yet it's all very simple. A few gentlemen who have links with the I.G. Farben works [the huge chemical company in Frankfurt] have scented which way the wind is blowing in Leuna. They want to take advantage of our present situation in order to reintroduce their I.G. Farben ideology. This is not a job for Leuschner or Selbmann or Ziller. Mielke must restore order. One must find the four or five I.G. Farben agents, *ja?* There aren't more than that of them. Once they've been found, things will quiet down in Leuna and the word will get around to the agents in other factories. Then all will go well with the plan; then all will go well with our economic policy; then all will be fine at Leuna and everywhere else— right? So I think Mielke should be sent down immediately, and then we'll see what happens next."

Mielke had accordingly been dispatched to the scene, where it had not taken him long to unearth half a dozen "I.G. Farben agents" who were promptly dragged off to jail. The "agents" in other factories immediately ran for cover, as Ulbricht had predicted, and there was no further talk of strikes or other anti-Party activities.

A few months later the man who had first tipped off his Party colleagues to the Leuna disturbances, Ernst Wollweber, lost his job as minister of state security. His crime, like his predecessor's, was to have harbored doubts about Walter Ulbricht's political and economic omniscience. He had faltered and chosen a weak rather than a strong line. But no such fault could be found in Erich Mielke, who had accordingly been chosen, in November 1957, to succeed him as minister of state security.

Walter Ulbricht had been fighting to survive for far too long in the quicksands of political intrigue to be able to relax his vigilance. But it was reassuring to realize that in Erich Mielke he had a tough minister of state security on whose loyalty he could count. Under Mielke's energetic direction, the ministry had been expanded to include fourteen thousand secret service employees, who were aided and abetted by one hundred fifty thousand paid informers in East Germany and fifteen thousand agents in the West. There was now not a citizen in the DDR who could claim not to be under the surveillance of at least one *Spitzel*. [4] Mielke's arm was also a long one—as he had proved by the more than two hundred spies, *agents provocateurs*, and *"saboteurs"* his SSD agents had managed to kidnap on West Berlin territory and bring back across the boundary into the Soviet sector.

Unfortunately this was nothing compared with the number of rebels and recalcitrants who were now fleeing the German Democratic Republic every day. The latest wanted list, established for the guidance of the Volkspolizei, contained more than forty thousand names of persons who had escaped arrest by indulging in *Republikflucht* ("flight from the Republic"), a crime punishable by anywhere up to five years imprisonment. It was all very well to have thrown a gigantic dragnet over seventeen million people, but too many escaping fish kept wriggling through.

This was not for any want of zeal on Erich Mielke's part. In 1952 the twenty thousand members of the Grenzpolizei (Grepos), the East German Border Police, had been transferred from the Ministry of the Interior to the administrative control of the Ministry of State Security. Being more exposed than ordinary Vopos to the lures of the capitalistic West, it was only logical that the

---

[4]*Spitzel*. German slang for an informer who is ordered to spy on colleagues, friends, neighbors, and even his own family.

Grepos should be subjected to particularly sharp political surveillance, lest they take advantage of their proximity to the
interzonal border to cross over into the Federal Republic. Each
Grepo was consequently required to report on the behavior of
his teammate—for there were always two border guards per
watch—and he had standing orders to shoot if his comrade tried
to make a run for it.

Although the desertion rate remained embarrassingly high,
the 1,381-kilometer border between the eastern (Soviet) and the
western (British and American) zones of occupation had been
fairly effectively sealed off, with the help of minefields, police
dogs, and a five-kilometer area that no one was allowed to enter
without a special pass. A recent directive issued to the
Grenzpolizei had been particularly explicit in recommending
measures to make the interzonal border even more hermetic
"through the erection of open, camouflaged and covered searchlights, barriers and technical installations for watch-towers, wire
barriers and obstacles, trip-wires, wire concertinas, tree-trunk
barricades, control strips and walls directly touching the border,
and if possible a second control strip farther back in the border
area. . . . "Controls," the directive had concluded, "must be carried out day and night, they must be carried out without prior
notice of time and place."

Yet these stringent measures had clearly failed in their purpose. Although the number of roads leading into West Berlin
from the surrounding countryside had been reduced in 1952
from 227 to 131, nothing remotely resembling a *Todesstreifen*
("death strip") existed along the 163-kilometer periphery of
Berlin's western sectors, where they touched the Soviet zone.
At the corresponding check points, there were Volkspolizei and
Customs posts, but the controls for the most part were perfunctory. The same held for the 22 vehicular and the 66 pedestrian crossings that existed along the 46-kilometer demarcation
line separating the Soviet from the three western sectors of
Berlin. Tram and bus communications between East and West
had been cut in 1952, but the subway and the elevated railway
still functioned normally for the entire area of Greater Berlin.
The easiest way of remedying this situation was to apply the
same stringent measures of control to the 163 kilometers of pe-

ripheral border separating the British, French, and U.S. sectors of Berlin from the surrounding Soviet zone of occupation. To be truly effective, however, such an "iron ring" around the city's western periphery would have to be extended around East Berlin as well. For with freedom of pedestrian, vehicle, and subway movement within Greater Berlin guaranteed by the four occupying powers, there was virtually nothing to keep an East German, once he had reached East Berlin, from crossing over into one of the western sectors. But the construction of a hermetic *Todesstreifen* between East Berlin and East Germany would inevitably reinforce the validity of the Four-Power agreements, which specified that Greater Berlin, unlike other German cities, was a separate metropolitan area with a juridical status of its own.

For Walter Ulbricht, as for his pistol-loving minister of state security, such a notion was heresy. There could be no question of legitimizing agreements that were defunct now that the DDR had been recognized as sovereign by the Soviet Union. Something else would have to be found to close the gaping hole in Erich Mielke's net, a hole through which dissidents, malcontents, misfits, hooligans, reactionaries, and counterrevolutionary elements of every hue—in a word, all who had succumbed to the blandishments of Western propaganda and who could not adapt themselves to conditions in the Workers-and-Peasants-State—were now pouring like shoals of frightened fish.

5

In the chancellor's office in Bonn, as usual, all seemed quiet, unruffled, serene. No storms, no matter how tempestuous, seemed able to disturb the thick-carpeted tranquillity of this room, beyond whose windows one could see the leafy trees of the Palais Schaumburg's garden and sense the faint shimmer of the Rhine. The familiar objects were there, exactly as they had been the last time that Hans Kroll, ambassador to Russia, had called: an old grandfather clock; the painting of a Greek temple against a bright Hellenic sky (a personal gift of its artist, Winston Churchill, to Konrad Adenauer); two old prints of Rome, given to him by Alcide de Gasperi; a fourteenth-century sculptured Madonna, presented to him by his cabinet on his seventy-fifth birthday, and near one window, a revolving globe, offered to him on his eightieth; and another painting, of a mountain landscape, above the polished cabinet behind his desk. Only the desk seemed to have changed—or, more exactly, the documents and reports piled on its shiny surface, as well as the Rhöndorf roses in the delicate, decanter-shaped vase.

The chancellor himself seemed sprightlier than ever, for all his five-and-eighty years. His parchmentlike, Tibetan face betrayed no trace of anxiety—to the considerable surprise of his ambassador, who had left Moscow with a feeling of vague alarm after learning from his American colleague, Llewellyn Thompson, that John Kennedy had been "floored" by Khrushchev's aggressive behavior and inflexibility.

So highly did Konrad Adenauer regard the exceptionally gifted envoy who stood before him that the previous February he had even thought of making him state secretary (the number two man) in the West German Foreign Ministry. He had been talked out of it by his old friend Heinrich Krone, parliamentary leader of the Christian Democrats, who had pointed out that Kroll, given his outspoken nature and heretical views, would soon be at serious odds with Heinrich von Brentano, the anything-but-adventurous foreign minister of the Bonn Republic.

A native of Upper Silesia, Hans Kroll had long been attracted by things Slavic, as Germans of the East so often are. Although he had no sympathy for communism, he was thoroughly at home in Russian, a language he had mastered during a tour of duty in the early 1920s as embassy secretary and consul in Moscow and Odessa. This skill had enabled him over the past four years to establish a unique rapport with the most forceful member of the ruling Kremlin team.

More than Russophilia had been needed, however, to tame the irascible Nikita. And if there was one person who was well placed to know what it felt like to be floored by Khrushchev, it was Hans Kroll. At one of his first public appearances in

Moscow—an Independence Day reception given by the Indian embassy—Khrushchev had advanced on him without warning, seized him by his jacket lapel, and begun shouting, "Your government has rejected my peace offers! So you want another war? You want to march on Moscow for a third time? The Federal Republic is arming and trying to obtain atomic weapons! Your policy is guided by militarism, a spirit of revenge, revisionism!"

While the other guests had looked on in stupefaction, Kroll had kept reminding himself of the advice Adenauer had given him before he had left Bonn for this new post: "Whatever happens, remain cool. Don't let yourself be provoked. As you will discover, Khrushchev, though wily and intelligent, is also impulsive and wrathful. But even if he resorts to insults, you must try to get on with him."

Even his detractors had to admit that Hans Kroll had succeeded in this last respect to a quite extraordinary degree. Almost as short, though not as stout as his assailant, Kroll on the occasion of their first major confrontation had let Khrushchev work his long diatribe up to a crescendo: "So here is your Federal chancellor! In one hand he holds a cross, in the other an atomic bomb! And he claims to be a good Christian! But with such intentions he hasn't a hope of reaching paradise. For such men another place has been foreseen!"

At this point Kroll had stopped him. The West Germans wanted peace as much as the Russians, he had pointed out. But they weren't going to accept a *diktat*; they weren't going to be browbeaten into accepting another Treaty of Versailles. Startled by the vigor of this counterattack, Khrushchev had finally asked in an almost peevish tone, "So our treaty proposal doesn't interest you?"

"Why yes," Kroll had replied, "there's one article in it we can accept. The one in which you propose to renounce reparations payments." Khrushchev's eyes had brightened as he burst into laughter.

It hadn't taken Kroll long to realize that many Soviet leaders, notwithstanding their ideological commitments, really preferred dealing with the more relaxed and expansive West Germans than with the secretive representatives of the German Democratic Republic. Khrushchev in particular made no bones about it. During their very first meeting in his Kremlin office, he declared that friendly relations between Russians and Germans—"the two most important peoples in Europe"—were essential to the future well-being of the continent. But when Kroll pointed out that there was one major obstacle to any such détente—Walter Ulbricht, whose callous despotism was responsible for maintaining a state of permanent tension between East Germany and the Federal Republic—Khrushchev had listened glumly and made no effort to contradict him. At diplomatic receptions he obviously preferred the company of the "brutally frank" Hans Kroll to that of the totally colorless Rudolf Dölling, a dour Sudeten German whom Ulbricht had chosen to represent the DDR in Moscow.

Just eight months before, during the traditional November 7 reception in the Kremlin's glittering St. George's Hall, Khrushchev had pointedly ignored Walter Ulbricht, Otto Grotewohl, and almost all the other Communist leaders who had traveled to Moscow to celebrate the anniversary of the October Revolution of 1917. After exchanging a few words with Wladislaw Gomulka of Poland, Khrushchev had buttonholed Hans Kroll, as he had so often done in the past, and drawn him over to one side, along with Mikoyan and Alexei Kosygin. If, Khrushchev suggested, Chancellor Adenauer really showed a willingness to normalize Soviet-German relations, then one thing was certain: He would win the next elections, due to be held in September 1961, hands down. Kroll had asked the Soviet leader if he really wanted the chancellor to win. Khrushchev, without a moment's hesitation, had answered Yes. Mikoyan and Kosygin had hastened to agree. Adenauer, they insisted, was the only German big and strong enough to be able to get his people to accept the bitter pill they would have to swallow in the interests of lasting peace.

Not content with this, Khrushchev had then come up with a large glass of vodka, placed it in the ambassador's hand, and insisted that they drink a toast. Kroll, who had been suffering from circulatory problems, asked if they couldn't drink a toast out of smaller glasses. But Khrushchev was adamant. They were going to drink, and out of *these* glasses. He got Mikoyan and Kosygin to back him up, adding, "I will bet with you, Mr. Ambassador, that you will empty your glass." Then raising his voice so that everyone within earshot—including Ulbricht and Grotewohl—could hear, he cried, "Comrades, I ask you to drink with the German ambassador, and to the health of Federal Chancellor Adenauer."

Kroll was too experienced a diplomat not to realize that there was as much calculated flattery as genuine sentiment in the compliments and attention he kept receiving from different Soviet leaders. But he was convinced that the only way to achieve a reunification of Germany—a reunification that would automatically solve the ticklish problem of Berlin—was by improving relations with the Russians. Arranging trade deals and credits and having West German industrialists visit the Soviet Union wasn't enough; he wanted his government to respond to each Soviet overture, even if it meant entering into bilateral negotiations. Only the Germans, he believed—and by that he meant the Bonn government—could reasonably be expected to defend the fundamental interests of all Germans, east as well as west of the Elbe. To expect the British or the French to do so was naive. Their interests were different, if not diametrically opposed—notably on the reunification issue. As for the Americans, they had demonstrated a singular capacity for slovenly diplomacy at Teheran in 1943, with the London accords of 1944 (which had first defined the future occupation zones and the "island" of Berlin in postwar Germany), and at the Yalta and Potsdam conferences of 1945.

Given the marks of special favor accorded him by the top men in the Kremlin, it was imperative, Kroll felt, that Bonn seize the olive branch and open direct negotiations at the highest level. But back home he had run into a stone wall. A long after-dinner conversation had left the cautious Heinrich von Brentano only half convinced. Konrad Adenauer was equally skeptical. Direct negotiations with the Russians were out of the question. The Americans would be alarmed—they were so touchy about such things. The Austrian precedent of 1955 was misleading and did not apply to an entirely different set of circumstances in Germany. To agree to a peace treaty first—a peace treaty that would leave West Germany partially disarmed—in the expectation that it would be followed by a promised reunification, was too risky to be satisfactory.

All Kroll had been able to obtain was the chancellor's agreement to start a personal exchange of letters with Khrushchev. The effect in Moscow had been almost electric. So much so that during the New Year's festivities of the preceding January, Khrushchev had dragged Kroll out into the Kremlin Grand Palace's winter garden, had plied him with champagne and encouraged Kosygin and Mikoyan to toast him as "the ambassador of *all* the Germans." Khrushchev had followed up in April by inviting him to his Crimean dacha at Gagra, where, between games of badminton and dips in his heated pool, he had finally declared that to spare Chancellor Adenauer undue embarrassment, he would not sign a separate peace treaty with the German Democratic Republic until the West German elections were over. He might even wait until after the Soviet Communist Party Congress, scheduled for October. "Or perhaps even until the spring of 1962," he had added reflectively, as he and Kroll sat on the spacious terrace, enjoying the warmth and the magnificent view over the sunlit sea.

The next day Khrushchev had arranged to have Kroll driven to the airport with a lavish bouquet of Crimean roses for his wife. The West German ambassador's visit to Gagra—the first ever made by a foreign envoy—was given unusual prominence in *Pravda*, and for days thereafter he was pestered for more details by members of the Moscow press corps. His fellow ambassadors—the United States' Llewellyn Thompson, Britain's Sir Frank Roberts, France's Maurice Dejean—all agreed that Khrushchev's apparent willingness to delay the signing of a separate peace treaty until October, and perhaps even until early 1962, was of major significance. This would give the West time to work out a coordinated strategy for dealing with the Berlin crisis.

Then had come the summit meeting in Vienna. Kroll had not yet been able to obtain the Soviet leader's own account of the meeting, but he was familiar enough with Khrushchev's domineering ways to fear the worst. Khrushchev's visit to the United States in 1959 had similarly aroused vain hopes. Neither the overpublicized Camp David meeting nor the tour of Roswell Garst's hybrid corn farm in Iowa had made any appreciable dent in his Communist fanaticism. But the boomerang effect of the

Vienna meeting could be far more troubling for the future peace of the world.

Konrad Adenauer, on the other hand, was extraordinarily sanguine. Kennedy, he felt, had stood fast on the essentials, and had made it clear that the United States was not going to renege on its Berlin commitments. The mere fact that the two leaders had met seemed to him auspicious and likely to open a hopeful new phase in international relations. Khrushchev in the past had always stressed the fact that John Foster Dulles was out to destroy communism. With such a determined adversary, a modus vivendi was difficult, if not impossible. Kennedy was more elastic and easygoing in his attitude to foreign countries, and thus more likely to concur with Khrushchev's conception of peaceful coexistence. One could thus envisage the prospect of a general and properly supervised disarmament, and of a definite détente between East and West.

Foreign Minister Heinrich von Brentano seemed to share the chancellor's buoyant optimism, whereas Kroll was frankly skeptical. He didn't feel that speculations about differences in attitudes between Dulles and Kennedy were going to get them anywhere. But if the chancellor was really committed to his ideas about Kennedy and Dulles, he should try them out on the Soviet leader.

Von Brentano once again seemed shocked by the suggestion. "Mr. Ambassador, you don't seriously mean that Mr. Adenauer should meet Khrushchev?"

"Yes, precisely, and why not?" was Kroll's reply. "That's exactly what I mean. In such a serious situation all possibilities must be considered."

Adenauer, looking more impassive than ever, refused to commit himself. He did not share his foreign minister's indignation nor his ambassador's enthusiasm for a personal meeting with Khrushchev. The suggestion was again allowed to die a quiet death.

The conversation soon broadened to include other Western leaders. The suspicions he had long harbored against Macmillan were unjustified, the chancellor now explained. He had come to the conclusion that the British prime minister was a "soft speaker" but a "hard actor." In that case, Kroll suggested, why not ask him to write a personal letter to Khrushchev, spelling out the British government's firm resolve on the Berlin question? "What matters is not what we think of Macmillan, but far more what Khrushchev thinks of him." Adenauer and von Brentano agreed that this was not a bad idea and might be worth pursuing.

The fact that at Gagra, Khrushchev had indicated that he would not sign a separate peace treaty with East Germany until October at the earliest struck Adenauer as significant and reassuring. He too was now convinced that nothing dramatic would happen before the conclusion of the West German elections. Kroll, however, was less sure. The Americans, so Llewellyn Thompson had indicated to him in Moscow, were now going to have to rearm on a massive scale. The Soviets were bound to react with a similar effort of their own. All this meant a deteriorating climate in which the unsolved problem of Berlin could lead the world to the brink of war at any time.

But there was no shaking the chancellor's tranquil optimism. This was one of his rosy days. He recalled the impression Kennedy had made on him during his visit to Washington in early April, shortly before the Bay of Pigs disaster. "He seems to be clear-headed. He is of course still very young and he has a lot to learn. But I am convinced that he will be reelected. After that," he continued in the same tranquil vein, "Vice-President Lyndon Johnson will succeed him. Which means that we can count on the continuity of American policy for a period of twelve years. And as I get on very well with Johnson, I will certainly be able to work with him."

Kroll at this point could not repress a laugh.

"What do you find so funny?" inquired Adenauer dryly.

"But Herr Bundeskanzler, from now until then there are still eight years to go."

"Well," was the imperturbable reply, "and what then?" The chancellor, after all, was only eighty-five, and the idea that he would still be running the Federal Republic at the age of ninety-three did not strike him as either improbable or strange.

6

The mid-June sun was beginning to disappear behind the gabled rooftops, lengthening the shadow cast by the equestrian statue of Duke Carl August over the warm cobbles of the Platz der Demokratie, as Erika Horn made her way toward the river. She didn't want to leave Weimar without a farewell walk over the Sternbrücke. A peculiar thrill came over her each time she glimpsed the almost perfect ovals formed by the stone bridge's graceful arches and their shimmering reflections. Their charm never failed to work on her, even when the reflections were pitted by falling raindrops or ruffled by the wind.

Was it because the bridge was off the beaten track, undisturbed by the tedious babble of guides herding their flocks of shuffling sightseers from one famous landmark to another? Or was it because it led on to the park, still peopled, in her imagination, with the glamorous ghosts of the past? Both, perhaps. Here, in any case, even when there was no one else in sight, she never felt alone. Always vividly present were the gracious Duchess Anna Amalia, the devoted Wieland, the cranky and disgruntled Herder; and even that silk-stockinged sot, Graf von Stolberg, unable to contain his astonishment over Their Highnesses' acceptance of untitled commoners: *Man geht mit ihnen um, ganz als wären's Menschen wie unsereiner* ("They [that is, simple burghers like Goethe or Schiller] are treated here exactly as though they were people like ourselves"). How she and her classmates had laughed when their teacher had quoted that idiotic remark, as a commentary on the society that had produced it.

Now, as she watched the bridge's reflections, she felt something of that "peace which passeth all understanding," as Paul had put it in one of his Epistles—Epistles which her brother, Joachim, and she had had to read at home with their mother, since at school they were dismissed, along with Christ and the New Testament, as the ridiculous superstition of the ignorant and unreformed. And yet the "peace" which *they*—the teachers, newspapers, and Party members—had forever on their lips, as though it were another Marxist invention—was something that passed *their* understanding in a quite different sense. None of them could understand any need to get away from everyone and everything for a while, to be alone with one's thoughts and reveries. For them this kind of withdrawal was and would always be a manifestation of antisocial behavior. But Goethe had understood this need, which was why he, who could have chosen any number of bigger and more glamorous capitals—like Maria Theresa's Vienna, the Berlin of Frederick the Great, or Saxon Dresden—had preferred this diminutive and heavily indebted duchy, with its thirty-four square miles of surrounding land.

O Weimar! dir fiel besonder Los!/Wie Bethlehem in Juda, klein und gross. ("Oh, Weimar! Chosen for a special fate!/Like Bethlehem in Judah, small and great.") The great poet had not wanted to become involved in the national rivalries and dynastic squabbles of his day; he had preferred the placid backwaters of the little Ilm. Yet even here he had been pursued by war. First the Prussians and then the French, after the battle of Jena, had invaded the innocent little town, emptying the cellars, chasing the squealing womenfolk, and using the furniture for firewood—as they had done in Goethe's own *Gartenhaus* by these very waters.

This, she had been taught at school, was how imperialists always behave. Violence and destruction come as naturally to them as looting and plunder. This was how the Nazis had behaved in the Soviet Union, how British and American flyers had behaved in reducing Dresden (that "Florence on the Elbe") to burnt stone and ashes in February of 1945. And not only Dresden. In that same month, Weimar too had been hit—"imperialist" bombs falling on the old Renaissance guild houses of the Marktplatz and so weakening their beautifully sculptured façades that they had later been torn down completely. Goethe's *Gartenhaus*, as well as his later home on the Frauenplan; Schiller's ocher-hued house with the curiously broad, single-panelled shutters on the ground-floor windows; the tall-roofed Wittumspalais in which Anna Amalia had made her home; the National Theater in which Franz Liszt had staged the world premiere of Wagner's *Lohengrin* in 1850—all had come in for their share of destruction. The imperialists had even unloaded a bomb or two on the old town church with its Lucas Cranach altarpiece and the organ on which, for five fruitful years, Johann Sebastian Bach had practiced and performed some of his finest compositions.

"How can these imperialists be so savage?" she had asked her mother not once but many times after learning about all these dreadful things at school.

Her mother, with a sad shake of her head, had been wont to reply, "My child, war is a form of madness; and in time of war even the wisest lose their heads."

Erika was only three when these events had happened—too young to recall most of the destruction. But she still had a vivid recollection of the heaps of masonry around which she and her mother had had to pick their way when walking through the cobbled streets. Even more vivid was her memory of the almost ceaseless hunger that had stalked them for months, indeed, years thereafter. Her father, who had been drafted into the Wehrmacht, had been killed on the Russian front in 1944, and his *Drogerie*—where soaps, combs, brushes, towels, perfumes, bathrobes, and every imaginable kind of shoe and floor wax and furniture polish were dispensed—later had had to be sold.

Aided by a meager widow's pension, Erika's mother barely had had enough to keep herself and her two children alive during their early years of schooling. She even had had to sell their old Bechstein piano, inherited from a music-loving aunt before the war. She had sold it to a Russian officer who had heard her playing it one day as he was passing the house. He had walked over and knocked on the front door. Joachim had rushed to his mother's side, crying, "Mother, mother, don't open! Don't open!" Even as children they knew what happened when one let Russians into one's home—or so they thought. For then the strangest thing had happened. Instead of pounding on the door with all his might and shouting and swearing bloody murder, as Russians so often did when they came reeling out of their officers' club, this one had said in an almost meek and surprisingly intelligible voice, *"Ich auch liebe Schumann—spielen Sie bitte weiter!"* ("I too love Schumann—please play on!"). He had repeated the phrase several times, first behind the door and then by one of the windows, which happened to be open since it was a warm summer evening, rather like the present one. Not knowing what to do, their mother had resumed her playing, nervously at first and then with growing confidence as she realized with relief that she was not about to be assaulted by a drunken barbarian. When the little concert had ended, he had even thanked her with almost exaggerated politeness, clicking his boot heels in comically Prussian style and making a slight bow.

This visit was the first of several, all equally embarrassing for their widowed mother, who could already imagine the neighbors' caustic tattling. But notwithstanding the bouquets he brought or the stilted compliments he paid her, it finally dawned on her that it was not her person but the piano that really interested this Schumann and Tchaikovsky lover. And so, after considerable haggling over the price, the piano had been sold and driven away in a weather-beaten Soviet army truck. Her mother steadfastly had refused to tell her how much she had got for the piano. All she had said at the time was, "I might as well sell it to someone who has some appreciation for music, for if I refuse, they can always requisition this house and take it away for nothing." But the loss of her treasured Bechstein had been bitterly felt for years. "And I who had such fond hopes—" she would sometimes say to her daughter, running her hand through her blond curls, "such hopes of having you take lessons in the Franz Liszt Hochschule" (the music school for advanced students and performers which was housed in the pillared palace of Weimar's one-time princes).

Erika, in any case, was not musically gifted. She had an eye for beauty—or so her mother assured her—but when it came to using pencils or brushes, she lacked the steadiness of hand that had enabled her brother to get a job at a nearby porcelain factory. How she had labored, seated on a camp stool by the riverside, to capture the lovely arches of the Sternbrücke and their quivering reflections. But the proportions were never right, the curves were clumsily drawn, and the water looked like anything but water.

Not until her fifteenth year had she begun to realize for what she might be destined. For her birthday her mother had given

her a little camera. She had spent hours wandering through the
old streets and squares, taking snapshots of her favorite façades
and roofs, choosing the moments when the angle of the sun was
most favorable for bringing out certain sculptured details. Encouraged by the photographer from whom she bought her film,
she began experimenting with orange, red, and yellow filters to
enhance the dramatic effect of cloud cumuli and sunsets.

Her adolescent efforts were so promising that one day the
photographer had offered her a job. "I can't pay you much, but I
can teach you what I know. And I badly need someone who has
an eye for effects to help me with my darkroom work."

Erika had jumped at the opportunity, feeling that she had
discovered a vocation at last. Her mother too was pleased,
saying once again, "Didn't I always say you have an eye for
beauty?"

For the first few months she was allowed to work in peace as
she mastered the art of developing negatives, making prints and
enlargements, reducing or heightening contrasts through careful
shadings of exposure. But the bitter disappointments were not
long in coming. The trouble was that she and her employer got
on well—too well to suit the local FDGB (trade union) officials.
He had long resisted efforts to incorporate him in the photographic guild, run by Party hacks who knew nothing about photography. To have resisted their repeated overtures was bad
enough; to have taken on an apprentice who was equally "nonso-
cial" in her outlook and enthusiasms made it worse.

Erika, who had hoped to forget her unhappy years of schooling, now found her past being held up as a reproach. To be sure,
at the Volksschule she, along with every other girl and boy in
her class, had been forced to join the *Young Pioneers* and to
parade around in blue scarfs and caps, white shirts, and black
skirts or trousers. Every morning when the flag was raised above
the schoolyard, they had been taught to spring to attention and
to salute, with the right hand held so high that the fingers
touched the crown of the head. They had been trained to sing
revolutionary songs and martial chants in well-regimented
unison. The drill, as much mental as it was physical, had included long propaganda sessions. Martin Luther was exposed as
a traitor and a sixteenth-century capitalist because he had dared

oppose the Anabaptist socialism of the "progressive" Thomas Münzer. The Right Reverend Otto Dibelius, the bishop of Berlin and Brandenburg (who had his episcopal seat in West Berlin), was denounced as a bomb-loving villain bent on leading astray the peace-loving and progressive youth of the DDR. Konrad Adenauer—another worshipper of atom bombs—was the Evil One on earth, a twentieth-century incarnation of Satan. God did not exist: No high-altitude flyer had ever bumped into him majestically seated on his nimbused throne. There had been the outings to nearby Buchenwald—sometimes in buses, more frequently on foot—where the abominable iniquities of the Hitler-Fascists were revealed to them in harrowing detail, and where they were lectured on how different things now were in the Workers-and-Peasants-State. And finally, as a supreme climax to all those years of indoctrination, they had been made to attend a Dedication of Youth ceremony that was intended to replace the traditional confirmation ceremonies of the church with a kind of youth rally festival, at which trumpets blared, drums were rolled, battle songs were sung, and the heroic strains of Beethoven's *Egmont* Overture, emphasized the import of the gift books and certificates distributed to the most deserving.

But after six years of youthful militancy, Erika had decided she had had her fill. She was damned if she was going to join the FDJ on reaching the age of fourteen, although her brother, Joachim, had, afraid that not joining would jeopardize his chances of advancement.

At sixteen it was still not too late to join the FDJ, she was informed by Party activists, who now dropped in to the photography shop for a chat, or else summoned her and her employer to a trade-union meeting. The pressure was maintained for months, but neither of them gave in. Frustrated in their direct approach, the union officials then resorted to more subtle forms of persuasion. The high-quality film or paper needed for their work suddenly ceased to be available from the wholesale suppliers in Wolfen. Lenses and filters could no longer be replaced; they found themselves having to make do with increasingly outmoded equipment.

Regularly, at meetings with union officials, it was drummed

into them that "by 1965 we'll have overtaken West Germany," and apparently in every field of activity. In 1958 there had been a lot of cheering in the press and on the radio when rationing at last was done away with. But now, three years later, it was back with a vengeance—with no meat in the butcher shops, butter rationed to 250 grams a week, and coupons even having to be reissued for potatoes.

Politically, the situation was as bleak as ever. The prospect of free elections and a reunification of Germany had all but vanished from the horizon. The previous year, Weimar had acquired a new mayor—Luitpold Steidle, an ex-Nazi who had surrendered to the Russians at Stalingrad (where he had supposedly "seen the light"), and who had later ingratiated himself with the authorities as a prominent member of a Communist-manipulated front. Such a man was in no mood to bite the hand of his patron and protector, Alois Bräutigam, the Party secretary for their district, who was usually referred to in the Horn household as the *Oberschwein* ("top pig") or Gauleiter of Erfurt.

At home they had often discussed the possibility of emigrating as a family to the Federal Republic. But Joachim was too keen on his work in the porcelain factory and their mother too devoted to the few remaining family portraits and pieces of furniture to contemplate a change. Besides, they had heard from friends and kinsmen that life in the Federal Republic—which had had to absorb ten million refugees from the lost provinces of East Prussia, Silesia, Sudetenland, and the territories beyond the Oder—was not all milk and roses.

Erika's employer had recently confessed to her that he had had it. But whether this meant that he was planning anything specific she did not know. That question was one she did not dare discuss even with him; there was always the chance of their being overheard by somebody who could denounce them to the authorities for attempted *Republikflucht*.

She herself had made up her mind to leave. Walter Ulbricht, in a newspaper interview, had recently announced that "never will Bonn rule all of Germany." Backed by Russian tanks and soldiers, like those stationed just outside of Weimar on the road to Buchenwald, Ulbricht's DDR seemed here to stay. She had no prospect of succeeding as an independent photographer under these circumstances. Waiting passively for the man of her life might prove equally disillusioning. Either he would turn out to be a Party sympathizer—which would bring on a fatal quarrel sooner or later—or he would find his chances of advancement blocked in whatever career or trade he had chosen.

Sorrowfully she retraced her steps from the little river, making a detour through the quaintly cobbled Seifengasse ("Soap Street"). She had not yet dared broach the subject to her mother. Indeed, so much had she dreaded this moment that she had put it off week after anguished week. But she couldn't put it off any longer. Joachim had been sent to Dresden for a month of special training in ceramics but was due to return the next day. Winning over her mother would be difficult enough, but against their combined strength she could not prevail.

Not until after supper—a frugal meal of carrot soup and spinach, accompanied by a slice of cheese—did she pluck up enough courage to break the news. There was a moment of long silence during which Erika could hear their breathing. Her mother sat very still on the couch next to her, her eyes seemingly fixed on the grandfather clock on the other side of the room. Then they filled, and two tears rolled slowly down her cheeks.

"Oh, mother!" cried Erika, seizing her two clasped hands. "I've changed my mind. I'm not going! I can't bear to see you suffer like this. Please, please, forget everything I've said."

"No, my child," said her mother, pressing her daughter's hands so tightly that it hurt. "No, you must go. You are right. I know it, we all know it. There is no future for you here. Don't worry about me. Joachim will take care of me. In any case, I'm too old to try to start all over again. But you who are young must make a better life for yourself over there."

The next day, seated in the train that was carrying her north toward Berlin, Erika watched the fields and valleys recede, the woods flash by in bursts of greenery. But her thoughts were elsewhere. As though reflected in the windowpane, her mother's tear-streaked face kept looming up before her. Bravely she had sought to stifle her feelings, but Erika could guess what was going on inside her: She was reliving that dreadful moment in 1944 when the news had reached her that her beloved

Thomas had died on the eastern front. Thomas Horn—the unfamiliar father Erika had never really known except from photographs. And now her mother was losing her only daughter.

After an infinitely painful silence, a few words had trickled from that pathetically twitching mouth. "Twenty-eight years, my child . . . twenty-eight long years this has lasted, and the end is not yet in sight."

Erika was barely twenty—her whole life was eight years less than the total span of human suffering her mother had accumulated under successive tyrannies. Yet it was she who was now running away. The thought made her miserable.

Beyond the train window the moving landscape suddenly dissolved, and she realized she was crying.

7

To emphasize the solemnity of the occasion—the highlight of this Thursday, June 15—the rows of tables laid out across the vast banquet hall had been covered with white linen, glasses, and an imposing array of beer and mineral-water bottles. The assembled newsmen could thus wet their throats before directing their questions to the stage, where, flanked by massed flags and flowers, half a dozen red-draped desks had been pushed together to form a dais.

Targeted by batteries of television floodlights, six men were now seated behind the altarlike desks, beneath the emblem of the German Democratic Republic: an upright hammer intersecting the angle formed by a pair of compass dividers. Some were familiar, others virtually unknown to the 350 journalists who had crowded into the hall. The small, intense, dark-haired figure on the extreme left, as one looked at the stage, was Hermann Axen, the forty-five-year-old editor of the daily *Neues Deutschland*. His neighbor was a distinctly older, white-haired expert in diplomacy, Gerhard Kegel, who had been a member of the East German delegation to the Foreign Ministers Conference at Geneva in 1959. At the other end of the podium, his beady eyes magnified by round bifocals, sat the spidery Gerhard Eisler, chairman of the East German State Radio Committee. A former Comintern official who had managed to elude a four-year prison term for Soviet espionage in the United States by smuggling himself aboard a Polish steamer, this Goebbels of the DDR, as his enemies liked to call him, had coined the AMI, GO HOME! slogan of the early 1950s. Next to him, looking appropriately thoughtful with his fluffy gray hair and knitted brows, was Albert Norden, the regime's official philosopher. The center of the podium was occupied by the youngish-looking Kurt Blecha, a Nazi-party member turned Communist who headed the governmental press office. But it was the person seated to his right who was the focus of attention. The familiar goatee and rimless glasses needed no introduction. They belonged to the man who had recently taken a leaf from Nikita Khrushchev's book by making himself the chairman of a new State Council, a post that placed him at the head of the country's administrative as well as Party apparatus.

It was not often that Walter Ulbricht exposed himself to western as well as eastern newspapermen, and he was taking no chances. He wanted to create the impression that he was only a first among equals and thus the spokesman for a collective leadership.

In this same banquet hall, then part of his vast Air Ministry, Hermann Goering had often wined and dined his fellow pilots and bombardiers. Notwithstanding its cyclopean dimensions—it was a good quarter mile long—the headquarters building had miraculously escaped destruction during the many Allied air raids that had flattened most of the other official edifices on the once proud Wilhelmstrasse. Renamed the House of Ministries, it had undergone a postwar transformation as the administrative home of four East German departments: Forestry, Trade, Water Supply, and Agriculture.

Although he had little taste for public encounters of this kind—in this respect too he was the exact opposite of Nikita Khrushchev—Ulbricht was determined to force the pace of their offensive. Bonn was already beating a retreat in the face of Soviet pressure. After first declaring that until 1959 both the upper and lower houses of the federal parliament had regularly met in Berlin without arousing objections from the USSR, the West Germans had suddenly backed down. The president of Bonn's upper chamber, Franz Meyers, had let it be known that the Bundesrat would not after all be meeting in Berlin on June 16.

This, for Walter Ulbricht, was new proof of what he had been contending all along: that if unrelenting pressure were brought to bear on the Allies, they would eventually give way. It was a waste of time treating these gentlemen with kid gloves. Much more could be obtained by kicking them resolutely in the shins.

Before answering individual questions, Walter Ulbricht began with a few introductory remarks. A peace treaty for Germany and a solution of the West Berlin problem were on the agenda for 1961. The Soviet proposals were contained in the memorandum that the chairman of the Council of Ministers of the USSR (Khrushchev) had handed to the president of the United States in Vienna. They had been approved the day before at the meeting of the Central Committee. Since the Vienna meeting, Ulbricht claimed, his office had been swamped with questioning letters, which was why he had decided to call this press conference. The USSR was offering Germany a great opportunity for a "German rebirth"; the peace treaty would be a major contribution to the cause of peaceful coexistence and German reunification.

Most of this information was old hat and of no interest to the members of the Western press. The first questions, and especially those put to him by East German correspondents, elicited the same standard replies. The German Democratic Republic was deeply interested in the Kennedy-Khrushchev meeting in Vienna because it served the cause of peace. The DDR was ready to enter into negotiations with the Federal Republic "tomorrow or the day after." It was ridiculous to claim that the proposals contained in the Soviet memorandum were a *diktat*. The Soviet memorandum was full of positive and constructive proposals, and so on.

More interesting was the answer, or more exactly the answers, made to a three-pronged query from the correspondent of the West German weekly *Spiegel*. How would a

free-city solution for West Berlin affect the economic and
financial aid provided by the Federal Republic, the ability of
refugees to enter West Berlin, and control of the access
routes? The free city of West Berlin, Ulbricht reassured his
questioner, would be free to make whatever economic or
financial agreements it wished with any country of the world.
But, he went on, moving to the second point, "the enticing of
human beings away from the capital of the DDR belongs to
the methods of the Cold War. Many espionage agencies—
West German, American, English, French—which are based
in West Berlin, are involved in *Menschenhandel.* [5] For us it
goes without saying that the so-called refugee camps in West
Berlin will be closed down, and that those persons who are
involved in Menschenhandel will leave West Berlin."

The third part of the query was astutely side-stepped. Movements between the two parts of Germany (East and West) must
be controlled by law, as was the general international practice.
Any East German wishing to settle in the Federal Republic
could do so by obtaining the permission of the Ministry of the
Interior of the DDR, just as any West German could move to
the DDR with the permission of the Federal Republic's Ministry
of the Interior.

The next questioner was Norman Gelb, of the Mutual Broadcasting System. "Mr. Chairman, the American Senator Mansfield proposed yesterday that the whole of Berlin, East *and* West
Berlin, should become a free city placed under the protection of
an international organization. What do you have to say about
this?"

The question was easily disposed of. "I do not know Senator
Mansfield and his statement," was the answer delivered in the
familiar high-pitched voice. "I adhere to the official declarations
of the United States government. For the time being they
suffice. Besides, the capital of the German Democratic Republic
is not something that is negotiable."

Norman Gelb was followed by Annamarie Doherr, the short,

---

[5]*Menschenhandel.* Literally translated, this term means "man trade." But the typically East German term carries strongly perjorative overtones of slave trade, dra-
gooning, underhanded recruiting, and so forth.

plump correspondent of the *Frankfurter Rundschau,* a newspaper known to be favorable to the West German Socialists. "Mr.
Chairman, does the creation of a 'free city,' as you term it, mean
that the state boundaries of the German Democratic Republic
will be erected at the Brandenburg Gate?"

The question was a sharp one and of vital interest to all. If
West Berlin was to become a free city, was it to be severed from
the Soviet sector by a state frontier similar to the interzonal
border—one which might one day become as impermeable and
difficult to cross as the five-kilometer "death strip" that now
divided East from West Germany? Ulbricht's eyes behind the
rimless lenses betrayed no emotion. "I understand your question as implying that there are people in West Germany who
would like to see us mobilize the construction workers of the
capital of the DDR for the purpose of building a wall. I am not
aware of any such intention. The construction workers of our
capital are for the most part busy building apartment houses,
and their working capacities are fully employed to that end.
Nobody intends to put up a wall. I have said it before: We are in
favor of regulating the relations between West Berlin and the
government of the German Democratic Republic through a
treaty. This is the simplest and most normal way of settling these
questions."

The correspondent for the London *Daily Mail* wanted to know
if the travel rights for all Germans, East or West, should not be
"anchored" in the projected peace treaty. The reply was
breathtaking to those unaccustomed to the tone of the eastern
press. "The freedom of movement of Germans inside of Germany is presently being hindered by the West German government. Citizens of the German Democratic Republic who have
been coming to West Germany, who have been having normal
conversations with West German citizens and making family
visits, are presently being arrested in West Germany in ever-increasing numbers. This means that West Germany has erected
an iron curtain." Adenauer, Ulbricht went on, to back up this
curious contention, had even spoken out against sport meetings
between East German and West German athletes. But this kind
of veto would automatically disappear once a peace treaty was
signed—a peace treaty that would automatically put an end to

"the free movement of the militarists and of the espionage agencies of Herr Strauss."

A *Daily Telegraph* correspondent wanted to know if Walter Ulbricht would be prepared to hold independently controlled elections or a plebiscite in East Germany, such as the West Germans were prepared to hold in the Federal Republic on the question of German reunification. The reply revealed a subtle dialectician who knew all the answers. A plebiscite, to be meaningful, had to serve the cause of peace. "We are therefore in favor of a plebiscite on the subject of general and complete disarmament in Germany. We are for a plebiscite on the subject of a peace treaty, on the subject of negotiations between the two German states. This is the real issue."

John Peet of *German Democratic Report*, an English-language fortnightly put out in East Berlin, asked Ulbricht what he thought of recent American reports of armored columns being readied in West Germany, ready to stage a breakthrough at Helmstedt if there was any interference in normal autobahn traffic. "What madness!" replied Ulbricht, raising his hands in disbelief. "We simply will not and cannot believe that the USA will feel the need and ambition to be branded before the whole world as aggressors against the DDR and the Soviet Union. This we regard as not possible."

Ellen Lentz of the *New York Times* then asked him if the Tempelhof Airfield, in the case of an agreement, would be "put out of action." The blunt question provoked laughter in the hall. "This does not depend on me," was the subtle reply. "Perhaps the airport will close itself down. . . . Think of the West Berliners. Today they are constantly disturbed by the noise of airplanes, and they are exposed to the danger of planes crashing into buildings, as happened in Munich" (a reference to an American C-53 that had crashed in the center of Munich in December of the previous year).

The *Spiegel* correspondent returned to the attack, trying to pin Ulbricht down on the question of airline passenger controls for persons seeking political asylum. This question too was fielded with aplomb. The DDR, being a sovereign state, would exercise its right to stamp the passports of persons flying in or out of its territory, just as British officials did at the London airport. But when an East German correspondent followed with an obviously prepared question about the one billion marks a year that the DDR was losing thanks to the "trouble-making" of western radio stations, the chairman of the State Council did not mince his words. "I am for simply settling the bill by seeing to it that a peace treaty is signed and the trouble-making RIAS radio station is liquidated.[6] That would be the simplest thing to do. Then the score would be settled. Then all would be in order."

The press conference ended as it had begun, with another Ulbricht statement—this time a short diatribe against the Bonn "militarists" who were clamoring for atomic arms, employing Hitler pressure tactics, and planning to march on the Oder. To these ritual phrases the foreign journalists only listened with half an ear. What mattered was that Walter Ulbricht had publicly committed himself and his regime to the silencing of West Berlin's radio stations and the closing down of its refugee centers.

At six o'clock that same evening, the television viewers of East Germany saw the face of Nikita Khrushchev flash into focus on their screens. The chairman of the Soviet Council of Ministers was broadcasting his own account of his Vienna meeting with John Kennedy. It was a long account—far longer than the U.S. president's relatively brief "Report to the Nation" of June 6—and it repeated the familiar Soviet arguments in favor of disarmament and the rapid conclusion of a German peace treaty. "Peace treaties were signed more than fourteen years ago with Italy and other states that fought on the side of Hitlerite Germany. The United States, Britain, and other countries concluded a peace treaty with Japan in 1951. Yet the governments of these same countries will not hear of concluding a peace treaty with Germany."

There were the usual invectives against the "massive provocations" by enemies of peace—the latest example being the Bundesrat meeting that was to have been held in West Berlin,

---

[6]RIAS. *Rundfunk im amerikanischen Sektor*—the American-financed radio station in West Berlin.

even though West Berlin "was never and is not a constituent part of the Federal Republic of Germany." But such provocations were not going to deter the Soviet Union from signing a peace treaty with East Germany, if necessary. Control over the access routes to West Berlin would then be turned over to the German Democratic Republic, the result being that "if any country violates the peace and crosses another's borders—by land, air, or water—it will bear full responsibility for the consequences of aggression and will be duly repulsed."

For East German listeners, the conciliatory tone of the concluding section, in which Khrushchev said that the Vienna meeting had been profitable and that he had gained "the impression that President Kennedy appreciates the great responsibility that reposes on the governments of two such mighty states," mattered far less than the blunt assertion made in the middle of the speech: "The conclusion of a peace treaty with Germany cannot be postponed any longer."

The television projection of Ulbricht's press conference, which followed at 8:00 P.M., spelled out his point even more clearly. A Soviet peace treaty with East Germany would mean the closing down of the refugee camps and DDR control over the air lanes, in addition to that already exercised over the railroads and highways crossing East German territory.

All over the Soviet zone frightened citizens began packing their belongings. Many others had already "flown the coop." For the week of June 10–16, Federal Republic officials noted with concern that the number of refugees registered at Berlin's Marienfelde and at other camps in West Germany showed a startling rise: a total of 4,770 persons for seven days.

8

In his upstairs editorial office, in the dark sandstone building that had once housed the clerks and accountants of the Deutsche Zentralbank, Hermann Axen had reason to be pleased. *Neues Deutschland*'s offensive against the Frontstadt of West Berlin was now eliciting the support of anti-Brandt and anti-Adenauer defectors. Judged by any standards, proletarian or capitalistic, the Karl-Heinz Falk story, which filled most of the second page of its June 21 edition, was a journalistic coup, one more resounding blow to the tottering prestige of "Espionage Minister" Ernst Lemmer and his "head-hunting henchmen" at Marienfelde.

It was five years almost to the day since Axen had been appointed editor-in-chief of the DDR's leading Party newspaper, largely on the strength of his success in helping Erich Honecker indoctrinate the FDJ movement. But after moving into the newspaper's office on the Mauerstrasse just south of Unter den Linden, the forty-year-old agitprop expert found that there was little he could teach a staff of editorial hatchetmen well versed in the arts of socialistic agitation and propaganda. It was axiomatic that the DDR and the Soviet Union should be portrayed as peace-loving while the Federal Republic was represented as in the ruling grip of militarists and revanchists. Still, none of them had foreseen the propaganda boon that was offered to them in the spring of 1958, when the Adenauer government had first formulated a request for atomic weapons.

Over the years Hermann Axen and his sharpshooters had set up a series of sitting ducks to sustain the regime's conviction that the Adenauer government was Nazi-infiltrated. One of their favorite targets had long been Dr. Theodor Oberlaender, a former German consul in the USSR, as well as Nazi party member and Wehrmacht officer, who had been the Federal Republic's minister for refugees. He had later been replaced by Gerhard Schröder, a one-time schoolteacher who had taken the Nazi party oath in the mid-1930s in order to keep his job, and who had since risen to become Bonn's minister of the interior. Then there was Hans Globke, the secretive state secretary of the chancellery, who was considered by many to be Adenauer's *eminence grise.* As an official of the Third Reich's judicial apparatus, it had fallen to Globke to write a legal commentary on the racial decrees that had been promulgated at the Nuremberg Congress of 1935—for which he had been branded for life as a "Jew-murderer" who had worked hand-in-glove with Eichmann for the liquidation of all European Jews.

Although the Eichmann trial provided an ideal opportunity for reopening fire on the chancellor's valued assistant, *Neues Deutschland*'s number one *bête noire* was no longer Globke or Adenauer or even that dangerous "atomic warrior," Defense Minister Franz-Josef Strauss. The paper's number one target for abuse was now Ernst Lemmer, the affable if somewhat elephantine minister for all-German affairs.

Regularly labeled a "Gestapo confidante" or a "Goebbels agent," Lemmer was detested by the Ulbricht regime for several reasons. As a prewar Berlin correspondent for Swiss and Belgian newspapers, he had made no secret of his anti-Soviet sentiments. After the war he had added insult to injury by trying to organize a truly independent Christian Democratic party in the Soviet sector of Berlin. Now here he was, federal minister for all-German affairs. And whereas Adenauer was sometimes suspected of indifference to the plight of his East German compatriots—most of them being Protestants or Socialists, if not both—Lemmer was known to be with them heart and soul. His ministry administered Marienfelde and other refugee camps, which acted like beacons for dissidents and malcontents bent on fleeing the DDR; and it was funds from his ministry that helped to finance the *Informationsbüro West*, a press agency specializing in bulletins and feature articles about conditions in East Germany, based on interviews with refugees. To show such interest in the internal affairs of the German Democratic Republic was highly suspect, grounds enough for calling him "Espionage Minister" Lemmer.

Just five days before, in its June 16 edition, *Neues Deutschland* had got all worked up over the fate of a thirty-three-year-old electrical mechanic named Willi Bornschein, who had been arrested on May 12 by West German counterintelligence agents while visiting his sister in Württemberg. Although no reason for the arrest was given, members of his family had decried it as illegal and ten thousand fellow workers from his office-machine factory near Erfurt had been mobilized to protest this "arbitrary" act—which afforded new proof to the obstinate and unbelieving that it was the Federal German authorities, not those of the DDR, that were obstructing interzonal travel.

All this was good newsworthy stuff, new grist for *Neues*

Deutschland's propaganda mills. But what Hermann Axen now had before him was even better. It was the story of a West Berliner who had decided to go east. A West Berliner, furthermore, who had been employed at the Marienfelde refugee camp in counterespionage. Here then was one more rock to throw at "Espionage Minister" Lemmer's already battered image.

The man's name was Karl-Heinz Falk. At Marienfelde he had worked for four years with a unit mysteriously designated as *Vorprüfung B-1* ("Preliminary Examination Bureau 1"). This unit was part of the Office for the Protection of the Constitution (the West German equivalent of the FBI), which, Falk claimed, was heavily engaged in foreign espionage activities.

The procedure was simple. Once the western intelligence agencies were through interrogating the incoming refugee, the Vorprüfung B-1 boys took over. The refugee was "persuaded" to provide detailed information about factories, administrative offices, party structures and personnel, mass organizations, and other institutions of the DDR. This information was then sent to the Federal Republic's counterintelligence headquarters in Cologne, where it was processed and condensed, to provide the Bonn government with guidelines for new disturbance measures against the DDR.

A favorite West German intelligence technique was to make lavish promises of aid if the refugee agreed to talk. For example, a Frau Ursula Stenzel, who had abandoned her home on the Grünberger Strasse, gave her interrogators detailed information about the state-run Elektrokohle utilities plant in East Berlin. She was then told to report to an address on the Fehrbelliner Platz, in the British sector, where instead of the promised reward she was solicited by recruiting officers for West German Counterintelligence. With the information thus hopefully provided, all refugees from the DDR could be "filed" and brought under the permanent surveillance and control of the Federal Republic's secret police agents.

The West German counterintelligence people and most of the Marienfelde personnel treated East German refugees as second-class humans, as pawns for their political purposes. Some refugees, according to Falk, were even infiltrated into Willy Brandt's Social Democratic party, to act as informers for

Adenauer's Christian Democratic Union. This had happened to the thirty-seven-year-old Giesbert Bartrow. He had left East Germany in September 1960. After being interrogated by Klaus Franke (a former naval officer who had served on Admiral Dönitz's staff), and after giving him precious information about mass organizations in the DDR, Bartrow had been hired as a counterintelligence front man, put to work informing on other refugees in the Askanischer Platz camp, and then infiltrated into the Social Democrats' party apparatus in West Berlin. The same had happened to the fifty-four-year-old Georg Türker, from Pankow, who was now employed as a Cologne counter-intelligence agent among the Social Democrats of Neukölln.

Most of the Marienfelde counterintelligence people were ex-Nazis, Fascists, or militarists. Egon Schweigk, who headed Vorprüfung B-1, had once directed a Wehrmacht spy school in Ortelsburg, East Prussia. His assistant, Paul Nagrotski, had served in a Wehrmacht department specializing in enemy defections. Hans-Joachim Weist was a former SS man and expert in antipartisan warfare. And as for Elizabeth Bergert, she was none other than a former Hermann Goering secretary.

No, Falk concluded, it had all been too much for him—the callous, antihumanistic activity of these counterintelligence people, who were brazenly indulging in a daily Menschenhandel with DDR fugitives. This was why he had left the poisoned atmosphere of the West in order to breathe more freely in "democratic" East Berlin.

The interview had ended pretty much as it had started—with a general statement from Karl-Heinz Falk to the effect that the Bonn *Ultras* (ultrareactionaries) and the "Brandt clique" were opposed to a free-city solution for West Berlin, because West Berlin would then cease to be an *Agentensumpf* ("spy swamp") and a Frontstadt of the Cold War. To this *Neues Deutschland*'s editors needed only to add the final, culminating phrase: "West Berlin should no longer be a spy swamp and the powder keg of a new war!"

Yes, all things considered, this was a good story. It struck just the right note. And if Hermann Axen felt any regrets, it was that *Neues Deutschland* couldn't publish a first-class exposé like this every day of the week.

On this same Wednesday, June 21, Nikita Khrushchev's portly form again flickered onto the television screens of East Germany. He now appeared in the dress uniform of a Soviet lieutenant general, the rank he had acquired as a political adviser on the Stalingrad and Ukrainian fronts during World War II. The occasion was the twentieth anniversary of the start of Hilter's blitzkrieg offensive against the USSR. The commemorative ceremony, staged in the Lenin Hall of the Grand Kremlin Palace, was so elaborate that only fragments of it could be shown to East German television viewers, but they included the solemn moment when a colonel and two other veterans of the battle of Berlin appeared with the Red Army flag they had triumphantly hoisted over the gutted Reichstag in late April of 1945.

The Soviet leader used the occasion to review not only the origins of the "great patriotic war," but also the causes of the Cold War that had followed. It was the Western powers that were ultimately responsible. They had put the "Hitler-Fascist military machine" up to destroying the USSR. Truman had justified this policy by suggesting, "If we see that Germany is going to win, then we should help Russia, and if Russia starts winning, then we must help Germany. May as many of them as possible be killed in this way."

This diabolical duplicity had forced the Soviet Union to sign a nonaggression pact with Adolf Hitler. But it had not saved the countries of the West from being subsequently assaulted by him. Their sudden collapse had encouraged the German imperialists to attack the USSR in the hope of destroying the first socialist state in the world. The result was the bloodiest war in history, in which millions lost their lives. Unfortunately, the lessons of this war had not been learned. Many former Wehrmacht officers and war criminals had gone scot-free and since risen to occupy leading positions in NATO. Sixteen years had passed since the war was ended, and yet there was still no signed peace treaty. The artificial postponement of a peace treaty now threatened everyone with a third world war—"in which not dozens but hundreds of millions of people would be killed."

On June 22 it was the East Germans' turn to commemorate the historic anniversary, with a mass meeting held in the

Werner Seelenbinder Halle. Behind the huge dais—a good fifty yards broad—the red banner of the Soviet Union, with its hammer and sickle, and the black, red, and gold banner of the DDR, with its hammer and compass dividers, had been carefully unfurled and pinned against the blank wall on slanted flagstaffs to suggest the invincible onward surge of the proletarian cause. Beneath, in large red letters, was the latest slogan of the day: HER MIT DEM FRIEDENSVERTRAG! FORT MIT DER HERRSCHAFT DES DEUTSCHEN MILITARISMUS! ("Up and Onward with the Peace Treaty! Down with the Domination of German Militarism!").

Television viewers saw a bespectacled Walter Ulbricht, looking distinctly stiff in his double-breasted suit, indulge in a ceremonial handshake with the Soviet ambassador, Mikhail Pervukhin. The chairman of the DDR's State Council was accompanied by Hermann Matern; Friedrich Ebert, lord mayor of East Berlin; Willi Stoph; Erich Honecker; Albert Norden; Paul Verner, party boss for East Berlin's eight boroughs; and two lesser Politburo members. But the hero of the hour was the minister of national defense, Gen. Karl-Heinz Hoffmann. With his well-combed wavy hair, thick circumflex brows, eyes that could be narrowed to mean slits, and a suitably resolute jaw, he seemed made for the theatrical role he was being asked to play.

In his wonderfully ham-handed speech, the catastrophes of the past were used to smear the criminals of the present. Adenauer's Bonn Ultras behaved and talked like Hitler and the Hitler-Fascists. But the Brandt team was no better. The Potsdam agreement of 1945 was to have banished militarism from the soil of Germany forever. Yet at their Bad Godesberg Congress of 1959, Brandt's German Socialists had cravenly capitulated to the Ultras, agreed to West German rearmament, and thus "stabbed the working class in the back." Brandt had even let himself be photographed in the uniform of a Bundeswehr Panzer officer. Nevertheless, as in 1945 and again in 1952, the magnanimous Soviet Union—this time in the person of Nikita Khrushchev—was offering the West a great opportunity for securing world peace. So let the two German states sit down together and start negotiations.

Neues Deutschland followed up, on June 24, with another broadside against the "campaign of lies" that was being organized by "Goebbels agent Lemmer." His latest crime was to have ordered his camouflaged spy outfit, Informationsbüro West, to publicize the food shortages that were creating unrest among the personnel of the Hennigsdorf Locomotive Works (where the June 1953 East German workers' strike had first been launched). The West Berlin "powder fuse" must be resolutely cut before a new world war was ignited. If there was now imminent danger of war and aggression, it was because there was not one but a thousand Globkes at work in Bonn. Napoleon had occupied Prussia 150 years before, and look what had happened to him! The "destroyers of the Four-Power accords" (that is, the Western powers) had no right to remain in West Berlin eternally. Their occupation status had no basis in law whatsoever. "It is purely and simply an arbitrary act," the article stated. "The Western occupation troops came to Berlin not through any right of conquest, but only because Berlin was the seat of the Allied Control Council." After one more swipe at the "Hitler generals" in NATO, the "Ribbentrop diplomats" in the United States, and the "Hitler *Blutrichter*" ("blood judges") in Bonn, the article concluded trenchantly, "West Berlin belongs by law to the DDR, which surrounds it on all sides."

The next day, East Germany's leading daily noted with satisfaction that in the West certain enlightened souls were beginning to face facts. Khrushchev had already commented favorably on Senator Mansfield's support for the free-city idea (although he had scoffed at its possible application to all Berlin). Now here was the London *Economist* urging a realistic recognition of the Oder-Neisse line. Lord Altrincham, the diplomatic correspondent of the *Guardian*, had gone even further and was advocating diplomatic recognition of the German Democratic Republic. In the Federal Republic the Public Transport Union, the second largest trade union in the West German Labor Federation, had come out openly against atomic arms for the Bundeswehr, while Thomas Dehler, a leader of the Free Democrats and the vice-president of the Bundestag, had called on Chancellor Adenauer to negotiate and to accept the peace offers of the Soviet Union.

All this was most encouraging. In the West the voices of reason were beginning to be heard, and the hard-liners were crumbling. It was time to give the screw another twist.

On June 28 the East German government announced in its official gazette that as of August 1 all foreign aircraft flying over its territory would be required to register with an East German "safety center" prior to entry and exit, and that all radar-equipped planes would need advance authorization before being allowed to penetrate the airspace of the sovereign DDR.

At the end of this same week, another 4,169 fugitives from East Germany were registered at Marienfelde and other reception centers in the West.

9

For those who had heard of its hospitable basement, the Henneckes' squat, red-roofed house was not difficult to find. Those coming from the east had only to board the elevated Stadtbahn train at one of the stops in the Soviet sector, while those from the south or west could get on at Potsdam or Babelserg and ride the S-Bahn to the Zehlendorf station, in the southwestern corner of West Berlin. From there it was easy walking distance through several tree-lined streets to the house with the downstairs spare room and the empty cellar.

Ever since Whitsunday, which had fallen on May 21, they had been turning up, singly or in pairs, with suitcases and parcels that gradually had taken over the spare room of Frau Hennecke's large basement. The visitors who brought these "gifts"—everything from woolen blankets to disassembled bicycles—sometimes were friends but more often were strangers who had been informed through some mysterious grapevine (that is, friends of relatives or relatives of friends) that their things would be quite safe with the jolly, white-haired Frau Hennecke, and that they need have no fears of being robbed or dispossessed of the belongings they were anxious to bring out of Ulbricht's DDR prior to their own departure.

Among the friends who turned up—a good half a dozen times—were a florist and his wife from Frankfurt-on-Oder. They always appeared with the same two suitcases, which were duly emptied of steamer rugs, featherbedding, winter dressing gowns and coats, in a specially designated corner of the cluttered spare room. Theirs promised to be a complicated moving operation, for in addition to three children—aged nine, seven, and five—the couple had a sixty-two-year-old mother and an eighty-nine-year-old grandmother to support. There could be no question of leaving any of them behind in East Germany. They had found it increasingly difficult to keep their little flower shop going, despite a steady demand for funeral wreaths, for they had lost their greenhouses and a nursery garden, which were still visible through binoculars on the other, now Polish side of the Oder.

Quite different was the case of another of these basement users—an optometrist and watchmaker from Jena. Financial reasons alone could not have prompted him to leave the DDR, for to judge by his fine suits and luggage, he earned an unusually good salary. At the sight of the paper bags into which they would have to repack their clothes, the watchmaker's wife would break down and start to cry, and the normally good-natured Frau Hennecke would have to remind her that she belonged wherever her husband chose to go.

The most ingenious and determined of them all, however, was a machine-tool maker from Wittenberg named Otto Seidel, who had relatives in the Federal Republic. He had turned up unannounced one day, accompanied by a pregnant wife and two children. Inside their bulging suitcases and parcels were not only winter clothes, linens, and an eiderdown, but, as the expectant mother confided to the wide-eyed Frau Hennecke, parts of a sewing machine that her deft-fingered husband had personally dismantled. Neither of them could tell just what awaited them in the West, so it was better to be prepared for hard times.

They had decided to leave the DDR for several reasons. The machine-tool maker was fed up with the constant raising of work norms that forced him to increase his output, even if quality was sacrificed, or face a reduction in pay. Food supplies, explained his wife, were so erratic that it was virtually impossible to plan the next day's meal, since she never knew just what kind of meat (if any) or vegetables she would find in the shops. But the deciding factor had been the increasing reluctance of the authorities to grant interzonal passes to persons wishing to visit friends or relatives in the Federal Republic. Everywhere in Wittenberg, but particularly at Otto Seidel's factory, the same disturbing rumors could be heard: This was just the opening wedge in a systematic drive to "close the hatch." The new child was expected toward the end of June, which meant that they had little time if they were to get out at all.

The four of them had reappeared at Frau Hennecke's house a fortnight later, again weighed down with suitcases and bundles, including more parts of the sewing machine. And then, again without warning, they returned, this time for good. Frau Hennecke and her husband treated them to a supper of hot goulash and noodles, with all the butter they wanted for the accompanying slices of brown bread, after which they walked the Seidels to the Sundgauer Strasse station, where they were to take the S-Bahn to the Marienfelde refugee camp. Frau Hennecke was afraid that the pregnant mother might be seized by labor pains before reaching her destination. But her fears fortunately were groundless, and the mother was able to make it to the lower-level platform without mishap.

It had begun to rain once more. Queued up before the entrance to the Marienfelde refugee camp, the latest arrivals from the East looked more than usually forlorn. The luckier ones huddled under umbrellas; the less fortunate stood stoically in line under dripping hats and raincoats. Most of them carried a single suitcase, a knapsack, or a couple of market bags—all they had dared bring over on the underground or the S-Bahn railway for fear of being hauled out onto the platform and searched by suspicious Vopos.

The bright red, blue, and yellow parasols that only yesterday, when the sun had been shining, had given the camp an almost festive look, were no longer to be seen. The young boys had abandoned the soccer field, and there were no squealing children soaring upward on the swings or slipping down the athletic poles on the day-nursery lawn. All, save the newcomers who had yet to gain admission, were now crammed indoors in crowded waiting rooms and corridors, waiting to be examined by some camp doctor or nurse or interrogated by Allied intelligence officers and officials representing the three major West German parties: Socialists, Christian Democrats, and Liberals.

Just beyond the entrance to the main reception building, the newcomers filed past a warning sign:

VORSICHT
bei Gesprächen (Spitzelgefahr)
bei Einladungen (Menschenraub)
bei Schriftverkehr mit der Ostzone
Sektorengrenze beachten

BE CAREFUL
during conversations (danger of snooping)
with invitations (danger of abduction)
in corresponding with the East Zone.
Heed the sector boundary.

Caution was the watchword even here, since the southern limits of the camp actually bordered the Soviet zone. For his personal security, each refugee was given a number to which he was expected to respond, so that no family name need be used when issuing a summons by ordinary voice or loud-speaker. This was to protect the families or friends they had left behind in East Germany from possible reprisals, and to shield the newcomers from the molestation of other East Germans hastily dispatched by DDR officials to "persuade" a particularly popular mayor or trades-union official to return to his demoralized community. Because the full screening process could last as long as twelve days, such emissaries had a fair chance to catch up with their victims. But the Marienfelde authorities had no intention of facilitating such interceptions.

Located near a trotters' racetrack and a well-known monastery, The Good Shepherd, the Marienfelde reception camp had grown over the years to the point where it could accommodate a maximum of three thousand refugees. The surroundings were typically suburban: unpretentious cottages and villas, a number of low-budget housing units, a few factory warehouses, and a quilted patchwork of small garden plots cultivated by owners or tenants who for the most part lived elsewhere.

Five hundred employees were now needed to man the medical centers, screening offices, and mess halls, which occupied eight out of twenty-five apartment blocks spread over the camp's square mile of lawns and lanes. There was a hospital to treat cases of tuberculosis and malnutrition and the less frequently encountered victims of venereal diseases. Food for the transients was prepared outside the camp in several catering kitchens and brought to Marienfelde in insulated containers. For breakfast and supper, each refugee received a fixed ration of bread, butter, sausage, and jam; a hot midday meal was served in the central dining hall in successive shifts.

Most of the fugitives had brought over East German marks, which they could change into West marks at the unfavorable 4-to-1 exchange rate. In addition, each was given a token amount of pocket money, varying from three to five West marks a week—enough to finance several trips to the sausage and Coca-Cola stand, which a vendor was authorized to operate during the daylight hours. For a surprising number of East Germans, Coca-Cola was synonymous with "freedom"; it was a legendary beverage they had heard of but never actually tasted.

A curious metamorphosis came over many of these refugees by the fourth or fifth day in camp. Persons who at first seemed silent or depressed suddenly found their tongues again— when they realized that there was no longer a danger of being overheard and reported to some Party official.

All this was familiar enough to Marienfelde's processing personnel. What was new was the increased human pressure, which was beginning to approach the feverish tempo of June and July 1953. Almost half the new arrivals were under twenty-five, and this too was new and strange. The "vacation refugees"—those who chose to leave East Germany at the conclusion of the school year—were no longer waiting for the month of August; they were coming over now. Rumor had it that the DDR authorities were about to issue new *Kennkarten* on the Soviet model: identity cards that would keep the bearer from traveling outside his registered district. Others had left as a result of Khrushchev's threatening speeches. It was commonly believed that he was going to sign a separate peace treaty with Ulbricht on August 1. After that, anything could happen. They were getting out while they could.

An eighteen-year-old carpenter from a village near the town of Cottbus (forty miles west of the Polish border, in southern Brandenburg) was about to be conscripted into the Nationale Volksarmee for an eighteen-month period. "So I beat it with a friend. I hope nothing happens to the parents we both left behind," he added glumly.

"I want to give my children a religious education," explained a worker from Güstrow, in Mecklenburg. "I want them to believe in God and not become Communists."

A twenty-four-year-old mechanic from Thuringia told how he had become involved in an argument with some Russian officers and soldiers. It had ended with his telling them to get the hell out of Germany and to take Ulbricht with them. A Party official had come up and warned him that the time would soon come when such public utterances could no longer be made. Rather than risk a prison sentence, he had headed for West Berlin.

Another skilled mechanic had come to join his wife, who had already fled to West Berlin. He had had to wait to finish his term in the Nationale Volksarmee, but even though there were excellent job openings in the East, he was fed up with life in the Soviet occupation zone.

Similar reasons were given by an unusually large and well-knit family—a grandfather, grandmother, two widowed daughters, and two grandchildren—who had managed to come out together. The two middle-aged daughters had been earning fairly good salaries working for a state-controlled food store; one of the grandsons was a trained gardener. They all could have gone on living in the Zone without fear of arrest, but they couldn't stand the travel restrictions placed on them. It had reached the point where the mere expression of a desire to visit a Western country could lead to denunciation and arrest for *Republikflucht*.

10

June melted into July with no letup in international tension. A *Newsweek* report that the Pentagon was working on contingency plans for the evacuation of American civilians from bases in France, Germany, and West Berlin set off new tremors of anxiety all over the continent. Refusing to yield to a sudden heat wave that sent the temperature soaring, the U.S. Berlin Command issued a stern Order of the Day, banning the wearing of bikinis or shorts in housing areas, shopping centers, and other public places. On a pre-Independence Day visit to the beleaguered *Frontstadt*, Gen. Bruce Clarke, commander of the U.S. Seventh Army, congratulated the parading GIs on their "devoted service," after warning them that they could not be "too well prepared for the missions that lie ahead."

From East Berlin came mysterious reports about a secret meeting of the Party's Central Committee, at which "peace plans" for Berlin and Germany had been discussed. *Neues Deutschland* called once again for "special vigilance" against all attempts at provocation by West German "militarists," while Karl Maron, the East German minister of the interior, commended his police forces on the success of their July 1 Vopo Day.

Bonn countered this new propaganda barrage by issuing a detailed report on the paramilitary units that were stationed in and around East Berlin in defiance of the Four-Power agreements: the forty-five hundred shock troopers of Erich Mielke's Wachregiment, equipped with armored cars and stationed in Adlershof; thirty-seven hundred Garrisoned Police, armed with light and heavy infantry weapons and directed from a Nationale Volksarmee headquarters in Treptow; thirty thousand factory militiamen, who could be mobilized at short notice to man machine guns, mortars, and even light tanks; a military intelligence headquarters in Lichtenberg, which maintained four thousand agents in the Soviet sector alone; and last but not least, the names of fifteen factories that were engaged in illicit arms production in East Berlin.

The entire Soviet zone now seemed to be seething with uncertainty, unrest, and discontent. At the Hennigsdorf Locomotive Works, just beyond the northwestern periphery of the French sector, restive workers were reported to have drowned out speeches made by Party activists on behalf of the Soviet peace plan by breaking into a massive singing of the "Internationale." "Once this escape hole to freedom is closed," a middle-aged man from Leipzig told Ellen Lentz of the *New York Times*, "we might just as well take a rope and hang ourselves."

In an effort to keep the pressure down, Bonn's chubby, cigar-smoking minister for all-German affairs, Ernst Lemmer, called on his fellow citizens of the Federal Republic to rise to the occasion with a positively "Christmas" fervor, by sending millions of food packages to the underfed and rationed inhabitants of East Germany.

In Warsaw the executive committee of a World Lutheran Federation—represented by delegates from East Germany, Czechoslovakia, Hungary, Estonia, and Poland—issued a call for world peace and announced plans to set up a powerful radio transmitter to broadcast from Addis Ababa.

Addressing a Tory party rally at the Marquess of Lansdowne's Bowood estate, Harold Macmillan reminded Khrushchev and the Soviet Union that the West could not countenance "acts of force" in Berlin or "interference with Allied rights. . . . Let there be no mistake. This is an issue upon which the peoples of the Western world are resolute. It is a principle they will defend."

Undeterred by riots in North Africa, angry farmer demonstrations in central and southern France, and threatening letters sent to town and village officials by Frenchmen hostile to his Algerian policy, Charles de Gaulle continued his tour of Lorraine, riding bareheaded in an open car under a blazing sun. "We are on the eve of a serious international crisis," he told the printers and textile workers of Epinal, in the Vosges. "France, like the entire free world, is threatened by a certain block in the East which is full of ambition and pretension," he lectured the inhabitants of Nancy, who had crowded into the eighteenth-century Place Stanislas to hear him. "Do they want peace or do they want war? Perhaps in the near future things will be clarified."

From Long Beach, California, former Vice-President Richard Nixon added his voice to the international clamor by telling five thousand American Legion veterans, "It is fortunate that President Kennedy made it clear that there will be no compromise on Berlin. We must support President Kennedy for more funds for military strength. We must support a strong statement on Berlin, backed up by military strength."

John Kennedy himself chose to spend the long Independence Day weekend on Cape Cod. He made the trip by air—sixty-two minutes in a military jet from Andrews Air Force Base to Otis, Massachusetts, followed by another eleven minutes in a helicopter which deposited the president, his wife, brother Bobby, and daughter Caroline on a sunken lawn near the three gabled houses of the Kennedy compound in Hyannis Port. The president was accompanied by his personal physician, Janet Travell, who had prescribed a rest cure and no golf playing, to allow him to recover from the muscle strain he had contracted during a tree-planting ceremony in Canada.

Most of Saturday morning, July 1, was spent in a bathrobe and pajamas, but the prescribed rest cure did not keep John Kennedy from conducting government business over the telephone. A long-distance talk with Secretary of Labor Arthur Goldberg about the maritime strike was followed by an intelligence briefing by the president's military aide, Gen. Chester Clifton. Much of the discussion was devoted to the explosive situation in Kuwait, where a British marine infantry brigade had just been landed to protect the oil-rich sheikdom from the predatory claims of Iraq's new revolutionary leader, Gen. Abdul Karim Kassem.

Although the crisis in the Persian Gulf was primarily Harold Macmillan's problem, the Berlin crisis was essentially Jack Kennedy's responsibility. In March, some weeks before the Bay of Pigs fiasco, he had asked Dean Acheson to prepare a report on NATO and the German question. The report, finally handed to the president three weeks after his return from Vienna, pulled no punches. The prime aim of Khrushchev's diplomacy, so Acheson argued in his crisp, incisive style, was to test the new administration's determination to stand up to an aggressive Soviet foreign policy. The conflict over Berlin was thus essentially a test of wills. If the Soviet Union could pressure the United States into hedging on its vital commitments to the people of Berlin, there would ensue a crisis of confidence that would shake the NATO structure to its foundations. There was consequently nothing to be gained and much possibly to be lost by agreeing to enter into negotiations over the Berlin question. Any eagerness to negotiate would be interpreted in Moscow as a sign of weakness, an indication that the United States was not prepared to risk a nuclear war for the welfare and safeguard of two million West Berliners. The only way to impress Khrushchev was with action—a rapid buildup of U.S. nuclear and conventional forces in America and overseas.

The strengthening of conventional forces in Germany was of paramount importance in Acheson's opinion. If Khrushchev went ahead and signed his separate peace treaty with East Germany, the United States should simply stand pat on the existing procedures governing the use of the access routes to West Berlin. If these rules and rights were tampered with, the United States should be ready to send an armored corps, or two full tank divisions, up the Helmstedt autobahn to make clear that it meant business. The mere existence of such an armored force would give everyone—Russians as much as East Germans— pause. It was thus the best guarantee against any decisive change in the status quo.

This advice was a far cry from that which Harold Macmillan had offered the young American president in London. The tone of Acheson's report, in its adamant opposition to negotiations, was almost Gaullist. Although well argued and perhaps even based on sound premises concerning Khrushchev's real intentions, it was altogether too negative for a young president who called himself an advocate of change and who fancied that under his administration things were going to be different. Although he was determined to build up America's conventional forces— depleted to the danger point through the Radford-Dulles doctrine of "massive retaliation"—John Kennedy did not wish to be accused of pursuing a policy of purely "negative" resistance, as John Foster Dulles had done.

There was also a personal factor. Dean Acheson was not secretary of state any longer, and although the younger man had gone out of his way to consult the older one about key cabinet appointments, Kennedy had no intention of letting Acheson become a kind of grand vizier, the real power behind the throne. Eisenhower had delegated control over foreign affairs to a virtually omnipotent secretary of state, John Foster Dulles. But John F. Kennedy was determined to be his own secretary of state. He needed to be advised and seconded by someone who had had considerable State Department experience, who was not too opinionated and self-willed, who could be counted on to serve him loyally. The soft-spoken, level-headed, unexcitable Dean Rusk seemed to fit all these requirements.

In March 1961, on the eve of his departure for Europe, where he was to see Macmillan, Adenauer, and De Gaulle, Acheson had called on the president, who had taken him out into the White House garden so that they could enjoy the warm spring sun.

"Do you know anything about this Cuba proposal?" Kennedy had suddenly asked, as they sat talking on a wooden bench.

"A Cuba proposal? I didn't know there was one," was Acheson's reply.

Kennedy had then filled him in on the essentials—an invasion of Cuba to be pulled off by fifteen hundred trained exiles. "Well, this is the proposal and I've been thinking about it seriously—to that extent it's serious, you can say—I've not made up my mind about it yet, but I'm giving it serious thought."

Acheson was appalled enough by the little he had heard to remark, in the half-humorous, half-cutting tone that came so naturally to him, that he didn't think it necessary to "call in Price Waterhouse to discover that fifteen hundred Cubans aren't as good as twenty-five thousand Cubans"—the intimation being that with an invading force twelve or fifteen times as strong, the scheme might stand a chance of success, but that otherwise it was a certain "bust."

The subsequent "bust" had made a shattering impression on the European statesmen Acheson had later seen during his European trip. They had had high expectations in the new president but now no longer knew quite what to think. On his return to Washington, Acheson had made a speech to a group of Foreign Service diplomats, in the course of which he had remarked that the Europeans he had talked to had had the impression of watching a gifted young performer practice with a boomerang, which to their spellbound horror had returned to knock out the performer. The caustic simile had irritated Kennedy. But not being a person to nourish grudges, he had quickly relented, realizing that Acheson's only fault was to have been proved too right in his reaction to the Cuban "adventure."

The same Dean Acheson who had shown caution on the Cuban question was now prepared to be a paragon of boldness on the issue of Berlin. The program he was advocating as a reply to Khrushchev's belligerence called for a partial mobilization of the country. This was more than Kennedy had bargained for. The people of the United States were simply not prepared for anything so drastic. The West Europeans, to judge from State Department reports, were even less prepared for a policy of military muscle flexing. De Gaulle was paralyzed by an unsettled Algerian problem and a major crisis in Bizerte, to say nothing of mutinies and dissension in top French-army ranks. Harold Macmillan, who had taken a dim view of the armored corps idea when it had first been propounded by Pentagon officers in 1959 and who was grateful to John Foster Dulles for having "buried" it (or so he thought) shortly before his death, was now horrified to see it resuscitated as Washington's best answer to the autobahn access problem. Indeed, he was so appalled by the proposal that he was soon calling all American contingency planning on the Berlin problem "absurd."

Within the State Department, opinions were divided, but few were willing to line up unequivocally behind the Acheson report. Dean Rusk was noncommital. The department's leading Russian expert, Charles Bohlen; its legal counsel, Abram Chayes; and the head of the Policy Planning Commission, George McGhee, all considered it dangerously provocative. Only Foy Kohler, the assistant secretary of state for European affairs who had recently been appointed head of a "Berlin task force," showed any enthusiasm for it, but his opinion was considered suspect by many members of the White House staff because of his previous association with Richard Nixon and the Eisenhower administration.

The same divisions of opinion were to be found at the Defense Department. Paul Nitze, the assistant secretary for international affairs, was generally favorable to the hard-line Acheson approach, while his superior, Robert McNamara, was not. In the Senate the Democratic majority leader, Mike Mansfield, was opposed, as was William Fulbright of the Foreign Relations Committee. In the White House itself, the hard-liners were represented by the president's military adviser, Gen. Maxwell Taylor; his personal army aide, Brig. Gen. Chester Clifton; and Walt Rostow, deputy secretary of the National Security Council. But these three men were a distinct minority and wielded less influence than did Kennedy's main speech writer, Theodore Sorensen, and McGeorge Bundy, his special assistant for national security affairs. The White House eggheads—those whom Joseph Alsop had taken to calling "soft-boiled eggheads"—were unhappy about the Acheson approach, which struck them as much too negative. They included Jerome Wiesner, the president's scientific adviser; Arthur Schlesinger, Jr., the speech-writing historian-in-residence; Carl Kaysen, a Harvard economist who had joined Bundy's staff; and another Cambridge (Massachusetts) professor named Henry Kissinger.

On Wednesday, July 5, John Kennedy returned to Washington still undecided about the Acheson report. That same day, the counselor of the Soviet embassy, Georgi Kornienko, called on Arthur Schlesinger in an effort to ascertain the president's thinking on the Berlin problem. The result was a long and fruitless discussion which ended with Schlesinger voicing American wariness over Soviet "guarantees" regarding West Berlin and with the Soviet diplomat replying, "Well, if you do not consider those guarantees adequate, why do you not propose your own guarantees?" The Russians, apparently believing at this point that the hard-line Acheson program enjoyed the president's favor, were now, so Schlesinger reasoned, making new overtures to avert a head-on confrontation.

Fearing that Kennedy might adopt the main lines of the Acheson report after all, Schlesinger went to work the next day with Abram Chayes, of the State Department, on a memorandum advocating the exploration of other than military courses of action. Kennedy was impressed enough by the arguments to ask Schlesinger to expand them into an unsigned memorandum that he could use for the important discussion of these issues, scheduled for July 8 at Hyannis Port, with Dean Rusk, Robert McNamara, and Gen. Maxwell Taylor. The five-page memorandum was completed in time to be stuffed into the president's black alligator briefcase prior to his takeoff for Cape Cod.

The main thrust of the memorandum was that the Acheson approach was much too narrow because it was essentially tailored to a Soviet blockade of the Berlin access routes and offered no ready-made answers to other possible forms of Soviet action. The issue was debated at great length the next morning when John Kennedy received Dean Rusk, Robert MacNamara, and Gen. Maxwell Taylor on the sunporch of his Hyannis Port house, and later when they boarded the fifty-two-foot cabin cruiser *Marlin* to continue the discussion on the fantail.

When host and guests returned to shore, no final decisions had been made. But Kennedy's military aide, Brig. Gen. Chester Clifton, jolted them all with the latest news from Moscow. Khrushchev had just made another tough speech—this time to say that he was canceling the projected troop reduction of 1.2 million men, that because of the hostile attitude of the West toward peaceful negotiations, he was going to increase the Soviet military budget by one-third. He had not even waited to find out if the Acheson program was going through. He was clearly out to intimidate Kennedy by resorting to the same shock tactics he had used in Vienna.

Later that same Saturday afternoon after the visitors had left, Kennedy reread the Chayes-Kissinger-Schlesinger memorandum, particularly the concluding paragraph in which the authors had criticized the tendency to put the issue in black-or-white terms. "Are you chicken or not? When someone proposes something that seems tough, hard, put-up-or-shut-up, it is difficult to oppose it without seeming soft, idealistic, mushy. Yet, as Chip Bohlen has so often said, nothing would clarify more the discussion of policy toward the Soviet Union than the elimination of the words 'hard' and 'soft' from the language. People who had doubts about Cuba suppressed those doubts lest they seem 'soft.' It is obviously important that such fears not constrain free discussion of Berlin."

This was also John Kennedy's feeling. He did not wish to be

surrounded by yes men; he wanted everyone to speak his mind. But the fact remained that Dean Acheson, who had not been afraid to take a soft line on Cuba, was now as hard as nails on the subject of Berlin. It was easy to criticize him and to claim that his national mobilization program was an "over-response" to the situation. But the former secretary of state had been proved right on Cuba, and in dealing with Nikita Khrushchev he might possibly be right again.

11

It was one thing to realize that thousands of Soviet zone farmers had preferred to seek refuge in the West rather than see their farms collectivized; it was quite another to drive through the rich province of Mecklenburg and to see with one's own eyes the thousands of acres of untilled land that the stubborn farmers had abandoned. In every town through which he drove on his way to Rostock, where he was to cover the opening of Baltic Week, Thomas Reiche of the Associated Press was struck by the long queues outside the food stores. The fertile agricultural region that had once supplied butter and potatoes to all Germany no longer seemed able to supply itself.

This situation was the delayed consequence of Walter Ulbricht's decision to complete the collectivization process he had begun in 1952 and halted one year later in the wake of mass upheavals. For six years thereafter, East Germany had stumbled along on two uneven legs, one-half of its farms collectivized, the other half still in the hands of individual owners. But whereas the Land-Production-Cooperatives (LPGs) had required ever-increasing state subsidies, the private farms had prospered. This was an intolerable situation for the Party planners, who were out to prove that collectivization was the wave of the future.

And so, in February 1960, Ulbricht had resumed the drive to collectivize East German agriculture. Bus loads of Party activists armed with megaphones were dispatched from the cities to harangue the ignorant peasantry about the backwardness of their ways: "Do you want peace or do you want war? Those who want peace will join the LPGs."

The drive had been pushed with determination and a bland unconcern for the consequences. Ten weeks after it was launched, the drive was considered completed, and the regime confidently announced that all agriculture in the DDR was now collectivized—with 19,000 LPGs employing 931,000 members and cultivating a total area of almost 11 million acres.

What was not said was that the new drive had encountered fierce opposition once again. Some farmers immediately fled to the West. Others paid lip service to the new ideals but worked a strictly eight-hour day, like their fellow workers in the cities. Many others waited until the harvest was in and then decamped with their earnings. Entire families, indeed entire communities, fled, leaving empty farms and cattle sheds, empty town halls and taverns. Nobody really knew just how many had left, but rumor had it that this year as much as one-fifth of the arable land in East Germany was lying fallow.

Thomas Reiche could well believe it as his eyes swept the desolate fields, where not a farmer, horse, or tractor was to be seen for miles. In the villages and towns where he stopped, he heard the same complaints. What was the point of the regime's making such a fuss over Yuri Gagarin's forthcoming visit to Berlin? It was a publicity stunt, no more, intended to impress them with the technical superiority of the communist system. But they would do better to let the farmers till the soil and tend their livestock as they had done in the past.

The regime, of course, put the blame for the poor harvest on an unusually rainy summer and attributed the high mortality of livestock to various animal diseases. Lotte Ulbricht was now urging LPG farmers to reduce the death rate by giving shelter to ailing piglets in their kitchens, as they had done before being collectivized. But the farmers, having lost all incentives, didn't see why they should sacrifice their comfort for the sake of pro-duction targets set by city bureaucrats who couldn't tell a bull from a heifer.

A story making the rounds had it that in the Mecklenburg village of Demnin a kolkhoz chairman had bawled out the fore-man responsible for pig production: "What, six more piglets dead! What's going on? Did this kind of thing happen when you owned your own farm?"

"No, never," was the prompt reply.

"Then how do you account for all the deaths that are taking such a toll of our stock?"

The foreman scratched his head and declared with a puzzled frown, "Damned if I know, Comrade Chairman, damned if I do. The only thing I can think of is that . . . well . . . maybe they've been committing suicide."

It was a dismal joke, in keeping with the dismal mood of the Pomeranian, Brandenburg, and Mecklenburg farmers Reiche managed to question. And not only the farmers felt this way. Everywhere the people he met seemed to be on tenterhooks, sitting on packed suitcases, ready to head for West Berlin the moment they thought the border was going to be sealed. The young vacationers who had come to spend their holidays on the Baltic made no secret of their flight plans, any more than did a Grepo he talked to near the West German border. Three of his comrades had recently received special commendations for the excellent performance of their duties. A few days later they had slipped aboard a ferry bound for Trelleborg, Sweden, and there had asked for asylum.

"I'm all for their leaving," Reiche was told by a well-paid shipyard worker in Rostock with whom he struck up a conversation. "In fact, as far as I'm concerned, let 'em all clear out! The more the merrier. Let 'em all go. What difference does it make? It will even help solve the supply problem, don't you see? . . . Hell, man, it's obvious! The fewer mouths we have to feed, the more food there will be for the rest of us."

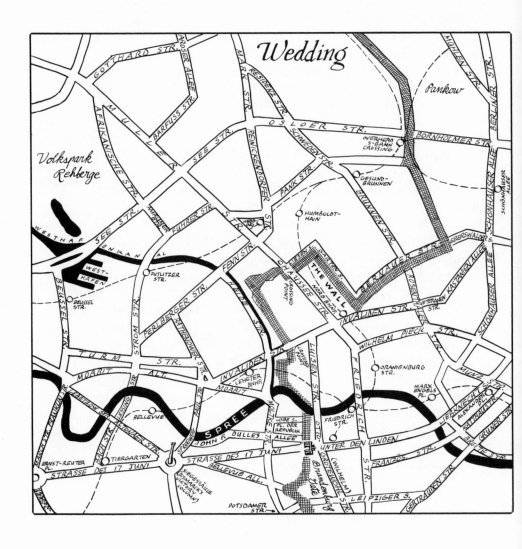

PART TWO

THE PANIC

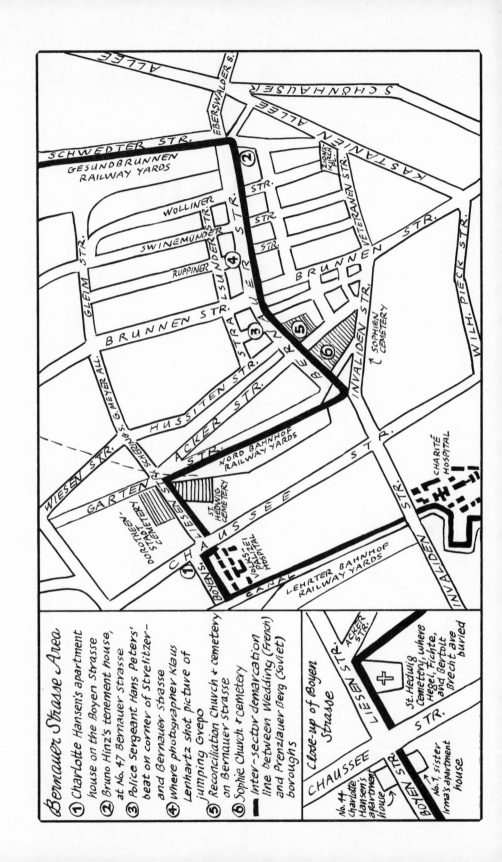

Bernauer Strasse Area

① Charlotte Hansen's apartment house on the Boyen Strasse

② Bruno Hinz's tenement house, at No. 47 Bernauer Strasse

③ Police Sergeant Hans Peters' beat on corner of Strelitzer- and Bernauer Strasse

④ where photographer Klaus Lenhartz shot picture of jumping Gvepo

⑤ Reconciliation Church + cemetery on Bernauer Strasse

⑥ Sophie Church + cemetery

▬ inter-sector demarcation line between Wedding (French) and Prenzlauer Berg (Soviet) boroughs

Close-up of Boyen Strasse

St. Hedwig Cemetery, where Hegel, Fichte, and Bertolt Brecht are buried

No. 4 Charlotte Hansen's apartment house

No. 7 sister Irma's apartment house

1

On July 12 Konrad Adenauer flew to Berlin in a U.S. Air Force plane. Although it had been eighteen months since the chancellor's last visit to the city, news of his arrival was enough to send *Neues Deutschland* into a spluttering rage. It was one more in a long series of provocations undertaken by this die-hard "apostle of the Cold War" against the peace-loving DDR.

For the aging chancellor such trips were relatively few and far between. Born and brought up in Catholic Cologne, Adenauer had never much cared for the capital of Protestant Prussia, a city forever associated in his mind with the energetic *Kulturkampf* ("cultural war") that Bismarck had launched in the early 1870s to combat the influence of the Catholic church. It was a distant and somewhat alien outpost where spike-helmeted overlords had long indulged their passion for saber-rattling. Indeed for this dyed-in-the-wool Rhinelander, all the flatlands east of the Elbe were a kind of *Kartoffelland* ("potato country"), the westernmost fringe of the Asiatic steppe. So ingrained was this conviction that in 1946, when there was much debate as to just where Germany's postwar capital was to be established, Adenauer had come out in favor of Frankfurt-on-the-Main on the grounds that the venerable Frankish city was located on "age-old German soil," which was more than one could say for Berlin.

The chancellor's intimate conviction was that Germany, like ancient Gaul, was divided into three distinct parts. There was the Germany of the schnapps drinkers of Prussia; there was the Germany of the beer drinkers of Bavaria; there was the Germany of the wine-drinking Rhineland. Of the three, he had once wryly remarked, only the wine drinkers were sober enough to rule the rest. This was why he had virtually boycotted his Christian Democratic party's first postwar meetings in Berlin. Only when he felt that the seriousness of the situation demanded it—as in November 1948, at the height of the blockade—could he get himself to leave his beloved Rhineland to fly to the embattled Frontstadt. He had done so in June 1953 shortly after the East German workers' revolt, and now that the storm clouds were gathering anew over the eastern horizon, he was flying up again.

The prime purpose of Adenauer's visit was to attend a private meeting of the Berlin *Senat*—the twelve-man government responsible for administering the three western sectors under the overall jurisdiction of the Allied commandants. The Senat in turn was responsible to a kind of lower chamber, or house of representatives, composed of 133 members, 78 of whom were Socialists and 55 Christian Democrats. Under the pressure of Khrushchev's ultimatum of November 1958, the two parties had formed a coalition government, headed by a Socialist governing mayor (Willy Brandt) and a Christian Democratic deputy mayor (Franz Amrehn).

To find himself once again face to face with Willy Brandt must have been a strange experience for Konrad Adenauer. With the two previous governing mayors, the chancellor had managed to maintain good, if not cordial, relations. Although both had been Socialists of a more or less agnostic hue (Ernst Reuter had even been a Communist), neither had made any serious attempt to extend his political influence to all West Germany. But in November 1960 the Social Democratic party had decided that the relatively young (he was not quite forty-seven) and personable governing mayor of Berlin was the person best fitted to be its candidate for the chancellorship in the Federal election campaign of 1961. This decision created an awkward situation. In West Germany, Adenauer's CDU and Brandt's SPD were openly opposed, whereas in threatened West Berlin, they were allied in a coalition government.

As members of the Bundestag in Bonn, Adenauer and Brandt had had plenty of time over the years to take each other's measure. Grateful as he was to the chancellor for the stalwart support he had always given to the principle of lavish federal aid on behalf of West Berlin, Brandt had been amused to discover how unfamiliar Adenauer was with the local Berlin scene. Once during a meeting with the Bundestag's Foreign Affairs Committee, Adenauer had passed him a note that read: "Bulganin is very much interested in Berlin. He has asked me if Kempinski's (the Kurfürstendamm's most fashionable hotel) is still standing. He always ate well there in the past." "And did you know if Kempinski's is still standing?" was Brandt's tongue-in-cheek riposte.

During a visit to Berlin in 1957, when Brandt was president (or speaker) of the local House of Representatives, the ailing mayor, Otto Suhr, had accompanied Adenauer to Tempelhof Airfield. The Federal chancellor and the governing mayor had been helped into the back seats, while Brandt climbed in up front next to the chauffeur. As they drove out of the Rathaus square, Adenauer had said to Suhr, "You must do everything possible to get well again. Here you are irreplaceable, and you know you enjoy my full confidence."

"What you say is very nice, Herr Bundeskanzler," Suhr had answered. "But when the time comes that I can no longer fulfill my duties, Willy Brandt will take over my office."

"About that I have my doubts," remarked Adenauer crisply. "And I'll tell you what he's after: *he* wants you out of the way."

A moment of troubled silence had followed, and only then did the chancellor notice that Willy Brandt, whom he had apparently taken for some Secret Service man, was seated next to the chauffeur. But more than this was needed to throw the old man off his stride.

"Ach, there sits the Herr Präsident," Adenauer had exclaimed, without a trace of embarrassment. "Now tell me, what are you really interested in, Herr Brandt? As you know, I am interested in garden design and the cultivation of flowers."

Half turning in his front seat, Brandt had shot back, "I am interested in political biographies"—a pointed reference to the "authorized" and thus anything but critical biography that Paul Weymar had recently written about Adenauer.

Just a few months earlier, in the spring of 1961, Brandt had called on the chancellor at his Bonn office, after reading the text of a strong Ash Wednesday speech that Adenauer's defense minister, Franz-Josef Strauss, had delivered in his rough-handed style. "We have a right to ask Herr Brandt, What did you do during the twelve years you were abroad? What we did here in Germany, that we know!" Stung by the insinuation that in preferring prewar exile to life under the Nazis, he had been unpatriotic, not to say treasonous, Brandt had asked the chancellor if he felt that this was the proper level on which the coming election campaign should be fought. Adenauer's imperturbable reply had left him open-mouthed: "But Herr Brandt, I have no idea what it is you want. If I had something against you, I would say it to you right out."

Now they sat opposite each other in the cabinet room of the Schöneberg City Hall. The chancellor began the session with a brief review of the international situation. No one knew exactly what Khrushchev was going to do next. He had been making bellicose speeches—enough to alarm Ambassador Kroll in Moscow. But after his latest blast, he had calmly left for a holiday in the Crimea. He had even assured Kroll that he wouldn't carry out his long-standing threat and sign a separate peace treaty with Ulbricht until the autumn at the very earliest, that is, after the election campaign in West Germany. It could thus be hoped that the burning question of Berlin would be left out of the campaign.

Speaking next, Willy Brandt emphasized the importance of the five-point program to which the two coalition partners in the Berlin city government had agreed in January 1960. There must be no tampering with the legal rights of the Western Allies to remain in West Berlin. West Berlin must be judicially, financially, and economically linked to the Federal Republic. There must be no restrictions on the free access of persons and goods to Berlin. Any new agreement reached on Berlin by the occupying powers must be founded on the freely granted consent of the Berlin population. Finally, Berlin must fulfill its historic role as a *Treffpunkt* (central meeting place and forum for all Germans). These five basic points were unanimously endorsed.

Of more immediate concern was what was likely to happen in the coming weeks, with the exodus from East Germany beginning to assume the proportions of a flood. The refugees pouring into Marienfelde and other reception centers seemed possessed by a fear that Ulbricht was about to close the escape hatch. Only the day before, Otto Winzer, deputy foreign minister of the DDR, had made a speech in Rostock reiterating the East German government's determination to assert control over all air traffic between the Federal Republic and West Berlin. A statement like that was enough to precipitate the flight of thousands of jittery East Germans.

Willy Brandt clung to his conviction that as much as they might rant and rave about the "spy swamp" of West Berlin, Ulbricht and his colleagues were not likely to attempt a total seal-off of the three western sectors. West Berlin, for most of the inhabitants of the East, was a kind of safety valve, and if that valve were ever to be jammed, the result could be another explosion comparable to the one of June 1953—an event Khrushchev would almost certainly prefer to avoid.

The governing mayor was fortified in this conviction by an incident that had occurred one month before during an official visit made to Berlin by Heinrich Luebke, president of the Federal Republic. Toward the end of a banquet being given in his honor in this same city hall, an official connected with a West German intelligence agency had appeared with a top-priority report indicating that the East Germans were about to close off all the access routes leading into West Berlin. The Western Allies had immediately been alerted, a few observers had been dispatched to East Berlin to check on road and railway movements into the city, others had been posted at strategic points with binoculars, and they had all spent a tense weekend waiting for the ax to fall. But nothing had happened. No attempt had been made to block the twenty-two vehicle and the sixty-six pedestrian crossing points between the Soviet and western sectors, or the streets, roads, or pathways linking the western sectors to the Soviet zone. The report had turned out to be one more rumor, like the hundreds of others that were now circulating over the length and breadth of the DDR.

In the five weeks that had passed since then, however, the situation inside East Germany had deteriorated so dramatically that the DDR authorities were now taking drastic measures. All the incoming refugees spoke of reinforced police controls on highway and railroad travelers making for Berlin. They were being asked their reasons for wishing to reach the city, and those suspected of *Republikflucht* were being summarily detained on the highways or hauled off the trains.

Only the day before, on July 11, Vopos stationed on Route 96 just south of the university town of Greifswald on the Baltic had stopped the chauffeur-driven car of the Right Reverend Friedrich Krummacher. The bishop and his wife were on their way to attend a five-day *Kirchentag*—a Protestant "church day" rally scheduled to begin in the western sectors of Berlin on July 19. This annual event, expected this year to draw thirty-five thousand Protestant believers from all parts of Germany, had been forcefully denounced on July 8 by Lt. Gen. Fritz Eikemeyer, commander of the East German Volkspolizei. The Ulbricht regime had first tried to browbeat the Protestant hierarchy into holding the Kirchentag rally in Leipzig, where East German believers would not have been exposed to the corrupting temptations of the West; and when the church hierarchy refused, Vopos stationed on highways and in train stations were ordered to turn back all East Germans found carrying Bibles, considered to be proof that they were headed for West Berlin. Bishop Krummacher, of Greifswald, had not only been turned back; the Vopos had confiscated his identity card, along with his wife's, which meant that they could no longer travel anywhere.

Even more serious than the antireligious harassment was the campaign against the Grenzgänger that the East German authorities were now launching. In 1951 the number of Grenzgänger living in the East but working in the West had actually exceeded one hundred thousand, while the number of West Berliners going to work in the East amounted to forty-two thousand. The numbers had since shrunk significantly, but even so, the fifty-three thousand East Berliners who continued to work in the western sectors were four times more numerous than the thirteen thousand West Berliners who were still willing to work in the East.

It was this imbalance that the Ulbricht regime now seemed determined to redress through a campaign of deliberate intimidation launched with the announcement, on July 7, that all East Berlin Grenzgänger would have to register with their local labor offices and obtain permission to go on working in the West. The Soviet sector's city hall had followed up this directive four days later with another one limiting purchases of cars, motorcycles, motor scooters, television sets, refrigerators, washing machines, and boats in East Berlin shops and stores to persons able to produce certificates showing that they were gainfully employed in East Berlin. The East German authorities were thus trying to compensate for a continuing loss of skilled workers and technicians fleeing to the West by retrieving the East Berliners who were working in the western sectors of the city.

The Schöenberg City Hall meeting produced two decisions. Instead of returning to his Ministry of All-German Affairs in Bonn, Ernst Lemmer was to remain in Berlin to supervise the handling of incoming refugees, who would now have to be flown to the Federal Republic at the rate of one thousand a day. And in a gesture of solidarity toward the severely rationed inhabitants of East Germany, the Federal government was going to make a formal offer of five thousand tons of butter as its contribution to the solution of the present crisis.

The two decisions were announced the next morning by Konrad Adenauer at a press conference during which he deftly sidestepped pointed questions regarding Allied plans and future countermeasures. Asked what he thought of the idea of trying to organize a mammoth end-of-war conference, to which all fifty-two of the nations that had declared war on Nazi Germany were to be invited, the chancellor replied, not much. The proposal, made by Willy Brandt and endorsed by Sen. Hubert Humphrey during his recent trip to Berlin, was dismissed by *der Alte* as a "sheer waste of time."

The first reactions from the East were not long in coming. Within hours, the offer of five thousand tons of butter was rejected in an ADN news bulletin as a propaganda statement and ridiculed as being woefully insufficient to meet the needs of the DDR's high butter consumption. The rejection was accompanied by a new announcement, issued this time by the deputy mayor of East Berlin, to the effect that from now on no West Berliner could have any repairs made in East Berlin unless he paid for them in West German marks or in eastern marks obtained at the official exchange rate of 1 to 1.

The following weekend the refugee rate made another upward bound as close to three thousand East Germans registered at Marienfelde.

2

Hans Kroll, who had been summoned back to Bonn for a meeting with other West German ambassadors, was for once in complete agreement with his boss, Heinrich von Brentano. The British had again let down the Allied side. Blithely choosing to ignore the possible diplomatic repercussions, they had invited Yuri Gagarin to Britain and given him a royal welcome. The Soviet spaceman's visit, coinciding with a Russian trade fair, had been one long triumph. Although not officially a guest of the British government, he had attended a reception given by Prime Minister Harold Macmillan, and the next day, July 14, he had lunched at Buckingham Palace with Queen Elizabeth and Prince Philip. The working men of Manchester who, like the schoolboys of London, had turned out to cry "Tovarich!" and to cheer him whenever he appeared in public could be forgiven their ignorance; but Whitehall officials knew perfectly well that less than two weeks before, Khrushchev had told Sir Frank Roberts, Her Majesty's ambassador to Moscow, that the USSR could blow Britain from the face of the map with eight atomic bombs. Yet here was John Bull deliberately turning the other cheek.

The Bonn Foreign Ministry was so upset that it ordered its ambassador in London, Herwarth von Bittenfeld, to lodge a protest with the Foreign Office. The protest was received with frigid displeasure. For Brentano, the British were running true to form. They had always been too soft in their dealings with the Soviets. All of this was disconcerting. At a time when the Western Allies should be closing ranks against a common danger, they were more divided than ever.

Meeting informally in Brentano's hillside villa on the Venusberg, overlooking the misty hills and ruined castles of the Rhine, the ambassadors spent two days discussing the international situation. Kroll, who did most of the talking the first day, dwelt at length on his personal meetings with Khrushchev and hazarded the guess that the chances of peace were better than

100

50–50. Basically, the Soviets were out to sever the constitutional and economic ties linking West Berlin to the Federal Republic, and on this point the West had to maintain an intransigent position.

Such also was the opinion of Wilhelm Grewe, a law professor turned diplomat whom Adenauer had appointed ambassador to Washington. As reserved and academic as Kroll was outgoing and garrulous, Grewe had not had an easy time of it. The uncertainty and wobbliness that had begun to manifest itself in U.S. diplomacy under Christian Herter seemed to have increased under Kennedy and Rusk, causing the West German ambassador to file increasingly critical reports. The bright-eyed champions of the "New Frontier" were not at all to his liking. Adenauer had had to chide his ambassador for being overcritical in his reports, but *der Alte*'s displeasure had not altered Grewe's conviction that there was not an authentic hard-liner in the White House. Exactly what would happen when the crunch came and Khrushchev signed his separate peace treaty with Ulbricht's DDR was anybody's guess, but he was frankly pessimistic.

Two days after this inconclusive exchange of viewpoints, Adenauer again received Kroll in his Palais Schaumburg office. The eighty-five-year-old chancellor was in a relaxed mood, clearly looking forward to his forthcoming holiday on Lake Como, where he was going to rest for two weeks before plunging into the fray of the West German elections.

"Well, how goes the world?" was his opening query.

"Not too badly, in my opinion," replied his ambassador. "We shouldn't give way to hysteria. There won't be a war. Khrushchev has no intention of letting a war compromise the main aim of his life, which is to make the Soviet Union into the world's leading industrial power, and to give peace and well-being to the Soviet people."

Adenauer agreed that there would be no war over Berlin. He then moved on to one of his pet themes: the need for controlled disarmament, without which nothing else really mattered. The armaments race was absurd, but since Khrushchev had just increased his arms expenditures, the American president had no choice but to do the same. The speech that Kennedy was to make the following day in Washington would probably be a tough one—the delayed consequence of the failed summit meeting in Vienna.

Yes, agreed Kroll, "but to these official speeches Khrushchev will have to reply publicly. He too can't afford to lose face, particularly on the question of Berlin, where he has committed his personal prestige. If one wants to get reasonable decisions out of him, one must have recourse to personal and confidential conversations (like the ones he himself had had in the Crimea) without interpreters," he added significantly. He then reiterated his plea for a summit meeting between the chancellor and Khrushchev once the West German elections were over.

On this point Adenauer was as wary as ever. The Americans, with their "Rapallo complex," would take it badly. "You can't imagine how touchy they are on the subject. The influential and highly regarded Senator Fulbright has just declared publicly that the American government had recently let its policy making be too much influenced by me. This is obviously absurd, but one has to take this American viewpoint into account."

The encounter, once again, thus ended in a draw.

Kroll left shortly afterward with his wife for a summer vacation in Bavaria. Before leaving for Italy, Adenauer told a group of German reporters that the Berlin crisis would not reach as dangerous a point as had been feared several weeks before. Not until mid-November would Khrushchev be ready to negotiate about Berlin, for the Congress of the Soviet Communist Party, due to convene on October 17, was certain to keep the men in the Kremlin busy for three to four weeks.

In the distant Crimea a rotund and beaming Khrushchev continued to thrash the waters of his specially constructed swimming pool, between the perusal of dispatches and talks with his advisers about the simmering crisis in Berlin. In distant Washington, *New York Times* columnist James Reston wrote in a Sunday editorial:

Berlin is regarded here for the moment not as a military emergency but as a political opportunity. It may develop into a military crisis around, of all times, Thanksgiving, but for the time being it is being used to get a lot of things done that President Kennedy wanted to do anyway, but could not get done without the lash of Khrushchev's threats.

3

The hard-line Acheson program, calling for the proclamation of a national emergency and the call-up of one million draftees and reservists, was allowed to die a quiet death at a special meeting of the National Security Council held on Wednesday, July 19. Acheson, who attended the meeting, found himself opposed by his one-time protégé, Dean Rusk, who felt that a precipitated effort would probably alarm rather than reassure the United States' allies. Robert McNamara was even more negative. Any military buildup should be orderly and sustained rather than abrupt and panicky, he argued, and a congressional resolution would provide a less dramatic but equally effective way of expanding the armed services.

Kennedy himself no longer needed convincing. His economic advisers had been warning him that the proclamation of a national emergency would set off panic buying and send prices soaring all over the country. From Moscow Llewellyn Thompson had been bombarding the State Department with dispatches predicting a violent Soviet reaction to anything resembling a crash program. A less blatantly advertised program of muscle building was more likely to impress the Russians as a token of determination and resolve.

It was one thing to bury the Acheson program; it was another to find something suitable to replace it. At a meeting of the recently created Berlin Task Force, which now met daily on the seventh floor of the State Department under the chairmanship of Foy Kohler, Acheson had told Abram Chayes, who had volunteered to draft a different "scenario" aimed at defusing the Berlin crisis, "Abe, you'll see. You try, but you will find that it just won't write." This, obviously, was a challenge to the president, who felt that Harold Macmillan was right in advocating, and Charles de Gaulle wrong in condemning, eventual negotiations with the Russians. Indeed, in his private conversations, Kennedy made no bones about it. If the Russians went ahead

103

and signed a separate peace treaty with Ulbricht's DDR—
something they might well do if not restrained by the prospect of
eventual negotiations—the United States was not going to war
over the question of whether East German officials should have
the right to examine the papers of U.S. personnel traveling on
Reichsbahn trains or driving up and down the Helmstedt–Berlin Autobahn.

The Russians, curiously enough, had reached much the same
conclusion. The Soviet ambassador in Washington, Mikhail
Menshikov, was no longer the same "Smiling Mike" he had been
in February 1958, when he had first been appointed to his post
and had surprised everybody by a diplomatic affability no Soviet
envoy had displayed since the days of Maxim Litvinoff. Like his
boss in Moscow, he was now all threats rather than all smiles. At
a cocktail party given at the Iraqi embassy on July 14, he got into
an argument with an American guest who had been insisting on
America's determination to fight for Berlin. "I do not believe
this," he bluntly declared. "I have talked to many people in this
country. My reports are objective. They have to be. Many of the
Americans I have talked to do not want to fight. They do not feel
the way you do. . . . In the final analysis, and when the chips are
down, the American people won't fight for Berlin."

The incident, reported by Warren Rogers, diplomatic correspondent for the *New York Herald Tribune*, was splashed over
the front page of that newspaper's Sunday edition. James
Reston, in a *New York Times* column published on that same
day, July 16, described Ambassador Menshikov as being

if anything, even more extreme and menacing than anybody else.
Menshikov has been saying to diplomats in Washington that the decision to make a separate peace treaty with Communist East Germany
has been taken in Moscow; that he was present when it was taken; that
such a peace treaty would end all Western rights in Berlin; and that any
attempts by the West to enforce its rights would start a nuclear war.

The next day—Monday, July 17—Walt Rostow, an M.I.T.
economics professor who had joined the White House staff as
McGeorge Bundy's assistant for national security affairs, happened to lunch with the Soviet ambassador. He soon discovered

that what he had read in the previous day's newspapers was no exaggeration. Menshikov scoffed at the idea that anyone in the West was prepared to die for Berlin. If the crisis intensified, the West Germans would begin to flee their country as fast as the East Germans were now fleeing theirs. The French? Totally unreliable, despite De Gaulle, who in any case was powerless to act effectively. The British? Totally lacking in determination; all they wanted was to be able to live in peace on their little island.

"Don't underestimate the British or their will," Rostow reminded him. "That was exactly the mistake Hitler made, and it's what landed him in a world war in which Germany was finally destroyed and occupied. Democracies aren't like dictatorships. They don't react in the same ways, and nothing is easier than underestimating just how courageously democratic citizens are capable of behaving in times of crisis."

Menshikov shook his large, round head. All this reasoning was very fine, but what had happened in 1939 or 1940 no longer applied. Hitler did not possess nuclear weapons, and this fact made all the difference.

There were two chinks of light in this otherwise somber conversation. The first was an intimation that the East Germans would not block Allied access to West Berlin after the conclusion of a separate peace treaty, but would make the rights of future access conditional on some sort of recognition and on the cessation of offensive activities in West Berlin. The second was Menshikov's bland assertion that a German peace conference would be held during the last two weeks of November.

All this, naturally, was passed on to the president. It did little to lighten the load he had to bear. If the Soviets were growing so cocky, it was, he felt, in no small part due to the scandalous length of time it had taken the State Department to answer the Berlin memorandum that Khrushchev had handed to him in Vienna on June 4. The delays, Dean Rusk and Foy Kohler kept explaining, were due to the need to consult the three major Allies—Britain, France, and West Germany—about the wording of the official reply. But these explanations only made Kennedy more fretful. If this was the business-as-usual pace at which Western diplomacy was going to operate, then clearly they were in for trouble. The Russians would be able to run circles around them, and the West would find itself losing each new diplomatic round.

On July 19 Robert Kennedy, who had been giving some thought to these matters, asked Walt Rostow if the Berlin problem couldn't be handled a bit like an issue in U.S. campaign politics; that is, couldn't they think up some neat theme or simple slogan around which most of the countries of the free world could rally? John Kennedy had decided that the crisis was serious enough to warrant a major television address to the American people. The date had already been set: Tuesday, July 25—less than a week away.

Rostow, who had not been given the names Walt Whitman for nothing, responded with a memorandum urging firmness, regardless of the hesitant mood of the United States' allies. Washington, not London or Bonn, had its finger on the atomic trigger. Each nation naturally possessed just so much stomach for a war-facing situation; the capacity of European nations for this kind of nervous test was—and should be—lower than that of America's, simply because they had suffered far more from wars over the past half century. He concluded by saying that the Western Allies might stay the course united, or the crisis might abort at a relatively early stage. In any case, they should be prepared for a somewhat lonely stage, and—in a reference to the film *High Noon*—the United States should accept this lonely responsibility without throwing its sheriff's badge in the dust the moment the crisis subsided.

The president had asked two economists—Paul Samuelson and Seymour Harris—to estimate what might be the inflationary or other effects on the U.S. economy resulting from substantially increased defense spending. Harris's estimate was that it would do the economy more good than harm. The expansion already under way, stimulated in part by an earlier decision in March to boost defense spending, promised to add $14 billion to the Gross National Product and to bring in $4 billion in additional revenue. Kennedy had decided to fix the figure for new defense appropriations at $3.2 billion. This brought the total increase since January to some $6 billion over and above the level originally set by the outgoing Eisenhower administration. He felt that this was a burden that the U.S. economy could carry in its stride and which the members of Congress would be willing to accept.

By an appropriate coincidence Gen. Douglas MacArthur was the president's luncheon guest on Thursday, July 20. In the afternoon Kennedy closeted himself with two of his speech writers—Theodore Sorensen, his special counsel, and Arthur Schlesinger, Jr., the Harvard historian—to discuss certain points in his forthcoming television speech. This working session was followed by an informal meeting attended by Dean Rusk; Defense Secretary Robert McNamara; Gen. Lyman Lemnitzer; Gen. Maxwell Taylor, the chief military adviser for the White House; and Edward Murrow, head of the U.S. Information Agency. Those present were asked to think up striking phrases that might be incorporated into the president's television speech once Sorensen had completed the first draft, which he was scheduled to do over the weekend.

That evening Kennedy sent off three cabled dispatches—to Konrad Adenauer, Charles de Gaulle, and Harold Macmillan— outlining the main elements of U.S. policy on Berlin, as he saw them, and mentioning the main points he intended to make in his television speech. The $3.2 billion increase in defense spending was intended to give the United States the military capability of moving six additional U.S. divisions to Europe by the end of 1961, should the situation seem to warrant it. The number of bomber aircraft placed on an alert status was likewise to be increased by 50 percent. However, he pointedly added, the Soviet challenge to the West could only be met if "the NATO members make a comparable effort."

The Friday morning, July 21, edition of the *New York Times* carried an interesting follow-up on the earlier stories about Soviet Ambassador Menshikov. Interviewed by Harrison Salisbury in New York as he was about to board a transatlantic liner, Menshikov began by hedging; the remarks he had made at the Iraqi embassy cocktail party had been off the record. He had been accosted by an American superpatriot who had declared, "Please inform your government that we will fight for Berlin." To which Menshikov had answered, "Nobody can keep you from committing suicide if you want to." Salisbury, however, was insistent: What was the ambassador's *on-the-record* opinion on

the subject of American willingness to fight over Berlin? After
hesitating for a moment, Menshikov finally gave it: "I don't think
it is in the interest of the American people to fight for the interests of West German militarists, revanchists, and Fascists."

There was some comfort to be derived from the realization
that the Soviet ambassador was sailing home for a leisurely six-
week vacation. The masters of the Kremlin would not have taken
the risk of letting their ambassador leave Washington for this
length of time if they were anticipating a major confrontation in
late July or August. Khrushchev himself had left for his dacha
near the Crimean resort of Sotchi, and a couple of days before,
the *New York Times'* Moscow correspondent, Osgood Carruth-
ers, had reported that there were scant signs in the USSR of
civil-defense preparations.

On Monday morning, July 24, a meeting was held at the
White House to discuss the first draft of the forthcoming television address, which Theodore Sorensen had prepared over the
weekend. Edward Murrow suggested adding a two-fisted sentence to the effect that one cannot negotiate with those who say,
"What's mine is mine, and what's yours is negotiable." This sop
to the hard-liners, who, like De Gaulle, felt that negotiations
with the Soviets would yield nothing, was accompanied by a sop
to the soft-liners suggested by McGeorge Bundy: a sentence
recognizing the "Soviet Union's historical concerns about their
security in Central and Eastern Europe." Gen. Maxwell Taylor,
for his part, had already suggested another bit of hard-line rhetoric: "I hear it it said that West Berlin is militarily untenable.
And so was Bastogne. And so, in fact, was Stalingrad. Any spot is
tenable if men—brave men—will make it so."

From the White House meeting, which broke up shortly after
one o'clock, Theodore Sorensen had himself driven to the May-
flower Hotel, where he had a luncheon date with his brother
Tom, now the number three man in the U.S. Information
Agency, and James O'Donnell, a former *Newsweek* and *Saturday Evening Post* correspondent who had given up journalism to
work for George Ball, under secretary of state for economic
affairs. In July 1945 O'Donnell had flown to Berlin to set up a
German bureau for *Newsweek*. He had later lived through the
blockade of 1948–49 and eventually established residence there.

becoming in the process an "old Berlin hand." He had been instrumental, during a labor conference held in Berlin in 1959, in introducing Tom Sorensen to Willy Brandt, thus helping to pave the way for Brandt's visit to the White House in March of 1961. And in the early stages of the 1960 election campaign, Jack Kennedy, who had known him at Harvard, had had O'Donnell prepare a memorandum on Berlin outlining the origins and history of the Four-Power agreements governing the occupied city.

"Well," said Theodore Sorensen, as they sat down to lunch, "just look at this—it ought to make even hard-liners like you and (Marguerite) Higgins happy." With that he handed over the reworked draft of the president's scheduled speech.

O'Donnell went through the text carefully and was initially impressed. On first reading it looked like a tough speech. The lines about the "untenability" of Berlin that Gen. Maxwell Taylor had suggested were followed, for example, by this solemn warning:

We do not want to fight—but we have fought before. And others in earlier times have made the same dangerous mistake of assuming that the West was too selfish and too soft and too divided to resist invasions of freedom in other lands. . . . We cannot and will not permit the Communists to drive us out of Berlin, either gradually or by force.

This was good Kennedy rhetoric, showing the same Irish spunk which had caused him to declare, in an interview published in *Harper's* magazine at about the time of the first Khrushchev ultimatum of November 1958, that to his mind, "the fate of Berlin is as important as the fate of Paris, London, or even New York."

The text also contained a trenchant accusation which John Foster Dulles would have been hard put to improve on:

The world is not deceived by the Communist attempt to label Berlin a hot-bed of war. There is peace in Berlin today. The source of world trouble and tension is Moscow, not Berlin. And if war begins, it will have begun in Moscow and not Berlin.

For the choice of peace or war is largely theirs, not ours. It is the Soviets who have stirred up this crisis. It is they who are trying to force a change. It is they who have opposed free elections. It is they who have rejected an all-German peace treaty, and the rulings of international law. And as Americans know from our history on our own old frontier, gun battles are caused by outlaws, and not by officers of the peace.

Yes, these were fighting words, in the fighting Kennedy spirit. And yet, as O'Donnell went through the text a second time, curiously flabby bits showed up next to the stronger passages. "We have previously indicated our readiness to remove the actual irritants in West Berlin, but the freedom of that city is not negotiable." What were these "actual irritants" in West Berlin? A free and unfettered press? Free radio stations? A freely elected parliament where properly elected representatives could speak their minds without fear of arrest? The existence of free air flight lanes over the DDR that fugitives from the East could use to seek asylum in the West? From the East German point of view, all these were irritants that had to be removed in order to "normalize" the situation. Merely to suggest that such irritants existed was to concede that there was a measure of truth to Walter Ulbricht's propaganda, and to give him and his Soviet mentors one more club with which to bludgeon Uncle Sam.

Nor was it clear just what was to be gained by adding in the next paragraph:

We recognize the Soviet Union's historical concern about their security in Central and Eastern Europe, after a series of ravaging invasions, and we believe arrangements can be worked out which will help to meet those concerns, and make it possible for both security and freedom to exist in this troubled area.

Was this a tacit admission that the militarists and munitions manufacturers in West Germany were once again on the warpath and thus a threat to Russia's perennial security? What a boon for the press lords of the East! This was precisely the impression *Pravda* and *Neues Deutschland* had been striving to promote for weeks.

But what worried O'Donnell most was the repeated references to West Berlin as opposed to the whole of that city. Only in one place, near the beginning of the speech, was passing reference made to the overall validity of the Four-Power agreements governing all four sectors of Berlin: "Berlin is not a part of East Germany but a separate territory under the control of the Allied powers." Elsewhere the emphasis was placed on America's commitments to the two million inhabitants of West Berlin, and to them alone. In essence, this speech, as written, bade farewell to the Four-Power agreements of the past and invited the Soviets to do as they pleased in their sector of the city.

To this objection the Sorensen brothers gave the standard reply. The Russians had *in fact* for years been doing exactly as they pleased in their sector of Berlin. What, then, was the good of staking out exaggerated claims that none of the Western Allies were in a position to enforce? It was difficult enough to get ordinary American citizens to accept the need for a buildup of U.S. forces in Europe in order to safeguard the welfare of two million West Berliners. To ask them to risk a major confrontation with the Soviet Union over the lot of a million *East* Berliners as well was simply asking too much.

The argument, which went on for a good hour, ended in disagreement. Ted Sorensen refused to believe that the Four-Power agreements were that important, since the Russians had been violating them for years and getting away with it; and he was shocked when O'Donnell suggested that he beef up the text by simply omitting the word *West* in front of *Berlin* in most of the places where it occurred.

"Look," he protested, "I can't monkey around any more with the text of this speech, which is to be delivered by the president of the United States. It's been read and approved by a dozen different people, and subject to a few minor changes and added flourishes, this is it." On that note the luncheon broke up.

The criticism voiced by Harold Macmillan, to whom Kennedy had sent five densely typed pages of the initial draft, was of a different order. He took issue with the section devoted to civil defense and to the need to protect the American civilian population from the menace of nuclear destruction. He wondered if

Kennedy couldn't possibly "avoid emphasizing too much the need for air-raid shelters. In our little island they would be impossible and useless."

This judicious advice also went unheeded. When the atomic chips were down, it was he, John Fitzgerald Kennedy, not Charles de Gaulle or Harold Macmillan, who would have to make the truly agonizing decisions that might lead to an all-out nuclear war. He could not afford to be off-handed or to disregard Khrushchev's threats. At Vienna the rollicking Ukrainian's bomb rattling had frankly shaken him, and he wanted the American people to share his concern and to appreciate his sense of responsibility for their fate. One day when Paul Fay, whom he had named assistant secretary of the navy, had telephoned him, Kennedy had asked if he had got around to building his bomb shelter. "No," laughed Fay. "I built a swimming pool."

"You made a mistake," was the stern rebuke.

The next day after a formal luncheon and an afternoon reception for Sir Abubakar Tafawa Balewa of Nigeria, Kennedy retired upstairs to his bedroom. The television address was scheduled for 10:00 P.M. He took a hot bath to ease the chronic pains in his spine and then had his supper brought in on a tray. In the middle of the meal, he summoned Evelyn Lincoln, his secretary, and dictated a new ending to his scheduled speech. In it he specifically referred to the possibility of a conflict with the Soviet Union leading to mass destruction on both sides.

What makes this so somber is the fact that the Soviet Union is attempting in a most forceful way to assert its power and this brings them into collision with us in those areas, such as Berlin, where we have long-standing commitments. Three times in my lifetime our country and Europe have been involved in wars and on both sides in each case serious misjudgements were made which brought about great devastation. Now, however, through any misjudgements on either side about the intentions of the other more devastation could be rained in several hours than we have seen in all the wars in our history.

A brief peroration followed in which Kennedy declared that there was "no easy and quick solution to the present crisis. We are opposed by a system which has organized a billion people and which knows that if the United States falters their victory is imminent."

At 9:30 the president made his way downstairs to his office in the west wing of the White House. The electricians and television crews were finishing the installation of the cameras and floodlights trained on his desk and on the map of Germany that had been unfolded on the wall behind. Walking into Evelyn Lincoln's office to the right, he picked up a copy of the added paragraphs. He then walked into the Cabinet room, and sitting down at his usual place at the long table, made a few last-minute changes.

At ten o'clock he was ready to face the cameras, seconded by his naval aide, Comdr. Tazewell Shepard, who stood behind him with a blackboard pointer to indicate the areas of immediate conflict mentioned in the speech.

Three months before, Jack Kennedy had had to go before the television cameras to explain his painful decision to back out of the Bay of Pigs fiasco. The crisis, although serious—especially for his personal prestige—was nonetheless essentially local. But the crisis he was now facing was of worldwide dimensions. In Moscow, East Berlin, and all the capitals of the Soviet block, as in the capitals of the West, his every word would be weighed and examined for clues to his thinking, character, and future reactions. John Fitzgerald Kennedy did not need to be told that this was the most important speech he had yet been called upon to deliver.

4

Forty minutes later a profusely perspiring president emerged from the Oval office. Close to sixty persons—a few privileged correspondents (including the head of the local TASS news agency), a score of photographers, some Secret Service men, and a few members of the White House staff—had crowded their way into the office, which soon felt like an oven. The air conditioning had been turned off to improve the quality of the microphonic pick-up, and the strain of having to read a carefully prepared text under the hot glare of two floodlights had caused an unusually tense and nervous Kennedy to flub one or two or his lines (saying "unpressed" where "unprecedented" was intended, for example).

The earnestness of his delivery, however, made a generally favorable impression on his audience. Within hours the White House was being deluged with telegrams indicating an overwhelmingly favorable listener response. Most of the newspapers in the country praised a speech that had been firm but not truculent in tone. Encouraging too was the response from Capitol Hill, where the Republican minority leaders, Charles Halleck, representative from Indiana, and Everett Dirksen, senator from Illinois, held a press conference to voice their support for the president's call for an increased defense effort.

In London, as Drew Middleton wrote in the *New York Times*, "the British are slowly and uncomfortably awaking to the bitter realities of the developing crisis over Berlin." The Foreign Office gave the speech its emphatic endorsement. Conservative newspapers were full of praise for the speech, but so, surprisingly, was the *Daily Herald*, normally favorable to the Labour party; Kennedy, it wrote, had "made it as clear as words and precautionary deeds can make it that there will be no surrender to Russian threats or to Russian force over Berlin. It is not just the safety of a city that is at stake. It is the safety of the whole West."

When it came to deeds, the picture was less rosy. Confronted with an economic crisis, an unfavorable trade balance, and a weakening of the pound, the British government had announced a projected cut in the country's defense expenditures. During a brief stopover in London, Robert McNamara had been assured by Harold Watkinson, the British defense minister, that Britain intended to bring its Army of the Rhine up to its prescribed strength of fifty-five thousand men. But how was this pledge going to be honored at a time when British reinforcements were pinned down in the Persian Gulf, whither they had gone to defend Kuwait against Iraqi saber rattling?

In Paris there was the same discrepancy between official praise and practical impotence. French newspapers, like the government, were more concerned by the military flare-up in Bizerte, Tunisia (recently occupied by French paratroopers), than they were by the American president's long-range plans for increasing the United States defense effort.

There was praise for Kennedy's speech in The Hague, as there was in Rome, a few days before the Moscow visit that Premier Amintore Fanfani and Foreign Minister Antonio Segni were due to make in early August. Only from Ottawa, among Western capitals, was any criticism forthcoming, the Canadians expressing disappointment over the U.S. president's failure to come out with "specific proposals" for negotiating the Berlin crisis.

From Cadenabbia, on Lake Como, where he was vacationing, Konrad Adenauer sent Kennedy a telegram expressing his warm thanks. The West German press was almost unanimous in its commendations, and the Berlin *Kurier* even called it "a great speech." In a formal statement issued from the Schöneberg City Hall, Mayor Willy Brandt declared that "anyone who bears responsibility and thinks responsibly will be deeply impressed by the measures for the strengthening of military security which the American president has made known. No less important are his references to the need for an offensive diplomacy."

More surprising was the initial reaction in East Berlin. Passing over the tougher sections of the speech, *Neues Deutschland* stressed the "willingness to negotiate" it expressed, while finding it regrettable that Kennedy should have offered no solution to the Berlin problem. A few hours of reflection were enough to make Hermann Axen and his editorial colleagues realize that stronger words than these were needed to express the East German government's official displeasure over the stronger passages of the speech. In a much longer article published in its next issue, on July 28, Kennedy was criticized for sounding "warlike tones" and for waging a "war of nerves" against the Soviet Union in a foredoomed attempt to keep the USSR from signing a separate peace treaty with the DDR. The article also doubted Kennedy's readiness to remove any of the "irritants" he had mentioned—such as the "sabotage and man-training centers" in West Berlin, and of course the RIAS broadcasting station, described once again as a *Störzentrum* ("disturbance center") directed "against the DDR and other socialist countries. What is an American radio station doing in the capital of the DDR? Is it Mr. Kennedy's intention, in the name of equality, to allow the DDR to open a radio station in Washington, D.C.?" The editorial concluded with another broadside against the "anachronistic occupation rights of the Western powers," which flouted all accepted notions of international law.

Even sharper were the reactions in Moscow. Mincing no words, TASS denounced the president's speech as a symptom of the "war fever" that had overtaken Washington, adding that it had "nothing in common with a genuine concern for the protection and 'freedom' of West Berlin, which nobody has been or is threatening." Soviet officials, contacted by Seymour Topping of the *New York Times*, were even blunter: "He threatened us. That does not work in the Soviet Union any longer. If he wants war he can have it."

Most volatile in his condemnation was Khrushchev. Kennedy's chief disarmament negotiator, John J. McCloy, who had flown to the Crimea to see the Russian premier, was treated to a long tirade in the familiar Nikita style. Kennedy, he declared, had issued an ultimatum and all but openly declared war on the Soviet Union and its allies. But no amount of warlike bluster was going to deter the Soviet Union from signing a separate peace treaty with East Germany. If the Western powers refused to recognize the new realities and the sovereignty of East Germany, and if they insisted on shooting their way through to West Berlin, they would be well advised to remember that the USSR enjoyed a crushing superiority in tanks, guns, and men, and that it was far closer to the field of battle.

This fruitless bellicosity was playing into the hands of Khrushchev's scientists and engineers, who were building a one-hundred-megaton bomb. They already had rockets powerful enough to lift and propel it all the way to the United States. The one thing that troubled them was their inability to test it. "I cheered them up by telling them that the United States would soon start testing again, and that then they would get permission to go ahead with their own bomb. 'So don't piss in your pants— your chance will come soon enough.'"

If war came, Khrushchev concluded, the outcome would be

decided by rocket warfare, and it so happened that the Soviet Union had more and bigger rockets than anyone else. So what was the point of calling up a few American reservists and trying to impress the Soviet Union in this fashion? Basically the arms race was ridiculous. But if it ever came to war, one thing was certain: John Kennedy would be the last president of the United States, and he would have no successor.

On July 26, the day before this outburst, Walter Heller, chairman of the White House Council of Economic Advisers, flew to Bonn, where he had been invited to speak to a group of industrial and financial leaders. His arrival at such a delicate moment was not made to please certain of the Christian Democratic Union's leaders—including Adenauer and former Finance Minister Ludwig Erhard—who had not forgiven the former U.S. military government official for having signed a report urging the retention of rigorous controls over the West German economy.

Having already left for Lake Como, Konrad Adenauer was spared the embarrassment of having to receive Walter Heller. The task was left to Franz Etzel, who had succeeded Ludwig Erhard as finance minister, and to Adenauer's bosom friend and adviser, the Cologne banker Robert Pferdmenges. A dinner arranged by the U.S. ambassador, Walter Dowling, enabled Heller to meet a dozen influential Germans, and the next day, Friday, July 28, he lunched in Frankfurt with the directors and staff members of the Bundesbank in Frankfurt.

Virtually every German he talked to voiced the same sentiment: "Thank heaven there's leadership in the White House once again!" The firmness of Kennedy's tone, the logic of his speech, the careful balance between determination and conciliation, the plans for the long haul—all were unanimously praised. The differences of opinion began over the immediate prospects, and what the West should do about them.

The most forceful and forthright in airing his opinions on this subject was Axel Springer, publisher of *Bild Zeitung* and *Die Welt*, a one-time Socialist who had risen to become West Germany's leading newspaper magnate. Under no circumstances, he argued, should the Western powers accept a separate Soviet peace treaty with East Germany in exchange for a new agreement guaranteeing Allied access rights to Berlin. Such an agreement would amount to tacit abandonment by the West of the city's Four-Power status. Barbed-wire barriers would be put up to seal off West Berlin completely from East Germany; the pressure thus exerted would cause the people of West Berlin to lose heart and to begin flying their children out to the safety of the Federal Republic before emigrating themselves. West Berlin would end up a hollow shell.

It was also Springer's belief that the most effective Allied riposte to a separate peace treaty would be an embargo on West German exports to Ulbricht's DDR. These exports represented only a small percentage of total West German output but were of major importance to industrial production in East Germany.

Finally, there was the explosive situation in East Germany. A popular uprising in response to a separate peace treaty or blockade was something that had to be reckoned with. Springer, and in this view he was not alone, insisted that "another Budapest" was in the making. In Washington, as elsewhere, advance planning and analysis were needed on the key question of what might happen if the Western Allies intervened in East Berlin. The prospect was unpleasant, but it had to be faced.

These impressions and reactions, recorded in a two-page memorandum, quickly found their way to John Kennedy's desk. They had been preceded by a press conference that Willy Brandt staged in Bonn on July 28, a few hours before Heller flew back to Washington.

Brandt had nothing but praise for John Kennedy's televised speech, contrasting its "positive tone and content" with the (by implication negative) statements recently emanating from official Bonn circles. Kennedy had placed the West's struggle with the Soviet Union in its worldwide perspective, whereas Adenauer had tried to limit the confrontation to the particular problem of Berlin. Kennedy had indicated a willingness to enter into negotiations on the general problem of Germany, whereas the Adenauer government was merely standing pat. Kennedy's suggestion that a local plebiscite be held to decide the question of the continued presence of Allied troops in Berlin was a serious proposition, whereas the "seemingly similar" idea Adenauer had toyed with the previous year was intended as a "private poll" and would have been pointless. Whereas Kennedy had solicited and obtained the support of other American parties for a joint national effort, the Adenauer government had covered itself with self-praise, "bowed down before itself in awe and homage," and refused all dealings with the opposition.

The reaction of Konrad Adenauer's Christian Democratic Union was prompt and sharp. A government spokesman issued a statement declaring that there was a complete meeting of minds between Bonn and Washington. CDU members went further, accusing Brandt of trying to start a quarrel between West Germany and her allies.

Thus, less then seventy-two hours after its delivery, a speech that was intended to forge a common front against a threatening Soviet Union was being used for partisan purposes in Germany.

5

The campaign in favor of a separate peace treaty with the Soviet Union was now in full swing from one end of the German Democratic Republic to the other. On July 27 Friedrich Ebert, the pliably pro-Communist lord mayor of East Berlin, told a large workers' rally at Frankfurt-on-the-Oder that a peace treaty was the only way to halt the warlike preparations of the militarists in Bonn. In the old university town of Wittenberg, where in 1517 Martin Luther had pinned up his Ninety-five Theses and thus launched the Reformation, the deputy chairman of the provincial council, Heinrich Homann, took the cold warriors to task for a particularly "dirty maneuver" in trying to make it seem as though a peace treaty would be a danger to world peace.

In the port of Wismar, on the Baltic, this burning issue was also the first item on the agenda at a dockworkers' rally held in the Mathias Thesen shipyards. The occasion was one of the regular monthly meetings that were organized by the state-controlled workers union and which traditionally began with a review of the current political situation. The pattern did not vary on this Friday, July 28—a particularly crucial Friday, as the twenty-four-year-old shipbuilder Eckhard Lemm was to discover.

The session began with a few introductory remarks concerning the Thirteenth Plenary Session of the Party's Central Committee, held on June 14, at which the latest Soviet proposals for a peace treaty and a free-city solution for West Berlin had been officially endorsed. The assembled workers were then asked to express their opinions.

One of Lemm's fellow workers spoke up, voicing a question that was on everybody's mind: "Why should only West Berlin become a free city? That's unfair. If it's going to be a free city, then it should be all Berlin."

"Why should East Berlin not be included?" repeated the union official. "Because everything there is normal. But the agents and espionage organizations are located in West Berlin. They are hampering our buildup and development and must therefore disappear."

Another shipyard worker objected that Berlin, by the terms of the Potsdam agreement, had been placed under a Four-Power status, which the East could not simply do away with, since the Western powers also had a right to be in West Berlin.

"The Western powers have long since forfeited their right to remain in West Berlin," retorted the union official. "As events have shown, they have broken the Potsdam agreement over and over again. In the East, on the other hand, the Potsdam accords have been strictly adhered to."

This seemed to Eckhard Lemm a bit too cut and dried. "That's not exactly so," he spoke up. "When the Western powers signed the Potsdam agreement, they obviously weren't thinking of communism developing in Germany. If they broke the agreement, then so did the East. If you look at it that way, then you can say both sides broke it. The West took a turning to the right, and the East to the left. It's a moot point which turned first and turned the most."

Other workers now joined the debate. The conclusion of a peace treaty in the present situation would only perpetuate the division of Germany for years and perhaps forever, one said.

"The West German militarists are feverishly preparing a third world war," insisted the union official. "The conclusion of a peace treaty will knock the war torch from their hands. That is why this is the number one task today. Later it will be possible to discuss German unification. That would be a job for both German states."

This stock reply failed to satisfy the listeners. They could not understand how the mere signing of a peace treaty with the Soviet Union could restrain the militarists in Bonn if they were really bent on war. A peace treaty, by itself, wouldn't add or subtract a single soldier from the twenty Soviet divisions already stationed on East German soil.

Feeling less and less sure of his position, the union official began hedging. Finally he admitted that he lacked the information needed to clear up all these questions. But at the next month's meeting, he promised, a high union or Party official would be present who would be able to provide satisfactory answers to all these questions and objections.

To Eckhard Lemm, this promise had an ominous ring. It would not be one but more likely a whole crew of Party officials who would descend on the next meeting, after having been fully briefed about what had happened at the last one. He had already climbed out on a limb in daring to challenge the accepted party line on the "violations" of the Potsdam agreement, and from now on he could be had up at any time for *Staatsverleumdung* ("state slander") against Ulbricht's DDR.

That evening he and his wife decided the moment had come. They must leave with their child for West Berlin.

6

At the Marienfelde reception center, doctors, interrogators, and a small corps of social assistants were working overtime to process the refugees streaming in from all parts of the Soviet zone. The daily average once again was over one thousand—what it had been for most of July.

In West Berlin there was widespread indignation over the latest outrage perpetrated by the East German authorities in their campaign of intimidation against the border crossers. On Sunday, July 23, Frau Ruth Markert, the thirty-eight-year-old mother of six children, had been rushed to an East Berlin hospital after suffering a hemorrhage due to a miscarriage. On learning that her husband was a Grenzgänger, the hospital authorities had refused to admit her, saying that since he earned his living in the West, he could not expect free medical treatment for his wife in the East. The anguished husband had then raced his limp wife to an emergency hospital in West Berlin, where she died from loss of blood within minutes of admission.

There seemed to be no limit to the ferocity with which the Ulbricht regime was now prepared to persecute the "criminals" and "parasites" undermining the DDR. But the greater the pressure brought to bear, the greater the panic urge to get out "before the door is bolted." Some were farmers who had refused to go along with the collectivization drive. Many more were workers or technicians, fed up with a system that placed incompetent functionaries in key factory or workshop positions simply because they were reliable Party hacks. The result was a maddening inefficiency, summed up in the phrase that kept coming back to the interrogators like a leitmotif: *"Nichts klappt!"* ("Nothing works!").

Even the relatively privileged had begun to despair. The thirty-five-year-old wife of a machine-tools grinder told how by working as a draftsman in a blueprint bureau, she had supplemented her husband's five-hundred-marks-per-month salary so that they could live comfortably and build up a savings account. They had been able to buy a washing machine, a record player, and handsome furniture for their five-room apartment in a Workers' Residential community. It had looked at first like a good deal—the rent was only fifty marks a month—but they had soon discovered that there were strings attached. To be allowed to occupy such an apartment in a country still suffering from an acute housing shortage, they had had to make a contribution of twenty-five hundred marks—about five months' pay—in unpaid work time to the state. While prices of commodities had been rising, real wages had been sinking because of the Party's insistence on raising work norms each time a production goal was reached. "As for consumer goods," she added, "it isn't a question of what you want. You have to take what's offered or go without buying. In the end we decided it just wasn't worth the sweat and effort—particularly since Ulbricht seems determined to close the hatch to West Berlin. Then we'd have been sitting over there like jailbirds in a prison, and they could have done with us as they pleased."

A senior hospital doctor who had been earning a princely four thousand marks a month—enough for him to afford a house of his own and a car in which he could roam almost at will over wonderfully empty highways—told how the attitude of his patients would change once they were alone with him in the X-ray room or elsewhere. "I still have cheek scars dating from the dueling escapades of my youth as a student at Jena. A reactionary fool, you in the West would say on seeing these scars. But over there, when my patients spotted these scars, they'd say to themselves, 'Hah, scars—ergo, he's not a Communist!' Then they'd let their hair down and say what they really thought of the Party and the rest of it."

He too was fed up with the endless dissembling, with people going around loudly saying *"Freundschaft!"* ("Friendship!")— the stereotyped greeting that had replaced the former *"Heil Hitler!"*—when they met in public places, or cold-shouldering the priest when they passed him in the street, even though the night before they had been ringing his doorbell. "I'd rather earn my living working as a minor assistant in a free country than go on enduring that!"

A sixty-four-year-old mason explained his own reasons for "getting the hell out." On July 10 he had been forced to attend a National Front meeting devoted to the coming *Kirchentag* gathering in West Berlin. All present were urged to take active part in the signature-collecting campaign that was being launched to denounce this "act of provocation" in West Berlin. As a Catholic, he did not feel himself in the least concerned by this Protestant event, and besides, as he pointed out to those who began to pester him, the Kirchentag was a purely religious affair and had nothing to do with politics. He was immediately taken to task by activists. They insisted that he sign the protest and help recruit other signatories. He resolutely refused to do either. Finally he was warned that he would have only himself to blame for the consequences of such an uncooperative and anti-social attitude. The warning was enough. Two weeks later he headed for the West.

Ursula Bünning, a twenty-one-year-old switchboard operator from Dessau, described in harrowing detail how the previous April, during a trip to Berlin, she had been hauled off the S-Bahn at the Schöneweide station and sent back to Dessau on the grounds that she was trying to flee the Republic. Her identity card was taken from her, and she was interrogated at length by an official of the State Security police. Her employers made it clear to her that she had incurred the Party's wrath and that she would have to mend her ways. It was high time she joined the Democratic Women's League of Germany (DFD) to show what a model of progressive womanhood she could become. The last time she had only planned a visit; this time she made it over to West Berlin for keeps.

In the German Democratic Republic even as mild an offense as asking for a raise could now get one into trouble. Such was the story told by a twenty-five-year-old worker employed in a state-run paper mill. On asking for a raise, he was informed by officials of the factory's Personnel Department that to qualify for higher wages, he would have to do a new stint of service in the Nationale Volksarmee—in addition to the eighteen months he had already served. He decided then and there that he had had all he could stomach. Fed up with having to stand in line for hours for even the most basic foodstuffs, his wife agreed that the time had come to look for work and food elsewhere.

Similar was the complaint of an exasperated engineer employed by the Karl Marx Locomotive Works in suburban Babelsberg—Germany's "Hollywood," as it had been known in prewar years for its abundance of film-making studios. Building locomotives was apparently not enough to keep the managers of this particular plant suitably occupied, so they had set up a Central Commission for Patriotic Instruction to recruit young "volunteers" for the Nationale Volksarmee and the factory militia. The engineer had had all he could take of parade-ground drill, rifle practice, and lectures on the need for worker vigilance. "But that wasn't all. They then insisted that I sign a petition calling for a Soviet peace treaty and a so-called free city of West Berlin. That clinched it. I wasn't going to stick around any longer, for West Berlin is the Zone's one and only hope."

Anton Kleinschmidt, a fifty-nine-year-old sales manager in a state-run department store, explained why he had finally chosen to leave Leipzig, where he had lived and worked for thirty years. He had always sought to remain apolitical, but in Ulbricht's DDR this was enough to make one politically suspect. Realizing that his rise to a position of importance had only made him more vulnerable to the curiosity of Party agents and officials, he had decided to get himself and his family out while he could.

To evacuate an entire family from the DDR was no longer an easy matter. He had first put a long-distance call through to a friend living in the Pankow district of East Berlin, asking him to drive down for a weekend visit. Since it was a Friday evening, the suggestion wouldn't sound too odd if the line happened to be tapped. Fortunately his friend understood immediately what this invitation really meant. Four hours later he turned up in Leipzig, and under cover of nightfall Kleinschmidt bundled his wife, daughter, younger son, and three small suitcases into his friend's Trabant.

He and his older son left the next morning on the 6:27 express to Berlin. They managed to get on the train without seat reservations, which led to a lively—and, as it turned out, providential—altercation with a grumpy ticket collector, who reached their compartment just ahead of a Vopo lieutenant who had to cool his heels in the corridor while the ten-mark supplementary fare receipts were laboriously filled and handed out. Able at last to examine Kleinschmidt's identity card and then his son's, the Vopo lieutenant asked the standard question now directed at all Berlin-bound passengers in the DDR: "Where are you going?"

Kleinschmidt had his story ready. "I'm just back from a health cure at Bad Brambach [a little resort town in the Karl-Marx-Stadt region of southern Saxony], and I'm going to spend my remaining ten days of vacation with friends who live in Woltersdorf, near Erkner [the latter being a suburban town situated on the eastern fringe of Berlin]. My son also has a few days of vacation left, so he's coming with me."

The Vopo lieutenant had probably never heard of Woltersdorf, but the ease with which Kleinschmidt had managed to rattle off the name was enough to still his doubts, and he didn't even bother to check the contents of the two suitcases in the luggage rack.

For the rest it had been a fairly easy "flight." His Pankow friend cleared the Mahlsdorf check point, south of Berlin, thanks to his East Berlin registration number, while hundreds of cars, motorcycles, and motor scooters with Zone license plates were stopped by the Vopos, and many of them doubtless turned back. From Pankow, where they had been briefly reunited, the various members of the family left separately on different subway or S-Bahn trains to reach the Gesundbrunnen station in the French sector.

Some of the escapes sounded little short of miraculous. Eight entire families living on one small Leipzig street had decided to leave in the space of one week. It was an act of collective folly, but they had all made it safely to the West. "The Vopos came with five men in the express train," one of the fugitives recalled, "but the corridors were so jam-packed with people that they just couldn't get through. Four of them gave up, saying they were through with checking people's papers. So they stood there for half an hour arguing among themselves. Finally the fifth Vopo said, 'All right, then, let's go through the train just once and then we'll have done our duty.' That was the last we heard of any controls."

Another couple from Leipzig had operated a beauty parlor in the city—a family enterprise in its third generation. The husband had shown no desire to become a Party member, but the authorities hadn't been able to keep him from clipping his clients' hair. His wife, however, had found it impossible to keep her little cosmetics shop going: the powders, creams, and eyebrow pencils were no longer to be had.

Realizing that they could no longer work individually, they cooked up an ingenious scheme for gulling the authorities. "We'd been married five years and we still hadn't had a honeymoon—that's the line we gave to the Party. We'd been working so hard to build up the business and to satisfy the clients that we just hadn't had time for a honeymoon. But now we wanted to celebrate our fifth wedding anniversary in style by going off on a honeymoon trip. So off we set, traveling through the DDR like newlyweds, visiting friends and relatives, and so on. In the train some Vopo plainclothesmen looked at our papers. We told them that we were on a honeymoon and going to visit an uncle in West Berlin, and they said, 'All right, we wish you a lovely delayed honeymoon trip!' "

Poignant, in comparison, was the tale told by an older woman. She and her husband had traveled all the way from near the Silesian border to reach East Berlin. They had then decided to cross over to the West on the elevated S-Bahn, traveling on the same train but separately. It was agreed that if something happened to one of them, the other was to ride on as though nothing had happened. Her husband had been dragged off the train by plainclothes agents, but she had come on through safely to West Berlin.

She had waited a day or two, with no news. Then she had received word that her husband had been arrested. The Vopos sent to check on their apartment, had battered their way in through the locked front door and found everything wrecked—chairs, piano, the precious cabinet porcelain, and the one valuable painting. Enraged at the thought of losing all these treasures, her husband before leaving had laid about him wildly with an ax, smashing everything he could and deaf to her stammering entreaties: "Heinrich! Heinrich! Leave them alone! They're lost to us anyway!"

His farewell fit of fury had merely aggravated his guilt. Now he would have to languish—who could tell for how long?—in one of Ulbricht's godforsaken prisons.

7

For Walter Ulbricht, too, these were troubling times. While Nikita Khrushchev could bask in the fragrant sunshine of his Crimean dacha, he had to stick close to his desk, impotently presiding over an economy that was sliding inexorably downhill. The only outing he could permit himself—on July 22, when he traveled to Leipzig and harangued some fifteen hundred municipal employees in the nearby township of Markkleeberg—was more like an ordeal than a holiday. He had to deliver the sobering news that the DDR could not import more foodstuffs because its exports of high-quality equipment barely sufficed to pay for vitally needed raw materials.

Although he was too smart to say so openly, Walter Ulbricht could not help ascribing many of his woes to his Soviet mentors. If Khrushchev had only kept his promise and signed a separate peace treaty with East Germany in the spring of 1959, things would never have reached this critical pass, and the hammer-and-compass-dividers emblem of the DDR would probably now be flying over the western sectors of Berlin. But the repeated threats and deadlines had proved so much Ukrainian bluff; and in late March, when he had gone to Moscow to attend a top-level meeting with other Communist party leaders of the Soviet bloc, he had been given the brushoff once again. The moment was not yet ripe for the signing of a separate peace treaty; Khrushchev and Mikoyan, the prime movers of Soviet policy, wanted first to take the measure of the new president of the United States and to prepare the terrain, psychologically, by putting a man into space before the Americans. In this way, they argued, the Soviet Union could maneuver itself into a position of unchallengeable strength and prestige, and browbeat the Western powers into negotiating on its own terms. It had all sounded wonderfully logical and convincing, but there was a fatal flaw in the scenario. By the time the Western powers got ready to negotiate—they were now talking about the late autumn, after the West German elections of September and the Soviet Communist Party Congress of October—the DDR would have bled itself to death.

The number of defections told only half the bitter story, which was that most of the 3.5 million East Germans who had chosen to defect since 1946 were able-bodied men. Women now accounted for 54 percent of the DDR's total population and 45 percent of its work force. There were even factories where 80 percent of the personnel were women. One citizen in five was too old to work, and the proportion of working adults to the old-age pensioners and children they had to support had reached the disturbing ratio of 4 to 3.

Not to be outdone by Khrushchev, who was already informing

the world that the Communists would soon be "burying" the capitalists, Ulbricht, at the Fifth Party Congress held in July 1958, had confidently predicted that the DDR would be reaching and even surpassing West Germany in the per-capita consumption of foodstuffs and important consumer items by 1961. He now preferred not to be reminded of those heady words, for in the three years since then, the gap between East and West had perceptibly widened instead of shrinking. Continuing defections, added to other economic headaches, had made a shambles of successive Five- and Seven-Year plans.

The wholesale exodus of peasants from collective farms was frustrating enough. But truly crippling for a country bent on making itself into an industrial power—a country which before the war had accounted for 36 percent of the German Reich's mining and industrial output; 40 percent of its textiles, cellulose, and paper production; 35 percent of its optical and precision instruments; 30 percent of its chemicals; and 20 percent of its motor vehicles, heavy and light machinery, and electrical goods—was the mass exodus of its technical elite. Over the past dozen years, seven hundred university professors and instructors and sixteen thousand schoolteachers had preferred to emigrate to West Germany. Five thousand doctors, dentists, and veterinary surgeons had also left the Workers-and-Peasants-State, as had seventeen thousand scientists, engineers, and highly qualified technicians. In 1960 one doctor in every ten had chosen to defect to the West. One could no longer speak of a "brain drain"; it was beginning to resemble a cerebral hemorrhage.

The continuing flight of highly trained engineers and factory technicians was particularly ominous. Although they formed a privileged class—one that had acquired the title of *Intelligenz* in the country's state-run factories—they and their families were deserting in droves. It wasn't simply because many of them were Lutherans or Catholics and couldn't stand a regime bent on turning their children into atheists and agnostics. Many who were not religiously inclined were also leaving, disgusted with a system of foreign spoliation that had been subtly maintained.

The Russians, of course, had made no bones about it in the early occupation years. The Germans—which is to say the East

Germans who were in their grip—were going to pay for the immense wartime damage inflicted on the Soviet Union by Hitler's Wehrmacht and SS. Accordingly, 213 key industrial plants, as well as the uranium mines in Silesia, had been taken over and made to work for the Soviet Union. Between 1945 and 1957 they were estimated to have provided Russia with the equivalent of $25 billion worth of goods and equipment—two and a half times the amount of reparations that Stalin had demanded at Potsdam.

This milking of the East German economy had continued until 1957, when the DDR was finally admitted to COMECON (the East European equivalent of the West's Common Market). The 213 "mixed" companies were then returned to German management. But the process of economic spoliation had not ceased for all that; it had merely been perpetuated by other, more subtle means.

The most obvious was a currency reform which from one day to the next had devalued the East German mark from two to five marks to the ruble. The practical result of this devaluation had been to halve the value of what East Germany had been exporting to the Soviet Union, which alone amounted to more than half the DDR's total exports.

More insidious, because less obvious, was another form of exploitation practiced in the name of the primary interests of the USSR. Just four months before, in March 1961, Bruno Leuschner, the Politburo member responsible for economic planning, had been forced to announce a radical cutback in East German aircraft production. Six aircraft factories, which had been developed at an investment cost of one billion East German marks and which were supposed to develop an East German turbojet airliner, had been partly converted to the manufacture of incubators, luggage racks, and television antennas before having to cease all aircraft production in order to concentrate on hydraulic equipment, machine-cutting tools, and conveyor belts.

In the West the experts had concluded that this sudden conversion was due to sloppy planning, and to a lack of qualified aeronautics engineers and first-class capital equipment. The truth was radically different. A shift to rocket construction in the Soviet defense industry had plunged a number of Russian bomber factories into a state of semi-idleness. So it had been decided to make use of their plant capacity by having them turn out the BB-152 and BB-155 jetliners that were to have been manufactured in East Germany.

Much the same fate had overtaken the state-run Bergman-Borsig works in Leipzig. This huge plant had traditionally specialized in the output of big turbines. But not long after East Germany's entry into COMECON, the directors had been ordered to obtain approval for their production plans from the competent officials in the Soviet Union. The plans had finally been returned with all sorts of revisions, and it had been made clear that the manufacture of large turbines was henceforth to be entrusted to Russian factories. The Bergman-Borsig works were to be overhauled and adapted to the construction of small turbines. But—and for a number of Bergman-Borsig engineers this had been the last straw—the Soviet master planners did not wish to see the plant's big-turbine facilities dismantled. They wanted the engineers in Leipzig to continue the research and development of big turbines, and to keep them supplied with blueprints, designs, and the initial testing results. Only after the new models had been tried and tested was the job of mass producing the big turbines assigned to plants in the Soviet Union.

In the spring of 1958 Anastas Mikoyan had turned up in East Berlin and undertaken a first-hand tour of the different sectors. The striking contrast between the feverish building activity visible in the West and the mountainous heaps of bomb-blasted rubble still marring the landscape of the Soviet sector had prompted the peppery Armenian to get off some acid remarks, which Ulbricht, for all his sangfroid, had found hard to swallow. After all, who, if not the Russians, were ultimately responsible for this drain of vitally needed manpower from the ruthlessly despoiled and debilitated East to the prosperous and thriving West? He, Walter Ulbricht, was expected to plan and to accomplish miracles while being systematically deprived of the necessary means.

The development of the Nationale Volksarmee had encountered similar difficulties. Most of the old Wehrmacht officers had been weeded out as politically unreliable, and in

June·1960 the NVA cadet school that had been set up on the Soviet model in the town of Naumburg had been dissolved. Officers of the NVA were now being trained in Soviet military academies. For lack of qualified manpower, the Nationale Volksarmee was reduced from seven to six planned divisions. Rather than put in eighteen months of voluntary service, thousands of young men had been disgracefully decamping to the sanctuary of West Berlin. Close to thirty thousand of those who had agreed to enlist had subsequently fled to the West, along with several thousand Grepos—a desertion rate unequalled by any other army in the world.

Recent efforts to check the rot had proved conspicuously unsuccessful, notwithstanding new restrictions on travel to West Germany, which was virtually declared off-limits for all East German citizens because of the polio epidemic that was now ravaging the Federal Republic. The number of Vopos detailed to check identity papers on trains and highways had been doubled, tripled, and finally increased sixfold, all to no avail. The tens of thousands of East Germans who were now quite lawfully leaving their normal places of work and residence for the seaside or some other resort had complicated the maddeningly difficult task of distinguishing bona fide from bogus vacationers, and although hundreds of suspects were being hauled off the trains and S-Bahns every day, hundreds more were still slipping into West Berlin. The campaign to intimidate the border crossers had so far proved a flop. Three weeks of intensive propaganda in the papers and over the radio had made only the slightest impression, and less than one Grenzgänger in ten had so far consented to give up his or her job in the West and go to work in East Berlin.

Police pressure was clearly not enough. What was needed was action of a broader and bolder scope—such as the closing of the air corridors to this scandalous traffic in refugees. But would the Russians allow it? The answer to that question did not lie in East Berlin. It lay in Moscow—toward which, on this early Monday morning of July 31, Walter Ulbricht was flying.

8

For weeks, for months, for years, Siegfried Schäfer had been thinking and worrying about this moment—the moment when he would have to pull up his stakes, say good-by to everything he had spent years of effort to acquire, and leave Leipzig with his wife and daughter. But now, as he watched his wife, Lotte, light the little candles on the birthday cake, he knew that the long-awaited, and at the same time dreaded, moment had come. Walking over to the radio-record player, he turned up the volume so that the gay dance music could be heard through the thin walls of their four-room apartment. The neighbors must be persuaded that this birthday party was real rather than a bogus binge intended to mask the first phase of an escape.

After kissing his wife and daughter good-by, Schäfer let himself out through the front door and trotted down the stairs, trying to look as casual as possible. If he bumped into any of the neighbors, he had to give the impression that he was going out for a moment on an errand. To be seen walking out of the apartment house with a suitcase was much too risky. It would have attracted unhealthy attention. This kind of elementary slip could give one away at the very start, as many would-be escapers had learned to their cost. Once caught in the act of Republik-flucht, the chances of pulling off a second, successful escape were drastically reduced. At worst, one could be sentenced to several years in prison; at best, one's identity card would be taken away by the authorities and replaced by a temporary *Ausweis* stamped Invalid for Berlin. And from then on, one was kept under special surveillance by the regime's ubiquitous informers.

As it happened, he met nobody on the stairs. Half an hour later he reached the main Leipzig railway station, where a friend was waiting with his suitcase. They shook hands briefly but warmly, wondering when, if ever, they would see one another again.

The platform next to the Berlin train was teeming with uni-

133

formed Vopos and others who looked too purposefully casual to be anything but plainclothes agents. Surprisingly, Schäfer was not asked for his identity card. The Vopos and plainclothesmen were apparently under orders to watch for suspects but not to detain any passengers until they were actually on the train.

As he walked up the platform, Schäfer passed a car that had been reserved for the police. A dozen Vopos were standing near it. They were doubtless the ones who would be traveling to Berlin on this same train. Tall and powerfully built, Schäfer was not normally a nervous man; but he found it impossible to keep his heart from beating faster.

Two cars farther up, Schäfer climbed onto the train. The compartments he passed were discouragingly full, but he managed to find a vacant seat on the corridor side. The atmosphere in the compartment was tense. Each traveler seemed to be watching his neighbors in the same wary silence.

In an effort to calm his nerves, Schäfer stepped out into the corridor and lit a cigarette, but he couldn't help noticing how his fingers were trembling.

As more passengers climbed on in a last-minute scramble for vacant places, Schäfer returned to his seat. The whistle blew and the packed train moved out of the station. Shortly thereafter, a lieutenant and three Vopos filed past on their way up front. Trying to look unconcerned, Schäfer stared at the open page of the book he had taken out of his raincoat pocket. But the lines swam before his eyes.

In the compartment no one spoke. How many of his companions were vacationers, travelers on bona fide business, and how many would-be escapers like himself? Schäfer wondered. He recalled the questioning look on the face of his factory foreman when, several days before, he had explained that he wanted to take a few days off to celebrate his forty-fifth birthday. How much better it would have sounded if he could have said it was his fiftieth. To ask for special leave in the middle of July—one of the year's busiest building months—was a pretty bold thing for a construction engineer to do. But the foreman had given his consent. If he had said no, Schäfer and his wife would have had to devise an entirely different escape plan.

Two Vopos came down the corridor, escorting a downcast culprit toward the central car, where he was presumably going to be locked up. What was it that had aroused their suspicions or given the game away? Schäfer flicked the page in front of him, pretending to read, but the words were as meaningless as ever.

The Vopos came back up the corridor and disappeared into the car ahead. A few minutes later Schäfer heard their boots and voices in the corridor; they were opening compartment doors and forcing the passengers to open their suitcases.

Finally they reached his compartment. The passengers were asked for their identity papers. Schäfer produced his *Kennkarte*.

"Where are you going?" asked one of the Vopos.

Schäfer explained that he was going to East Berlin to visit an aunt who lived in the Lichtenberg district. There was an inheritance problem he urgently needed to discuss with her.

"How long are you planning to stay?"

"Six days."

"And your factory knows about this?"

"Of course. They wouldn't have let me go otherwise."

"Is that your bag?" asked the Vopo, pointing to the small suitcase that Schäfer had lodged in the luggage rack above his head.

Schäfer nodded.

"Well, let's see what's inside."

Schäfer pulled down the bag and opened it in the corridor. One of the Vopos bent down and went carefully through the contents. The suitcase contained a suit, four shirts, a pair of pajamas, socks, underwear, and a few toilet articles.

"How long did you say you were staying?"

"Six days," answered Schäfer, trying to sound calm.

"Four shirts for six days?" said the Vopo, raising his eyebrows. "Don't you think that's a lot?"

Schäfer had to think fast. This was something he hadn't anticipated. "My wife is a maniac for cleanliness," he improvised. "She can't stand the idea of my going around with dirty cuffs or collars, so she always packs more shirts than I need."

The Vopos laughed and let Schäfer close his bag. His identity card was returned, while attention was concentrated on the other suspects in the compartment. Several suitcases were opened, but none of them contained any incriminating evidence.

Schäfer went back to his simulated reading. He could hardly

hold the book; he was almost afraid to turn the pages. He thought of his wife, whom he had left behind in Leipzig and who would be taking another Berlin-bound train like this one tomorrow. Traveling together would have been too risky, so she was taking a late-morning train after drawing some money from the bank, while Monika, their daughter, was being driven to Berlin by car.

It was a strange feeling to be sneaking away like this, abandoning everything he had worked to attain over the past twenty years. He should have left years before, when there was less to leave behind and when it would have been easier to start all over. But like his friends and almost everyone else in Ulbricht's DDR, he and his wife had been convinced that "it can't go on like this forever," and so they had kept postponing their departure. He had known for a long time, of course, that he was not in the Party's good books. He and Lotte were too attached to their Lutheran pastor and their Evangelical faith for that. This had created trouble for him at his building-materials factory, where he had been called in more than once by *Agitprop* officials and told to watch his step if he expected better pay or advancement. A former schoolmate who had since become a Party member had even taken him aside one day and said, "Siegfried, be careful—that's all I can say: *be careful!*"

Since his competence in engineering was appreciated by the state-controlled construction firm that employed him, Schäfer took these warnings with a grain of salt. They were part of the everyday strain of existence, one of the things one had to learn to live with. But the pressure had ceased to be an everyday affair when they had begun to apply it to his daughter, who had been very active in Young Parish activities. A few weeks before, she had been approached by Party officials and ordered to inform on young people she knew who might be planning to flee the DDR. For the normally patient Siegfried Schäfer, this was all that was needed to turn a vague idea into an immediate plan of action.

Twenty minutes out of Berlin, the express slowed to a halt. They had reached Schönefeld, near Königswusterhausen— probably the most detested railway station in the DDR because of the thoroughness with which passengers from Magdeburg or Thuringia were crossexamined and searched before being allowed to proceed. Schäfer had heard alarming reports about the swarms of Vopos who boarded the incoming trains at this point, subjecting everyone to a pitiless inspection. Although he managed to sound convincing in repeating the story he had concocted about an aunt and an urgent inheritance problem, thirty less-fortunate souls were hauled off the train before it was allowed to continue on its way.

In East Berlin Schäfer did not call on his aunt but spent the night in an inexpensive lodging house. He would let his aunt know of his real plans and intentions once they had been realized, not before.

The next morning, to kill time, he went for a long walk as far as the Rathaus and the Marx-Engels-Platz. Berlin seemed to have succumbed to the same poster frenzy as Leipzig, for there was hardly a major edifice that had not been festooned with red slogans proclaiming the present or future victories of the regime. DER SOZIALISMUS TRIUMPHIERT, WIR SIND DIE STÄRKEREN! ("Socialism Is Triumphing, We Are the Stronger!"), a crimson streamer barked at him from a blank, bullet-scarred wall. UNSERE TATEN STÄRKEN DIE DEUTSCHE DEMOKRATISCHE REPUBLIK UND SICHERN DEN FRIEDEN ("Our Deeds Strengthen the German Democratic Republic and Ensure the Peace"), boasted another rain-soaked wall overlooking a bombed-out lot. DEN BONNER ULTRAS KEINE ATEMPAUSE—ALLE KRÄFTE FÜR DEN ANSCHLUSS EINES FRIEDENSVERTRAGES! ("No Respite for the Ultras of Bonn— Spare No Effort for the Conclusion of a Peace Treaty!"), cried a long, ribbonlike banderole from under the overhanging eave of an apartment building. This last exhortation—about the conclusion of a peace treaty—was now visible everywhere, like some incantatory formula whose magic powers could be unleashed by sheer force of repetition.

In the early afternoon Schäfer returned to the Ostbahnhof to wait for his wife. The incoming express from Leipzig was packed. Safely lost in the stream of outpouring passengers was Lotte, clutching her little suitcase which the Vopos for some reason had not bothered to examine.

It had been agreed that they were not to wait for their daughter Monika, who was traveling to East Berlin by car and who would join them at Marienfelde. Once again, for security reasons the Schäfers separated, Seigfried leaving his wife seated on a station bench while he boarded the S-Bahn for West Berlin. At the Friedrichstrasse station, the last stop in the East, the Vopos boarded the train in force, hauling out passengers carrying suitcases or suspiciously large bags. The number of suspects was so great that they did not have time to concern themselves with Schäfer and his overnight case.

Lotte was less fortunate. While Siegfried waited at the Lehrter Bahnhof—the first S-Bahn station in West Berlin—at first hopefully and then with mounting anxiety, she was pulled off the train at the Friedrichstrasse station and taken to a police shack, where the contents of her little suitcase were meticulously searched. Why was she going to West Berlin? she was repeatedly asked. To friends living in the Charlotten-burg district, she kept replying. The Schäfers had rehearsed this story thoroughly and well; these friends actually existed, although they had no idea their names were now being used to facilitate an escape. Where, and how, and when had Frau Schäfer first met them? Why was she visiting them now? One searching question followed another, in a determined attempt to break her down.

When she finally appeared on the Lehrter Bahnhof platform four hours later, Siegfried had almost given her up for lost. Collapsing into his arms, she burst into tears of happiness and relief. "They went on and on and on, my nerves were about to crack—I never thought I'd make it!" she kept repeating. "I still can't believe I'm here."

At the Marienfelde reception center they were soon joined by their daughter, Monika. Her own trip had been un-eventful. The car she traveled in had been waved through the check point, and she had come over on the S-Bahn without being stopped or searched.

It took her parents days to recover from the nerve-wracking tensions of their escape. Each time he was asked to tell an interrogator or a member of the press exactly how he had made it to Berlin, beads of perspiration would form on Sieg-fried Schäfer's reddish brow, as though he were physically reliving his experience. "You know, my hands were trembling so while I sat in that compartment that I was afraid to turn the pages of my book for fear of giving myself away." Instinctively his voice would drop to a whisper, and then catching himself, he would add, "You know, I can't get used to speaking openly and freely, without weighing every word. It's something I'm going to have to learn again."

9

Seldom in his life had Walter Ulbricht felt more like an outsider than now, as he had himself chauffeured around Moscow in a luxuriously curtained limousine. The Berlin crisis seemed almost light-years removed from this sweltering metropolis, where tourist groups could be seen gaping at the haze-shrouded university skyscraper or fanning themselves in the sightseeing boats that glided silently up and down the Moskva River. Seemingly impervious to the ninety-two-degree heat, the smartly dressed guards in front of Lenin's mausoleum maintained their slow, stiffed-legged strides as queues of thirsty Muscovites formed before the drinking fountains on the sidewalks for cupfuls of carbonated water. The newsstands offered a plentiful supply of papers prominently featuring the new and much-publicized Communist Party Program ("the biggest revision of Marxism since early Bolshevik times," commentators in the West were already calling it). Suntanned bathers frolicked near the Kremlin in the shimmering blue waters of a huge open-air swimming pool, or stretched out indolently beneath the sun, listening with half an ear to the strains of Soviet jazz being played over loudspeakers.

A firm believer in the virtues of daily exercise, Walter Ulbricht would have liked to join the swimmers, but his Lenin-like goatee would have given him away. It was a bit galling to realize that he had had to fly in secretly and remain as incognito as possible, along with his deputy premier, Willi Stoph, and his two diplomatic advisers—Lothar Bolz, the foreign minister, and Bolz's deputy, Otto Winzer. Nikita Khrushchev, on the other hand, could return to his capital at a leisurely pace, stopping on the way to visit a tractor-and-harvester-testing institute in the Kuban and a kolkhoz near Kharkov. Although he could now be put up at the East German embassy, Ulbricht was reminded a bit of the 1938–40 period of his life, when he and his future wife, Lotte Wendt, had lived cooped up in the Hotel Lux—a ponderously overdecorated piece of late-czarist architecture—where members of the Komintern lived in daily dread of having their rooms ransacked and of being dragged off on unspecified charges by the nocturnal search squads of Stalin's NKVD. This time he ran no such dangers. But the fact remained that he was not officially supposed to be in Moscow—at a time when Khrushchev and other Soviet leaders were due to play host to the Romanian chief of state and to the premier and foreign minister of Italy.

Even for a person of Nikita Khrushchev's bustling energy, this moment was an exceptionally busy one, so that the amount of time he could devote to Walter Ulbricht was limited. On Monday, July 31, he and Andrei Gromyko had to receive nine African delegates who wanted Moscow to condemn France for the recent occupation of Bizerte. Tuesday morning was devoted to talks with Gheorghe Ghiorghiu-Dej, secretary general of the Romanian Communist party, and members of the important delegation he had brought with him from Bucharest.

Before receiving Ulbricht, Khrushchev had himself briefed on the latest developments in the United States and West Germany by his ambassadors to those two countries—Mikhail Menshikov, who was now in Moscow, and Andrei Smirnov, who had hastily been recalled from Bonn. Neither seemed to think that the Western Allies would do much more than issue token protests if the Soviet Union went ahead and signed a separate peace treaty with the German Democratic Republic. Kennedy, in his recent television address, had tried to sound tough, but the influential head of the U.S. Senate's Foreign Relations Committee, William Fulbright, was already sounding a different note regarding the Berlin refugee problem. ("I don't understand why the East Germans don't close their border, because I think they have a right to close it.") Chancellor Adenauer, also trying to sound tough, was suggesting that the most effective riposte to a separate peace treaty would be a full-scale economic embargo on

West European exports to countries of the Soviet bloc. But this proposal had so far gained little support in Paris, London, and Washington, and even less elsewhere. There remained the possibility of a limited embargo—imposed on the German Democratic Republic by West Germany—but even this seemed doubtful.

As it turned out, much of the briefing was beside the point. What Ulbricht now wanted, in addition to a separate peace treaty, was immediate and energetic action to stem the refugee flow. Every day the Western Allies were flouting the sovereignty of the DDR by flying out hundreds of its citizens without Ulbricht's being able to do anything about it. This situation was intolerable not only for the DDR but also for the Soviet Union, whose international prestige was likewise being challenged.

Khrushchev did not take kindly to this suggestion. It was one thing to issue a decree, as the East German government had done, indicating that from August 1 on, all Western aircraft using the air corridors would have to register with an air-traffic control center in East Berlin; it was another thing to enforce it. If Ulbricht thought that he could call on Soviet fighters to enforce this decree, then he was seriously mistaken. Even at the height of the Berlin blockade of 1948–49, when the countries of Western Europe were in a pitifully weak economic and military condition, Stalin had carefully refrained from using Soviet fighters to halt the airlift. You can hold up a convoy at a check point for a considerable length of time; you can arrange to have a bridge suddenly "collapse," effectively closing off an autobahn for days or even weeks at a time. The same tricks can be played with river barges and railway traffic. But the one place it cannot be done is in the air. Any attempt to interfere with American, British, or French airplanes flying East German defectors out of West Berlin would be an act of war. One plane shot down would be enough to touch off a conflagration comparable to the assassination of Grand Duke Franz Ferdinand at Sarajevo in 1914.

In an important document that Khrushchev had just released, the Communist party of the Soviet Union had formally abandoned the idea that war between capitalist and socialist states was inevitable. The atomic bomb had not existed at the time of the 1917 Revolution, and this consideration could not simply be ignored. He had publicly committed himself to a policy of peaceful coexistence and to having the strongest country of the socialist camp, the Soviet Union, overtake the most powerful country of the capitalist camp, the United States, in most areas of industrial production by 1970. This contest was the kind he was interested in winning in order to demonstrate the inherent superiority of communism over capitalism. The Soviet Union had already shown the world what it was capable of achieving by being the first to hoist a sputnik and then a man into space; and there were more surprises of this kind in store for the Americans, who had yet to master the technique of capsule recovery, as they had recently demonstrated in the Atlantic, where their astronaut, Maj. Virgil Grissom, had had to swim for his life while his open capsule sank. What was needed, therefore, was continuing pressure of this kind to bring them to the negotiating table, and to make them realize that a free-city solution for West Berlin was in the best interests of everybody.

Did this, asked Ulbricht, mean that Comrade Khrushchev had scrapped the idea of signing a separate peace treaty with the German Democratic Republic? And how could he, after having spoken about its necessity and imminence, now suddenly abandon the project completely?

The Soviet government had no intention of abandoning the campaign in favor of a separate peace treaty with the German Democratic Republic, replied Khrushchev firmly. But it was determined first of all to explore all possibilities of negotiating a new status for West Berlin with the Western powers. On the subject of negotiations, the Western powers were basically divided. The object of Soviet diplomacy was to exploit these differences, and to mobilize world opinion—and notably the Afro-Asian countries in the United Nations—in favor of negotiations and a free-city solution for West Berlin. The premature signing of a peace treaty might do more harm than good, consolidating rather than dividing the capitalist powers.

Try as he might, Ulbricht could not conceal his disappointment. Basically, these arguments simply restated those that had been presented to him when they had met in late March. But in the meantime the situation had changed in one dramatic respect. The German Democratic Republic was now losing one thousand defectors a day. The rate might reach two thousand, three thousand, or—who could say?—perhaps even ten thousand a day unless something drastic was done about it and done soon.

At this point Ulbricht received unexpected support from Anastas Mikoyan. Speaking as an economic specialist, Mikoyan had to concede that Comrade Ulbricht was right on one particular point. He had studied the figures on East German defectors, and there was no question about it: the German Democratic Republic was losing its technical and industrial elite at a catastrophic rate. The country's ambitious industrial plans could not possibly be realized in such a situation and would have to be scrapped. This was bound to make for an unstable and unsettled situation, one that could not be tolerated for very long in a socialist country. A complete economic breakdown might even result, with incalculable consequences for not only the German Democratic Republic but for all the other Popular Democracies. The counterrevolutionary elements would once again raise their heads, as they had in 1953 and 1956, endangering the peace and security of Central Europe. The continuing exodus of traitors and defectors from the German Democratic Republic would have to be stopped and stopped fast—whether a separate peace treaty was signed now or later.

Khrushchev for once seemed perplexed. The situation was undeniably different from what it had been in March—there was no argument about that. Something drastic was going to have to be done about it. But what?

If the Soviet Union was not prepared to close the air corridors to DDR defectors, then, Ulbricht replied, the only alternative was to seal off West Berlin from East Berlin and the surrounding territory of the DDR. Although a formidable task, it undoubtedly could be carried out—as they had already proved by making the 1,380-kilometer frontier with West Germany impassable.

Ulbricht and Willi Stoph then reminded their listeners that such a master plan had been elaborated as far back as 1952 by Wilhelm Zaisser, then responsible for state security. The scheme had first been conceived as a form of diplomatic retaliation and was to be put into effect once the parliaments of France and the Federal Republic of Germany had ratified the European Defense Community (EDC) project. In fact, parliamentary ratification of the EDC had taken far longer than expected, despite heavy American pressure, and in the end the French had rejected it. The moment for executing the master plan had never come, although it had been given a dress rehearsal on December 5, 1952. That day, all cars bearing West Berlin number plates had been stopped at the sector crossing points and refused admission to East Berlin. Similarly, East Berlin cars had been stopped from entering West Berlin—except for a few with special passes. The interruption of intersector traffic had lasted for twenty-four hours—long enough to prove that it was a relatively simple police job.

The most difficult to achieve in practical terms was a complete seal-off for pedestrians as well as motor vehicles. Early in 1953, Waldemar Schmidt, who then headed the Volkspolizei (he had since been promoted to the position of deputy mayor of East Berlin) had undertaken a detailed inspection of the West Berlin borders with Vassili Chuikov, commander of the Group of Soviet Forces in Germany. The conclusion they had reached was that the job could be done, although it would take time to make it absolutely impermeable. The chief difficulty lay in the distances involved, since the intersector border zigzagging through the center of Berlin was 46 kilometers long, while the peripheral border, between the western sectors and the surrounding territory of the DDR, extended for a total of 111 kilometers.

Here, too, a start had been made in 1952, when the more than 200 streets and roads connecting the western sectors of Berlin with the surrounding countryside had been reduced to 131. Closing these 131 crossing points—which included bicycle paths as well as streets, roads, and highways—would be a simple matter. Schlagbaum barriers with guardhouses could be erected on streets considered vital for continuing traffic, while the remaining streets could be barricaded with barbed wire or walled off completely. The real problem was what lay between—the intervening spaces, which were often more like open country than built-up communities. Here, obviously, a lot of wire fencework would have to be erected.

There was general agreement that the measures to be taken were too drastic and far-reaching in their implications to be settled bilaterally among themselves. Ulbricht's proposal—made from Berlin almost two weeks earlier—that a new meeting of the Warsaw Treaty countries be convened had been accepted. Obviously, the Western powers, which were trying to act in unison, would be doubly impressed if on the subject of Berlin all the Warsaw Treaty countries spoke with one voice. Comrade Ghiorghiu-Dej, secretary general of the Romanian Communist party, was already in Moscow, as was Todor Zhivkov, secretary general of the Bulgarian Communist party, who had recently called on Khrushchev in his Crimean dacha. Gomulka of Poland, Novotny of Czechoslovkia, and Janos Kadar of Hungary were expected to arrive within the next forty-eight hours.

That left only the Albanians, whom Khrushchev and Mikoyan would just as soon have left undisturbed in Tirana. The previous November, they had had a terrible row with Enver Hoxha and other prominent members of the Albanian Politburo, who were outraged to be accused of anti-Soviet activities. One of the Albanians had gone so far as to suggest that Khrushchev wasn't a Marxist, while Khrushchev had asked Hoxha to stop shouting and foaming at the mouth. The Russians had refused to deliver two submarines for the Albanian navy; the Albanians had retaliated by closing the port of Vlorë (the Italian Valona) to Soviet submarines. Nevertheless, officially they were still members of the Warsaw Pact group. It would only make matters worse if they were not invited to attend this hastily convened session of the Warsaw Pact countries. But if they chose to attend, the Albanians would have to be kept out in the cold and not admitted to any of the top-secret sessions.

The plenary meetings in any case would have to stick to general principles, leaving the technical problems to the more private sessions of the Consultative Political Committee. Tomorrow—Wednesday, August 2—Khrushchev was going to be kept busy playing host to the Italian premier and foreign minister. They would meet again in plenary session on Thursday evening to decide on a common course of action.

10

For six days the tension had been mounting steadily until it had become unbearable. On his return from a two-week holiday, which he and his wife, Herta, had spent with friends at Schmalkalden, a peaceful resort town in the pine-covered Thuringian mountains, Karl Behrens had found two letters waiting for him from the Bernau Town Council. In the first, fairly politely worded, he was asked to come to the Rathaus for a "talk"; in the second, sent one week later, he was summoned to appear without delay.

On July 28 he had gone to the town hall. The waiting room, presided over by a framed photograph of Walter Ulbricht, was already full of people who had received summonses like his own. Behrens recognized several of them. Then it dawned on him that they were all Grenzgänger like himslf. He now knew what to expect. Comrade Losensky, mayor of Bernau, had recently had a leaflet distributed in which the inhabitants of the town were asked to bring their influence to bear "frequently and effectively" on those wayward citizens who still stubbornly preferred to work in West Berlin.

After a long wait, Behrens's name was called, and he was ushered into a small committee room. Three men were seated at a table; a fourth, acting as a secretary-clerk, had a typewriter in front of him. Behrens recognized one of the three men as a Party official and a member of the Bernau Town Council, but the other two were strangers.

"Have a seat," said the town council official, indicating a plain wooden chair in front of the table. He made no move to introduce the strangers seated to the right and left of him. "Behrens," he began, leafing through an open file in front of him, "we have called you in for a little exploratory talk. But before we get on to that, what do you mean by not answering the first summons? It was sent to you a good two weeks ago."

"I couldn't answer it because I wasn't here."

"What do you mean you weren't here?" shouted one of the strangers in a threatening voice. He was a thick-necked fellow with a sallow face and pale, almost colorless eyes. He too was obviously a Party official, perhaps even a *Stasi* working for the SSD.

"I was away on vacation. With my wife and son."

"On vacation, eh?" said the thick-necked fellow. "Ah, yes, spending your ill-gotten gains! But where? Not in Adenauer's war-state, by any chance?"

"No, we were at Schmalkalden, in the district of Erfurt."

There was a moment of silence, but it did not last long.

"Schmalkalden!" repeated the thick-necked stranger in a sarcastic voice. "Comrades, did you hear that? This *Kursschwindler* was enjoying the good life at Schmalkalden! Occupying living quarters that should have gone to reward honest, meritorious workers!"

"Intolerable!" agreed the other stranger, tapping the table with a pencil. "A *Nutzniesser* like this shouldn't be entitled to vacations!"

Behrens protested. Although a Grenzgänger, he wasn't an "exchange swindler," since he exchanged the western marks he earned at the official rate. (This assertion was not strictly true, but he would have been in serious trouble if he had said anything else.) By the same token he wasn't a *Nutzniesser* living off the toil of others, since the western marks he earned went to help the DDR's trade balance.

But there was no placating his questioners. As a Grenzgänger he was automatically a parasite. "It's people like you who are sapping the lifeblood of the DDR!" they kept repeating.

"All right, then," said the town council official, finally tiring of this game. "But let's look at your record for a moment. Until 1957 you led an honest life and held different jobs over here— that is, in democratic Berlin. Now what was it that suddenly made you change your ways?"

Behrens explained that he had found an excellent job as an engine tuner in a big automobile repair workshop in the French sector. The pay was better than anything equivalent being offered in East Berlin. He would have liked to add that the work conditions were also more pleasant—everyone spoke his mind, and there were no political meetings that one was forced to attend—but he didn't dare.

"What do you mean the pay is better?" shouted the pale-eyed bully. "Are you saying the Workers-and-Peasants-State doesn't pay its workers properly?"

Behrens tried to explain that this was not what he had meant.

"Then what did you mean?" asked the second stranger. "That you have let yourself be bought by the capitalists, who are out to undermine our planned economy by robbing us of our mechanics and technicians?"

Behrens protested once again. He'd given twenty years of his working life to the DDR, and he didn't see why he was betraying it now by choosing to work in West Berlin. It wasn't illegal, as far as he knew. He and thousands of East Berliners had been doing it for years.

"But they won't be doing it much longer," declared the town council official. "Things are going to change. And if you want to save yourself a lot of trouble, you'd better start right now looking for an employer in democratic Berlin. We're prepared to give you a few weeks, but that's all."

"One month," nodded the thick-necked bully.

"August being a holiday month, we might lengthen it to six weeks," said the second stranger. "Or even eight. But you must agree to it now."

"Agree to it now!" exclaimed Behrens. "What do you mean?"

"What we mean," said the town council official, "is that you must give us your promise under oath that you are going to give up your job in West Berlin and start a new, honest worker's life in the DDR. Once we have that assurance, and have it in writing, you will be left alone."

"Here is a sheet of paper," said the second stranger. "All you have to do is to write out your pledge and sign it. It doesn't have to be long. One sentence will do. 'I, the undersigned, Karl Behrens . . .' "

"Now just a moment," broke in Behrens. "What you're asking of me is a lot. It's not something I can be rushed into. I've got to think this thing over."

It was pointed out to him that in his own interest it would be better if he signed now. But Behrens refused to do so. He said he needed time. Among other things, he wanted to discuss it with his wife.

"Your wife's opinion has no bearing on this question," the Party official reminded him. "This is a question of patriotic duty. If you refuse to sign, you will be assuming an enemy-of-the-people attitude. It will mean that you would rather throw in your lot with the Bonn Ultras and militarists than work for the peace-loving DDR."

Behrens realized that he was fighting a losing battle, but he still refused to sign.

"You're asking for trouble," the Party official warned him.

Two days later it started. Behrens's wife, Herta, began receiving visits from neighbors who all developed the same theme: It was unpatriotic, it was treasonous, to go on working for the capitalists. She also received a call from the house superintendent, whose job it was to keep an eye on all the tenants and to report all goings-on to the Party (much as the hated *Block-leiter* had done in Nazi times). His tone was distinctly hostile. He termed her husband a "people's parasite" and warned that if he went on working in the West, the authorities would have the Behrens thrown out of their apartment.

These incidents were nerve-wracking enough, but worse was to come. On the evening of August 2, Karl Behrens was homeward bound from his automobile workshop in the French sector when he got the shock of his life. On the platform of the little Bernau station a huge signboard had been erected. *DIESE GRENZGÄNGER SIND KRIEGSTREIBER!* ("These Border Crossers Are Warmongers!"), it proclaimed in frightening capitals. Beneath the sign were listed the names of five "warmongers." One of them was his own.

The following afternoon, after his return from West Berlin, Karl Behrens received a telephone call from an electrician who had agreed to teach his son the rudiments of his trade. He said that he had to talk to him urgently. Behrens went to see him immediately. The electrician said he was sorry, but he had no choice; he'd received instructions to terminate his son's apprenticeship forthwith.

Early the next morning, a Friday, Karl Behrens left as usual for his job in West Berlin. His wife and son left on a slightly later S-Bahn train, as though on a shopping expedition. But their destination this time was the Marienfelde refugee camp, where it had been agreed they were to ask for temporary asylum.

11

In the midst of the growing tension, one man at least had not lost his Blimplike calm: the head of British intelligence in West Berlin. Replying to a letter sent to him by the *Manchester Guardian*'s Terence Prittie, whose attention had been drawn to a report of unusually heavy truck traffic on the north–south highways leading into East Berlin, he informed his friend that he was taking his family to the Costa Brava on August 22 and that they would be back in Berlin by September 13.

I am hoping very much that the sun will shine while we are there and that nothing will happen to prevent the trip.

At present the wretched Grenzgänger are having a miserable time and Marienfelde is bursting its seams but West Berlin is as confident as ever: Bank deposits are normal for the time of year; the Bourse is steady, and there isn't a room to be had in even the smallest pensions for the period of the Radio Exhibition later in the month.

I believe the present crisis will end in anticlimax after the Federal elections—just as the 1958 one did after the French and Berlin elections. This is naturally a Bishopsian theory and bears no resemblance to anyone else's ideas on the subject, but I have a maddening habit of being right on most occasions!

12

On this Thursday morning Hermann Fink rose early, as he had done for most of his fifty-one years, and made ready to go out into the fields of the collective farm which had been established the previous year in his native Thuringian village of Kranlucken. He had no idea what new vexations the authorities might have in store for him, but being by nature an optimist and stubborn in his ways, he refused to let the prospect of new troubles spoil his breakfast of hot milk and coffee, rich brown bread and butter, and a bit of sausage.

His was the third generation to occupy this farm, one of the oldest in the village, and he was determined to hang on to what he could of it so that his twenty-one-year-old son Willy or one of his other two children could go on cultivating the land when the time came for him to retire from active work. The only question was, How much would there still be left for them to till and harvest when the time finally came? From a total of more than ninety acres, which is what Hermann Fink had owned before the collective had been established in the late spring of 1960, he was now down to barely forty that he could still call his own. This tract was less than half of his original land holdings, but it was something—like the thirteen head of cattle, the two horses, and the twelve pigs he had been allowed to keep, largely because of the sizable reserves of fodder he had managed to stow away in his barns.

All things considered, the previous summer had not been too bad. Each of the local farmers, having plowed and sown his fields before the collective was set up, had been allowed to reap his crop individually. The really nasty surprise had come in the autumn, when they were informed that none of them would be paid for the work they had put in on the collectively cultivated land. They would have to live off what they had been able to raise on their remaining plots. What little enthusiasm there had been for working the surrounding lands collectively dried up completely, and the grumbling was general through the following winter and the spring.

To soften the resistance they had encountered during the first collectivization drive of 1952–53, the authorities had granted East German farmers the right to work the collectivized lands on an eight-hour-a-day basis, like their working brothers in the factories. At Kranlucken the farmers had made the most of this concession—to the dismay of the authorities who here, as elsewhere in the DDR, were now vociferously denouncing the "eight-hour ideology."

The authorities had no less rashly introduced a clause into the official statutes theoretically entitling each member of an LPG collective to give notice if he wished to opt out at the end of the first working year. On June 30 Hermann Fink accordingly had given notice, as had thousands of other collectivized farmers throughout the DDR. At Kranlucken his example had been promptly followed by twenty-eight others—more than half the village's total of forty-seven farmers.

From that day on, Hermann Fink and his family had known no peace. As the leading farmer in the village, he was set upon by the mayor and by activists brought in from outside, who accused him of having egged the others on. They drove into his farmyard and out into the fields with vans and trucks equipped with loudspeakers and subjected him to nerve-wracking lectures in favor of the LPG collectives. On one occasion he found himself surrounded by fifteen Party agitators who turned the loudspeakers up so loud that nobody could understand a word. Each onslaught ended with the same insistent demand: He must renounce his intention of leaving the collective. But each time he refused. In this struggle of wills he wasn't going to be the loser.

This morning, however, was different from the others. This time it wasn't random Party agitators who were waiting for Hermann Fink as he left his farmyard for the fields. Four leather-coated agents of the SSD were waiting to pick him up. His son Willy, who had been working as a mechanic for harvesting machines in a neighboring village, had knocked somebody over with his motorcycle and then tried to make a run for it, they told him. Hermann's presence was needed at the "hearing."

Seated between two plainclothesmen, Hermann Fink was driven to a Grenzpolizei barracks at Geisa. There he was taken to a room and left under the watchful eye of an armed guard. Half an hour later seven plainclothes officials burst into the room and began bombarding him with accusations. He was an agent of the West—that much they knew. Who were his bosses? Who were his employers? Who exactly were the people who had been giving him missions and assignments?

Fink stared at them baffled. An agent of the West? He who'd never been to the West in his life, who'd never been given an order or assignment of that kind by anyone? What was this all about? What did it mean?

"What does it mean?" shouted one of his tormentors, seizing Fink's shirt with his two hands and ripping it in the process. The Kranlucken farmer was cuffed about and hit in the face a number of times, but to no avail. He was not going to admit that he was an agent for people he'd never seen.

The "hearing" completed, he was led outside and told to climb into a canvas-coated truck. It was dark inside, and he was not allowed to peer out. A few minutes later the canvas flap was raised, and his son Willy climbed in next to him.

"What happened to you?" the father began, only to be silenced by one of the plainclothesmen seated opposite.

"You'll have time to talk about it soon enough."

One look at his son's face was enough to make Fink realize that he'd been through the same treatment.

They were driven through the countryside for about an hour, without the slightest idea of where they were headed. Finally the truck stopped. Farmer and son were ordered to climb out. They found themselves in a field. Not far away were two photographers, and near them two Grepos holding their guns ready.

One of the plainclothesmen now addressed them. "It is an honor for these two members of the Grenzpolizei to have the honor of expelling these two Western agents back to where they came from."

A couple of swift kicks and the barked order "Run for it!" sent Hermann Fink and his son running across the field and into a nearby wood. Beyond the trees, they came to a ten-meter stretch of unplowed land. Only after they had crossed it did they realize that they were no longer in East Germany. They had just crossed the border into the Federal Republic.

Three days later, after being interrogated at length by West German and Allied officials, father and son were prevailed upon to hold a most unusual press conference in Bonn. Their story confirmed reports that all over the DDR, farmers were trying to opt out of their collectives en masse. But why the authorities had picked on Hermann Fink and his son, had them photographed as "enemies of the state" and "agents of the West," and then forced them to commit a crime—flight from the East German Republic—punishable by two years in prison, was anybody's guess. Frau Fink, a second son, and a daughter were, in any case, being forcibly retained in the DDR as hostages.

In West Berlin people shook their heads in wonderment. The Ulbricht regime was resorting to methods of intimidation that were bound to increase the existing panic.

13

Returning to Berlin even more hurriedly than they had left, Walter Ulbricht and Willi Stoph were back on German soil in the wee hours of Friday, August 4. They were driven through the night to the Wandlitz compound, where Ulbricht summoned Erich Mielke, Bruno Leuschner, and Erich Honecker to his villa.

The newcomers were given a quick rundown on what had happened in Moscow. The first plenary session of the Warsaw Pact powers had got off to a bad start thanks to the Albanians, who had sent a delegation from Tirana headed by Politburo member Ramiz Alia. Khrushchev, being in the chair, could not take the offensive himself, so it had fallen to Ulbricht, as the first speaker, to denounce the disruptive behavior that Comrades Hoxha and Shehu had displayed the previous November and to demand that the Tirana delegation be excluded from these new deliberations. Admitted to this first session as observers, the Chinese had lodged a protest but in vain. All the first secretaries of the Warsaw Pact countries had followed suit in demanding the exclusion of the Albanians, who had walked out in a huff.

The substantive discussions had not gone too well either. The Russians once again were blowing hot and cold on the question of signing a separate peace treaty with the DDR; and Khrushchev had personally vetoed the idea of using force to keep the Americans, French, and British from using the air corridors to fly DDR fugitives out of West Berlin. Ulbricht had even had trouble obtaining general agreement to the only feasible alternative: sealing off West Berlin. Permission to go ahead had been granted tentatively, subject to two conditions. The Warsaw Pact partners wanted to be sure that the DDR's military and police

forces were now strong enough to hold the lid down in East
Berlin, since no one wanted a repetition of what had happened
in 1953. They also wanted to know how well the DDR could
cope with an economic siege if Adenauer and the West Germans
decided to retaliate by halting all interzonal trade.

It was now a race against the clock. The answers to these two
questions had to be brought back to Moscow on this same Friday
evening in time to be approved by the Kremlin prior to the start
of the third and final session of the Warsaw Pact meeting,
scheduled for Saturday afternoon. None of those present in Ulbricht's villa could expect to get much sleep this night. Mielke,
as minister of state security, and Honecker, as the Central
Committee secretary responsible for national security, were to
help Willi Stoph prepare a report on the reliability of available
forces, with precise estimates of the number of troops and which
units of the Nationale Volksarmee, the Grenzpolizei, and the
factory militia should be brought into Berlin during the seal-off
operation to forestall a revolt. Leuschner, as chairman of the
State Planning Commission, was to decide which areas of the
East German economy were likely to be hardest hit by a sudden
halt in West German deliveries of vitally needed chemicals,
high-grade steels, and specialized machinery.

The two reports would have to be ready by 10:00 A.M. At 10:30
they would meet in another top-secret session with a few key
colleagues—including Paul Verner (head of the Party apparatus for East Berlin) and Karl Maron (minister of the interior)—who could be trusted to keep their mouths shut. Karl-
Heinz Hoffmann, the defense minister, and other senior
officers would be informed when the time came to prepare the
seal-off. But for the time being and for the sake of secrecy, it
was essential that the number of privileged insiders be kept to
a minimum.

Notwithstanding his precautions, Ulbricht's recent absence
had been spotted by close observers of the East Berlin scene
who had noted his failure to show up at a hastily improvised
reception for Kwame Nkrumah, president of Ghana. By
Friday morning the *Frankfurter Allgemeine Zeitung* and the
New York Herald Tribune were simultaneously claiming that
Ulbricht had made a secret trip to Moscow to see Khrushchev

about the refugee crisis. According to rumors now making the rounds in Bonn, he had been spotted in the grandstand at a soccer match between the Blue-White Amsterdam and the Moscow Dynamo teams on Wednesday afternoon.

His hurried return to Berlin might lead to more speculations, particularly if it was followed by an important meeting of Politburo members at his official residence. An exceptional midmorning meeting in the Wandlitz compound would set tongues wagging in half a dozen ministries and Party offices. To meet in the new Central Committee headquarters on the Werderscher Markt would be equally risky. The projected meeting must be held in some totally unexpected place, far from inquisitive eyes. The choice fell on the Ministry of Public Health, located on the Wilhelmstrasse and within easy walking distance of Unter den Linden. Anyone wondering why so many Politburo members should be converging on this building could be given a ready answer: This was an emergency meeting to decide what needed to be done to protect East Berlin and the DDR from the polio epidemic which, according to *Neues Deutschland* and other East German papers, was now ravaging the Federal Republic.

A few hours later Walter Ulbricht was seated once again behind his office desk in the Niederschönhausen Schloss, an eighteenth-century country house situated in the northern Pankow suburbs. Before proceeding to the midmorning rendezvous on the Wilhelmstrasse, he wanted to catch up on the latest local developments. The "open letter" that Friedrich Ebert had addressed to Willy Brandt on July 31, proposing that representatives of the two city governments meet to discuss a solution to the problem of border crossers, had been rejected without comment by the West Berlin Senat.

The three Western commandants, in identical notes sent to their Soviet opposite number, Col. Andrei Solovyov, in Karlshorst, had protested the recent measures taken against the border crossers, claiming that they violated the Four-Power agreement of June 20, 1949—an agreement designed to "promote the normalization of life in Berlin and to facilitate the movement of persons between Berlin and the rest of

Germany." Brandt, running true to form, had commended the commandants for their action.

The campaign against the head-hunters and the man-traders of West Berlin was proceeding apace. Factory committees were being formed in many state-run plants to demand sterner measures against these criminal elements, and a number of Western agents who had been caught red-handed trying to recruit workers and technicians for the Western monopolists had been brought to trial and were being given stiff sentences.

The drive against the border crossers also had been put into high gear. Already barred from buying East German cars, motorcycles, refrigerators, and television sets unless they could produce certificates proving that they worked in democratic Berlin, they were now being informed that they would have to pay for their rent, gas, electricity, water, and local taxes in West marks. Parents wishing to place their children in nurseries or kindergartens would have to provide proof that they worked in democratic Berlin. Border crossers faced eviction from their lodgings if they maintained their stubbornly antisocialist and uncooperative stand. *Neues Deutschland* and other DDR papers were being swamped with letters from indignant readers wanting to know how much longer the government was going to tolerate the abuses of these *Schmarotzen* ("spongers") and *Speckjäger* ("bacon chasers") who were out to get the best of both worlds.

All this was fine. The Party apparatus was functioning as it should. But the gap between intention and achievement was as enormous as ever. The Grenzgängers' response to this well-coordinated pressure was worse than mediocre. So far less than one thousand border crossers—according to the figures provided by Mielke's SSD and Friedrich Ebert's city hall authorities—had agreed to give up their jobs in West Berlin. That number amounted to less than one in fifty, if one counted only those who were officially registered in the West, or less than one in a hundred, if one added all the unregistered cleaning women and odd-job men who crossed over several times a week to do housework in West Berlin.

The situation with regard to the defectors who were leaving

the republic was no brighter. At certain S-Bahn stops beyond the city limits, the human traffic had been reduced to a trickle since hundreds of travelers had been intercepted and their identity cards taken from them. But many defectors were now evading the final railway checks by getting off at the next-to-the-last S-Bahn stop and walking for several kilometers through woods, fields, or casually guarded streets into East or West Berlin.

The number of fugitives, while showing no rise over the preceding three days, had shown no tendency to decline below the 1,100-a-day level. One of them was a particularly prominent citizen of the DDR—Dr. Pfeiffner-Bothner, medical director of the Volkspolizei Hospital, situated less than 200 meters from the French sector's Wedding district. Taking advantage of the weekend, he had driven over to West Berlin in his private car with his wife, two children, and mother-in-law on Saturday, July 29—the eve of Ulbricht's departure for Moscow. Not until Monday had his absence at the hospital been noted. In the West he was now being hailed as a number one witness against the Ulbricht regime.

The rot was spreading relentlessly, and unless it was soon stopped, the infection would invade every corpuscle and cell in a mortally stricken DDR.

At 10:30 A.M. the chosen few met in a carefully vacated office in the Ministry of Public Health to discuss the reports that had been hastily prepared during the night and early hours of the morning. The first, read by Bruno Leuschner, elicited little discussion. Since Khrushchev had assured Ulbricht and Stoph that the Soviet Union would stand behind the DDR economically as well as militarily, it was up to the USSR and its COMECON partners to supply the substitute materials needed to keep East German factories going.

The composite report on the reliability of the Nationale Volksarmee, Grenzpolizei, and Volkspolizei units which Willi Stoph presented was quite another matter. There was general agreement that the 8,200 Vopos and specially trained riot police and the 3,700 Garrisoned Police actually on hand could not begin to cope with the formidable job of stringing out

barbed wire, patrolling long stretches of border, and maintaining law and order in a restless capital, even though they
would be backed up by more than 12,000 factory militiamen
and the 4,500 hand-picked volunteers of Erich Mielke's
Wachregiment. As many as 40,000 more men might have to
be brought in from the outside to snuff out any sparks of revolt
before they spread to other regions of the DDR. Two newly
formed brigades of the Grenzpolizei were readily available, as
well as five battalions of alert police—three of them based at
Basdorf, the other two at Potsdam. They could count on some
of the 10,000 soldiers and on most of the 150 tanks of Col.
Horst Stechbarth's First Motorized Rifle Division, whose
units were spread out along the southern periphery of Berlin
from Potsdam to Alt Glienecke. But to make doubly sure that
the situation did not get out of hand, these forces would have
to be reinforced by thousands of hard-bitten Saxon militiamen
from the industrial centers of Halle, Chemnitz, and Leipzig.
As a final precaution—and this job was one for Honecker, who
had helped to organize and build up the FDJ—some of the
border-surveillance work would be assigned to Free German
Youth units, composed of eager young Communists who
would be thrilled to put their military training to practical
use.

Stoph's conclusion left no room for doubt. Eight years earlier, the Nationale Volksarmee had not existed, and all the
regime had been able to rely on in the crisis of 1953 had been
insufficiently trained Garrisoned Police units. Since then, unreliable officers and noncoms had been dismissed in large
numbers, and a disciplined army, strictly trained and drilled
on the Soviet model, had come into being.

The answer to the question raised in Moscow was an un-
equivocal Yes. Standing shoulder to shoulder in this hour of
grave crisis, the dedicated fighters of the NVA, the KVP, the
Grenzpolizei, the Kampfgruppen, the Wachregiment, and
the FDJ could crush all attempts at counterrevolution without
having to rely on the fraternal aid of their Soviet comrades-
in-arms.

[7]KVP. *Kasernierte Volkspolizei* ("garrisoned police"). East German officials habitu-
ally use these abbreviations—and NVA for Nationale Volksarmee, FDJ for Freie
Deutsche Jugend—rather than the full appellation.

For the operation to be successful it was absolutely vital that the preparations be made to look like a concerted police action aimed at insulating the western sectors of Berlin from the surrounding territory of the DDR. Forty kilometers of barbed wire already had been brought in from Perleberg, near the West German border, and stored in a training camp at Basdorf, just off Highway 109, over which it could be trucked into Pankow at the very last moment. Similar stocks of chicken-wire fencing and concrete uprights were being amassed in other field depots along the periphery of the city. Slabs of concrete and pressed rubble had been piled up in abundance at many building sites in East Berlin, and it would be a simple matter to move them up to the intersector border for the second phase.

The final question to be settled was the exact date and hour for the operation to be launched. Although here too the Russians would have the final word, it was up to those present to make a definite proposal. The answer was soon found. To undertake a seal-off operation in the middle of the week, when it would directly affect fifty thousand Grenzgänger crossing from East to West, to say nothing of the thirteen thousand West Berliners who crossed over every day to work in democratic Berlin, would be asking for a border-line explosion. The logical time to act was over a weekend, when most Berliners would be taking it easy. Since it couldn't be the upcoming one—now only twelve hours away—they would have to try for the one after.

By the early hours of Saturday, August 5, Ulbricht was back in Moscow with precise replies to the questions that Khrushchev and other Communist party heads had wanted answered. At another secret Kremlin session, the two reports were examined and accepted in principle. The Soviet Union would provide economic help to the German Democratic Republic, the other countries of the Warsaw Treaty bloc would do their bit to keep East German industry from collapsing for lack of vital metals and other key materials. The seal-off operation would be put into effect the following weekend and, to achieve a maximum of surprise, in the dead of night.

On Saturday morning Khrushchev received the Tunisian ambassador, Sadok Mokkadam, for an hour and a half. Afterward he had to accompany the Italian premier and foreign minister to the airport. Before they parted he told his guests that the behavior of Italy and other West European states over the Berlin question reminded him of the story of a hunter who went out one day with a friend to catch a bear. During their search the two hunters were separated. Finally one of them called, "Hey, I've got him!"

"Then bring him here!" shouted his companion.

"I can't," came the reply, "the bear won't let me go!"

Not until midafternoon could the leaders of the Warsaw Treaty bloc resume their deliberations on a plenary basis. By this time, however, the major problems had been dealt with. The Russians were going to take steps to impress the world with their military might and determination.

Although the Soviet forces in Germany were going to be placed on a special alert and combat footing, just in case, it was unlikely that they would have to intervene militarily against the Western powers. However, it was made bluntly clear to Ulbricht that his soldiers and policemen were not to overdo it. They could barricade the sector borders on their side of the boundary, but they were not to provoke the Western Allies by encroaching on the territory of the western sectors. Soviet advisers and KGB officers from the army's political branch would, in any case, keep a close eye on all phases of the operation.

It only remained to complete the preliminary draft of the declaration that was to be issued in the name of the Warsaw Treaty states when H-hour struck, as well as the joint communiqué that was to be released in a few hours to explain the purpose of this sudden gathering of Communist party leaders. The second statement—a minor masterpiece of diplomatic eyewash—declared that the first secretaries of the central committees of the Warsaw Treaty states had met to reaffirm their desire for a German peace treaty with both German states which would guarantee West Berlin's future as a "free demilitarized city." All the participants were inflexibly determined to achieve a peace settlement with Germany before the end of the year.

To the Albanians who had returned to Tirana in a rage, as to most other outsiders, it looked as though the Kremlin summit had heaved yet again and brought forth a mouse.

14

While the Communist party leaders of Eastern Europe were debating the future of Berlin behind closed doors in the Kremlin, the Parliament in London officially adjourned at the close of a "gruelling session," as the *Daily Telegraph* described it. On Friday evening Harold Macmillan addressed the British people in a special BBC broadcast before leaving for his country home in Sussex. He began by speaking of Berlin, where, he had to confess, his hopes had often been dashed and he had suffered cruel disappointments. "Everyone knows that Russia is a great, powerful country. Everyone knows that Mr. Khrushchev is a strong leader. What we are all wondering is whether he can prove to be a statesman too."

More than ever the white-haired premier was convinced that it was imperative to try to bring the Soviet Union to the conference table as quickly as possible. His foreign secretary, the Earl of Home, had just left to attend a meeting in Paris with other Western foreign ministers (Dean Rusk, Couve de Murville, and Heinrich von Brentano), and he was going to press for negotiations as strongly as he could, but without going so far as to alienate the French, who were almost certain to oppose any such initiative at the present time. There were, however, grounds for cautious hope. From reports the Foreign Office had received from the Earl of Scarborough, who had been representing the United Kingdom on the Allied "working group" formed to deal with the Berlin problem, it now seemed that the Americans—in particular Abram Chayes, the State Department's legal counsel, and Foy Kohler—had reached the same conclusion. To open negotiations with the Soviet Union was likely to do more good than harm in defusing the crisis. Dean Rusk, who had just flown in from Washington, was expected to take the same line.

The next morning Macmillan summed up his own and the

Foreign Office's position on the subject in a letter written to Queen Elizabeth, who had left London for her estate at Balmoral.

On the question of Berlin, the third great issue which is our concern, Your Majesty will have seen from recent telegrams that the Americans are, as I expected, getting off their high horse. They would, of course, like to put the blame for this upon us, but I think the Foreign Secretary has with great skill protected himself and our country from this accusation. In spite of the efforts of journalists known to be very close to the White House, the vigour of the attack upon us has much decreased, and I think they will find it difficult to pretend that the President's desire for negotiation is due to the weakness of the Allies. I think they are more likely to claim it as a mark of his pre-eminent statesmanship. However, I have always thought about American Presidents that the great thing is to get them to do what we want. Praise or blame we can leave to history.

15

In his commandant's office, located near the Tegel airfield in the large, walled-in compound of the Quartier Napoléon (as the former barracks-headquarters of the Hermann Goering division was now called), Gen. Jean Lacomme was wondering whether he could risk leaving Berlin for a few days to attend the Bayreuth Festival. During his thirty-two months of service in Berlin, he had steadfastly refused to take extended leaves, limiting his absences to four days, no more. Nobody was more keenly aware of just how woefully weak were the 2,500 French soldiers and the eighteen AMX tanks under his command, when compared with the twenty Soviet divisions stationed on East German soil. But what he lacked in military strength he could at least try to make up for in vigilance. This, he felt, was the minimum he owed to a city to which he had grown sincerely and surprisingly attached.

Personally, Lacomme did not much care for Wagner. But his

music-loving wife was of another mind. Somehow, through the uncertainties and shifting tensions of the international situation, they had let one entire festival go by. Now she was full of reproaches: "This is our last chance. If we don't go now, we'll never go again."

If only he could have foreseen that the summer of 1961 would be marked by a new and unprecedented spurt in the refugee flow, he would have arranged to skip the Bayreuth Festival as he had done in 1959. But how could such developments be anticipated that far ahead? This crisis was not the first of its kind that he had lived through. One thing he had discovered over the past two and a half years was that there were cyclical variations in the East German refugee flow, which tended to decrease each time the Ulbricht regime relaxed its dogmatic drives to regiment its citizenry. This time the authorities of the DDR seemed hellbent on maintaining the pressure, but who could tell if they might not end up once again relenting, as they had done in the past?

In August of 1958, when he had been appointed commandant, Jean Lacomme was already fifty-six years old, and he knew that this assignment was likely to be his last abroad. Just why he had been chosen for this post—he who had spent most of his military life in non-European theaters of operation—he had no idea. It was certainly not due to any fondness in his family for the Germans, who had killed his father at the battle of Verdun. Lacomme had never been an ultra-Gaullist, so this post could not be considered a reward for loyalty. To be placed in command of two thousand men, even in an advanced outpost like Berlin, was not much to brag about in any case. Seven signatures of approval had been needed for his appointment, and they included that of the minister of foreign affairs as well as that of the prime minister (Charles de Gaulle)—which presumably meant that they had been unable to discover any traces of violently anti-Gaullist sentiments or behavior in his military past. Of course, they may have decided that this Berlin post was as good a military "siding," as any onto which to shunt an officer who was fast approaching retirement age.

Most of Jean Lacomme's military life, after his graduation from the Saint-Cyr Academy in 1924, had been spent in Indo-

china, Morocco, Algeria, and Equatorial Africa—more than
enough time to earn him the appellation of "bloodthirsty colo-
nialist" in *Neues Deutschland* and other organs of the DDR.

Under the circumstances, it was surprising how genuinely
attached to this city he had become. If chance had presided over
his appointment to this outpost, it was also a bit by chance that
the French had been given jurisdiction over the two northern-
most boroughs of West Berlin—those of Reinickendorf and
Wedding, which were distinctly more proletarian than middle-
class in their demographic make-up. He felt as much at home
among the working men and women who earned their daily
bread at the huge Siemens electric plant or at the Borsig
Locomotive Works (near which he lived) as he probably would
have among the better-housed and better-clothed residents of
Zehlendorf and Dahlem, in the U.S. sector. His mother had
been a schoolteacher and his father an accountant, and it was
with a stout Socialist family in Thuringia that he had gone to stay
for four months in 1932 to pick up the rudiments of German,
which now stood him in such good stead. Berlin, for those
humble provincials, was already a "spot of perdition" and a place
to be avoided in those crucial watershed months when the ill-
fated Weimar Republic was being consumed from within by the
ultraanationalistic cancer of Hitler's Brownshirts.

The curious thing about this baleful "sink of iniquity" was that
as long as the elections had been free, the city's inhabitants had
never given Hitler and his henchmen a clear-cut majority vote.
The betterheeled residents of Zehlendorf and Dahlem might
have voted massively for the Nazis, but certainly not the prole-
tarians of Reinickendorf and Wedding—the Saint-Denis of
Berlin, as Lacomme liked to call it. In the spring of 1959, when
he had been summoned back to Paris for consultations, De
Gaulle had startled him with the question, *"Alors, comment
vont vos Prussiens?"* Lacomme, who curiously enough bore a
slight resemblance to De Gaulle—his head relatively small
compared with his large body—had had to explain to his haughty
superior that there were few "Prussians" and even fewer Junkers
in the French sector of Berlin. Many, if not most, of its inhabitants were of proletarian stock. In the 1932 elections, 33
percent of the borough's citizens had voted Communist—a large

enough proportion to win it the name of *das rote Wedding* ("red Wedding"). Under Hitler many of these Communists had been forced to join the brown-shirted *Sturm-Abteilungen.* The Nazis often called these browbeaten storm troopers *Beefsteak-Genossen* ("Beefsteak Comrades"), for although their uniforms were brown, deep down within them they remained stubbornly red. Some of the hardier Weddingers had even been known to sport red carnations in their buttonholes on May 1, Europe's traditional Labor Day. It had taken the rape-and-loot rampage of the Red Army's "Mongolian horde" in 1945, the tactics of Walter Ulbricht's SED, and Khrushchev's first Berlin ultimatum to cut this Communist vote to an insignificant 1.9 percent in the most recent elections of December 1958.

De Gaulle had seemed so intrigued by what Lacomme had to tell him that their conversation had lasted three quarters of an hour instead of the scheduled fifteen minutes. In practical terms, however, this tête-à-tête at the Elysée Palace had proved as fruitless as the morning staff conference that had preceded it. France had not yet left the integrated NATO structure, and General Norstad, with the backing of the Eisenhower administration, was pressing for a unified command in Berlin. *"Il y aura un commandement unifié à Berlin,"* De Gaulle finally had decreed, *"quand le feu aura parlé."* It was one of those sibylline phrases that sounded splendidly Napoleonic when first heard, but which appeared increasingly hollow when more closely examined. Just what did De Gaulle mean by, "There will be a unified command in Berlin when the guns have spoken?" What guns? Whose guns? Would an exchange of fire between East German Vopos and West Berlin policemen mean that the "guns had spoken" and that a unified command was thus justified (under U.S. leadership, since the Americans, with six thousand men, had the largest Western garrison)? The answer to this question was not forthcoming; and De Gaulle's later decision to remove France from the integrated NATO structure ("Let Norstad have his [air] battle over Germany, I want mine over France!") was proof that the stiff-necked president of the French Republic was not interested in a unified command in Berlin or anywhere else unless it was one he could personally boss.

For the time being the question was academic. The crisis had not yet assumed wartime proportions, and Grepos and Schupos were not exchanging shots across the sector boundaries. The refugee flow was still running at an alarmingly high level, but in the last couple of days the rate seemed to be dipping. The French commandant's deputy, Comte Bernard Guillier de Chalvron, had made it clear that, crisis or no crisis, he was returning to France for his summer holidays. He planned to leave Berlin on Saturday, August 12, barely one week away. If he and his wife were to take in the Bayreuth Festival, they would have to leave now, so that he could be back at his post before Chalvron departed.

Gen. Jean Lacomme decided he would risk it. By car Bayreuth was little more than a three-hour drive. If anything dramatic happened while they were at the festival, he could have the chauffeur drive them back in their Mercedes 300. Although his own tastes in classical music ran to Beethoven, Mozart, and Bach, he agreed with his wife that it would be a shame to let that scoundrel Ulbricht keep them from hearing *Die Meistersinger* sung in the sanctum of Wagnerian sanctums.

16

A few hours after the early-morning release of the Warsaw Treaty powers' communiqué, another Soviet sputnik was launched into space. The news, broadcast over the capital's radio stations at 10:40 A.M., Moscow time (seven hours ahead of eastern standard time), made the first page of the late Sunday morning, August 6, edition of the *New York Times*.

The Russians, once again, had scored a first. The five-ton spacecraft, piloted by Maj. Gherman Titov, was more than twice as heavy as the four-thousand-pound capsules in which Alan Shepard, in May, and Virgil Grissom, in July, had made their brief suborbital trips to the upper stratosphere; and whereas their flights had lasted fifteen and sixteen minutes respectively, Major Titov had already been aloft for a full hour and a half when the news was flashed from Moscow, and he was continuing to circle the globe once in every eighty-eight minutes.

Nikita Khrushchev, who could converse by special radio hookup with the globe-girdling astronaut, had reason to be pleased and proud. He hadn't been idly boasting when he had told Ulbricht and other Communist party leaders that the Americans were in for new cosmonautic surprises. The Soviet Union, already manufacturing rockets with a thrust of eight hundred thousand pounds—ten times more powerful than those that had lifted the two American spacemen from the earth—had again demonstrated its enormous technical advance in space exploration and had afforded new proof of the inherent superiority of the communist over the capitalist system.

The glad tidings were soon being broadcast from street-corner loudspeakers all over Moscow, between recordings of rhythmic march songs and patriotic chants. Although less rhapsodic in their rejoicing than when Yuri Gagarin's first orbital flight was announced on April 12, many pedestrians stopped to listen to scientists and academicians vie with each other in extolling this exemplary achievement.

The Soviet Union's allies hastened to follow suit. In Warsaw the news was considered sensational enough to warrant an extra edition of the daily *Tribuna Ludu*. In East Berlin, factory sirens wailed and automobile horns began to blare each time it was announced that Major Titov's *Vostok II* was passing triumphantly overhead.

The first reactions in Washington were contradictory. Pentagon officials shrugged off the news as militarily of no particular significance. But elsewhere there was an uneasy feeling that the Americans were falling seriously behind in the space race, belying Jules Verne's confident prediction that they would be the first to reach the moon. "It is almost incredible," was the comment of Sir Bernard Lovell, director of the Jodrell Bank Radio-Astronomy station in Great Britain, "and it underlines in a vivid way the advance of Soviet science and technology. I am far from being pro-Russian in any political sense, but I think one of the greatest dangers in the world today is to doubt their position and their strength in science and technology."

This statement, needless to say, was music to Khrushchev's ears. He wanted the world to know that the Soviet Union was now, scientifically as well as militarily, the most formidable power in the world—even though, as Botho Kirsch, the *Frankfurter Rundschau*'s Moscow correspondent, pointed out, on this same Railwayman's Day (intended to laud the glorious achievements of Soviet railroad transportation), some thirty thousand tons of urgently needed vegetables, furniture, and building materials were rotting or gathering dust in unloaded freight cars, thanks to the bureaucratic chaos reigning in the distribution sector.

Now that Russian cosmonauts were blazing new trails through the heavens, what did it matter if grumbling housewives had to stand in line for hours to buy a few hard-to-find tomatoes? New proof of the invincible forward march of Soviet science and technology was afforded on Monday morning, August 7, when the news was flashed that Maj. Gherman Titov had landed safely somewhere near Saratov after completing 17 orbits and covering 696,000 kilometers—the distance to the moon and back—in 25 hours.

Never one to waste his time, Walter Ulbricht spent this same Monday morning at a camp near Biesenthal, some ten kilometers north of Bernau, where Grenzpolizei units were undergoing summer training. He wanted to brief a number of senior officers from the Ministry of the Interior, and it suited his designs to do it in the country, in order to distract attention from what was being planned in East Berlin itself.

Karl Maron's Ministry of the Interior had already taken a significant step in this direction by having the State Printing Office in Leipzig prepare multicolored passes for distribution to local Volkspolizei offices. Any resident of the Soviet zone now wishing to travel to Berlin was required to obtain one of these passes from his employer or police station, so as to be able to present it, when challenged, along with his identity card. Rumor soon had it that the different colors had been deliberately chosen by the authorities to represent different areas of East Germany, so that an examining Vopo could tell at a glance just where the traveler came from. Such information was in fact quite superfluous, for every East German identity card carried a roman numeral indicating the district in which it had been issued. But hundreds of thousands of East Germans were now persuaded that these multicolored passes were being issued as part of a systematic plan to seal off Berlin from the rest of the Soviet zone.

Walter Ulbricht was not out to contradict this impression. The clamp-down on human traffic between East Berlin and the Zone was to be backed up by a general tightening of controls all around the outer periphery of Greater Berlin. Volkspolizei and Grenzpolizei units assigned to guard this periphery were to be progressively strengthened over the next few days by the cancellation of leaves and the last-minute recall of noncoms and vacationing soldiers. The barbed-wire fences already erected along various stretches of the 111-kilometer demarcation line between the western sectors of Berlin and the surrounding Zone were to be reinforced. The general tightening of controls would, however, be gradual, to keep the rank and file from getting the wind up. For the time being, Grenzpolizei soldiers and noncoms were to be told by their political officers that the bales of barbed wire and the concrete posts being stockpiled in their barracks areas were going to be used to fence in their encampments. If questions were raised about the watchtowers and the searchlights that were being set up at certain points along the city's western periphery, they were to be explained as being needed to protect the territory of the German Democratic Republic from the incursions of revanchist elements operating out of the NATO Frontstadt of West Berlin.

That same evening Nikita Khrushchev appeared again before his country's television cameras, to deliver his much-awaited reply to Kennedy's address of July 25. The balding Soviet leader read the transcript in front of him with studied care and restraint, only occasionally raising his eyes from the text. He was obviously speaking not for himself but for the entire Central Committee, of which he was the first secretary.

The speech began with a few sentences of praise for Maj. Gherman Stepanovich Titov and the "remarkable scientists, designers, engineers, and workers" who had made possible "this great achievement gratifying our Soviet motherland." He then spoke at considerable length of the new Seven-Year Plan, listed a whole series of achievements in the fields of industrial production and agriculture, before roundly asserting that the Communist party's new draft program had won the approval of the entire Soviet people.

As a result of these many achievements in space and on the ground, the superiority of a socialist over a capitalist economy was no longer being proved by theoretical arguments. "The material evidence of this reality is already clear," he went on, blandly ignoring the dramatic evidence to the contrary emanating from East Germany. It was what he had said to Kennedy when they had met in Vienna in early June; it was what he had repeated to the other Communist party leaders hastily summoned to Moscow a few days before. Let history settle the issue between the two. He was personally convinced that the socialist economic system would triumph over the capitalist system because it was "more viable and progressive."

After again excoriating the "suicidal mania" of the military hotheads and bluntly declaring that the Soviet Union now had sufficient weapons to destroy American military bases all over the world, Khrushchev expressed the hope that the more sober-minded would soon gain the upper hand in the counsels of the West. This was followed by a highly significant passage which was as close as he could come to disclosing his and his East German partners' real intentions.

The imperialists feel that the present situation gives them a convenient loophole, with the aid of which they can thwart the German Democratic Republic's development as a socialist state. They are using West Berlin as a springboard for subversive activities against the German Democratic Republic and other socialist countries. They have been infiltrating their agents in order to keep the military situation there at white heat. The imperialists' sole concern is to enlarge that loophole and to weaken the German Democratic Republic. But they are being told: "Stop, gentlemen! We know very well what you want, what you are after. We are going to sign a peace treaty and close your loophole into the German Democratic Republic."

The speech, which it took Khrushchev an hour and forty minutes to deliver, ended with an assurance that the Allied access routes to Berlin would not be affected in any way should the Soviet Union have to sign a separate peace treaty with the German Democratic Republic. But the Western powers must understand that nothing would deter the Soviet Union from signing a German peace treaty with or without their active participation. Should the need arise, they (the Russians) were even prepared to "increase the numerical strength of the army at the western frontiers by transferring divisions from other parts of the Soviet Union." The leaders of the West would thus be well advised to renounce their reckless plans and agree "to sit down like honest men around a conference table."

The speech, spread over the first pages of *Neues Deutschland*, next to photos of Gherman Titov, inspired Hermann Axen's editorialists to dithyrambic heights of praise and abuse:

But the scum of human evolution living west of the Elbe River would like to spoil the worldwide rejoicing over Titov's feat. . . . We hope that the nuclear warriors around Strauss have meanwhile reconsidered their plans for conquering the world. . . . German workers are proud of being led by men with strong characters like Walter Ulbricht. . . . The Soviet astronauts have shown everyone that the strongest power in the world is standing by our side.

In Paris the latest Soviet space exploit, followed by Khrushchev's truculent oration, captured the headlines, completely overshadowing the inconclusive conclusion of the foreign ministers' conference. *Kroutchev: "J'AI ASSEZ DE FUSÉES POUR ECRASER LE MONDE ENTIER!"* ("Khrushchev: 'I have enough missiles to crush the entire world!' ") was one Paris newspaper's jarring headline.

Before flying back to Britain, where he was to report to Prime Minister Macmillan at his Sussex home, the Earl of Home told reporters that the Soviets were only interested in whittling away Western occupation rights and turning them over to the East Germans. There was no earthly good, he warned, in looking upon negotiations as an incantation that can be repeated as though it will solve everything. If from the start there is no real hope of an agreement, then negotiations are worse than no negotiations at all. . . . It is quite clear that Mr. Khrushchev is playing a game of political poker, and we cannot and ought not to disclose our hands, our cards.

But his own countrymen, to judge by the Tuesday morning press in London, were deaf to this judicious warning, the public clamor for negotiations—now, immediately, without delay—having apparently been stimulated rather than discouraged by Khrushchev's latest exercise in bomb rattling.

Although the reassuring words about Allied access routes being unaffected were what most impressed Kennedy and his White House advisers, this solemn televised speech was differently interpreted by listeners in East Germany. For the first time Khrushchev had spoken publicly of a "loophole" that must be plugged; and although this particular passage was curiously omitted from the English text later released by TASS, there was no way of removing it from the spoken address.

In Berlin the consequences were almost immediately apparent. The news (now officially confirmed, after first being denied) that Ulbricht had made a trip to Moscow had already persuaded 3,268 East Germans to crowd into the Marienfelde refugee center between noon on Saturday and four in the afternoon on Monday. Over the next twenty-four hours the human tide rose even higher, to reach a record level of 1,741—the highest that had been recorded so far in 1961.

On Sunday Ernst Lemmer, Bonn's minister for all-German affairs, had appeared on West German television and reiterated an earlier plea. He was asking the inhabitants of East Germany to think twice before streaming over to the West. Like his predecessor Jakob Kaiser, he said, he had steadfastly discouraged West German industrial firms from sending scouts to comb the refugee camps for technical talent. For the East German authorities to speak of a government-sponsored "man-trade" was an arrant lie. Indeed, in 1960, when East German doctors were fleeing en masse, he had publicly appealed to them to remain at their posts, notwithstanding the cruel hardships, so that the bedridden in East German hospitals could continue to receive proper medical attention.

Ernst Lemmer, for all his good intentions, was wasting his breath. Appeals to calm now sounded absurdly out of place to the frightened inhabitants of the DDR. From their newspapers and radio broadcasts they learned that the USSR was prepared to move new divisions to the western borders of its empire; workers in Soviet defense factories were "spontaneously" demanding an eight-hour instead of a seven-hour workday so that their peace-loving country could give a "smashing reply" to the enemies of peace who were "fanning war hysteria and brandishing weapons"; "sabotage radio stations" like RIAS in West Berlin were going to be put out of action once a separate peace treaty with the USSR was signed, and to cap it all, the East German Volkskammer was being convened in extraordinary session on Friday, August 11, to discuss this peace treaty question.

By 4:00 P.M. on Wednesday, another 1,926 refugees had streamed into Marienfelde—almost 200 more than the previous day's record-breaking total.

In Bonn, as in Washington and other Western capitals, it was now feared that to fill the yawning gaps in manpower, the Russians might resort to a massive injection of workers and technicians from other Communist states to "colonize" Ulbricht's depopulated and demoralized Workers-and-Peasants-State.

As always in periods of mounting tension, the weirdest rumors were rampant. According to some, peddled by "authoritative sources," Ulbricht had returned from Moscow looking more than usually grim, because Khrushchev had refused him permission to seal the borders with West Berlin. According to other reports, engineer units from the Nationale Volksarmee were replacing rusted barbed wire and clearing a 50-meter-wide "death strip" around the 111-kilometer border separating the western sectors of Berlin from the surrounding Soviet zone. Once cleared of weeds and bushes, the death strip was to be fenced off with stakes and barbed wire supplied to the DDR by West German firms under the terms of the interzonal trade agreement. Watchtowers equipped with powerful searchlights were being similarly erected by units controlled by Erich Mielke's SSD along lakes, rivers, and canals at points where they neared, formed, or crossed the established lines of demarcation.

The various reports were mutually contradictory—unless one assumed that Ulbricht had decided to go ahead on his own, regardless of Khrushchev's opposition. Of the two, the reports about strange doings along the outer periphery of West Berlin seemed the more plausible, confirming the unanimous predictions of Western intelligence experts. Indeed, one of the few points of real agreement to have emerged from the recent foreign ministers' and NATO delegates' meetings in Paris was that if and when the seal-off was put into effect, it would be around the periphery of Greater Berlin rather than through the center of the disputed city.

17

Cheering crowds lined the highway leading into Moscow as the motorcade drove majestically into Red Square, where white guidelines had been painted on the asphalt to channel the marchers in a massively prepared welcome parade for Titov. The sun shone brightly on this festive Wednesday afternoon, and seldom had Nikita Sergeyevich Khrushchev looked jollier than as he embraced Gherman Titov and Yuri Gagarin on the black marble rostrum of Lenin's mausoleum, publicly hailing them as "celestial brothers."

In his answering speech, Gherman Titov sounded the familiar themes. He could have landed his *Vostok II* spaceship anywhere he chose; his twenty-five-hour flight was "a victory of unmatched power for scientific purposes in the name of progress"; but he also reminded his listeners that the Soviet people now had the means to "crush an aggressor should the enemies of peace launch another war," adding that "as a combat pilot I am ready to fulfill my mission to the Communist party and the government."

The impressive parade lasted for two hours, and that same

evening the new idol was honored with the firing of a rare
twenty-one-gun salute. But the highlight of this Wednesday was
the vast Kremlin reception held in Saint George's Hall, to which
two thousand Soviet scientists, engineers, military men, and
Party leaders had been invited, along with members of the Diplomatic Corps.

Once again they were in for a surprise. Shortly before President Brezhnev was due to pin the Order of Hero of the Soviet
Union on Gherman Titov's chest, Khrushchev, with a champagne glass in his hand, launched into an impromptu speech.

"Fools! What do you think you are doing? Is this your vision of
the future?" he asked, addressing himself rhetorically to the
"partisans of war" in the West who were trying to intimidate his
country. The peace-loving Soviet Union was in favor of universal
disarmament and would gladly see all weapons of mass destruction sunk to the bottom of the oceans. But the world being what
it is—full of military hotheads, lunatics, and "suicide cases"—
the Russians had had to spend money on rockets and nuclear
bombs that were not made "for slicing sausages. . . . We will
use them only if attacked," he went on. However, he wanted
everyone to know that his scientists had assured him that they
could build monster bombs and rocket warheads with an explosive power equal to 100 million tons of TNT!

He then raised his glass to propose a toast to the gravity-de-
fying pilot of *Vostok II*. "The Americans are not launching sput-
niks. Theirs jump up and fall into the ocean. But we are glad,"
he added generously, referring to Virgil Grissom's recent
mishap, "that the American flyer didn't drown!"

"Gentlemen capitalists, don't be offended!" Khrushchev went
on, now addressing himself to the U.S. chargé d'affaires, John
McSweeney, and to other Western diplomats. "Every duck
praises its own pond. And why not? This is an event that shook
the world."

Although relatively brief by Khrushchevian standards, this
speech shook the chandeliers. For the chairman of the council
and first secretary of the Central Committee was not yet through
boasting of his country's invincible might. He particularly
wanted his warning words to reach the ears of the stiff-necked
saber rattlers on the Rhine. Persons of his age had lived through

two or three wars. But "we never bowed when the Germans came close to Moscow and Leningrad. Do you think we will bow down now because of Adenauer? If Adenauer with his Bundeswehr thinks he can achieve reunification through war and we are attacked, then there will be no German nation left. All Germany will be reduced to dust. We are not threatening anybody, but we are not going to tremble like cowards!"

These fighting words, strangely at variance with the accompanying photos showing a grinning Nikita hugging the two Russian astronauts on Red Square, again filled the front pages of newspapers in the West.

In West Berlin a singularly harassed Kurt Exner, the city hall senator responsible for social affairs, was forced to issue a desperate plea to all available doctors and nurses, asking them to volunteer a few hours of their daily time to help their hopelessly overworked colleagues at Marienfelde. The deputy mayor, Franz Amrehn, announced that he would not be campaigning for his Christian Democratic party in the Federal Republic, the local situation being far too critical for him to be able to leave Berlin. A senior judge of an East Berlin court of appeals explained that he had fled the DDR because the show trials now being organized against random "head-hunters" and "slave-traders" were a grotesque mockery and caricature of justice.

During a Wednesday evening television show witnessed by millions of East Germans, Gerhard Eisler, deputy chairman of the DDR's State Radio Committee, vented his scorn on refugees and fugitives, terming them "fools and dunderheads." And cathedral pastor Karl Kleinschmidt, of Schwerin, paid his own homage to Caesar by terming the fugitives criminals and urging the authorities to close the doors to the West without delay.

Undaunted by intermittent downpours which sent rivulets of water swirling along the sidewalks, 1,709 East Germans had checked into the Marienfelde refugee center by 4 P.M. the following day. Conditions within the DDR, many of them reported, had reached a state bordering chaos. There were not enough farmhands to bring in the harvest, not enough doctors to handle patients in crowded waiting rooms. Many streetcars were being driven by women to replace the men who had fled to the West; and in the Baltic port of Rostock, as in Potsdam, fifteen-year-old schoolboys were being pressed into service as ticket collectors. Many government departments and HO[8] department stores were having to close at noon for lack of sufficient personnel. The Workers-and-Peasants-State, which was to have overtaken the Federal Republic in per-capita production by the end of 1961, was now on the verge of wholesale collapse.

18

Seated around the table for a late-morning cup of coffee in what had once been Field Marshal Keitel's villa in residential Dahlem, the three Allied military liaison officers found themselves reduced to speculations. Shortly after eight o'clock each of them had been informed by a telephone call from the Soviet External Relations Branch that Col. Gen. Ivan Yakubovsky, commander in chief of the Group of Soviet Forces in Germany, would be pleased to see the three mission chiefs at his Wünsdorf-Zossen headquarters at 4:30 P.M. on this Thursday, August 10. Such a summons—quite different from the lower-level contacts maintained to clear up scraps involving Allied and Russian soldiers—was a relatively rare and thus puzzling event.

The senior of the three in rank was Brigadier Thomas Pearson, a tall, jovial former airborne officer who had been posted to Berlin the previous October after finishing a tour of duty as chief of staff of the British forces in Cyprus. The senior in terms of service—thirteen months in Berlin—was Col. Ernest von Pawel, a former cavalry officer from Kansas who had worked with the European Advisory Committee in wartime London and had helped plan the occupation of postwar Ger-

[8]HO *Handels-Organisation* ("trade organization") is the official title of East Germany's state-run department stores.

many. The third and most conspicuous of the three—a burly, balding giant—was Col. Michel Barré de Saint-Venant, a French Air Force officer who believed that any pilot worth his salt should be at the controls of his machine. Like his British and American colleagues, he was almost invariably tailed by a Russian car each time he toured the Soviet occupation zone—a zone so full of restricted areas that it resembled a leopard skin. When the shadowing grew too irksome, the one-time dogfighter would change places with his chauffeur and put his Mercedes 220 through a dizzying series of gyrations. More than once he had had the satisfaction of seeing his less skilled pursuer skid off the road or plow into a field while he continued his terrestrial reconnaissance undisturbed.

At 3:30 P.M. the three mission chiefs and their Russian interpreters were off, headed for the Wünsdorf-Zossen headquarters—a ninety-kilometer drive through Potsdam and then east and south. After skirting the shimmering lakes, the fountained gardens, and the pergolas of Frederick the Great's Sans-Souci, the three cars passed the forbidding walls of several old Prussian garrisons, now used to quarter the men and materiel of the Tenth Tank Division and a Soviet heavy-artillery outfit. Farther south they joined the uncompleted Ring-Autobahn, which was once intended to encircle Berlin completely. The rain, which had lashed the city for several hours in the morning, had momentarily let up, and save for a few passenger cars and an occasional lumbering truck spewing blue-black diesel smoke, the moist Magdeburg–Frankfurt-on-the-Oder autobahn was deserted.

At the Zossen exit they turned off and headed south over a two-lane, black-tarred road—the same Reichsstrasse 96 that Field Marshal Gerd von Rundstedt had once caustically christened *der Weg zur Ewigkeit* ("the road to eternity"), because it led to the heavily camouflaged headquarters of the Wehrmacht's general staff, from which many a German officer had been dispatched to his doom. Overrun by the Red Army during the final weeks of World War II, the former Wehrmacht complex had been considerably enlarged since then and now encompassed two hundred square kilometers of off-limits territory, stretching from Zossen in the northeast to

Treuenbrietzen and Jüterborg in the west and south—an area large enough to garrison an entire army corps, the headquarters of an air force army, and an antiaircraft missile site.

Some distance beyond Zossen, a red and white *Schlagbaum* barrier came into view, lowered horizontally across the road. At the sight of the lead car's distinctive license plate—blue cyrillic letters and a painted stars and stripes—the sentry came tumbling out of the guardhouse to lift the metal barrier with one hand while he steadied his shoulder-slung Kalashnikov sub-machine gun with the other. The three cars drove on between two tall wire fences marking the limits of the vast Soviet enclosure.

One kilometer farther on, the three cars had to slow again before a second, more imposing *Schlagbaum* barrier. They were waved through without a stop, and two hundred yards beyond they drove under a third hastily raised barrier up to the carefully guarded headquarters. The dozen Wartburg staff cars parked near the gleaming white building were immediately identifiable as part of the Nationale Volksarmee.

To Colonel von Pawel the presence of all these NVA vehicles was a bad omen. "If this means that Yakubovsky is going to tell us to bow to Ulbricht's directives from here on out, there's going to be trouble," he remarked to his interpreter. They were under instructions to deal only with Soviet officers and to avoid actions that might enhance the status of the puppet East German government, which the United States, like France and Britain, refused to recognize.

On the terrace steps there was an exchange of salutes and a brief shaking of hands with the bare-headed Soviet officer who was waiting to greet them. But there were none of the usual amenities. The atmosphere on this Thursday afternoon was crisp, businesslike, almost tense. Accompanied by their interpreters, the mission chiefs filed in through the large glass doors, crossed the carpeted hall, and followed the guide up the stairs to the second floor, where they were led down a corridor and into a kind of outer office. A captain—wearing the standard Soviet blouse, blue breeches, and black boots— came out from behind a desk to shake hands and take their hats.

They were joined a moment later by the Soviet chief of staff, an unusually dapper, gray-haired Byelo-Russian named Ariko, who led the way into the commander in chief's office. Colonel von Pawel, who followed him as the doyen of the three Allied mission chiefs, was surprised not to be greeted at the door by Yakubovsky's bone-crushing handgrip. But today the massive three-star general was standing stiffly at the farther end of his office near the large executive desk. Next to him, looking slightly dwarfed by Yakubovsky, although he himself was no midget, was a balding, tub-shaped officer whom von Pawel immediately recognized. There was no mistaking the round Ukrainian peasant's head and the five-pointed marshal's star on the jutting shoulder pads. Ivan Koniev, the sixty-two-year-old "conqueror of Dresden and Prague," as he was known to his countrymen, had resigned his post as commander of the Warsaw Treaty forces in July of 1960 and withdrawn from the public scene. Now, without a word of warning, he was back—near the city he had helped Zhukov to storm in the late spring of 1945.

Obviously enjoying the effect of surprise, Koniev invited the mission chiefs to take their places at the long conference table. "Gentlemen, my name is Koniev," the stocky marshal began, with a faint twinkle in his deep-set blue eyes. "You may perhaps have heard of me."

There was a ripple of amusement as the Russian words were translated for the benefit of the visitors. "You are of course accredited to the commander in chief of the Group of Soviet Forces in Germany. Well, I am now the commander in chief, and it is to me that you will be accredited from here on out." He wanted the liaison officers to inform their respective commanders in West Germany of this change at the top. His friend, General Yakubovsky, who had served under him during the battle of Berlin, was staying on as his deputy. Well, that was all he had to say. But he would welcome any questions the military liaison officers might have to put to him.

So this was the bombshell ultimatum the visitors had dreaded! The announcement was as cryptic as it was laconic. Colonel von Pawel hardly knew what to say. The dozen questions he would have liked to throw at the marshal ("What

persuaded Khrushchev to send you here?" "What are you
going to do about Ulbricht?" "What are you going to do about
the refugee problem?") died on his lips. Instead, he found
himself getting off the usual banalities: The commander in
chief of the U.S. Army in Europe, General Clarke, would
certainly expect him to convey his greetings and would look
forward with pleasure to their meeting at a later date.

Brigadier Pearson, who followed, said much the same thing
on behalf of his own British forces commander. The French
mission chief, however, refused to be daunted by Koniev's
jaunty chin and challenging blue eyes. "Unfortunately," he
declared, "I am in no position to extend a greeting to you on
behalf of General Crespin, the commander in chief of the
French forces in Germany, for the good reason that he is
unaware of your presence and assumption of command. If it
had occurred to you to give us advance warning, monsieur le
Maréchal, we would have had time to refer the matter back to
our superiors, and we would have received the necessary instructions."

Leaning forward over the table on his elbows, Koniev
cocked two plump fingers at the Frenchman. "Ah, you are
trying to be clever and play the diplomat? But here we are
among soldiers. And as one soldier to another, let me tell you
this, so that you can repeat it to your general: I have always
reminded my officers that a commander should *never* be taken
by surprise."

This jovial reprimand was greeted by general laughter. The
marshal then rose and invited his guests to empty a glass or
two of champagne with him. A few hypocritical toasts were
proposed and drunk.

Later, standing by a window overlooking the parking lot,
Colonel von Pawel pointed to the long line of Volksarmee
vehicles and remarked that Marshal Koniev was obviously
being kept busy with so many people to see.

"Yes," replied the marshal blandly, "I had hoped we could
all meet together at the same time—that would have sim-
plified things enormously. Unfortunately, I discovered that
this was not possible."

Von Pawel nodded. He felt obliged to point out that such a

meeting would have proved most embarrassing, "since we have no desire to meet people we do not officially recognize."

Koniev laughingly responded, "I've been away from Germany for so long that I thought you had resolved this problem long ago."

It was close to 6:00 P.M. as the mission chiefs and their interpreters drove out of the vast Soviet complex. At the first autobahn *Parkplatz* they pulled off the highway and in among the trees for a hurried conference. The Kremlin was deliberately stressing the importance of Koniev's appointment, but precisely what it meant none of them could say for sure.

Climbing back into their cars, they drove on down the autobahn as far as the Potsdam turn-off, expecting at any moment to see a string of Volksarmee sedans speed past them. But the only thing that overtook them on the almost empty autobahn was a brief shower of rain, which left the potato and beet fields on either side looking more desolate than ever.

Walter Ulbricht spent this same Thursday afternoon haranguing the workers at the Oberspree Cable Works near the river in the southern part of the Soviet sector of Berlin. He turned up shortly after 2:00 P.M. for a combined pep talk and question-and-answer session, dressed in a light double-breasted summer suit, which contrasted with the short sleeves and overalls by which he was soon surrounded. At the factory entrance, select members of two work brigades presented him with flowers and set speeches about their collective achievements and their iron determination to increase output even more.

The factory officials then led him on a guided tour through the cable-making plant, while some fifteen hundred workers from the main shift were ordered to assemble in the high-voltage hall. Dressed in overalls and the wooden shoes they wore as protection against the molten metal, they flocked into the hall until they were squeezed up against each other like sardines. A few enterprising souls sought relief from the crush by clambering up the struts of the cranes; others managed to perch on top of the twelve-foot cable rollers.

Walter Ulbricht's appearance was greeted by a ritual ovation, after which the Party functionaries and factory officials
accompanying him sat down on chairs that had been lined up
to receive them.

"Comrades," began the chairman in his high-pitched voice,
"I have come to visit this factory today to tell you about my
recent trip to Moscow and to explain to you why it is imperative that a peace treaty be signed without delay between
the German Democratic Republic and our glorious and com-
radely ally, the Union of Soviet Socialist Republics." The
Western powers, so the orator claimed, had violated both the
Yalta and Potsdam agreements, thus rendering them null and
void. Neither the artificially aroused "war hysteria" in the
United States nor "threats from NATO" could forestall the
signing of a peace treaty. "Nobody," he went on, his voice
growing shriller, "can stop Socialism, and nobody can run
away from it. Not even those who have fallen into the clutches
of the slave-traders, who have left our Republic by running
away into the arms of West German militarists, thereby
hoping to find happiness. But No, they cannot flee Socialism!
Nobody can run away from Socialism, and one day they will
say: 'What fools we were to run away from Socialism and into
the arms of NATO!' "

To Kurt Wismach, seated on top of a tall cable roller, his
wooden clogs dangling out over the heads of the Party officials
seated just below, it all sounded tiresomely familiar. For
weeks, indeed for months, the newspapers and the radio had
been full of this stuff about a peace treaty. There was now
hardly a wall or a prominent façade in East Berlin that did not
carry its red or crimson streamer, insistently demanding the
quick conclusion of a *Friedensvertrag*. And here was the Party
chairman sounding off on the subject in his ridiculously shrill
voice, pronouncing his *b*'s like *p*'s and his *d*'s like *t*'s, like the
Saxon he was.

Kurt Wismach was proud of the fact that he was a native-
born Berliner. He had been brought up in Kreuzberg, a relatively poor quarter which had suffered terribly from wartime
bombing, lying as it did between the Tempelhof airfield and
the administrative heart of the Third Reich. In the last year of

the war, when he was barely sixteen, he had been drafted into
the *Volkssturm*—a barrel-scraping assortment of adolescents
and quinquagenarians, hastily conscripted, armed, and flung
into the desperate battle to save the Thousand-Year Reich.
The Reich had gone under, and he had been captured on the
western front by Montgomery's soldiers. He had escaped
from a British prisoner-of-war camp and had made it back to
Berlin, only to discover that his father had been killed in the
war and his family's Kreuzberg flat had been bombed to bits.
Forced to find new lodgings, his mother had moved in with
relatives living in Köpenick, a wood- and water-bounded
suburb that would have been a perfect place in which to live
had it not been located on the wrong side of the Spree and
well within the Soviet sector. But life was too hard in those
Götterdämmerung days for him to contemplate moving his
mother out to the more expensive West.

The young Kurt Wismach had obtained a job as a molten-
metal worker in the Oberspree cable factory. It was hard,
dangerous work, for he had to manipulate a pair of long-handled tongs, steering the white-hot ingots into steadily narrow-
ing channels until the cooling metal assumed the form of wire.
Often the metal strips would jump out of their runways, sometimes so suddenly that they would burn holes through the
protective apron and even scar his flesh before he had time to
react. He had been scarred more than once, for the anti-
quated equipment in those first postwar years left a great deal
to be desired, and scant attention was paid to safety rules
when it was a question of working extra hours to meet the
"requirements of the plan."

After three years of waiting, his mother had obtained permission to move into a tiny backyard cottage. It was little
more than a shed—just two rooms and a kitchen—but it was
better than having to share an apartment with two other
families, as they had been forced to do up until then. They
could have obtained roomier lodgings if he had joined the
Party and become an activist, but he could not bring himself
to do so. The only time he had ever engaged in demonstrations was on June 17, 1953, when he had joined the striking
workers, marched with them to the Alexanderplatz, and

shinned up one of the masts to tear down the Red flag, now a symbol for a new form of proletarian exploitation.

"The real reason why the Bonn government refuses to consider signing a peace treaty at the present time," the nasal voice was saying, "is that it wants to turn the German Democratic Republic into an advanced bastion and parade-ground for NATO directed against the socialist states. . . . The signing of a peace treaty will remove the last arguments of the West German revanchists. . . . The problem of West Berlin will be resolved, because the peace treaty will do away with all occupation rights throughout the territory of the German Democratic Republic, upon which West Berlin is located. The DDR will then exercise all sovereign rights on its territory."

The peace treaty . . . the DDR . . . sovereign rights . . . West German revanchists—the same themes that had been dinned into them for weeks were now being repeated, as though by a worn gramophone needle. Save for the Party toadies and the armed militiamen who liked to show what good Socialists they were by swinging their fists and stamping around with rifles, Kurt Wismach knew of nobody in the factory who cared much for Walter Ulbricht. Although he headed the Workers-and-Peasants-State, he'd probably never held a tool, still less a pair of metal-handling tongs, in his life. He was the totally colorless product of a colorless machine which had its agents everywhere: among the trade union officials, in the women's brigades, in the FDJ. They were the ones who demanded extra shifts to build socialism or to display a militant solidarity with some oppressed cause. They were the ones who tacked up lists showing the number of overtime hours each worker had labored for socialism. If your name was low on the list, there was no hope of obtaining a permit for a TV set from the trade union clerk. The overtime zealots could count on getting the necessary permit within a month or two; the rest, like Wismach, had to wait for several years. The same went for vacations. The longest holiday he had ever been granted was for twenty-four days, but he had never made it to a beach or other resort. The necessary railway passes, tickets, and hotel rooms were reserved for the bigwigs and other Party fry along with their families.

"The open border with West Berlin now costs us one billion marks a year," the shrill Saxon voice continued. "The *Menschenhandel* and the kidnappings cost us two and a half billion marks a year. Every citizen of our State will agree with me that we must put a stop to such conditions. . . . We must secure the peace in order to insure our economy against all disturbances. First peace must be assured and then we can advance toward the accomplishment of our other tasks."

Peace . . . peace . . . peace. The *Spitzbart* seemed to be able to talk of nothing else. It had become a Party obsession, invading every sphere of public and even private life. Wismach was reminded of the Sunday when he had gone out to watch a bicycle race. The next morning when he opened the newspaper, he discovered that he and hundreds of others had not watched the race for the sheer fun of watching an athletic contest; they had gathered to "demonstrate for peace," for, believe it or not, this cycling event had been a "peace race."

"Should the need arise, the borders of the DDR facing the West German Republic will be militarily protected by troops of the Nationale Volksarmee as well as by the troops of our Soviet friends. This will dampen the aggressiveness of Bonn. For hostile activity there can be no freedom. This would mean freedom for warmongers."

Maybe the dolts who used *Neues Deutschland* as their Bible could swallow this, but not those who listened to Western radio broadcasts. Just the other day, Wismach had heard Ernest Lemmer, Bonn's minister for all-German affairs, begging his listeners in the East to stay put and not flee to the West. It almost sounded like a plea on behalf of the *Spitzbart*'s detestable regime. A curious "warmonger," this Lemmer.

Like almost everyone else in East Berlin, Wismach listened to Western programs, both on radio and television, even though it was an offense for which he could be arrested. It was a standing joke at the factory: One would listen in silence to an anecdote or piece of news that a fellow worker had picked up on a Western program, and then demand in a mock threatening tone, "Say, Comrade, just where did you hear that?" *Comrade*—the term that had once denoted endearment and the solidarity of the working class—had now come to mean "spy" or "Party informer."

After eight harrowing hours spent struggling with inadequate equipment—the breaking of a screw or the tangling of a cable could bring the production process to a total halt—Wismach would come home to find that the neighbors' kids had been asked in school if anyone at home watched West Berlin television. At the kindergarten level the question was often put more insidiously by a teacher who would suggest with a smile: "Now why don't we all play what we saw on television last night." Children whose parents had been watching West Berlin programs would innocently fall into the trap. Now that he had a son of his own, Jeorg, Wismach was more conscious than ever of such pitfalls and dangers.

"The warmongers . . . the 'Cold Warriors' in West Berlin and Bonn," the litany continued. But apparently there were others who were fed up with these clichés. To make his point, Ulbricht quoted one of them. A woman comrade had asked, "Wouldn't it be better if the DDR abolished its military protection measures? Then in all probability no one would harm us."

This disarming piece of naiveté touched off a burst of laughter from the crowd. "Now I must tell this woman," the Party chairman continued, "that she has no understanding of West German militarists. . . . We cannot throw away our weapons. . . . Our borders with the West German Republic must be protected militarily by troops of the Nationale Volksarmee as well as by the troops of our Soviet friends."

This reassuring news was greeted by vigorous applause, particularly loud among the functionaries seated below Wismach's legs.

"Another Comrade asked me: 'Is there no other way of solving the problem than the one suggested by Khrushchev and adopted by the Volkskammer in its Peace Plan?' But no, there is no other way! There are people who have been proposing facile solutions. A woman employee here recently asked a Party member if it wouldn't be a good idea to hold free elections throughout Germany. Then everyone could decide exactly which way he wanted to go."

Kurt Wismach could restrain himself no longer. He began

clapping enthusiastically. Walter Ulbricht paused. There was a deathly silence, and it seemed to Wismach that a thousand eyes were suddenly trained upon him. He stopped clapping and shouted, "Even if I am the only one to say it: Free elections!"

"Now just a moment!" cried Ulbricht, glowering over his rimless glasses and angrily shaking his goatee. "We're going to clear this up right away!"

"Yes!" Wismach shouted back, "and we'll see which is the right way!"

"Free elections!" screamed Ulbricht. "What is it you want to elect freely? The question is put to you by the Working Class. The question is put to you by the People."

There were shouts of "Hear, hear! Right you are!" from the faithful, who began clapping to cover up the chairman's discomfort. In the sea of faces and bodies before him Wismach could detect ripples of movement made by Party comrades who were trying to push their way toward his cable roller. The Spitzbart's casual mention of "the People" made him madder than ever.

"Have you the slightest idea what the People really think?" he shouted defiantly.

The veins stood out on Ulbricht's forehead as he waved his fist and ranted against the various elections—each one more crooked than its predecessor—that had been held in the 1920s and 1930s. And what had been the result? World War II. "Now I ask you: Do you want to travel along this same road?"

"*Nein, nein!*" shouted the Party faithful, breaking into frantic applause. Most of Wismach's fellow workers kept their hands by their sides. But Ulbricht's tirade proved an unexpected blessing, for it kept the Comrades who wanted to get at Wismach from forcing their way too noisily through the packed throng.

"The one lonely heckler thinks he showed special courage," Ulbricht angrily concluded. "But one doesn't need courage for that. Have the courage to fight against German militarism!" (Bravos and more applause.) "Whoever supports free elections supports Hitler's generals." And on that heroic note the Party chairman stormed out of the hall.

The Party faithful flocked out after him. Clambering down

from his cable roller, Wismach was surrounded by friends and fellow workers who clapped him on the back as he made his way to his post. No one tried to molest him.

But the next day when he reported for work at 2:00 P.M., he was summoned to the management offices. Three men and a woman were waiting for him. "We have come from the Central Committee," one of them declared.

Wismach refused to be rattled. Only two of the four, he finally decided, were actually Central Committee members; the others were probably Party officials from the Oberspree Works' political department.

The heated discussion that followed lasted for three tiring hours. The Comrades were bent on finding out if Wismach belonged to an *Agenten-und-Menschenhändlerzentrale* ("agent- and-man-traders center") in the West. Wismach said he did not. All right, they finally conceded, maybe he didn't actually belong to one, but he had participated in the work of existing agents' networks. Wismach denied this accusation too. There was a lot of bitter arguing about comparative social and economic conditions in the DDR and the Federal Republic, but what really infuriated them was the "ruffianlike" way in which Wismach had shouted at the Party chairman.

"How dare you use the familiar *Du* when addressing the first secretary of the Party!" cried one of the Central Committee members.

"You deserve a punch in the nose!" bellowed the other.

"Do you mean that literally?" demanded Wismach, drawing himself up to his full six feet.

They glared at each other briefly, and then the Central Committee member relented. "I meant it symbolically," he explained.

Wismach would have to do penance, the Comrades insisted. He would have to sign a written statement, retracting the ill-considered words he had uttered at yesterday's meeting. After that, he would have to accept a less well-paying job for a period of six months to prove through work and hardship that he had reached a "correct political awareness." Wismach refused to sign such a statement. He'd said exactly what he thought, and it wasn't only what *he* thought; it was what just about every other worker in the factory was thinking. This was a fact that his interrogators, like the Party chairman, would have to realize.

In the evening, when Wismach returned home, he noticed that a gray car was following him. Later he noticed that a man was standing outside his house. That same night he made up his mind to take his wife and child and leave East Berlin.

19

Once again nothing had been left to chance. On the Speaker's desk, where on the stroke of ten Dr. Johannes Dieckmann was to open the Nineteenth Plenary Session of the Volkskammer, a pile of letters and telegrams had been assembled to impress the parliamentarians, the members of the Diplomatic Corps, and the honored guests (among them Richard Crossman, of the British Labour party) with the importance of this historic moment. The former businessman and small-time politician—who had been "persuaded" after the war to help found a bogus Liberal party so that East Germany could be made to look like a genuine, multiparty democracy—did not have to read more than two or three of the messages before everyone realized that they were predictably alike and keyed to the same overriding theme: the fight for peace.

Outside on the pavement of the Luisenstrasse, a bare quarter of a mile from the old Reichstag building, groups of factory workers, administrative employees, peasant women, and housewives were waiting to greet the parliamentarians with beseeching posters: Give Us More Protection Against Bonn's Head-hunters! Protect Our Republic Against These Slave-Traders!

On the other side of the sector boundary, however, the "head-hunters" and the "slave-traders" were finding it increasingly difficult to accommodate the flood of persons hell-bent on delivering themselves into bondage. Disturbed by the sight of hundreds of refugees huddled without shelter in the

pouring rain, the British commandant, Maj. Gen. Rohan Delacombe, ordered a section of Welsh engineers to put up emergency army tents on the soggy grounds of Marienfelde. Drier
and less cramped quarters were also to be made available in the
locker rooms under the grandstand of Hitler's Olympic Stadium,
in the British sector.

In West Berlin's dark stucco city hall, officials were harassed
by rumors of all kinds, which had been given new urgency by
the bombshell announcement of the appointment of Marshal
Koniev to command the Soviet forces in Germany. Like the
NATO intelligence experts, most of them were persuaded that
Ulbricht and his Soviet mentors were going to have to do something drastic to halt the refugee flow: They were going to have to
close the border around the outer periphery of Berlin. But a few
were beginning to sound a different note.

One of them was a veteran Social Democrat named Werner
Ruediger, who lived in the Prenzlauer Berg district of East
Berlin. Sentenced to twenty years in jail for political crimes—
doubtless because he was a singularly outspoken Socialist—he
had been miraculously released from his confinement and had
been able to represent his borough in the West Berlin city parliament. Politically, Ruediger was the champion of revolutionary
ideals and methods that were no longer fashionable in Willy
Brandt's SPD entourage, so that few people took him seriously
when he began issuing warnings that Ulbricht was getting ready
to close the intersector boundary with barriers of barbed wire.
They were going to do it, furthermore, this coming weekend.

Vague reports of this kind had begun circulating on Thursday,
the day of Koniev's arrival. Twenty-four hours later they were
increasingly precise and specific. Informants from East Berlin
reported that large quantities of barbed wire had been secretly
stored in the warehouses of a meat-packing plant in Lichtenberg. Prefabricated concrete slabs had been quietly shifted from
construction sites farther east and concentrated at three points
not far from the border of the U.S. sector. Contingents of NVA
troops, normally stationed outside of Berlin, had been brought
in under the cover of night and housed in KVP barracks.

True? False? The harassed city hall officials frankly did not
know.

Precautions had been taken against the onset of a new blockade, which was considered more than likely if Khrushchev
went ahead and signed a separate peace treaty with Ulbricht.
The accumulated reserves of canned and packaged goods were
now sufficient to last for an entire year. Ration cards for vital
foodstuffs had been printed in advance. Nothing had been neglected. Cement, sand, gravel, tar, and even sizable quantities
of stone and reinforcing metal strips had been shipped in to keep
the West Berlin construction industry going should river-barge
and railway connections with West Germany be cut, as they had
in 1948-49.

Preoccupied by the ever-mounting tide of refugees, many city
hall officials felt frustrated by the increasingly long absences of
their boss, Willy Brandt. Only twice in the preceding fortnight—on August 3, and again on August 7, when he had let
himself be interviewed by Harry Gilroy of the *New York
Times*—had Brandt touched down briefly in Berlin. All his energies seemed to have been absorbed by the political campaign
in the Federal Republic, which was about to reach a new peak of
intensity with a major SPD rally in Nüremberg.

On this Friday, August 11, Brandt was once again out of town,
although not entirely for electoral reasons. He had gone to Bonn
to be briefed by Heinrich von Brentano about the results of the
recent foreign ministers' conference in Paris. The Adenauer
government was not yet prepared to follow his suggestions, but
at least it was not ignoring him entirely, which was encouraging.

Encouraging too was the up-to-the-mark readiness of the U.S.
Army's Berlin garrison. There was to be no sloppiness or letup in
discipline in these hot August days. The brigade's daily bulletin
announced that there would be rifle practice for the troops on
Rose Range from 8:00 A.M. to 5:00 P.M. every day from Monday
to Friday. "Is is essential that fruits and vegetables eaten raw
be properly decontaminated," it warned. "All female de-
pendent personnel are requested to cooperate in the ob-
servance of the proper dress and decorum when patronizing
community facilities. . . . It is desired that shorts (except
knee-length Bermuda type), two-piece sun-suits with halters
and similar items of abbreviated attire will not be worn.

"Keep your immunizations up to date," the bulletin con-

cluded. "Drink water only from army-approved sources or
purify it with iodine tablets or by boiling. . . . In civilian restaurants eat only well done meats and cooked vegetables."

GIs stationed in Berlin might not be campaigning in the
jungles of the South Pacific or the malarial swamps of southern
Italy, but their commanders too were taking no chances.

In the fisherman Kollow's house on the rain-swept Baltic
shore, Klemens Krüger sat by the radio. East Berlin's
Deutschlandsender kept playing military marches. It was
what they had known under Hitler—march music, special announcements, request performances for pieces played by the
Nationale Volksarmee band. Foreign Minister Bolz and Defense Minister Stoph had just made speeches in the Volkskammer. Both spoke of head-hunters, of man-stealers, of kidnappers, and of the many West German intelligence services
which were supposedly the cause of the floodtide of refugees.
For a doctor—so the East German press claimed—they were
offering three thousand marks; for a farmer, one thousand; for
an artisan, two thousand. The German Democratic Republic,
to judge by these speeches and announcements, was one vast
swamp of espionage agents and recruiters armed with glib
tongues and plenty of banknotes.

"Following the example of the people-owned Berlin
Light-Bulb Factory, which founded an Anti-Manhunt Committee on Tuesday," Krüger read in the *Ostzeezeitung*, "all
workers in all regions of the Republic are currently taking up
the fight in their enterprises against this abduction campaign."

There was another pause for the latest news flash: The
Volkskammer had unanimously approved a kind of Full
Powers Act, granting Walter Ulbricht the right to take what-
ever measures he saw fit against the "man-hunters."

New Russian divisions—so the latest rumor had it—had just
moved into the DDR, and Marshal Koniev had assumed overall command. Koniev, the German-hater! The news height-
ened the prevailing malaise.

Word suddenly spread that a shipment of potatoes had arrived. The women scampered off with their empty market

bags to the town square, where the potatoes were doled out under the watchful eye of the Volkspolizei. No one was to take a snapshot of the queuing women.

Later in the evening, Krüger watched Sholokhov's *And Quiet Flows the Don* on television. Then Walter Ulbricht was shown addressing workers in some East Berlin factory about the peace treaty. Krüger found his high-pitched Saxon voice unpleasant. He seemed totally lacking in self-assurance. He too seemed a bundle of nerves. He spoke of the crushing blow that must be dealt to the Ultras of Bonn. A blow thanks to which peace would be assured.

"What exactly are . . . these Ultras?" asked the fisherman Kollow with a puzzled frown. "The Spitzbart is always talking about them, and nobody knows what he means."

Krüger tried to explain that the Ultras were dyed-in-the-wool reactionaries, but his words were lost in the wave of laughter with which the people seated around the television greeted the sight of Ulbricht's listeners. The workers' skeptical, disbelieving faces remained on the screen for a full minute at a time—stern, unsmiling faces against whose wooden impassivity Ulbricht's words seemed to dissolve into smoke, like blank cartridges.

That night Krüger slept badly. He was kept awake by the boisterousness of drunken vacationers staggering down the street. Particularly obnoxious were a group of rowdy youngsters who kept bawling the same stupid refrain: *"Berlin bleibt frei— Trinkt Coca-Cola!"* ("Berlin remains free—Drink Coca-Cola!").

Before dropping off to sleep, Krüger heard a loud voice on the radio, so loud that it could be heard through the intervening wall. It was the voice of a RIAS broadcaster. Thanks to Ulbricht's threats, the flood of refugees from East Germany had suddenly surged over the three thousand mark.

In Moscow the television cameras were again trained on the familiar rotund face as Nikita Khrushchev rose to address the assembled company at this Friday afternoon's Soviet-Romanian friendship meeting. It was his third major address in five days, and in some ways the most threatening and bellicose of all.

Often departing from his prepared text, the Soviet leader trained his guns on Italy and Greece, which, as allies of the United States, would find themselves in the line of fire were an atomic war to break out because of a failure to sign a German peace treaty which would end World War II.

It is well known that military bases are not located in deserts. In Italy they are reportedly located in orange groves, and in Greece in olive groves. Perhaps there are some who expect that certain cities will be proclaimed open cities, as it was possible to do during the last war. But one should not allow oneself to indulge in such illusions.

In a future thermonuclear war, there would be no difference between the front and the rear; and if necessary, atomic bombs would be dropped on the Acropolis and other historical monuments in Greece.

Most of the speech was in the same free-swinging vein. In Washington, generals and politicians were now talking of developing a neutron bomb capable of destroying all forms of life on earth. "Yes, Comrades, this is what these people are thinking. They are acting according to the principle of robbers. They want to murder a man without staining his suit with blood, so that they can later use the suit."

While welcoming the conciliatory statement made by President Kennedy in the previous day's press conference in Washington ("We hope we will be able to achieve a peaceful solution of these problems"), he ridiculed the idea that any of the Western powers were prepared to fight and to die for the freedom of Germans in West Berlin. "But this is a fairy tale. There are 2,200,000 people living in West Berlin. But if a war is unleashed, hundreds of millions will perish."

Adenauer was again singled out as a menace to world peace, but this time Macmillan, too, came in for his share of abuse.

Imperialist colonizers are used to high-handed tactics. . . . They are, one might say, used to making India and other Asian and African peoples shake with fear by roaring like a lion. But times have changed.

The roar of the British lion does not make anybody shake with fear today. The Egyptians have already twisted this lion's tail and flung him aside.

Later that same evening at a glittering Kremlin reception held in St. George's Hall, Khrushchev accosted the ambassadors of the West. He seemed in a buoyant mood, almost as though someone else had just threatened the world with nuclear fire and destruction. When Sir Frank Roberts, the British ambassador, twitted him on his anti-British statements, reminding him of how others who had dared twist the lion's tail had been made to bite the dust, Khrushchev grinned; he was as sure as they that there would be no war over Berlin. He was glad to be able to drink toasts to the cause of peace with the diplomatic representatives of Great Britain, France, and Canada, and he regretted only that United States ambassador, Llewellyn Thompson, could not be with them because he had been recalled to Washington for consultations.

As for himself, he added, he was planning to leave that very weekend for the Ukraine, proceeding from there to his dacha in the Crimea. He was going to enjoy two weeks of mid-August holidays before returning to Moscow in early September to play host to Prime Minister Nehru of India.

The message was clearly meant for the chancelleries of the West. Anastas Mikoyan was leaving on Sunday for a ten-day trip to Tokyo, while Khrushchev was leaving for Sochi, on the Black Sea. For the next two or three weeks the two most influential men in the Soviet Union were going to be absent from the Russian capital. The gentlemen capitalists could relax. Between now and early September nothing cataclysmic was going to occur.

20

It had been too wet and sunless to have been a really first-class holiday, but the three weeks that Hans Magdorf had just spent on the Usedom peninsula, ten miles west of where Klemens Krüger was vacationing, had at least enabled him to forget the monotony of his job as a trade union official in a large bread-making factory in East Berlin. The mere fact that he had been allowed three weeks on the Baltic coast—a privilege not granted to everyone—and that he could travel there and back in his small Trabant sedan was a suitable reward for Party loyalty. In all his thirty years it had never occurred to this pudgy, fair-haired bachelor to doubt the Party's superior wisdom, which is why he had been entrusted with the delicate task of supervising the morale, welfare, and "security" of the factory's 750 employees. He could even flatter himself with having found a comfortable nest where the work—so much less demanding than that of the stokers and bakers—was often limited to choosing and changing the records for the soft music piped from his little office phonograph to the loudspeakers scattered around the factory.

Now, as he motored south on Highway 109 through the evergreen woods and flatlands of Pomerania, he began overtaking long columns of Volksarmee trucks headed in the same direction. Each highway intersection was policed by Volksarmee soldiers carrying packs and field equipment. The sight of all these trucks and soldiers did not strike Magdorf as unduly strange. This Prenzlau-Milmersdorf area, fifty kilometers north of the capital, was often used for military maneuvers.

After twenty minutes of convoy hopping, he left the last lead truck behind. The highway was now clear, and in three quarters of an hour he would be sighting the first suburban villas and warehouses of Pankow. Relaxing his grip on the wheel, he let the little car bound forward, happy at the thought that he would soon be able to embrace his mother in her modest Köpenick flat.

For Hilde Tauer it was by now second nature. Monday through Friday the forty-six-year-old seamstress would leave the cold-water flat that she and her husband occupied in the midtown district of Friedrichshain and cross over into the U.S. sector to sew and stitch dresses, jackets, blouses, trousers, and curtains for West Berlin families. Dressmaking was her profession; by it she supplemented the meager pension received by her husband Heinrich, who had suffered a severe head wound from a piece of shrapnel during the last months of the war.

So adept had she grown at commuting that not one of the neighbors in their apartment building realized that she worked in the West. By leaving her home at 6:30 in the morning, she gave them the impression that she was going to work in some East Berlin garment factory. Her West Berlin customers were not always pleased to see her turn up at their homes when it was not yet eight o'clock; she had to explain to them that she was not free to choose her hours of clandestine work. For such indeed it was, and in more respects than one. A secret pocket she had sewn into her jacket permitted her to bring back copies of West Germany's leading tabloid, the flashy, photo-filled *Bild Zeitung* (her husband's favorite newspaper), without arousing the attention of the police at the Friedrichstrasse station. Into the waistbands of her skirts she had also sewn smaller fob pockets to conceal the West marks that she earned from her sewing.

In recent weeks the police controls at the Friedrichstrasse station had grown increasingly strict, and Hilde Tauer had seen many passengers with their bags hustled off the trains. To make herself as inconspicuous as possible, she rode in the smoking car, usually filled with commuting workers who were not so closely examined since they carried no luggage.

Three days before—on Wednesday, August 9—the painters had invaded their three-room apartment and turned the place upside down. In the process, the radio had been disconnected, so that neither she nor her husband had heard the broadcast extracts from Ulbricht's speech at the Oberspree Cable Works. Friday she had stayed home to clean up the mess left by the painters, while her husband took the S-Bahn into the U.S. sector, where he picked up a copy of the *Bild Zeitung*. He had hidden it carefully on the return trip, which had lasted an un-

usually long time—the Vopos, had gone through every car, removing any passenger found carrying anything heavier than a
handbag.

"I don't like the look of it," Heinrich had told his wife that
evening, pointing to the newspaper. "More and more *Flüchtlinge* going over every day! Marienfelde is swamped already.
Soon they'll have to start camping in the Grünewald." But Hilde
was too busy with housecleaning to pay much attention.

The housework still was not finished by Saturday noon, when
they set out for West Berlin to call on Heinrich's sister Anna,
who lived in Neukölln. On the busy Karl-Marx-Strasse they
stopped to buy creamed cottage cheese and linseed oil, neither
of which were available in the Soviet sector, although when
combined with boiled potatoes, they made a dish much prized
by poor Berliners.

They also picked up a copy of the *Bild Zeitung* before dropping in on Heinrich's sister. The tabloid's glaring headlines—
another record-breaking rise in the refugee flow—made Heinrich unusually irritable. He got into an argument with his sister,
and finally left in something of a huff in the early afternoon. At
the Warschauer-Brücke subway stop (at this point an elevated
station), he and Hilde had to show their identity cards to the
Vopos. The train was jam-packed, and on every side they could
hear passengers muttering their apprehensions.

Back home Heinrich pulled out the newspaper he had carefully folded into an inner pocket and said, "Just look at those
headlines! I tell you, something's going to happen. It just can't
go on. In fact, if you ask me, I think this may be the last trip we'll
be making to the West."

"Oh, don't be so gloomy and upset!" his wife replied, trying to
cheer him up. "And anyway, what can we do about it? We've got
enough right here to keep us busy."

Neither of them had ever thought of fleeing to the West,
where life was so much more expensive. And this wasn't the
moment to leave everything behind, just when they had had
their apartment completely repainted. That evening they were
able to sup in a living room that was almost back to normal. The
meal was untroubled by the latest news, for the radio was still
disconnected.

Klemens Krüger strolled along the beach. By the water's edge the campers were busy brushing their teeth and rinsing their knives, forks, and plates. Most of them were young, many wore sideburns. Some were soaping their faces, hands, and legs. Others, huddled in a group, were sitting half-dressed in the shallow water in order to make the blue jeans they were wearing—recently bought in the HO department store—still narrower and softer.

A couple of days before, so Krüger had been told, several hundred of these youngsters had stormed the local *Heim der Intelligenz* (a state-run guest house) shouting, "We are hungry, we too are intelligent!" Before the Volkspolizei could intervene, they had devoured and drunk everything they could lay their hands on, while the inmates had fled in panic.

As far as he could judge, these youngsters were more like anarchists than revolutionaries. Their opposition wasn't based on any fundamental or political considerations. What they wanted was a kind of American way of life with perhaps a few socialistic overtones.

Almost every day in this vast, six-mile-long camp area there had been scuffles with the Volkspolizei, bursts of rebellious violence, and black-market deals. The newspaper was full of scorn for a *Club der Glatzköpfigen* ("Shave-headed Club"), which had raised hell, fomented a revolt, and actually stormed the police station. The *Glatzköpfigen* had been flung into jail and pilloried as "man-robbers," "perverts," "subversive elements," and so on. "Led astray by American gangster films they saw in West Berlin," read the newspaper headline next to a photo showing two bald-headed youths. The accompanying caption described them as "Faces of Bonn agents." "This is how they look," the article declared:

The brutal mugs of those whom Espionage-Lemmer has hired for his criminal handiwork. These bandits from West Berlin were infiltrated as *Glatzkopf*-gangs into the bivouack area of this region in order to terrorize the populace, stir up unrest, harass our State, and unleash a man-hunt which is supposed to drive them into the snares of the Bonn spy networks. The scoundrels are being haled before the court today.

Our citizens demand stiff punishment for elements such as these. . . .
The West Berlin swamp must be drained.

Krüger continued his stroll through the flat countryside. Extending as far as the horizon, the vast cornfields, which had not
yet been reaped even though it would soon be mid-August,
looked unweeded and gone to seed. He and his companion
passed groups of peasants who were calmly seated by the roadside talking. This experience too was a novel one for Krüger.
Never before had he seen Pomeranian peasants engaged in
midday palaver during harvest time. "Ever since they became
LPG farmers," his companion explained to him, "they've gone
over to an eight-hour day. At 8:00 A.M. they are summoned to
the LPG courtyard by a bugle, and from there they march out
in close formation to the fields. At 5:00 P.M. they drop their
hoes, pitchforks, or whatever else they may be carrying and
take off as punctually as masons."

That evening Krüger went to see a movie. During the
weekly news review, Walter Ulbricht appeared on the screen.
His face generated a burst of laughter.

"Look at the Spitzbart!" cried the youths seated behind
Krüger. The noisy laughter and the taunts grew bolder and
bolder. Suddenly the lights flashed on. Two Vopos appeared
and walked down the aisle, examining the blank faces on
either side. There was not a smirk to be seen.

"Who was doing that shouting?"

No one spoke up.

The Vopos wheeled about and marched slowly back up the
aisles. The moment they left, the lights dimmed and the
mocking laughter was resumed.

Later that same evening Krüger invited two of these young
lads to have a drink with him. "We're not for Adenauer," they
explained. "The political setup in the Federal Republic is for
the birds. It'll do for our parents. They live off illustrated
magazines that have been smuggled in; they read human-
interest stories about Soraya; they eat up the news about each
new royal wedding; they'd like to have Adenauer as their chief
of state. What we want is a Socialist state, a bit like what

they've got in Poland, or, even better, Scandinavian social-ism."

Krüger found them surprisingly well informed. They were very critical, but they weren't all-out adversaries of the Ulbricht regime.

However, a young woman who had joined them was not so noncommittal. "What do you mean? What will happen when Ulbricht closes the border? Won't the level of terror here increase tremendously? Won't everyone who dares open his mouth be hauled off to jail?"

No one answered her question. But it expressed the apprehension now weighing on every mind.

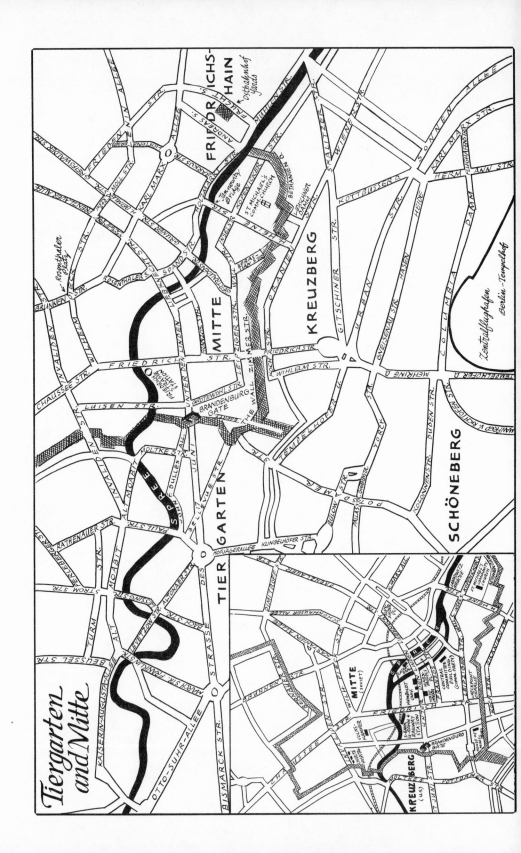

PART THREE

AUGUST 13, 1961

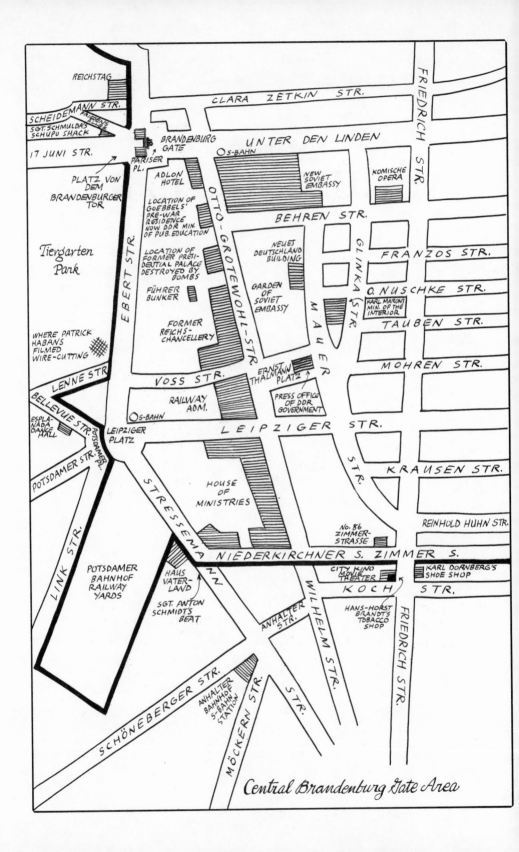

Central Brandenburg Gate Area

1

After the drenching downpours earlier in the week, this Saturday afternoon seemed hot, with the temperature climbing to twenty-four degrees centigrade as the cloud-shadowed sun began to descend. The Wannsee beaches in southwest Berlin were crowded, as were those of the pine-girt Müggelsee in the Soviet sector. White sailboats veered and tacked up and down the long, undulating reaches of the Havel. Greens and fairways were alive with softly padding golfers, like the American commandant, Maj. Gen. Albert Watson, who spent several hours pitting his carefully calculated shots against those of his opponents from West Berlin's Blue-White Club.

In the city center, along the flag- and streamer-spanned Zimmerstrasse, now closed to traffic for the Kreuzberg *Kinderfest*, excited children from the Soviet and U.S. sectors crowded into sidewalk tents for their share of cakes and ice cream, or waited outside under the balloons clapping their hands and scrambling with delight whenever upper-floor tenants threw them wrapped candies from their windows. Dog fanciers congregated at the Katzbachstrasse stadium to watch the whippet races and to admire an exhibition of prize German shepherds. The more musically inclined flocked to the Hohenstaufenplatz to laugh at the puffed red cheeks of the heavily blowing band, moving on as evening began to fall, to the Kreuzberg Park, where acrobats and clowns tumbled and tottered about the vaudeville stage for the benefit of circus lovers willing to pay one mark and fifty pfennigs.

For many West Berliners, of course, this weekend was no picnic. The more generous and public-minded—church workers, members of civic clubs, simple volunteers (including a number from the Allied occupation forces)—spent a tiring afternoon at Marienfelde and other centers feeding the hungry and trying to help harassed mothers calm their fretful babies. The two thousand refugees who had poured in since the previous

207

evening had swamped all available facilities. School classrooms had to be cleared of desks and filled with cots, church naves and transepts transformed into dormitories, as camp beds were placed edge to edge to accommodate the human flood.

Elsewhere, however, life went on much as ever. The sight-seers who had paid five marks at the Severin & Kühn offices on the Kurfürstendamm noticed nothing unusual when their beige-brown bus crossed into the Soviet sector around 4:30 in the afternoon. There were the customary restrictions against the taking of snapshots through the bus windows of bridges, bar-racks, and other "strategic" buildings, but the tourists were en-couraged to use all the film they could on the heroic statuary of the Soviet War Memorial in Treptow Park. Only to the bus driver, who knew the course by heart, did there seem anything novel in the sight of cranes and concrete slabs in places where there had been little or no sign of construction activity before.

The onset of night was greeted with a gay firework display over Kreuzberg Park—to the delight of not only the assembled youth but also the well-heeled couples who were now swaying to the rhythms of Romano Tessoni's combo on the roof terrace of the Berlin Hilton. To the west, visible through the reflections of the broad plate-glass windows, rose the bombed-out hulk of the Kaiser Wilhelm Memorial Church, with its rebuilt pillar of red-dish blue stained glass—a looming pinnacle of darkness against the river of light leading down the Kurfürstendamm. In the distance the turquoise green cupola of the eighteenth-century Schloss Charlottenburg seemed to hang magically upturned, like a jeweled chalice, while looking north, one could make out the winged angel atop Bismarck's Victory Column and the toothy smile of the new Congress Hall, better known to Berlin wits as "the pregnant oyster." On the eastern fringe of the light-less Tiergarten, the experienced eye could detect the somber, wedding-cake mass of the gutted Reichstag next to the stiff, spartan lines of the floodlit Brandenburg Gate. The two neighboring structures—one in the British sector, the other in the Soviet sector—marked the invisible frontier between two worlds. The dark ocean of the Tiergarten, to the left, was matched to the right by vast smudges of obscurity. Dark wounds that had not yet healed, they covered East Berlin like a quilt, vestiges of a ruinous war that the Ulbricht regime had not wished or been able to remove.

On the periphery of these two worlds, some three miles east of the Hilton roof terrace, police Sgt. Anton Schmidt was once again patrolling the strategic corner where the Niederkirchner-strasse ran into the Stresemannstrasse. The first of these two intersecting streets, once known as the Prinz-Albrecht-Strasse, had acquired a sinister reputation in the 1930s, for on its north-ern side was Heinrich Himmler's Gestapo headquarters. The dread building, like so many others in this central area of Berlin, had been bombed into oblivion during wartime air raids. Now, across the intervening fields of ruins, Anton Schmidt had an unobstructed view of the long House of Ministries, where his old Luftwaffe boss had once reigned. The street that had once borne Hermann Goering's name had been rechristened the Stresemannstrasse after the war in memory of the statesman whose Locarno Pact, had it but been respected, might have spared Europe and Berlin the catastrophes that finally overtook them. For almost three hundred yards to the north and west, this street cut through the Soviet sector. But because it led directly to the Potsdamer Platz and northward to the Branden-burg Gate, it was used by many West Berliners for north–south traffic, with little or no hindrance from the Vopos, who had set up their check point slightly to the east of this important artery.

Due to the proximity of the Soviet sector, the bombed-out buildings on the western fringe of the Stresemannstrasse had not been rebuilt. Instead, like wooden cabins along a windswept beach, a string of vending booths had sprouted among the ruins. The makeshift stands were even occasionally visited by a Vopo, who as the evening wore on and the traffic lessened would saunter casually across the Stresemannstrasse, as though on a tour of inspection, and then calmly buy himself a Coca-Cola. These Vopos, on the whole, were a friendly lot—that is, when they were Berliners. More than once Schmidt had been quietly approached and asked if he could buy toothpaste, soap, and razor blades. Indeed, relations of late had been so friendly that just two nights before, Schmidt and a young colleague from the West Berlin Customs Service had amused themselves kicking a soccer ball across the invisible sector boundary; each time, the ball came sailing back, neatly jack-booted into the U.S. sector by the playful Vopos.

At the upper end of the Stresemannstrasse on this warm Saturday night, there was much the same relaxed coming and going. Along the western fringe of the Potsdamer Platz, another bombed-out area haunted by the gray ghosts of gutted buildings, workers and employees from East Berlin ambled from one stand to the next, while others crowded into the makeshift cafeterias, drinking schnapps, beer, and the Coca-Cola they could not buy in bars located in the Soviet sector. The numerous pinball machines kept the young clients in a state of swearing frustration, while the jukeboxes ground out the latest hits—"Roses from Athens," "Salomé," "Danke schön für die Blumen"—sung by a Swiss-Italian crooner with the incandescent name of Vico Toriani.

One mile to the north of the Brandenburg Gate, at the *Kneipe* forming the corner of the Bernauer- and the Ackerstrasse, many of the beer and schnapps drinkers were playing skat, a card game much favored by middle-aged Berlin burghers. The wives and young ones these card-loving menfolk had left at home were seated opposite their television screens watching Jean Renoir's film version of Maupassant's *Picnic*, although some may have preferred the East German channel to see how the packers at the RAFENA works in Radebaul were celebrating the production of their millionth television set with the help of folk-costumed dancers from Prague.

In his apartment on the Prenzlauer Allee, in the northeast section of the Soviet sector, the East German bicycle champion Harry Seidel began rigging up his indoor television antenna. Although his set was connected to a roof-top aerial, it was prudently turned toward the east, lest some young Communist or Vopo be tempted to climb up onto the roof and put it out of action. But behind the carefully drawn curtains of his living room, nobody could stop him or his wife from enjoying the Dutch comedian Lou Van Burg, as much a favorite with them as with millions of West German viewers.

On this Saturday night the movie houses too were doing a brisk business, and none more so than those conveniently located near the sector borders. These cinemas traditionally catered to East Berliners, who for an admission fee of one mark and twenty-five pfennigs (in eastern currency) could enjoy two-fisted westerns or more sophisticated foreign films, like *Under Paris Skies*, which the Aladin movie house, on the western side of the Potsdamer Platz, was showing on this particular night. The more daring could even venture farther afield to the Passage cinema, in the working-class quarter of Neukölln, to see *The Devil Plays the Balalaika*, an anti-Soviet film devoted to the brutalities of a prisoner-of-war camp in Siberia.

Nor was this nocturnal traffic a purely one-way affair. Many West Berliners had crossed into the Soviet sector to take in a play—one of those presented by Bertolt Brecht's famous Berliner Ensemble, for instance; to chuckle at the latest antiregime jokes at the Distel, East Berlin's leading political cabaret; or simply to visit—as did Grepo Horst Ewald's West Berlin friends, who were often to be seen at the Rialto bar, in the northeast Pankow district, emptying steins of beer until the wee hours of the morning.

The gourmets of East Berlin, particularly those who fancied spicy Romanian or Hungarian dishes, had once again invaded the Bucharest, on the Alexanderplatz, and the Budapest, on the Stalinallee, where Armenian cognac, Soviet champagne, Polish vodka, and Bulgarian wines could be obtained for outrageous prices.

More fortunate than the severely disciplined Ivans, who were discouraged from fraternizing with the fair sex of East Berlin, the Green Jackets and the Tommies of the First Welsh Regiment were living it up in the NAAFI dance hall in the British sector. There was music and gay entertainment too for the French *bidasses* who were prancing around the dance floor of the Maison du Soldat with the Gretchens and Lottes of their choice. The GIs, not to be outdone, were making the most of this weekend in service clubs and well-stocked bars, where the atmosphere was noisy and the Lili Marlenes were in plentiful, heavily lipsticked supply. To them, as to most of the city dwellers they were officially protecting, this Saturday night must have seemed like any other.

Gone were most of the weathercocks that had so stirred

E. T. A. Hoffmann's sense of the fantastic, like the delicately carved fountains that had once made Albrecht Dürer's Nuremberg the pride of Renaissance Germany. But like a bruised and battered Phoenix rising from its wartime ashes, the old Gothic city was alive and humming once again, as banner-waving Socialists pressed through its narrow streets and filled its taverns with their boisterous clamor. On the cobbled squares, imported brass bands thumped, trumpeted, and tootled for the divertissement of the tens of thousands of political pilgrims who had flocked here from all parts of the Federal Republic to participate in the *Deutschland Treffen* ("Germany Rally"), which was to usher in the final phase of the Social Democratic party's electoral campaign.

Most of the party's big guns had gathered for the event, which had begun on Saturday morning with a big meeting in the modernistic Exhibition Hall. The speeches, as was to be expected, were full of exalted rhetoric varying from the ponderous and platitudinous to the simplistic and sublime. For party chairman Erich Ollenhauer, the main danger inherent in another Christian Democratic victory was not so much the advanced age of Chancellor Adenauer as the ever-growing influence and power of his "gray eminence," Franz-Josef Strauss. A victory for the Christian Democrats would be a defeat for democracy. It would open the way to the "reckless power and elbow politics" of Adenauer's defense minister and expose the country to perilous adventurism.

Willy Brandt was more forceful in his denunciations. The Christian Democratic party, he declared, was intellectually stagnant and spiritually bankrupt. It had become the party of conformity, lazy-mindedness, and stupidity. Having nothing more of its own to offer, it had taken to borrowing shamelessly from the Socialists.

At the open-air rally on the marketplace, which followed in the early afternoon, there was a lot more of the same. Chancellor-candidate Willy Brandt declared that Germany was passing through the most critical moment in her postwar history. But this did not mean that party differences had to be suppressed. One had only to look at the United States to see how a healthy democracy could reconcile basic agreement on foreign-policy issues with vigorous debate at home. The Christian Democrats, however, were trying to stifle rather than promote debate. Under the aegis of their aging chancellor, they had staked out a claim to rule by divine right, even though theirs was a superannuated style of government marked by selfishness, self-satisfaction, misuse of power, calumny, and slander. Typical was Chancellor Adenauer's refusal to debate the great issues of the day on television or in any other public forum with his challenger.

This statement, in which Adenauer's "negativism" was implicitly contrasted with Nixon's "fair play" in agreeing to televised debates with Kennedy during the U.S. presidential campaign of 1960, touched off a lively ovation. So did the harsh words that followed, obviously inspired by the criticism leveled at Willy Brandt for his frequent absences from Berlin. True, as the SPD's candidate he had been touring West Germany in recent weeks. But what of Konrad Adenauer? "In the first six months of this year, he ruled for two and a half months from Cadenabbia. I, on the other hand, spent thirty-five days in the Federal Republic campaigning for Berlin and telling people what its future is to be."

No, it was time to end such slanderous innuendos and to call a spade a spade. The inhabitants of the Federal Republic "want a change in the relationship between the rulers and the ruled. They do not wish to be treated like witless children. . . . Even Herr Adenauer must understand at last that in this election campaign he is a candidate and nothing else."

The listeners massed on the cobbled marketplace cheered their heads off. This was the stirring talk they had come to hear. These were the fighting words they craved. With a leader like Brandt, the SPD could march forward to victory.

As dusk fell over the war-scarred battlements and the new slate roofs of the reconstructed Altstadt, the squares resounded to the joyous thump and trumpeting of imported bands. Just what the outcome would be on September 17, when the election returns came in, no Nuremberger knew or seemed to care. For on this festive evening there was a feeling of future triumph in the air, marked by fireworks and balloons and banners proclaiming: "*Voran mit Willy Brandt!*" ("Forward with Willy Brandt!").

From the Stresemannstrasse construction site where he worked from Monday morning to Saturday noon, there were exactly six S-Bahn stops to Emil Goltz's home in East Berlin. The first five were in the U.S. sector, where less than a minute was generally allowed for passengers to get on or off. But at the sixth stop, Treptow Park, the halt had now lengthened to two minutes or even more, to give the Vopos time to go through the train's six cars and haul off any East Berliners suspected of returning from the West with excessive amounts of contraband.

So far Emil Goltz had managed to avoid molestation on his S-Bahn journeys to and from work. Like the fifty thousand other border crossers who traveled daily from the East to work in the West, he carried a special certificate, in addition to his personal identity card, indicating that he was a Grenzgänger and as such was allowed to "import" a limited amount of consumer goods for his personal use. Several years before, he had succeeded in smuggling in a radio and a small television from West Berlin without getting caught. But that was as far as he had dared go.

It had been seven years since he had given up his job with the East Berlin Bau-Union and gone to work for a West Berlin construction firm, and he had no reason to regret it. The combination of high wages from the West and low rents in the Soviet sector made it possible for him to support his wife, Anna, and their nine-year-old daughter, Beate, without his wife's having to get a job. But now, as he walked from the Treptow Park station to his home on the Graetzstrasse, a couple of blocks from the U.S.- sector boundary, Goltz wondered how long his good luck was going to last.

The first warning had come during the last days of July, when five other border crossers working for the same West Berlin construction firm told him of the pressure that was being brought to bear on them by local Party officials. All of them owned small suburban houses situated just beyond the city limits in the Soviet zone; and all of them had been given to understand that if they wanted to hang on to these pieces of property, they would have to seek new employment in East Berlin.

The second warning had been much more direct. Goltz had crossed over into the Neukölln district to enjoy a late-afternoon drink with some friends in the U.S. sector when he was stopped on his way back by a particularly zealous Vopo who had him unbutton his jacket. Tucked into the inner-lining pocket was a copy of *Hör Zu*, West Germany's leading radio-and-television weekly. The Vopo had escorted him to the nearest police station, and there he had been ushered into the frowning presence of a Political Indoctrination officer.

"So you've been smuggling forbidden publications into democratic Berlin," said the officer as he examined Goltz's identity card and border-crosser's certificate. "A Grenzgänger! And in the building trade! Building barracks for the Bundeswehr, eh, Herr Goltz? Barracks for the troops that are preparing an armed aggression against the DDR! Has it never occurred to you that this activity might be treasonous, a punishable offense?"

"Barracks!" snorted Goltz. "You call those barracks—those housing units we're building over there in Kreuzberg for workers and employees? For workers and employees—not for millionaires or Bundeswehr generals or captains or Feldwebels or any other kind of soldier! As you know perfectly well!" he concluded in a burst of anger which he made no effort to control.

Fortunately, the sharp exchange had ended there. The officer had simply handed back Goltz's papers without a word.

The third and potentially most serious warning had been delivered only a couple of days before in the form of a written summons instructing him to report for registration as a Grenzgänger at the Treptow borough town hall. The date indicated for his appearance and registration was August 14, a Monday, now just two days away. Goltz didn't like the sound of it. But if the authorities were going to keep him from working in West Berlin, then no matter what his wife might think or say, he was going to move with his family to the West.

There was a pot of steaming coffee waiting for him when he walked into the apartment. His wife poured both of them a cup as they chatted about this and that. He didn't want to cast a shadow over the rest of this Saturday by starting another argument. In a few hours, Anna and Beate were leaving for Thuringia to spend a two-week vacation with relatives who lived near Erfurt. Emil unfortunately could not accompany them; his vacation didn't come until late autumn or winter.

Anna went into the bedroom to pack. By 6:00 P.M. all was ready. Picking up the two suitcases, Goltz led the way downstairs and over to the Treptow Park station. The eastbound platform seemed surprisingly empty of Vopos; there was not one in sight. Not that it made much difference, since the three of them were headed for the Ostbahnhof, where mother and daughter were to board the train for Erfurt.

The railway cars were already filling up with other vacationers when they arrived. The atmosphere was almost festive, although Beate nearly cried when the moment came to kiss her father good-by.

Standing on the platform, Goltz kept waving to his little daughter, who was barely tall enough to get her forearm out of the lowered window. The departing train, instead of heading west, was headed south and east—one of the many anomalies of divided, postwar Berlin. Rather than expose their citizens to additional temptations by letting westbound or southbound trains roll directly through the British and U.S. sectors, the DDR authorities had preferred to reroute them along a circuitous detour through Königswusterhausen.

Half an hour later Goltz was back at the Treptow Park station. Once again he was surprised by the absence of Vopos. "An ideal evening for smuggling," he thought to himself as he headed home. Why were the East Berlin authorities now relaxing their grip?

He felt too tired to give the matter further thought. The one thing that interested him was going to bed and getting a good twelve-hours' sleep. He wouldn't have to get up until ten o'clock the next morning, and he could then dawdle as much as he liked while treating himself to three eggs and four cups of strong coffee. After that he would take a late-morning stroll and maybe drop into a nearby tavern for a glass of beer with some skat-playing friends. Even in the DDR, Sunday was a day of rest.

Before leaving for the Plänterwald Cafe, Ursula Heinemann changed into a dress. At seventeen she was a remarkably pretty girl, with a slender figure, soft brown eyes, long auburn hair, and high cheekbones inherited from her partly Byelo-

russian mother, which gave her an alluringly Slavic air. Danc-
ing was Ursula's passion, and at the Plänterwald she was never
short of partners.

This evening was going to be an early one, as she explained
to her mother. She hoped to be back by 10:30 at the latest.
That would allow her six hours of sleep before she rose at 4:45
the next morning and hurried to catch her S-Bahn train at the
nearby Schöneweide station. It was a thirty-five- to forty-
minute ride over to the Savignyplatz, and from there a short
walk to the Plaza Hotel, near the Kurfürstendamm, where her
work as a waitress began at 6:00 A.M.

All things considered, it wasn't a bad life, and the pay—400
West marks a month—was princely by East Berlin standards.
That is, if she was careful. Just two weeks before, she had
thoughtlessly opened her handbag at the request of a Customs
official at the first S-Bahn stop inside East Berlin, forgetting
that it contained almost an entire month's salary. Un-
impressed by the story she improvised to explain away the
presence of the incriminating banknotes ("They were given to
me by a cousin of mine who lives in West Berlin"), the gray-
uniformed Customs official had confiscated the 350 West
marks, handed her a receipt, and told her to be on her way if
she wanted to avoid further trouble. The receipt of course was
worthless: Any attempt to reclaim the impounded sum would
have exposed her to disciplinary measures and possible imprisonment.

Opening the apartment door, Ursula paused for a moment
to see if there was anyone on the landing. The new apartment
building, located in the wood- and garden-surrounded community of Johannisthal, was part of a block of recently built
housing units inhabited for the most part by Party officials.
The apartments were considered fine enough to constitute a
reward for faithful service, and the tenants, whether genuine
fanatics or simple opportunists, expressed their gratitude for
the privilege of living here by hanging flags from their
windows and balconies each time the Workers-and-Peasants-
State celebrated a holiday. Most of the neighbors were
middle-aged couples, models of middle-class conformism. But
a couple of doors away lived a particularly aggressive couple

who seldom missed a chance to make some nasty remark about Ursula's "provocative" appearance. They seemed to regard her good looks, gay scarves, and form-fitting sweaters as insults to the spartan integrity of the working class. The last time they had run into each other, on this very landing, the wife—a pudgy-faced matron—had given her a syrupy smile and purred, "Wait a little, *Fräuleinchen*, times will change for you too. And then you will sing a different tune, my pigeon."

Seeing nobody outside, Ursula closed the apartment door and hurried down the stairs. Situated south and east of the Soviet Garden of Remembrance, not far from the Spree River, the Plänterwald was something of an exception as East Berlin cafes went, having recently acquired a combo imported from Scandinavia, whose repertory consisted for the most part of hit tunes from the West. The evening fare was usually hot enough to attract West Berlin jazz lovers, who would drive over in their Mercedes or Opels and often end the evening in fist fights with less opulent youths from East Berlin, infuriated to see the invaders successfully wooing their girlfriends with expensive cocktails or chilled bottles of Soviet champagne.

After letting herself be rock-and-rolled all over the dance floor by a succession of young men, Ursula sat down to rest at a table with former school friends. There was the usual gossip and only casual mention of the *Torschlusspanik* that seemed to have seized on so many inhabitants of the DDR.[9] Ursula for her part had no intention of being panicked into fleeing to the West. At the "house meetings" held every two weeks for all occupants of her apartment building, she had been criticized more than once for working in the British sector and had been advised to seek employment in East Berlin. A local FDGB trade-union official had even called on her one day at her parents' apartment and suggested that she would do well, if she wanted to get ahead in the hotel business, to apply for a job in Czechoslovakia or Romania, where hard-working German boys and girls were in much demand. But, probably because she was still a minor, she had been less exposed to badgering than her stepfather, an electronics expert who had

---

[9]*Torschlusspanik.* The graphic term, meaning "closing-door panic," was then on everybody's lips.

taken a job with a light-bulb factory in West Berlin a year or so before.

At ten o'clock she rose to go home. One of her former school-mates, Ingrid Imgard, a plain-faced girl with large horn-rimmed glasses, left with her. The night was agreeably warm, and as they walked back toward Johannisthal, the Köpennicker Landstrasse seemed undisturbed by anything except the sound of their chatter.

Ever since he had started working as an industrial engineer at the VEB Montage-Bau in Treptow—a factory specializing in the manufacture of steel-girder armatures for factory buildings and industrial plants—Georg Maurer had consistently declined to become involved in Party, or what was more euphemistically called "social," activities. Each time he was approached by a SED member, he gave the standard reply: He was an engineer by training and profession. He understood nothing about politics; he was interested only in doing his job as competently and efficiently as possible, so that the state-controlled Montage-Bau plant could fulfill the production quotas established by the Plan.

Although not always satisfied by these evasions, the Party activists had been willing to leave him alone, after some mild words of remonstrance. But when approached for his signature to a factory petition requesting the immediate creation of an "action committee against the man-trade," George Maurer knew he could not so easily refuse. The purpose of this committee was to urge the government to take even more drastic measures against the "speculators," the border crossers, and the "agents" of the Western intelligence services who were undermining the economy of the DDR by robbing it of its trained workers and technicians. The campaign against the Grenzgänger had by now reached such a crescendo—with daily broadsides in the press and on the radio—that he realized it would be folly to resist. So he signed the petition, like the three hundred others employed in the firm, just to be left in peace.

If there was one thing Georg Maurer wished to avoid at this particular moment, it was to attract the attention of the Party.

He wanted to remain as inconspicuous as possible for the next few days.

As a degree-holding engineer of twenty-seven, he knew that he held as good a job as he could reasonably expect to obtain for his age and educational achievements. But he had discovered that in West Berlin, the pay was higher for the same kind of work. And people on the other side weren't subjected to this mounting sense of insecurity, to this feeling that at any moment the ax was going to fall, cutting off all further access to the West.

The hard thing had been persuading his wife, Carola, that they *must* leave East Berlin with their eighteen-month-old daughter before it was too late. It had taken weeks, indeed months, of argument and discussion. But for the almost accidental fact that they had been unable to obtain precious baby foods and especially Milkena (a pharmaceutical substitute for ordinary breast milk) in East Berlin and had had to make frequent trips to the West to buy them, Carola might never have agreed to the idea. Like many East Berliners, she took the existence of a free West Berlin for granted, and she had difficulty imagining that access to it might one day be denied them. She was almost umbilically attached to the part of the city in which she, like Georg, had been raised. In East Berlin there was not the feeling of living on an island surrounded by a kind of hostile sea, from which so many West Berliners suffered; for any East Berliner could travel beyond the city limits into the neighboring countryside and return with a minimum of trouble, whereas this privilege was denied to all West Berliners. There was also the vital question of lodgings. The small flat they occupied in the Karlshorst residential area was anything but palatial, but the rent was cheap. In West Berlin, on the other hand, she was afraid they would have to pay a small fortune for anything comparable.

Georg had finally managed to convince her that a higher salary would enable him to pay the higher rents encountered in the West. After using his spare time to canvass a number of industrial firms in West Berlin, he had signed a contract for a new job in early July. He was to report for work on September 1. This interval would give his new employers time to find him a suitable apartment, and it would give him time to enjoy several weeks of paid vacation—and an ideal opportunity to move his family to the West.

Several times a week since then, Georg Maurer had ridden the S-Bahn over into West Berlin, bringing with him small bundles of personal belongings, which he deposited with friends. Now, on this Saturday, August 12, he was making one more trip to be sure that all had been properly taken care of by his future West Berlin employers. Unfortunately, the man he wanted to see most of all was not in his office. But he was told not to worry; Everything was being attended to, so that he, his wife, and child could make their move the following week.

Back at his apartment, Georg Maurer watched his wife feed their little daughter. Little Ilse's gums were swollen; It looked as though she was beginning to cut new teeth.

"Don't bother about me," urged his wife, who knew that he wanted to go to the movies. "Go on your own, Georg. It will do you good. It will help keep your mind off all these problems."

Georg needed little urging, although he felt like a cad leaving his wife at home. The film, a Russian one, was neither particularly good nor bad, but as she had said, it did occupy his mind for several hours.

As he emerged into the open air, he found himself wondering if he would ever set foot in this movie house again. It was close to 10:30 P.M. on Saturday, the twelfth. Just two sunrises away —barely thirty-six hours hence—he would be returning to his factory to collect three weeks' holiday pay. His Montage-Bau employers wouldn't be expecting him back until the end of the month, and he couldn't help smiling at the thought of how helpful they were being in financing his move to West Berlin.

Along one side of the large staff room, a cold buffet had been laid out, with sausages and hams, platters of cold veal, bowlfuls of Fleisch and potato salad dressed in mayonnaise and pickles, as well as salmon sandwiches, caviar temptingly smeared on strips of buttered bread, and yellow ovals of neatly halved boiled eggs. Behind another white-linened table, several waiters stood ready to replenish empty glasses with bubbling champagne from the Crimea, to measure out

Dornkaat, schnapps, or vodka to those with a taste for stronger stuff; and to pass out cups of steaming coffee. The officers invited to this Saturday evening surprise party at the Nationale Volksarmee's headquarters at Strausberg, some thirty kilometers due east of Pankow, would not have to return to their billets and command posts with empty stomachs. Their genial host, the wavy-haired and somewhat dandified Gen. Karl-Heinz Hoffmann, knew how to "sprinkle" the occasion.

Although the primary purpose of this curious party was to brief the regimental commanders and the political officers of the Nationale Volksarmee and Grenzpolizei units stationed in and around Berlin, most of the NVA's top brass were present to emphasize thesolemnity of the moment. Prominent among them was Hoffmann's deputy, Lt. Gen. Kurt Wagner, whose military credentials were not exactly striking, but whose political loyalty to his fellow Saxon, Walter Ulbricht, was unimpeachable. The bald, bespectacled Friedrich Dickel had in his younger days commanded the famous Ernst Thaelmann Battalion of the international brigades in the Spanish civil war before rising to become chief of the NVA's planning and logistics staff. Discreetly present too was one of the Defense Ministry's most formidable workhorses, Ottomar Pech, a former Wehrmacht soldier who had been taken prisoner by the Russians on the eastern front. From his important job as commander and trainer of the Ministry of State Security's alert-watch unit, he had since moved on to head the cryptically designated "Administration 2,000," a special section created to coordinate the activities of the National Defense and National Security ministries.

In the last few days a great deal had been accomplished, as Pech was particularly well placed to know. Large quantities of concrete uprights had been secretly brought in from the Eisenhüttenstadt industrial area, on the Oder River, and stockpiled in the main courtyard of the Niederschönhausen Volkspolizei barracks in Pankow. Behind the forbidding walls of the huge SSD compound at Hohenschönhausen, on Berlin's eastern periphery, prisoners awaiting trial had been denied access to the workshops, where sawhorse street barriers were now being constructed at a feverish pace by several hundred Volkspolizei second lieutenants rounded up from different parts of East Germany. The barbed wire with which these "Spanish riders" were spiked and garlanded had been obtained from firms in West Germany. To avoid diplomatic complications and possible reprisals, the minister of state security had ordered the labels to be ripped off and burned in a workshop furnace under the supervision of SSD officers.

The military aspects of the operation, of course, lay beyond the scope of Erich Mielke's secret-police responsibilities. They had been carefully worked out with the NVA's Russian advisers. To limit the risk of shooting incidents with the Western Allies—for there was no telling just how they would react—the police units charged with blocking the intersector border were going to be issued two five-bullet clips of blanks, and three clips of live ammunition for their carbines. The first clips were to be fired, if necessary, for purposes of warning or intimidation; the others were to be used only if absolutely necessary in self-defense. Grenzpolizei soldiers and noncoms armed with Tommy guns were to be issued limited quantities of ammunition, to be carried in the canvas satchels attached to their leather belts. The only ones to be plentifully supplied with live ammunition were the Kampfgruppen factory militiamen; the two crack Wachregimente—one belonging to Hoffmann's NVA, the other to Mielke's SSD; and the tankmen of Horst Stechbarth's First Motorized Rifle Division, whose task it would be to keep the restive East Berliners cowed through an impressive show of force.

After being offered a cinematographic divertissement—a morale-boosting film designed to demonstrate the class-conscious combat readiness and invincible might of the armed forces of the Socialist countries—the regimental commanders and political officers invited to Strausberg were treated to a short speech by their bemedalled host. H-hour was at hand, Heinz Hoffmann explained, and a major operation was about to be launched to seal off all but a few of the roads and streets connecting West with East Berlin and the outlying suburban towns. Each Grenzpolizei and NVA unit was being given a specific area to cover, but in the interest of maximum security, the precise orders and instructions would not be made known to the various regimental and battalion commanders until after midnight. In the meantime, all Grenzpolizei and NVA units involved were to be alerted and the men given an explanatory pep talk by their Polit-officers.

The political officers were then instructed to rejoin their units. The regimental commanders, on the other hand, were invited to stay on, to help themselves to more caviar sandwiches and sausages, and to down a few more thimblefuls of schnapps or vodka. After two hours of blood-warming libations, they were finally released and speeded on their respective ways.

It was now fifteen minutes past midnight, on the early morning of Sunday, August 13, 1961. H-hour had almost struck, and the great city-splitting operation was about to begin.

2

Most of the East Berliners who had crossed to the western side to play the pinball machines or to enjoy a glass of Schultheiss beer had by now returned home, leaving the Potsdamer Platz more deserted than ever. A few minutes later, when Manfred Bauer, of the Berlin Bear City Tours, drove his bus load of nightclub revelers around the dark, empty square ("just to give them a sobering shock," as he liked to put it), the chatter and the laughs abruptly petered out at the sight of this unlit no man's land. Watched over by two solitary Vopos stationed on the square's eastern rim, this eery expanse of nothingness looked like a graveyard without graves; and it was with a feeling of relief that bus driver and passengers turned their backs on it, heading for the bright lights of the Anhalter S-Bahn station, which they passed on their way to their final nightclub destination—the noisy Resi dance hall, in the bleak, although less bomb-flattened quarter of Neukölln, not far from the Tempelhof airfield.

The lights were also shining brightly in the broad, many-windowed building on the Mauerstrasse, just south of the Soviet embassy, where a special night shift was now putting the Sunday edition of *Neues Deutschland* to bed. The Saturday-morning edition had played up the Volkskammer session ("The Time for Decisive Measures Has Come!") and included lengthy extracts from the speeches delivered by Dr. Johannes Dieckmann, Foreign Minister Lothar Bolz, and Acting Premier Willi Stoph. The first Sunday edition had contained more tirades against "kidnappers" and *Menschenhändler*. But at the surprisingly early hour of 10:00 P.M., most of the night-shift employees were informed that they could go home since their work was done. Gratefully they picked up their jackets and handbags and made for the exits.

A hand-picked few were told to stay on. They were the ones who enjoyed the special confidence of Hermann Axen, the editor in chief. Feverishly they went to work preparing a second Sunday edition. Unlike the first, which was already rolling off the press, this one carried the full text of an important proclamation issued by the governments of the Warsaw Pact powers.

At the Borsig boiler and electric-generator factory in Pankow, where he worked in the export department, Klaus Brückner was often jokingly referred to as "Ahmed," because his unusually dark hair and intense look made him resemble the Algerian rebel leader, Ahmed Ben Bella. He tended to shrug off the ironic appellation with a frown. Admittedly, he was something of a rebel; he had resisted the Party's repeated efforts to enroll him as a card-carrying member of the SED. But he had little use for political causes of any kind. The militant fanaticism he had encountered in his late teens as a member of the Freie Deutsche Jugend had left him with a deep-rooted distaste for uniform wearing and indoctrination. The insistent slogan-mongering, the incessant war of words against "class enemies" and "western spies," the denunciation of parents daring to question the infallibility of the beloved *Vorsitzender* ("Chairman")—the incantatory word that had replaced *Führer* in the Party lexicon—all were too reminiscent

of the Hitlerjugend's mind-warping methods of indoctrination.

Anxious though he was to remain apolitical, Klaus Brückner
could not avoid the constraints imposed on him as a factory
employee. In 1955 everybody in the Borsig works—from
janitors and tool cutters to the upper echelon of engineers,
scientists, and managers—had been forced to join the factory
militia, which the Party had recruited to prevent a recurrence
of the workers' uprising of June 1953. The result was a distinctly apathetic amalgam of manual workers and white-collar
specialists of varying sizes, shapes, and ages.

The training, to begin with, was intermittent and entrusted
to outsiders—discharged *Volksarmisten* and Volkspolizei
officers—who kept all weapons carefully locked up at district
police headquarters. Sometimes an entire shift would be
called out and put through its paces for a whole day, the work
thus lost having to be made up in extra hours; at other times,
they had to devote a weekend, including Sunday, to target
practice and parade drill—the latter regarded as vitally important for "shock workers" who were expected to march in
rigorously Prussian step past the Marx-Engels-Platz reviewing stand and up the Stalin-Allee on May Day and the January
15 anniversary, commemorating the assassination of Germany's two proletarian martyrs, Karl Liebknecht and Rosa
Luxemburg.

At noon on this Saturday, August 12, Klaus Brückner had at
last been able to leave his invoice files and account books,
having completed a forty-four-hour week. Earlier in the
month he had sent his wife and three children to the Baltic
resort of Herringsdorf for a two-week vacation. Accommoda-
tions had been provided for them at cheap boarding-house
rates by the state-run trade-union federation, but he himself
had not been able to join them. The seven hundred East
marks he earned each month were simply insufficient.

What Klaus Brückner could not or would not spend on a
vacation, he was, however, quite willing to spend on drinks
and Peter Stuyvesant cigarettes. Since the latter were not
available in the Soviet sector, he would when in short supply
hop into his car, a second-hand DKW, and drive up the Wol-
lankstrasse, slowing to flash his identity card at the Vopo on

the sector boundary. Farther up the same street, in the French sector, was a bar called Der Italiener. Near it stood a slot machine from which Brückner could extract half a dozen or more packs of Peter Stuyvesants to tide him over the next few days. Since the slot machine was geared to West German coins, he had first to trade in twenty or thirty East marks at some nearby cafe or sidewalk booth to obtain the necessary 1-mark coins at the costly 4- or 4.5-to-1 exchange rate.

His other weakness—hard liquor—Brückner usually indulged at the Rialto bar, a spacious Pankow beer hall with room enough for eighty tables and a three-man orchestra. One of these tables, situated in a cozy corner, was regularly reserved for Brückner and his friends.

It was for the Rialto that Brückner now headed after spending most of this Saturday afternoon with his father and mother, who had generously plied him with cream cakes and cups of coffee. In his wallet were the one hundred East marks he had taken from a night-table drawer in his bedroom before leaving his apartment—a sum he figured would cover the drinks he would want to buy for his friends. Although he was allowed to read selected West Berlin newspapers for the foreign-trade information they contained, Brückner had paid little attention that morning to anything except the financial pages. He also had ignored the *Neues Deutschland* headlines and lead articles announcing the arrest of four new "headhunters" who had sold their mercenary souls to American and West German "man-hunting" agencies. Bad as the news might sound, he wasn't going to let it spoil his Saturday evening with the boys.

His four beer-hall companions—technicians like himself —were equally determined to forget the world and its woes, as they tossed back their schnapps and kept ordering another round. The atmosphere was growing steadily more jolly when one of the three musicians walked up and tapped Brückner on the shoulder. He let himself be led off to one side. Located not far from the Polish, Romanian, Czechoslovakian, and Bulgarian embassies, the Rialto was often frequented by East-bloc diplomats and strangers with disturbingly long ears. In a public place like this, one had to be careful.

"You know what I've just heard?" the accordionist told him,

whispering into his ear. "Long Volksarmee convoys are converging on Berlin. Coming from Prenzlau and headed south. I was just told it by a client. Claims to have seen them with his own eyes." Brückner thanked him for the news and regained his seat.

"What's new?" demanded his neighbor, a chemist.

Brückner repeated what he had just been told.

The chemist laughed. "Is that all?"

Brückner nodded.

"Prenzlau," repeated the chemist. "You know where that is? Sixty kilometers—no, not even—from Neustrelitz and that big maneuver area."

It was common knowledge to almost everyone in East Berlin. Sixty miles north of the capital, Neustrelitz and its surrounding plains and forests were a vast training area frequently used by Soviet and Volksarmee units for joint exercises in the field.

"Relax," insisted the chemist. "They're just out on another of their night maneuvers."

With that the subject was dismissed. Another round of schnapps was ordered, and nobody at the table gave further thought to the matter.

Kurt Gohlke couldn't honestly say that the evening had been a success. For several days his sister Greta's boyfriend, an American MP sergeant, had been warning them that the East German regime was about to seal off the sector borders. This was no rumor—he had it from a sure, top-secret source—and there wasn't a minute to be lost if they wanted to tip off friends or relatives in East Berlin. The clamp-down, the sergeant insisted, was being planned for this weekend!

The thirty-year-old Gohlke was not personally affected. The West Berlin insurance company for which he worked as a janitor was located on the safe southern side of the Zimmerstrasse, and he occupied an apartment on the Potsdamer Strasse, also in the U.S. sector. But an uncle living in Köpenick would find himself trapped if, as the MP sergeant claimed, Ulbricht was now going to lower the bar between East and West Berlin.

Feeling it his duty to warn his uncle, Kurt Gohlke had

ridden the S-Bahn over to Köpenick. "You say they're going to run down an iron curtain through the very heart of this city?" his uncle had exclaimed. "Why, you're out of your mind! I tell you, it can't be done. Even Ulbricht wouldn't dare try such a damn fool thing as that. Don't forget, Berlin is still under Four-Power jurisdiction, and that's something Ulbricht can't change. I'm not surprised your MP sergeant can't name his source. It's a lot of hot air, that's what it is! Like so many other rumors we've been hearing!"

When Kurt Gohlke finally left shortly before midnight, it was with the tranquil assurance that nothing would have changed in another week's time and that he could come back next Saturday and help his uncle empty another bottle. There was no sign of any impending action as the elevated S-Bahn train carried him back through Karlshorst and Rummelsburg toward the center of Berlin.

But at the Friedrichstrasse station, where he got off to change from the upper to the lower level, he saw a number of Vopos placing wooden barriers across corridors leading to the main station concourse. On the underground platform, forty or fifty men in uniform were milling around aimlessly, apparently waiting for instructions. They made no effort to board the north–south S-Bahn train when it finally rolled into the station.

At the Unter den Linden stop, the train did not halt as it usually did. It rolled on at a steady, although somewhat slower speed through the big Potsdamer Platz station, where usually there was a minute-long stop to enable the Vopos to board the cars and to drag out luggage-carrying passengers. This time the Vopos were otherwise employed. As the train rolled slowly through the station, Gohlke saw them piling up concrete posts and wooden barriers. How they had reached the station platform, he had no idea; presumably they had been brought into the station by a workshop train and then dumped onto the platform for the Vopos to pick up.

The train finally slowed to a halt at the Anhalter station, the first stop inside the U.S. sector. Gohlke left the train at the next stop, where the S-Bahn emerged from underground. He was feeling a bit lightheaded from the schnapps he had imbibed. He did not even suspect that he had just ridden the last S-Bahn train that was to travel between East and West Berlin.

Dealing with refugees was not exactly a new experience for Heinrich Albertz, the fifty-year-old Protestant pastor turned politician whom Willy Brandt had picked in 1959 to run his Berlin City Hall staff. Born in Silesia and brought up in Saxony, where he had begun his theological studies, he was something of a refugee himself, having been gradually severed from his homeland by the vicissitudes of politics and war. The Nazis, who had taken a dim view of his socialist inclinations, had jailed him in 1943 for daring to speak up for the pacifist pastor Martin Niemoeller. Two years later Silesia had been carved up, with a good slice of it (including his native city of Breslau) going to Poland. Having already tasted the bitter fruits of one dictatorship, Albertz had felt no urge to submit to another in the Soviet zone of occupation; instead, he had preferred to spend the first postwar years in Lower Saxony—the area encompassing Hamburg and Bremen—where he had worked in the state administration for the resettlement of those who had lost their homes and most of their possessions. Even so, the crisis now confronting him at the Marienfelde refugee camp was as bad as any he had ever had to face.

From his office in the Schöneberg Rathaus, Albertz called George Muller, the deputy political adviser (and thus the number three man) of the U.S. mission in Berlin. A Vienna-born American, Muller spoke German fluently, and had served for several years as the American liaison officer between the Berlin city government and the U.S. mission. At Marienfelde, Albertz explained, they had run out of food for the refugees. Was there anything the Americans could do to help?

Muller put in several telephone calls, then rang Albertz back. It wasn't much, but he had managed to pry several thousand C-rations away from the U.S. garrison's stocks. Albertz thanked him. Several thousand C-rations were better than nothing.

How they were going to get through the next few days, Albertz did not know. All available seats were booked on flights out of Berlin, and the refugee centers were overflowing. *"Die Sache kann auf die Dauer nicht so weiter gehen"* ("This can't go on forever"), Willy Brandt had observed several days before, disconsolately shaking his head. Ulbricht was going to have to do something—but what? A report from West Berlin police headquarters at Tempelhof indicated that unusually heavy movements of military trucks had been noted in East Berlin. What did it mean?

"I don't know what your plans are," Albertz told his assistant, Dietrich Spangenberg, as they left the Rathaus together. "But I'm going to stay home tonight in case anything happens."

"I think I'll do the same," said Spangenberg, who was supposed to go to a party.

A little later FLora Lewis walked into George Muller's office in the U.S. headquarters building on Clayallee. Married to Sydney Gruson, the *New York Times* correspondent in Bonn, she had come to Berlin to help him cover the *Frontstadt* scene. "Well, what's cooking?" she inquired.

All Muller could tell her was that the refugee flow had reached such alarming proportions that they were bringing out C-rations to keep them fed. Koniev's assumption of command, followed by the Volkskammer session, seemed to indicate that drastic action was imminent.

One possibility that had longed worried the Western allies was that the Soviets and East Germans might decide to stir up trouble in the western sectors as a diversionary maneuver. They could pack the S-Bahn trains with thousands of factory militiamen disguised in civilian clothes, have them gather at carefully selected points ready to start street riots and disorders on a massive scale. Even if the Russians and East Germans did not intervene to restore order with their troops, the uproar would blacken West Berlin's image as an island of freedom. It thus was imperative to keep a sharp eye on both the elevated S-Bahn and the subway. But there was nothing on this Saturday evening to suggest such a camouflaged invasion.

The next time Albertz called it was to report something

rather different. For reasons he could not explain, the S-Bahn was no longer functioning as it should. The trains were still running toward the east on the sinuous east–west line which crossed the Spree River some distance to the north of the ruined Reichstag building, but they had stopped going west.

The fourteen members of the U.S. military liaison mission had spent Saturday afternoon, like their British and French counterparts, touring the Soviet zone in a vain endeavor to probe the military intentions of Marshal Koniev and his division commanders. If the Russians were up to something, they were certainly playing a close hand. When Col. Ernest von Pawel drove out to the U.S. mission's house at Potsdam in the early afternoon, he was informed by his subordinate, Lt. Col. David Morgan, a Russian area specialist, that if anything, the Soviet garrisons seemed quieter than usual. Few Soviet officers or Russian families were to be seen in the Potsdam residential area, and their favorite haunts along the lakes and rivers seemed to have attracted less than the usual number of amateur fishermen.

The one thing that aroused the two colonels' attention during a subsequent drive through the countryside was a temporary bridge that a Soviet engineer company was erecting across a tributary river. The small country road with which it was connected led directly to the Potsdam compound where the Tenth Soviet Tank Division was garrisoned. But the Soviet soldiers engaged in the bridge-building operation seemed so lackadaisical and the officer in charge so indifferent to the presence of two U.S. colonels that the latter were left wondering if this Saturday-afternoon assignment wasn't some punitive or training exercise imposed on a lackluster unit. For a scant five hundred yards from this spot was a permanent bridge over this same waterway.

Shortly after their return to their Potsdam house, another mission tour team came in with a similar report: They too had come upon a Soviet engineer detachment engaged in setting up a temporary bridge not far from a permanent one. Just what this coincidence signified nobody could figure out.

At 11:00 P.M., however, things began to move. Calling from

the Potsdam house, where he had elected to spend the night, Lt. Col. David Morgan told von Pawel that he could hear the steady roar of tanks moving in large numbers down the road. He had tried to drive onto Highway 10, an old road linking Neu Fahrland and Potsdam, only to be stopped by a Soviet officer, who had informed him that for his own safety he would not be allowed on the highway until the tank columns had passed by.

In the little town of Basdorf, straddling Highway 109, the Grenzpolizei's First Motorized Brigade was now settling down for the night. To allay any possible suspicions and to achieve a maximum of surprise, its commanding officer Lt. Col. Hans Wahner, had deliberately granted weekend leaves to a few of the thousand soldiers serving under his orders. But the twenty-year-old Horst Ewald was not one of them. In his Feldgrau uniform, with the distinctive green band around his garrison cap, this blond, blue-eyed peasant's son from the province of Brandenburg, to the west, looked every inch the legendary, 100-percent Aryan prototype of Nazi manhood. During his three-year term of service, which was now approaching its end, he had been subjected to a lot of propaganda—of a different, post-Nazi brand—by political officers.

Although the barracks were located just off the main street, which led through the town to Wandlitz, Horst Ewald had never set foot inside the exclusive compound, where the Party bigwigs had their luxurious villas. These were almost completely hidden from view by a six-foot-high concrete wall, itself screened by the trunks and foliage of beech trees and low-limbed firs. It was a standing joke among the enlisted men of the First Motorized Brigade that their unit was "Ulbricht's last guard"—the intimation being that in the event of another uprising comparable to the workers' revolt of June 17, 1953, they would be called upon to defend the boss of the Socialist Unity party. So far Ewald and his buddies had been permitted only fleeting glimpses of Walter Ulbricht's rapidly driven limousine. More familiar because slower moving was the special diesel coach that was used to carry Acting Premier

Willi Stoph from the village railway station to Berlin and back
to Basdorf, where a black bullet-proof sedan would be waiting
to transport him to the safety of the compound. But curiously
enough, Ewald had never seen Karl Maron, minister of the
interior and the nominal head of the Grenzpolizei, although
he was one of the compound's privileged denizens.

Their training being essentially of a military nature, the
soldiers of the First Motorized Brigade had spent a lot of time
in the field bivouacking or maneuvering, sometimes alone,
sometimes in conjunction with Soviet army forces, which
maintained a major tank pool farther north around the town of
Bernau. In these maneuvers, coils of barbed wire were often
used for obstacle-course and firing-range exercises, so that
Ewald had not been surprised to see truck loads of coils being
piled up in their barracks area during the second half of July.
So much barbed wire had been stocked that it eventually
covered one quarter of the soccer field. What had intrigued
him, as it had his colleagues, was not so much the quantity of
wire amassed as its provenance, for the wire carried labels
indicating that it had been manufactured in West Germany. It
had occasioned a good deal of sarcasm at the expense of "those
greedy Western capitalists" who were ready to manufacture
anything provided it reaped them rich profits.

On this Saturday evening Ewald and his Grenzpolizei colleagues had returned to their barracks as usual for a 10:00 P.M.
lights out. One hour later they were aroused by the sudden
blowing of a siren, signaling an emergency alert. This signal
meant that they had to climb into full field uniform, complete
with steel helmet, and carry a full pack and Kalashnikov submachine gun. They were also issued loaded drums containing
seventy-two rounds, which they were instructed to attach to
their belts. The drums in their Kalashnikovs, however, were
not loaded.

No explanation for this sudden emergency was offered beyond
the vague statement that their destination was Berlin. Outside,
they stood by as coils of barbed wire were heaved into waiting
trucks.

By midnight all was ready. Headed by Volksarmee jeeps, the
long column headed south for Berlin, a half hour's drive away.

As the column of trucks rolled heavily up the Prenzlauer Allee, lights began flashing on above, curtains were ripped back, and the windows in the dark façades of houses and apartment buildings were suddenly alive with peering heads. Like Horst Ewald, they had no idea of what was up but had reason to fear the worst.

In most of the nearby cafes the clients were hard at it playing games of skat when police Sgt. Hans Peters reported for duty at Police Station 52, on the Stralsunder Strasse, near the easternmost extremity of the French sector's Wedding district. This promised to be another uneventful summer night—one more to add to the hundreds he had already spent here, patrolling the point where the Strelitzer Strasse cut across the Bernauer Strasse into the Soviet sector.

After three hours of strolling up and down, with an occasional pause to talk to the West Berlin Customs officer who was on duty with him, Peters returned to the Day Room at Police Station 52 to eat a sandwich and drink a cup of coffee. At midnight he was back on the job, pacing up and down the largely empty street. Most of the windows were dark, indicating that the sober burghers of the Bernauer Strasse had already gone to bed. "No," Peters reflected, "this is not exactly an exciting beat."

But then, quite unexpectedly, something began to stir. Up the Bernauer Strasse from the right, where the street ran into the fenced-off railway yards of the dismantled Stettin station, came throngs of excited men and women. Their words—loud, angry words that Peters could hear long before they had drawn abreast of him—were accompanied by angry gesticulations. As they passed, one of them, somewhat older than the rest, stopped to explain to him that he and a group of West Berliners had bought tickets and been admitted to the platform of the Stettin station S-Bahn when the loudspeakers had informed them that no more trains would be running that night.

"The swine are up to something once again!" cried one of the pedestrians, shaking his fist in the air.

Peters hurried back to the Stralsunder Strasse police station to report what he had just seen and heard. Then he returned to his beat. The swarm of thwarted commuters had moved on, taking its tumult with it, and except for a few stragglers the Bernauer

Strasse was quiet. The upstairs windows were dark once again.

Yes, Peters reflected, this was a quiet, indeed a boring beat. It was a far cry from the life he had led some eighteen years before as a Feldwebel in the Luftwaffe's tough paratrooper corps, which had fought the British and Americans to a standstill more than once at Cassino and elsewhere. But still, he could thank his lucky stars that he was alive today. And relatively free.

In his office on the Schönhauser Allee, Adam Kellett-Long was struggling with a new dispatch. Reuters being the only Western news agency allowed to operate in East Berlin, the young British journalist suffered from a slight feeling of isolation, although there was nothing to keep him from crossing the border into West Berlin to hobnob with his colleagues of the Western press.

At present he had a deadline to meet. The special Volkskammer session on Friday, and the importance accorded it by East Germany's radio stations, had convinced him that something was going to happen. He had accordingly filed a long dispatch outlining the kinds of action the Ulbricht government could take to stem the refugee flow. Should the reinforcement of existing police controls on roads and railways leading into Berlin prove inadequate, the East Germans could try to seal the eastern sector of the city from the Soviet occupation zone. Or they might try severing the city down the middle. The first action would involve a major fence-building operation around the periphery of East Berlin; the second, an even more formidable undertaking, would involve building a wall through the very heart of the city. Walter Ulbricht, however, at his news conference of June 15, had specifically denied any intention of building such a wall.

To the Reuters desk men in London, the idea that the East Germans could consider walling themselves off from the other sectors of Berlin sounded preposterous. The mid-August heat had got the better of their man in East Berlin. He had succumbed to the prevailing refugee hysteria. For what, in strict fact, had happened? Nothing. Saturday had come, and a good part of it was gone without producing any hard evidence to substantiate such alarmist reporting. Something in a more sober vein was needed for the Sunday press. So Kellett-Long was asked to file a second, "climbing-down" dispatch.

Dutifully the young Reuters correspondent set off in his car for a tour of East Berlin. It looked as though his London bosses were right. Everything on this Saturday evening was calm. There was no sign of any impending action. A few strollers in the ill-lit streets; lovers embracing or walking arm-in-arm under the trees; the cafes full of skat players; older people walking sedately home after a visit with friends or several hours of cinema or theater entertainment—there was absolutely nothing unusual to report.

To make doubly sure, he stopped to pick up the early-Sunday-morning edition of *Neues Deutschland*. It contained nothing of exceptional interest beyond the routine denunciations of "head-hunters" and *Menschenhändler*. There was no getting around it: He would have to sit down at his typewriter and bat out that "climbing-down" story.

He was well into his dispatch when, some time after midnight, the telephone rang. *"Ein kleiner Vorschlag,"* said a voice in German. *"Geht nicht ins Bett heute Nacht!"* ("A small suggestion—don't go to bed tonight!"). There was a click, then silence. The stranger had hung up.

Climbing back into his car, Kellett-Long decided to make one more reconnaissance. From his Schönhauser Allee office he drove to the Marx-Engels-Platz and then up Unter den Linden. Some distance from the Brandenburg Gate he was halted by a solitary Vopo, waving a flashlight. This was as close as he could drive to the sector boundary, he was informed. No reason was offered. Kellett-Long turned his car around. As far as he could determine, his was the only vehicle around and there were no other Vopos visible. All very odd, even disconcerting.

Driving south from Unter den Linden, Kellett-Long tried approaching the sector border again, up the Leipziger Strasse toward the Potsdamer Platz. This time he was waved to a halt by a red light wielded by a uniformed soldier. *"Die Grenze ist gesperrt,"* ("The border is closed"), the *Volksarmist* declared, without further explanation.

Clearly, something was up, although in the streets there was no sign of overt activity. Back at his Reuters office, Kellett-Long began typing out a brief report on what he had just encountered. Shortly after 1:00 A.M. the East German ADN ticker tape suddenly burst into life. For the next ten minutes it beat out the text of a fairly long proclamation just issued by the governments of the Warsaw Pact states to the effect that they had been forced by the obstinacy of the Western powers in refusing to sign a peace treaty to introduce "reliable supervision and real control" over the sector boundaries of Berlin. This, as Kellett-Long knew, could mean anything or nothing. What mattered was what followed.

It was not long in coming. At exactly 2:00 A.M. the ADN ticker tape resumed its feverish chatter—this time with the text of an official decree issued by the Council of Ministers of the German Democratic Republic. This communiqué was only one of a whole series that were hammered out from that moment on with no letup.

3

The night watch at the Brandenburg Gate was usually a dull, routine affair. For the six uniformed members of the *Schutzpolizei* ("Schupos" for short), the tour of duty began at 8:00 P.M. and finished twelve hours later. These six men, belonging to West Berlin's "Protection Police," a kind of border-control force, were assisted by three or four Customs officials, who were supposed to check incoming and outgoing vehicles for contraband of all kinds.

Nothing on this evening of August 12 led patrol squad leader Franz Schmulda to suspect that this night shift might differ from the usual. Shortly before 8:00 P.M., he reported for duty at Police Station 28, responsible for the Tiergarten area. Several members of his squad were already waiting for him, and shortly afterward they were joined by Wachtmeister Rudi Schulze and a strapping, twenty-one-year-old athlete named Peter Schröder. Together they were driven to the little wooden shack which served as combination restroom and armory for the members of this particular beat. Equipped with a telephone, a table, a few chairs, and a locker containing six French K-36 carbines (for use in emergencies), it was located just off the recently rebaptized John-Foster-Dulles-Allee—a tree- and park-lined stretch of roadway that ran almost parallel and a little to the north of the mighty West–East axis which the kings of Prussia had laid out several centuries before from the village of Charlottenburg in the West to the Hohenzollern Stadtschloss (city-palace) in the East.

When, in September of 1944 and in anticipation of Hitler's eventual defeat, the city of Berlin had been carved up by Allied planners into three distinct areas of occupation, the Soviets had been granted the right to occupy the eight boroughs of East and Central Berlin. They included the district known as Mitte, the Middle—the traditional nerve center of administration not only for the Prussian monarchs but also for the republicans of Weimar and Hitler's Third Reich. The only major government building left outside of the Soviet sphere of occupation was the monumental Reichstag, a statue-decorated chunk of nineteenth-century masonry erected in the *fin-de-siècle* heyday of the Bismarckian Reich, which was little more than a gutted shell when Soviet soldiers finally hoisted the red flag over its smoking ruins in May of 1945. The Reichstag, along with the Tiergarten area and other boroughs lying to the north and west, became part of the British occupation sector. But everything to the east—including Berlin's proudest thoroughfare, Unter den Linden; the State Opera and Theatre; Frederick the Great's Stadtschloss (or what was left of it); and the Wilhelmstrasse, along which were located the new Reichschancellery, Ribbentrop's Foreign Ministry, Goering's Air Ministry, and Hitler's subterranean *Führerbunker*—fell to the Russians. Most of the Potsdamer Platz ended up likewise in the Soviet sector. So, one kilometer to the north, did the Brandenburg Gate, the sector boundary at this point following the tram tracks in a semicircle through the Hindenburgplatz—the name given to the esplanade to the immediate west of the gate.

Through the powerful lenses of his binoculars, Wachtmeister Rudi Schulze could peer deep into the Soviet sector, as far as the Karl-Marx-Platz. It was here, some twelve hundred yards to the east, that Walter Ulbricht on May Day of 1955 had sat with a soapy smile on his goateed face as his Garrisoned Police, now elevated to the status of a Nationale Volksarmee, had jackbooted their way past the reviewing stand, in brazen defiance of the Four-Power agreements banning the presence of uniformed German soldiers in any part of occupied Berlin.

Into one of his pale blue tunic pockets police Sgt. Peter Schröder had slipped a packet of Western cigarettes, even though he himself was a nonsmoker. They were intended for a Vopo with whom he had struck up a conversation a couple of nights before. His relations with the Vopos—across the tram-track boundary which both sides respected—had generally been cordial. Most of them were, like himself, young Berliners who had been drafted into the KP—a paramilitary force made up of unmarried policemen who were garrisoned in barracks. They carried Tommy guns as well as the regulation pistol with which Schulze, Schröder, and the West Berlin Schupos were armed.

The Vopos seemed eager to talk to their Western counterparts, usually waiting for the opportune moment, after their superiors had finished their spot checks and roared off on their motorcycles or in their chauffeured jeeps. Politics were seldom if ever discussed, by a kind of tacit agreement. Only when the Vopos on duty spoke with the telltale Saxon accent would Schröder and his Western colleagues avoid prolonging the conversation. Natives of Ulbricht's homeland, the Saxons were instinctively distrusted, and not least of all in East Berlin, where their often fanatical loyalty to East Germany's goateed dictator had won them the appellation of "the fifth occupation power."

On this Saturday evening there was a fairly normal flow of traffic through the Brandenburg Gate until midnight, when it began to taper off. Most of the passing cars bore West Berlin license plates. A few Allied military sedans were waved through with a minimum of fuss. The pedestrians used the colonnaded porticos to the left and right of the gate, where their identity cards were subjected to the same perfunctory examination. Brilliantly floodlit from both sides, the gate's six Doric columns looked more like a theater backdrop than a traffic check point, bathed as they were in a kind of luminous aura which seemed to rise to the underbelly of the clouds.

Back in the Schupo shack, police Sgt. Peter Schröder was glad to rest his aching feet and to sip the strong, steaming coffee from the thermos bottle his wife had prepared for him.

At midnight Schröder and his friend Rudi Schulze sallied forth to relieve their buddies, who had been on duty since 10:00 P.M.. Schulze, as the more experienced of the two (he was thirty years old and the father of three children), was supposed to supervise the area closest to the Brandenburg Gate, while Schröder's beat covered the Soviet War Memorial, several hundred yards to the west. Each had a small sentry box equipped with a field telephone directly linked to squad leader Schmulda's Schupo hut.

There being nothing to report from the War Memorial area, Schröder returned to join his friend Schulze and the two Customs officials on duty with him near the corner formed by the John-Foster-Dulles-Allee and the broad asphalt expanse of the Strasse des 17. Juni.

Shortly before one o'clock, large flocks of pedestrians began pouring through the colonnaded porticos of the Brandenburg Gate. Schulze and Schröder went forward to find out what was going on. They were met by entire families, so upset that many were in tears. They were on their way home to West Berlin when their S-Bahn train had stopped at the Friedrichstrasse station, and the platform loudspeakers had told them that this stop would be the last. The traffic between East and West Berlin had been discontinued on both the elevated S-Bahn and the U-Bahn subway, and they would have to make it home as best they could by other means.

Schulze hurried back to his little sentry box to report the news to squad leader Schmulda, who relayed the information to the duty officer at the Tiergarten police headquarters.

More pedestrians emerged from the templelike wings of the Brandenburg Gate. At the Schupo hut Schmulda plied them with questions while telephoning for taxis to take them home.

All brought disturbing tidings from the Soviet sector. Some claimed to have seen columns of tanks in the outskirts of East Berlin; others spoke of large troop movements and of masses of soldiers assembling on the Marx-Engels-Platz. Soviet or East German tanks? Russian soldiers or Volksarmisten? They were unable to say.

In the middle of the hubbub, an S-Bahn employee appeared with even graver news. Although he worked for the East German–directed S-Bahn, his home was in West Berlin. The upper end of the Wilhelmstrasse, just north of Unter den Linden between the Spree and the Clara-Zetkin-Strasse, he reported, was lined with trucks parked bumper to bumper. Many of them were hitched to trailers loaded with tarpaulin-covered guns. Other stranded S-Bahn travelers said they had seen tanks—at least thirty of them stationed on the Wilhelm-strasse, in the empty lot where Hitler's Reichschancellery had once stood. They were Soviet T-34s, they claimed, for their crews spoke a language they couldn't understand. Schmulda transmitted each new report to the Tiergarten duty officer.

The tempo of events seemed to be calming down a bit when, at about a quarter to two, Wachtmeister Rudi Schulze telephoned again from his sentry box to say that he could hear the continuous roar of truck engines coming from somewhere beyond the Brandenburg Gate, although he could see no sign of unusual traffic. Shortly after this report, the six floodlights mounted on two white masts in the Hindenburgplatz suddenly went out. The street lights on Unter den Linden continued to glow dimly, but the Brandenburg Gate was plunged into darkness.

Schulze was too busy trying to make out what was happening beyond the Gate to be startled by this "economy measure," which is what he first thought it to be. He saw a single truck pass between the gate's Doric pillars and advance a short way into the Hindenburgplatz. Out of the truck sprang a dozen men whose gray uniforms and forage caps, so far as Schulze could make out, were those of the East German Betriebsampfgruppen, or factory militia. The twelve men, armed with Tommy guns, posted themselves in front of a traffic lane, a bare ten yards from where Schulze was standing.

They stood there while another squad of Kampfgruppen militiamen came through the central span of the Brandenburg Gate carrying wooden sawhorses and barricades.

Schulze summoned his younger colleague Schröder over from where he was posted, forty yards away, near the Reichstag building. Schröder arrived just in time to see a ghostly line of trucks advancing up Unter den Linden with shaded headlights. With the spectral precision of a slow-motion *danse macabre*, the trucks peeled off to right and left before reaching the Gate.

Schulze darted back to his sentry-box telephone to report what he had seen, while Schröder stood in the middle of the roadway, transfixed by the sight and sound of soldiers unloading their metallic gear. Through the colonnaded porticos on each side of the Brandenburg Gate they came, their hobnailed boots echoing hollowly on the paving stones. Some carried rifles, others machine guns that were quickly mounted on tripods, their neatly aligned muzzles pointed ominously toward him.

Squad leader Schmulda now left his shack for a first-hand look at what was going on. Although he had seen a lot of grim action on the eastern front during World War II, he almost lost his nerve at the sight of those prone riflemen and gunners, who were only waiting for an order to open fire. He and his five Schupos had only their Smith & Wesson revolvers with which to defend themselves—one bullet in the barrel, five in the drum: six shots in all for each of them. They would all be mowed down long before they could reach, let alone load, the carbines kept in the shack's gun locker.

While Schmulda doubled back to the hut to renew contact with Tiergarten police headquarters, his five Schupo squad members watched in mute awe as more East German soldiers poured out onto the Hindenburgplatz. Suddenly they found their tongues. "Say, what's going on?" they shouted. "What the hell are you up to anyway?" But their questions seemed to fall on deaf ears until out of sheer exasperation they found themselves yelling, "Speak up, you bastards!" But the bastards went about their business without a word.

The gray-clad Kampfgruppen had by now disappeared,

leaving the sawhorse barriers behind. These were moved to form two lines of hurdles, perpendicular to the two extremities of the Brandenburg Gate and across the north–south axis of the Ebertstrasse.

A few military trucks drove onto the Hindenburgplatz, where they were unloaded. Out spilled mysterious bundles of wire. Then came long white objects, soon identified as concrete posts. Although squad leader Schmulda only realized it later, these posts were the tarpaulin-covered "artillery pieces" that an excited S-Bahn employee claimed to have seen on the trailer trucks parked bumper to bumper on the Wilhelmstrasse.

At the intersection formed by the Heidelberger- and the Elsenstrasse, where the U.S. sector ended and the Soviet sector began, there at first had been nothing unusual for police Sgt. Paul Erdmann to report. Each time the door of the Heidelberger Krug was opened to admit another thirsty client the loud jukebox music would flood out into the street. Then the silence would return, after a final farewell greeting or an oath proferred by a tottering drunkard homeward bound.

Not all these Saturday-night patrons were from West Berlin by any means. Quite a few were East Berliners who made a regular habit of visiting this noisy, smoke-filled bar. But the news some of them insisted on giving the police sergeant as they now emerged from the Heidelberger Krug was anything but usual—for them at any rate. Treptow Park, they claimed, had been turned into a military camp, with thousands of bivouacking Volksarmee and Russian soldiers. A lot of them had even been seen in military trucks, parked for some reason near the park's S-Bahn station.

Erdmann paid little heed to this Saturday-night-early-Sunday-morning gossip. Next to the huge Soviet War Memorial in the middle of the park was an extensive barracks complex that had long housed elements of Ulbricht's Garrisoned Police. Nor was the forty-six-year-old police sergeant unduly surprised when, some time after midnight, the Vopo patrol on the Elsenstrasse was suddenly doubled from four to eight policemen.

The first to be surprised, a couple of hours later, was his colleague, police Sgt. Joachim Arzleben, who had taken up his post four blocks away on the corner of the Harzer- and the Bouchéstrasse. Two trucks suddenly appeared, driving slowly up the ill-lit Bouchéstrasse toward him. The lead truck halted a bare ten yards from where he was standing, near the invisible demarcation line between the Soviet and U.S. sectors. Out of the truck clambered fifteen helmeted soldiers, whom Arzleben quickly identified as Grepos, brown-uniformed members of the East German Border Police. Moving back to the second truck, the fifteen-man detachment began unloading coils of barbed wire.

Hurrying to the emergency call box on the Harzer Strasse, Arzleben reported the information to Neukölln Police Station 215, then returned to his post. The sector boundary had been drawn in such a way that the houses on the left side of the Bouchéstrasse, as Arzleben looked up it from the Harzer Strasse intersection, were in the Soviet sector, as was the left-hand sidewalk and roadway. The houses on the right side of the street, like the sidewalk in front of them, were in the U.S. sector. The two East German trucks were thus parked on territory assigned to the Soviet sector, and it was onto this territory that the Grepos were unloading their coils of barbed wire. They worked quietly and methodically, paying no attention when Arzleben approached to watch them. He heard them converse in calm, unemotional tones and realized that they were not Berliners. Some of them were Saxons; Others, as far as he could tell, were from Thuringia.

Four blocks away, police Sgt. Paul Erdmann was confronted with a similar spectacle. The Elsenstrasse being an important thoroughfare leading to a bridge across the Spree, it was blocked by about forty Grepos, who dismounted from their trucks with their Tommy guns at the ready and the bayonets on their carbines fixed.

News of their arrival was not long in penetrating the noise- and smoke-filled interior of the Heidelberger Krug. The patrons began trickling out, their weekend jollity abruptly silenced by the unnerving sight of all those helmeted soldiers. The silence then gave way to exclamations of surprise, soon followed by angry insults. The drunks, less inhibited than the rest, even staggered across the Heidelberger Strasse to taunt the Grepos. *"Ihr Penner! Ihr Scheisskerle! Ihr lackierte Affen!"* ("You bums! You shits! You lacquered apes!"), they bawled. "What in God's name are you doing?"

No answer was forthcoming. Stolidly, impassively, the Grepos stood their ground, forming a thorny hedge of bayonets.

Armed with nothing more than a French pistol and exactly six bullets, police Sergeant Erdmann found it difficult to handle the steadily growing crowd now swollen by West Berlin Grenzgänger who wanted to go to work in the Soviet sector. The farther side of the Elsenstrasse was closed to them, as it was to everyone else. Each time the crowd surged forward, the Grepos forced it back across the street with fixed bayonets. The impotent mob then began to take out its frustration against the solitary policeman in its midst. "What are you waiting for?" angry bystanders shouted at him. "Why don't you bring up police reinforcements and teach those Communist bastards a lesson?"

"Just wait till the *Amis* get here!" cried others, in a more hopeful vein.

But the Americans seemed in no hurry to appear.

A mile and a half to the northwest, much the same kind of uproar had now descended on the corner where the Bethaniendamm and the Köpenicker Strasse meet. Originally a canal and an offshoot of the Spree, the Bethaniendamm in the early years of the Hitler regime had been drained, filled with earth, and transformed into a gently curving boulevard graced with trees and bushes. The caprices of international diplomacy had placed its inner, northern rim of buildings in the Soviet sector, while the southern arc of the crescent was included in the U.S. sector. But here, as almost everywhere else, the demarcation line had never been hermetic. The inhabitants of the northern rim could cross to the other side without hindrance, and from the windows of his modest two-room apartment, fifty-year-old Kurt Sedlacek could watch children from both sectors playing hide-and-seek in the bushes, while young lovers strolled along the sandy paths or embraced on the benches.

President John F. Kennedy greets Soviet Premier Nikita Krushchev on June 3, 1961 at the start of their Vienna conference. (Wide World Photos)

Walter Ulbricht at the opening session of the Sixth Communist Party
Congress in East Berlin in January of 1963. (Wide World Photos)

Many of those who took action quickly had little trouble escaping. *Above:* The doors leading to the Bernauer Strasse in the western sector were locked, but for a while one could still use the windows. (German Information Center N.Y.) *Below:* The Lenné-strasse "breakthrough," as filmed on August 13 by Patrick Habans of *Paris-Match*.

On the days following August 13 the East Germans began the job of plastering the cracks in the wall. *Above:* Barbed wire being lowered to prevent underwater escape. *Opposite, top:* Tank traps at the Potzdamer Platz. *Opposite, bottom:* Garden houses in the Klemkestrasse allotment gardens being cleared to create a "no man's land." (German Information Center)

Above and below: Uniformed police supervise the building of the wall. *Opposite:* Bars of barbed wire, soon to be replaced by bricks. (German Information Center)

Above: Armed Grepo, symbol of August 13. *Opposite:* East German
water cannons face British MPs at the Brandenburg Gate. (UPI Photos)

The seal-off proceeds inexorably. Brick replaces barbed wire. Houses become part of the wall. (German Information Center)

The Brandenburg Gate seen through massed barbed wire. A border guard patrols. (German Information Center)

A West Berliner throws a wreath into a cemetery across the wall. (German Information Center)

Vopos on the newly strengthened wall at the Stresemann-strasse. (German Information Center)

Observation tower at the border in Lichtengrad. (German Information Center)

Vice President Johnson at a mass rally at the City Hall, August 19, 1961. *Above:* With Mayor Willy Brandt. *Below:* With General Lucius Clay. (Wide World Photos)

Above: Nearly three years after August of 1961, the East Germans continue to improve the wall's effectiveness. Here, houses used for cover by escaping East Germans are being demolished. *Below:* A more peaceful aspect of the wall. (German Information Center)

Chancellor Konrad Adenauer at Tempelhof airport on August 22, 1961.
With him are Willy Brandt, Deputy Mayor Franz Amrehn (with eye-
glasses) and next to him, Ernst Lemmer, Minister for All-German
Affairs. (Wide World Photos)

The East German hierarchy celebrating the tenth anniversary of the building of the wall, on August 13, 1971. From the left, Erich Mielke, Generals Hoffman and Varennikov, and Paul Verner. (Landesbild-stelle, Berlin)

Saturday nights for Kurt Sedlacek were always something special. A truck driver employed by the West Berlin Sanitation Department, he was a man of relatively simple tastes—like the many workers from the Soviet sector who preferred the sparkling Schultheiss beer they could buy in the pubs of the West. Sometimes, with his friends, Sedlacek would move from one bar to the next—for there was no dearth of bars along the Köpenicker Strasse—and listen as East Berliners sounded off against their masters. The genuine *Schnapsbrüder* ("brandy buddies"), who liked to lace their beer with slugs of hard liquor, would occasionally stick it out until the pubs closed at 4:00 or 5:00 A.M. The Vopos and East German Customs officials would let them stagger home as they had earlier let them pass, without bothering to check their identity cards—their curiosity reserved for citizens carrying suspiciously large parcels or suitcases.

On this particular Saturday Kurt Sedlacek had asked his wife to join him while he made the usual rounds. Sometime after midnight they pushed their way into the Costa Rica, a raucous dive packed with Saturday-night revelers. The normally taciturn Sedlacek was beginning to mellow when he heard someone shout, *"Die Schweine laden Stacheldraht ab!"* ("The swine are unloading barbed wire!").

There was a general push toward the door. A moment later Sedlacek and his wife were outside. In the bright headlight glare of two East German trucks—one blocking the Bethaniendamm, the other the Köpenicker Strasse—a number of brown-uniformed Grepos were playing out coils of concertina wire. Others, armed with carbines, faced the crowd.

To Sedlacek the spectacle seemed unreal, theatrically floodlit as it was by the trucks' intersecting beams. Like actors moving on and off the stage, people kept crossing from one sector to the other, simply skirting the slowly lengthening stretches of barbed wire. The Grepos did not try to stop them. The air was full of insults, to which they paid no attention. Those who had shouted themselves hoarse would stagger back into the Costa Rica, to tank up once more before returning to the attack. The smoky dive was even invaded by a few latecomers from the East, attracted by the early-morning hubbub. Among them Sedlacek recognized a familiar face. "Stick around," his friends advised him. "Don't go back yet. Wait to see what's going to happen. If you go back, you may well regret it. What makes you think this barbed wire isn't here to stay?"

But the East Berliner refused to believe it. He had been crossing from one sector to the other for so long that he couldn't believe things could ever be different. "All right," he said, "and what if they are laying out a lot of barbed wire? That doesn't mean they are going to block these streets indefinitely. They want to discourage border crossers and fugitives." But he wasn't a Grenzgänger, and he wasn't planning to flee. He was quite happy where he was. So he was going back. "You'll see," he insisted, "I'll be back here next week."

Sedlacek and his friends shook their heads, but there was no holding him back. Courageously, if a bit unsteadily, the East Berliner walked away, around the barbed wire and the line of Grepos. Then, with a wave of the hand, he vanished. The clients of the Costa Rica were not to see him again for a long time.

It was about twenty minutes to two when police Sgt. Hans Peters began to realize that tonight was not going to be one more sleepy Sunday morning. He happened to be looking down the Strelitzer Strasse, a singularly unlovely street lined with weather-beaten tenement houses, when half a dozen trucks came roaring toward him with their headlights blazing. About eighty yards away, they halted as suddenly as they had appeared. The tailgates were lowered, and a moment later the street was full of soldiers—helmeted soldiers who seemed to be heavily armed. Separating into two squads of half a dozen men, the soldiers trotted up both sides of the Strelitzer Strasse lugging dark objects that turned out to be machine guns.

Reacting with the instincts of the war veteran that he was, Peters pulled his Smith & Wesson revolver from the holster, slipped a bullet into the barrel, and headed for the cover of a nearby doorway. Peering out from behind the protective stone, he saw the two squads of Communist soldiers squat down and then sprawl out over the sidewalks behind their tripod-mounted machine guns, which were aimed into the French sector.

Two other squads approached, carrying coils of barbed wire. They were flanked by soldiers armed with Tommy guns. Reaching the invisible demarcation line separating the Soviet and French sectors, the squads began to cordon off the street they had just come up.

Only now did Peters realize that no invasion of the French sector was intended. From a nearby telephone booth, he alerted his superiors.

The street-sealing operation had been so smoothly carried out that no one seemed to have been disturbed. No lights flashed on; not a window was opened. The unsuspecting burghers of the Strelitzer Strasse slept on.

Later, as it began to dawn, Peters could finally identify the soldiers posted behind their strands of barbed wire. They were brown-uniformed Grepos, and seemed extraordinarily young. They were also so tight-lipped that not one of them would talk to him.

At West Berlin police headquarters, in one of the long barracklike wings of the Tempelhof air terminal, all had seemed calm when Lt. Hermann Beck had turned up at 4:30 on Saturday afternoon to take charge of the telephonic nerve center connecting Tempelhof with police headquarters in the twelve boroughs of West Berlin.

The first hours passed without special occurrences, as was noted in the police register. A bathing enthusiast had suffered a sudden cramp and drowned in the Wannsee. There were several automobile accidents to record. A drunken motorcyclist whose wild careenings had scared the daylights out of motorists and pedestrians was finally caught by the police and locked up for the night in a station cell. Yes, it was all routine.

Midnight passed, then one o'clock. They were now well into Sunday, August 13, and things seemed to be quieting down. Lieutenant Beck decided that he might as well stretch out for a little nap on the cot in his office.

He had just pulled off his trousers when the telephone

buzzed. He noted the time—1:54 A.M. It was the duty officer calling from Spandau police headquarters. The elevated railway train from East Germany, which should normally have continued toward the center of Berlin on the main east–west S-Bahn line, had stopped at the Staaken station, straddling the western limit of the British sector. The passengers had been ordered out of the cars by loudspeaker instructions and told to reclaim their fares at the ticket window. The empty train had then returned into the Soviet zone. "S-Bahn traffic will be interrupted until further notice," the platform loudspeakers were now periodically repeating.

Beck barely had time to jot down this information before the telephone buzzed again. It was 1:55, he noted. The night duty officer responsible for the French-sector boroughs of Wedding and Reinickendorf was reporting the discontinuance of S-Bahn traffic at the Gesundbrunnen station for both incoming and outgoing trains. This announcement was being made over the station's loudspeakers.

Beck was still recording the second message when a third call indicated the interruption of S-Bahn traffic at the Bornholmer Strasse station, on the intersector border between Wedding and Pankow. He felt singularly stupid, seated in his shorts and frantically jotting down each new message, but he could no longer leave the desk. The three ticker-tape machines in the next room were now chattering wildly, while the telephone buzzed uninterruptedly.

At 2:07 A.M.—exactly thirteen minutes after receiving the first call—Lieutenant Beck was informed by Tiergarten police headquarters that East German trucks full of Vopos had just driven up to the Ebertstrasse—the north–south artery linking the Brandenburg Gate to the Potsdamer Platz. This report was followed almost immediately by a second one from Tiergarten headquarters. Twenty-three East German troop carriers had been sighted assembling on the Pariser Platz behind the Brandenburg Gate. A sizable number of motorcycle troops also had been observed.

There was not a moment to be lost. Beck seized the third telephone reserved for top-priority calls and dialed the home number of Günter Dittmann, who headed the Organisations-Abteilung. A major operation was obviously under way, he reported. He wondered if he shouldn't alert Erich Duensing, head of West Berlin's Schutzpolizei.

"Sure, call Duensing at once," Dittmann answered. "I'll be with you as soon as I can."

One minute later Beck was through to Duensing.

"What's up, Beck?" was Duensing's terse reaction to this middle-of-the-night summons. A former Wehrmacht general, Duensing was a no-nonsense Prussian and something of a martinet. Less than medium height, he made up in temper what he lacked in size.

Beck gave him a quick rundown on the reports now flooding in from all sides. Duensing asked what measures he had taken. Apparently satisfied with what he heard, he told Beck that he would be at police headquarters in half an hour.

At the Tempelhof nerve center, the messages continued to pour in, leaving a bare-legged Hermann Beck barely time to draw his breath. He was relieved to see Dittmann walk in, soon followed by the Schutzpolizei's tight-lipped boss. But so relentless was the pressure of incoming calls that it was another hour before Lieutenant Beck could dash over to the cot and pull on his trousers.

Before the war, the Esplanade, located on the southeastern fringe of the tree-filled Tiergarten, had been one of Berlin's deluxe hotels, the equal in elegance of the better-known Adlon. Like the Adlon, it had come in for its share of Allied bombs. After the war, rather than attempt to rebuild an edifice located precariously close to the Soviet-sector boundary, the owners had preferred to transform the remains of their once-fashionable hostelry into a dance hall. Here, dressed in trailing gowns and ballroom slippers, in black ties and dinner jackets (and even occasionally in tails), West Berlin couples often came to spend an evening, emerging onto the terrace between the fox trots and the waltzes to look at the shrubbery concealing the bleak expanse of what had once been the flowered gardens of Hitler's Reichschancellery.

Undisturbed by the distant strains of music, Hans Redlin had gone to bed in his wing of the Esplanade at a relatively early hour on Saturday evening. His job as janitor really began in daytime, and tomorrow being Sunday, he knew he could sleep late.

But at 2:30 in the morning while it was still dark outside, he was awakened by the insistent barking of his dogs, a German shepherd named Greif and a squat-legged dachshund named Billy. At night they were locked up in a little courtyard, through the railings of which the Potsdamer Platz across the way could be seen. Sometimes when lovers or loiterers ambled past, the two dogs would growl or let out a bark or two. But this time their barking continued unabated, and even seemed to grow in fury.

Groping for his slippers, Redlin got up and shuffled over to the window. The open space below, normally illuminated by two ornamental lampposts, was now harshly floodlit; and in the glare of the projectors, Redlin could make out the shadowy forms of Vopos busily digging up the pavement. Others were unrolling bales of barbed wire and bringing up concrete posts.

Calling to his wife, he told her to get up. "Come over here and look! I think they're sealing off the border!"

Leaving his wife at the window, Redlin pulled on his clothes and made his way downstairs. He had left East Germany in 1958, unable to stand it any longer, but bad as the situation was, he had never thought it would come to this.

Outside, the Potsdamer Platz was full of trucks and soldiers. To the left on the farther side of the Bellevuestrasse, the Grepos, who had taken off their cartridge belts so that they could move more freely, were already sinking concrete posts into the grass- and weed-covered earth of the Tiergarten. Walking up and down in front of them were guards cradling their Tommy guns. East German trucks kept bringing up more posts and bales of barbed wire.

With Redlin on the sidewalk in front of the Esplanade were a number of late-night dancers looking singularly effete in their evening clothes as they watched this most unsabbatical exhibition of hard labor. Their comments were alternately frivolous and critical, and interspersed with labored wisecracks, which often made it sound as though they were watching a second-rate circus performance. But the jibes reached a new, sarcastic pitch when one of the dancers darted across the Bellevuestrasse and tore a small tag from a recently deposited bale of barbed wire. Returning to the sidewalk of the Esplanade, he held up his trophy for his elegant friends to see.

"Look, kids, look at this! Those s.o.b.'s are using barbed wire imported from England!"

Redlin too was granted a privileged peek at the little rectangular tag. There was no doubt about it: On it was printed the name of a British firm.

Not a light was burning in the dark stucco city hall as Franz Amrehn stepped out of the Mercedes police van that Erich Duensing had hastily dispatched to his Dahlem home. The entrance doors were shut and bolted, and only after Amrehn had repeatedly pressed the button did a sullen night watchman finally appear to unlock the door and let him in. Hurrying upstairs to his office, the deputy mayor telephoned several secretaries and switchboard operators, telling them to report immediately for emergency duty. In the absence of Willy Brandt, the calm, affable, articulate lawyer who headed the local Christian Democratic Union was the number one German in West Berlin.

Five minutes later, Amrehn emerged from the lifeless building and told the driver to take him to the Brandenburg Gate, where police president Johannes Stumm was apparently carrying out a front-line inspection. A small crowd of West Berliners were already gathered before the Gate watching the East Germans going about their barricading business, but there was no sign of Stumm; he had already moved on to the Potsdamer Platz, five hundred yards to the south.

The driver turned the police van into the north–south Ebertstrasse. In the gray predawn light they could already recognize the black-clad figures on the left as East German firemen who had been issued black-lacquered Wehrmacht helmets instead of the usual brassy headgear. Strung out along the sidewalk, next to the underbrush and thickets which had been allowed to sprout at random in this bombed-out no man's land, they were hammering at the ground with pneumatic drills.

As they came abreast of the Vossstrasse—the east–west

street on which the proud entrance of Hitler's Reichschancellery had once stood—they were waved down by a Grepo who reminded them that all of the Ebertstrasse's roadway as far as the western curb belonged to the Soviet sector. They would have to turn back.

Turning around, the driver drove the van back a hundred yards, then turned left onto the Lennéstrasse. Cutting across the southeastern end of the Tiergarten, he now approached the Potsdamer Platz via the Bellevuestrasse. They found the sixty-six-year-old Johannes Stumm leaning against a railing that the Grepos had put up along the eastern edge of the Platz to indicate the boundary separating the Soviet sector from the adjacent British and U.S. sectors. With Stumm were a number of West Berlin newsmen and photographers. Beyond the railing was a cordon of gray-overalled Kampfgruppen, armed with Soviet sub-machine guns, posted there to protect the Grepos as they staggered up with eight-foot concrete posts and began levering them into position in the recently drilled holes. Across the square, a seemingly endless line of trucks could be seen slowly moving up the Leipziger Strasse to have their cargoes of white posts and metal bales unloaded. The East Germans were preparing to place most of the Potsdamer Platz off-limits behind a wire-mesh fence, itself protected by concertinas of barbed wire.

The piece of ground on which Amrehn and Stumm were standing was part of the U.S. sector, but no American troops were visible. Several military sedans with U.S. Army personnel inside drove up, crossed the Potsdamer Platz, and disappeared into the Soviet sector, while others—or perhaps the same ones—returned periodically from the East. Their occupants did not bother to dismount, still less remonstrate with the Vopos.

"I wonder what they're up to," said Amrehn.

"I suppose they're driving to Karlshorst to lodge a protest with the Soviet commandant," was Stumm's innocent suggestion.

Little did they realize that they were anticipating events by more than fifty hours.

4

The first of the Western Allies to be alerted were the British,
responsible for the maintenance of law and order in the central
western sectors. They, too, were taken by surprise. Several
Royal Military Police officers had even chosen this evening to
throw a stag party at the British Officers' Club for fifteen West
Berlin police officials from the Tiergarten borough. The atmosphere was so jolly and the whisky so plentiful that a number of
Schutzpolizei officials had trouble making it home when the
party finally broke up between 2:00 and 3:00 A.M. One of the
victims was the police officer in charge of Tiergarten Police
Station 28. He could not be reached when needed—a discovery which threw Erich Duensing into an icy rage.

The officers involved were, fortunately, exceptions. The
British, on this warm Saturday night, continued to patrol the
twenty-mile border between their sector and the Soviet
zone—a largely wooded area interspersed with stretches of
thinly populated farmland. Shortly after midnight, when Corporal Blakey and Lance Corporal Bray of the Royal Military
Police drove up to Check-Point Bravo 3—where the westbound Heerstrasse becomes the main Berlin–Hamburg
Highway 5—neither the patrol they were relieving nor the
Schupos and Customs officials on duty had anything unusual
to report. Proceeding northward in their radio-equipped
Land Rover, the two policemen reconnoitered the sector-
Zone border as far as Check-Point Bravo 8, where the British
sector ends and the French sector begins. Here, too, all was
quiet and uneventful.

Turning around, the two military policemen headed south.
On reaching Check-Point Bravo 5, they were informed by
West Berlin Schupos that the platform lights had been
switched off at the nearby Staaken railway station, and that an
East German who had wanted to return with his son to his
home in the Soviet sector had been told that he could go no

255

farther. The stranded passenger claimed to have seen East German troops and tanks, and even Russian soldiers, near the railway station.

Corporal Blakey used the patrol car's radio-telephone to contact Lt. Col. Richards, head of the Royal Military Police in the British sector. Richards jumped out of bed, dressed, and made it to Staaken at top speed, reaching the check point shortly after 2:00 A.M.. On the East German side of the border, NVA soldiers and Grepos were unloading barbed wire, concrete posts, and horizontal slabs.

Richards used his own radiotelephone to alert the British commandant, Maj. Gen. Rohan Delacombe, and his aide-de-camp at the villa they occupied near the Gatow airfield. The East Germans, he reported, were getting ready to block the Staaken railway line, but as far as he could tell, they were undertaking defensive rather than offensive measures. U.S. military intelligence, which he had contacted, had nothing to report, nor were there any reports of similar action from the eastern limits of the British sector. Since the situation was distinctly odd, he was going to drive to the Brandenburg Gate to see just what the East Germans were up to.

With his blue roof light flashing and his police siren wailing, Richards managed to cover the almost straight, fifteen-mile stretch to the Brandenburg Gate in ten minutes. The sight that greeted his eyes was in striking contrast to the sleepy emptiness of the avenues he had roared up. From trucks drawn up on the Hindenburgplatz, NVA soldiers and Grepos were busy unloading pneumatic drills. Compressors and earth-moving bulldozers were being brought up for what was obviously a major operation. He noted with a feeling of relief that the East Germans were staying carefully on their side of the sector boundary. Had they wished to, they could have rolled straight into the British sector virtually unopposed.

Using his radiotelephone once again, Richards gave the British commandant an on-the-spot description of what was happening at the Brandenburg Gate. What the East Germans were doing did not seem aggressively inspired, but to make sure, he was going to try to enter East Berlin via the Pots-damer Platz to see what was going on in the Soviet sector. If possible, he would report back while touring East Berlin, although he might have to observe radio silence for reasons of security.

He then transmitted the same information to Bernard Ledwidge, the British political adviser, who had just been pulled out of bed in his turn by a call from William Whalley, deputy public safety officer for the British sector. Since it was Ledwidge's duty to inform the Foreign Office in London, he asked Richards to keep in touch, to the extent that it was possible. In the meantime, he was going to get dressed and leave for his office in the British headquarters building, near Adolf Hitler's Olympic Stadium.

At his house in Dahlem, around the corner from American headquarters on Clayallee, George Muller, the deputy U.S. political adviser, had been trying to figure out the meaning of the S-Bahn interruptions. After conferring over the telephone with the deputy head of the U.S. mission's Eastern Affairs section, he decided that the best way to find out would be to send someone over to reconnoiter the Soviet sector. The choice fell on Richard Smyser, a member of the Eastern Affairs staff, and on his colleague Frank Trinka, who happened to be the mission's duty officer that night.

It was still dark when Smyser's Mercedes convertible reached the dimly lit Potzdamer Platz around 3:30 A.M., although not dark enough to conceal the shadowy forms of armed soldiers unloading equipment and stretching out concertinas of barbed wire. Passage across the square itself was already blocked, but Smyser was determined to go through.

"We are members of the Allied occupation forces, which have jurisdiction over all Berlin," he kept repeating to the Vopos and then to the officer who came up to see what all the arguing was about. Finally the officer relented, as much as to say: "We're not interfering with Allied rights, we're just acting to stop the *Schmutzmacher* 'dirty dogs' who have been fouling up everything by their dishonest behavior."

The Vopos were ordered to roll back the barbed wire sufficiently to let the Mercedes go through. Smyser and Trinka spent the next quarter of an hour exploring the streets south and then north of Unter den Linden. Everywhere military convoys were moving up with troops and equipment, while startled onlookers in pajamas and dressing gowns stared down from upstairs windows. Near the sector boundary the equipment being unloaded included steel poles and concrete pedestals. Farther back, nine or ten streets from the boundary, the gaping lots formed by wartime bombardments were slowly filling up with armored personnel carriers, half-tracks, and radio-communication vans.

Smyser next headed for the Friedrichstrasse station. Except for East German trucks, the streets so far had seemed deserted, but here a milling throng of several hundred pedestrians were trying to force their way into the station and up the stairs to the east–west S-Bahn platform past a score of armed Vopos. They were obviously unaware of the fact that all S-Bahn traffic had momentarily been halted. Smyser managed to elbow his way inside the station and halfway up the stairs to the elevated level. But access to the train platforms was solidly barred, even though the Vopos seemed none too happy about pushing back the vociferous and shouting mob. Many women were in tears; others sat despondently on suitcases, not knowing what to do.

Eventually an East German official appeared with a pile of printed leaflets, which he began distributing, while a colleague pasted up another on a bulletin board. It was an official proclamation issued by Karl Maron, the East German minister of the interior. In accordance with a decision taken by the government of the German Democratic Republic, street traffic between West and East Berlin was henceforth being limited to thirteen cocrossing points. Citizens of the DDR wishing to visit West Berlin would need special passes, obtainable from their local Volkspolizei office, while citizens of the DDR who did not actually work in Berlin were requested to refrain from traveling to Berlin until further notice.

An accompanying leaflet, issued by the East German minister of transport, indicated that S-Bahn traffic between West Berlin and suburban localities in the DDR was being suspended. S-Bahn train connections between the eastern and western sectors were being cut, except for the main east–west

line linking the Friedrichstrasse station to the Lehrter Bahnhof in the British sector. At the Friedrichstrasse station,
eastbound passengers would not have to show their papers
and could enter the S-Bahn trains from Platform C. But all
westbound passengers would have to show their passes before
being admitted to Platform B, now the terminus for S-Bahn
traffic across the western sectors of Berlin. Five of the six
underground stations on the north–south S-Bahn line, which
connected the French and U.S. sectors, were being closed
down, including the Unter den Linden and Potsdamer Platz
stops. Only the sixth, at the Friedrichstrasse station, was
being kept open. Similar measures were being introduced to
sever east–west connections for the U-Bahn subway network.

What this meant, in effect, was that henceforth Berlin was
to have two separate systems of subway and elevated-railway
communications. In East as in West Berlin, traffic would operate
on a "pendulum" basis, trains stopping at the last preboundary
destination and then reversing their direction. The only difference—and it was a big one—was that whereas traffic
movements in West Berlin would be confined to the three
western sectors, in East Berlin S-Bahn trains would continue
as before to their terminal stops in the Soviet zone.

Before returning to the parked Mercedes, the two Americans picked up an early morning copy of *Neues Deutschland.*
This, the second, special edition that had been run off the
presses shortly after midnight by a hand-picked skeleton
crew, contained the official text of the declaration made by the
governments of the Warsaw Pact powers.

From the Friedrichstrasse station Smyser and Trinka drove
back across Unter den Linden and down to the Potsdamer
Platz. But this time they could not get through. There were
now two lines of barbed wire instead of one, and there was no
point even trying to argue with the Vopos.

Smyser drove back toward Unter den Linden. Turning left,
he headed for the Brandenburg Gate. The broad expanse of
the Pariser Platz had not been sealed off with barbed wire, but
there were many parked trucks, soldiers, and police around to
keep East Berlin pedestrians from approaching the gate. The
convertible was stopped once again, this time by a Vopo

officer who treated the two Americans to a long harangue about the "peace-loving, Fascist-fighting forces" of the DDR, which, being an independent state, had every right to introduce whatever measures it saw fit to protect and secure its frontiers.

These measures, Smyser and Trinka retorted, did not concern them as members of the Allied occupation forces. Since East Berlin was placed under the jurisdiction of the Soviet occupying power by the terms of the Four-Power agreements, Smyser insisted on seeing a Soviet officer. The Vopo officer declared that this was unnecessary. They, the East Germans, were running this show, and besides, there was a member of the Central Committee in the guardhouse who could decide on their case.

With that he disappeared into the templelike pavillion to the right of the gate. The invisible and possibly nonexistent Central Committee member must have given his subordinate the nod, for the latter returned with a final warning about respecting the sovereignty of the DDR. Their brief lecture completed, the Vopos waved the Mercedes through.

At his headquarters office near the Olympic Stadium, the British political adviser, Bernard Ledwidge, telephoned through to the Foreign Office's resident clerk in London to warn him that something serious was happening in Berlin and that emergency telegrams would soon be on their way.

From the Soviet sector, which he too had entered through the not-quite-sealed-off Potsdamer Platz, Lt. Col. Richards was keeping Ledwidge informed of what was going on. The East Berlin police had tried to tail his military police car several times, but the chauffeur managed to shake them off. Finally, while passing in front of the Ministry of the Interior, on the Mauerstrasse, Richards had noticed someone handing out leaflets. He had the chauffeur park the car around the corner, then went back, stood dutifully in line, and picked up copies of the new traffic-controlling proclamations. These confirmed what he had already reported: that the East Germans were not planning offensive operations.

The first British cabled report went out shortly afterward,

reaching London around 4:00 A.M. Although outpaced by the
wire services, which had been grinding out dispatches for
more than an hour, Ledwidge got the official news to
Whitehall hours before it was to reach the State Department
in Washington.

Not that it much mattered in this mid-August, midholiday,
midelection season. While West Berlin, like so many other
cities, slept, East Berlin was a beehive of activity. For more
than three hours now, Paul Verner's SED headquarters on the
Dimitroffstrasse had been issuing telephonic orders to
Hundertschaft commanders scattered through the eight
boroughs of the Soviet sector. They were to alert their deputies and the factory militiamen assigned to their "hundreds"
and have them gather at given assembly points to be issued
arms and ammunition from the Volkspolizei officers in charge.
Their martial resolution steeled by pep talks and a stirring
Order of the Day from Walter Ulbricht ("Give the jackals one
in the face and they'll crawl howling back to their holes!"), the
Comrade Fighters of the Kampfgruppen were now being
driven up to the "front" in Volkspolizei trucks.

Not all these Comrade Fighters were workers in the strictly
industrial sense. The Ministry of Trade and Supply had contributed its white-collar contingent. So had the Academy of
Sciences. And so, too, had *Neues Deutschland*, from the same
evening shift that had been dismissed a few hours earlier with
the unusual tidings that the day's work was done.

At the Potsdamer Platz they wheeled an old water-cooled
Maxim machine gun into position, as though they were about
to fight it out with the handful of pistol-armed Schupos stationed on the fringes of the Tiergarten. Another Kampfgruppen unit lugged its machine gun to the top of the Brandenburg Gate, setting it up by the right wheel of the
quadriga—as was duly noted by M. Sgt. Franz Schmulda and
his five-man squad when the first light of dawn began to dis-
sipate the darkness at 4:00 A.M.

A number of western journalists had by now reached the
scene. One of them was *Reporter* magazine's George Bailey,

whose article "The Disappearing Satellite" had made such an impression on Jack Kennedy a few months before that Kennedy had asked one of his subordinates to check on the accuracy of its devastating refugee statistics. Bailey had been pulled out of bed at 3:30 by a telephone call from his friend John Daley, of the American Broadcasting Company, who had decided to take his new bride for an evening taxi ride to admire the dark, burned-out shell of the Reichstag and the floodlit splendor of the Brandenburger Tor.

On hand to watch the show when Bailey reached the border, was a sorry-looking group of late revelers and early risers, some cameramen and journalists, a few gray-haired charwomen, two bar girls, and one West Berlin policeman. Some of the women were crying; the others watched in silence. Not far away, looking quite incongruous in his plum-colored dress uniform, was a Volkspolizei captain. A cigarette dangled from one corner of his mouth, and there was a smile on his face as he hammered at the surface of the Ebertstrasse with a pneumatic drill.

The master plan to cut Berlin in two was proceeding on schedule—without a hitch, and without any hindrance from the other side, which had been caught not only napping but in bed.

5

By a coincidence which later struck many Berliners as sure proof of a tipoff, Edward R. Murrow had chosen to spend this Sunday, August 13, in West Berlin. The famous CBS news commentator, whom President Kennedy had picked to head the United States Information Agency, had left Washington a couple of days before on a tour of USIS offices in Europe.

Waiting to meet him at Tempelhof at 10:00 P.M. on Saturday were Albert Hemsing, the press and information officer and acting director of the local USIS office, and Robert Lochner, the bilingual son of a famous prewar American correspondent who had recently been named to head the RIAS radio station.

From the air terminal they drove to the U.S. mission's Wannsee guesthouse, where Murrow was briefed on the latest developments in Berlin and the surrounding Zone. Given the shortness of his projected stay, arrangements had been made to have him meet an East Berlin schoolteacher, who was to come to the U.S. sector on Sunday morning to describe the mood of his compatriots and to explain why so many were now fleeing to the West.

Toward midnight Murrow, complaining of an upset stomach, said he would like to call it a day. Albert Hemsing had already gone home to be available to the U.S. newsmen whom the gathering crisis had attracted to Berlin.

Lochner had not been in bed for more than an hour when he was awakened by the ringing of his telephone. A member of the night monitoring staff at RIAS was calling to say that the East Berlin radio stations had interrupted their night program to broadcast a proclamation, issued by the Warsaw Pact powers, and several East German ministerial decrees, indicating that they had decided to close the borders between East and West Berlin.

This new alarm, Lochner quickly realized, was not a bogus one, as had been the case with two previous alerts that had kept him on tenterhooks for several nights. At the RIAS offices the ticker tapes were already confirming what the monitoring staff had picked up from the radio stations of the East, while Albert Hemsing was being bombarded by U.S. and German newsmen's eyewitness reports of what was happening along the intersector border.

The night program was promptly altered, and arrangements were made to have news flashes broadcast every half hour. The first one had barely gone out over the air when the disc jockey caught himself just in time. The next scheduled recording was to have been a sentimental tune called *"Machen wir's den Schwalben nach"* ("Let Us Imitate the Swallows"). Realizing how sardonic this would sound after the news of border closings, he quick-wittedly picked another, less carefree song.

Robert Lochner meanwhile had been calling various members of his staff, telling them to get over to RIAS in a hurry. He also tried to get through to Allan Lightner, head of the State Department mission in Berlin, but maddeningly there was no answer.

Only after an hour of insistent ringing was Lochner able to get through. A sleep-drugged voice answered at the other end. Worn out by an unusually tiring Saturday, the U.S. mission chief had disconnected the portable telephone by his bedside so as not to be disturbed. Now he listened incredulously to what Lochner had to say.

Press and Information officer Albert Hemsing had been encountering resistance of a different kind. Tied down at home by a ceaseless stream of telephone calls from questioning correspondents, he used a separate line to query the officer on duty at U.S. military headquarters on Clayallee: What could the army people tell him from their own sources of information? After several such calls, he rang the major once again to ask -if General Watson, the U.S. commandant, had been alerted.

"No, sir, not yet," was the matter-of-fact reply, "though we've been debating about whether to wake him up."

"Listen," said Hemsing, trying to keep his cool, "if you don't call the general *immediately*, I will, do you understand?"

Bowled over by such insistence—after all, it was Sunday and not yet 4:00 A.M.—the duty officer said that he would call the general.

At the RIAS station on the Kufsteiner Strasse, the disc jockey continued to select sober songs and melancholy music. Every half hour the music was interrupted for a special news flash. Farther to the West, beyond the Elbe, the radio stations of the Federal Republic continued their programs as scheduled. Their standing instructions called for uninterrupted music from midnight until daybreak.

Outside it was still dark. Most Berliners slept on, their radios turned off, while in West Germany the few night owls who had their sets switched on listened with untroubled contentment to the lullabies of pining sirens and crooning troubadours.

The lights were on in many upper-floor windows when

deputy mayor Amrehn returned from his brief reconnaissance of the sector border. The gray stucco city hall was in a fever; in Willy Brandt's absence no one quite knew what to do.

The three Allied commandants having been alerted—or so it was assumed—by their respective liaison officers, Amrehn got to work on the text of a City Hall communiqué that was to be broadcast over RIAS and Sender Freies Berlin. Brandt's assistant, Heinrich Albertz, was meanwhile trying to contact his boss, while on another line Rudolf Kettlein was calling his press-office chief, Egon Bahr, in Nuremberg.

"How do I get back to Berlin fast?" was Bahr's immediate query.

One of his press-office secretaries consulted a timetable. The first flight, as far as she could see, was from Munich. In offering this information she inadvertently sent Bahr off on a Sunday-morning wild-goose chase. Hiring a taxi, Bahr had himself driven from Nuremberg to the Munich airport, where he was told that there *was* no early-morning airplane to Berlin, and that he had missed the normal Nuremberg–Berlin flight, which would have had him arrive in time for breakfast.

Getting through to Willy Brandt proved more difficult. He and a number of SPD friends were now headed northward on the Munich–Kiel express. Pulling out a Bundesbahn timetable, Albertz tried to figure out where the train might now be—sometime after four o'clock in the morning. The nearest stop, according to his calculations, was Göttingen. The city-hall switchboard operator was instructed to put through a top-priority telephone call to the stationmaster of the old university town. The call went through, but it was too late. The train had just pulled out of the station and was headed for Hanover—one hour and 108 kilometers away.

A telephone call was promptly made to the main dispatcher's office at the Hanover Hauptbahnhof, while another was put through to the Hanover police. They were to intercept Brandt's train and tell him that Ulbricht's Vopos and Volksarmisten were now sealing off the sector boundaries of Berlin.

The two maroon railway coaches that Willy Brandt had

hired for his "whistle-stop" campaign tour of West Germany consisted of a sleeper with the usual number of compartments and a lounge car, which had but two compartments—one for the Socialist Kanzler-Kandidat, the other for his campaign manager, Klaus Schütz. Schütz had thoughtfully brought along a few bottles of whiskey to extend the choice of liquor for those who might have had their fill of Moselle wine or Münchner Löwenbräu, and this welcome addition had undoubtedly contributed to the general euphoria of this train ride.

The last 36 hours had been a bit of an ordeal, even for a seasoned campaigner like Brandt, who had logged 22,000 kilometers and made 503 speeches in the two-month period from May 7 to July 8. There had been no slackening of the pace since then. But this Nuremberg rally had been a great success, and now they could all relax in their shirt sleeves with the feeling of having richly earned the next morning's outing—a cool, hair-ruffling cruise up the Kiel fiord aboard a Baltic steamboat, with plenty of beer and sausages, fried sole, and cream-and-dill-dressed eel to keep them happy while the band thumped, puffed, and tootled their favorite tunes.

In addition to the deceptively youthful Klaus Schütz, the company included Kurt Neubauer, a member of the Berlin House of Representatives and deputy chairman of the local SPD chapter; Brandt's campaign assistant Winfried Starr; and a Social Democratic public-relations man named Klaus Voigdt.

Having retired sometime after midnight, the men were all sleeping soundly when the Munich–Kiel express braked to a stop inside the Hanover main station. A railway official boarded the lounge car to awaken Willy Brandt. Sitting on his bunk, Brandt stared dazedly at the official, who brought him an urgent message from Herr Albertz in Berlin. The Regierende Bürgermeister must give up his trip to Kiel and return posthaste. The East was sealing off the sector borders and had halted S-Bahn and U-Bahn traffic.

Brandt dressed as quickly as he could. He then shook Klaus Schütz awake, telling him to get the others out of bed while he went to call Albertz from the stationmaster's office.

A couple of minutes later a tieless Klaus Schütz entered the second coach and began waking the other members of the party. "Get dressed as fast as you can. We're heading home. The East has closed the border in Berlin!"

There were protesting grunts, followed by oaths and exclamations of hungover dismay. The blinds were fumblingly raised. "Hannover Hauptbahnhof," read the sign. The clock read 5:17. The station looked gray; the people on the platform bustled past as in a dream. The sleeper was not moving. In fact, the two campaign cars had already been uncoupled from the Munich–Kiel express.

While the two maroon cars were shunted off onto a siding, the frustrated holiday makers shaved and dressed. Hot coffee and rolls were waiting for them in the lounge car. Brandt, returning from the stationmaster's office, joined them shortly afterward. He seemed surprisingly composed, with no trace of a hangover. He had just talked to Albertz. In Berlin they had already taken the necessary first steps. Members of the Senat had been summoned to an emergency session in the morning, to be followed by a meeting with the Allied commandants in the Kommandatura building. Albertz and Amrehn had broadcast a message saying that the governing mayor was returning posthaste to Berlin.

Brandt began jotting down things that needed to be done and preparing his first statement for the press. Klaus Schütz was sent out to commandeer taxis to take them to the airfield. The others gave free rein to their fury against Ulbricht. Particularly upset was Kurt Neubauer, who still had his home in East Berlin. After putting in several telephone calls of his own, he returned looking much relieved. "Thank God!" he said. "They're safe." His wife and son had spent the night away from home with friends living at Heiligensee, a truck-garden area on the northern periphery of the French sector.

At the Langenhagen airfield there was a forty-five-minute wait. Brandt led the way into the air-terminal restaurant. Urging his companions to have a hearty breakfast—there was no telling what pressures they might have to endure once they were back in Berlin—he went to the Pan American office to put in another long-distance telephone call to Heinrich Albertz.

He returned a little later, shaking his high-domed head.

"Dreadful! The city on both sides of the border is still asleep. They started in the middle of the night, when almost everybody was in bed. There are still only a handful of people who know what's going on."

Finally their flight number was called over the public-address system. The Pan American airplane they were to board had just flown in from Tempelhof with a full load of refugees and August vacationers. One of them, recognizing Brandt as he walked past, exclaimed, "Ah, here comes our Regierender Bürgermeister," adding with pompous fatuity, "and we, Herr Bürgermeister, are on our way to enjoy our vacations!"

Brandt nodded curtly and walked on without a word.

6

Hans Magdorf was awakened by an insistent rapping on the outer door. Propping himself up on his elbow, he stared at his alarm clock. It was 5:00 A.M. Five o'clock on a Sunday morning! Who would want to wake him at this hour? He did not have to switch on the bedside lamp, for it was already light outside—the gray light of a Nordic dawn. And probably the beginning of another sunless day.

Slipping his feet into his slippers, he padded out of his bedroom into the living room beyond. "Who is it?" he asked when he reached the front door.

"Karl," came the answer.

Magdorf unlocked the door. His friend and neighbor Karl Gunkel was already fully dressed and visibly uneasy.

"They've closed the sector border!" he blurted as Magdorf let him in.

Magdorf had often wondered what had drawn him to befriend this unassuming window-washer for whom he, as a convinced Communist, should have felt nothing but loathing. For Gunkel was that most despicable of creatures—a Grenz-gänger, against whom the radio had been inveighing for

weeks. One of Magdorf's duties at his Lichtenberg bread factory had been to urge stokers and bakers to berate any Grenzgänger they happened to know. But when he came home to
his two-room apartment on the Belforter Strasse and thought
of the even smaller flat Gunkel occupied in the same building,
he just hadn't had the heart to chide him.

Breathlessly Gunkel explained how he had got up at the
crack of dawn to go wash the windows of a primary school in
West Berlin. "I got on my bike and headed for the Leipziger
Strasse, intending to pedal across the Potsdamer Platz into
the American sector. But I couldn't get close to it. At the
intersection of the Leipziger Strasse and the Wilhelmstrasse I
found the street barred by a huge flock of Vopos and Grepos
backed up by trucks and Volksarmisten. The Vopos stopped
me and told me to turn around and go home. Instead, I
pedaled as fast as I could up the Wilhelmstrasse toward Unter
den Linden, where I hoped I could get across. Nothing doing.
The Pariser Platz was chock-full of trucks, with armed men
everywhere. They would have pulled me off my bike and
arrested me on the spot. I wasn't going to risk it. I decided to
come back here. I figured maybe you might have some idea of
what's going on."

But Magdorf knew nothing. The fact that he was a Party
member had cut no ice with the master planners who had
conceived and were now supervising the execution of their
city-splitting operation. He was obviously too small a cog in
the SED machine to have merited the top-secret confidence
accorded to the few.

Going into his kitchenette, Magdorf turned on the radio he
had installed on a cupboard shelf. The Deutschlandsender
was playing Shostakovich's "Storming Youth," sung by a Freie
Deutsche Jugend choir.

Finally there was a fade-out, followed by a special bulletin.
It began with an elaborate preamble. The governments of the
Warsaw Pact powers had long striven to terminate the abnor-
mal situation that had existed since the end of the war against
Germany by signing a general peace treaty. But the Western
powers had shown no interest in such a treaty, preferring
instead to turn West Berlin into a hive of espionage and agita-

tion centers designed to undermine the peace-loving German Democratic Republic. The governments of the Warsaw Pact powers had therefore been obliged to introduce reliable supervision and real control over the sector boundaries of Berlin—it being understood that these measures would not affect the traffic and access routes between West Berlin and West Germany. The announcement ended with a statement to the effect that the need for these new measures would lapse once a peace treaty with Germany was signed.

The martial music now returned. Ten minutes later the Warsaw Pact powers' communiqué was repeated—as it was periodically for the next hour or two. Magdorf turned the radio dial to Sender Freies Berlin and then to RIAS. Both stations confirmed the news of the official seal-off decree.

Slumped in an armchair, Gunkel was a picture of dejection. Magdorf did his best to cheer him up. These were temporary measures, solely aimed at the Grenzgänger, he sought to persuade him. Once they had accepted the idea that they must work in the sector where they lived, thus ceasing to be profiteers, these emergency measures would be scrapped and the Berliners would be free to cross the sector boundaries from East to West and vice versa just as they had been doing for years.

On the side of the Potsdamer Strasse opposite to where he lived, Karl Fabian ran a shop that specialized in leather goods. Because the shop was a mere hundred yards from the Potsdamer Platz, most of his customers were East Berliners, though not all of them by any means were interested in leatherware. Many dropped by to pick up second-hand copies of West German magazines—like the women's monthly *Constanze* or the weekly *Spiegel*—of which he sold hundreds of copies every month. Concealed under jackets or raincoats, this literary contraband was smuggled easily enough into the Soviet sector. "You will see," he had told the man to whom he had sold his shop license a few weeks earlier, "you may not sell much leatherware, but you'll do a brisk business in magazines, that I can guarantee."

Years of service in the Wehrmacht had helped Karl Fabian

to develop a taste for early rising. He even claimed that staying in bed too long was enough to induce a serious headache;
and in a head like his—with its prominent, Boris Karloff forehead—that sounded like a particularly painful experience.

On this particular morning, Karl Fabian rose even earlier
than usual, his slumber disturbed by a disquieting sound.
According to his alarm clock, it was only a quarter to six, when
nothing should have been stirring on a tranquil Sunday morning. Slipping out of bed, he tiptoed to the open window and
leaned out. His ears had not deceived him. Those were hobnailed boots grating on the cobblestones, and now he could
see who were wearing them. Three hundred feet away, a line
of helmeted soldiers in brown uniforms barred the street;
moving in and out between them were men in overalls working on the paving stones with crowbars.

"Lisa," he said, going back to the bed and shaking his wife
awake. "Get up! They're sealing off the border!"

Ten minutes later the two of them were in the street. By the
time they joined the small crowd of West Berliners who were
facing the helmeted soldiers, the paving stones had been
pried loose and the holes enlarged, and the men in overalls
were lifting white concrete posts into the gaping cavities.

The crowd of bystanders was already a noisy one. "You dirty
swine! You slaves! You lackeys of the Russians! You belly-
crawling cowards!" they shouted, as though their insults were
going to induce instant petrifaction. Karl Fabian decided to
reserve his lung power for better things.

Presently, British, American, and French officers began
appearing, sometimes alone, more often accompanied by
West Berlin police officers. They conversed among themselves, then returned to their military vehicles and drove off.
Later, two U.S. Army sedans drove up with what looked like
top brass. There was more head nodding and conversing.
Then they, too, climbed back into their sedans and disappeared.

Once again the crowd was on its own, facing the helmeted
soldiers and the men in overalls. Not a single Allied tank, not
an armored car, not even a patrol, had come up to contest this
flagrant breach of the Four-Power agreements. The Allied

officers had simply driven up and subjected the East Germans to close inspection, as though they were examining a new species of giraffe, or a troop of exotic baboons.

Like the West Berliners next to him, Karl Fabian felt himself slowly burning up inside. All around him he could hear rumblings of discontent. He kept pressing his wife's hand but could find no words of encouragement. "If they're allowed to finish this job," he told her grimly, "then you can take my word for it—nothing, *nothing* will make them reopen it. I know their mentality."

Moving over to the steps of the Esplanade to get a better view of the barricaded Potsdamer Platz, Karl Fabian found himself rubbing shoulders with bystanders who seemed particularly worked up.

"I saw it!" one of them insisted. "I saw it with my own eyes! An English label, I tell you! From a bale of English barbed wire!"

"And they call themselves protecting powers!" another person in the group exclaimed. That still doesn't keep the British from selling them the wire to fence us in!"

"I tell you," Karl Fabian muttered to his wife, "this is a put-up job."

"What do you mean?" she asked.

"I mean, the Allies *knew* this was going to happen. That's why they're not doing a damn thing and won't be doing a damn thing—except maybe going to church to pray for this thing to disappear!"

The bedroom door was opened, then closed.

"You must get up immediately," Krüger heard a voice break into his sleep.

He opened his eyes. No, it wasn't a dream. Kollow the fisherman was standing by his bed. There was a worried look on his face.

"Ulbricht has closed the sector borders. With police, Volksarmee, barbed wire, and tanks. You must leave. There's going to be a war. The Western powers can't take this lying down."

A war? A war? Krüger leaped out of bed. Outside it was

broad daylight—a bright mid-August morning, not unlike those he had known during the prewar summer of 1939.

Still half asleep, he staggered down the stairs and into the living room. Kollow's daughter was seated in front of the radio. Her son had fled to the West some six months before. Her husband, as usual, was somewhere out at sea, fishing.

"What's going to happen?" she asked. "Is there going to be a war? My young one will get caught up in it if there is."

The radio was humming softly, tuned far down. They were listening to Sender Freies Berlin. Several friends crowded in from outside. Kollow had gone out and hauled them out of bed. They were from East Berlin and Saxony. With them was an elderly man from Thuringia.

"So the Spitzbart finally dared do it!" he said. "Now he wants all of Berlin."

They listened to the news. Armored cars at the Brandenburg Gate. Tanks in East Berlin. Infantry units at the sector border. And then—the governing mayor of Berlin, Willy Brandt, was on his way to Berlin in an airplane. He was expected to arrive around eight o'clock. The Senat was due to meet in emergency session.

The listeners sat around the radio in silence. There was a mounting feeling of excitement but also a sense of sinking hope.

"Will the Western powers intervene?"

"If they're going to intervene, then they must do it immediately," said Kollow.

"But the Allied troops haven't yet been placed on the alert."

"They've got to clear the barbed wire away with their tanks. Not a shot will be fired, I tell you. The Volkspolizei haven't been ordered to shoot, that's certain. But if they (the Western Allies) don't do it now, they won't be able to later on."

Kollow was a man of experience. He had fought in two world wars, and he listened regularly to all the news broadcasts he could pick up. He turned the dial to the Deutschlandsender. The room filled with the sound of triumphant march music, the steady thump of Prussian drums and clashing cymbals. There followed greetings and congratulatory messages for the Volksarmee soldiers and police on the sector border.

"Soon the red flags will flutter over all of Germany," exulted the announcer.

Krüger went back upstairs and lay down again. Through the open windows he could hear the voices of radio broadcasters coming from all sides: voices worked up to almost fever pitch, accompanied by nerve-wracking march music. There wasn't a house nearby in which the radio hadn't been switched on. Krüger listened. He could make out RIAS. He could distinguish the Norddeutscher Rundfunk, Sender Freies Berlin, and the voice of the Deutschlandsender announcer boldly proclaiming: "The warmongers and revanchists in Bonn will now have to give up their machinations once and for all." There was the usual stuff about "Hitler-generals, Fascists, Ultras—"

Suddenly it dawned on Krüger that this August 13 was going to mark a decisive turning point in postwar German history. He could no longer think of sleeping. Stripped of its dreamlike veil, the naked truth now stared him in the face. Germany was being split—and this time all the way.

Seated in his car near the U.S. liaison mission's Potsdam house, Lt. Col. David Morgan had had to wait a long time for the Soviet tanks to rumble past. Not until one o'clock in the morning could he finally drive onto Highway 10 and start trailing the last armored column as it headed south and east. They passed through successive villages until, slowing down to a crawl, he saw the last tanks in the column disappear off the road into a wooded bivouac area.

Later, with Col. Ernest von Pawel, who had driven out to Potsdam to join him, Morgan made a second reconnaissance of the area, which was immediately south of Berlin. Both were astonished at the speed and diligence with which Soviet mop-up crews had acted to clean the highway of muddy tank tracks and other telltale marks. In some of the villages through which they drove, cobblestones and bricks had even been carefully put back into position, and only a practiced eye could tell that along this road an entire armored division had moved from its usual garrison into a forest area where it was now almost entirely hidden from view.

Another mission tour soon came in with a similar report—this time about a Soviet mechanized infantry division that had moved into position north of Berlin. Other reports followed, until the pattern became clear.

At 7:30 A.M. Colonel von Pawel repaired in person to the Emergency Operations Center, located in the basement of U.S. headquarters on Clayallee, to report the news to the American commandant, Maj. Gen. Albert Watson. Four Soviet divisions had moved out of their usual garrison areas and Berlin was now surrounded.

7

After picking up fellow cameraman Harry Thoess, Peter Dehmel drove his Volkswagen toward Tempelhof Airfield. The National Broadcasting Company, for which they worked, had decided to feature a major story on East German refugees and had sent David Brinkley to West Berlin to oversee the on-the-spot coverage. The network wanted the film and accompanying script *soonest*.

At 6:00 A.M. there was a rapid fade-out in the music coming over the Volkswagen's little radio as the time signal ushered in the news. A dramatic announcement followed.

Dehmel and Thoess looked at each other in amazement. This was the first inkling they had had of what was happening at the border. There was not a moment to be lost. Tempelhof and the refugees waiting to be loaded onto westbound planes could wait.

Leaving the Volkswagen parked on the Potsdamer Strasse, well within the U.S. sector, Thoess and Dehmel walked the rest of the distance on foot. A long line of Vopos and Grepos in blue and khaki overalls were stretched across the western fringe of the Potsdamer Platz and up the Ebertstrasse tearing up the asphalt and the sidewalk with picks and pneumatic drills. The two photographers began shooting the scene from a distance, then came steadily closer with their movie cameras. The workers paid not the slightest attention.

Continuing to film, Dehmel and Thoess began walking up the Ebertstrasse. The area to the right, both before and after the Vossstrasse, was an extensive wasteland, much of it covered by underbrush and trees. This had once been the heart of the Third Reich, and as such it had come in for a devastating pounding from the sky. Rather than rebuild the eastern side of the Wilhelmstrasse, the East Germans had decided to leave this central area, covering all of four square miles, in its desolate and unreconstructed condition. While the immediate vicinity of Hitler's Führerbunker had been fenced off and placed out of bounds, the rest of this wasteland had been left open to anyone who wanted to roam through its weeds and scrub and into the British sector. This freedom of movement was now being drastically curtailed by the erection of a chicken-wire fence, almost eight hundred yards long.

After reaching the Brandenburg Gate, Dehmel and Thoess retraced their steps, still shooting film as they proceeded. It was almost two hours before they were back at the Potsdamer Platz. In the front row of Western onlookers, and particularly conspicuous because of the dark suit he was wearing in defiance of the August heat, was a thick-set man with a tall, sloping forehead whom Dehmel immediately recognized as the governing mayor of West Berlin.

At Tempelhof, Brandt had come down the ramp of the Pan American airplane looking positively stony-faced. He had shaken hands briefly with police president Johannes Stumm; his City-Hall assistant, Heinrich Albertz; and Deputy Press Officer Kettlein, before speaking a few words into the microphones of a waiting radio team.

The ride to the border was uncomfortable for everyone. His lips grimly pursed, Brandt refused to say a word. They drove up the Mehringdamm, the Hallesches Ufer, and the Linkstrasse, past bombed-out houses and the ruined walls of an old hotel. To the right, behind the skeletal façades of half-destroyed buildings, were railway yards belonging to the Soviet sector.

Getting out of the Mercedes, Brandt walked up to the Vopo workers, who were tearing up the pavement of the Potsdamer Platz with pneumatic drills. *"Hört mal! Was soll das?"* ("Now look here! What's the meaning of this?"), he remonstrated.

But the blue-denimed workers continued to drill, dig, and shovel as though he did not exist.

"Furchtbar!" ("Dreadful!"), muttered Brandt, between his teeth. *"Entsetzlich! Schrecklich!"* ("Atrocious! Terrible!"), he kept repeating. The sight of all these East Germans calmly tearing up the roadway without a single Allied soldier in sight seemed to leave him paralyzed.

After several minutes of speechless watching, Brandt returned to the Mercedes and had the driver take them up to the Brandenburg Gate before going on to the City Hall. During the drive, once again not a word was spoken. It was impossible to know just what was going on in Brandt's mind. Stumm felt most uncomfortable, as did Kettlein. Their normally articulate Bürgermeisgue seemed to have lost his tongue.

From his upstairs office Brandt telephoned his wife, Rut, who was in the small duplex villa they occupied by the lakeside of the Schlachtensee. Satisfied that all was well at home, Brandt asked to be left alone. The door to the Bürgermeister's office was closed and remained shut for a good fifteen minutes, while the members of his staff looked at each other wonderingly.

At 4:45, when the alarm clock had sounded, Ursula Heinemann had dragged herself from bed. After slipping on a blouse and skirt, she had gone into the kitchen and prepared herself a quick breakfast of coffee with a boiled egg and a slice of buttered bread and marmalade. By now it was such a familiar routine that she could do it all in about a quarter of an hour. It was five minutes to the Schöneweide station, and even if she had to wait a few minutes for the next S-Bahn train, she could be reasonably sure of reaching the Savignyplatz by 5:50, in time to start her morning shift as a waitress at the Plaza Hotel at 6:00 A.M.

The sun was rising over the eastern horizon when she reached the Schöneweide station hall. Walking briskly over to the ticket counter, she dropped three ten-pfennig pieces in the metal trough. Beyond the glass partition the ticket collector shook her head and pushed the three coins back at her. She was a fat, unlovely woman whom Ursula had often seen on duty at this early-morning hour. Normally her plump face was expressionless as she took the coins and handed back a ticket. But this time there was a malicious gleam in her eyes as she said, *"Nein! Nein!* Take your pfennigs back! It's all over now with trips to West Berlin!"

Ursula stared at her uncomprehendingly.

"What's come over you today?" she cried in exasperation. "Give me my ticket! I have a train to catch!"

The woman shook her head once more, adding some unintelligible phrase. At that moment Ursula heard the sound of boots on the stairs leading up to the S-Bahn platform. Five black-uniformed Trapos (East German Transport Police) appeared, each armed with a rifle and a fixed bayonet. In a flash the grim truth dawned on her, and she began to panic. They were coming to arrest her, here and now, as a Grenzgänger caught red-handed trying to leave for West Berlin!

Without stopping to retrieve the three coins in the metal trough, she ran across the hall and out of the station as fast as her legs could carry her. She kept running and didn't stop until she was back at the Johannisthal apartment building. She was so out of breath that she could hardly see. She pressed one button, then another, then all of them. What did it matter on a day like this!

Soon startled voices began sounding through the buzzer. "Who is it? What is it?"

"They've closed the border! They've closed the border!" she repeated hysterically, continuing to shout the news after the front door latch had been released. "They've closed the border!" she panted as she hurried up the stairs.

In a moment all the apartment doors were open and the landings and corridors resounded with startled exclamations.

Ursula's stepfather was standing on the threshold to greet her. "They've closed the border!" she repeated once again, brushing breathlessly past him. She had never liked him and made little effort to hide it now.

The stepfather seemed transfixed by the news. "I knew they'd do something!" he muttered.

"Oh, my darling!" said Ursula's mother, coming out of the bedroom and taking her into her arms. She cried. Ursula cried. Everybody seemed to be crying. Outside on the landing an old woman was wringing her hands and wailing. She had a daughter (she'd never mentioned it before) who lived in West Berlin.

"I knew they'd do something!" the stepfather kept muttering in a kind of trance.

The first to pull herself together was Ursula's mother. "Since you're already dressed," she said, "be an angel and go down and get us a liter of milk, would you? The can is in the kitchen in its usual place."

Ursula picked up the can and almost ran down the stairs. She was so worked up that she couldn't walk at a normal pace. Her fear had given way to fury, a kind of pent-up rage she did not know how to express. She wanted to do something, break something—anything!

Her feelings, she soon discovered, were shared by others. The milk shop was already filled with seething housewives, made all the angrier by the appearance of five middle-aged Vopos, who had queued up complacently for their share of milk. They were newcomers from Saxony, recently reassigned to East Berlin and lodged in a nearby housing complex.

Just as Ursula was about to be served, one of the housewives turned on the Vopos. "You shit-faced Saxons!" she exploded. "You're always the first to make life miserable for the people! *Ja*, always the first! You were all for Adolf Hitler, and now you're all for Spitzbart and the Ivans!"

"Shut up!" ordered one of the Vopos, "or you'll see what will happen to you!"

"You dare tell us to shut up—you who don't even know how to speak German properly! Well, take this, you big-mouthed thin oaf!" And with that she heaved the contents of her milk can into the Saxon's face.

In a moment the air was full of flung milk as other housewives followed suit. The outnumbered Vopos fought back, trying to intercept the milk cans and turn their contents on the heavers. Ursula did not hesitate. She heaved the milk in her can at the nearest Vopo. The Vopo let out a curse as Ursula splashed out of the shop and began running homeward.

Back at the apartment she explained a bit shamefacedly what had happened. There were no reproaches. On this Sunday, August 13, the Heinemanns had to drink their coffee black. Lunch was a disaster. Ursula's mother was so nervous that she let the roast burn in the oven. None of them, in any case, felt much like eating as they sat in the living room glued to the radio and the television set.

All were agreed that the Saturday-night housewarming had been a roaring success. There had been plenty of beer and wine, and for hours on end the floor of the Goebenstrasse apartment, in the Schoeneberg district of the U.S. sector, had shaken under the impact of breathless couples rocking and rolling to the rhythmic strains pouring out of the Blaupunkt radio set. It was a young people's party, which is why Willi Schenck's mother had preferred to stay sedately home in the third-floor apartment she occupied on the Zimmerstrasse. Willi's father, too, was absent, for he had to be at work early Sunday morning at the Friedrichstrasse station, where he was a dispatcher for the East-controlled Reichsbahn. But Willi's younger brother Heinz was there to join in the fun with his banjo.

By 5:00 A.M. everyone felt pleasantly exhausted, and the hostess, Willi's wife, Annette, was so worn out that she could hardly stand.

"Go get some sleep," Willi urged her, giving her a kiss. "Heinz and I and the *Skrupellose* here will accompany our friends back to the Potsdamer Platz."

Skrupellose was the nickname of a burly, blond-haired fellow with a taste for hard liquor and barroom brawls whom Willi Schenck had befriended as an adolescent. Although he was only twenty, the "Unscrupulous One" already had his name on the police records of West Berlin.

Born and brought up in the rough-and-tumble Prenzlauer Berg district of East Berlin, Willi had undergone years of

Communist indoctrination, but it had made little impression on his essentially carefree disposition. His parents, who had twice been bombed out during the war, had continued to occupy the cheap apartment they had been lucky enough to find on the central Zimmerstrasse, even though their side of the street was technically part of the Soviet sector. None of the eight other families living in the same apartment house were militantly Communist, and Frau Schenck, like her son Heinz, who had a room on the same floor, did not feel guilt-ridden or threatened because they were Grenzgänger.

Politically they were neutral and, like so many Berliners, only vaguely conscious of the barriers dividing the Soviet from the other sectors of the city. The two boys had even managed to live through the tumultuous upheavals of June 17, 1953, without taking any particularly active part in them. They had simply been enthralled spectators. Standing on a mound of uncleared rubble in the middle of this war-blitzed landscape, they had watched an angry crowd set fire to the wooden Customs shack on the corner of the Friedrichstrasse. One of the demonstrators had severed a fire hose with an ax stolen from a fire engine. The Party's district headquarters on the Mauerstrasse had then been ransacked, and when a witless SED member had tried to reason with the wreckers—women as well as men—they had knocked him down and trampled him to death. All in vain, of course. Order had been brutally restored by Soviet tanks, and a drastic curfew and the "shoot-onsight" proclamation of martial law had kept the Schencks and thousands of other East Berliners at home for a couple of days.

Willi's wife, Annette, on the other hand, was a West Berliner. Because of the difference in civil statutes and marriage laws—in West Berlin one reached majority at the age of twenty-one—she had eloped to the East at eighteen and married Willi Schenck before a local justice of the peace. Her parents had been outraged but had finally relented; and in March 1961 the forgiven son-in-law had agreed to give up his job as a linotypist with a small East German newspaper and to find similar employment in the West. For a month the young couple had shared a rented room until, with the help of Annette's father, they had been able to move into a two-and-a-half-room apartment on the tree-lined Goebenstrasse.

Not all those invited to the housewarming were West Berliners, by any means. Five of them were old school chums of Willi's who still lived over in the East, and there was also a girl from an outlying community in the Soviet zone. It was they whom Willi Schenck, his brother Heinz, and the Skrupellose were going to escort back to the Potsdamer Platz.

The sun was already up, and there was an early-morning freshness to the air when the nine of them poured into the street and made for the nearest bus stop. Shortly after midnight as he left the City-Kino Cinema, where he worked in the projection room, Heinz Schenck had noticed an unusually large number of Vopos gathered in the East Berlin part of the Friedrichstrasse. But he had not given it much thought.

After a short wait the double-decker bus rolled up. They climbed to the upper deck, and since the bus was almost empty, pushed forward and filled the two front rows of seats.

The street up which they traveled on this early Sunday morning seemed almost as empty as the bus they were riding in. But after turning into the Potsdamer Strasse, they noticed an unusual commotion. Several vendors were hawking the early-morning edition of the *Berliner Morgenpost*, and the copies were being ripped from their hands by anxious clients. No wonder. There, in stark black letters on the accompanying billboards, was the news: EXTRA! OSTBERLIN ABGERIEGELT! (Extra! East Berlin sealed off!).

Stumbling down the curving stairwell, the nine astonished housewarmers piled out of the bus at the next stop and bought a copy of the newspaper. They kept passing it back and forth, incredulous, as they walked in the direction of the Potsdamer Platz. Soon it came into view, with its familiar, war-silhouetted landmarks and the electric signboard across which marched the latest news in big luminous letters. Located on the western fringe of the square and aimed toward the East, it was meant to emphasize the freedom attached to the very name of West Berlin. But now, with most of the square obstructed by barbed wire, the news that was being flashed seemed pathetically superfluous.

Joining the throng of bystanders, the nine partygoers

looked on open-mouthed. It was several minutes before any of them could react.

"For God's sake!" cried Willi to his eastern friends. "Don't you realize—this is it? This time they mean business. This is no joking matter. If you cross over now, you'll have trouble getting back."

But the easterners were unconvinced. The most anxious to get back was the girl from the suburban town in the Zone. Her mother was at home, and at a moment like this she just had to be at her side. She couldn't leave her in the lurch.

There was nothing the Schencks could say to make her change her mind. Finally she shook hands with her hosts and friends. Looking distraught and pale but resolute, she pushed through the line of bystanders and walked on through the Grepo check point. The guards did not even bother to check her papers; it was those headed the other way who interested them. Her friends saw her figure shrink as she crossed the broad square, but not once did she turn to wave good-by. At the Leipziger Strasse terminus she boarded the streetcar and disappeared from view.

Willi's school chums soon followed suit. They all had families in East Berlin, and they wouldn't hear of staying in the West.

Only after the last of them had passed through the Grepo check point did Willi suddenly realize that his own parents might also be in trouble.

"*Ach, du Scheisse!*" he cried, gripping his brother Heinz's arm. "Maybe they're blocking the Zimmerstrasse, too!"

Hailing a taxi, they had the driver take them to the Friedrichstrasse. Since the shortest route via the Stresemannstrasse was now blocked by Grepos and barbed wire, the taxi had to make a detour around the Potsdamer Hauptbahnhof marshaling yards and approach the Zimmerstrasse from the south.

People living on the Zimmerstrasse knew that the street marked the boundary between the Soviet and U.S. sectors. But how much of the street belonged to the Russians and how much to the Americans nobody seemed to know, and for years people living on the U.S. side had made a practice of parking their cars along either curb. The Vopos usually made no fuss. For them, as for most Berliners, the invisible demarcation lines were the work of foreign occupants, and to the extent that this blindness was tolerated by their superiors, they preferred to treat them as nonexistent.

Now, however, everything was changed. The streamer-strewn Zimmerstrasse, which only a few hours before had seen youngsters from the Soviet and U.S. sectors joyously intermingling for the Kreuzberg *Kinderfest*, was cut in two by rolls of barbed wire stretched along the northern sidewalk. In front of the barbed wire, pacing up and down in the middle of the street, were the jackbooted guards of East Berlin. A sullen crowd was massed along the southern sidewalk. On the other side of the street, beyond the barbed wire, were the hapless East Berliners. Among them, standing in front of number 86, was Frau Schenck. She was talking to a neighbor, and both women were in tears.

Approaching the barbed wire, Willi and Heinz Schenck began pleading with their mother. Look, it wasn't all that high; all she had to do was step over the loose coils and she would be safely in the West.

"Oh no!" she cried. "I can't, I can't!" Their father hadn't come home yet; she had to wait for his return from his job at the Friedrichstrasse station (a ten-minute walk from where they were standing). Besides, it would mean leaving behind everything they owned. And where were they to live? Father was in poor health, and in West Berlin they would be homeless.

"*Quatsch!*" broke in the Skrupellose, who had been listening in silence to their argument. "I have friends who live in number 12 over here on the western side, and I'm sure they can put you up."

Frau Schenck shook her head in an agony of indecision.

While the young Heinz went on pleading with her, the Skrupellose drew the older Willi to one side. "Look, it's no use arguing with her. What you and Heinz have got to do is simply grab your mother at a moment when the Vopos have their backs turned and lift her over that damned wire. After all, it's only knee-high.

"Now listen," he went on, "I'm going back to get my gun (a
Walther pistol that the Skrupellose claimed to have found one
day in some empty lot), and I'm coming back to help you and
Heinz lug the furniture out of your parents' apartment and
over to the West. And if any of those *Scheisspenner* try to stop
us, they're going to get a bellyful of lead."

Willi Schenck by now was so worked up over the sight of
the Vopos strutting up and down the street that he accepted
the proposal. What the hell! Something had to be done and
fast!

The Skrupellose disappeared through the throngs of sullen
bystanders as Willi came up and whispered into his brother's
ear. They waited until the guards had passed; then, trampling
on the loose strands of barbed wire, they stepped forward,
seized their mother by the arms, and dragged her over the
obstruction to their side of the street.

"Oh, Willi! Heinz! What have you done! What have you
done!" But she made no effort to resist or to go back.

The two sons, who were also in tears—but tears of relief—did
their best to console her. But it was not easy.

"Oh, my poor Ulrich!" she kept repeating. "What is going
to happen to him now?"

The Skrupellose soon came running back with the news that
everything was arranged. His friends had a room for her.

The two sons escorted their weeping mother as far as the
doorway of number 12, where she was welcomed by sympathetic neighbors who took charge of her and began plying her
with drink.

"Mother, just give us the key," said Willi. "We're going to
see what we can rescue from the apartment."

In addition to his Walther pistol, the Skrupellose had managed to coax three knuckle-dusters out of his underworld
friends. Thus armed, the three of them set out on their rescue
operation.

The Grepos had unrolled a second concertina of barbed
wire along the Zimmerstrasse. Fortunately, it was no higher
than the first. Also, as luck would have it, the guards were
now busy reinforcing the obstructions at the key Wilhelmstrasse and Friedrichstrasse intersections, and there was

nobody guarding the stretch of wire opposite number 86.

Stepping boldly over the wire, the Skrupellose and his two companions entered the house and climbed to the third floor, where young Heinz Schenck had a room next to his parents' apartment. They wrapped glassware, pieces of china, framed photographs, candlesticks, silver, and assorted knickknacks in dresses, sheets, and blankets and carried them downstairs and over the wire.

The three of them then went back and emptied the dressers and wardrobes of all the clothes they could carry. They then concentrated on the smaller pieces of furniture, carrying them down the stairs and into the cluttered hallway of a house situated on the other side of the Zimmerstrasse. They were going to move the stuff to number 12 once the apartment-emptying phase of the operation was completed.

In all, they made four expeditions, growing bolder with each trip. Tramping up the stairs for the fifth time, they realized they would have to call it a day. The bed, sofa, wardrobe, dresser, remaining table, and two armchairs were simply too heavy to be handled.

"But I'm damned if we're going to leave all this to those swine!" cried the Skrupellose. "I'll tell you what, let's put a match to this stuff and burn the lot! It will be that much less for those *Scheisspenner* to get their dirty hands on."

Emboldened to the point of recklessness, the two Schenck brothers almost agreed to the wild scheme. But Heinz, who had lived next door, quickly thought better of it. "No, we can't do that. Remember, there are other people living here. If we set fire to this apartment, the whole house might burn down."

"I guess you're right," said the Skrupellose reluctantly. But his face brightened a moment later. "All right, so we can't burn what's left. But what's to keep us from wrecking it—just so those bastards don't get it?"

As though possessed, the three of them went to work smashing everything they could. They overturned the wardrobe, tore its mirrored door from the hinges and shattered the glass. They used a carving knife to rip the mattress, bedstead, and the sofa's upholstery. They broke the back of the armchair, pounded the table's legs into splinters. Kitchen and dresser drawers were emptied and all the crockery smashed.

Their mission of destruction finished, the three wreckers descended toward the street. As they rounded the final landing, they came face to face with a young Vopo officer who was coming up the stairs.

"Hey, scram!" cried the Skrupellose, whipping out his pistol. "Beat it! Make yourself scarce! Get out of here and fast, or we'll knock the stuffing out of you, do you hear?"

The Vopo heard, all right. Pivoting on his heel, he ran down the stairs and disappeared into the street.

When the three of them came out onto the sidewalk, there was no sign of him. He must have run to the next corner in search of reinforcements.

Sure enough, after they had negotiated the barbed wire for the last time and were safely on the southern side again, they saw the officer march back up the Zimmerstrasse with half a dozen Vopos. When they reached the entrance to number 86 the Skrupellose let them have it.

"*Ihr Dreckschweine!*" he bellowed at the top of his lungs.

The Vopo officer turned, recognized the trio, and shook his fist in vain.

It was a good ten minutes before the officer reappeared. He did not seem too pleased by what he had seen upstairs. But to make sure that this piece of "DDR property" was not subjected to further raids, three Vopos were stationed outside number 86.

8

In Bonn Hans Globke, the state secretary in charge of the chancellery office, had been alerted shortly before 6:00 A.M. by a telephone call from the hard-pressed Franz Amrehn in Berlin, followed by another from Ernst Lemmer, federal minister for all-German affairs, who had been campaigning for the

Christian Democratic Union in Baden-Würtemberg.

Although he knew that on weekdays, Adenauer often rose before six to take a cold dip and an early-morning cup of tea, Globke was reluctant to interrupt the old man's Sunday rest too soon. The chancellor, recently returned from his two-week holiday in Italy, had spent a tiring Friday and Saturday delivering campaign speeches, and Globke felt that he deserved another hour of sleep before having to face this latest crisis.

Shortly before seven, Globke telephoned to Adenauer's Rhöndorf villa, several miles upstream on the eastern bank of the Rhine. Never one to waste words, *der Alte* told him to report at nine o'clock with Horst Osterheld, head of the chancellery's foreign affairs section.

The two men reached the little garden gate a few minutes before nine. The quaint Rhenish village, with its Grimm's fairy-tale houses and its frescoed inns, seemed silent and asleep, although some of its devout inhabitants had already attended early-morning mass in the little steepled church. More than seventy stone steps led up to the chancellor's hillside villa, zigzagging between rock-garden beds of fragrant roses—rare species varying in hue from soft yellow to pale scarlet. In the late 1930s, when he could devote time to gardening, having been forced into retirement as lord mayor of Cologne by Hitler and his brown-shirted Nazis, Adenauer himself had carried the stones for many of these terraced beds up the winding path. Even now, at the age of eighty-five, he would hold long discussions with his gardener about the tending of his quince, apricot, and walnut trees or his Japanese Pavlovnia, or debate the proper placing of a cherub-decorated fountain brought back from Italy.

Dominated by the legendary Dragon Cliff of the Siebengebirge, with a broad living-room window looking south toward the undulating Eifel Mountains, this slate-roofed house was Konrad Adenauer's personal retreat, whose privacy he defended as zealously as the river barons of the past had defended their hill-perched castles. To be admitted to this sanctum was a rare privilege indeed.

During the long talk they had had three days before at

Cadenabbia, Adenauer had told Dean Rusk that the most effective Western response to a new Soviet threat to West
Berlin would be a total embargo on trade with the countries of
the Eastern bloc. But a full-scale trade embargo, to be effective, had to be undertaken by all the NATO countries, and
that was bound to take time. In the nature of things, it was a
long-term countermeasure, whereas this new challenge was
immediate. Besides, the access routes to West Berlin were
not yet directly menaced, and the communiqué issued by the
Warsaw Pact powers had even contained an assurance that
they would not be affected.

The immediate question, therefore, was what the chancellor himself should do. Should he or should he not leave immediately for Berlin? At eleven o'clock, when Sen. Thomas
Dodd of Connecticut turned up at the Rhöndorf villa for a
meeting which Globke had hastily arranged, Adenauer was
still undecided. The senator, as ardently anti-Communist as
the chancellor, was planning to fly to Berlin. But Adenauer
could not bring himself to go with him. His presence in West
Berlin at this moment would merely exacerbate the crisis; it
would be interpreted as a signal of encouragement to the restive East Berlin inhabitants, who might well rise in spontaneous revolt against the Ulbricht regime, as they had done in
June 1953. This was one thing he wanted to avoid, since it
could easily lead to a blood-bath.

For the time being, the chancellor was not moving from the
Rhine. He wanted to discuss the situation with his foreign
minister, Heinrich von Brentano, and with the ambassadors of
the Allied powers. Any unilateral action on his part might be
misinterpreted and severely judged, since the Federal government's jurisdiction did not officially extend to West Berlin.
The Federal government could only act after consultation and
agreement with the Allies. The West must maintain a very
firm stand against this Communist action, while at the same
time acting with circumspection.

Neither Globke nor Osterheld could prevail on the chancellor to change his mind after the U.S. senator had left. Nor was
Adenauer's old friend, Heinrich Kron, the parliamentary
leader of the CDU, destined to be more successful when the

discussions were resumed in the afternoon. Adenauer was not going to Berlin—not now at any rate.

By 7:00 A.M. there was not an intersector crossing point in all Berlin that was not the scene of angry confrontations. One of the most tumultuous was the Bornholmer Strasse, connecting the Prenzlauer Berg and Pankow districts of East Berlin with the equally proletarian Wedding borough in the French sector. When Lothar Böhm, a young East Berliner who was an active supporter of Willy Brandt's Social Democratic party, drove up in a car, he found the metallic bridge spanning the S-Bahn tracks blocked by barbed wire and sixteen tough-looking factory militiamen, commanded by Vopo officers. Four of the militiamen faced the jeering crowd to the west; the remaining twelve had their weapons trained on the even bigger and angrier crowd to the east.

The younger and more impetuous of the demonstrators began pelting the Kampfgrüppen militiamen with stones. The militiamen riposted with tear-gas grenades, which had people crying and coughing long after the acrid, suffocating smoke clouds had drifted away. While many East Berliners retreated, others hastily covered the smoke bombs with paper bags and began tossing them back. Coughing and weeping in their turn, some of the militiamen actually dropped their Tommy guns and sought momentary refuge on the western side of the borderline—to the dismay of their officers, who had difficulty summoning them back.

On the Behmstrasse, running under the Gesundbrunnen S-Bahn tracks, the violence was such that East Berlin fire engines had to be brought in to disperse the rioters. But the firemen, not relishing this unpopular assignment, aimed their arching jets of water over the demonstrators' heads.

Not until eight o'clock, when a convoy of Vopo reinforcements rolled up, could the border guards begin to gain the upper hand. Now anyone daring to shout an insult or refusing to obey an order was seized, pushed into a truck, and taken to the nearest police station. The Vopos were assisted by civilians with red brassards on their sleeves—reliable Party members who had been alerted during the night and granted auxiliary police powers.

Near the Bornholmer Strasse a baker who had risen early to prepare cakes for young East Berliners who were to take part in a Free German Youth initiation ceremony went to the threshold of his shop in his undershirt and slippers. Unable to contain himself, he shouted that all this police violence was a *Schweinerei* ("swinish thing"). He was denounced by two red-brassarded informers and dragged away by Vopos, while the cakes intended for the FDJ novitiates burned to charcoal in the ovens.

A resolute old woman who brought her full market bag down on a soldier's helmet so hard that his knees buckled was likewise seized and dragged away. The same fate overtook a fourteen-year-old boy who, when informed that he would not be permitted to travel to West Berlin to visit his grandmother for her eighty-fifth birthday, called a Vopo officer a *Rindvieh*. The "dumb ox" had him struck and pushed with rifle butts toward a waiting police truck.

While sound trucks with loudspeakers toured the streets calling on the populace to remain calm—the measures being undertaken were for their own good—Lothar Böhm gradually gathered the impression that much of the commotion was being fomented by Party agitators bent on having potential trouble makers arrested before they could work up crowds to riot pitch. He was soon to discover that he was mistaken in only one respect. Many of these agitators were members of Erich Mielke's SSD. At 9:45 his turn came. He had thrown no stones or bottles, he had not shouted a single insult, but the mere fact that he was an active East Berlin member of Willy Brandt's SPD was enough to brand him a spy. The plainclothesmen who arrested him had, in fact, been shadowing him for hours. He ended up in an overcrowded SSD cell not far from the Alexanderplatz.

Equally unfortunate was Erich Lowitz, a fifty-two-year-old cabinetmaker who had developed a hatred for things Soviet after six years as a prisoner of war in Russia. Although he had actively participated in the antiregime revolt of June 17, 1953, he had continued to work in a Prenzlauer Berg furniture factory and to live in East Berlin. The sight of NVA soldiers pushing back the crowds with bayonets while Soviet-made T-34 tanks pointed their gun barrels at Walter Ulbricht's own subjects was more than he could take. Just three blocks from his home, he ran into a platoon of helmeted soldiers marching ponderously toward the border.

"You filthy swine!" shouted the former Wehrmacht trooper. "Now it's us you don't hesitate to shoot!"

He was seized by the platoon sergeant and two of his men. With a sub-machine gun pointed at his ribs, Lowitz was ordered to march along with them. Shortly afterward, a Volkspolizei patrol car was flagged down, and he was turned over to the custody of the East Berlin police.

At about the same time, Col. John R. Deane, commanding the U.S. Army's Second Battle Group, drove back down the Friedrichstrasse after completing a second reconnaissance of the Soviet sector. His main concern had been to ascertain how many tanks were now in action and just who—NVA or Soviet crews—were manning them.

"What are you going to do?" he was asked by an Associated Press reporter.

"I'm going to church with my wife."

"What, today?" exclaimed the flabbergasted newsman.

"I go to church every Sunday," was the pious officer's reply.

Service on the east–west S-Bahn line had been resumed some time after dawn, but at the key Friedrichstrasse station, a hastily constructed partition now cut the central platform in two. Passengers coming in from the East and discovering to their surprise that the through line was now a terminus could gain access to the westbound platform beyond the partition only by producing the necessary passes, which few of them had. There were no problems as yet for West Berliners, as twenty-year-old Klaus Haetzel of the *Telegraf* newspaper discovered when he rode into the station on a train he had boarded in the U.S. sector shortly after seven in the morning. The station was teeming with guards of every kind, as well as hundreds of thwarted fugitives who had not heard the morning news on the radio. At the foot of the stairs leading to the upper platforms, a line of black-uniformed Trapos, their arms linked and their booted legs apart in a stance reminiscent of Himmler's SS, barred the way.

Outside the station other guards blocked access to the two entrances leading to the north–south U-Bahn line. Since this subway line began at a northeastern terminus in the French sector and ended at the Alt-Mariendorf terminus on the southern fringe of the U.S. sector, Ulbricht and his city splitters had decided to let its trains run unhindered through the six central stations situated in East Berlin. The entrances to five of them were now closed, while access to the sixth, at the Friedrichstrasse, was denied to those who did not have the proper papers.

"Traitors! Russian lackeys!" cried the furious mob as the unhappy-looking Vopos barred the way. Haetzel was surprised to see the West German novelist Günter Grass leaning on the guardrail in his shirt sleeves. With his drooping, almost Stalinesque moustache, he looked more than usually saturnine. For half an hour journalist and novelist stood side by side watching the pathetic scene. Only once during that period did the Vopos agree to break ranks—when a squat grandmother of about sixty-five forced her way resolutely forward and told one of the guards that they would have to let the two small boys accompanying her return to their parents in West Berlin. But not until she had raised her voice and actually seized him by the lapels of his pale green jacket was the startled Vopo willing to relent.

If there was less turmoil at the Potsdamer Platz, two S-Bahn stations farther south, it was simply because the seal-off measures there were even more stringent. Berliners trying to approach the square from the east found the Leipziger Strasse completely blocked by barbed wire and tanks. Here, too, there were heated arguments and jeers. Every now and then the crowd would lapse into grim silence as a wire-encrusted sawhorse barrier was moved back to let FDJ girls in blue blouses and black skirts come forward with bouquets of summer flowers. The Free German Youth of Ulbricht's DDR was paying official homage to their heroic tankmen and defenders.

What Karl Gunkel had already discovered at five o'clock in the morning was now everywhere the case. Finding the broad Chausseestrasse crossing point into the French Wedding district too well guarded, the East Berlin journalist Karl-Heinz Wendland decided to try his luck farther south. Boarding the S-Bahn at the Friedrichstrasse station—which he was allowed to do since he was headed east rather than west—he got off seven stops later at the same Schoeneweide station where Ursula Heinemann had been so disagreeably upset a few hours before. Heading west on foot through park grounds and small garden plots, the journalist soon reached the Teltow canal. There was not a Vopo or an NVA guard in sight, and he had no trouble swimming across the eighty-meter stretch. There were still holes in Walter Ulbricht's net, but they were steadily shrinking.

Another who managed to escape—through the very center of the net—was Kurt Kasischke. This tall, gaunt, fifty-year-old Wehrmacht veteran was on a Sunday- morning stroll when a neighbor told him what was happening along the intersector border. He returned immediately to his one-room flat, not far from the bomb-scarred cathedral and the Marx-Engels-Platz, and picked up his meager savings—exactly three hundred East marks. He was prepared to lose his tiny apartment in the East but not his job as a night watchman in West Berlin.

He now made for Unter den Linden, an area he knew well. For three years, between 1938 and 1940, he had paraded up and down this world-famous avenue as a member of the crack Wachbataillon Berlin. Many were the times when he had had to stand rigid guard at the entrance to the Neue Wache mausoleum, situated between the Prussian Finance Ministry and the Zeughaus War Museum.

As Kasischke approached his old guardsman's stamping ground, he saw that the former Zeughaus Armory—since transformed into a museum of contemporary history—was now guarded by proletarian sentries decked out in gray forage caps and overalls. He quickened his pace. But on reaching the corner of the Friedrichstrasse, a good quarter of a mile from the Brandenburg Gate, he was stopped by a police cordon and could go no farther.

Turning north toward the Friedrichstrasse station, Kasischke managed to walk up several side streets running more or less parallel to Unter den Linden until he found himself on the northeastern edge of the Pariser Platz, in full view of the Reichstag building to the right and the Brandenburg Gate to the left. Straight ahead less than two hundred yards away was the Schutzpolizei shack, where squad leader Franz Schmulda had had such a hectic time of it in the wee hours of the morning.

The Pariser Platz was now crammed with military trucks, buses, command cars, armored troop carriers, and helmeted soldiers, some of whom had been accosted by East Berlin civilians. Cars, most of them with West Berlin or Allied license plates, were still passing through the extreme right-hand arch of the Brandenburg Gate. Beyond, a gap had deliberately been left between the sawhorse barriers and the stake-mounted strands of wire that had been loosely strung out near the demarcation line.

Making a diagonal approach, Kasischke was stopped by a strapping Vopo who told him to move back into the Pariser Platz, east of the Gate. Although a bachelor, Kasischke told the Vopo that he had come forward to see if his wife was on her way back from a short errand into West Berlin. He was expecting her at any moment.

Perhaps emboldened by his example, another group of East Berliners now approached the demarcation line. Leaving Kasischke for a moment, the Vopo marched impatiently toward them. Kasischke did not hesitate. Walking forward as unconcernedly as he could, he passed beyond the loose-strung wire into the British sector. He could hardly believe his luck. With three hundred East marks—now worth less than sixty West marks—he was anything but rich. Gone was his one-room flat. But not his job as a night watchman. The Marienfelde camp, to which a kindly West Berliner was soon driving him in his automobile, would take care of the rest.

When it came to crossing to the other side the frontier guards were in a privileged position. One such escape—so discreet that it hardly merits that appellation—was personally witnessed by Joachim Lipschitz, the West Berlin senator of the interior. At a Bernauer Strasse crossing point, he overheard this curious exchange. A young Vopo in his early twenties was questioning a West Berlin Schupo. "Is it true that you guys get a so-called head bonus for every East Berliner you talk into switching over to West Berlin?"

"Listen," replied the Schupo, "the dough I'd get from your coming over to our side wouldn't be enough for me to buy myself a box of matches."

The Vopo needed no further persuading. Soon afterward in a nearby bar he was being treated to a round of "Liberation schnapps" by West Berlin's senator of the interior.

Less discreet was the escape made not far from this same spot by a Grenzpolizei sergeant, who had been given the job of barb-wiring the Swinemünder Strasse, a street now angrily alive and swarming with protesters. Forced back against the barrier they had strung up a few hours before, the Grepo sergeant and his four men would have succumbed to the sheer weight of numbers had Volkspolizei reinforcements not suddenly appeared and begun to push back the crowd with rubber truncheons and rifle butts. The insults and exhortations now turned into roars of wounded rage.

The sergeant lit a cigarette to steady his nerves. But it was no good. He was sickened by the sight of Vopos using their rifle butts on unarmed civilians who were simply protesting the severing of their own street.

Lighting a second cigarette and then a third—partly to calm his nerves and partly to allay the suspicions of his fellow Grepos—the sergeant slowly approached the strands of barbed wire. He was not afraid of being shot by his colleagues, for they were under strict orders not to aim their weapons at the western sectors. They could shoot at a fugitive only if he was standing far enough inside the border so that a stray bullet could not accidentally kill someone in the West. Besides, he knew it would take time for them to unlock their safety catches.

Ten yards from the barbed wire the sergeant began running. A moment later he was in the air. His boots cleared the wire, but in his breathless concentration on the obstacle he lost his grip on his submachine gun, which clattered noisily to the ground. He was greeted with cheers on the western side and immediately taken into custody by friendly Schupos.

Not far away, three East Berliners who had heard that the Vopos guarding the Ackerstrasse had not been issued live ammunition for their submachine guns decided to make a dash for it in a West Berlin Volkswagen. The car came roaring down the street, scattering the startled Vopos and ripping away the flimsy barbed-wire barricade.

Sometime after ten o'clock, Walter Ulbricht left the SED headquarters building, where he and many of his Politburo colleagues had spent a sleepless night. The Western Allies were not moving. Not a tank, not an armored car, not even an infantry platoon had been sent up to the intersector border to remove the sawhorse barricades or the concertinas of barbed wire. The Allies had not lifted a finger to prevent his engineers from blocking the S-Bahn tracks at the peripheral border stations. They had not tried to stop them from blocking the S-Bahn tracks on the Treptow Park bridge and the U-Bahn tracks on the Oberbaumbrücke spanning the Spree. They had not even protested the closing down of seventy-five of the city's eighty-eight intersector crossing points. The "jackals," as he had predicted, were lying low.

In East Berlin, Erich Mielke's agents, Karl Maron's Vopos, Walter Borning's Kampfgruppen, Erich Peter's Grepos, Paul Verner's red-brassarded assistant commissars, and the carefully selected NVA units had the situation under control. Concentrated at key points, Horst Stechbarth's tankmen were ready to crush the slightest manifestation of revolt.

Climbing into a shiny black Zis limousine, which took a discreet sixth or seventh place in a convoy of twelve cars—he was not one to take risks when traveling—Walter Ulbricht had himself driven north to the Rosenthaler Platz and from there on toward his Niederschönhausen Schloss in Pankow. Khrushchev in Moscow, Koniev at Wünsdorf, Pervukhin at the Soviet embassy on Unter den Linden could go to bed. The DDR was proving to the skeptics that it was a strong Socialist state fully capable of handling its own problems. Nine hours had passed and he had won the first round.

9

It was close to ten o'clock when the three Western commandants and their staffs finally gathered at the Allied Kommandatura building on the Correnplatz, in the suburban Dahlem area of the U.S. sector, to decide on what immediate steps should be taken.

The meeting was devoted mostly to deciding what couldn't be done. The U.S. commandant, Maj. Gen. Albert Watson, who occupied the chair by virtue of an automatic system of monthly rotation, had nothing to suggest. He was a relative newcomer who had been posted to Berlin the previous May after having made his way up the military ladder as a field artillery officer. The fact that he had exactly six 105-millimeter howitzers at his disposal, in addition to 27 tanks (less than one for every mile of sector boundary he had to cover) did not put him in a mood for military adventurism.

The same was true of the British commandant, Maj. Gen. Rohan Delacombe, a chubby-cheeked Sandhurst officer (known as "Jumbo" to his friends) whose past encounters with the enemy—in Norway, Italy, and France—had left him with no taste for a kamikaze operation. With three thousand men at his command, a handful of tanks, and not even one artillery piece, he was not prepared to do battle with the thousands of tanks and guns that the Russians could mass against them.

The doyen of the three in terms of Berlin service, Gen. Jean Lacomme, was in much the same position. Although he nominally commanded a pitifully small force of two thousand five hundred men, he had to gain advance clearance from Paris for any action or utterance of importance. He was also handicapped on this fateful Sunday morning by the absence of his deputy and chief diplomatic aide, Count Bernard Guillier de Chalvron. Feeling himself entitled to a well-earned respite,

Chalvron had left two days before with his family on a fifteen day vacation.

The only person present who dared recommend bold action was the U.S. deputy political adviser, the short, dark-haired, Vienna-born George Muller. He had recently filed a report entitled *Treffpunkt Berlin* ("Meeting Place Berlin") to combat the capitulationist mood of those in Washington who had written off East Berlin as irretrievably lost. The gist of his argument was that although the Soviets had set up a separate administration in their part of the city, they had left many strands of metropolitan existence more or less intact. Freedom of movement for border crossers and others was one example. The elevated S-Bahn continued to function between the four sectors and the surrounding Soviet zone. Direct telephone communications had been cut in 1952—to call someone in East Berlin, one had to telephone via Copenhagen—but the gas, electricity, and sewage networks had been largely unaffected. Although the Four-Power agreements had been repeatedly violated, the Soviets had respected Berlin's special status to the point of allowing the West German SPD to maintain offices in East Berlin—a privilege not enjoyed by Socialists in the Soviet zone, who had been forcibly pressured into a shotgun merger with the Communist-dominated SED. In return, of course, the Western Allies and the City Hall authorities had been forced to grant the same privileges to Ulbricht's SED in West Berlin. This situation exemplified Berlin's exceptional status and magnetism—as did events like the annual industrial fair; the "Green Week" exhibition of agricultural machinery; and the recently condemned Kirchentag, which drew thousands of East German visitors to West Berlin.

Although it was not yet clear just how permanent the latest East German measures were going to be (there had been previous traffic interruptions, notably during the East German currency reform of 1957) Muller felt that the Western Allies had to react vigorously and imaginatively to this new assault on Berlin's residual unity. Since the Soviets and the East Germans had been depicting Berlin as the powder keg of a possible new war, it was logical to demand the immediate convening of a Four-Power conference in Berlin. Nothing would be more embarrassing to the Russians than those blocked streets and avenues if the city had to accommodate a major diplomatic conference with alternating sessions in its eastern and western halves.

This diplomatic move, however, had to be backed up by military action; otherwise, the Soviets would have every reason to brush the proposal aside as a meaningless diversion. Allied tanks should therefore be brought up to the intersector boundary to crush the sawhorse barriers and the concertinas of barbed wire under their caterpillar treads. Or, if that was too risky, Allied foot soldiers properly equipped with leather gloves and clippers and supported from behind by tanks and armored cars should be sent forward to remove the barbed wire from selected crossing points.

These military proposals were ruled out on the grounds that they would be both risky and ineffective. Even if they did not lead to head-on confrontations with East German tanks, there would be no way of preventing the East Germans from laying out a new line of barbed wire and sawhorse obstacles one hundred or two hundred yards farther back, well within the Soviet sector. To penetrate that deeply into Soviet territory would be inviting trouble. The troops sent in might even be cut off and arrested for "provocative acts" and "peace-disturbing misbehavior." Any tanks sent to their rescue would be just as vulnerable, for over and against every Allied tank sent over the sector border, the Russians and East Germans could mass fifty or a hundred.

After an hour's discussion, Willy Brandt was ushered into the commandants' conference room along with his deputy, Franz Amrehn. Brandt, whose previous encounters with the Allied commandants had been held informally in his City Hall office or in one of their private homes, had never before set foot in this mahogany-paneled chamber. He was startled to see the portrait of a Soviet general hanging on the wall. Gen. Alexander Kotikov had been the Soviet commandant in 1948, when Stalin had put an end to the periodic meetings of the Four-Power Kommandatura by ordering his military representative in Berlin to boycott future meetings. The general's portrait had been allowed to hang there in the hope that the Russians might one day be lured back and to sustain the official validity of Berlin's Four-Power status.

Although there was no Russian present now, this was a most uncomfortable moment for those who were. Only two weeks before, Brandt had been telling people that West Berlin was an indispensable safety valve for the inhabitants of East Berlin, and that the authorities of the DDR would not dare block it for fear of a popular explosion. Now they were doing just that. The Allied commandants, like everyone else in the West, had been taken by surprise; but at least they had been on hand, whereas he had had to be dragged off the Munich–Kiel express and rushed back to Berlin by airplane. The situation called for bold and imaginative action, which none of the commandants were empowered to undertake. At best they were agents, at worst the pawns of slow bureaucratic mechanisms that they could do no more than jostle. Maj. Gen. Albert Watson had neither the prestige nor the four stars nor the political acumen that had enabled Gen. Lucius Clay to stand up to the war-weary Russians in 1948 and 1949. Although he was the U.S. commandant in West Berlin, he was subordinate militarily to the commander of the U.S. Army in Europe and politically to the State Department.

Maj. Gen. Rohan Delacombe was in much the same position and committed, in any case, to the standard Whitehall policy of not rocking the boat. As for the French commandant, Gen. Jean Lacomme, with the best will in the world he could do little. His every word and gesture first had to be cleared with the Quai d'Orsay, and in practice that meant with Foreign Minister Maurice Couve de Murville. The three years Couve had spent in Bonn as French ambassador had apparently convinced him that he knew all that was worth knowing about Germany and Berlin. "Don't get upset," he had reassured François Seydoux, who had succeeded him as French ambassador in Bonn after Khrushchev had issued his first Berlin ultimatum of November 1958. "All this will blow over. Nothing will happen." For Lacomme, who was holding the fort in isolated West Berlin, this complacency was a shade too Olympian.

No less troubling for Lacomme was the French foreign minister's condescending attitude toward Willy Brandt, who had
made a special effort to recruit foreign support for West Berlin
in the face of Khrushchev's repeated threats and ultimatums.

Seated across the conference table from Gen. Albert
Watson, Willy Brandt was now subjected to a number of questions by the Allied commandants. Had he contacted the Federal government in Bonn? What had been its reaction to the
news? What, if anything, was it proposing to do? How was the
West Berlin population reacting to this latest crisis? What did
he personally think was likely to happen?

It was soon Brandt's turn to ask the commandants what *they*
were going to do. Speaking for his colleagues, Gen. Albert
Watson replied, "Our respective capitals have been informed.
Our governments will make the necessary decisions."

Brandt was anything but happy over the blandness of this
answer. It was imperative, he declared, that the Allies react
vigorously to Ulbricht's seal-off measures. The decision to
impede free communications between the eastern and western halves of Berlin having been announced in the name of the
Warsaw Pact powers, he suggested that the Allies protest not
only to Moscow but also to the other capitals of the Warsaw
Pact. Just what such a protest could be expected to achieve,
the governing mayor was not able to say. It was not a particularly felicitous suggestion, and in any case it far exceeded the
limited scope of the commandants' authority.

More to the point was Brandt's second suggestion: that the
Western Allies send patrols up to the sector borders to bolster
the sagging morale of the West Berliners by at least showing
the flag and a bit of military muscle. To his surprise even this
mild request was turned down. General Lacomme had his
hands tied, and the British were adopting a wait-and-see
policy before committing themselves. Everything depended,
once again, on the Americans. But the Americans did not
intend to go it alone. More at home on the golf links or the
polo field than in this nebulous, half-diplomatic–half-military
situation, Gen. Albert Watson was not going to stick his neck
out and undertake bold action on his own. He was going to be
a disciplined subordinate. He was going to play it by the

numbers and await instructions from Washington. In Washington it was not yet 6:30 A.M., and they would probably have to wait several hours more before knowing what the State Department or the White House was prepared to let them do. For the time being, therefore, all the U.S. commandant could promise was a routine protest to be delivered by the three Western Allies to Colonel Solovyov, the Soviet commandant in Karlshorst.

Brandt listened in his chair, dumbfounded. But then what could one expect of a totally inexperienced two-star general who had had only ten weeks to familiarize himself with a highly complex and tricky situation? If anyone was to blame, it was the people in the Pentagon who had decided on a change of U.S. commandant at this singularly inopportune moment.

Sitting back in his chair, Brandt let his deputy, Franz Amrehn, take over. At the Berlin Senat session that had preceded this meeting with the commandants, everybody had been struck by Brandt's unusual listlessness. He had let others do the talking and suggesting; he seemed to have lost his tongue as well as his nerve and his will. He seemed stunned, in the grip of a traumatic shock that had left him half-paralyzed. Amrehn, on the other hand, seemed to have been galvanized by the challenge.

More forcefully than Brandt, Amrehn now put in his own plea for Allied action. Like George Muller before him, he could afford to make bold suggestions since the supreme responsibility was not his. But his lawyer's eloquence left his listeners unmoved. The commandants were not going to undertake anything rash or provocative. The East German seal-off measures, although a flagrant violation of the Four-Power statutes, had so far been defensive in nature. A strong Allied reaction might be all that was needed to transform an essentially defensive operation into something far more serious and offensive. The commandants were not prepared to take this risk. They had orders to defend the western sectors against all forms of attack; beyond that they could not and would not go. This might be rough on all Berliners, in the East as well as in the West, but they would have to grin and bear it.

As the meeting broke up, Brandt could not conceal his disenchantment. Speaking in German and through an inter-preter—rather than in English, which he spoke fluently—he remarked that if this was all the Western commandants were going to do, *"dann lacht der ganze Osten von Pankow bis Wladiwostok!"* ("the entire East was going to laugh from Pankow to Vladivostok!")

More than three thousand miles to the west and five hours behind in time, Washington was even slower in waking to the crisis. For many congressmen and public officials, this was a weekend to spend in the country. Wilhelm Grewe, the German ambassador, who had speaking engagements in upper New York State, spent a peaceful Sunday visiting Niagara Falls with his two eldest daughters. Robert McNamara, secretary of defense, had left town, as had his aide, Paul Nitze, who had flown to Maine to enjoy the cool sea breezes of Bar Harbor. Hervé Alphand, the French ambassador, was treating himself to a holiday in Italy, while the president's personal assistant and head of the National Security Council, McGeorge Bundy, had left with his wife for Manchester, Massachusetts.

Kennedy himself had left Washington at five o'clock on Friday afternoon, lifted off the White House lawn by helicopter and thus transported to Andrews Air Force Base. The fifty-minute talk he had had with Dean Rusk shortly before lunch, during which the secretary of state had reported to him on the results of his recently completed European trip, had not been alarming enough to prompt any sudden change of plan.

Saturday had been spent at Hyannis Port in a relaxed holiday spirit. The president had gone sailing in one of his yachts with his Choate School roommate, Lemoyne Billings, while the three-and-a-half-year-old Caroline set out with her mother on the cabin cruiser *Marlin*. The afternoon had ended with a cocktail party, and that evening, after the young ones had been put to bed, the older members of the clan had gathered in Ambassador Joseph Kennedy's living room to watch a sixteen-millimeter film. It had begun shortly after 9:30—the very moment when, in far-away Berlin, Vopos and Grepos were starting to unload their coils of barbed wire.

Not until two and a half hours later did the first reports begin to reach the heat-drugged American capital—by which time most Washingtonians were either asleep or preparing for bed. It was midnight, eastern standard time, when the Berlin Task Force duty officer, John Ausland, received a telephone call at home from the State Department's recently created Operations Center informing him that according to wire-service teletype dispatches, something serious was happening in Berlin. An expert on East Germany who had served in diplomatic posts in Frankfurt, Belgrade, and Berlin, Ausland asked his informant to keep in touch.

At 4:00 A.M. the person on duty at the Operations Center rang again. He had just received a brief message through military channels: The East Germans were blocking all movement between East and West Berlin. Ausland immediately telephoned to Frank Cash, a former consul and second secretary with the U.S. embassy in Bonn, who was running the Berlin Task Force in the absence of its director, Martin Hillenbrand, who was on summer leave.

"I'm going to the Operations Center," Ausland told him.

"All right," said Cash. "I'll join you there later. But first I've got to see my family off at the airport at seven o'clock. They're leaving on vacation."

On reaching the Operations Center, Ausland telephoned to Col. Bur Showalter, who had been given the job of maintaining liaison between the Pentagon and the State Department. Showalter made it over as fast as he could. From the Operations Center he put in a long-distance telephone call to the duty officer at the U.S. European Command in Paris. But the duty officer in Paris could tell him nothing new.

As the minutes ticked away, Ausland sat there with the uneasy feeling that something very serious was happening in Berlin and that he should be doing something about it. He would have liked to telephone through directly to the U.S. mission in Berlin, but he would have had to use an open line which ran through East Germany and that was known to be tapped.

Around six in the morning, a telephone call came in from the duty officer at the White House. The communications machinery in the White House basement, which included a ticker tape and a special line to the Pentagon, had alerted him to the gathering crisis in Berlin. Like the U.S. Army major who had hesitated to disturb General Watson some seven hours before, the White House duty officer was reluctant to wake the president so early on this Sunday morning. He said he was going to call Hyannis Port at 8:00 A.M.. The president was thus allowed to sleep on while at the Berlin Kommandatura, Willy Brandt and the three Allied commandants were debating what to do.

Before hanging up, the White House duty officer suggested that they have something ready for Pierre Salinger in case a press conference had to be improvised at short notice in Hyannis Port. Soon a call came in from Walt Rostow, who had just reached the White House. The three-point memorandum that Ausland had prepared for the press struck him as all right, but he suggested a further point, which was added.

Having seen his family off at the airport at 7:00 A.M., Frank Cash hurried to the State Department. When he reached the Operations Center, Ausland asked him for the Berlin contingency plans. Cash had told him on the telephone that these plans were in the Duty Office safe, but Ausland, who had only recently returned to Washington from a tour of duty abroad, did not have the combination. Cash pointed to a briefcase he had brought in with him. Opening it, Ausland rummaged around until he came upon a folder appropriately marked "Division of Berlin." But when he opened the folder, he got a shock: it was absolutely empty.

A week or two before, James O'Donnell had bumped into Karl Mautner, as the latter came down a State Department corridor with an armful of papers.

"What are you carrying there?" O'Donnell had asked Mautner, a member of the Berlin Task Force who had served for years as the State Department mission's liaison officer with the Schöneberg City Hall. Mautner explained that these were contingency plans for Berlin.

"Karl," said O'Donnell, shaking his head, "if I know the Berlin situation and the people dealing with it, you've got a plan there for everything except for what's going to happen."

"That's right," Mautner had agreed with a chuckle, before proceeding on his way.

But now it had ceased to be a laughing matter. What planning the Berlin Task Force had managed to achieve in the short span of its existence had concerned other contingencies. This one—the division of Berlin, the splitting of the city into two almost hermetic halves—although foreseen, had been neglected, while attention was focused on Soviet and East German threats to the Allied access routes to West Berlin. Misled by Khrushchev's bombastic warnings and obsessed by memories of the 1948–49 Berlin blockade, the State Department specialists had, in the classic general-staff tradition, been preparing to refight the last war.

10

For two hours they had been sitting around in the fisherman Kollow's living room, now filled to bursting with relatives and friends. Anxiously they awaited the hourly news bulletins. A blond, somewhat portly woman from Erkner, near Berlin, was crying, but nobody paid attention to her tears. They were too busy airing their various opinions on the West, Adenauer, Strauss, Kennedy, NATO. "They can't let us down. They've promised. They will help us."

"Who promised it?" asked Krüger.

"Adenauer," said somebody.

"Strauss," insisted another.

"Kennedy," declared a third.

Klemens Krüger shook his head in disbelief as indignant voices rose around him. They quoted sentences from Adenauer; they quoted sentences from Strauss; they quoted sentences from Kennedy. Every word they could seize upon in any number of Western speeches had been transmuted into promises firmly lodged in their minds. They had heard them over RIAS; they had heard them almost daily over the Freies

Berlin broadcasting station. Now the pledges must be honored.

"What, then, is the point of your 'policy of strength'?" they objected. "Why on earth did you rearm? If you're now incapable of taking on Walter Ulbricht's feeble army, then you might just as well pack your bags and clear out!"

"That would mean war," Krüger pointed out. "Atomic war."

"And what of it?" they replied. "We'd rather perish in an atomic war than go on living under Ulbricht."

Klemens Krüger held his peace. Those were dangerous words, poisoning the air like some malignant growth. Fear and hysteria were evident on every face. Hatred of the system, the despair of the marooned.

Another news flash came over the air. Brandt had just reached Berlin. The listeners could hear his voice, speaking from the airfield. It sounded hoarse and strained yet calm. Everyone could feel the pressure now bearing down on this man.

Krüger finally left the room to go for a stroll along the beach. A strong northwest wind was blowing hoarsely through the tall beech trees, as hoarse as Brandt's voice on the Tempelhof airfield.

The campers had not yet evacuated their area, having decided to stick it out until the police drove them away. "That was a bunch of lies about the dysentery," they told Krüger. "There's been no dysentery here. They just want to force us to go home so there won't be an uprising. Any kind of human gathering is a danger for that crowd."

The woods resounded with the roar of motorcycles and two-stroke DDR automobiles. Behind them they left blue clouds of oil-stinking exhaust fumes.

In the early afternoon everyone crowded back into Kollow's living room. The meeting of the Berlin Senat was broadcast. Brandt was on the air once again: "And even if the world be full of devils, we will not recoil one step!"

His brief address was moving. It brought tears to the eyes of the listening women, who held handkerchiefs before their lips.

But it was still only the voice of Willy Brandt—who had only a couple of thousand civilian policemen at his disposal.

"Where is Adenauer?" asked Kollow. "Why doesn't he speak up? Why isn't he in Berlin yet? And Kennedy?"

"Off on a weekend," said Krüger.

"And Macmillan?"

"He's probably playing golf."

"And Strauss?"

Krüger lapsed into silence once again. How could he know just where the West German defense minister was and how he was spending this particular time of day? But as a citizen of the Federal Republic, he realized that he was being held responsible for everything the West might now be doing or planning to undertake. It was an uncomfortable feeling.

Of the many bomb-scarred streets in the northern Kreuzberg district, few were more dismal and depressing than the Sebastianstrasse, a street which, like many of its neighbors, straddled the Soviet and U.S. sectors. This area had been subjected to such a thorough wartime pounding that on the street's southwestern side only one structure had survived: a weather-beaten tenement which still bore the number "72." Its gray brown stucco peeling from the walls, it stared out over a bleak landscape of vacant lots and heaps of rubble on which everything from rotting mattresses to twisted metal had been piled. A nearby apple tree that had miraculously survived the blitz still offered its friendly branches to transient pigeons and perching sparrows, but there was little else to relieve the surrounding desolation. The field of view was virtually unbroken as far as the first East Berlin apartment blocks, beyond which, even farther east, one could discern the shadowy bulk of a power plant dominated by a tall, chalk-white chimney belching coils of black smoke.

Given any choice, Klara Michaelis would gladly have moved elsewhere—as would most of the other working-class tenants who had been crammed into this overcrowded tenement. But the wages paid her by the Lorenz radio factory, even combined with her truck-driving husband's earnings, weren't enough to cover a move to better quarters. Before the war she had lived in Danzig, since occupied by the Poles; and like many who had lost their homes, she was glad to have a roof over her head.

But now suddenly it was as though the war had caught up with them again. It had begun with an ear-splitting din which had awakened the two of them in the early hours of the morning. There was no mistaking the sound of the pneumatic drills at work under their windows. The scene below was spectral, like some nightmarish film set. Under the glare of floodlights, East German soldiers were digging holes at intervals of five yards in the middle of the broad sidewalk on their side of the street. These were the holes into which concrete posts were to be slipped so that nine-tenths of the street could be wired off and the inhabitants of number 72 limited to a narrow passageway between fence and façade.

Going downstairs, the buxom Klara Michaelis sallied forth into the Sebastianstrasse and began plying the green-uniformed soldiers with questions.

"Who are you anyway?" she kept repeating, between bursts of pneumatic hammering, "and where are you from?"

Won over by her forthright manner, the soldiers finally began to talk. They belonged to a Kasernierte Volkspolizei unit normally stationed in Dresden. They didn't like this job one bit, but then what were they to do? Orders were orders; they weren't here as volunteers.

Like everyone else, they'd been taken by surprise, one of them explained. "We'd been sent out for a few days of training in the field when with no warning, they herded us into trucks with our military gear. At first we thought it was part of some field maneuver. But as we moved farther and farther away from the training area, we began to think differently, and finally, by looking closely at the road signs, we figured out that we were headed north toward Berlin. We were finally dumped out not far from here, and it was only then that they explained what we had to do."

The Dresden Vopos were clearly unhappy over this assignment. The conversations struck up between reluctant soldiers and worried tenants grew increasingly open and less inhibited as the morning wore on.

"To hell with it!" one Vopo finally declared. "This is dog's work. I'm quitting. Let 'em get someone else to do their dirty work for 'em!"

His example was soon followed by others. Gradually the pneumatic drills ceased their mad hammering, and around 1:30 P.M. a restful silence descended on the area. Drills and shovels were left lying on the pavement. Some soldiers sat down to rest, others joined discussion groups.

The "break," lasting half an hour, was abruptly terminated by the appearance of a number of Vopo officers who hurried up and began to lecture the men. At first the soldiers refused to move, but then, fearing the dire sanctions that their mutinous behavior was sure to bring down on them, one after another they got to their feet and resumed their drilling. The attempt to fraternize had been frustrated, and the disappointed West Berliners now began to boo and jeer.

Living across the way, in a half-destroyed tenement which had obstinately refused to collapse, was an elderly couple well known to Klara Michaelis. She saw them walk up to several Vopo officers and begin asking questions. Approaching in her turn, she heard the officers reassuring them: "You've got nothing to worry about. All this is temporary. The barbed wire here is meant to stop illegal passage into the American sector. It's not meant for honest people like you. You'll eventually get a pass and be able to come and go as you please."

Looking relieved, the aged wife and husband wandered back to their half-bombed house. But on the western side there was a sudden clamor. A Kreuzberg worker who had been watching the scene in gloomy silence suddenly erupted. Pulling his Communist party card from his wallet, he shook it under the nose of a Vopo officer: "Here, you swine, you can take it and shove it up your ass! I've got no goddamn use for it anymore!"

With an angry gesture he flung the card down by the Vopo officer's boots. His face flushing with anger, the officer lunged forward and grabbed the West Berliner by the arm. But the disgusted Communist, a robust man in his early forties, was having none of it. Wrenching himself free before he could be dragged over to the Soviet side, he gave the officer a shove that sent him reeling backward into one of the newly drilled holes. There was a loud oath as the two boots and breeches disappeared below the level of the pavement.

The officer's misfortune was greeted with laughter from the West Berliners. Even his green-uniformed Vopos could not repress their titters. But a moment later he was out of his hole and shouting more angrily than ever, while brushing the dust and dirt from his uniform. The laughter and the titters died as, hesitantly, the pneumatic drills resumed their deafening chatter.

To twenty-year-old Patrick Habans of *Paris-Match*, this territory was totally unfamiliar. He didn't speak a word of German, but that had not kept his boss from waking him up at 5:30 A.M. to say that he must leave immediately for Berlin to help their on-the-spot photographer get them pictures of the seal-off operation.

Traveling first class in an Air France Caravelle, Habans landed at Tegel, in the French sector of Berlin, shortly before one o'clock. There had been a forty-five-minute stopover in Frankfurt, and on the way up the flight corridor, two Soviet MIG fighters had approached the plane and escorted it for a few minutes before wheeling away. This had not kept the young photographer from enjoying a first-class luncheon snack, washed down with a little wine.

Twenty minutes later he was off, at the wheel of a rented Mercedes. A reservation had been made for him at the fashionable Kempinski Hotel on the Kurfürstendamm, but since this trip was his first to Berlin, he hadn't the foggiest idea of how to get there. Soon he found himself on a broad artery headed due east. Ahead of him loomed the Bismarck Victory Column, and beyond it in the distance the Brandenburg Gate.

Turning right at the next intersection—known to Berliners as the *Kleiner Stern* ("Small Star") because of the roads radiating off it—he drove through the Tiergarten in the hope that it would bring him out somewhere near the Kurfürstendamm and the Kempinski Hotel, where he wanted to unload his suitcase and contact his fellow photographer, Klaus Bier. Reaching a kind of small, tree-bordered square, he stopped his Mercedes and examined his map, hoping to find his bearings. Across the way he noticed a long chicken-wire fence. Beyond it, her back pressed against the wire, was a young girl being kissed by a young man. Or rather, he was pretending to kiss her, for Habans now noticed that although his arms encircled her, one of the young man's hands held a pair of clippers with which—yes, there could be no doubt about it—he was cutting the diagonally strung chicken-wire strands.

Instinctively he reached for his camera, quickly mounting a telescopic lens. He snapped a couple of pictures, then decided that his position was too exposed. He didn't want to attract the would-be lovers' attention to his conspicuous Mercedes. Driving on a couple of hundred yards, he left the Mercedes by the roadside and came back through the trees until he was once more opposite the lovers.

The chicken-wire fence he was looking at was situated on the eastern side of the Lennéstrasse, forming one side of a triangular area bounded by the Bellevuestrasse and the Ebertstrasse. It had been erected only recently by the kind of work squads that Peter Dehmel and Harry Thoess had filmed so exhaustively between 6:00 and 9:00 A.M. Now, as Patrick Habans began his own filming, the Lennéstrasse seemed virtually deserted, perhaps because it was the lunch hour. Beyond the wire mesh, however, many people were moving back and forth, as though out for a Sunday stroll. Every now and then the young wire cutter would interrupt his work, perhaps fearful of being denounced by some informer; but a couple of minutes later he would be back with his beloved to continue his strange game of pseudo passion.

Cutting the higher and lower strands was a singularly awkward job for someone masquerading as a lover, but the young man managed to do the job well enough to be able to open a gap in the fence. He then whistled, and suddenly out from behind the low trees and underbrush came scores and eventually hundreds of people who obviously had been waiting for this very moment. The younger ones in particular began pushing their way through the gap. But what amazed Habans was the number who stayed behind, simply standing around to watch the fun. Holding the wire open for them to slip through, the young man kept pleading with his fellow East Berliners to avail themselves of this chance of escaping. But only a handful—perhaps not more than fifty or sixty—took advantage of this opportunity, whereas the crowd behind, so it seemed to Habans, now numbered in the thousands.

Vopo guards soon came running up, finally aware that something unusual was happening. The gap in the wire was immediately closed, and fresh bales of chicken wire were brought up to reinforce the damaged section. The crowd to the east of the wire mesh was gradually dispersed by guards with fixed bayonets. The fun was over.

New work details appeared on the Ebertstrasse. The chicken-wire fence running along the former Reichschancellery garden was now reinforced by a second, more advanced barrier of wire jutting across the street as far as the sidewalk on the western side. The Ebertstrasse, until now a major north--south artery for West Berlin motorists, was thus severed, and like a twice-garroted jugular, condemned to die.

The scene that the young French photographer had just witnessed was now being reenacted in endless variations up and down the intersector border and, indeed, all over East Berlin. For every person ready to chuck everything and get out, there were several hundred who preferred to stay put. Some—including border crossers like Hilde Tauer—sat in their apartments, too paralyzed to move. Others were convinced that the seal-off measures were only temporary, similar to the brief closure of the street crossings, which had occurred during the June 17, 1953 uprising, or the one-day closure imposed on intersector traffic during the currency reform of 1957. Still others were certain that the Western Allies were not going to take this lying down.

In the Bernauer Strasse area, the question on everybody's lips was: *"Was machen die Amerikaner?"* ("What are the Americans doing?"). "When are they coming to put an end to this *Saustall?"* Although this was the western limit of the French sector, it did not occur to anyone to ask what the French were going to do about this "pig-sty" situation. It was taken for granted that they would follow the American lead, if and when it came.

The more resourceful had meanwhile discovered that by slipping through backyards and entering the houses on the eastern side of the street, they could walk through an inner corridor, open a front door, and step out into the freedom of the Bernauer Strasse. Since the entire street surface, including the eastern sidewalk, belonged to the Wedding borough, no East German guards could station themselves anywhere on this mile-long street. All they could do was station Vopos in the backyards and side streets, thus frightening would-be fugitives away or forcing the pluckier ones to invent convincing tales about the relatives or friends there whom they absolutely had to see.

In front of the Esplanade dance hall and on the Bellevuestrasse, it was no longer a score or two of late-night revelers but two to three thousand West Berliners who were now massed on the Tiergarten side jeering the Grepo work squads as they hammered into the pavement with pneumatic drills. *"Keine Butter, keine Sahne, aber auf dem Mond eine rote Fahne!"* ("No butter, no cream, but on the moon a red flag!"), they chanted in rhythmic unison, mocking Gherman Titov and the Russians' latest exploit in space.

When Robert Lackenbach, *Time-Life*'s Berlin correspondent, reached the scene around 3:00 P.M., his first impression was that the crowd, held back by three worried Schupos, was going to surge across the street at any moment in a mass assault on the militiamen standing guard over the drillers. Although armed with Tommy guns, the Kampfgruppen factory men did not look as hard boiled as he had expected. The drillers looked positively unhappy, but so scared were they of their Vopo or Grepo officers that only when they were not around would they dare exchange a few words with the nearest West Berliners.

11

At the sprawling U.S. embassy at Mehlem, a pile-supported structure incongruously joined to a slate-roofed Schloss on the western bank of the Rhine, there was not a trace of frenzied commotion. Although urgent messages had been coming in from Berlin from 9:00 on, they had failed to disturb the duty officer's dominical serenity. He read them as they came in, then laid them aside, apparently persuaded that all the fuss-and-feathers up there in the former German capital would rapidly subside.

Not until early afternoon did it begin to dawn on this phlegmatic diplomat that something unusual might be happening along the banks of the Havel and the Spree. It might not be a bad idea, he finally concluded, to alert the ambassador. A telephone call was put through to the ambassador's residence, but he was not at home. Immediately after lunch, Walter Dowling had left for a nearby playing field, where a "Little-League" game was to take place between an embassy team and a group of West German softball enthusiasts. It took the messenger some time to locate the scene of this encounter, with the result that the message was finally delivered just as the ambassador was about to toss out the opening ball. Walter Dowling scanned the message hurriedly. His presence was urgently needed at the embassy; serious things were happening in Berlin.

Walter Dowling pocketed the message with his left hand while his right hand tossed out the opening ball. The signal was greeted with cheers from participants and spectators, and the game began as the ambassador made a discreet and largely unnoticed withdrawal.

On reaching the embassy, Dowling put in a telephone call to Allan Lightner in Berlin to get the latest on-the-spot report. Shortly thereafter a call came in from Washington. It was Foy Kohler on the line advising him to "play it cool." Walter Dowling could congratulate himself on having done just that.

It was close to 9:00 A.M., Washington time, when John Ausland, at the State Department's Operations Center, finally got
through to Foy Kohler, assistant secretary of state for European affairs and now head of the Berlin Task Force. The news
that the East Germans were systematically interrupting traffic
across the sector boundaries in Berlin left Kohler remarkably
unmoved. A soft-spoken Ohioan with friendly brown eyes, he
had served in a number of Balkan and Near Eastern capitals
before being sent in 1946 to Moscow, where he had risen to
the rank of minister at the U.S. embassy. Accident rather than
design had made him something of a Russian expert, but
unlike certain other members of the Berlin Task Force, he
had never held a diplomatic post in Germany.

After listening to the draft of the press release that Ausland
had prepared with the help of Walt Rostow, Kohler added a
fifth and final point. Ausland then asked if he would be coming
in to the Department, where Dean Rusk was due to turn up at
ten o'clock.

"Oh, I don't think so," was Kohler's nonchalant reply. "You
and Frank [Cash] can handle it."

"But people are going to be asking us what we're going to
do," objected Ausland.

"That's to be expected," answered Kohler calmly. "But
whatever happens, we must play it cool and not be rushed into
making rash statements."

Kohler was only presuming what had been decided a few
days earlier at the foreign ministers' conference in Paris. A
threat to West Berlin's life lines, on the ground as well as in
the air, would be considered a casus belli. Anything less than
that would not.

This point of view was also held by the secretary of state,
who thumped into his office shortly before ten. In November
1957, when the Soviets had sprung their first Sputnik campaign on a startled world, they had momentarily caught Uncle
Sam off balance, by issuing late Friday or early Saturday
communiqués cleverly calculated to make the Sunday papers.
The only way to counter these methods, the State Department had discovered, was to have the senior officials drop
into their offices on Saturdays and even Sundays, ready, if

necessary, to improvise a quick countercommuniqué designed to snatch the Sunday headline away from the latest
Soviet blast.

The Bureau of European Affairs, to complicate matters, was
at this time woefully understaffed. Its jurisdiction covered not
only Germany, the Balkans, and the Soviet Union, but in
addition, Canada and all the European possessions in the
Caribbean. When William Tyler, the deputy assistant secretary of state for European affairs, reached his office on this
Sunday morning, his desk was already cluttered with incoming cables—the more important of which he had to carry
up to Dean Rusk, whose seventh-floor office was directly
above his.

Although obviously preoccupied by the news from Berlin,
the secretary of state seemed anything but rattled. Indeed,
his attitude was so noncommittal that when Tyler emerged
from his office a few minutes later, he had no idea what course
of action Rusk intended to propose or to pursue.

For the secretary of state,· this was an awkward moment.
Four months before, the Bay of Pigs fiasco had revealed a
glaring failure in U.S. intelligence analysis. Kennedy had
reacted by instructing his brother Robert to undertake an
investigation of the CIA with the help of Gen. Maxwell
Taylor, the former Army chief of staff. Their efforts had been
vain—to judge by the spectacular failure of intelligence analysis in this new crisis. To be sure, the CIA this time was not
wholly to blame. It had been the unanimous feeling of all the
NATO intelligence experts who had just met in Paris that the
Soviets would not try to build a wall or death strip through the
very heart of Berlin.

Still, this was cold comfort. At his Friday-morning press
conference, Pierre Salinger had intimated that the president's
decision as to whether or not to leave for Hyannis Port would
depend on his midday meeting with the secretary of state.
Members of the Washington press corps might well conclude
that Rusk, in reporting on his recent trip to Europe, had been
deceptively reassuring in playing down the Berlin crisis.
What was he now to say to the president? And what was he to
say to the U.S. mission people in Berlin, who had been bombarding him with cables?

In a last-minute change of mind, Foy Kohler turned up at the State Department after all. From the Operations Center, where he conferred briefly with Frank Cash and John Ausland, he went straight to Rusk's office. The five-point memorandum that Ausland had prepared with his and Walt Rostow's help was already on the secretary's desk, but so far he had done nothing about it.

"Before we try contacting the president," said Rusk, "we must call Allan Lightner in Berlin to get a clearer picture of what's going on there."

The answer to this question was not long in coming. In Berlin the three Western commandants had continued their discussion of the situation after Brandt and Amrehn had left. All three felt that something had to be done. But what? One suggestion—made by the British political adviser, Bernard Ledwidge—was that all three commandants climb into their official cars and drive into the Soviet sector to lodge an oral protest with the Russian commandant, Colonel Solovyov. This action would be the simplest and quickest way of "showing the flag." Unfortunately, there was no guarantee that the Soviet commandant would be on hand to receive this oral protest. This being a Sunday, he would probably have absented himself deliberately from his Karlshorst office. The three Allied commandants would be received with shrugs by an ignorant Russian sentry, or by an evasive duty officer, who would tell them that they would have to come back tomorrow. Their joint attempt to make an impression on the Soviets could thus easily end in their looking ridiculous.

The possibility of issuing a written protest to the Soviet commandant had to be abandoned for other reasons. Both General Watson and General Delacombe felt that they could undertake such an initiative without requesting prior authorization from their respective governments. But the unfortunate French commandant could only take such a step with the specific authorization of the Quai d'Orsay. And Couve de Murville, as it happened, was not even in Paris.

There remained one possibility: to issue a protest statement for the form, as it were. A protest statement that could be handed to the press and thus disseminated over the ticker tapes and radio waves. This action would cut no ice with the

Soviets, make no impression on Ulbricht and his henchmen, but it would at least amount to something. It would be a token protest and better than a silent acquiescence with what was going on. General Lacomme agreed. This he could agree to without asking for prior approval from Paris.

The three political advisers—Howard Trivers for the United States, Bernard Ledwidge for Britain, and Serge de Guenyveau for France—withdrew for a quick lunch at the U.S. officers' mess hall to discuss the terms of the press release. From the mess hall they moved up to Trivers' office, where they put the finishing touches to a joint text, which was then translated into German. All that was needed now was the official clearance from each of the three commandants.

For Trivers, who had his office in the same building with General Watson, this posed no problem. But the British and French political advisers had to return to their respective headquarters. It was accordingly agreed that each would telephone the clearance through to Trivers, who would then release the joint Allied text. But just as Bernard Ledwidge and Serge de Guenyveau were about to leave Trivers' office, they were informed that Washington was on the line to Allan Lightner.

The person at the other end was Foy Kohler, who was calling from the office of the secretary of state. Lightner explained what was going on as succinctly as he could. Everything said was being recorded over the open line by the East Germans and doubtless the KGB as well, but at this point what did it matter? He ended by saying that the three political advisers had just completed a joint protest, which the Allied commandants were going to release to the press at six o'clock.

"Let me hear it," said Kohler.

Lightner read the prepared text over the insecure line.

"Well, the secretary is right here," Kohler replied. "Let me tell him about it." There was a long moment of silence and then Kohler returned to the receiver. "I have strict instructions for you, Al, *not* to issue anything in Berlin. You can't go ahead on this thing. Anything that's going to be said on this issue has to come from the capitals. As a matter of fact, we'll get something out ourselves this afternoon."

That was the end of the conversation. It was also the end of the prepared statement. Sitting down heavily behind his desk, Allan Lightner ran his hand repeatedly through his tousled gray hair—a sure sign that he was upset. Usually it was the Americans who were annoyed because the British or the French or both refused to go along with some U.S. proposal. Now the shoe was on the other foot, and it was the Americans who had reneged at the last moment. Howard Trivers, who had to inform his opposite numbers of Washington's last-minute veto, felt no happier. The British and French political advisers shook their heads and withdrew in silence, sparing him needless commentary.

Without intending to, the American secretary of state had just betrayed his underlying distaste for the troublesome Berlin problem. He wasn't going to take any risks or initiatives with an issue that the president was determined to handle in person. This suited Rusk's essentially placid and often inscrutable personality, which was to earn him the nickname "Buddha."

It also suited his personal inclinations. A few days before, at the end of the foreign ministers' conference in Paris, Rusk had flown down to Rome to hear what Amintore Fanfani and Antonio Segni might have to tell him of their impressions of Khrushchev. From Rome, Rusk had flown north to Milan to spend the night in a Rockefeller Foundation villa at Bellaggio, not far from where Konrad Adenauer was staying. Since he had been invited to call on the chancellor, Rusk had asked his ambassador in Bonn, Walter Dowling, to accompany him. As they flew north, Dowling undertook to brief his boss on recent German developments. But Rusk would continually interrupt, nodding toward the porthole window as they overflew the Apennines and saying, "Look at those mountains! My, just look at that view!" Nothing else seemed to interest him. Only at the very end of the journey, when they were already on board the little steamer that was to take them across the lake to Cadenabbia, did Rusk cease to be a sightseer and suddenly become the American secretary of state, even asking a couple of questions about Adenauer and the forthcoming elections.

Although not as anti-German as certain members of Kennedy's entourage, Dean Rusk was irked by a problem which was an irritating thorn in his diplomatic flank. "When I go to bed at night," he would say, "I try not to think about Berlin." He would never have admitted it publicly, but he really cared little for Germany or the Germans. He had little understanding of their language and was, on the whole, unfamiliar with their way of thinking, even though he had spent a semester at the University of Berlin in 1934. From 1942 to 1945, the fortunes of war had taken him to the China-Burma sphere of operations, and although James Byrnes had called on him in 1946 to help draft the statutes that were to govern future U.S.-German relations, the Orient had continued to be his main area of responsibility.

At heart Rusk was an Anglo-Saxon, and this colored his attitude toward a wide segment of foreign affairs. Unlike Jack Kennedy, the son of a wealthy Irish-American, Dean Rusk had spent the first years of his life on a "one-horse, two-holer" farm near Woodstock, Georgia. He had had to work his way up from the bottom, and had done so brilliantly, graduating as a Phi Beta Kappa student from Davidson College in North Carolina before winning a Rhodes scholarship. The three years he had spent at Oxford, free at last from the pressures of financial constraint, had made an indelible impression on him, instilling a profound respect for genteel scholars who cultivated understatements and dry wit and who were not dogmatically inclined or excessively temperamental.

"You know," he once remarked to one of his associates, "it's wonderful to deal with the British. It's like putting on an old shoe." With Latins, on the other hand—whether from South America or Europe—Rusk tended to feel ill at ease. They were too volatile to suit his sober tastes, and he could not get too worked up over the crises provoked by their periodic tantrums. This was as true of De Gaulle's France as it was of Franco's Spain or of Getulio Vargas's Brazil. Indeed, Rusk's fundamental lack of interest in France was so pronounced that not once in four years, so one of his principal subordinates recalls, was the secretary of state willing to sit down for an hour for a really searching discussion of French affairs.

Toward the Germans and their murky problems his feelings were even more mixed. People capable of producing a madman like Adolf Hitler were capable of anything. He had had a close-up glimpse of National Socialism, having elected to pursue his studies in Berlin in 1934, when the führer and his goose-stepping lieutenants were already in power, and it had left him much soured on all things German. Rusk even liked to recall how once while rowing on the Havel he had tied his boat to the riverbank in order to go for a stroll. He had returned to find his boat gone, or more exactly, stolen—a typical example of German "lawlessness."

The Germans might be scholars, but they were certainly not gentlemen, and the less thought one gave to them the better it would be. There were, to be sure, a few stalwart characters among them—like Konrad Adenauer—but they were egregious exceptions.

12

It had been a nightmarish morning for Emil Goltz, the border-crossing construction worker who had been looking forward to a leisurely Sunday breakfast. Instead, his twenty-year-old cousin Norbert had awakened him by pounding on the door a good hour before his intended rising time with the news that the streets were full of soldiers and Kampfgruppen militiamen and that the sector border was being closed.

At first Goltz had refused to believe it. Then, sinking into an armchair, he had listened to the radio in stunned silence. He felt wretchedly stupid; this was something he should have foreseen. The warning signs were there. It was obvious that they were going to do something to stop the panicky refugee flow, and yet he had done nothing about it; he had let his wife and daughter go off on holiday, even carrying their suitcases to the station and kissing them good-by, as though everything was normal and there was absolutely nothing to worry about. And now here he

was, alone in Berlin, with Anna and Beate two hundred kilometers away in mountainous Thuringia.

In his hurry to dress, he had forgotton all about breakfast and
his usual morning shave. Outside, small groups of people were
gathered here and there to discuss the latest developments. But
each time Goltz and his cousin came near, the chatter would die
abruptly. How typical! thought Goltz. And how stupid! Taking
him for a possible Spitzel—he who had preferred to go work in
the West rather than be forced, for job-keeping reasons, to join
the FDGB workers federation or the GSDF.[10]

Instead of heading for the nearest border crossing, only a
couple of blocks away on the Elsenstrasse, he had let his cousin
take him into a crowded tavern, where most of those present
seemed interested only in drinking themselves into a state of
amnesic stupor. At one table a party of eight border crossers had
even ordered expensive champagne from the Crimea, apparently determined to "burn" the money they had earned in the
West as quickly as possible.

But that was only a beginning. His cousin Norbert had insisted next that they call on various relatives, and before he
knew what was happening, Emil Goltz found himself being
dragged from one family living room to the next and exposed to
tiresome doses of speculative twaddle. The leitmotif was: What
are the Allies doing? When are they going to intervene? All this
was fine and well; indeed, it echoed his own feelings. But there
was something a bit too smug about all these people comfortably
seated around their radio sets waiting for the Western Allies to
do something when they themselves couldn't be bothered to go
down to the sector border to see what was going on.

Not until early afternoon was Emil Goltz able to free himself
at last. Climbing into a streetcar, he rode as far as the telegraph
office near the Ostbahnhof, from which he dispatched a terse,
two-word telegram to his wife: *Was nun?* ("What now?"). He
wasn't asking Anna to come racing back to Berlin with their.
daughter Beate—that would have been risking trouble. But he

---

[10]GSDF—*Gesellschaft für Sowjetische-Deutsche Freundschaft* ("Society for
Soviet-German Friendship").

felt sure that Anna would understand what he really wanted her to do without his actually having to spell it out. By now news of the border seal-off must have reached them down there in Thuringia.

This essential chore accomplished, Goltz undertook a reconnaissance of the sector border. He was stopped by a cordon of soldiers and Vopos from approaching the corner of the Bouchésstrasse and Heidelberger Strasse, but elsewhere he found the surveillance far more casual. Once again he cursed himself for his short-sightedness. It would be easy to escape this evening, once night fell. But he wasn't going to do it alone, leaving his wife and daughter in the lurch.

After the departure of his window-washer friend, Hans Magdorf had decided to have a first-hand look at what was going on along the French sector border. The small bachelor's flat he occupied on the Belforter Strasse was situated in an area of the Prenzlauer Berg borough where all the streets were named after German victories won during .the Franco-Prussian War.

Twenty minutes later he found himself on the Ruppiner Strasse, up which any East Berliner previously had been able to walk, with a perfunctory flashing of his identity card before the check-point Vopo, crossing the intersecting Bernauer Strasse and entering the French sector. The street was now blocked on the eastern as well as the western side by two angry crowds. For Magdorf, convinced Communist though he was, it was a shock to see those coils of barbed wire guarded by young Grepos carrying submachine guns, who were themselves backed up by older Kampfgruppen militiamen armed with carbines.

No less upsetting to Magdorf was the sight of East Berlin housewives queuing up on the Brunnenstrasse in front of the few bakeries and grocer's shops that were open on this Sunday morning. Although the queues were orderly, they were unnaturally long, and there was something fearful and panicky about them. The women looked grim. There was a tension in the air that Magdorf did not like at all.

He decided then and there to head for his Lichtenberg bread factory, some three miles to the east. When he finally reached it, around two o'clock in the afternoon, he got another shock. The front gate was guarded by about forty Kampfgruppen workers, armed with Wehrmacht carbines and Soviet submachine guns. Stranger still, they were not part of the factory's own *Hundertschaft;* they were armed workers from the nearby state-run Lichtenberg Metallwerke. The bread factory's own militiamen, as Magdorf soon discovered, had been sent down to guard the barbed-wire barricades across the Elsenstrasse, blocking access to the U.S. sector.

The authorities were taking no chances. Fearing an outbreak of unrest or even a riot among the bakers, they had detailed Kampfgruppen workers from another factory to maintain and, if necessary, restore order. The strangers had installed themselves at the factory's main gate, had taken over the central switchboard, the SED party office, and even Magdorf's small radio room.

The atmosphere inside the factory was almost as tense as in the vicinity of the Bernauer Strasse. The workers were sullen, all but turning their backs each time a Party member passed by.

Magdorf himself was buttonholed by the factory's SED secretary, who told him that he was expected to indulge in a bit of *Agitprop.* Dutifully, Magdorf went to work, using his dialectical talents to convince groups of skeptical workers that the border closures were peace-preserving measures.

The workers he accosted looked singularly unconvinced. A charwoman who normally liked to chat with Magdorf while sweeping up now deliberately avoided him.

Later in the afternoon a stoker, who had been summoned to the factory on special Sunday duty to tend one of the kilns, gave violent vent to his feelings. "So here we all are, back in the same old *Ka-Zets!*" he shouted, using the initials *K* and *Z*, which in German designate a *Konzentrations-Lager,* or concentration camp. "Like what it was in Hitler days! I'm fed up with it all! I'm not going to work! Let the goddamn ass holes arrest me if they want to!"

When a factory foreman tried to pacify the furious stoker, he was almost beaten up for his pains. Two burly janitors had to be summoned to deal with him. They dragged the struggling worker to a cabin near Magdorf's radio room, where the "madman" was locked up. Several Party functionaries then went in to work on him, goading him into even more reckless and self-incriminating oaths. Finally, two secret-police agents of the ubiquitous SSD appeared in their shiny leather topcoats and hauled him off to prison.

He was released after two days of confinement, as Magdorf was later to discover, because his captors were convinced that a man who swore and blasphemed so openly must be genuinely mad.

Posted on the southern side of the Friedrichstrasse intersection, Willi Schenck had been waiting for hours for his father to return from his railway dispatcher's job. The border was still obstructed by two parallel concertinas of barbed wire, but Willi was afraid that at any moment new rolls might be laid out, impeding further passage from the northern to the southern side of the Zimmerstrasse.

At exactly 4:30 P.M., he caught sight of the old man walking slowly down the Friedrichstrasse. An incongruous trenchcoat—this was, after all, the month of August—obscured the dark blue Reichsbahn uniform, and in his right hand, as usual, was the weather-beaten briefcase into which, each morning, he tucked his black-bread-and-goose-fat sandwiches. With bated breath, Willi watched as his father was stopped by a Vopo at one of the police cordons strung across the street. Satisfied that he really did reside on the Zimmerstrasse, the Vopo let him proceed.

As the old man rounded the corner, Willi came up to the barbed wire and shouted to him: "Father, Father, here quick—you must jump! Jump over to this side! We're all waiting for you! Quick! Jump!"

But the father, although he recognized his son, stood rooted to the spot. The cancer that had been undermining his body seemed to have sapped his will as well.

Desperately Willi pleaded with him. "Quick! Jump! Jump! Mama is with us! She's waiting for you!"

Tears started to trickle down the old man's cheeks as at last he began to grasp the situation. But it was already too late. Briskly rounding the Friedrichstrasse corner, two Vopos came up and pushed him back from the barbed wire.

"Leave my father alone!" shouted Willi Schenck. "Leave him alone, or I'll bash your goddamn heads in!"

The Vopos paid no heed as they shoved and prodded the old man on along the northern sidewalk toward number 86.

Willi Schenck stepped back as though about to spring over the first barbed-wire concertina, but he was caught by his brother Heinz and the Skrupellose. They dragged him back before he lost his head completely. Suddenly he stopped shouting. The old man was now inside the house on the other side, and all hope of escape was gone.

The two brothers spent a miserable half-hour waiting to see their father reappear. It had not occurred to them that he might have to witness the havoc they had wrought on his apartment. What a shock to the old man to see all that splintered wood, the disemboweled upholstery, the shattered glass!

He finally emerged looking like a broken man. The Vopos escorted him to the corner and up the Friedrichstrasse. Where they were taking him, the sons had no idea. Not a word was uttered between them. What was there to say?

13

Four months before, the Bay of Pigs fiasco not only had taken Washington by surprise; it had found the White House unprepared and poorly organized to meet the crisis. New American administrations traditionally need a shake-down period to adjust to the realities of executive power-wielding, often so different from what the incoming president has known in the past. John Kennedy's was no exception. He had entered the White House confidently persuaded that he could run the executive branch of government more or less as he had run his senatorial office, only to discover the hard way that this could not be done.

His predecessor, Dwight Eisenhower, had developed an elaborate staff system designed to ease the burdens of office by delegating large areas of responsibility to the more important members of the cabinet. At the State Department, John Foster Dulles had virtually been his own boss, as was "Engine Charlie" Wilson at the Department of Defense, and George Humphrey at the Treasury. Such coordination as existed was provided by the White House chief of staff, Sherman Adams; the Boston banker Robert Cutler, who headed the National Security Council; and the fraternal links binding Dulles to his brother Allen, who ran the CIA. Although this highly compartmentalized system suited Ike's easy-going, golf-loving temperament, it was ill-suited to rapid action in emergencies.

In his well-intentioned desire to obtain greater "flexibility" by shaking up an overcompartmentalized system of government, John Kennedy had gone from one extreme to the other. He had inadvertently thrown the executive baby out with the bureaucratic bath water. Having installed his chief secretary, Evelyn Lincoln, in a side office to the right of his own oval office and Kenneth O'Donnell, his appointments secretary, in another office to the left, the new president let it be known with disarming informality that the White House was, as it were, an "open house"—open to all constituents and particularly to members of the press. There was to be none of the bureaucratic rigidity and stuffiness of the Eisenhower years. The Washington press corps—the majority of its members at any rate—loved it, not realizing that in the process of "loosening and livening things up," certain vital executive organs—like the Planning Board and the Operations Coordinating Board of the National Security Council—had been casually abolished.

When Gen. Maxwell Taylor, who had helped Robert Kennedy investigate the causes of the Cuban debacle, was invited to become the president's personal military adviser, he was secretly appalled by the unmilitary chaos he found reigning at the topmost echelons of the new administration. So careless and disorderly were the ways of the White House staff that he could walk into almost any office, request and obtain a sheaf of top-secret papers, and then leave without having to sign a receipt form indicating exactly where the papers had gone.

The administrative confusion was compounded by Kennedy's determination to be his own secretary of state, and by his habit of telephoning directly to any State Department or Pentagon official he thought might have an answer to the question that happened to be troubling him. Instructions, sometimes fairly important ones, were also transmitted in this informal way, with consequences that were often as embarrassing as they were confusing to subordinates accustomed to more orthodox procedures.

The first to realize that this chaotic situation could not long endure was the president's special assistant, McGeorge Bundy. From the wreckage of the National Security Council setup—under Robert Cutler a most elaborate affair—he rescued a veteran Foreign Service officer named Bromley Smith, who had served under George Marshall and Dean Acheson. Aided by a score of hard-working assistants who were given the job of dealing with emergencies as well as preparing reports on long-range problems involving the country's security, Bundy, Walt Rostow, and the NSC's new executive secretary, Bromley Smith, established a modest but efficient communications center in the White House basement, using Signal Corps equipment and teletype facsimile repeaters. Known as the "Situation Room," it was linked by secure telephonic circuits to the State Department, the Pentagon, the office of the Joint Chiefs of Staff, and the Atomic Energy Commission.

By August of 1961 the casual chaos of the early Kennedy months had given way to a fairly effective system of administrative coordination. Each morning the president's military aide, Maj. Gen. Chester Clifton—or, if he was off duty, the Naval or Air Force aide—would bring in the "president's check list," a beige binder containing the latest CIA reports. The items were presented on the left side of each page in a kind of newspaper-headline style, and the substance of each report filled several paragraphs on the right. If Kennedy left for Hyannis Port on Friday afternoon, as he liked to do during the hot summer months, the CIA folder, along with any material Bromley Smith might feel was necessary, was flown to Cape Cod on Saturday and again on Sunday morning. In addition, urgent messages could be transmitted over the telex circuit linking the White House communications center to the basement of the Yachtsman's Motel in Hyannis Port, where a ticker tape and other telegraphic devices had been installed and were maintained by a crew of Signal Corps specialists.

For reasons that are still obscure, the first message about the crisis in Berlin, which the White House duty officer had promised to transmit to Hyannis Port at eight o'clock in the morning, failed to get through to John Kennedy. Or if it was delivered, the message was so vague that it seemed unimportant. Shortly after 10:00 A.M. the president and Mrs. Kennedy left their gabled cottage and drove to the St. François Xavier Church in Hyannis Port for Sunday-morning mass. According to Kenneth O'Donnell's presidential appointments book, they left the church thirty-five minutes later and were back at the cottage by a quarter to eleven.

Shortly afterward, John Kennedy, accompanied by Jackie, Caroline, and other members of the family, set out on the *Marlin* for a midday cruise. The weather could hardly have been better. There were few clouds in the sky, and there was a refreshing ten-knot breeze blowing from the north. This time their destination was Great Island, where they were to have lunch at the Mellon Beach House with John Walker, director of Washington's National Gallery of Art, and his wife.

The cabin cruiser was not far out to sea when a Signal Corps messenger came running up to General Clifton, who was acting as the president's onshore duty officer, and handed him a brown envelope. "This looks important," said the breathless messenger. Inside the envelope was a yellow teletyped message from the White House Situation Room saying that Berlin had been cut in two by the East Germans.

Picking up his walkie-talkie, Clifton called the Secret Service man on the Kennedy cabin cruiser. "Hello, this is Watchman," he began, using his designated code name. "I've got a top-priority message from Washington. You must turn the president around and have him come back to shore."

The Secret Service man hesitated, but Clifton was insistent. The message was accordingly delivered to the president.

The *Marlin* changed course and headed back toward the wharf, where Clifton was waiting to take the president to his cottage in his motor-powered golf cart. After glancing at the telex message, Kennedy told Jackie and the other members of the party to continue with their picnic plans and to proceed to Great Island without him. He would remain on shore.

From the cottage's informally furnished living room, a call was immediately put through to the State Department via the White House communications center. A moment later Dean Rusk was on the line explaining the situation in Berlin. The East Germans had halted all subway traffic between the East and West, had closed most of the crossing points, and were putting up barbed-wire fences and barricades all along the border. But just how permanent this clamp-down was intended to be, nobody at this point could tell.

And the Russians? Kennedy asked. The Russians, Rusk explained, were keeping a low profile. None of their soldiers seemed to be involved in the border-blocking operations—at least for the time being. Russian tanks had taken up positions around Berlin, but as far as could be ascertained, they had not been brought into East Berlin in any significant numbers. The Russians were leaving it to Ulbricht's police and army units to do the dirty work. So far the Russians had undertaken nothing that could be construed as an aggressive move. The Warsaw Pact powers had even issued a proclamation declaring that the Western access routes would not be threatened. He therefore felt that the best course would be to avoid doing anything of a provocative nature, anything that might prod the Soviets into dangerous counteraction.

There was also the latent danger of a mass uprising in East Berlin, which the Russians would have to drown in blood, as they had done in 1953. Any incendiary statements made by the three Western Allies might be all that was needed to put a match to the powder. He felt it was essential to "talk the fever out of this thing"—which is why he had vetoed a protest statement that the three Western commandants were about to issue in Berlin.

Rusk then read the statement he had prepared with Foy Kohler on the basis of Ausland's original memorandum. The East German authorities, it declared, had taken severe measures to deny their own people access to West Berlin. "These measures have doubtless been prompted by the increased flow of refugees in recent weeks." The refugees had not been responding to "persuasion or propaganda from the West, but to the failures of communism in East Germany. . . ." The Communist authorities had denied the collective right of self-determination to the people of East Germany. . . . But the available information indicated "that the measures taken thus far are aimed at residents of East Berlin and East Germany and not at the Allied position in West Berlin or access thereto." The statement ended by declaring that a limitation on travel within Berlin was a violation of the city's Four-Power status, and that the latest "violations of existing agreements will be subject to vigorous protests through the appropriate channels."

Rusk proposed to issue this statement to the press, with the president's approval of course. John Kennedy gave his approval.

His talk with Rusk completed, Kennedy got on the telephone, called his defense secretary, Robert McNamara, his national security adviser, McGeorge Bundy, and his brother Bobby, among others. He wanted them to know that the situation was under control. The danger he had feared above all else—a direct challenge to the Western access routes—had not materialized. The Soviets seemed to be going out of their way to avoid a head-on confrontation. This was the essential point; the rest, as far as he was concerned, was of secondary importance. This being the case, he didn't see the need to shorten his weekend stay at Hyannis Port. He would return to Washington on Monday morning as usual.

Inside the Schöneberg City Hall the confusion and uproar of the morning had by now given way to gloom. Everybody had been caught off guard—the Allies; the West Germans and their BND Intelligence system; and, not least of all, the many city-hall officials who had blithely ignored the latest warnings. No one in the West seemed in real control of events. Macmillan was holidaying in northern England, Kennedy was in Hyannis Port, De Gaulle was at Colombey-les-deux-Eglises, in the French Champagne. The only Western leader who had been at all close to his capital when the lightning struck was Konrad Adenauer; but beyond the issuance of a noncommittal statement, the canny old man was doing nothing.

The general feeling of frustration was shared by the Allied commandants and their political advisers. The capitals of the West—London, Paris, Washington, and even Bonn—seemed totally inert. The Foreign Office so far had said nothing— thirteen hours after the start of the seal-off operation. The Earl of Home, vacationing in Scotland, had not seen fit to interrupt his holidays any more than had Macmillan; and in London the task of coordinating policy had been left to the prime minister's personal assistant and, at times, interpreter, Philip de Zulueta, a French-speaking Briton of Basque origin. The dominant feeling in the Foreign Office was above all to "keep the Americans from going off half-cocked" and even to keep them from issuing "bombastic statements."

The situation in Paris was no better. Both the premier, Michel Debré, and the foreign minister, Maurice Couve de Murville, were vacationing—although Couve had by this time decided to return to Paris in the evening. François Seydoux, the French ambassador to the Federal Republic, had inter- rupted his holiday in Brittany but would not be back in Bonn until late Sunday night at the earliest. Eric de Carbonnel, the head of the Quai d'Orsay's Political Affairs Department, was also vacationing, as was his able assistant Jean Laloy, who was enjoying the stimulating air of the Savoie Mountains above Grenoble.

Ernst Lemmer, the Federal minister for all-German affairs, had by this time returned to Berlin from the Black Forest. Heinrich von Brentano was back in Bonn. His friend Eugen Gerstenmaier, president of the Bundestag, had been con- tacted at his hunting lodge in the Eifel Mountains shortly after the conclusion of the Sunday-morning service and had im- mediately suggested that he and Brentano fly together to Berlin. Brentano, however, had said that he could not leave the Foreign Ministry at such a moment but that Eugen should by all means go.

Telephoning to the nearest military base, Gerstenmaier had a Bundeswehr helicopter carry him to the Frankfurt airport. His reaction was in striking contrast to Adenauer's, but un- fortunately it could have no bearing on the situation. The president of the Bundestag exercised no jurisdiction in Berlin, and there was not a uniformed West German soldier on the spot to whom he could have issued orders, even if he had been empowered to do so.

In the suffering, severed city, somebody had to speak, and that man inevitably was Willy Brandt. In the course of the afternoon he made several radio declarations, and at 6:30 he addressed an emergency session of the West Berlin City Parliament. The session had been announced at such short notice that many seats in the small assembly hall were empty. The governing mayor's speech was full of feeling and compassion for the plight of those who were being locked into a concentration camp, full of ringing phrases about the outrageous violation of human as well as juridically established occupation rights. "The cold concrete posts which now split our city have been rammed into the heart of German unity and into the living organism of our city!"

Almost every word he spoke was true and to the point, but words could not make up for deeds at this critical moment. Nobody knew it better than Walter Ulbricht. All afternoon, at half-hour intervals, blue-shirted boys and girls from the Free German Youth movement or juvenile members of the Young Pioneers had been tramping up to the leather-helmeted tankmen stationed on a vacant lot near the Friedrichstrasse and offering them bouquets of flowers, soft drinks, and assorted pastries. The offerings made, the well-rehearsed groups burst into patriotic chants—like *"Die Partei hat immer Recht"* ("The Party is always right")—which the radio stations of East Berlin had been repeating at hourly intervals.

The final treat was offered by Walter Ulbricht himself when he turned up unexpectedly, accompanied by an imposing array of NVA officers, senior Party officials, and plainclothes SSD agents. There was a note of triumph in his voice, as he exhorted the tankmen to new heights of proletarian valor. On this memorable day they had struck a mighty blow against the capitalists and sent them reeling back. Thanks to their presence near the border, the threatened homeland had been saved from the machinations of its enemies. But the watchword still must be vigilance and an iron-hearted determination to crush the republic's foes whenever and wherever they dared raise their ugly heads.

When James O'Donnell finally reached the upper floors of the State Department, shortly after 10:00 A.M., they were abuzz with rumors and interrogations as people buttonholed each other in the corridors to ask, "What's the latest news?" Since the official State Department dispatches coming in from Berlin first had to be scrambled and then unscrambled by cryptographic specialists, they could not compete in speed with the wire services, which were delivering the hot news as it poured in.

O'Donnell himself had been one of the first to be informed, thanks to a long-distance telephone call he had received from his journalist friend Peter Boenisch in Berlin. Boenisch had wanted to know how Washington was going to react, but there was nothing O'Donnell could tell him at that early hour, since most people on his side of the Atlantic were still in bed. He had promised to call back as soon as there was something to report. Later, before leaving his Georgetown apartment, he had had a chat with another journalist friend, Marguerite Higgins, who had fled the heat of the Potomac for the refreshing sea breezes of Cape Cod. "I'm going down to the Department to talk to George Ball," he had told her. "But as soon as I get back this afternoon, I'll ring you."

While Dean Rusk remained closeted with Foy Kohler in the sanctum of sanctums, word went out that an emergency staff meeting was being called. At this hastily improvised meeting, several experts from the Department's legal section began propounding the thesis that the desperate measures now being taken by the Ulbricht regime could not be considered really offensive or dangerous enough to warrant a sharp American reaction. They were only laying claim to what was already theirs, and in doing so they were revealing how vulnerable and unpopular this regime really was. The seal-off action along the sector boundaries could only be regarded as "a major setback and defeat for communism."

When O'Donnell heard this, he snorted, "It's nothing of the sort. This is a flagrant violation of the Four-Power statutes, and if we let Ulbricht get away with this, it's going to shake the Germans' confidence in Uncle Sam and rattle the whole NATO structure to its foundations."

George Ball, with whom he began discussing the question in the corridor while the meeting continued inside, was inclined to agree. A cosmopolitan American who had spent his childhood in England, he had always tended to be a "hardliner" when it came to defending Western interests in Europe, and he made no secret of the pro-European feelings which caused him to view De Gaulle's French chauvinism with a jaundiced eye. As under secretary of state for economic affairs, Ball had no direct responsibility for the Berlin problem. Nor had he intended doing more than drop in on the emergency staff meeting. But O'Donnell, being an "old Berlin hand" as well as one of his speech writers, was determined that Ball should go in there and fight. "You must get in there, George, and alert those idiots to the fact that this is not a great day of victory. The only victor today is Ulbricht and his jackbooted goons!"

In the midst of their discussion, they were joined by George McGhee, who headed the twenty-man Policy Planning Council. A Rhodes scholar like Rusk, McGhee was a Texas geologist and oil man turned diplomat who had once served as assistant secretary of state for Near Eastern, South Asian, and African affairs, and as U.S. ambassador to Ankara. He knew nothing about Berlin beyond what he had picked up from others in recent weeks, and he seemed to think that the best way of "taking the fever" out of the Berlin problem was to create an international access authority composed of representatives of neutral nations acceptable to the Soviets and Ulbricht's DDR as well as to the Western Allies, which would be responsible for administering the access routes and thus able to prevent future blockages on the autobahns leading to Berlin. He tended to agree with what Sen. William Fulbright had said a few days before: Whether we liked it or not, the Russians were the masters in their sector of Berlin. Allied interference in the Soviet sector was a dangerous game and could only lead to trouble. The legal grounds for such action, as Abram Chayes, the State Department's legal counsel, had explained, were debatable at best, since for years each of the four occupying powers had implicitly assumed sovereignty over its allocated sector.

O'Donnell, who had been in and out of Berlin for the better part of fifteen years, felt himself getting hot under the collar. He had tried but failed to get Ted Sorensen to understand that the Four-Power agreements, which provided the Western Allies with the juridical basis for their continued presence in Berlin, applied to all four occupation sectors. Adenauer and the West Germans had respected these statutes and the special status of Berlin by establishing the provisional capital of the Federal Republic in Bonn. Ulbricht and the East Germans, on the other hand, had repeatedly violated these same statutes, with all but open Soviet backing, by proclaiming East Berlin to be, both de facto and de jure, the capital of the German Democratic Republic. From the start the fundamental aim of Soviet policy in Berlin had been to limit the application of the Four-Power statutes to the three western sectors, this being an important first step on the road to a free-city solution. To acquiese in this new violation of the Four-Power agreements, one which simply made a mockery of them, was to undermine the legal position of the Western powers and help the Soviets to gain new ground at the expense of the West. Once Berlin was severed into two radically different halves, the Berlin question, and thus the German question, was closed for the foreseeable future. The Berliners, both eastern and western, were bound to feel themselves betrayed. And thus could be born a new *Dolchstoss* ("stab-in-the-back") theory which might poison and bedevil future relations between Germany and the United States.

The head of the Policy Planning Council, however, was of a different mind. Finally O'Donnell could contain himself no longer. "McGhee," he exploded, "you and your crowd of mandarin idiots are trying to put a fourth color into the American flag!"

For a moment it looked as though the two Irish-Americans were going to take their jackets off and go to it, but George Ball stepped in and dragged his protégé away.

Ball eventually went into the staff meeting, while O'Donnell drifted downstairs to the cafeteria, where he had a cup of coffee with Lothar Loewe, a former Axel-Springer journalist who now worked for one of West Germany's major television networks. Loewe had been up since four o'clock in the morning, vainly trying to find out how the State Department and the Kennedy administration were going to react to Ulbricht's challenge. Nine hours later he was none the wiser. O'Donnell told him the little that he knew. The under secretary of state for political affairs, Chester Bowles, and other "experts" were peddling the line that the seal-off operation in Berlin represented a "moral victory for the West" and a "major defeat for the Communists." This being so, Uncle Sam didn't have to do anything; he could simply rest on his laurels.

Around 2:30 in the afternoon, George Ball emerged from his office, and he and O'Donnell took the elevator to the ground floor. Ball was disconsolate. He, too, felt that the United States should be doing something about the dramatic situation in Berlin. The staff meeting had produced a lot of talk but little else. The only official reaction was a weak-kneed communiqué which the Department's spokesman, Roger Tubby, had issued after it had been approved by the president. If the United States had wanted to encourage Ulbricht to persevere, it could hardly have done better.

"Come on over to the house and have a drink," Ball suggested, when they reached the ground-floor lobby.

"Thanks," said O'Donnell, "I'd sure like to, but I think I ought to wander over and see what those CIA clowns have been doing all weekend."

"Fine, do that," said Ball, as they moved from the air-conditioned building out into the sultry August heat.

They were about to part when Dean Rusk came through the door and tripped lightly down the steps and into his waiting limousine. He was dressed in a searsucker suit and carried a Panama hat. But there was no sign of a briefcase.

"Where's he going?" asked O'Donnell.

"He's off to Griffith Stadium to watch the ballgame," said Ball, shaking his head. It was clear that he didn't approve. But then that was Rusk's way. The president had agreed that they should play it cool. This was as good a way as any of manifesting that decision.

14

One mile to the southwest of the Plänterwald Cafe, where Ursula Heinemann had spent a carefree Saturday evening, forty-nine-year-old Harald Grabowski had been watching the fencing off of the intersector border from the vantage point of his truck garden. The boundary at this point followed a ditch, known as the Heidekamp Graben, whose moist, moatlike bottom was an ideal breeding place for frogs.

The first to turn up in the morning had been steel-helmeted Grepos armed with carbines, who had fanned out along the ditch's one-kilometer length to intercept escapers. Nationale Volksarmee engineers in field-gray uniforms had then come up with picks and shovels and begun digging holes for the sinking of concrete uprights. The engineers seemed a singularly listless bunch, and not until midday, when they were replaced by Grepo work details, was the slightest enthusiasm shown for this post-and-barbed-wire-erecting job.

Grabowski saw more than a dozen East Berliners escape across the ditch, egged on by garden owners on the U.S.-sector side, who alternately jeered, cheered, and encouraged Walter Ulbricht's soldiers to follow suit and flee. A blond girl in her mid-twenties lost both shoes as she waded across the ditch. One of Grabowski's neighbors offered her another pair so that she would not have to travel to Marienfelde barefooted. But the girl refused, saying that she had already smuggled out many of her clothes and personal belongings during the preceding week.

A few hundred yards farther on, the intersector border joined the Teltow Canal, following it for a distance of four miles. Here, accompanied by her mother and stepfather, Ursula Heinemann spent this late Sunday afternoon wandering from one vegetable plot to the next, past bungalows and lawn-flanked cottages, among whose flower beds an execrable porcelain dwarf was occasionally to be seen leering out above the stems and blossoms.

Near the canal itself a number of foxholes had already been

dug by NVA soldiers, who were crouched down inside them. But along other stretches the surveillance was virtually nonexistent. Scores of East Berliners had come up to "watch the fun," standing by while young boys and girls made their final preparations behind garden hedges or leaf-covered fences.

Among those preparing to escape, Ursula recognized several former schoolmates. One group was hard at work in a truck garden building a raft out of logs and random pieces of timber. It took them an hour of hard work to rope and nail the thing together. Then, as the daylight began to fade, they crept out of their truck garden and wheeled their precious Mopeds down the embankment onto the raft. The waterlogged craft managed to sustain the weight as the valiant swimmers pushed and pulled it toward the farther shore, in the U.S. sector.

Her mother and stepfather finally returned home, but Ursula stayed on far into the evening, sometimes acting as a sentinel, occasionally offering help. She even clambered down the slippery enbankment to the water's edge to help a girl who was having trouble with the plastic bag in which she had wrapped a few personal belongings. The girl seemed at a loss as to how to attach it to her body so that her arms would be left free for swimming. Ursula attached the bag to one of the bathing-suit straps. But she made no move to follow as the girl splashed off toward the other side. She still clung to the idea that something—she didn't know what, but something—was going to happen, and that when all the fuss had died down she would be allowed to go back to work at her Kurfürstendamm hotel.

Considerably less sanguine was Georg Maurer, the Treptow Montage-Bau engineer, who had spent the early afternoon with his wife Carola reconnoitering the central Friedrichstrasse area. Realizing that further procrastination might be fatal—the confusion could not be expected to last forever—they had ridden the S-Bahn back to Karlshorst and had gathered all the money, small valuables, and jewels they possessed, packing them into a small satchel. Then, as though going out for a Sunday stroll, they lifted their little daughter Ilse into her carriage, locked the apartment door, and headed out on foot through the wooded Königsheide toward the garden plots bordering the Teltow

Canal. Georg explained to Carola that if they couldn't get across a bridge into Neukölln, they would try their luck swimming the canal. Fortunately, it was not wide and had practically no current.

The four bridges spanning the canal were all heavily guarded. They would have to swim for it. Leaving the baby-carriage by a hedge, they threaded their way through the garden plots as twilight turned into darkness.

On the way they met an East Berliner who happened to live near the garden-plot area. He immediately guessed what they were up to and volunteered to help. He told them to remain hidden behind some fruit trees. In the course of the day he had seen eight different groups come down to the canal; they had all swum across and made it safely to the other side. The Maurers stood a good chance, too, provided they were careful. The important thing was not to get caught by one of the armed patrols that periodically came up the dirt path skirting the eastern bank of the canal.

Satisfied that the coast was clear, the friendly gardener beckoned them on. Gripping the child, Georg moved forward, followed by his wife. Cautiously they slipped and slid down the steep embankment and into the cold water. Neither of them took their clothes off. As the water level rose, almost to their chins, they pushed out from the bank. Unable to use his arms, which were holding the little Ilse above the water, Georg pushed himself forward as best he could with froglike kicks. Carola swam immediately behind, ready to catch the child if he tired.

The night-time splashing had attracted a number of West Berliners, who leaned down with outstretched arms to pull them up to the top of the embankment. Georg and Carola collapsed on the stonework, thanking their lucky stars that the canal was not as closely watched on the eastern side as on this one.

Shortly afterward the two dripping parents and their little child were bundled into a West Berlin patrol car and driven to the Marienfelde refugee camp. It was a strange way to start a holiday, but at least they were free.

As dusk fell on the Baltic, the atmosphere began to sour in Kollow's living room. News had finally come in from America.

Foreign Minister Rusk had spoken—of negotiations. Negotiations? The listeners could not believe their ears. What was the point of negotiations now?

"Above all, no panic," Adenauer was reported to have counseled in Bonn. No panic? How come no panic? If this wasn't grounds for panic, then what was?

"But this is only a first step. Don't you people over there get it?" they kept harrying Krüger, now become the representative for the entire Federal Republic.

It suddenly dawned on Krüger that if everyone in the room was gripped by fear, it was not so much of war as of the forthcoming terror of the Ulbricht regime. No reassuring word from Bonn could possibly free them from this dread.

"Perhaps in Washington and Bonn they knew about this action even before it began," suggested Krüger.

His words touched off an uproar. There were cries of indignation from all sides. "That's impossible! That would be a breach of promise! No, no, that would be betrayal!"

"There will be protests, no more, you can be sure of that," added Krüger, deliberately throwing cold water on their illusions. This might be the best therapy, it occurred to him, for the looming collapse in their spirit of resistance.

The remark brought on a sudden silence. Kollow, the aging fisherman, planted his elbows firmly on the table and looked Krüger in the eye. "So they've written us off?"

"That's not what I meant. But what should they do, risk a war for the sector boundaries? A third world war?"

"Then they should have done less talking. Not a word about German reunification. It would have been a lot better. So it was all empty talk?"

"No, no," protested Krüger.

The blond woman from Erkner burst into tears once more.

"Of course they've written us off," said Kollow. "The folks over there think only of their own security. For them, well-being is everything. Who among them still thinks about us? As far as they're concerned, we can go on paying—for them, for the whole war that was lost. For sixteen years now we've been paying for it, and we're going to have to tighten our belts once again."

Krüger climbed the stairs feeling utterly dejected. The night over the Baltic was dark. From an HO restaurant he could hear the strains of a Strauss waltz. What was it somebody was celebrating—the victory or the definitive defeat of the Germans begun on this somber Sunday of August 13, 1961?

On the western side of the blocked Berlin border, the temperature had been mounting steadily all afternoon as the crowds were reinforced by new and late arrivals on the scene. This Sunday had begun in a kind of eerie quiet, disturbed by the mysterious sound of motors and military boots; it was now ending in noisy tumult on a massive scale.

At eleven o'clock in the morning, Manfred Bauer had still been able to drive his bus load of sightseers through the right-hand archway of the Brandenburg Gate for a tour of East Berlin. But by six in the evening, normal access to the Gate had been blocked by a crowd of West Berliners, thousands strong. Many of them carried signs that read: *Es gibt nur ein Deutschland!* ("There Is Only One Germany!") and *Deutschland bleibt deutsch!* ("Germany Remains German!").

Several armored cars and water-cannon trucks advanced through the archways of the Brandenburg Gate to back up the string of nervous Vopos stationed just east of the sector demarcation line. The sight of these ungainly slit-eyed vehicles further infuriated the West Berliners. The Grepo officer in command ordered his trucks to use their cannons. The jets of water were answered with howls of rage and a barrage of stones. Some of the East German guards retreated in confusion under this unexpected pelting. But the retreat was checked by the appearance of several companies of helmeted soldiers who were sent forward between the pillars of the Gate.

At the Potsdamer Platz, a quarter of a mile to the south, the factory militiamen guarding the barbed-wire barricades also had to be reinforced against another howling mob of West Berliners, who were chanting slogans and singing *Deutschland über alles*. Behind the mob, standing on the platforms of their trucks and the roofs of their police vans, Schupo officers and noncoms anxiously surveyed the scene. Through their field glasses they spied a familiar goateed and bespectacled face—that of Walter Ulbricht. Accompanied by his usual retinue of army, Party, and security officials, he was making a front-line visit to the square. He apparently did not much appreciate what he saw and heard, for he departed as suddenly as he had come.

The East Berlin radio stations meanwhile had broadcast a warning to West Berliners telling them not to come within one hundred meters of the intersector border; otherwise, they could expect immediate countermeasures. The news, which spread like wildfire from mouth to mouth, exacerbated the crowds at many border points. By 8:00 P.M. the six hundred "rowdies" (as they were to be called by *Neues Deutschland*) assembled on the Bethaniendamm were so worked up that forty of them pushed aside the barriers and stormed into the Soviet sector. Smoke bombs, tear gas, and truncheons had to be used to drive them back. In the confusion of the retreat, one of the invaders was caught by the Vopos and dragged away out of sight.

By 8:30 P.M. the six hundred "rowdies" had swollen to several thousand. When Vopo officers began warning them through megaphones that their men would open fire unless they scattered, the Kreuzberg district chief had his Schupos disperse the turbulent crowd.

At about the same moment another crowd of fifty Kreuzberg youths, massed on the corner of the Stallschreiberstrasse—not far from the solitary house inhabited by Klara Michaelis—trampled down a section of barbed wire, enabling five East Berliners to escape. Half an hour later as night was falling, an unidentified East Berliner was shot down some fifty yards from the barbed-wire barrier slicing the Bethaniendamm crescent. West Berliners watched in stunned silence as the Vopos carried away the body. It was, as far as West Berlin police authorities were later able to ascertain, the first time a shot had actually been fired. It was not to be the last.

The main focus of tension, however, remained the Brandenburg Gate. Afraid that the situation was going to get completely out of hand—a bare thirty meters separated the howling mob of West Berliners from the thin Vopo cordon beyond the demarcation line—Erich Duensing finally ordered his Schupos to block all approaching cars at the "Kleiner Stern" intersection, eight hundred meters west of the Gate. Motorists could no longer get through, still less bring up reinforcements for the mob, which continued to be strengthened by pedestrians sneaking up through the trees of the Tiergarten.

To Molly Kaye, the novelist and wife of Brigadier Goff Hamilton, who reached the scene after sundown, it looked as though "every television camera crew and news reporter in the world" had converged on this explosive flash point. There were spotlights everywhere, many of them trained at the blinking faces of young East German guards a short distance away.

"Haengt Ulbricht! Der Spitzbart muss weg!" ("Hang Ulbricht! The Goatee must go!") shouted the mob of West Berliners, most of whom looked like students. But shout, curse, and encourage as they might, the Vopos opposite would not move. Only one of them could pluck up the courage to desert in full view of the television cameras. He was received with shouts of jubilation. But the rest stayed put, as though rooted to the spot by some paralyzing spell. They were probably not afraid of being shot at from behind if they made a run for it, for the floodlights were too strong and the general confusion too great. But they knew that they would be leaving behind parents, kinsfolk, and friends who could be held hostage and be made to pay for their "crimes" in fleeing the Republic. Ten years of relentless indoctrination had not made all of them fanatics by any means, but it had struck them dumb with fear.

15

Ever since the early hours of this Sunday, when he had first heard the news, Edward Murrow had been nervously chain smoking. The virtually nonstop discussions he had had later with Allan Lightner, senior U.S. Army officers, intelligence officials, and the newspaper magnate Axel Springer, had stirred his curiosity and fighting spirit. He wanted to get out and see for himself just what was going on, what Berliners on both sides of the border were doing, saying, thinking, feeling.

Shortly after 4:00 P.M. he climbed into a black Chevrolet sedan along with Robert Lochner of RIAS, and James Hoofnagle, public affairs officer of the U.S. embassy in Bonn. Their first destination was the Potsdamer Platz, where they came upon Daniel Schorr, who was standing near the coils of barbed wire, microphone in hand, treating his CBS radio listeners to an on-the-spot description of how the East German work squads were fencing off the square. Spotting Time-Life correspondent Robert Lackenbach, whom he had known during the London blitz, Murrow got out to exchange a few words. The worried creases in his forehead seemed to deepen as Lackenbach told him that the West Berliners were in a boiling rage and might explode at any moment.

From the Potsdamer Platz the sedan drove south around the railway yards and past the yellow brick ruins of the Anhalter station to the Friedrichstrasse check point, where the Vopo guards waved them through and into the Soviet sector. The sedan had some trouble driving northward through streets teeming with policemen, soldiers, Kampfgruppen militiamen, and crowds of gesticulating civilians. Finally they reached the Wilhelmstrasse, where they got out and walked the remaining distance to the surviving wing of the Adlon Hotel to have a bite to eat and a glass of beer.

In this same hotel, then one of the choice meeting places of Berlin, William Shirer had spent many hours watching the creeping spread of the Nazi dictatorship. Now another totalitarian machine was busy imprisoning and cowing its captive populace. From where the Americans were seated in the restaurant, they could hear the chatter of pneumatic drills at work on the Eberstrasse. When the time came to settle the bill, the waiters insisted on being paid in West marks or dollars. Clearly afraid of being overheard, they refused to be drawn into a discussion when Hoofnagle questioned them about the value of the East mark relative to the West mark or the dollar.

Back at the Wannsee guesthouse, Murrow let it be known that he was delaying his departure scheduled for the next day.

"Mr. Murrow," Hoofnagle protested, "you are no longer a war correspondent. You are the director of the U.S. Information Agency, and your job is in Washington." Murrow shook his head, as he lit another cigarette. No, he was staying right here.

Sometime after 10:00 P.M., they were joined by Albert Hemsing, the U.S. mission's press and information officer. Murrow began questioning him. How were these seal-off measures going to affect the people of Berlin? How many crossed over from East to West and from West to East on an average day? Two hundred and fifty thousand was Hemsing's startling reply. Fifty thousand of them were East Berliners who worked in West Berlin; twelve to thirteen thousand more were West Berliners who had jobs in East Berlin. Many other East Berliners who weren't registered with the West Berlin authorities—mostly charwomen and the like—also came over regularly to work in West Berlin. Others came over on shopping errands; to buy items such as newspapers and cigarettes; or to take in a movie they couldn't see in the East. And how many West Berliners had relatives in the East? asked Murrow. Most of them, was Hemsing's answer. There was hardly a Berliner who wouldn't be affected directly or indirectly by the splitting of the city.

"I wonder if the president realizes the seriousness of this situation," said Murrow. He decided to draft a personal report. Joseph Phillips—like himself an old newspaper hand before rising to become USIA's area director for Europe—sat down before a typewriter and began batting out the dictated sentences. Murrow paused every now and then to check the accuracy of the facts and figures with Hemsing. The burden of the message was simple: In sealing off the intersector border, the Communists had taken a step that had profoundly shaken West Berlin morale. The action was causing great human anguish and suffering. It directly challenged the credibility of American guarantees regarding the freedom of West Berlin. Energetic action was therefore needed to avert a major crisis of confidence and a catastrophic collapse in local morale.

While the others sat around enjoying a late-evening drink, Murrow took the rough draft and rewrote it completely. What emerged after two hours of concentrated effort was pure Murrow—a message that was plain, direct, compelling. There was no beating about the bush, no bureaucratic waffle.

At about two o'clock on Monday morning, it was ready to be shown to Allan Lightner, who, as head of the U.S. mission, had the right and the duty to see all outgoing messages. It was a pure formality, for Lightner shared Murrow's sense of urgency. A few hours later, after being scrambled in the U.S. mission code room, the report was on its way to the White House.

Ed Murrow's mind was made up. He was staying on to see what was going to happen next. The USIA's worldwide network wasn't going to collapse if he made it back to Washington a day or two later than expected. His place was in Berlin. There was no other place on the globe, at this crucial juncture, where he was more badly needed to get the message across to the people in high places back home.

On the other side of the Atlantic, another determined American was also pleading for action. After leaving the State Department, James O'Donnell had driven to Chevy Chase to call on a friend of his who worked for the CIA. A Silver Star veteran of World War II who had learned German as a prisoner of war, this friend had served in the American military government and was, generally speaking, a hard-liner who tended to be skeptical of John F. Kennedy and the champions of the "New Frontier."

On this hot Sunday afternoon the "hard-liner" was mowing his lawn. He took O'Donnell inside for a drink. What should they do in Berlin? The question, he reported, had been debated at great length within the Agency, and the conclusion they had reached was that they had best do nothing. If the Allies, or more exactly the Americans, tried to put an end to this barbed-wire-spreading business, the East Germans could pull back a hundred yards and start all over again. If there was a second attempt to interfere, they could pull back another hundred yards, and so on. Sooner or later the Russians were bound to intervene to put an end to Western encroachment in the Soviet sector. True, the Americans might score an initial success against the East Germans, but when the Red Army intervened, they would have to give way or risk escalating a local shoot-out into a full-scale world war. Not to mention the possibility of a new June 17, 1953, explosion. What would have been gained? Uncle Sam would have proved to the world that he was ready to stand up to the pip-squeak Walter Ulbricht but in a hurry to run for it when faced with his Big Brother. The end result would be a shattering psychological defeat.

O'Donnell remained unconvinced. "Didn't anybody make the point that the Soviets have a legal right to have armed forces in Berlin but that Ulbricht definitely does not?" he asked.

Yes, replied his friend, he had made the point, but it had cut no ice. Ulbricht had been parading his military and paramilitary units through East Berlin for years in defiance of the Four-Power agreements. It was too late now to try to force him to give up a "right" he had been exercising illegally since 1955.

Back at his Georgetown apartment, O'Donnell found several telephone messages waiting for him. The first was from Marguerite Higgins in Chatham. He picked up the receiver and called her long distance.

"What's going on?" she asked. He had to tell her, nothing much. The State Department had issued a weak-kneed communiqué. Kennedy and Rusk had apparently decided to do nothing. Ulbricht was thus being allowed to get away with murder, and there were people in the State Department who were practically cheering him on.

"You know who our neighbor is up here?" said Marguerite after they had talked for several minutes. "Gen. Lucius Clay."

Marguerite Higgins's husband, Gen. William Hall, was also an "old Berlin hand." He had served as General Clay's air intelligence officer, and, like his future wife and Jim O'Donnell, both of whom he had befriended in Berlin, he had lived through the heroic months of the 1948–49 blockade. He was now living in retirement. Being neighbors as well as friends, he and Clay saw each other frequently.

General Clay, with whom Marguerite Higgins had already

spoken by telephone, shared her impression that the "appeasers" in the State Department had won out once again.

"I'm going over to see him," Marguerite Higgins said, "and then I'll call you back."

Twenty minutes later she was on the line again. But this time General Clay was at her side. O'Donnell had not talked to the general for ten years, but Clay remembered him well from the days when O'Donnell was covering Germany for *Newsweek* and the *Saturday Evening Post*.

"What do you think I should do?" Clay asked after the initial amenities had been exchanged. Both Maggie Higgins and Bill Hall felt that his presence was needed in Berlin. "I'm thinking of volunteering to the president to go back there in the old Frank Howley job."

O'Donnell welcomed the idea of Clay's returning to Berlin; it would be a badly needed shot in the arm for the inhabitants of the western sectors. But things had changed greatly since the late 1940s, when the tough-minded and tough-talking Howley had endeared himself to West Berliners by his truculent refusal to kowtow to the Soviets. "The commandant in Berlin is only a major general. You are a retired four-star general, and I don't see how a former military governor of Germany can go back in a much lower position." The important thing, however, was to let the president know that he was available if wanted. The easiest way of doing this, O'Donnell added, was through Maggie Higgins, since she was a close friend of Robert Kennedy.

One hour later Marguerite Higgins was back on the wire. She had talked to Bobby Kennedy, she explained, and in principle he had expressed his agreement to the idea of sending General Clay to Berlin. He had promised to take the matter up with his brother Jack. The trouble was that Clay was a Republican. He couldn't be sent to Berlin alone; he would have to go with a Democrat to make it suitably bipartisan.

At 9:00 P.M., Washington time, Peter Boenisch called again from Berlin. He gave O'Donnell a sober yet moving description of what had been going on during Sunday afternoon and evening. What had most struck him and many others was the significantly low profile of the Russians. They were like chess players cautiously moving their pawns forward. There were practically none of them to be seen at the sector boundaries; they had left everything to Ulbricht's Vopos and Kampf-gruppen. They obviously wanted to see how much Ulbricht and his men could get away with. Boenisch was personally convinced that there was a tremendous amount of bluff in-volved, as had been the case in 1948 when Stalin had started to interrupt traffic to and from West Berlin. The Americans at first had done nothing, and because they had done nothing, Stalin had been encouraged to increase the pressure by clos-ing all the access routes and blockading West Berlin. So the vital question was: What were the Americans going to do *now* to test Ulbricht and his Russian mentors?

The only news O'Donnell could give him was that General Clay had volunteered to return to Berlin. O'Donnell felt that Willy Brandt should be informed. "Give him the message that Clay has volunteered. It will help the morale of the Berliners, even if the news is first released in Berlin rather than here in Washington.

Boenisch, glad to hear that Washington was planning to do something at last, promised to transmit the news to Willy Brandt. He accordingly telephoned Egon Bahr, the city gov-ernment's press officer. Bahr, who had been under relentless pressure ever since he had returned to Berlin from Munich, listened with half an ear. It was close to 3:00 A.M., Monday, August 14, and he was dog tired. All this talk about Margue-rite Higgins and James O'Donnell, General Clay and Robert Kennedy, sounded more like vague journalistic gossip than hard fact. Besides—and here Boenisch agreed with him—sending Clay to Berlin was no answer to their immediate problems. What was needed was action on the spot, and now. Another twenty-four hours and it would be too late. They would all, including Clay, be confronted with a fait accompli.

Yes, Bahr assured Boenisch wearily, he would pass the news on to Willy Brandt. With that he put down the receiver and thought no more about it.

PART FOUR

THE AFTERMATH

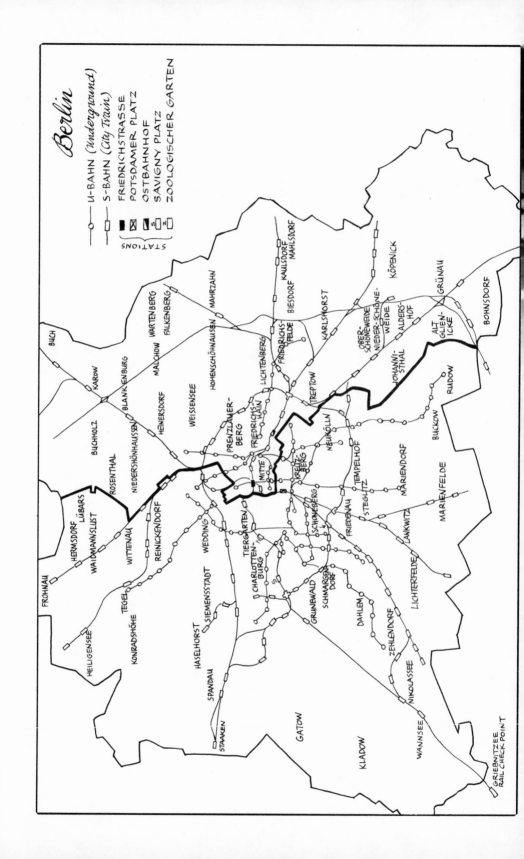

1

After the upheavals of the previous day, Berlin seemed a deceptively quiet city in the early hours of this Monday morning. Most of the demonstrators had finally gone to bed, worn out from so much shouting, and at 3:00 A.M. the West Berlin Schupos had been able to remove the police cordon they had established on the Strasse des 17. Juni at the level of the "Kleiner Stern" intersection. But a few hardy souls were still gathered behind the rope barrier just west of the sector boundary as the dawn spread its gray light over a sullen overcast of cloud beyond the Brandenburger Tor.

When Klaus Lehnartz, a free-lance photographer who had come racing back from Holland, drove up to the Potsdamer Platz at 5:00 A.M., he arrived in time to see East German Transport policemen going about the grim task of sealing the two stairway accesses to the underground S-Bahn station with bricks and mortar.

One of the thirteen intersector crossing points that had officially been left open the previous day, the Brandenburg Gate was still being used by occasional cars when Willy Brandt drove up later in the morning. Accompanying him in an obvious show of solidarity were Erich Ollenhauer, chairman of his own Social Democratic party; Eugen Gerstenmaier, president of the Bundestag; and two other parliamentary leaders from Bonn. As they stood near the demarcation line unhappily surveying the scene, Gerstenmaier suggested that the Bundestag be called into immediate session—right here in the Reichstag, the parliamentary symbol of Germany's erstwhile unity. The convening of a special parliamentary session in the still-gutted Reichstag would have posed quite a problem. But nothing came of this suggestion, now overtaken by a startling occurrence. Realizing that this was the chance of a lifetime, a young East German guard ran forward and leaped over the low barbed-wire-encrusted barrier. He made it safely to the West without a shot being fired by his colleagues or the tough Kampfgruppen militiamen behind them. There would have been hell to pay, as he knew well, had any of them opened up and hit the president of the Bundestag or the governing mayor of West Berlin.

On the other side of the border the atmosphere was as depressing as the early-morning drizzle, which lasted from 6:00 to 9:00 A.M. At the Friedrichstrasse station, clusters of thwarted fugitives sat on their suitcases looking completely stunned. The Vopos and NVA soldiers paid scant attention to them as they screened the few passengers who claimed a right to enter West Berlin through a four-foot-wide "sluice-gate" that was guarded by a good thirty uniformed watchdogs. All told, somthing like three hundred soldiers and policemen had been posted inside the station to deal with a possible tidal wave of border crossers, while outside, six T-34 tanks covered the main access streets, their guns occasionally swiveling as though about to open fire.

The East German authorities could have spared themselves these formidable precautions. In fact, only a handful of the fifty thousand border crossers who used to make the regular weekday trip to and fro still dared to try their luck. Most of them, like Hilde Tauer, stayed at home glued to their radios and television sets.

To David Martin of the London *Daily Mirror*, East Berlin was like a ghost city, so numerous were the closed and shuttered shops. The British correspondent had his passport checked a dozen times by Vopos or Kampfgruppen guards who kept him covered throughout with their carbines or machine pistols. "What can they do when they have guns pointed at their heads?" commented his taxi driver, referring to the border crossers. "Under Hitler we had many concentration camps, but now there is only one—East Berlin."

Many East Berliners who had naively assumed that these measures were temporary ones designed to thwart the "traffickers"—particularly East German peasant women who had been wont to journey into West Berlin with baskets of eggs, poultry, and butter to be sold on the local "gray market" for

West marks—began to have second thoughts in the face of this imposing show of force. Rudi Schuetze, an East Berlin soccer fan who had spent the night of August 12 and 13 staggering drunkenly back and forth between the U.S. Kreuzberg and the Soviet Treptow boroughs with some joyous teammates, found his Adlershof construction factory teeming with gray-uniformed Kampfgruppen who obviously meant business.

Elsa Sahl, who had spent much of the previous day trying to find some way of slipping over into Wedding with her husband, had a similar experience when she reported for work at the Oberspree Cable Works. The chief of her department turned up in a gray Kampfgruppen uniform and had his subordinates assembled for a discussion of the government's latest measures. These, he made it clear, had to be approved unanimously by all those present. Woe to anyone who might have the nerve to disapprove. Trouble makers of this sort would be pitilessly dealt with. "Those who don't care for them will get their snouts pushed in! That's tough language, yes, but it's the language of the working class!"

A prominent Social Democrat named Wolfgang Dammerow—who, now that the direct S-Bahn line had been cut, had to travel from his parents' home at Staaken all the way around the northern periphery of Berlin on the outer railroad ring to reach his Friedrichshain flat—was in for a similar surprise. When he turned up at the Grenzgänger Registration Office, which had been set up on a makeshift basis at the OSRAM light-bulb and electrical-equipment plant, he found the nearby Warschauer Strasse in a state of turmoil. Factory militiamen in gray and blue overalls were everywhere, arguing with East and West Berliners (the latter having come over with their identity cards to see relatives and friends). "You don't know what you're doing!" the younger members of the crowd kept shouting. "You ought to be inside the factory manufacturing your goddamn light bulbs instead of playing policeman outside! Why, you pigs are no better than the Nazis!"

The taunts finally got under the skin of these hard-bitten Communists, some of whom had survived imprisonment in Nazi concentration camps. One of them grabbed his young detractor by the collar and slapped him hard across the face.

The young man retaliated with his fists, and there was a general free-for-all as two other lads joined the fray. Other militiamen hurried up and dragged the three away while the crowd jeered and booed. The infuriated Kampfgruppen militiamen then got armed Vopos to help them clear the avenue entirely, establishing five police cordons over the three-hundred-meter stretch separating the S-Bahn station from the Oberbaum bridge.

Employed in a state-run house-painting enterprise, which boasted the progressive name of *Vorwärts* ("Forward"), thirty-two-year-old Rolf Kasten, like his colleagues, did little actual brushwork on this bleak Monday. The Lichtenberg housing project on which they were working was left in its semipainted state as everyone discussed the seal-off measures in low, bitter voices. Even the foreman, Party member though he was, seemed singularly subdued and depressed— probably because he realized that his daughter, who lived in West Berlin, would no longer be able to bring over his favorite cigarettes.

For the hitherto ardently Communist Hans Magdorf, there were few surprises in store. When he returned to his Lichtenberg bread factory on this Monday morning, he found the atmosphere not much changed from what it had been on the previous day. The stokers and bakers were going about their chores in a sullen silence which, once again, made him feel uncomfortable. The Party secretary summoned him to his office and told him to select some light and lively tunes to "cheer the Comrades up a bit." In his little radio cubicle, Magdorf picked out a few records that seemed to him appropriate. One of them was George Gershwin's "Rhapsody in Blue," as interpreted by the Czechoslovakia Radio Orchestra.

As the day wore on, Party agitators appeared with a prepared statement and blank sheets of paper on which workers were invited to sign their names. The statement approved the drastic seal-off measures undertaken by the government of the DDR and ended with a pledge printed in thick black letters: "Our Soldiers and our Kampfgruppen mounting guard along the state borders of our Workers-and-Peasants-State need bread. WE WILL MAKE MORE BREAD FOR THEM!"

As far as Magdorf was able to determine, there was not a stoker or a baker present who failed to sign the pledge. They knew what would happen to them if they didn't sign.

In the evening, after the list of absentees had been drawn up and registered in the books of the Personnel Office, the names of all those who had failed to report for work on this Monday, August 14, were forwarded to the State Security Service—that is, to the headquarters of Erich Mielke's secret police.

The seal-off operation had been carried out with such secrecy—and haste—that certain Grepo and NVA units were not fed anything for fifteen, eighteen, or, in a few cases, twenty-four hours. Horst Ewald and other Grepos of the Basdorf-based First Motorized Brigade, posted in front of the House of Ministries to guard the Wilhelmstrasse–Zimmerstrasse intersection, were more than a little disgruntled over the wretched quality of the food that was finally dished out to them from hastily improvised canteen kitchens. Nor were they enchanted by their new billets, since they had to spend Sunday night sleeping on a schoolroom floor.

Everywhere Politofficers were hard at work trying to convince the men that this "anti-Fascist bulwark" was being erected to thwart the warlike plans of Adenauer, Strauss, and the Bonn Ultras. But few were the Grepos, Vopos, or NVA enlisted men who were ready to swallow these glib truths. When one of them, a Nationale Volksarmee soldier who had spent the night in a bivouac tent, was asked by a westerner what it was that was being cooked for his lunch in the steaming cauldron nearby, he answered, "Our freedom!"

Groups of FDJ girls continued to march up with bouquets of flowers for the "heroic fighters" at the front, as though to sweeten the bitter pill that East Berliners were being forced to swallow. And a bitter pill it was. Thousands suspected of being potential trouble makers had been arrested by Erich Mielke's agents. The SSD's central headquarters at Hohenschönhausen, like its grim Magdalenenstrasse jail, were so jammed that thirty-two prisoners were now pressed into cells normally expected to hold half that number. Among the unfortunates was a former lieutenant colonel of the Volkspolizei who had been arrested for "sabotage" because he had been unable to provide sufficient food for the Volkspolizei, Grenzpolizei, NVA, and Kampfgruppen units for which he was responsible.

To keep the East Berlin population from becoming swollen with would-be fugitives and other turbulent elements streaming in from the Soviet zone, NVA units, backed by tanks and armored cars, had been ordered to block the incoming roads with barbed wire and transversal trenches. At Erkner, on the city's eastern periphery, only persons with identity cards showing that they were residents of Berlin were allowed through; the others were pushed back several hundred yards from the barriers by Vopos. Party members who tried to persuade the non-Berliners to return to their homes met with spirited resistance. The altercations grew so heated that a special detachment of riot police had to be brought in to disperse the protesters. The most vociferous of the demonstrators were bundled into Volkspolizei paddy wagons.

The entire Soviet zone had by this time been placed on semiwar footing and in a state of siege. Telephone communications between East and West Germany had been abruptly severed at 4:00 A.M. Monday morning. Postal and telegraph services between the two were likewise discontinued. East German barges were prohibited from using waterways that passed through West Berlin. West Berlin pedestrians could still enter East Berlin by flashing their identity cards, but they had to be on their guard; "Worker Fist" goon squads now roamed the streets provoking arguments and beating up anybody who ventured to criticize the latest "anti-Fascist" decisions of the Party.

In West Berlin the prevailing mood was one of critical disbelief. Few could understand how or why the three Allied commandants had let thirty hours go by without a word of protest. Their troops had been placed on alert, but, confined to barracks as most of them were, they had remained conspicuously invisible. It was almost as if their commanders had decided that patrolling the intersector border was essentially a West Berlin rather than an Allied responsibility. In a word, the so-called protectors were passing the buck to their protégés.

The old wartime grudges, born of the city's terrible bombardments from 1943 to 1945 and later nourished by the passivity of the Western Allies in the face of Soviet "salami" tactics and the steady whittling away of Four-Power agreements and guarantees, began to surface once again. In this crisis the Allies were proving to be spineless.

Particularly irate were the workers in West Berlin factories, many of whom had border-crosser friends who were now prisoners in the East. At the huge Siemens electric-equipment plant, in the British sector, five hundred workers went on strike, demanding that several notorious members of Ulbricht's SED be fired immediately; only after they had been given firm assurances that their demands would be met were they willing to resume work. Others, quitting their machines and work benches in scores of different factories, formed delegations which converged on the Schöneberg Rathaus. "We Want Countermeasures!" read the hastily scrawled signs. "Away with the Tanks and Barbed Wire! Against Arbitrariness and Terror! For Unity in Freedom!" And even, most hopefully, "Reunification Soon!"

Five or six thousand workers—many in overalls or wearing the hard hats of the building trade—eventually gathered in front of the dark stucco city hall. A worried-looking Willy Brandt had to come out to the hastily erected barrier by the steps to listen to their complaints. They were fed up with empty words and tame communiqués issued by distant governments and foreign ministries. They wanted action here and now. Why had nothing been done to close all the SED offices in West Berlin in immediate retaliation for the brutal crackdown on their Grenzgänger colleagues? Why were West Berliners being allowed to go to work in East Berlin, thus contributing their services to Ulbricht's detestable regime? Why were notorious Communists being allowed to go on working in West Berlin factories, while Ulbricht and his crew were stamping out the last lingering sparks of freedom in the Soviet sector? What about the S-Bahn trains that were being allowed to run back and forth inside West Berlin, even though they were run by Communist personnel? What was to prevent them from continuing to flood West Berlin with Communist agents of every kind? Above all, what were the Western Allies—the so-called protecting powers—going to do about it? "If the Allies can't help us in this situation, then we can't trust them any more!" cried someone, speaking for everybody in the crowd.

The harassed governing mayor shared their sense of outrage, their feelings of frustration. But the means at his disposal were limited. He did his best to calm them. Their demands would be given serious consideration. He would take up the matter of the S-Bahn with the protecting powers to see if it couldn't be placed under Allied administration.

At exactly 2:00 P.M., a fifteen-minute protest strike was observed all over West Berlin. Tools were laid down and humming wheels allowed to idle to a halt. Traffic was stopped in the streets, taxicabs refused to budge. It was an impressive gesture of solidarity toward their captive brethren in the East. But it was still only a gesture and not likely to impress the East German regime. The only ones affected by this fifteen-minute work pause were the inhabitants and the economy of West Berlin.

Expressing an almost universal feeling, the *Bild-Zeitung* tabloid—the only newspaper that appeared on Mondays in Berlin—warned that what had happened was only "the first of many blows to come. The Western powers also know this. It is up to them to react accordingly." In private conversations, the newspaper's dynamic publisher, Axel Springer, urged vigorous action, pointing out that this was the first time since the Prague coup of February 1948 that the Soviets had dared to gobble up another slice of Central European territory.

The West Germans who had flown to Berlin seemed, however, to be as irresolute as the Allies. Some, like Gerstenmaier, were for an immediate convocation of the Bundestag. But the parliamentary leader of the Christian Democrats, Heinrich Krone, arguing that the Bonn government must first be given time to decide on appropriate countermeasures, was in favor of a slightly later convocation.

Senator Joachim Lipschitz's bold suggestion that Allied tanks be brought up to flatten the flimsy barbed-wire barricades had got nowhere, and the more cautious governing mayor had by now concluded that there was nothing further to be expected of the three Western commandants. They were nothing but front-line pawns, incapable of independent action or initiative. What mattered was the attitude of the leaders behind them. But the leaders were taking it easy. De Gaulle was at Colombey-les-deux-Eglises; Macmillan was still vacationing in Yorkshire; Kennedy, when last heard from, had been out sailing off Cape Cod. His secretary of state, Dean Rusk, had spent Sunday afternoon watching a baseball game. Konrad Adenauer had chosen to remain in Bonn.

In a desperate effort to cheer up everybody, Senator Dodd of Connecticut was going around telling people, "I'm certain the Kremlin won't get away with this, just as it couldn't get away with the blockade." It was nice of him to say so, but even Harry Truman had been unable to keep Stalin from blockading Berlin for the better part of a year. In September 1948, when a mob of Communist toughs had been allowed by the Russians to storm the Berlin City Hall, then located in the Soviet sector, forty-six West Berlin policemen had been dispatched to the scene, only to be overwhelmed by the NKVD-trained mobsters. The Western Allies had done nothing. Not an Allied soldier had been sent over to aid the beleaguered policemen, most of whom ended up in East German jails. Many were those in the West Berlin administration who, like Franz Amrehn, felt that three companies of Allied infantry would have sufficed to put an end to the nonsense and to show the Russians that the West meant business. But the Western powers, then as now, had not moved. The real and increasingly irremediable division of Berlin and Germany had begun at that moment, and since then it had done nothing but widen. What was happening now was simply the final stage in the process.

If the West could so easily write off East Berlin as lost, then what faith could be placed in Allied guarantees about the security and integrity of the western sectors? The news that James O'Donnell had wanted conveyed to Willy Brandt—that

Kennedy was favorably disposed to the idea of sending General Clay to Berlin—had failed to reach the governing mayor, who had begun to have his doubts. Kennedy, in whose youthful energy he had placed such faith, seemed for the time being to have forgotten West Berlin's existence.

2

It was time to leave the Baltic coast, Klemens Krüger had decided. A war might still break out in spite of everything. East Germany's Deutschlandsender now spoke of Berlin as a mousetrap and praised the "brave fighters" on the sector border. The hesitations of the first hours were over. Victory jubilations, along with stimulating march music, came pouring out of the radio. One interview followed another—with soldiers, policemen, and Comrade Fighters from the red factory militia. "The Bonn Ultras are shaking at the knees!" an insolent voice announced. It was the voice of Eduard von Schnitzler, a former prisoner of war and BBC broadcaster who had become the East German radio's leading commentator. A little later it was Gerhard Eisler, proclaiming, "Whoever opposes us will be annihilated, at home as abroad."

"Their easy triumph has gone to their heads, and we're really browned off!" said old Kollow the fisherman.

There was a general feeling of despair. No one in the house dared laugh any more. Only now did Krüger appreciate what a free Berlin had meant.

"It was always a special occasion for us," explained Kollow to his guest. "Every Christmastime we used to travel to West Berlin. There we bought shoes, clothes, socks—all so very expensive for us, naturally. Still, we bought them. Then we went to the movies and bought a couple of illustrated magazines, which we smuggled back here. Now that's all over and done with."

Yes, it was all over and done with—that everybody knew. But there was still a nervous tension in the air, a lingering hope that the West was going to help. "There will not be a war over Berlin," Adenauer was reported to have said. Could he really have said that? They couldn't understand it. Nobody could understand such a statement coming from him.

"It isn't simply a question of Berlin," they explained to Krüger. "It's also a question of us. Have they forgotten about us completely? Why don't they at least cut off all interzonal trade? We're ready for any sacrifice, even if we have to starve."

But Erich Mende had just declared in Berlin that the interzonal trade agreement would not be abrogated. It was a two-edged sword. An abrogation of the agreement would boomerang against the inhabitants of the East.

"So nothing will happen," they sighed. "The people in the West think only of business."

The radio was left on all day. News flashes, commentaries, march music from the Deutschlandsender, light music from the radio stations of the West. Obviously nobody over there realized that this was a day of boundless grief for the seventeen million Germans here in the Zone; that it was worse even than June 17, 1953. As a citizen of the Federal Republic, Krüger tried to defend himself against the reproaches heaped upon him, but he was fighting a losing battle.

Many of the campers were now leaving. Their motorcycles and automobiles roared and growled through the town. They were leaving not out of fear of dysentery but from nervousness and anxiety about a possible war. The air buzzed with rumors. Russian armored divisions were reported to have hermetically sealed in Berlin.

Krüger went for a walk on the beach. The sea was restless, the horizon unclear. A couple of young lads came strolling toward him. Naked torsos over stovepipe jeans. Sideburns. They were talking about Ulbricht's latest measures and laughing. They couldn't take him seriously. For them he would always be a bugbear, a scarecrow.

3

Since early Sunday afternoon, the West German Foreign Ministry in Bonn had been in a dither. Most of the senior officials were back at their desks. But by early Monday morning it was clear that their feverish bureaucratic activity had achieved nothing of significance. The endless telephone calls had not had the slightest impact on events in Berlin.

When Hans Kroll, who had hurried back to Bonn from his interrupted vacation in Bavaria, was ushered into Heinrich von Brentano's office, there was little he could tell his boss. He had been away from Moscow for the past three weeks, and there was no new information he could impart about Khrushchev's intentions. He agreed with the foreign minister that severe countermeasures were called for. Brentano, however, was frankly pessimistic. The British were all for moderation, and even the Americans seemed anxious not to heat up the crisis.

This initial impression was confirmed when Brentano received the three Western ambassadors at 10:00 A.M. François Seydoux, back from Brittany, had nothing concrete to propose. His standing orders were to maintain an attitude of absolute intransigence on the question of Allied rights in Berlin. This intransigence, however, was purely verbal. The suggestion made by the Quai d'Orsay's leading Berlin expert, Jean Laloy, that the Western Allies should make their displeasure over the unilateral Soviet action known through a series of peripheral measures—the closing of airports to Russian airplanes, the halting of all trade negotiations—was allowed to die a quiet death by Eric de Carbonnel, the head of the French Foreign Ministry's Political Affairs department. There was to be no negotiating under duress with the Russians. But French troops and tanks were *not* to be moved up to the intersector border. France's policy was to maintain the status quo through thick and thin. The status quo had just been wrecked, but that made no difference. The important thing was to preserve the appearance of being as hard as nails and as solid as a rock.

Sir Christopher Steel, who, like Harold Macmillan, had long since seen through this diplomatic pose, had radically different instructions. The British had always believed in the virtue of trying to defuse the crisis through diplomatic negotiations. Sending British tanks or armored cars to the intersector border was out of the question. The Imperial General Staff had always considered West Berlin to be militarily untenable. This was no time to prove it by challenging the Russians.

Walter Dowling, the American ambassador, was in both a privileged and a more exposed position. His was the only country possessing enough military power to be able to stand up to the Russians. But Dowling was not by temperament a fighter. A soft-spoken southerner from Georgia, like Dean Rusk, he was a courteous and thoughtful rather than a forceful personality. Known to his friends as "Red" Dowling, because of the reddish hair which he wore combed and parted far down over the left ear, he wore crescent-shaped spectacles which made him look more like a university teacher than a professional diplomat. He had been ambassador to South Korea and had served briefly as assistant secretary of state for European affairs in 1959, but his real specialty was German-speaking Europe, for he had risen to be U.S. deputy high commissioner in both Austria and Germany.

Dowling had been much affected by the years he had spent in Vienna. One of the convictions he had acquired was that a settlement of the German problem along the lines of what had been accomplished in Austria, in May 1955, was no longer possible. The United States, he believed, had missed the bus on at least two occasions since World War II, and this had enormously complicated the problem, virtually nullifying the possibility of a satisfactory solution. The first mistake had been made by the Truman administration in refusing to heed Robert Murphy and General Clay's suggestion that an armored train be run through to Berlin in 1948. The airlift undertaken to circumvent the Soviet blockade had proved a costly and inconclusive substitute, since the prestige gained in the air had subsequently been squandered at the conference table, leaving the Allied position in Berlin as juridically weak as ever. The other mistake had been the failure of the Eisenhower administration to react intelligently to the June 1953 uprising in East Germany, when real pressure could have been brought to bear on the Russians to get rid of Ulbricht and to introduce a more humane regime.

Shortly after his appointment to Bonn in November of 1959, Dowling had met a Soviet diplomat named Timoshenko, whom he had previously known in Vienna. Timoshenko had begun reminiscing about the good old days. "Do you remember in Vienna when we used to say, 'Yes, we are going to get a state treaty'?"

"Yes, indeed," Dowling had answered. "But now let's see if we can't do the same thing here."

At that the Soviet diplomat had shaken his head sadly. "No, I'm afraid that's impossible. You missed your chance in 1952."

With the passage of time this, too, had become the U.S. ambassador's conviction. The West had missed its great chance in the 1952–53 period, and the only thing it could do now was to make the best of a bad job. Unlike Adenauer, Brentano, and Kroll, who talked endlessly of Germany's "reunification," Dowling was privately convinced that the two Germanies were here to stay.

All this, in a sense, was academic. The question to be decided now was what should be done in the face of the latest Soviet moves. There was first of all the question of Chancellor Adenauer. Should he fly to Berlin, as a number of persons had been pressing him to do? Dowling's opinion was that he should not. The presence in West Berlin of a person as prestigious as the federal chancellor might well destabilize the situation and encourage another massive uprising in East Germany. Since the Western Allies had no more intention of intervening now than they had in June 1953, the ensuing blood bath would result in a major loss of Allied face. The psychological consequences were incalculable. Twice before, the West had had to face this kind of dilemma: in Berlin in 1953, in Budapest in 1956. The resentment generated over a third failure to intervene in this kind of upheaval was certain to be profound. It was a risk that neither the chancellor nor the West as a whole could afford to take.

The question remained: What energetic countermeasures should be taken in retaliation for Ulbricht's seal-off action? At Cadenabbia, in Ambassador Dowling's presence, Adenauer had told Dean Rusk that a threat to Berlin could best be countered by a general trade embargo. Still, what had so far happened in Berlin was not an all-out threat to the Allied presence and to the vital access routes. If the Federal Republic were to impose a full-scale boycott on its trade with East Germany, Ulbricht might well retaliate by halting the rail and river-barge traffic needed to keep West Berlin properly supplied. Even if it was only a partial blockade and did not directly affect Allied access rights, it would be a major blow against West Berlin's economic viability. Sooner or later the Western Allies would have to break this blockade by force, with all the risks that might entail. It therefore seemed wiser, all things considered, to consider a trade embargo against the East as a kind of ultimate weapon, to be enforced *after*, not before, Ulbricht and his Russian mentors had instituted a full-scale blockade.

While these conversations were progressing at the Foreign Ministry, Konrad Adenauer was going over the latest dispatches in his chancellery office prior to the emergency cabinet meeting that had been called for later in the morning. Among the papers and reports handed to him by his secretary, Anneliese Poppinga, was one containing extracts from the fighting electoral speech that Willy Brandt had made at Nuremberg on Saturday. As he read the cruel passages in which his government was portrayed as a model of superannuated selfishness and complacency, as a haven of self-satisfaction, and as a promoter of calumny and slander, a faint twitch began to agitate the chancellor's scarred, Tibetan features. Then came the even more cruel passage concerning his absences from Bonn. During the first six months of this year, Brandt had declared, Konrad Adenauer had ruled for two and a half months from Cadenabbia. "I, on the other hand, spent thirty-five days in the Federal Republic campaigning for

Berlin and telling people what its future is to be."

In a voice of deliberately controlled anger, Adenauer said to his secretary, *"Dieser Mann muss still bleiben!"* ("This man must keep his mouth shut!").

Several hours later, after the emergency cabinet meeting, Konrad Adenauer told his staff that he would not be going to Berlin. He was going to Regensburg, as planned, to deliver another campaign speech that evening.

4

In Berlin, tempers had been rising steadily. By midday the West Berlin Schupos manning the rope barrier stretched across the broad Strasse des 17. Juni, opposite the Brandenburg Gate, were finding it increasingly difficult to hold back the crowd. Unable to approach the gate directly, many young Berliners were creeping up behind the shrubs and trees of the Tiergarten to throw stones at the Vopos and soldiers.

"Are you happy with your barbed wire? Is this the Spitzbart's latest gift to you?" they kept taunting the helmeted guards.

The latter finally riposted with jets of water and tear-gas grenades. Neither were particularly effective, for the mild northwest wind was against them, and some of the Vopos were visibly affected as the tear-inducing smoke drifted back into their faces.

While West Berlin Schupos armed with megaphones pleaded with the hotheads to move back, four East German armored cars advanced between the pillars of the Brandenburg Gate. The armored cars were followed by water-cannon trucks, which came close to the demarcation line and began dousing photographers and others who had managed to slip through the straining police line. Shortly afterward, a loudspeaker on the eastern side announced that because of West Berlin provocations, the Brandenburg Gate was being closed to both pedestrians and motor vehicles.

The crowd of West Berliners, worked up to fever pitch, seemed for a moment about to break through the thin Schupo police cordon. On the other side of the demarcation line were soldiers armed with fixed bayonets and Tommy guns, with armored cars in reserve. Stones as well as insults were flying through the air. A Vopo officer fired a couple of warning shots.

In the American headquarters building, William Whalley, British public safety officer, was conferring with his American counterpart, Alex Yaney, about the possibility of taking over and running the S-Bahn in the three western sectors, when he received a call from one of his colleagues. All hell was breaking loose in front of the Brandenburg Gate. Angry West Berliners were hurling stones at the Kampfgruppen and East German soldiers, and at any moment the latter might open fire. Johannes Stumm, the West Berlin police president, had thrown in the one hundred riot policemen he was allowed by the occupying powers to deploy without prior authorization. But the single Bereitschaft company was hopelessly outnumbered. Reinforcements were desperately needed. Whalley told him to give Stumm and police chief Erich Duensing the green light; they could order out all twelve hundred men of the riot police assigned to the British sector.

A few minutes later when he drove up, the former RAF officer found the approaches to the Gate in a state of turmoil. Erich Duensing was there and not much liking what he saw. The rage was too wild and uncontrolled, too much like mob violence to suit his sense of Prussian discipline. It was time to put an end to the nonsense.

Several companies of riot policemen were brought up. They looked curiously old-fashioned and pacific in their shiny black shakos and leggings, compared with the armed and helmeted contingents to the east. Forming a human chain with outstretched arms and hands firmly gripped to each other's pistol belts, the West Berlin riot policemen began pushing the mob back up the Strasse des 17. Juni and away from the Brandenburg Gate.

This enforced, step-by-step withdrawal took a full hour and a half and was marked by one serious incident. A Russian bus bringing soldiers to the Soviet War Memorial happened to drive up as the furious crowd was being pushed back, and the inevitable happened. Someone threw a stone, which smashed through one of the bus's windows. The driver, realizing that the mob would gladly lynch every occupant inside, took off in a hurry. A new police cordon had to be formed around the Soviet War Memorial to keep the two unhappy-looking Russian sentinels on duty before it from being assaulted in their turn.

In the end, the riot detachments, backed by British Military Police officers and men, had to establish an almost unbroken line over the quarter-mile stretch running through the eastern fringe of the Tiergarten as far as the Potsdamer Platz. The West Berlin riot policemen thus found themselves having to defend the border-line fencework and barbed wire put up by the East Germans. This was not at all to Senator Joachim Lipschitz's liking and he let Duensing know it. Duensing, however, was strongly backed by the British commandant, who had the final say in such matters.

Not long afterward, after almost being hit by a flying stone during another tour of the intersector border, Joachim Lipschitz began to have second thoughts about the virtues of letting his fellow Berliners let off steam. It was announced from City Hall that no more demonstrations would be permitted near the border, and that the police were henceforth under orders to disperse all unauthorized gatherings.

The second major gateway between East and West Berlin— the Brandenburg Gate—was now definitely closed. The number of authorized crossing points between the eastern and the western sectors was thus reduced from thirteen to twelve. Still the Allies did not move. U.S. troops were still kept at their barracks on a stand-by alert, while British antitank gunners, who had taken defensive positions in the Tiergarten well back from the Gate, were so well hidden by the surrounding greenery that they were virtually invisible.

Affected like everybody else were the sightseeing bus tours, now prevented from using their habitual point of entry into East Berlin. Affected, too, were Allied transit rights, which neither the East Germans nor the Russians had previously challenged. When three British officers drove up shortly afterward, intending to enter East Berlin, they were told that they would have to pass through the U.S. sector to the south and enter via the Friedrichstrasse. The primacy of the U.S. over the other two western sectors was thus subtly stressed, but it brought no protest from the British.

It turned out that two of the officers were from the British Army of the Rhine and did not belong to the British Berlin Command. "If I had known they were coming, I would have told them not to go to the Gate," explained Brigadier Goff Hamilton. "We do not want to provoke incidents at a time like this." The once proud British lion had lost not only his bite; he had even lost his roar.

Walter Ulbricht could afford to exult. His fondest expectations had, if anything, been surpassed. Making another lightning visit to the "front" in his familiar double-breasted summer suit, he told a group of Volksarmee officers assembled on the Potsdamer Platz that peace was now assured.

One of the NVA officers mentioned the fact that a U.S. general had recently been seen walking past.

"Then," answered Walter Ulbricht, "he saw that the Nationale Volksarmee stands at its posts and that everything is in order. Now that everything has been carried out in such a precise fashion, there is no longer any doubt about the exact working of the state apparatus of the Workers-and-Peasants-State. Let us hope that they may draw the conclusion that it is far better, during the preparation of a peace treaty, to negotiate in advance!"

5

He had had a bad night, there was no doubt about it, and now, as he walked through the Treptow Park, past rows of trucks and groups of soldiers, Emil Goltz felt prematurely tired, as though it were the end rather than the beginning of the day. The previous evening, after reconnoitering the border, he had sat in front of the television set for a couple of hours, trying to concentrate on the images flitting on and off the screen. But his thoughts were elsewhere, while his ears were expectantly cocked for the sound of Allied tanks moving up from the West to flatten the coils of barbed wire strung out along the Heidelberger Strasse and the Kiefholzstrasse with their treads. But nothing had happened. The barbed wire, on this Monday morning, was intact, along with the sawhorses, the Grepos, and recent Kampfgruppen reinforcements.

At the Treptow borough town hall, where he had to register as a Grenzgänger, he did not have long to wait before finding out what lay in store for him. As ill luck would have it, he was confronted by a Party believer named Wiedemann, with whom he had once worked at the East Berlin Bau-Union. The mere sight of his former hard-hat colleague walking up to his desk was enough to throw the normally taciturn Wiedemann into a rage. His face flushed crimson, his eyes blazed, as he recited the litany of Goltz's crimes. He had betrayed his working-class colleagues and the DDR by working for and thus enriching the capitalists of the West, while enjoying the advantages of life in democratic Berlin. In short, he was an opportunist, a two-faced profiteer, a drone, who seemed to think that he could go on "eating out of two mangers," indefinitely.

The tirade finally completed—it lasted close to a quarter of an hour without eliciting a word of objection—Wiedemann angrily thrust a slip of mimeographed paper across his desk. "Here, take this," he barked. "You are to apply for work immediately at the Berlin Bau-Union. This is your assignment order."

Goltz pocketed the order and left without uttering a word. He decided to follow Wiedemann's instructions—for the sake of appearances.

The Bau-Union's personnel bureau chief examined the mimeographed slip and told him to report for work the next morning.

"Tomorrow morning?" objected Goltz. "I'm sorry, but that's impossible. I haven't yet taken my annual vacation, and I'm entitled to two weeks. So I'm going to take them now, and I'll report for work when the two weeks are up."

The bureau chief eyed him severely. "Colleague, you'd do well to think again about this proposed vacation of yours. In fourteen days' time we may no longer have an opening for you."

Goltz said that he would think it over.

That afternoon, as he had hoped, his wife Anna returned from Thuringia with their daughter Beate. A long and troubled conversation followed, lasting well into the evening. Only reluctantly would she agree to his arguments and entreaties. Yes, life here was infernal, and it was probably going to get worse. Yes, they would have to find some way of slipping across the border; and maybe, as Emil said, it would be far easier if they acted now, or at any rate tomorrow. But she just couldn't bear the thought of leaving all these things behind. Maybe they didn't mean much to him, but to her they were a whole world of meaning, associations, attachment. Besides, how did they know just what was going to happen next? Wouldn't it be better to wait to see how things were going to develop?

Anna Goltz was unwilling or unable to imagine that these sawhorses and barbed-wire barricades could stay there indefinitely. Once things had calmed down they might simply disappear.

"Things are going to get a lot worse before they get better," Emil warned his wife. "What have the Western Allies done? Nothing, absolutely nothing! So why should Ulbricht and his crowd stop halfway now that they've got away with murder?"

To this his wife had no reply. She buried her face in her hands.

Getting up, Goltz walked over to the window. Outside, the light was fading from the sky, although the street lamps had not yet gone on. His mind was made up. Tomorrow he would devote the whole day to a thorough reconnaissance of the border, and by the time night fell, he would know exactly where he, Anna, and Beate could sneak across into the U.S. sector.

It was midafternoon on the Baltic. Three women were seated in Kollow's living room talking about their children who were in the West. Their eyes were red from weeping.

"Will we ever see them again?" they asked Krüger.

Once again the West German was at a loss as to what to say. What could he tell them? How could he know what might happen tomorrow? They looked at him questioningly, and then one of them said, "This is what we have brought down on Germany! What a situation!"

Until now they had traveled back and forth to West Berlin, and from there had flown illegally to the Federal Republic once or twice a year, as long as there was enough money for them to see their children. Each such trip was fraught with fear. If discovered or betrayed it meant prison. But even these risks were now a thing of the past.

Krüger was going to leave the next morning. He had packed his things. Old Kollow said to him, "Yes, it's better you leave. It looks damnably like 1939."

In the evening friends, acquaintances, guests were again seated in the living room. There was a lot of arguing. Some said, "The West will intervene." Others claimed the opposite: "Nothing will happen, absolutely nothing. The West will yield in Berlin, just as it yielded in Budapest. They'll keeping yielding ground until it's too late."

Krüger said nothing. The Freies Berlin broadcasting station announced the latest news. Everyone crowded around the radio. Declarations from Western statesmen, all speaking of negotiations. Bitter disappointment could be read on every face. The West Berlin police had driven the demonstrators back from the sector border to avoid incidents, the speaker explained.

"They should leave the Berliners alone," said a young man, employed in a land-registry office in Chemnitz. "If the Berliners start something, we'll all cut loose with them. We've got to get rid of those bastards once and for all!"

"And what about the tanks?" asked Krüger. "And the atomic bombs?"

"If we let ourselves be pressured by Khrushchev's atomic bombs, then the Federal Republic will soon be in the same fix as Berlin. You'll see."

Krüger now found himself sharing their fears and despair. That night his sleep was singularly troubled. Outside, the street resounded with people's voices, and in his fitful slumbers he fancied he heard them shouting, *"Berlin bleibt frei—Trinkt Coca-Cola!"*

Late that same evening the Foreign Ministry in Bonn received a telegraphed dispatch from Wilhelm Grewe, the West German ambassador in Washington. He had had a talk with Dean Rusk at the State Department and had also taken part in a meeting of the Ambassadorial Group that was supposed to coordinate policy on the subject of Berlin. The meeting had proved totally fruitless. Grewe's earnest pleas for vigorous countermeasures had been rebuffed. The diplomatic representatives of France, Great Britain, and the United States had not been willing to endorse even mild retaliatory measures against East German officials, who could continue to enter West Berlin as they pleased. Allied policy, if such it could be called, was to do nothing for the time being that might exacerbate the situation.

The dispatch sent shock waves through the West German Foreign Ministry. There was a feeling of having been let down, not to say betrayed, at this critical juncture. By now it was a universal sentiment. "Well, Mr. Ambassador, how do you feel about it?" asked the chauffeur who was driving Hans Kroll to the airport, from where he was to fly back to Moscow. "That's a fine bunch of Allies we've chosen for ourselves!"

Konrad Adenauer meanwhile had left for Regensburg, in northern Bavaria. Twenty-five thousand people, most of them members of the Christian Democratic–Christian Socialist Union, had crowded into a local sports ground to hear what the Old Man had to say in this hour of national crisis. The weather, once again, was deplorable, and while Adenauer and members of his entourage were protected by the stadium overhang, many persons in the crowd were forced to stand and listen in the rain.

The chancellor apologized for arriving late—he had been detained by the latest developments in Berlin. With the closing of the Brandenburg Gate, the Soviet zone had been turned into an even more hermetically sealed prison. The Four-Power agreements of the past had been torn to shreds at a time when Khrushchev was calling for the negotiation of new agreements. What a commentary on the Soviet Union's demands that [West] Berlin be made into a free city!

Adenauer then proceeded to develop his pet theme: that the West's most effective weapon against the Communist bloc was economic. If West Germany's NATO partners would agree to a total embargo on trade with the eastern bloc, then they would be able to extract concessions from the East.

These preliminary remarks completed, the Old Man launched into a frankly partisan speech. Herr Brandt had been "giving himself airs" in the enunciation of a new "style" in foreign policy which Adenauer, for his part, was unable to comprehend. The CDU-CSU coalition government, in the words of the chief opposition leader, "exhausts itself in idolatry and haughtiness, and takes refuge in lazy-mindedness and stupidity." "Now that's pretty strong stuff," the chancellor commented acidly, "and if Herr Brandt permits himself such things and calls that a new style, then I say: Under no circumstances do we want this new style!"

There were cries of "*Sehr gut!*" from the crowd. "And if I may be allowed to add something, ladies and gentlemen," the chancellor went on, "then I am of the opinion that if there is someone who has been handled with the greatest respect by his political opponents, then it is the Herr Brandt, alias Frahm."

Although this cruel sally was applauded by Adenauer's partisan supporters, it was a fatal blunder. To say that Brandt had been treated with respect by his opponents was to overlook the major onslaught on his patriotism that Franz-Josef Strauss had launched the previous spring. And to follow up by referring to the governing mayor of Berlin as "Brandt, alias Frahm"—a reference to his illegitimate birth—was to aim below the belt.

The phlegmatic chancellor had for once lost his sangfroid. He had allowed the remarks made by Brandt at Nuremberg to get under his usually thick skin and had answered them in kind. It was not the behavior that most West Germans expected of their chancellor in this tense and perilous hour—as they were soon to make clear.

6

Berlin, on Tuesday morning, was a stunned as well as stunted city. Acting once again in the dead of night, when traffic was at a minimum, Karl Maron's Ministry of the Interior had issued new regulations for cars with West Berlin license plates. From 1:00 A.M. on, they were required to show special permits to be allowed into East Berlin. West Berliners, the ministry explained, had been abusing freedom of movement across the border for espionage purposes. Pedestrians were further advised not to come closer than one hundred meters to the DDR's security forces and to avoid any unnecessary loitering in their vicinity, in the interest of their own safety

The neighborhood of the Friedrichstrasse station, still full of suitcase sitters, looked more than ever like an armed camp. The T-34 tanks had not moved, but to protect them and their crews from the potential wrath of East Berliners, many of them were now surrounded by concertinas of barbed wire. FDJ delegations kept parading around, bringing gifts of hot coffee and cigarettes to the fighters at the "front."

The mood of the East German authorities was jubilant, and Hermann Axen's editorialists could pull out all the stops. "IT'S GREAT HOW EVERYTHING WORKED OUT!" was *Neues Deutschland*'s triumphant headline. "Thank you, Comrades of the Volksarmee, thank you, Comrades of the Kampfgruppen! . . . If peace is endangered, Walter Ulbricht does not hesitate. He restores order by closing the door to further provocations on the part of the warmongers and *Kriegsstadt* hyenas."

Foremost among these "war-city hyenas" was Willy Brandt, who for far too long had been allowed to instigate and organize the man-trade and the abductions of bamboozled East Germans. "Compatriots in Neukölln and Wedding, Kreuzberg and Spandau, take this piece of advice: kick that Brandt fellow out once and for all!"

The compatriots in Neukölln and Wedding, Kreuzberg and Spandau, were, however, in no mood to kick Brandt out. Their fury at this point was focused on the Grepos and Kampfgruppen, and also on the listlessness of the Allies. The joint protest that the three Western commandants had been allowed to hammer out after sixty hours of diplomatic wrangling, and which they delivered to the Soviet commandant at Karlshorst, did nothing to lessen the prevailing discontent. It was all depressingly familiar—like the innumerable "flagrant violations" of the Four-Power agreements, which had previously been denounced, to no avail. Allied troops were being kept as far from the intersector boundary as possible, while riot-police detachments were now protecting the fencework and barbed wire in the central Brandenburg Gate–Potsdamer Platz area.

Inside the Schöneberg Rathaus, the sense of gloom was deeper than ever. There was a feeling that something had to be done, but in the absence of any Allied lead or action, nobody quite knew what. People were getting restive. Because the S-Bahn was run by the East German authorities, it was being boycotted by West Berliners, but this was not enough. The previous night a group of angry youths had invaded the Lichterfelde-Süd station and smashed every train window they could with clubs and iron bars. There was no telling what might happen next.

Although Willy Brandt and his associates knew that Edward R. Murrow had taken up the cudgels for them and sent a strong dispatch to Washington, it seemed to have had no more effect than the messages of the U.S. mission chief, Allan Lightner, who was also pleading for some kind of action. Kennedy, like Rusk, was maintaining a discreet silence. Macmillan was still shooting grouse in Yorkshire, while Lord Home enjoyed the air of the Scottish moors. De Gaulle, too, had not yet seen fit to return to Paris from his country house at Colombey-les-deux-Eglises.

Visibly despondent and unnerved by a feeling of abandonment in this hour of need, Willy Brandt finally agreed to Deputy Mayor Amrehn's suggestion that a huge protest meeting be held in front of the city hall on Wednesday afternoon.

Perhaps a demonstration might jar the sleepwalkers in Washington, London, and Paris into some kind of reaction. It would at least provide some kind of safety valve for the pent-up emotions of hundreds of thousands, not to say millions, of West Berliners.

But the prospect of facing such a multitude with nothing concrete to offer was a grim one. And here, just to complicate his task, was the chancellor of the Federal Republic publicly mocking his illegitimate birth! When the text of Adenauer's remarks at Regensburg was brought to Brandt during a meeting of the city-hall Senat, he was so upset that he had to leave the room. So this was der Alte's answer to the invitation that had been extended to him to attend the next day's mass meeting!

Brandt's reply, delivered not long afterward, was devastating.

Before the terrible events in Berlin last Sunday, I would have expressed my scorn at such bad manners after such an attack on the part of the Christian Democratic Chancellor-Candidate. I can only leave the German people to judge his behavior.

The German people now need unity as they have never needed it before over the past sixteen years. He who endangers that unity or deliberately shatters it becomes the aider and abettor of our enemies. No infamy will keep me from behaving as the need of our people dictates.

For Klemens Krüger, on the distant Baltic shore, the time had come to bid farewell to Kollow and the other members of his household. The women were crying. They implored Krüger to look after their sons in the West. He promised to do so.

A woman he didn't know came up with a letter in her hand. "My daughter is in the West, in Bielefeld, illegally. She mustn't come back. If it's ever found out, she'll be put in jail here for years. Also, there's no way any more of getting used to things as they are over here. Take this letter and post it the moment you reach the West. She must stay where she is."

The woman began crying. Krüger tucked the letter away. He couldn't bear the sight of all these tears.

"My God, you are returning to freedom," said one person in

the group, "while we must stay behind—in prison."

Krüger was again overcome with a feeling of overpowering guilt, as though he were personally responsible for everything that had happened so far or that was going to happen. Yet what had he done? In what way was he guilty? Had he perhaps not done all he could for them?

"Take me with you," pleaded one of the women, "in the trunk of your car. My God, how am I going to get out of here?"

Krüger looked at her. Her anguish was boundless.

"At the very first check point they'll drag you out of the car," he said. But something, he thought, had to be done. Counter-measures, drastic countermeasures, were needed. Nobody could endure what was going on here, knowing that nothing was going to happen.

Krüger waved once again to those he was leaving behind. Several of them ran after his car, waving and weeping.

On the autobahn he was met by long columns of Nationale Volksarmee and Russian troops—green and olive gray uniforms, steel helmets, unslung weapons—in a virtually unbroken chain of trucks. The specter of war haunted the highway. Everywhere passenger cars were being halted and checked by senior Volks-polizei officers. Krüger, too, was waved to a stop by the road-side. But as soon as the Vopos recognized his car's West German license plate he was waved on and allowed to proceed.

He met with the same politeness at the interzonal border.

"You are coming from Mecklenburg?"

"Yes."

"Then you can drive on."

Krüger crossed the border without even having to pay the autobahn toll or having to submit to another check. As a citizen of another state—the Federal Republic—which had nothing in common with the one he was leaving, he could be treated with the courtesy due to an alien.

Overruled in his bold suggestion that Allied tanks be brought up to flatten the still flimsy barbed-wire barrier, Joachim Lip-schitz, the energetic senator of the interior, was busy promoting other forms of action. Everything must be done to help the East Berliners now caught in Ulbricht's giant mousetrap. Although no longer allowed to drive in by car, West Berliners could still enter East Berlin on foot and come out just as easily by showing a West Berlin identity card to the Vopos stationed at the twelve remaining crossing points. It did not take many of them long to realize that by borrowing a couple of identity cards from willing accomplices, they could cross into the Soviet sector and provide relatives or friends with a West Berlin identity card that could get them past the border guards. There was a risk involved, for the photograph on the card did not usually correspond to the appearance of the bearer, but this risk was one that many East Berliners were now willing to take. The logical next step was to give this new species of border crossers unofficial backing by manufacturing new identity cards with photographs as varied as possible to fit a wide range of features.

Considerably less hush-hush was another scheme that Lipschitz also began promoting. The idea was to use loud-speakers to undermine the morale of Grepos and Vopos stationed along the border and to persuade them to defect. The first such sound truck—an old Volkswagen that the Social Democrats had been using in their district electioneering—made its appearance this Tuesday afternoon. The volunteers for the curious assignment read off the latest news dispatches, played a record or two, and sprinkled their brief broadcasts with anti-Ulbricht jokes.

The effects of this sonic bombardment were not instantly apparent. Even if they had wanted to, most of the Grepos and Vopos on guard duty were too terrified of their officers to dare attempt a dash for freedom. Many knew that they would be leaving behind relatives against whom the Ulbricht regime could exercise reprisals. The authorities were doing everything to foster this impression by meting out stiff sentences to anyone who dared protest. An East German ambulance driver who had been held up at a Potsdam intersection the previous Sunday while trying to drive a woman in labor to the nearest hospital was sentenced to two months in prison for shouting at a straggler from a slow-marching column of factory militiamen, "I'll help you out of the way, you lame-assed dog!" Erich Lowitz, the Wehrmacht veteran who had cursed a passing NVA platoon because they were ready to shoot their own countrymen, was sentenced by a People's Court to six years in jail for incitation to revolt.

The few East German border guards who had enough courage

to defect on this Tuesday probably needed no sound truck to inspire them. One of them was shot in midair while leaping over the barbed-wire fence barring the Ruppiner Strasse, but he survived and became famous overnight. The person who "shot" him was the West Berlin photographer Klaus Lehnartz, who happened to be walking up the Bernauer Strasse when his attention was drawn to a young helmeted Grepo, nervously fingering the topmost strand of wire. From the apprehensive glances he kept casting in the direction of two colleagues who were pacing up and down on the opposite sidewalk, Lehnartz realized that he was trying to pluck up the courage to make the fateful leap. Walking casually by and then retracing his steps, Lehnartz told the Grepo as he passed that he would train his camera on the guard's two colleagues who, being camera shy, would probably turn their backs. The Grepo said something in reply, but his words were lost in the rumble of a French army half-track driving down the Bernauer Strasse.

Providentially for Lehnartz, an amateur photographer now came up. Lehnartz asked him to train his lens on the two Grepos across the way. He did. When nothing happened, Lehnartz decided to approach the wire and to encourage the Grepo once again. But the young Grepo chose this moment to take a running jump. Lehnartz just had time to raise his camera in an instinctive reflex action and to release the shutter, thus snapping the photograph that was to be splashed over the pages of newspapers all over the world.

This Grepo, too, dropped his weapon—a Tommy gun—as he flew over the wire. It was retrieved by a West Berlin Schupo, who hopped nimbly out of a passing police van. In the ensuing confusion, Lehnartz managed to follow the defecting Grepo and his retinue to the police station. The Grepo, Helmut Kurzke, turned out to be a disgruntled Saxon who had been forced to stand guard for eighteen consecutive hours. He took out a fifty-East-mark bill and slapped it down on the table in front of the Schupos. "You see that? That's what I was offered this morning by one of our officers just so I'd stick it out a little longer. But what d'you expect me to do with fifty lousy East marks if I can't spend them as I want to at the border?" He then opened his mess gear and displayed its contents—several slices of buttered bread. At that, all present, including Lehnartz, dug into their pockets and made spontaneous donations. A Schupo was dispatched to the nearest food shop to buy some rolls, butter, cheese, and sausage for the ill-fed, fed-up Saxon.

As Lehnartz came down the stairs, more or less driven out of the police station by the Schupos, who didn't want journalists around, he had another surprise in store for him. The eastern part of the Ruppiner Strasse was now swarming with a score or two of Vopos, Grepos, and NVA officers and soldiers who had hurried up to investigate the incident. They were followed by several East Berlin photographers whose cameras (as Lehnartz later discovered) had been presealed by the authorities to keep them from extracting the film inside for their own journalistic or other purposes.

Since the barbed-wire barrier at this point had proved too flimsy an obstacle, it was decided to replace it by something more solid. Soon a work squad drove up in a truck that was loaded with concrete slabs. It was followed by a small, tractor-mounted crane. The crane began lifting the slabs into position. The walling in of East Berlin's inhabitants had begun.

7

Although the Marienfelde reception center was still crammed with refugees, the previous week's flood was now reduced to a trickle. On Monday several thousand fugitives from the East had registered, but most of them were persons who had come to spend the weekend in West Berlin and who had decided not to return when they found the border closed. According to the official figures, exactly twenty-eight refugees had made it over during Sunday night and early Monday morning. Some—like Georg Maurer, his wife, and child—had chosen to swim across the Teltow Canal. But one of them, a fifty-year-old Reichsbahn employee named Alfons Dubinski, had managed to sneak across the no-man's-land wilderness of the former Reichschancellery garden, to squirm his way under the hastily erected chicken-wire fence along the Ebertstrasse, and to duck across the ill-lit street into the protective shrubbery of the Tiergarten before the Grepos could catch him.

On Tuesday the number of persons checking into Marienfelde had dwindled to several hundred. Most of them, again, were East Berliners who had been spending the weekend with friends in the West. The number of actual escapees during Monday night was estimated to have been no more than forty-one, including eight women and two children. For the first time, East German border guards had opened fire on a couple caught swimming across a branch of the Teltow Canal toward the U.S. sector. Neither of the fugitives were hit, but this was a grim omen for the future.

Tuesday night saw several more groups swim to freedom across the Teltow Canal, including girls and women who did not know how to swim but who made it over safely with the aid of inflated inner tubes. There had been so much splashing in the process that several of the fugitives were privately convinced that the Vopos stationed to intercept them simply pretended not to hear.

Theirs, however, were destined to be the last collective swims to freedom. On Wednesday, searchlights and machine guns were installed at different points along the Teltow Canal and its branches. Similar measures had already been taken along the edges of Griebnitz Lake, spanned by the so-called Unity Bridge, which the Allied liaison officers used when they drove into the U.S. sector from nearby Potsdam. The steel-girdered bridge was blocked to East Germans by a cordon of army troops stationed 150 yards from its western end, while Grepo guards were assigned to watch the shore below. A motorboat equipped with a searchlight now patrolled the lake—as nineteen-year-old Aldin Lindig of Potsdam discovered when he settled on this escape route after vainly trying several others. Only by hiding in a clump of reeds until the patrol boat's searching beam had passed over his head was he able to launch out and swim the two hundred yards separating him from the Promised Land of West Berlin.

By Wednesday morning it was clear to all but a few dreamers that the clamp-down, far from being a temporary measure, was going to be permanent and pitiless. The U-Bahn rails leading to the Warschauer Brücke station in East Berlin, hitherto merely blocked by Vopo sentries, had been torn up by East German sappers in the course of the previous afternoon. Schulenburg Park, between Treptow and Neukölln, where children from East and West Berlin had once happily played together, was now cut in two by a guarded wire fence. Machine guns were being installed by the Glienecke bridge, as well as small rocket launchers for night flares.

Similar measures were being taken underground. When Uwe Kordt, using a culvert, climbed down onto the now deelectrified subway track near the Walter Ulbricht Stadium in the Pankow district, he found the way into the French sector barred by a sawhorse barricade, watched over by three Vopo guards and two police dogs.

At a number of points along the intersector border three-to-four-foot walls, composed of concrete or pressed rubble, were beginning to replace the flimsy barbed-wire entanglements. The fencework sealing off the Boyenstrasse-Chausseestrasse rectangle, just north of the Volkspolizei Hospital, was now two meters high and guarded by some 450 armed militiamen. The fencework barring the Potsdamer Platz was equally high, if not as long, and behind it Grepos could be seen goose-stepping and snapping smartly to attention each time a general appeared. Residents of the Bernauer Strasse, who had been able to walk out of their houses and into the French sector more or less at will, were being required to surrender their front-door keys to the Vopos, who had been ordered to bolt the doors. Some were even stationed in the passageways to keep an eye on what was going on inside.

A widespread power failure that Wednesday morning led many East Berliners to believe that rebellious workers had launched a general strike. But by early afternoon, the normal electric current was restored, dashing all lingering hopes of a major insurrection. At the Oberspree Cable Works, where she worked in the accounting department, Elsa Sahl heard workers complaining bitterly and comparing their present lot to that of the Warsaw ghetto under the Nazi occupation.

It was not only in East Berlin that people felt themselves

hemmed in and trapped. Many West Berliners were now seized by a sense of panic. If Ulbricht's men could cut the city in two without the slightest trace of an Allied reaction, then what was to keep his soldiers and tankmen from driving triumphantly on into the western sectors? Grocery stores were mobbed by panicky housewives who, fearing the imminent outbreak of fighting and a new occupation, were out to buy all the sugar, flour, and canned goods they could get their hands on. The same affluent but faint-hearted souls who had reacted to the first Khrushchev ultimatum of November 1958 by trying to get their furniture transported to the Federal Republic began besieging the moving-van companies, which were soon solidly booked for weeks and months ahead.

The less affluent were also getting jittery, as Robert Lochner discovered on this same Wednesday. Although his RIAS staff members remained unflinchingly at their posts—ignoring the East German Deutschlandsender's uninterrupted exultations over the paralysis and confusion in Allied ranks, the defeat of the Cold Warriors in Washington, Great Britain's abandonment of West Berlin, and so on—Lochner's own maid could not wait to clear out. She had served him for ten years, but after talking on the telephone to a friend in West Germany who assured her that the Russians were going to block the traffic routes to the Federal Republic, she packed her bags and flew back to her native Frankfurt.

A by-now-ritual visit to the intersector border, made on this Wednesday morning by Gen. Bruce Clarke, commanding U.S. Army ground forces in Germany, did little to boost local morale. A bareheaded Willy Brandt, his hair faintly ruffled by the breeze, accompanied the four-star general to the Brandenburg Gate. A water-cannon truck was stationed beyond the wire barrier ready to douse them, as several Western photographers had recently been doused, if they came too close.

As they were standing there, so Clarke later claimed, the governing mayor asked him, "General, how could we encourage that fellow to shoot water at me?"

"What for, Mayor?"

"Because I would get reelected for sure."

Perhaps Brandt was trying to brighten an otherwise routine

visit, the only immediate result of which was to authorize U.S. Army patrols to approach within a "baseball's throw" of the intersector border.

The prevailing mood in West Berlin was forcefully conveyed by the morning edition of Axel Springer's *Bild-Zeitung*. KENNEDY IS SILENT! MACMILLAN GOES SHOOTING! ADENAUER INSULTS BRANDT! were the mass-circulation tabloid's three challenging headlines. "Western diplomats," wrote the editorialist, "even think that Allied rights in Berlin were not directly affected. . . . For three days nothing has happened save for a paper protest from the Allied commandants."

Equally close to the popular mood and every bit as sensational was the headline run by *Der Kurier*, an early-afternoon newspaper generally sympathetic to Adenauer's Christian Democrats: MARSHAL KONIEV HAD INFORMED THE WESTERN POWERS! The article that followed claimed that on the previous Thursday, Koniev had invited the Allied military missions to the Soviet headquarters at Zossen-Wünsdorf for a talk. The exact details of their conversations were not known, but "the Allies were nevertheless informed that their rights would not be affected as a result of the measures being planned in Berlin."

The story—which, it was later discovered, had been deliberately leaked to the West Berlin newspapers by a Soviet agent—was immediately accepted as true by thousands of West Berliners. They were sure of it. This is why the Allies hadn't reacted the previous Sunday, or on any day since then. They'd been tipped off in advance that their own positions wouldn't be endangered. In short, the whole sordid business was a put-up job, secretly engineered by the Russians and the Western Allies behind the backs of their German victims!

By three o'clock that afternoon, when the mass meeting was due to begin, many factories and offices had closed for the day, deserted by their workers and employees. The entire population of West Berlin seemed to have made for the Schöneberg Rathaus. The square in front of the dark-stuccoed city hall had disappeared beneath an ocean of umbrellas—it was raining once again—and hundreds of signposts and banners. "Betrayed by the West!—We Demand Countermeasures! Enough of

Protests—Now Let Deeds Follow! Ninety Hours and No Action!
Silence! Many Are Still Sleeping! The Bundestag to Berlin!
Where Is the Chancellor—Vacationing in Italy? Kennedy to
Berlin! Munich 1938—Berlin 1961!" read some of the angry and
ironic slogans being waved above the dripping hats and umbrel-
las.

While waiting for the governing mayor to speak, the huge
crowd took up the rhythmic chant *"Howley soll her! Howley soll
her! Howley soll her!"* The man they were shouting for was
Frank Howley, the two-fisted colonel who had led the first U.S.
Army contingent into a completely Russian-occupied Berlin in
early July of 1945, and who had presented Marshal Zhukov and
his fellow conquerors with a fait accompli by defiantly hoisting
the Stars and Stripes over the six borough town halls of the
designated American sector.

Never had Willy Brandt had a more difficult speech to deliver. One word too much and the tense multitude, later estimated at three hundred thousand strong, would have surged
down to the Potsdamer Platz and the Brandenburg Gate, fancy-
ing that it could carry everything before it. One word too little
and the somber gloom of so many of his fellow West Berliners
could turn into panicky despair, completely undermining the
city's spirit of resistance.

Brandt had spent much of the previous afternoon and evening
with several of his close SPD colleagues drafting a personal
letter to Kennedy, who had told him the previous March in
Washington, that he could always appeal directly to the White
House if the need should arise. In the letter, Brandt had reminded the president that passive acceptance of the border closure amounted, in effect, to a tacit recognition of the "illegal
sovereignty of the East Berlin government." For this reason,
this was the most serious turning point in the city's history since
the blockade of 1948–49. The Soviet Union had already achieved
half its "free-city" objective through the unchallenged use of the
East German People's Army. The second act of the drama would
simply be a question of time. West Berlin, having lost its function as a refuge of freedom, would come to resemble a ghetto
unless energetic steps were taken to halt the drift and dis-
couragement. He was therefore asking the president to bring

the Berlin problem before the United Nations and to reinforce the U.S. Army garrison in Berlin as a demonstration of firmness vis-à-vis the Russians.

In his hour-long speech, delivered in a hoarse, emotion-choked voice, Brandt alluded to the letter, although he did not specifically divulge its contents. He compared the present crisis to the occupation of the Rhineland by the Nazis in 1936, adding, "The Man today is called Ulbricht!" (Cheers.) He wanted the representatives of all the nations of the world to come to Berlin to see for themselves what a "paradise" the Communist regime had created for itself behind its zoolike barriers of wire. (Cheers.) He was even prepared to let bygones be bygones and to welcome Dr. Adenauer to Berlin. (Mitigated applause.) Then he added meaningfully, "Berlin expects more than words; Berlin expects political action!" (Prolonged cheering.) The Allied commandants' joint protest was good, but it was not enough. (More cheering.) Finally, he appealed to all officials, army officers, and members of the Volkspolizei and Betriebskampfgruppen not to shoot at their fellow Germans. West Berlin, while strengthening its ties with the Federal Republic, would never abandon East Berlin or the people of East Germany.

Deputy Mayor Amrehn, who followed with a short speech of his own—intended to demonstrate the unity of West Berlin's coalition government, notwithstanding the election campaign—called on his listeners to remain calm and not to let their feelings rush them into rash actions that might do real harm. The mass meeting ended with a ritual singing of "Deutschland über alles," after which the pacified multitude dispersed.

Even his political opponents were willing to give the governing mayor credit for a masterly performance. The worst had been avoided, and a giant march, which could have turned into a blood bath, had been skillfully averted.

The performance left Brandt utterly exhausted. While solving some problems, his speech also had created new ones. The first was with Franz Amrehn, who was annoyed to discover that Brandt had undertaken to write a personal letter to the president of the United States without informing him, still less soliciting his advice. The authorities in Bonn were even more outraged at the "airs" the governing mayor was giving himself in bypassing the usual diplomatic channels and addressing himself directly to the master of the White House. But offended too was Kennedy himself, when he learned in the midafternoon of this same Wednesday that Willy Brandt had publicly aired the existence of a letter addressed to him which he had not yet received.

The letter, first drafted in German, had been turned over to Allan Lightner, head of the State Department mission in Berlin. It had had to be translated, put through the scrambler for cabled transmission to Washington, and then unscrambled at the other end. The process had taken an unusually long time, so that it was very late in the evening before Kennedy, who had retired to his bedroom, could actually read the letter intended for him.

In Berlin it was already 4:00 A.M., Thursday, August 17. Most of the city's inhabitants had long since retired, and few of them were around to watch another East German detail go to work on the Potsdamer Platz. By the time it had begun to dawn, a low three-foot wall made of gray concrete slabs had oozed its reptilian way across most of the square. Ulbricht once again had acted while his adversaries were sleeping.

8

Unknown to Willy Brandt, things had at last begun to move in Washington. Kennedy's first reaction to news of the seal-off had been one of frank relief. As he had put it to his appointments secretary, Kenneth O'Donnell, on Monday morning, after his return to the White House from Hyannis Port, "As far as I'm concerned, the crisis is over. If the Russians had wanted to attack us and cut off the access routes, they wouldn't be putting up barbed-wire barriers. . . . So I'm not going to get all that het up about it."

The president's first visitor on Monday morning had been Llewellyn Thompson, U.S. ambassador to Moscow. Thompson, who had been taking Khrushchev's bellicose threats with the utmost seriousness, agreed that playing it cool was the wisest course. Unpredictable though Khrushchev was, it did look as if he was deliberately acting to avoid a head-on confrontation with the United States, which was something to be thankful for.

Such was also the burden of the advice offered by George Kennan, who had a forty-five-minute talk with Kennedy on the afternoon of Tuesday, August 15—a day full of distractions, since it began with the customary White House breakfast with leading congressmen and was marked at noon by the president's departure for St. Matthew's Cathedral for the celebration of the All Saints' Day mass.

The feeling of the State Department's German experts was noticeably different. They had all held diplomatic posts in Germany, and some had even seen years of service in Berlin. There was virtual unanimity among them that some kind of action or reaction was essential. Uncle Sam couldn't simply sit back with folded arms, sadly shaking his head and saying, "Gee, I sure feel sorry for those poor guys over there in East Berlin, but what can I do about it?" A crisis of confidence among West Berliners and West Germans was bound to result if Washington did nothing. But what was Washington to do?

Some felt that the president or, failing that, the vice-president, should fly to West Berlin as a gesture of sympathy for the plight of the East Berliners and as a token of support for the anxious West Berliners. Another suggestion was that the United States should fly in a number of big C-135 transport planes filled with high-ranking American officials as well as troops. It was only natural, given his past experience and prestige as the organizer of the Berlin airlift, that General Clay be one of them. Another logical choice would be Gen. Maxwell Taylor, who had served for several years in Berlin before being appointed U.S. Army chief of staff and, more recently, the president's personal adviser on military matters. A third suggestion was that the five-thousand-man U.S. garrison in Berlin be reinforced with a contingent of U.S. troops, to be sent up the Helmstedt–Berlin autobahn.

The response to these various proposals was slow. Most of the State Department's senior officials—including Dean Rusk, Chester Bowles, Adlai Stevenson, Charles Bohlen, and George McGhee—wanted to take the heat out of the crisis by sitting tight and waiting for the commotion to subside.

By Monday afternoon Edward Murrow's strong plea for action had reached the White House, reinforcing Marguerite Higgins's earlier appeal, which Robert Kennedy had transmitted to his brother. The president, however, could not make up his mind, torn as he was by the contradictory advice he was receiving. The State Department's Russian experts—Charles Bohlen, George Kennan, and Llewellyn Thompson—were counseling extreme caution in dealing with a temperamental and volatile character like Nikita Khrushchev. The German experts, on the basis of instinct, experience, and the alarming reports they were receiving from Allan Lightner and the State Department Mission in Berlin, were counseling vigorous action to head off a major crisis of confidence.

The conflict was compounded by the equally contradictory advice that was being offered by the United States' allies. The Bonn government was demanding "vigorous countermeasures" without being able to reach any real agreement on what these might be. Even the idea of a purely West German and selective embargo—aimed at depriving the DDR of certain vitally needed machines, chemicals, and other products—was being openly opposed by politicians like Erich Mende and more quietly by Ernst Lemmer and the superhawk Franz-Josef Strauss.

The French were taking a firm, legalistic line, but they had carefully refrained from bringing French soldiers up to the sector border in Berlin. The British, for their part, were doing everything to soft-pedal the crisis, as though an attitude of lofty aloofness could snub it out of existence. Lord Home was still vacationing in Lanarkshire; in Yorkshire, Harold Macmillan continued to shoot grouse.

In Washington, too, there was some gunplay. The suggestion that the president fly to Berlin was shot down in flames by the marksmen in the White House, and as early as Tuesday morning, Henry Owen, deputy head of the State Department's Policy Planning Council, could inform the German desk boys that the C-135 airlift idea was "for the birds. But the vice-president idea is good." It was the first inkling they had had that Kennedy was seriously thinking of sending Lyndon Johnson to Berlin.

By Wednesday Gen. Maxwell Taylor, to whom General Clay had written a personal letter, was taking up the cudgels for his old army friend and informing the president that the former U.S. military governor and organizer of the 1948–49 airlift was ready and available for duty if there was anything he could do to help.

All this information, however, was private, known only to a few insiders. The official line being leaked from the White House was that the United States government was still resisting West German pressure for stringent action over the Berlin border closing. Elvis J. Stahr, Jr., secretary of the army, held a press conference at which he announced that the U.S. Army was placing 113 reserve units, totaling 23,626 men, on an alert basis. If all the measures planned were carried out—and this depended on the general world situation—then the U.S. Army would have reached a total strength of 984,000 men by June 1962.

In terms of its relevance to the present crisis, this announcement left something to be desired. In Bonn twenty university students sent President Kennedy a "Chamberlain umbrella" to stigmatize his passive reaction to the happenings in Berlin. The accompanying letter singled him out as "the worthiest recipient of this symbol of a fatal policy."

Charles de Gaulle had finally returned to Paris to preside over a meeting of the Committee of National Defense. At the conclusion of the meeting, it was announced that the crisis in Berlin made it necessary for France to move troops and aircraft from Algeria to Germany and the Rhine. But there was not even a suggestion that De Gaulle might be considering a reinforcement of the French garrison in Berlin. The communiqué issued from the Elysée Palace even betrayed signs of a camouflaged retreat, since it declared that France (hitherto adamantly opposed to any such idea) wished to negotiate with the Russians to reduce the existing tension.

Emerging from a third inconclusive meeting with his fellow members of the Ambassadorial Group, West Germany's Wilhelm Grewe had to admit that there was a "certain disappointment" in his country over the lack of energetic action on Berlin.

Pressed by journalists on this point, Lincoln White, the State

Department's official spokesman, said that there was no basic discord, no major disagreements between the United States and its allies. Other senior officials, speaking in a private capacity, claimed that the border seal-off in Berlin was a major propaganda setback for Russia.

At the usual morning press conference at the White House—which began on this Wednesday, August 16, at exactly 11:08 A.M., the same moment when three hundred thousand anxious West Berliners were listening to Brandt and Amrehn in front of the Schöneberg Rathaus—the normally loquacious Pierre Salinger was as buttoned-up as it was possible to be. No, he had no comment on the regular Wednesday-morning breakfast that the president had had with the secretary of state. The joint note delivered by the three Allied commandants to the Soviet commandant in East Berlin had been rejected. Was there going to be any U.S.-government reaction to this rejection?

SALINGER: There is none now. I would think that if there is anything, it would come from the State Department.

QUESTION: Is there going to be an official protest from Washington or from the Allied capitals about the closing off of the Berlin border?

SALINGER: I believe the matter has been handled by or through the normal Commandants in Berlin.

QUESTION: Will there be an additional note?

SALINGER: I can't tell you whether there will be or whether there will not be, but I don't know of any plans at present for one.

QUESTION: Pierre, has the president been in touch with Adenauer by letter, or by cable?

SALINGER: Not to my knowledge.

QUESTION: By phone or otherwise?

SALINGER: Not to my knowledge.

And that was that. John Kennedy might not be footing it across the Yorkshire moors in plus fours, gaiters, and a hunting cap, like Harold Macmillan, but he, too, was taking the crisis in a patently unhurried stride.

9

Shortly after dawn on Thursday, August 17, the British, who had so far limited themselves to setting up antitank guns in the Tiergarten, finally acted. At 5:30 A.M. a detachment from the Sixtieth King's Royal Rifles—popularly known as the "Green-jackets"—rolled down the broad Strasse des 17. Juni in army lorries and drew up opposite the Soviet War Memorial. The Russians, who normally maintained a twenty-man detachment in the rear part of the square-columned memorial to keep it from being vandalized by West Berliners, were taken by surprise. The two sentries stiffly mounting guard in front looked on in amazement, as did their colleagues, while British Tommies calmly unloaded concertinas of barbed wire. By eight o'clock the entire one-thousand-yard periphery was wired in, save for a gatelike gap in the back, through which the Russians could still come and go.

Two Russian officers, dispatched from Karlshorst, drove up in a staff car, which was allowed to pass through the Brandenburg Gate. They wanted to protest this indignity inflicted on the heroic bronze statue commemorating the Red Army's World War II victory over the Hitler Fascists. They were informed by a Royal Military Police officer that the action had been ordered by General Delacombe to protect the war memorial from possible assaults by angry West Berliners. The Russians replied that an action of this kind should first have been cleared with the Soviet military authorities. Then they climbed back into their army car and returned to East Berlin. Grumble as they might, there was nothing they could do about it. After all, less than five years before, this memorial to the "Unknown Plunderer"—as it was known to most Berliners—had been severely damaged by a raging mob, driven wild by the bloody suppression of the Buda-pest rebellion.

Later this same day, Sir Christopher Steel, the United Kingdom's ambassador in Bonn, flew to Berlin, where he had a forty-minute talk with Willy Brandt. The three Western Allies had finally managed to hammer out a joint protest at the

highest level, which their ambassadors in Moscow were delivering to the foreign minister of the Soviet Union. It called
on the USSR to "put an end to the illegal restrictions in
Berlin." Relieved to hear that the Allied capitals were doing
something, the governing mayor thanked the ambassador,
saying, "This is the right language at last."

At the press conference that followed, the British diplomat
refused to be drawn out on the subject of what specific
countermeasures the Allies might be preparing against the
illegal erection of Ulbricht's wall. He found the governing
mayor's speech of the day before "remarkably statesmanlike,
when you think of the pressure he is under." As for Allied
plans for taking over and running the S-Bahn in the western
sectors, this was a highly complicated matter.

Having delivered himself of these guarded comments, the
representative of the United Kingdom climbed into a sleek
sedan and headed for the Soviet sector. At the Friedrichstrasse check point, the gleaming limousine was waved
through by the Vopos without fuss or questions. "I was flying
the Union Jack—good old Victorian stuff, you know," Sir
Christopher explained after completing his inspection.

Notably less successful in their attempts to cross the border
on this same Thursday were Berlin's most prominent
ecclesiastics. The Right Reverend Otto Dibelius, Prostestant
bishop of Berlin and Brandenburg, and the Catholic arch-
bishop, the Most Reverend Julius Doepfner, whose homes
were in the West, were denied access to East Berlin, while
the president of the Evangelical church, Kurt Scharf, who
lived in the Soviet sector, was prohibited from entering West
Berlin.

At the twelve remaining crossing points, the controls were
growing steadily more stringent and the guards much
rougher. Many journalists and cameramen were flatly forbidden access to East Berlin, while the identity cards of West
Berlin pedestrians were now carefully checked against the
Vopos' wanted list.

Der Friedensvertrag kommt sicher, sagt Walter Ulbricht
("The Peace Treaty Is Bound to Come, Says Walter Ul-

bricht"), read the large sign posted over the heads of the information-bureau officials at the Friedrichstrasse station, not far from a red-and-gold placard proclaiming to the citizens of the Workers-and-Peasants-State that "Travel Brings Happiness."

The morale of East Berliners had plummeted "below zero," as one of them put it to a Western journalist. There were long queues of glum border crossers at the entrances to borough registration offices. Whereas in West Berlin there was now a serious dearth of skilled labor—certain businesses, like the garment industry, had been particularly hard hit—in East Berlin there was a sudden glut for the first time in years. Hotels and restaurants that had had to get along without doormen or sufficient waiters could now begin to offer less short-handed service. But it was a service offered without smiles.

"Do you realize to what extent we all hate this regime?" a correspondent of the *Berliner Morgenpost* was repeatedly asked as he toured the Soviet sector. But when he questioned people about the possibilities of an uprising, he was almost invariably told, "No, we are too closely guarded." East Berlin was swarming with Saxons, and Party precinct offices, like all the major factories, were guarded around the clock.

A day or two earlier, the houses on the eastern side of the Bernauer Strasse had been almost as porous as a sieve. Now they, too, were blocked. Caught trying to smuggle the wife of an East Berlin friend out through the corridor of his tenement house at number 47, the fifty-five-year-old border crosser Bruno Hinz was taken to the nearest police station by the Vopos. A meticulous examination of his identity card having revealed that he really did inhabit the house at number 47, he was released. On his way home, he came upon a Vopo stationed in the downstairs corridor. A little later he heard the sound of picks and shovels: A Kampfgruppen work squad was smashing a hole through the intervening wall and into the neighboring house in order to facilitate the movements of the police.

His good luck had saved him once, but there was no point in tempting fate a second time. As dusk fell, Bruno Hinz crept downstairs and found nobody about. For some reason the Vopo had left. Without wasting a moment, he picked up all the money he had; grabbed his wife, Erna, and his twelve-year-old son, Peterle; and hurried down the stairs. Using a second key he had prudently retained, he unlocked the front door, and a moment later they were all safely out on the sidewalk of the Bernauer Strasse, in the French sector.

A bare hour after their escape—so Hinz was later told—an entire Vopo squad returned to number 47, entering, as before, through the backyard. He was to have been arrested on several counts: as a suspect Social Democrat who worked in Wedding Town Hall and who maintained contact with other SPD members in East Berlin; and as an impenitent Grenz-gänger who had been caught red-handed in an act of criminal man-trade.

Only slightly better off than the other dwellers of their run-down tenement house—they were the only ones to own a television set—the Hinzes were left with nothing but the clothes they had on, while the Vopos, after banging open the apartment door, could help themselves to a Grundig radio, a silver bowling trophy, a weather-beaten teddy bear, and a Märklin electric train which the young Peterle had been given for Christmas.

On Monday, novelist Günter Grass had addressed an open letter to Anna Seghers, president of the German Writers Union of the DDR, describing how his Sunday morning breakfast had been ruined by the totally incongruous sounds of rumbling tanks, radio commentaries, and the inevitable snatches of Beethoven symphony music. He had journeyed over to the Friedrichstrasse station and from there proceeded to the Brandenburg Gate to witness "the unrecognizable at-tributes of a brutishly naked and stinking-of-pig-leather vio-lence." Grass hoped that having had the courage in the past to condemn Hitlerian methods, Anna Seghers would just as courageously condemn the tanks and the barbed wire being used to throttle Berlin—just as he was ready to go to Deggen-dorf, in Bavaria, and spit on the floor of the church that had recently given its blessing to anti-Semitic sentiments.

There was no reply from Anna Seghers, who was away on a

trip to South America. But as Ludwig Marcuse pointed out in a letter sent from Santa Monica, California, whereas Günter Grass was free at any time to go and spit on "the church of barbarism" in Deggendorf, Anna Segher would be clapped into jail "under the knout of highly trained prison wardens" were she to utter a word of protest against the current happenings in Berlin.

Unable to obtain an answer from Anna Seghers, Grass and his fellow writer Wolfdietrich Schnurre had composed a second letter on Wednesday, addressed this time to the East German Writers Union. Just as writers in the West had the duty to denounce the maintenance in office of people like State Secretary Globke, the Special (Emergency) Powers Law being prepared by Minister of the Interior Schröder, and the "authoritarian clericalism" of Adenauer's Federal Republic, so the writers of East Germany had the solemn duty to denounce the barbed wire, submachine guns, and tanks that had made life in the DDR unbearable. The letter ended with an appeal specifically addressed to the most eminent and honorable members of the Writers Union.

One of the writers specifically appealed to, Stephan Hermlin, lost no time in replying. How, he asked, could Grass and Schnurre condemn the "scope of the sudden military action of August 13" when an official spokesman in Washington (in fact, Dean Rusk, unnamed) had acknowledged that the rights of the Western occupying powers in West Berlin had not been affected by the measures undertaken by the German Democratic Republic? He, Hermlin, had not seen fit to send a telegram of thanks or congratulations to his government for the action undertaken, but he wanted Grass and Schnurre to know that these measures enjoyed his "unreserved and considered approval. Through this action they have, as is already evident, strengthened the Anti-Globke-State, they have taken a big forward step toward the achievement of a Peace Treaty, because it alone is capable of halting the world's most dangerous state, the Federal Republic, on its aggressive path."

Thus encouraged, the anti-Globke state continued to reinforce its anti-Fascist defences. A decree, issued by the Central Council of the Free German Youth movement, ordered the 1.7 million members of the FDJ to attend a special roll-call muster at 6:00 A.M. on Friday, August 18. It was their duty to become Volksarmisten ("People's Soldiers") by volunteering for two years of service in the Nationale Volksarmee.

Those who hastened to the recruiting offices were handed an eight-page questionnaire concerning the volunteer's past social-political activities. The first three pages were concerned with the volunteer's relations with the West. Did he have any relatives in the Federal Republic, in West Berlin, or in capitalist countries abroad?

If the answer is Yes, how long have your relatives lived there?

Have you yourself been in West Germany, West Berlin, or to a capitalist country abroad?

If the answer is Yes, when and for how long were you there?

To date have you had any contact (by letter and so forth) with West Germany, West Berlin, or any capitalist countries abroad?

Deserters from the Nationale Volksarmee and from the Kampfgruppen brought out reports of Ulbricht's latest plans. As of August 20, a second and more formidable "fortification" was to be built behind the first line of barbed-wire obstructions to make them virtually impassable. The factory militiamen who had been brought in from all parts of the Zone to help seal off the border and to keep the local populace in line, would gradually be withdrawn and replaced by trustworthy FDJ volunteers.

The third phase of the great seal-off operation—that entrusted to Erich Honecker—was about to open. The systematic regimentation of the anti-Globke state had begun.

10

At twenty minutes to one on Friday, August 18, Marguerite Higgins was admitted to the Oval Office of the White House for an off-the-record talk with her friend Jack Kennedy. "I have

good news for you," he informed her. "Not only have we decided to send General Clay to Berlin; we are sending the vice-president with him."

In fact, this information was not news for the New York
Herald Tribune columnist. She had been dining the previous
evening with General Clay, Sam Rayburn, and Lyndon Johnson,
when the vice-president had been called away from the table by
an urgent message from the White House. The idea of flying to
Berlin had not pleased Johnson one bit, and Sam Rayburn had
had to deploy all his eloquence to persuade his fellow Texan that
if the president himself couldn't go, then he, the vice-president,
was the person best fitted to show the American flag in
threatened West Berlin.

It was now too late to refuse, as Kennedy made clear to Johnson when they met for a Friday prelunch session in the Oval
Office. Gen. Bruce Clarke, commander of the U.S. Army in
Europe, had already been contacted at his Heidelberg headquarters and informed of the president's decision to reinforce
the Berlin garrison with an infantry battle group, and Walt
Rostow was working on the major policy statement that Johnson
would have to deliver in Berlin.

At 6:30 that evening, the president's senior advisers assembled in the Yellow Room of the mansion to discuss the final
details of the trip with Lyndon Johnson and General Clay.
McGeorge Bundy, who had been given the job of drafting a
reply to Willy Brandt's letter, was present, as were Walt Rostow
and Gen. Maxwell Taylor. Dean Rusk had brought along the
State Department's leading Russian expert, Charles Bohlen.
Robert McNamara, secretary of defense, was absent.

The draft texts of the two major addresses that Johnson was to
make in Berlin were discussed first. More controversial was the
question of the battle group that was to reinforce the U.S. garrison in Berlin. Certain of the president's White House advisers
had expressed misgivings that this "aggressive" action might
well provoke a strong Soviet reaction. Charles Bohlen tended to
agree with them, while Dean Rusk was noncommittal. Clay,
however, was emphatic in declaring that nothing could do more
to raise the morale of the West Berliners than this essentially
token gesture; no amount of Communist propaganda could con-

vince the world that the dispatch of fifteen hundred armed Americans posed an "intolerable" threat to the twenty Soviet divisions stationed on East German soil. General Taylor agreed, and so did the president.

Kennedy further decided, against the advice of his soft-liners, that every effort should be made to have the U.S. Army battle group reach Berlin in time to be officially welcomed by the vice-president. The one hard-line suggestion he backed away from was Clay's proposal that the vice-president fly into Berlin above the ten-thousand-foot level which the Russians, years before, had fixed as the ceiling for Allied planes using the air corridors to Berlin. That ceiling had been tacitly accepted by the three Western Allies in the early postwar years when they were using propeller-driven aircraft; it had become increasingly irksome for the pilots of high-altitude jets, who were used to flying above the weather. The legal arguments invoked were grotesque and even contradictory. If such aircraft were indulging in aerial espionage, they could obtain a closer view of the ground from seven thousand feet than from thirty thousand feet. Kennedy, however, decided that to challenge the Russians in the air at a time when they were being challenged on the ground would be overdoing it.

The meeting broke up shortly before 7:30. An hour and a half later, one of the three Boeing 707s that were maintained around the clock on instant alert at Andrews Air Force Base took off for Europe. On board the plane with the vice-president were General Clay and Charles Bohlen; three members of the State Department's Office of German Affairs; Johnson's personal press attaché, George Reedy; and a USIA official named Jay Gildner. Johnson had insisted on bringing along two secretaries—one of them too elegantly dressed to be considered a mere typist (she tended to leave such chores to her junior colleague)—while the State Department was represented by an unusually pretty blonde. The few journalists who had obtained permission to accompany the vice-president included John Scali, the Associated Press's senior diplomatic correspondent in Washington; Max Freedman of the *Manchester Guardian;* and Marguerite Higgins. The last to make the plane was Yoichi Okamoto, a Japanese-American who then headed the USIA's photographic services. At three o'clock that afternoon, Edward Murrow had telephoned him to say, "We're in the doghouse because there was no photographer along on Johnson's last trip to Southeast Asia." Okamoto had just one hour to obtain a passport from the State Department and the necessary inoculations before rushing home to pack a bag while a taxi waited to whisk him to the airport.

The flight had been improvised at such short notice that only the two major speeches Johnson was due to deliver had been prepared and approved by the White House. The three experts from the State Department's German desk were accordingly put to work drafting the "Golden Book" speech and other arrival statements which the vice-president would have to deliver in Bonn and Berlin. The penned drafts were then handed to the secretaries, who had their typewriters in the rear of the airplane. Indefatigable as ever, Johnson walked up and down the aisle, alternately egging on his staff and chatting with the journalists on board. At his insistence, the first draft of each speech was handed to Max Freedman, whose job it was to turn the State Department's "bureaucratese" into flawless prose.

Unencumbered by this laborious paperwork, General Clay sat in one of the airplane's four booths, exchanging reminiscences with "Chip" Bohlen and the already white-haired George Reedy. To find himself accompanied on this morale-boosting mission by a State Department watchdog who was a notorious soft-liner must have been a strange experience for the anything-but-dovelike general. In 1948 Bohlen had been one of the ten State Department advisers of ambassadorial rank who had recommended that the United States pull out of West Berlin, regarded as untenable in view of the recently begun Soviet blockade.

Clay, of course, was too much of a southern gentleman to remind Bohlen of his past faint-heartedness. But he could not resist the temptation of recalling how in 1948 he had been vir-tually alone among his military colleagues in arguing that West Berlin could be held against the Soviets. When Stalin had or-dered the closing of the Allied access routes, Clay had been summoned back to Washington and received at the White House by Truman and his advisers. Since nobody (save Under

Secretary of State Robert Murphy) was willing to back his scheme to run an armored train through to the beleaguered city, Clay had proposed to overcome the Soviet land blockade by flying in supplies. To his dismay, one after another of the president's advisers had ruled against it, saying that it was impossible to feed a population of two million by air. Convinced that he had lost this battle as well, Clay had got up at the end of the discussion and followed the others out of the room. As he reached the door, he happened to look back. Truman hadn't moved. He was still seated at his desk looking glumly at his hands. Then suddenly he looked up. Spotting Clay in the doorway, he said, quite simply, "General, you will get your planes." That single sentence had saved West Berlin, and probably altered, the course of history—although Clay was personally persuaded that if Truman had been bolder and supported the armored train idea, the blockade would have been called off, and later there never would have been a Korean War.

It was 9:30 A.M., West German time (4:30 A.M. Washington time), when the Boeing 707 landed at the Bonn-Cologne airport. Lyndon Johnson had been able to lie down for several hours in one of the front berths, but the three unfortunates from the State Department's German section—Frank Cash, Karl Mautner, and Henry Cox—had spent a sleepless night arguing with Max Freedman over the tenor of the vice-president's arrival speech and other statements. Inasmuch as the Federal Republic was now in the throes of an election campaign, particular care had to be taken to avoid words or gestures that might seem to favor Konrad Adenauer and his ruling CDU-CSU coalition over other West German parties.

From the airport, where they were met by Foreign Minister Heinrich von Brentano and Ambassador Walter Dowling, Johnson and his suite were driven down the autobahn and over the new Rhine bridge into the little town of Bonn. At the federal chancellery, the vice-president was taken upstairs to Adenauer's office, along with General Clay, Charles Bohlen, and Ambassador Dowling. For both Johnson and Adenauer it was like a meeting of old friends. The chancellor had always made a point of calling on Johnson, then leader of the Democratic party in the Senate, on each of the half dozen trips he had made to Washington during the Eisenhower years. Just five months before, when Adenauer had flown to Washington to meet the new U.S. president, Johnson had invited him to the LBJ ranch in Texas and treated him to a big barbecue feast, where king-sized steaks were served by farm girls dressed for the occasion in nineteenth-century German folk costumes. Johnson had placed a ten-gallon hat on the chancellor's venerable head and had presented him with a pair of silver spurs. Although the vice-president's folksy ways were a bit flamboyant for his own sober tastes, Adenauer had long admired Johnson's skill as a parliamentary tactician. Here was a down-to-earth politician, a supreme realist like himself. There was no trace in Lyndon Baines Johnson of the intellectual vanity that had moved John Kennedy to surround himself with eggheads who, however brilliantly they might have shone in university lecture halls, were apt to make fools of themselves in the less sheltered waters of politics, where what counted was the *Fingerspitzengefühl* ("finger-tip sensitivity") which permitted old pros like Johnson and himself to distinguish the politically feasible from the politically inept.

Charles Bohlen, on the other hand, was not somebody the chancellor could number among his friends. They had taken an almost instant dislike to each other in September 1955, when Adenauer had made a reluctant trip to Moscow to rescue thousands of German prisoners of war still held captive in the Soviet Union. Bohlen's past association with Franklin Roosevelt at Yalta and elsewhere had been enough to brand him in the chancellor's eyes as a softie who needed to be taught a thing or two about standing up to the Russians. The result had been a brief lecture, which the Russian-speaking American ambassador had had difficulty digesting.

Adenauer, on this Saturday morning, let Johnson do most of the talking. He was interested to hear what practical measures the Americans were going to take to shore up the sagging morale of the West Berliners. He was not altogether happy about the Allies' failure to give his pet idea of a collective Western boycott on trade with the Communist East a serious hearing, but he knew that foreign policy was not Lyndon

Johnson's specialty. Besides, Adenauer was in a poor position to criticize the "negative" behavior of the Americans, having so far failed to fly to Berlin himself. He was also too proud to raise the question directly and to ask the vice-president pointblank if he could accompany him to Berlin.

The job of sounding out the Americans on this matter was left to one of his Chancellery assistants, who put in a telephone call to the U.S. embassy. The first secretary, who took the call, had received no particular instructions, so the query was relayed to one of the German specialists who had flown over with Johnson. He told the first secretary that the question had been discussed in Washington at the White House level. Chancellor Adenauer was *not* to be allowed to fly to Berlin in the U.S. vice-president's airplane, since this would amount to an official gesture of support on behalf of the CDU-CSU coalition. The West German Socialists had never forgiven John Foster Dulles or the State Department for too openly favoring Konrad Adenauer in the elections of 1957. The new Kennedy administration was not going to be guilty of the same partiality; it was going to be strictly neutral throughout the election campaign. Besides, the vice-president's trip to Berlin was designed to stress the United States' continuing responsibilities in Berlin as one of the four occupying powers.

After the meeting in the chancellor's office, Charles Bohlen volunteered to break the news as diplomatically as possible to Foreign Minister Brentano. Adenauer was thus able to offer his guests a good lunch in a pleasant Rhine-wine-drinking atmosphere, and not until coffee was being served did Bohlen broach the subject with Heinrich von Brentano. After listening to Bohlen's explanations, Brentano walked up to the chancellor and suggested that, all things considered, it would be better if he did not accompany Mr. Johnson to Berlin. The chancellor had no choice but to acquiesce, which he did with stoic impassivity. The one German allowed to travel with the vice-president, it was decided, would be the Foreign Ministry's chief of protocol, Sigismund von Braun. But to make his displeasure clearly felt, Adenauer told his foreign minister to fly to Berlin on the first airplane he could catch.

It had been decided, for reasons of prestige and because it

was closer to Schöneberg City Hall, that the vice-president should land at Tempelhof, in the U.S. sector, rather than at the larger Tegel airfield, located near the northwest extremity of the French sector of Berlin. Since the Tempelhof apron was too short for the Boeing 707 on which they had crossed the Atlantic, the party was split into two groups. The less privileged climbed back into the 707, to be flown to Tegel, while the VIPs boarded a U.S. Air Force four-prop Constellation.

At Tempelhof, Johnson, Clay, and the two American ambassadors—Charles Bohlen and Walter Dowling—were greeted with a twenty-one-gun salute and the American and West German national anthems. Willy Brandt and a number of Berlin City Hall officials were waiting to welcome them. So was Heinrich von Brentano, whose last-minute appearance on the scene occasioned considerable surprise.

When the welcoming ceremonies were completed, the vice-president and Willy Brandt climbed into one of the U.S. mission's black Cadillac limousines. Preceded by a formidable motorcycle escort, the procession moved out through the airfield's northern gate and onto the Columbiadamm. Before proceeding to the Schöneberg Rathaus, situated a mile and a half to the west, the vice-president was to be driven northward to the Potsdamer Platz for a first-hand look at the barbed wire and the concrete wall. The local press having been alerted, many correspondents and photographers were gathered on the southwestern rim of the barricaded Platz, while a number of East German reporters and cameramen had congregated on the other side.

The protocol officials, however, had grossly underestimated the length of time it would take for the motorcade to reach the Potsdamer Platz. The sidewalks along the route were packed with Berliners of every age who surged forward around the leading cars of the convoy shouting, "Bravo, Bravo, Johnson!" General Clay, who was riding in the second limousine, received almost as much attention as the vice-president. The moment his hawklike profile was recognized through the open window, he was mobbed by young and old shouting, "*Der Clay, der Clay ist hier!*" The organizer of the 1948–49 airlift was smothered with flowers—a bouquet of thorny roses actually hit him in the face at one point—and his outstretched right hand was fervently wrung by so many that General Watson, who was sitting next to him, finally persuaded him to put out his other hand to keep his right elbow from being broken by the pressure of the throng.

Lyndon Baines Johnson was beginning to enjoy every minute of it. Even though he was among foreigners, he was in his element. In the thrill and excitement, he even felt free to alter the itinerary, blandly disregarding the significance of his appearance at the Potsdamer Platz. It had taken the procession more than twenty minutes to cover a distance they should normally have been able to cover in six or seven minutes, and progress toward the Schöneberg Rathaus was likely to be even slower. So it was time, he felt, to turn around and head for Berlin City Hall.

Getting out of the police car that was leading the procession, Dr. Walter Klein, the Senat's chief protocol official, hurried back to the black Cadillac to determine the reason for the unexpected stop. Inside, a disconsolate Willy Brandt was shaking his head in disbelief. But Lyndon Johnson was adamant. Yes, and what if they were only a hundred yards or so from the Potsdamer Platz? He hadn't been sent to Berlin to spit on the barbed wire or to tear it away with his bare hands. He'd come to reassure the inhabitants of West Berlin, and that's what he was going to do.

The motorcade turned and headed slowly west and south, in the direction of the Schöneberg Rathaus. The pace was still snaillike as cheering bystanders surged around the advancing limousines. Not content to shake hands through the open window, Lyndon Johnson got out, let himself be embraced by joyous women, kissed the babies that were handed to him, and even patted a dog. Disregarding the pleas of his Secret Service bodyguards, he walked several hundred yards before finally agreeing to climb back into his Cadillac. "Look at him!" commented Egon Bahr through his teeth. "He's already campaigning, getting ready for his election as the next president of the United States!"

The spacious square in front of the gray stucco Rathaus was so jammed with people that the motorcade had trouble squeezing up to the steps of the city hall. The avenues radiating from the square were awash with humanity. The windows, balconies, trees were crammed with applauders waving scarves, handkerchiefs, shawls, umbrellas, caps, hats, newspapers—whatever they had with them. Some brandished signs. One of them, written in English, read, "Use Your Own Eyes and Report to Kennedy."

Astonished by the turnout, George Reedy asked a German motorcycle policeman how many people the packed square and neighboring avenues could hold. The precise reply was 380,000.

Standing on the Rathaus steps beneath the colonnaded architrave, along which were strung out the heraldic crests of Germany's lost provinces, Willy Brandt delivered a short speech of welcome. He was visibly moved by the wild enthusiasm of the crowd. So was Lyndon Johnson when the time came for him to voice the words that had been prepared for him in Washington.

At this time when an unelected, unwanted regime is compelled to prevent the flight of the people who live under its domination by using barbed wire, armored cars, and guns, you have experienced a natural and human frustration. . . . But a solution will surely come. Self-determination, that word which the slave-makers fear as they fear no other, will also come to those to whom it is presently denied.

Few people in the crowd understood what he was saying in his broad Texas accent, but it made no difference. They cheered wildly, not bothering to wait for the German translation. What mattered was not his words but his physical presence among them.

General Clay added a few emotional words of his own, immediately swallowed up in another storm of ovation. Two bands—one German, the other a U.S. Army band—then struck up the two national anthems. After the last ringing notes and the final clash of cymbals, there was a momentary hush, followed by the deep boom of the city hall's Freedom Bell. Twelve million Americans had made donations to finance its construction, and their names were now preserved on a parchment scroll in a special belfry niche. In the packed square, the handkerchiefs had stopped waving; they were now wiping tears from trembling cheeks. Even among the dignitaries on the steps there were few dry eyes.

The vice-president next had to address a specially convened session of the Berlin House of Representatives in an upstairs chamber of the city hall. The speech, full of ringing phrases thought up by Walt Rostow, drew prolonged and repeated applause from the assembled deputies.

I come at a moment of tension and danger—in your lives, the lives of my countrymen, and the common life of the Free World. To the survival and to the creative future of this city we Americans have pledged, in effect, what our ancestors pledged in forming the United States: "our lives, our fortunes, and our sacred honor."

Heinrich von Brentano, in his answering speech, was less flamboyant, although in a moment of rhetorical exaggeration he reminded his listeners that the right to determine its future and to live in freedom "is today denied to no people in the world save the German." The concluding oration, also repeatedly applauded, was delivered by Willy Brandt, who recalled how moved he had been the previous March when President Kennedy had told him that the United States was "committed by treaty and conviction" to uphold the freedom of West Berlin. "We will not bend our necks beneath the yoke of a new dictatorship," he added, "irrespective of the color in which this dictatorship has decked itself out."

The evening ended with an impressive banquet held in the Rathaus's Brandenburg Hall. The sixty-yard-long table, laid for more than one hundred invited guests, sparkled beneath the candles and the chandeliers. In honor of the distinguished guest, the special Kronprinz service had been brought out, complete with its silver figurines of elephants and lions—a service which the city of Berlin had bought from a throneless Hohenzollern prince during the years of the Weimar Republic.

It was close to midnight when Lyndon Johnson finally took leave of his hosts on the Rathaus steps. A few hardy Berliners who had been standing outside for hours greeted his appearance with shouts and cheers. But the cheers were not aimed at the vice-president as much as at General Clay, and the shouts made it clear that the crowd wanted the general back on active duty and invested with special powers in Berlin.

This was not, as it happened, the last of the evening's surprises. Charles Bohlen, the veteran diplomat and interpreter whom Roosevelt had seated next to himself at the Teheran conference of 1943, now discovered that he would not be spending the night at Walter Dowling's ambassadorial residence on the Spechtstrasse in the leafy suburbs of Dahlem. The upstairs bedroom that had been prepared for him was to be occupied instead by the vice-president's senior secretary, Mary Margaret Wiley.

Mrs. Dowling was in for another surprise as well. When she asked the vice-president what he would like for breakfast the next morning, he answered lightly, "Oh, nothing much—some oatmeal and a bit of honeydew melon will do." It had not occurred to His Texan Lordship that in these northern climes honeydew melons might be as rare as kangaroos. But as luck would have it, there was a melon in the refrigerator.

11

Beyond the barbed-wire barriers, tens of thousands of East Berliners had spent this Saturday afternoon secretly watching Johnson's triumphant progress and the Rathaus square apotheosis on their television screens. Many others had carried on as usual, going for walks in the Wuhlheide or relaxing on the shores of Müggel Lake.

Among those who went out strolling was Ursula Heinemann, the seventeen-year-old border crosser who could no longer reach her former place of work at the Plaza Hotel. Six days of enforced idleness had been enough to convince her that no hoped-for miracle was going to oblige Walter Ulbricht to relent. She could no longer stand the atmosphere in the Johannisthal apartment building, where the fat-faced Frau who lived on the same floor gloated each time she caught sight of her, saying, "What did I tell you? Things from now on are going to be different for your kind."

On Thursday, Ursula's aunt—her deceased father's sister—
had come to call, accompanied by her husband, who was distantly related to the former Party leader Ernst Thälmann. She
herself had been a Communist from early youth on and had risen
to a position of some importance as a judge. But, as she explained to the Heinemanns, this barricading and wall building
were too much for her, and she had tendered her resignation.

"If you want a piece of advice from someone who's already in
her fifties and who's seen a lot of the world," the aunt had said to
Ursula, "then don't waste any more time. Get out and over to
the West as quickly as you can. Here everybody knows you've
been a Grenzgänger, and they (she meant, of course, the authorities) won't let you forget it. The moment they catch up with
you, they'll pack you off to some LPG farm in Mecklenburg or
Thuringia, and keep you there for as long as they want!"

Ursula had already reached this conclusion after recovering
from the initial shock which had kept at her home on Monday,
listening to the news with her friend Ingrid Imgard, too listless
and dispirited to move. The next day she had begun to pull
herself together. Deciding it was now too dangerous to try the
shortest escape route—across the Teltow Canal, where the
guards had been quadrupled—she and Ingrid took the train into
the Soviet zone and around to the town of Gross Glienecke, near
Potsdam. They wanted to see if they couldn't find a way of
sneaking across the border from the Zone into the U.S. sector
somewhere in this general area. They got themselves hired as
waitresses at a second-rate beer garden catering to NVA soldiers
and Grepos. Most of the Grepos and soldiers with whom Ursula
managed to strike up conversations admitted that they wouldn't
have the heart to shoot at a would-be escaper. But two tough-
looking guards from the backwoods of Thuringia said that they
would use their guns without a moment's hesitation.

"There's no point going back there tomorrow," Ursula had
told Ingrid that evening as they rode home on the train. "These
people have orders to shoot. I'm not going to risk it."

Even her mother was now reconciled to the idea of her escaping to the West. But how? Ursula could no longer sleep at night.
She felt trapped, like an animal that can hear the hunters'
footsteps inexorably approaching.

Saturday afternoon, she and her mother went for a walk. Heading northwest, they walked up the Südostallee, skirting the Königsheide woods to the left and passing the cemetery and the crematorium to the right. Beyond the cemetery they crossed the bridge spanning the Teltow Canal, both banks of which were in East Berlin territory at this point. They continued in the direction of Neukölln and the U.S. sector. A few hundred yards short of the intersector check point—one of the twelve still open to cars and pedestrians—they branched off along a dirt path leading through a number of cultivated truck gardens. There was no one on the path and the gardens were untended.

"Mother, wait here," said Ursula suddenly. "I'm going on ahead through this truck garden to see if there isn't a chance of getting through."

Opening a gate, she slipped into the garden and paused for a moment behind a fruit tree. Off to one side was a bungalow, but it appeared to be empty. Ursula now regretted having put on a conspicuous white sweater above her dark green slacks; it did not offer much protective camouflage. But this was no time to pull back.

Beyond the bungalow she came up against a barbed-wire fence. Getting down on her stomach, she began crawling under the lowest strand. She could feel one of the metal barbs tearing the wool over her shoulder blades. Turning, she tried to raise the wire with her left hand, ripping her wool sweater still more as she did so. She gashed her hand slightly against one of the barbs. Exhausted by the effort, she finally let her hand drop and felt the wire descend over her back. She was now halfway through. Wriggling forward, she tried to keep her bottom as far down as possible, so as not to have the barbs tear her slacks as well.

At last free of the fence, she remained still for a long moment, while she regained her breath. Her heart was pounding wildly. Ahead of her was a grass-covered moat, part of the same Heidekamp Graben which Harald Grabowski had seen being listlessly fenced off by NVA engineers the previous Sunday. In the intervening six days, a second barbed-wire fence had been erected along its western slope.

Once again Ursula set out to crawl under the lowest strand.

Struggling to disengage herself from the barbs, she scratched one of her wrists and both palms. Her sweater was severely torn. But she kept inching her way forward.

To the right she noticed a plume of cigarette smoke rising lazily in the warm afternoon air, but she was too intent on moving forward to pay much heed to it. Directly ahead was a sign reading *Grenze des demokratischen Sektors* ("Border of the Democratic Sector"). Crawling forward on her hands and knees, she passed the sign, and a moment later a young man popped up from behind a mound, saying, "Wonderful! You've made it! This is West Berlin!"

Ursula was ready to faint from relief. What a risk she had taken! The cigarette smoke she had seen must have come from a Grepo or NVA soldier seated in his camouflaged foxhole. He had almost certainly seen and heard her, but he had done nothing about it.

Taking her by the arm, the young West Berliner led her through a garden and out onto a sidewalk. Thirty or forty yards down the avenue to the right was the heavily guarded check point and the beginning of the Soviet sector.

The young man offered her a cigarette and had her sit down on the curb. She realized from the way he kept looking at her what a sight she must have seemed, with her scratched wrist and hands, lacerated sweater, and a small cut on the neck.

Soon a crowd was gathered around her, plying her with questions. Seeing a young lad come up with a bicycle, she asked him to do her a great favor: Could he take his bicycle, ride into the Soviet sector (something he could still do with his West Berlin identity card), and find her mother? She indicated the spot where she had left her, on the dirt path running off from the Südostallee.

The young lad said he would try. Pedaling off slowly in the opposite direction, he made a U-turn and then headed for the check point. He was back half an hour later with the reassuring news that he had found her mother and informed her that Ursula was safely across the border and in the U.S. sector.

Getting to her feet, Ursula dug into her pockets. Out came a handkerchief and an identity card, nothing more. The whole spur-of-the-moment business had been so unplanned that she hadn't taken the precaution of bringing along some money. A kind woman offered her two marks so that she could pay the necessary bus fares.

Like so many other refugees from the East, Ursula Heine-mann had to register with the West German authorities. But she did not have to spend the night at Marienfelde or any other reception center. At the Plaza Hotel, where she could now resume her work as a waitress, the management was glad to offer her free room and board.

12

At Seventh Army headquarters in Heidelberg, Gen. Bruce Clarke was hopping mad. For thirty-six hours the Pentagon had been bombarding him with cables specifying exactly how many rest halts the Eighth Infantry Division's First Battle Group was to allow itself while traveling on the autobahn from Helmstedt to Berlin, and other footling details of the same order. But not a word had been said about the ammunition the fifteen hundred soldiers were to carry. For Clarke, a crusty, front-line tankman who had helped Patton break out of the Normandy bridgehead in July 1944, this was a typical piece of buck passing on the part of higher headquarters. The boys at the top weren't going to stick their necks out. None of them were eager to take the rap if the GIs got into a firefight with the Russians on their way to Berlin.

With curly blond hair already turning gray, a fine aquiline nose, thick neck, and double chin, Clarke had the look of a Roman proconsul—a proconsul who had reason to be proud of his achievements. Often dubbed the "Sergeants' General" be-cause of his conviction that an army is no better than the sergeants who run its front-line units, he had taken a sloppy, spoiled, demoralized army of occupation and in ten months turned it into a snappy, well-drilled, combat-ready force. The unit he had chosen to reinforce the U.S. Army garrison in Berlin was typical in this respect. It had had less than six hours to hit the road, but with the help of helicopters that had brought some of its officers back from the British zone of occupation, where they had been acting as umpires in a war game, all fifteen hundred men were now bivouacked on a grass airfield near Braunschweig, ready to roll out the next morning for Berlin.

Then a message had come in from the U.S. embassy in Bonn, and Clarke had hit the roof once again. After informing him that the vice-president's party was on its way to Berlin, it had added that Johnson was planning to leave Berlin at 2:00 P.M. on Sunday afternoon.

Without wasting a moment, Clarke got on the telephone to Gen. Albert Watson in Berlin. He wanted the U.S. commandant to protest the needless precipitation of this departure to Lyndon Johnson and Ambassador Dowling "in my name." It was absolutely vital that the vice-president remain in Berlin long enough to be able to review the incoming battle group.

Watson agreed to transmit the message. But when, he asked, was the battle group due to arrive?

"Some time tomorrow," was all Clarke could tell him. It might be midday; it might be midafternoon; it might be evening. It all depended on how the Soviets would react along the length of the autobahn and at the two check points (one at Helmstedt, the other near the Potsdam entrance to West Berlin). "But I don't think there's anything more important than this operation going on over there in Washington on a Sunday afternoon." So why all this goddamn hurry? Clarke exploded, adding a few unprintable expletives for good measure.

At seven o'clock (2:00 P.M. Washington time) Clarke received a telephone call from McGeorge Bundy in the White House. Bundy was his usual cool, collected self.

"General, I understand you're chewing out everybody in sight because you're not happy to see the vice-president leave Berlin before the troops get in."

"That's putting it mildly, Mr. Bundy," Clarke replied. "The men will go all-out to get there on time to be received by the vice-president. I don't know what more important thing the vice-president could do than to be on hand to receive the troops with all the world watching the show."

"What time are you going to have all the men in Berlin?" asked Bundy.

"If I could guarantee that, we wouldn't be having a crisis, would we?" snorted Clarke impatiently. "Who can say where we may get stopped?"

Bundy promised to do what he could at the White House end. But how was Koniev going to react?

Clarke had had his Soviet opposite number informed of the U.S. decision to reinforce its Berlin garrison with a battle group of fifteen hundred men, who would be proceeding up the autobahn early on Sunday morning. The information had been relayed via the Soviet military liaison mission in Frankfurt, but there had been no reaction. Members of the U.S. military liaison team, led by Colonel von Pawel, had been cruising up and down the autobahn for telltale clues of military aggressiveness, but they had spotted nothing of interest. The Soviets, as usual, were giving nothing away.

For Col. Glover Johns, commander of the Eighth Infantry Division's First Battle Group, this proved to be a busy evening followed by a sleepless night. There was a moment of consternation when it was discovered that the fuel tankers on which the battle group depended had gone astray, and it took a lot of telephoning and some hectic reconnaissance by the group's scout cars to locate and guide them to the airfield. The consternation was followed by confusion as a flock of radio, television, and newspaper reporters invaded the bivouac area. They moved from tent to tent, snapping pictures, asking questions, improvising interviews. At the conclusion of a brief staff-and-commanders' meeting, Johns found that he, too, had to face the press, the flash bulbs, and the cameras.

After vainly trying to get a little shut-eye in his makeshift caravan—a tiny hut resting on a two-wheel trailer—Johns managed to shake off several television crews in time to take his place at the head of the column's first "serial," composed of two companies. At exactly 4:00 A.M. he raised his arm as the signal to move out, but the departure was delayed for five minutes by the unexpected bogging down of a mess truck.

The convoy reached the Helmstedt check point eight minutes behind schedule. Beyond the U.S. check point, several Soviet officers and soldiers could be seen examining the papers of German civilian drivers. All seemed routine. As far as Johns could tell, this Sunday was going to be peaceful. They weren't going to have to open the carefully guarded cases and pass out the ammunition.

The check-point MPs had been counting the vehicles and men in Johns's leading detachment. In all, there were 60 jeeps, trucks, and trailers and 276 men—amounting to two rifle companies with equipment and supplies. Farther down the highway, separated by a five-minute gap when the column was in motion, was the Combat Support Company; two more rifle companies; a maintenance and supply detachment equipped with heavy trucks full of high-explosive ammunition; an engineer company; and, drawing up the rear, a battery of 105 mm howitzers with their field artillery crews.

At exactly 6:30 A.M. the MPs waved Johns's column through the U.S. check point. He had been joined in the lead jeep by Major Luce, a Military Police officer who had been sent from Berlin to guide the battle group up the autobahn. As they came to the Soviet barrier, a short, squat Russian captain stepped forward. He seemed nervous and abrupt. He looked Johns up and down, then put his head back as though trying to take in the whole column at a glance. All right, he said to the interpreter, fifteen trucks were to move through the gate, and then they would count the men inside.

To Johns, who had never traveled to Berlin with his unit, this was an irksome procedure. His Movement Order carried the total number of men and the total number of vehicles in his battle group; it did not specify just how many men there were in each truck. The Russian officer began moving down the line of vehicles. To get a better view inside, he put his boot on a trailer hitch and was about to heave himself up when he was stopped by an American MP officer. The Soviets—according to detailed regulations that had been worked out and mutually accepted years before—were allowed to look into U.S. Army trucks but not to climb onto them. U.S. Army personnel, according to another regulation, could not be made to dismount once they had passed the Soviet barrier. It was thus left to the interpreter to try to count the number of U.S. soldiers seated beneath the olive-drab canvas in each truck. Even on a sunny day this was not an easy task.

Johns was beginning to lose patience. At this rate it would take the Russians a good minute of counting and checking to register the number of men in each truck. Since there were two hundred trucks in the battle group, they would need approximately three and a half more hours just to clear the check point.

Thinking it would speed things up, Johns suggested that his men dismount and be counted on the ground. The Soviet officer looked at him round-eyed. It was as though someone had just told him that the earth was really flat. It was too simple to be believed. But after a brief discussion with the interpreter he agreed to the suggestion. The GIs were ordered to dismount and stand by their vehicles. Carefully noting the serial number of each truck, the squat Soviet officer went down the line, jotting down the corresponding number of men on his register.

Having checked the fifteenth vehicle, the Soviet captain added up the total and began shaking his head. The number of men and vehicles recorded bore no relation to the figures on the U.S. Army Movement Order. Of course they didn't, Johns explained—for the simple reason that the figures on the Movement Order included the rest of the detachment, which was waiting beyond the Soviet barrier.

The other U.S. Army vehicles were now allowed through, while the first fifteen trucks advanced several hundred yards down the autobahn to make room for the others. A new count was begun, but again it yielded a discrepancy in figures. Johns suggested to the interpreter that all the men be lined up and counted at one go, rather than by vehicle, but the Russian officer was adamant. They had always counted by vehicle, and this was how they were going to do it today.

A new count was taken, and at the end of it the captain disappeared into a hut on the side of the road. A few minutes later he emerged with his total. Again it failed to tally with the American figures.

Johns by this time was fit to be tied. They had lost a whole hour haggling over figures, and at this rate they would never reach Berlin. To hell with established procedure! he decided. Pointing his index finger at the Soviet captain, who was still shaking his head with puzzlement, the American colonel barked at him, "Look here, my friend, I'm going through this with you one more time. But this time we're going to do it my way!"

Johns had his men line up in a single, unbroken file and then went down the line, touching each man on the chest as he sounded off his number. Every tenth or fifteenth man, he turned to the Russian captain and queried, "Right?" The Soviet captain then confirmed the figure in Russian. At the end of the line, both agreed on the total. But the total still did not agree with the figure given on the Movement Order. Somehow they had counted one man too many.

Johns was beside himself. For a moment he wondered if an MP sergeant had been included in the count when he shouldn't have been. But the interpreter now came to the rescue, suggesting that the extra man might be the colonel himself. His name appeared at the top of the U.S. Army Movement Order, but it was not included in the list of men under his command.

A few minutes later, the lead detachment was on its way up the autobahn, headed for Berlin. There were no further holdups during the 110-mile trip. The battle group was over-flown by a twin-engine Soviet jet 8 or 10 times. The second time, it came down over the middle of the autobahn at a height of 500 feet, the bomb-bay doors open and the cameras clearly visible.

The four-lane highway was dotted with East German Vopos. Two of them were stationed by every bridge and pathway. Some stood half-concealed in thickets or under-brush; others scurried into the woods or disappeared down an embankment as the battle group approached. A few casual observers lay stretched out in the grass or among the roadside weeds, binoculars and sketch pads by their sides.

In his liaison-mission car, Col. Ernest von Pawel had come to the conclusion that the primary mission of all these watchdogs was to keep East German traffic off the autobahn and the battle group as hidden as possible from native eyes. They were not entirely successful, for Johns and his men saw farmers in the fields, some of whom waved while others stared. A number of civilian cars passed by, headed in the opposite direction. Their occupants seemed overjoyed to see the convoy. Some waved; others pulled out handkerchiefs; all were smiling.

13

Lyndon Johnson had put in a busy morning, too. More fortunate than the commander of the First Battle Group, who had to content himself with one C-ration biscuit, he was able to breakfast pleasantly on oatmeal and honeydew melon. Shortly afterward, Willy Brandt turned up at the Dowlings' residence for a private talk with the vice-president and Charles Bohlen.

The main item on the agenda was the three-page letter, written on pale green White House stationery, which McGeorge Bundy had drafted in reply to Brandt's letter of the sixteenth. Johnson had been instructed to deliver it personally to the governing mayor of West Berlin.

Two things about Brandt's letter had particularly nettled Kennedy. The first was the lack of delicacy Brandt had shown in revealing its existence before it had been delivered to the White House. The second was Brandt's anything-but-diplomatic exhortation: Words are not enough; what we want are deeds.

To be sure, Kennedy had told Brandt that he should feel free to get in touch with him at any time should there be an urgent need to do so. But in bypassing the West German Foreign Ministry, during an election campaign when the United States government was bending over backward to remain neutral, he had landed them all in a diplomatic mess. The president appreciated the tremendous strains under which the governing mayor was laboring, but he hoped that this kind of misunderstanding could be avoided in the future.

The recent measures undertaken by the Soviet leadership and "their puppets in East Berlin" had aroused outrage and indignation in the United States. But the inhabitants of West Berlin would have to accept the fact that in the existing circumstances, nothing short of war—and war was out of the question—could achieve any material change in the situation. All the United States could do and was doing was to reinforce its Berlin garrison by fifteen hundred men.

A full paragraph in Kennedy's reply was devoted to the feasibility of tossing the Berlin problem into the lap of the United Nations. The president's feeling, and that of his advisers, was that such a move would have little immediate effect, although it might be worth considering later.

Equally negative was Kennedy's reaction to Brandt's request that the Western Allies proclaim a reinforced Three-Power guarantee to assure the security and continued independence of West Berlin. This request had given rise to much perplexity in Washington and Bonn. Brandt explained to his listeners that he had not been advocating the abandonment of Four-Power responsibility for all Berlin. But because the Four-Power agreements had been flagrantly violated by the recent seal-off measures, it was imperative that the Western Allies reiterate their support for West Berlin more unambiguously than ever. It was not enough to insist on freedom of *Allied* movement to and from West Berlin; the freedom of movement of *German* goods and *German* people was equally vital, and this could only be assured by strengthening the links already existing between the three western sectors of Berlin and the Federal Republic.

Lyndon Johnson soon made it clear that he was a bit lost in all this talk of agreements, essential guarantees, and vital requirements. He was more than willing to leave such diplomatic details to professionals like Bohlen and Dowling. What interested him at this point was discovering what West Berlin might have to offer in the way of gifts that he could take home to his friends in the States—everything from electric razors to old prints and engravings.

The people in the U.S. and West Berlin protocol sections were accordingly alerted, to their considerable dismay. This being a Sunday, the stores and print shops were all closed. The unexpected diversion did, however, give Charles Bohlen a chance to draw Brandt off to one side for a piece of friendly advice. In the future, instead of writing to the president, he should simply pick up the telephone and call the White House. It would be simpler and faster, leave no trace, and spare everyone the embarrassment of subsequent recriminations.

At eleven o'clock the private session came to an end, to the unconcealed relief of the restless vice-president. A Cadillac limousine was waiting outside to take him on another tour of West Berlin. The itinerary agreed upon was to take Lyndon Johnson through the Tiergarten to the modernistic Hansa Viertel (a stretch of green-lawned park dotted with different-shaped buildings designed by famous architects). They were then to visit a new utilitarian housing project in northern Charlottenburg before proceeding to the Marienfelde refugee camp. Some time in the afternoon, although no one knew just when, the vice-president would arrange to welcome the U.S. Army battle group as it rolled into Berlin.

If anything, the turnout on this Sunday morning exceeded the previous afternoon's tumultuous welcome. There was hardly an inhabitant of West Berlin who did not now know that Lyndon Johnson had arrived with General Clay bearing messages of support from the president of the United States. By the tens, by the hundreds of thousands, men, women, and children lined the avenues and streets along which the vice-presidential motorcade was expected to pass.

The triumphal column was preceded by a photography truck on which television cameras had been mounted to record each second of this historic moment. Since the weather was fine, Johnson repeatedly got out of his limousine to walk and to shake hands with his frantic admirers. Deaf to the remonstrances of his chief Secret Service bodyguard, he would walk boldly into the throng of bystanders, raise his arms and wave, then let his right hand drop behind his back and into the "goody bag" which another Secret Service bodyguard held open and ready just behind him. Seizing a fistful of ball-point pens, the vice-president would distribute presents to the lucky ones closest to him. More arm waving would follow, a few more steps would be taken, and then the vice-presidential hand would return discreetly once again to another bag. This time the Texas magician would come up with a fistful of cards: U.S. Senate visitors'-gallery passes adorned with a facsimile of the vice-president's signature.

Spurning the Cadillac limousine in favor of a Berlin City Hall Mercedes, which had a roll-back top enabling him to stand upright as they moved along, Johnson continued his triumphal drive through wildly cheering crowds. The supply of ball-point pens was beginning to run out, and the "goody bag" containing the Senate passes was well-nigh empty long before they were scheduled to reach the utilitarian housing unit in northern Charlottenburg. But at that moment—it was already 12:30—word was brought to the vice-president that the U.S. Army battle group had reached the Soviet check point near Potsdam and would soon be entering West Berlin. North Charlottenburg and its expectant inhabitants were immediately forgotten. Preceded by a motorcycle and police-car escort, the open Mercedes roared through a maze of unscheduled avenues and streets, headed for the Avus, a one-time automobile racetrack which Adolf Hitler, in the 1930s, had turned into the start of the Berlin–Cologne autobahn.

As they sped south and west with the wind blowing through their hair, Johnson told Brandt, who was seated next to him, that he would like to buy some of the famous china he had heard so much about that was made by—what was it called?—the people who had made plates and cups for the kings of Prussia. Ah yes, said Brandt, the Königliche Porzellan-Manufaktur. They were the ones who had designed the pale blue dishes that Frederick the Great was so fond of. Yes, they were still in business, although under a slightly different name: the Staatliche Porzellanwerke. But unfortunately, that this was Sunday and the china shops were closed.

"Well, goddamnit!" exclaimed Johnson, "what if they are! You're the mayor aren't you? It shouldn't be too difficult for you to make arrangements so I can get to see that porcelain. I've crossed an entire ocean to come here, and besides, wasn't it you who were saying a day or two ago that what you wanted was action, not words? That's the way I feel about it too."

Brandt said he would get the protocol people on the job as soon as possible. He realized that the vice-president had come a long, long way, and they were all mighty grateful and would do everything to please him.

On the Avus racetrack, the Johnson motorcade was stopped by a sizable crowd of Berliners who had either heard or seen that a reviewing stand was being erected for the incoming U.S. troops. The crowd was already so thick that it took the combined shouldering of General Watson and the Secret Service to clear a path for Lyndon Johnson to the small roadside podium.

Colonel Johns by this time had cleared the Soviet check point and been welcomed a few hundred yards farther on by Brig. Gen. Frederick Hartel, commander of the Berlin garrison; a U.S. Army band; and a flock of camera-wielding newsmen. On seeing General Watson pushing his way through the crowd, Johns jumped out of his jeep and hurried forward to meet him. The helmeted colonel, his name clearly marked on a white tab over the right breast pocket of his battle dress, was pushed and heaved onto the platform. There his hand was vigorously pumped by Lyndon Johnson, who improvised a few solemn words of greeting, to which Willy Brandt added a few of his own. The colonel had almost as much trouble regaining his jeep, so tumultuous and excited was the crowd. Preceded by an MP sedan, the advance guard of the First Battle Group then rolled past the reviewing stand and was soon engulfed by cheerers who broke through the police cordons, stormed across the autobahn's central sward, and pelted the delighted GIs with flowers.

The soldiers were headed for the McNair barracks in the southern Lichterfelde area, where they were to be fed. Arrangements had also been made for the vice-president and his party to lunch there in the officers' mess. The VIPs were served more quickly than the GIs, who had to queue up with their mess kits; and some of the hungry soldiers barely had time for a few mouthfuls before they were called to the parade ground to be addressed by the vice-president. Here they were treated to some honest-to-goodness Deep South oratory, tempered by a few diplomatic phrases ("We are the protectors of freedom, we do not intend to be provocative or belligerent, but we are prepared always to do our duty with honor"). It was a hot, sunny August day—too hot for some soldiers, who collapsed on the parade ground from sheer exhaustion.

After Johnson had finished speaking, General Watson read a

welcoming message he had just received from General Clarke in Heidelberg. Then Col. Glover Johns, who had spent part of his student days in prewar Munich, said a few words in German to humor the West Berlin officials. These ceremonies completed, the commander of the U.S. battle group was told that he and his men had to get back to their vehicles. What they had seen and experienced so far was merely a prelude; the real parade was about to begin.

Willy Brandt had meanwhile left for the Schöneberg Rathaus in the city-hall Mercedes, leaving the vice-president with the U.S. mission's black Cadillac sedan. Although it was only a short distance from the McNair barracks to the Marienfelde refugee camp, which he was supposed to have visited earlier in the day, Johnson blew his top when he discovered that he was going to have to climb back into a closed car.

"What the goddamn hell d'you mean you haven't got an open car for me to ride in?" he shouted at the U.S. major in charge of transportation. "I'm not going to travel in that thing," he went on, pointing disdainfully at the sedan, as though it were a hearse. "I'm going to ride in an open car so that the people of West Berlin *can see me*, do you hear?" The flustered major heard, as did everyone else within fifty yards. A few foul-mouthed insults sent the poor major running, but an adequate convertible could not be found.

There were still several thousand refugees at the Marienfelde reception center who had not yet been evacuated to the Federal Republic or found new lodgings in the western sectors. On hearing that the vice-president of the United States had reached the entrance to the camp, they went wild. The vice-president was mobbed, cut off from his Secret Service protectors and other members of his party, and so squeezed that he could hardly breathe. He finally made it through the excited crowd to a yellow Porsche, which had been commandeered for the occasion. Standing on the driver's seat, he improvised a short speech, which only a few of the bystanders could hear and even fewer understand. But they cheered their heads off all the same.

While the vice-president was being mobbed at Marienfelde, Charles Bohlen and General Clay undertook a quick tour of East Berlin. They found the streets full of Vopos and soldiers but otherwise astonishingly empty. The reason was simple: Most East Berliners, on this Sunday afternoon, had stayed home to listen to the radio, and many of them continued to follow events in West Berlin on their west-oriented television sets.

From Marienfelde, Johnson was driven to the U.S. Command headquarters on the Clayallee in Dahlem, where he was to officiate at a formal drive-past of the newly arrived battle group. Once again the vice-presidential motorcade was ambushed by an enthusiastic mob, and Johnson climbed out of his car to shake hands. A waitress came running out of a nearby tavern with a bottle of Schultheiss beer, which she insisted on presenting to the distinguished visitor from Texas. He had to take a swig then, on the spot. The crowd roared its delight. The bottle was accordingly opened and out foamed the agitated contents—all over Johnson's tie and jacket. There were gasped apologies, and then more wild cheering as the vice-president unconcernedly brushed off his moist jacket and took a good-natured swig before passing the half-empty bottle to the governing mayor of West Berlin, who was once again by his side.

By this time—close to 5:00 P.M.—Col. Glover Johns and his battle group were more or less in position behind a convoy of German motorcycle policemen and American MP sedans. The canvas tops had been rolled back, so that the GIs in their battle dress could be clearly seen.

The route had been carefully chosen to enable the second detachment of Johns's battle group, which had only recently made it through the Soviet check point, to link up behind the forward echelon. This second detachment had one hundred trucks and trailers and four hundred men. Johns managed to contact a few of its officers by radio to explain that they were about to take part in a formal parade. But the acclamations were so noisy and the crowds engulfing them so dense that few trucks got the message. As the lead jeep came abreast of the reviewing stand, Colonel Johns, who was standing upright, saluted the top brass and then hopped out to take his place on the platform next to the vice-president. The GIs in the first detachment's trucks sat erect and well behaved, although they couldn't help waving at the crowds each time another bouquet came sailing in. But the GIs in the second detachment showed no such restraint. Most of them were bunched forward, cheering and yelling as loudly as the crowds swirling around them. Many of the trucks rolled past the U.S. headquarters without a single soldier on board even noticing the reviewing stand, which was set back a certain distance above and behind the roadside crowd. A few, suddenly spotting the top brass on the platform, gaped open-mouthed, then shouted to their companions, snapped to attention as best they could, and saluted—to the obvious amusement of Lyndon Johnson, who spent as much time waving as saluting.

When the last vehicle had passed, Johns left the platform and had a siren-screaming MP sedan clear the way for his jeep so that he could head the column once again. The motorcade wound on for miles, moving up the entire distance of the Kurfürstendamm, and seemed to go on for hours—hours of frantic waving which grew so tiring that the soldiers had to keep changing arms. When Colonel Johns finally made it back to the barrack quarters that had been prepared for him and his battle group, his face muscles ached and his mouth was quite dry from hours of nonstop smiling.

In the middle of the ninety-minute parade, a young Berliner pushed his way to the reviewing stand with a piece of sculpture that he was intent on presenting to the vice-president. It turned out to be a bust of John Kennedy—the work of two amateur sculptors who wanted Johnson to take it back with him to Washington as a token of their appreciation of the U.S. president's support of West Berlin.

The drive-past completed, Johnson returned to the ambassadorial residence on the Spechtstrasse for an impromptu press conference. He soon tired of the questions being asked and withdrew, as if to the men's room, leaving Charles Bohlen to carry on in his place. Bohlen, who had spent the early afternoon motoring around East Berlin with General Clay and Allan Lightner, dispelled all lingering doubts about Uncle Sam's intentions. They were essentially pacific, he made clear, adding a bit too casually, "We are not going to take any risks in Berlin." This was just what Khrushchev and Ulbricht were hoping to hear.

Now that the newsmen had dispersed, Johnson could at last relax with his hosts, Ambassador and Mrs. Dowling, and Willy Brandt. This was as close to a tete-à-tete as protocol would permit. It also struck one member of the State Department mission as unwise to have the vice-president of the United States thus closeted with Brandt, the official standard-bearer of the Social Democratic party in West Germany, only twenty-four hours after his electoral rival, Konrad Adenauer, had been discouraged from coming to Berlin. West Berlin, after all, was ruled by a two-party coalition government. He accordingly contacted Deputy Mayor Franz Amrehn and informed him of what was going on. Amrehn immediately got through to Brandt, who told him that he didn't care if the pussy-footing Americans didn't want a Christian Democrat around; by all means come over! So over to the Spechtstrasse Amrehn came. Johnson, whisky glass in hand, was in a jocular mood.

"Say, Mr. Mayor," he exclaimed, pointing to a pair of loafers Brandt was wearing, "where did you get those nifty shoes? I want a pair just like them."

Brandt must have felt like groaning. First it was china from the Staatliche Porzellanwerke; now it was shoes from Leiser, Berlin.

"I'm sorry, Mr. Vice-President," he explained, as patiently as he could, "but this is Sunday and the stores are closed."

Johnson shook his head, half-amused, half-angry. "What was that you said the other day in front of your city hall? That you wanted action, not words, from the Allies? Now how about a little action on your part? And remember, when Kennedy had me dragged away from a dinner party to say I was to go to Berlin, he didn't ask if I wanted to come or not. He simply said I had to fly over in a hurry because my presence was needed here."

Once again this was not a suggestion. It was a command issued by someone who didn't understand the meaning of the word *impossible*. The harassed mayor had no choice but to go to the telephone, ring up his staff at City Hall, and instruct them to get hold of the Leiser shoe-shop owner, even if it meant dragging him from his supper. He was to go to his shop, collect a score of samples, in the 10½-to-11 range, and bring them to the U.S. ambassadorial residence on Spechtstrasse.

When Johnson heard that it might take a couple of hours before the shoes would arrive, he decided to make good use of the interim. "Let me invite you to dinner," he said to Brandt. The previous evening he had been the guest of the governing mayor and the Berlin parliament; now it was his turn to play the host. Mrs. Dowling had made plans for a small dinner party at home, but the vice-president had other ideas. He was going to invite them and their wives all to—well, how about the Hilton? It had a roof-top restaurant? Great! From that vantage point they could enjoy a fine view of nocturnal Berlin.

Robert Lochner had meanwhile gone home, leaving Johnson without an interpreter. "All right," said the vice-president, "but why don't we round up those German desk boys who came over on the plane with us? This will give them something to do."

Half an hour later, Frank Cash and Henry Cox, who had just returned from their own tour of East Berlin, were intercepted at their U.S. Army guesthouse by a first lieutenant who told them that the vice-president had decided to give a dinner for the governing mayor at the Hilton and that they were needed to interpret. They were bundled into a military staff car and driven to the hotel, where they borrowed an electric razor from the reception desk and ducked into the men's room to shave.

On the roof-top restaurant, a large rectangular table had been prepared for about twenty people. Willy Brandt had been asked to bring his wife, Rut, and Mrs. Amrehn had been invited to accompany her husband, Franz. It was some time, however, before they could all sit down, because at the last moment Johnson was called off to one side by a member of the City Hall protocol section, who informed him that the manager of the Staatliche Porzellanwerke had been contacted and that he had agreed to open his show room on the Kurfürstendamm for the U.S. vice-president. Accompanied by the protocol official and Mrs. Dowling, Johnson made a quick trip to the show room, where he picked out a simple service for the LBJ ranch in Texas and a more elaborate set of *rocaille* plates, which he wanted to have adorned with the vice-presidential seal. The manager, who had been dragged out of bed for this late-evening opening of his show room, was more than a bit perplexed. The simple service was no problem; it could be made available in a day or two, ready to be flown to the United States. But the other service would take weeks, perhaps even a month or two, before the intricate work could be completed.

These negotiations at an end, host and guests could at last sit down to dinner in the Hilton's roof-top restaurant. The seating arrangement, however, made no sense. The gentleman from Texas, with a regal disregard for protocol, decided to place Ambassador Dowling on his right and Mrs. Amrehn, who spoke no English, on his left. Brandt, who did not need an interpreter, was seated opposite, next to Henry Cox. Although the vice-president displayed a truly southern gallantry, rising to his feet each time Rut Brandt, who was pregnant, left the dining room, he naturally found it easier to talk to Ambassador Dowling than to his other neighbor, Mrs. Amrehn. She, in turn, found it difficult to follow General Clay's nostalgic reminiscences of the heroic airlift days of 1948–49. Henry Cox was thus asked to come around to their side of the table and to interpret for them.

True to his Texan style, Johnson had ordered southern fried chicken for everybody. Some of the guests were a bit startled to see their host seize a drumstick with both hands and gnaw at it with frontiersman gusto.

They were no less startled somewhat later to see the vice-president indulge in a bit of sharp, country-fair bargaining. Henry Cox, who had finally been allowed to return to his stone-cold chicken, had just had time to start on it when Johnson, favorably impressed by his linguistic proficiency, summoned him back. "Hey, boy," he beckoned to him across the table, "would you come over here and please tell this man how grateful I am to him for having opened his show room for me? I particularly appreciate his having done this on a Sunday."

The man in question was Werner Franke, the pint-sized director of the Staatliche Porzellanwerke, who had just been ushered into the dining room. He had brought an exact inventory list of the dishes the vice-president had ordered for the LBJ ranch. Johnson was genuinely touched by this mark of solicitude, and he wanted the little man to know it. Ambassador Dowling's German had apparently not been up to the task, so now he had Cox repeat the message not once but several times.

Not satisfied, Johnson dug into the pocket of his trousers and pulled out a fat wad of dollar bills—more ten-, twenty-, and fifty-dollar bills than Cox had seen in a long time.

"Now tell me, how much do I owe this man?"

"Nothing," was the translated answer. "He doesn't want to be paid now," Cox explained. "He'll ship everything you've requested to your ranch in Texas. There you can decide what you want to keep and send the rest back."

This unexpected largesse gave the vice-president an idea. "Say, tell him this, would you? I normally give out key rings to people who come to call on me in Washington. So what I'd like now is to have some ash trays made to order with the vice-presidential seal on them. Now ask him if he can take care of that order."

Cox translated the question. The answer from Herr Franke was Yes, he could take care of the order.

"Only tell him I don't want to pay more than thirty-three cents apiece for them," the canny Texan insisted.

Why thirty-three cents Cox was at a loss to understand. But he translated the figure, even giving the rough equivalent in Deutschmarks and Pfennigs. Herr Franke nodded. *Jawohl*, for the equivalent of thirty-three American cents he could turn out as many ash trays with the vice-presidential seal on them as the Herr Vice-President might wish.

"O.K., it's a deal," said Johnson, happily dismissing the *Porzellan* manufacturer and the helpful interpreter, who was allowed to return to his frigid fowl.

Toward midnight Johnson rose from the table saying, "I'd like to have a look at the Soviet sector." He walked over to the edge of the roof terrace with the other members of the party and stood there for a while gazing eastward into the night.

Flabbergasted by Johnson's seemingly tireless energy, one

member of the party accosted a Secret Service man. "Say, is this the way he usually carries on? He's not high by any chance?"

"Oh, no," the Secret Service man assured him, "the vice-president is just his usual bubbling self."

Johnson proved it again by informing the assembled company that he would be flying back to Washington in the early hours of the morning. He then returned to the Dowlings' residence. The Leiser shoes had been delivered. The dozen boxes were emptied, and shoes and wrapping paper spread all over the living-room floor as Lyndon Johnson tramped around trying on one pair after another. Finally satisfied, he ordered half a dozen pairs, to be sent on after him to Washington, and then went upstairs to pack. The job of fitting the proper shoes back into the proper boxes was left to Mrs. Dowling and a high-ranking military aide, who spent some embarrassing minutes crawling around on their hands and knees trying to tidy up the mess.

By the time the vice-president and Mary Margaret Wiley were ready to leave, it was almost 4:00 A.M. "Now, Mr. Vice-President," said Mrs. Dowling in her soft southern voice, "you can't leave at this hour without having some breakfast."

"Never mind about the breakfast," said Johnson, with a wave of his hand.

But she insisted. Even in Berlin she could show him a little southern hospitality. So he emptied another bowl of oatmeal before handing out more fountain pens to the servants who were lined up near the front entrance to say good-by.

The early departure hour upset the usual protocol. Military honors are not usually rendered between sunset and sunrise, and Johnson was inclined to go along with the usual procedure. His right hand was swollen and his right arm sore from shaking so many hands, and he felt he had taken enough salutes as it was. General Clay was forced to intervene. The vice-president was, after all, the symbol of America's determination to stand by West Berlin. He couldn't sneak away without a final farewell. "Mr. Vice-President, you just can't leave West Berlin without having the honors presented by the three Allied forces."

Johnson immediately relented, agreeing to postpone the takeoff until after dawn. Drawn up on the Tegel airfield to honor him as he walked toward his Boeing 707 jet were parade units of the French, British, and American garrisons, complete with military bands and pipers. The Schutzpolizei also had brought its band, which broke into the popular song *Das ist die Berliner Luft!* ("That Is the Berlin Air!) as the vice-president paused on the tarmac. Among Germans, the sprightly quality of Berlin's tree- and lake-rich air has long been a source of particular pride to the locals. Robert Lochner, who was back on the job as interpreter, sought to explain this by remarking, tongue-in-cheek, "Mr. Vice-President, the band is playing the West Berlin national anthem."

Johnson immediately stiffened, and assuming a frozen expression, he placed his right hand over his heart and faced the band. Looking much surprised, Willy Brandt and the other Germans who had come to see him off, shuffled to attention. And on this semivaudeville note the farewell ceremonies were concluded.

14

Although the Johnson-Clay visit was a real shot-in-the-arm for the demoralized West Berliners, it had virtually no impact in the East. Hermann Axen's *Neues Deutschland* compared it to "the take-off of a rocket at Cape Canaveral. It puffed and fizzled, but did not rise into the air. The reason for all this is the balance of world politics"—now irreversibly tilted in favor of the Socialist camp. "The DDR Saved the Peace Even from These People" was the headline over an article describing Col. Glover Johns as *"Der Killer aus Texas,"* a sinister gangster with the "face of a gallows-bird," whose thuglike troops had spent their time in West Germany raping and murdering the terrorized populace in their area of occupation. The same line was peddled to the Grepos and Vopos guarding the intersector border. The newly arrived GIs were all gangsters and pimps, they were told by their Politofficers, who added for good measure that Brandt's hope that they would come straight up and start tearing down the concrete wall and the barbed-wire barricades had been cruelly deceived.

Yielding to American pressure, on Sunday the British had reinforced their garrison with eighteen armored troop carriers and sixteen Ferret scout cars, which were shipped to Berlin on railway flatcars.

But more than this was needed to impress the East Germans who were now receiving open encouragement from Richard Crossman. In a *Sunday Telegraph* article, the Labour M.P. demanded that the United Nations be moved to Berlin, that Western troops be withdrawn, that "the subversive and sabotage campaign directed from West Berlin" be suspended, and that the East German regime be granted de jure recognition. Macmillan, for his part, was still relaxing in Yorkshire, while the Earl of Home, after traveling to London for a meeting with the French, U.S., and West German ambassadors, had returned tranquilly to Scotland.

The next day, newspaper readers were informed that Her Majesty's government had rejected an American request that the British garrison in Berlin be reinforced through the addition of one battalion. The primary purpose of the three thousand soldiers already stationed in Berlin was to maintain and improve local morale, "show the flag," and maintain internal security. Evidently satisfied that all three of these objectives were being achieved, Her Majesty's government saw no need to dispatch more troops to a vulnerable forward position where, if anything serious happened, they could easily be trapped. Whitehall, running true to form, was using purely military reasons to justify a policy of political passivity. Or was it impassivity? Some began to wonder when they learned that Harold Macmillan, at the close of his grouse-shooting holiday in Yorkshire, was preparing to move farther north for a second holiday in Perthshire.

In Berlin, meanwhile, the pressed-rubble-and-concrete wall was continuing its reptilian growth. It was oozing into every nook and cranny, mortaring up cracks, fissures, and neglected orifices with its hideous gray excrement. Under the menace of

Vopo and Kampfgruppen Tommy guns, reluctant masons were being compelled to brick up the ground-floor doors and windows of houses on the eastern side of the Bernauer Strasse. The inhabitants were ordered not to lock their apartment doors, leaving them open to police inspection at any time. The *laisser-aller* of the previous week was over; the reign of terror had begun.

Early on Tuesday morning Ida Siekmann, who had spent an anguished night wondering how she was going to get over to the West the next day to celebrate her fifty-ninth birthday now that the front door was walled up, heard the Vopos coming up the stairs and knocking on her neighbors' doors. Thirty-five feet separated her third-floor apartment from the ground, but try as she might, she had been unable to fashion a suitably strong rope out of her bed sheets. Now galvanized by panic, she pulled the mattress from her bed, staggered over to the open window, and pushed and pulled it over, letting it fall to the pavement. As the Vopos, hearing no answer to their knocks, began to pound on the illegally locked door, she clambered out onto the window sill, perched there for a moment, and then jumped. Missing the mattress, she hit the hard pavement and was knocked unconscious. An ambulance was hastily summoned, but the poor woman died of compound fractures and hemorrhages long before she reached the hospital.

A few hours later Konrad Adenauer flew to West Berlin in a U.S. Air Force plane for the official visit he should have made a week before. Willy Brandt was waiting to greet him at the Tempelhof airfield, but the atmosphere was glacial. There was not the flicker of a smile on either face as the two political antagonists shook hands.

Scattered crowds of Berliners lined the streets and avenues along which the official motorcade was to pass, but along with the subdued clapping, sarcastic signs could be seen with slogans like "At Last!" and "It Was About Time!"

At the Potsdamer Platz the chancellor dismounted and walked deliberately toward the first barbed-wire barrier until he was not more than four or five yards away. The concrete wall beyond was already six feet high, and behind it green-uniformed Vopos had been posted on wooden platforms so that they could keep an eye on what was happening on the western side.

In anticipation of this visit, the East Germans had also stationed a water truck not far behind. Its revolving turret, grotesquely decorated with roses and long-stemmed gladioli, followed the chancellor's every step. As the Old Man stood his ground not uttering a word, a loud-speaker on the eastern side opened up with jeering slogans: "Look at this wall and realize that it is the product of your policy! Now we will offer some tourist information to a senile old traveler and his three boys." The three "boys" who were accompanying Adenauer were Ernst Lemmer, federal minister for all-German affairs; Joachim von Merkatz, minister for refugees; and West Berlin's deputy mayor, Franz Amrehn. Songs followed making fun of Willy Brandt, referred to mockingly as "the Adenauer troubadour."

The same macabre performance was repeated at the Brandenburg Gate, where the loud-speakers blared, "Look at him! He can't even smile! Yes, dear Konrad, this is the result of your policy!" But at other stops along the intersector border, small clusters of East Berliners waved pathetic greetings from a distance.

After visiting the Marienfelde reception center, where certain of the refugees were bold enough to ask him why he hadn't come sooner, and after attending a meeting with members of the city-hall government, Adenauer made a short statement in which he reiterated his conviction that "the great economic potential of the West" could be used to apply an economic embargo on the "entire Communist bloc." He was, however, firmly opposed to military countermeasures.

That same day, two more Grepos managed to escape to the West by crawling on their hands and knees under a barbed-wire fence. Questioned by interrogators, they said that there was no danger involved. "Ordinary soldiers like ourselves aren't equipped with live ammunition. Only noncoms and squad leaders are issued it—sixteen rounds of live ammunition packed into magazines for their sub-machine guns. These magazines are sealed with lead and carried in satchels attached to their belts."

There was, however, little cause for rejoicing in the West over these defections, which were no more than pinpricks in the increasingly thick hide of Walter Ulbricht's DDR. Whipped on by "red Hilde" Benjamin, the East German minister of justice, the People's Courts were launching a regular witch hunt against "saboteurs" and those still daring to indulge in "man-trade" activities. East German farmers caught trying to flee to the West after setting their barns on fire in rage and resentment over the border seal-off received savage prison sentences, up to as many as a dozen years. Peter Hellwig, a twenty-one-year-old worker employed at the OSRAM light-bulb works in East Berlin, was sentenced to four years in prison for allegedly trying to help a friend escape. Jörg Schmidt, a twenty-one-year-old cameraman working for the Freies Berlin radio station, was given five years for trying to smuggle a girl into West Berlin with a borrowed identity card. A twenty-year-old storage worker named Gerhard Garow got seven years for two similar offenses. At the trials, given a maximum of publicity in the East German press, witnesses testified that Sender Freies Berlin was now a hotbed of anti-DDR plotting; that in the Schöneberg Rathaus fake identity cards were being peddled for two to three hundred West marks apiece; that the Catholic Students Union was up to its neck in "man-trade" contraband; and so on.

Now happily convinced that it had nothing to fear from possible military or economic countermeasures, the East German government added new injury to insult. Late Tuesday evening—but in time for the news to make the front pages of next morning's *Neues Deutschland*—Karl Maron's Ministry of the Interior issued three new decrees. The first put a brusque end to the West Berliners' last remaining freedom: the right to enter East Berlin by simply showing a valid identity card. Henceforth, West Berlin pedestrians would be subjected to the same conditions as motorists, and would be required to obtain special permits to be able to enter the Soviet sector.

The second decree reduced the still-unblocked crossing points from twelve to seven. Four of them were reserved for West Berliners. Two more were left open for citizens of the Federal Republic. The seventh and last—the Friedrichstrasse crossing point (soon to become world famous as "Check-Point Charlie")—was made the obligatory point of entry and exit for all non-Germans and diplomats.

The third decree gave formal backing to the warning that Maron's Ministry of the Interior had already issued to West

Berliners. But now they were *ordered* to stay one hundred meters clear of the intersector border. The order, furthermore, was applicable to all the inhabitants of West Berlin without exception. The East German authorities were thus trying to establish a buffer zone between their barricaded border and the western sectors of Berlin.

The provocation this time was too blatant to be taken lying down. In a rare display of unanimity, the three Allied commands hammered out a joint protest in record time, declaring these measures to be illegal and "further proof that the East German Communist regime cannot tolerate the maintenance of even the simplest contacts between families and friends." Speaking for the British, Brigadier Goff Hamilton declared, "The Western commandants have no intention of being told by the East where the West sectors begin and end. We will send our troops at any time and to any place we wish in our area of responsibility." At a press conference held at the Maison de France, on the fashionable Kurfürstendamm, Gen. Jean Lacomme was even blunter: "French soldiers do not let themselves be insulted by the policemen of East Germany."

At exactly 1:00 P.M. troops from the three Allied garrisons moved up to the intersector border. Along the Reinickendorf "front"—which is what it had virtually become—French armored cars began cruising up and down, while infantrymen took up positions on the Chausseestrasse, Brunnenstrasse, and other Wedding streets. In the central Tiergarten area, soldiers of the Durham Light Infantry began pitching bivouac tents under the trees between the gutted Reichstag and the wired-in Soviet War Memorial. Other units from the "Greenjackets" set up machine guns and mortars on the other side of the Strasse des 17. Juni. British armored cars were ordered to patrol up and down the Heidestrasse, west of the Lehrter Bahnhof railway yards and the Volkspolizei hospital. The Americans did the same. While startled Volksarmee officers, hastily summoned to the windows of the Haus der Ministerien, peered through their binoculars, heavy U.S. tanks, accompanied by armored personnel carriers, rumbled up the southern part of the Friedrichstrasse to within yards of the sector boundary. The lead Patton tank—carrying the name

"War Eagle" painted in bold letters—trained its gun muzzle straight up the Friedrichstrasse. U.S. infantrymen—equipped with carbines, automatic rifles, and walkie-talkies—were ordered to patrol the Kreuzberg and Neukölln borders on a twenty-four-hour basis, advancing to within thirty-five yards of the East German obstructions, if necessary.

Grateful West Berliners streamed up with words of thanks and armsful of flowers. When Willy Brandt came up for a first-hand look at the Friedrichstrasse check point, he was beaming. This was the kind of action he had hoped to see on August 13.

The East Germans, who finally brought up several armored cars, seemed for once to have been caught by surprise. Obviously put out by this sudden show of strength, a nervous Vopo officer advanced with a piece of chalk and drew a white line across the street to indicate exactly where the U.S. sector ended and the Soviet sector began. A U.S. officer then walked up and deliberately effaced the chalk line with the soles and heels of his shoes. The Volkspolizei officers and soldiers looked on speechless.

There was not much at this point that Walter Ulbricht could do about it. He had chosen this Wednesday to celebrate his victory by staging a huge Kampfgruppen parade up the wide Stalinallee. The parade was accompanied by the inevitable harangue, in the course of which Ulbricht declared that the "militarist" Brandt had to be removed, along with the "present Fascist military gang" that was running things in the Schöneberg Rathaus, and the administration of West Berlin entrusted to "peace-loving, sensible leaders."

15

One East Berliner who did not witness Ulbricht's parade or the sudden concentration of armor at the Friedrichstrasse check point was construction worker Emil Goltz. Each evening, for some days, he had been leaving his apartment on the Graetz-strasse, in the Treptow Park district, to reconnoiter the possibilities of making it over to the West, only to return home with a feeling of mounting frustration. For the first three days after the Sunday seal-off it would have been fairly easy for the three of them—his wife, his daughter, and himself—to slip across the not-too-well-guarded Kiefholzstrasse, but each time the moment came for action, his wife, Anna, had found some new pretext for postponing the attempt.

On Thursday, August 17, all hope of making it across the Kiefholzstrasse had to be abandoned. The kilometer-long stretch of boundary was now barricaded by formidable coils of barbed wire and hard-bitten Kampfgruppen. There were rumors that the Vopos were under orders not to shoot to kill, but Goltz was wary of such reports. He was convinced that the older, tougher, and more fanatical factory militiamen would have no scruples about opening fire on his wife, his nine-year-old child, or himself. He had miraculously survived the last months of World War II without getting a bullet or a piece of shrapnel in his hide, and he was in no mood now to risk being crippled for life by some trigger-happy militiaman bent on proving his heroic loyalty to the Workers-and-Peasants-State.

The daily arguments with his wife were taking an increasingly bitter turn. Just how long it would take before she finally saw the light, Emil Goltz had no idea. But it would probably be too long to matter. He would have to go it alone and make it over to the other side on his own. Once over, he would try to enlist the help of ingenious West Berliners to help Anna and Beate escape. One thing, at any rate, was certain: The longer he remained in East

Berlin, the greater risk he ran of being picked up for questioning by Vopos or agents of the SSD.

Instead of concentrating on the area close to the sector boundary, as he had been doing, Goltz decided to try something radically different. While the Friedrichstrasse station had become a double, back-to-back kind of terminus for S-Bahn trains—with eastbound trains using one platform and westbound trains another—interzonal or international trains still traveled on the old Reichsbahn tracks through to the British and U.S. sectors of West Berlin. Once aboard one of these trains, one did not have to get off or change until it made the regular single stop at the Zoologischer Garten station, near the Kaiser Wilhelm Memorial Church and the upper reaches of the Kurfürstendamm.

Leaving his wife and daughter at home, Goltz spent several evenings reconnoitering the Ostbahnhof station, which was just three stops away by elevated S-Bahn. Here the S-Bahn platforms were close enough to the main railway station for him to be able to watch the train traffic moving out toward the north and west. He soon made an important discovery. When the Moscow–Paris express rolled into the Ostbahnhof shortly after 10:00 P.M., it remained in the station for almost twenty minutes. The last three coaches, bearing shields marked "Moskau–Brest Litowsk–Warschau–Berlin," were uncoupled from the seven or eight other cars making up the train and shunted off onto a dark siding in the adjacent yards. While the express was thus being divested of its last three cars, the other seven remained unguarded on the platform. A solitary railwayman walked from one end to the other, striking the wheels and bogies with a long-handled hammer; but only at the last moment, a few minutes before the actual departure time, did the platform suddenly fill up with Vopos, posted there to check the passports and identity cards of passengers who were going to board the train.

There was thus an interval of ten to fifteen minutes during which it would be possible, so Goltz reckoned, to sneak up to the back of the train from the dark sidings and railway yards lying beyond the station's platforms and arched roof. By wedging himself in over the transversal connecting rods, which linked the wheel brakes just above the rotating axles, he stood

a fair chance of being able to ride into the British sector un-
observed. So curved and undulating was the track between
the Ostbahnhof and Zoo stations that all trains, including
through express trains, covered the seven kilometers at a
slow, milk-train pace. The undercarriage stowaway thus ran
little risk of being jarred out of his precarious position by
violent jolts, or hit in the face by flying pebbles.

To his wife, Goltz had made no secret of his intention of
fleeing to the West. But he had not told Anna just when or
how he proposed to escape. Nor did he do so now, on this
evening of August 23. But she must have guessed his intention; for as he opened the door, saying he was going out for
another evening stroll, she gave him an unusually long, fixed,
wordless look. He, for his part, would have liked to say good-
by, but he didn't dare. His attire, he later realized, must have
given him away. To blend into the darkness more easily, he
had put on a dark suit.

Once again he boarded the S-Bahn train at the Treptow
Park station. Three stops farther on, he got off at the Ostbahnhof. He sat down on the platform bench for a moment
and pretended to be busy tying his shoelace. The passengers
drifted toward the exit while the S-Bahn train moved on, leaving him a clear view of the main railway station. The Moscow–Paris express was already there, led by its black steam
engine, the coal-carrying tender, and the first three sleeping
cars in which privileged Muscovites could travel with a minimum of fuss from the banks of the Moskva to the banks of the
Seine. Goltz's timing was sound, but there was not a moment
to be lost.

Instead of following the other passengers out through the
exit, Goltz got up and walked deliberately toward the southeastern end of the platform. If anybody stopped him, he
would say that he was a Reichsbahn employee and thus entitled to cross the tracks. Fortunately he met no one. He
paused near the end of the platform to look around, but
nobody was watching him. He then hopped down onto the
level of the rails and walked toward the lightless yards.

Under the shelter of darkness, he turned right and began
stepping carefully over the parallel tracks until he found him-

self abreast of, or more exactly, one hundred yards behind the tail coach of the Moscow–Paris train. Its orange taillights were on, and it was silhouetted between the illuminated platforms to the right and left. But the last car had come to a stop just beyond the station platform, where it was relatively dark.

Advancing briskly, Goltz reached the end of the coach and ducked down between the wheels. He then heaved himself over the axles and onto the transversal crossbars linking the wheel brakes. Careful though his planning had been, he had not foreseen just how greasy and dirt-covered these connecting rods would be, and as he pulled and shoved himself forward with his hands and knees, he could feel the grime and the grease rubbing off on his dark suit.

He was now lying on his stomach, his hands holding the foremost brake rod. Uncomfortable though this horizontal position was, he was determined to hold on, come what might. From this position, slightly higher than the axles, he could see a few yards of illuminated platform, and he could hear the voices of approaching Vopos and the metallic clang of the railwayman's hammer as it struck against the wheels.

The Vopos' boots came so close that he could see them too. After a few tense minutes, there was a shudder and the train began to move. Goltz gripped the crossbar near his head and held on to it tightly. The iron rumbling of the wheels just below and to each side of him was painfully communicated to his ribs, thighs, and shins. Beneath him in the darkness he could vaguely distinguish the railbed sleepers over which they were passing.

A minute or so later another stretch of platform began to slide past. The Jannowitzbrücke station, no doubt. The train did not slow or stop, but continued at the same slow, rumbling pace through to the Alexanderplatz station. The train did not stop there either, nor at the Karl-Marx-Platz station, through which they rumbled shortly thereafter. Then, something like five minutes after they had started, the shoe-brakes clamped down on the wheels and they came to a gradual halt inside the Friedrichstrasse station.

Here, Goltz knew, he would have to endure a ten-minute wait. To his left he could see the illuminated platform and the boots of the Vopos standing guard. There was plenty of bustle and noise on the platform, and fortunately none of the Vopos thought of getting down on hands and knees to see if by any chance there was a stowaway hidden in the undercarriage.

After ten uncomfortable minutes they began moving once again. With deliberate slowness the train lumbered onto the railway bridge spanning the Humboldt basin. Once again Goltz caught sight of Vopo boots, worn by guards stationed on top of the bridge to catch any East Berliners who might be tempted to follow the tracks over and into the British sector. The train rolled on nonstop through the Lehrter Bahnhof; passed the extensive railway yards to the south, rumbled over the Spree River a second time and into the Bellevue station, then continued on through the Tiergarten station, without a halt. Goltz held on grimly. Although they were now in the British sector, this was no time to relax his grip and fall between the wheels.

A couple of minutes later the brakes were applied again with a loud, grating sound, and they slowed to a halt at the Zoo station. Pushing himself backward, Goltz eased himself to the ground and crept out from under the tail coach. All told, he had managed to retain his horizontal position for more than half an hour. He felt bruised and a bit cramped but otherwise not overly exhausted. Nor had his wits abandoned him at this crucial moment. Instead of walking forward, which might have alerted the train personnel inside, he walked back and away from the last car. His escape plan had worked exactly as he had hoped, and he wasn't going to give away the secret now, for if it could work for him, it could work for other East Berliners.

Several hundred yards farther on, he came upon some metal rungs leading down the railway embankment. A moment later he was in the street. It was 11:00 P.M. and he was in West Berlin.

At the nearest police station he was offered a cup of tea and a bar of soap with which to wash the dirt and grease from his hands and chin. The face that stared back at him from the washroom mirror was almost unrecognizable; it was that of a chimney sweep.

After spending the night at Marienfelde, where he was lent a jacket and a pair of clean trousers, he reported the next morning to his construction firm in Kreuzberg. He was received with open arms and exclamations of delighted surprise by foremen and fellow workers, who had just about given up hope of seeing him again. His employers even gave him an advance to help him get resettled in the West.

It was now August 24—St. Bartholomew's Day—a day he would long remember with mixed feelings. Over on the other side, beyond the barbed wire and the concrete slabs, his daughter, Beate, was celebrating her tenth birthday—without her Daddy.

16

On this same Thursday, two new incidents occurred at the Friedrichstrasse check point. After an East German water truck had doused a group of West Berliners who had come too close to the triple-tiered slalom-gate barrier, a U.S. tank rumbled up with its muzzle pointed directly at the offending vehicle. Later, three U.S. Army buses on a sightseeing tour were held up for an hour at the check point when the unarmed GIs inside refused to show their identity cards to the Vopos. A military sedan was refused admission on the same grounds. The Vopos were informed that in accordance with existing regulations, Allied personnel could be required to show their personal documents only to Soviet officers. The buses, after turning around, came back to the check point a few minutes later, and this time there was no fuss; they were allowed through immediately.

The East Germans were again testing the reaction of the Allies—and with good reason. The latest restrictions and the Western response to them had aroused mixed feelings in the capitals of the West. While many of those serving on the Allied staffs in West Berlin felt that the decrees of August 23 were deliberately designed to humiliate the Allies and to depress the shaken morale of the West Berliners even further, nobody in the

White House—with the single exception of Gen. Maxwell Taylor—favored forceful countermeasures to maintain the occupying powers' right to enter the Soviet sector through check points other than the Friedrichstrasse.

Whitehall, as usual, was for playing it cool. The August 24 issue of the London *Daily Mirror* described Berlin as "frightened and bewildered" by the sudden confrontation of military and police units along the intersector border. But the two adjectives could have been more aptly applied to the British public. Harold Macmillan predictably remained his usual phlegmatic self. Less than forty-eight hours later, he noted in his diary:

The Russian and East German pressure on Berlin is growing apace. East Berliners are literally "sealed off," and the crossing-places are few and well guarded. There is, actually, nothing illegal in the East Germans stopping the flow of refugees and putting themselves behind a still more rigid iron curtain. It is certainly not a very good advertisement for the benefits of Communism—but it is not (I believe) a breach of any of our agreements.

The prime minister, alas, was misinformed. He had not done his homework. He had never bothered to acquaint himself with the tortuous diplomatic history of postwar Berlin, and he had only the haziest idea of exactly what had been agreed to between the Soviet Union and the Western powers in the troubled 1945–49 period. He had preferred to leave "all this detailed stuff" to his close friend, Alec Home; and although Home knew the score, he had somehow failed to get the essential points across to his prime minister.

With a certain amount of reason, Harold Macmillan was persuaded that it was fatal for a political leader to "get too bogged down in detail." But there are problems that cannot simply be ignored or delegated to others, and Berlin was one of them. In the field of foreign affairs Macmillan's energies were concentrated on two principal and closely linked objectives. The first was his desire to have Great Britain join the European Common Market. The second was his desire to strengthen NATO by humoring De Gaulle into cooperating more closely with London and Washington. He was persuaded that because he had worked for months with DeGaulle in Algiers, in the 1943–44 period—he was the person who could do it. John Kennedy, for all his talent, was too young to be able to impress or influence the haughty, stiff-necked general. This task was cut out for an old-timer like himself. Whatever interfered with this primary concern—and Berlin did precisely that—was for Harold Macmillan an irksome distraction.

Such too, but for entirely different reasons, was the sentiment of Charles de Gaulle. Of the three Allied powers, France for some time had enjoyed the reputation of being the most adamant in resisting Soviet pressure on Berlin. It had even created a lot of bad feelings in both Washington and London. Whenever it was a question of being "moderate" or of offering the Soviets "reasonable concessions," the president of the French republic and his foreign minister seemed positively mulelike.

Logically, Paris's response to Ulbricht's latest provocations should have been firm, but it was precisely the reverse. The response, once again, was purely verbal. For having dared move his armored cars and soldiers forward to the intersector border without obtaining prior permission from the Quai d'Orsay, General Lacomme was taken stiffly to task. He had overstepped the bounds and exceeded his authority, and he was given to understand in no uncertain terms that this sort of thing was not to happen again.

For the unfortunate French general this was one more bitter pill to swallow. His was the smallest occupying force, even though the total length of intersector and sector-Zone border that his men had to patrol was as great as that of the British. The Americans had chosen to reinforce their garrison. The British had sent up a number of armored cars. But what had his own government done? Beyond words and statements, absolutely nothing. Not one soldier, still less a tank, had been sent up to reinforce the French garrison in West Berlin. The Americans had felt sufficiently concerned by the crisis to send over their vice-president, accompanied by General Clay. Paris had sent nobody. De Gaulle, who could have made himself the most popular foreign statesman in Germany overnight by flying to Berlin, had preferred to stay quietly at home.

The truth, which Gen. Jean Lacomme could only partially

appreciate from his particular vantage point, was that Berlin—
that city inhabited by "Prussians," as De Gaulle had remarked to
a surprised Lacomme and an even more startled Willy
Brandt—was, for De Gaulle, a mere *péripétie*, a regrettable
vicissitude that should not be allowed to interfere with the grand
designs of his diplomacy. He had never wished to confront the
Soviets head-on. The Russians had been the first to offer official
diplomatic recognition to his wartime government in London.
Also, no matter how trenchantly anti-Communist he might
sometimes sound in France, he needed a Franco-Russian alliance to offset the "hegemony of the Anglo-Saxons." An open
break with the Soviets would destroy the central pillar of his
policy. It would fatally cramp his diplomatic style, reducing him
on the European chessboard to the rank of a mere pawn. It
would force him willy-nilly to abandon all claims to a privileged
position, to a sacrosanct independence. In short, it would fatally
turn a proud and independent France into a passive and pliant
satellite of the United States.

The future of the European continent, Charles De Gaulle was
convinced, was essentially a continental matter. It could not be
entrusted to Great Britain or the United States, both of which
were insular and oceanic powers. The fate of Europe would
ultimately be decided by its three most important countries:
France, Germany, and Russia. André Malraux, the only person
in his entourage whose intellect the general genuinely respected, had also been saying it for years: Since France's peculiar genius was one of "synthesis," her national vocation should
consist in trying to reconcile those seemingly irreconcilable
antagonists—the communist and capitalist systems.

This reasoning, applied to the problem of Germany, was more
or less what De Gaulle had undertaken to expound to Khrushchev during their two days of conversation in Paris and at
Rambouillet in March of 1960. While agreeing with his guest
that never again should Germany be permitted to become a
menace to world peace—which is why she should under no
circumstances receive atomic arms—the president of the French
republic took issue with Khrushchev's methods, aimed at ex-
acerbating rather than tempering the present division of Germany.

You must admit with me that from the point of view of peace, nothing will have been accomplished as long as this great people [the Germans] would have to go on enduring an unbearable national situation. The solution we must find is not to pit two monolithic blocs against each other, but on the contrary to work towards détente, entente, and cooperation within the framework of our Continent. We will thus create among Europeans, from the Atlantic to the Urals, relations, ties, and an atmosphere which will first take the virulence out of the problems of Germany—and also of Berlin—which will subsequently lead the Federal Republic and your Republic of the East to move towards each other and to combine their efforts, and which will finally keep the Germanic whole—*l'ensemble germanique*—enclosed in a Europe of peace and progress where it can undertake a new career.

What, for a man capable of such Olympian dreams, could all this uproar and tumult in Berlin really mean? A *péripétie*, no more.

On Saturday, August 26, a flock of British reporters who had pursued Harold Macmillan all the way up to Perthshire, in northern Scotland, finally caught up with him on the golf links. At every tee, near every green, there was some impertinent whippersnapper ready to pop a question at him. What did the prime minister think of the latest developments in Berlin? Was he thinking of returning to London with Lord Home after the meeting they were due to have the next day? Did he consider the situation in Berlin dangerous, with all those guns being pointed at each other across the border? What did he think were the chances of a war breaking out?

By the time he and Lady Dorothy had reached the eighteenth green, Harold Macmillan was in a temper. How in heaven's name could he concentrate on his strokes while being pestered by this unmannerly mob? Resting his putter on his shoulder for a moment, the white-haired prime minister gave the assembled newshounds a piece of his mind. The Berlin crisis? "I think it has been got up by the press," he roundly declared, adding no less crossly, "Nobody is going to fight about it."

Speaking at Sheffield the next day, George Brown, the number two man in the British Labour party, remarked, "Either he is a sick man or, he is acting the goat." The London *Daily Mirror* followed up on Monday by asking: "Is Prime Minister Macmillan living in the same world as other people?"

It was a question that millions of Germans, on both sides of an increasingly hermetic border, had been asking themselves for several weeks.

PART FIVE
THE
CONFRONTATION

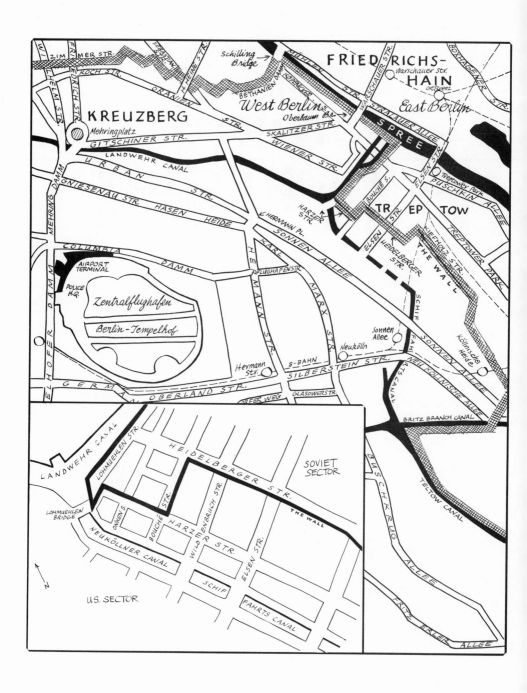

1

For East and West Berliners the month of August ended as tensely as it had begun. The good news, first released on Monday, the twenty-eighth, that Professor Walter Rudolph, director of the Institute of Dental Surgery at East Berlin's Charité Hospital, had managed to flee to the West, along with Dr. Gerhard Erdmann, a child specialist from the University of Rostock, was clouded the next day by a double tragedy in the Teltow Canal area. Two East Germans, attempting to escape, had failed to make it; the first was intercepted by Border Guards before he could get into the water, the second was shot while swimming and immediately sank.

Those who had fondly imagined that a policy of studied restraint would ease the pressure were once again in for a surprise. Not satisfied with walling in its own citizenry, the East German government had announced over the previous weekend that foreigners residing in East Berlin would have to get their governments to intervene on their behalf to enable them to leave the territory of the DDR. Their passports from now on would need a stamped exit visa—one more proof that the German Democratic Republic was fully sovereign in East Berlin and that the Western powers would have to recognize the fact.

Nor had the popular hue and cry for negotiations, particularly strong in Britain, done much to lessen the appetite of the Soviets. On the contrary, it seemed to have had the opposite effect. On August 23—when the twelve Berlin crossing points that were still open were reduced to seven—the Soviet Union delivered a harshly worded note to the three Western powers protesting the continued misuse of the air corridors to fly in "all kinds of revanchists, extremists, saboteurs, spies, and diversionists" from the Federal Republic. Six days later the Kremlin made known its decision to postpone the release from active duty of many reservists, and the next day, Moscow formally announced its intention of resuming the testing of nuclear weapons.

In the Crimea where he was still vacationing, Nikita Khrushchev told two visiting British members of Parliament that this kind of shock treatment was the only way to jolt the Western powers into negotiations on the German and universal-disarmament problems. "I have had enough," he bluntly declared. "I am going to do something about it. We are not going on with the present situation."

Kennedy, too, had decided to do something about it—even before receiving an urgent letter on the subject from Konrad Adenauer. The chancellor asked Kennedy to make no concessions to "further acts of force such as occurred in Berlin on August 13" and suggested that a fresh study be undertaken "of the nonmilitary counter-measures that might be taken when there is any threat, not as yet to access to Berlin or to the integrity of West Berlin, but to other important rights and interests of West Berlin." Adenauer made one more plea for economic sanctions against the entire Eastern bloc—a plea which Ambassador Wilhelm Grewe was going to back up with oral arguments, since he fully approved of the chancellor's thinking on the subject.

Adenauer's letter was delivered to Kennedy on August 30 by Wilhelm Grewe, who came to the White House with Foy Kohler. The half-hour talk that followed was probably not decisive; for Kennedy, under the insistent prodding of Edward Murrow and Marguerite Higgins, had already decided that action was needed to shore up the shaky morale of the West Berliners. At the 4:00 P.M. press conference held that same afternoon in the State Department's auditorium, the president announced that he was appointing Gen. Lucius Clay to be his personal representative in Berlin, with the rank of ambassador, because, as he went on to explain, "the situation in Berlin is a serious one, and I wish to have the advantage of having on the scene a person of General Clay's outstanding capacity and experience."

The announcement could not have come at a more timely moment. On this same Wednesday, a serious new incident had occurred in East Berlin as a direct result of the Ulbricht regime's insistence that its undisputed authority be recognized in the eastern part of the city. An army officer and three

sergeants traveling in a U.S. Army sedan were on a routine
tour of the Soviet sector when they were overtaken and waved
down by a mounted Volkspolizei policeman. While Allied vehicles traveling in East Berlin had to respect the normal traffic
rules and signals, they could not, according to the strict letter
of the Four-Power agreements, be halted for other reasons
except by the Soviet Military Police. The U.S. officer accordingly instructed his driver to resume speed, after the sedan
had almost slowed to a stop. Angered to see his flag-down
disregarded, the Vopo motorcyclist smashed his gloved fist
through the front side window of the American sedan, which
was finally brought to a halt by two East German police cars
farther down the Friedrichstrasse, within easy sight of
Check-point Charlie.

A heated argument ensued between the U.S. officer—
Captain Wirth—and the Volkspolizei officials. The captain,
sticking to his rights as a member of the U.S. Occupation
Forces, insisted on talking to a Soviet officer, and the Volkspolizei officers insisted on examining his papers.

The deadlock was finally broken when a U.S. Army tank and
five armored troop carriers moved up the Friedrichstrasse on
the U.S. side to within a few yards of the first East German
barrier. At that moment, as though by magic, a Russian major
appeared. Captain Wirth complained to him about the rude
behavior of the Vopos. The Russian officer shrugged his
shoulders, saying, "You had better protest to the Americans."
But he ordered the Vopos to let the U.S. Army car move on.

The incident, although trifling, had obviously been contrived to test the willingness of the Western Allies to defend
their residual rights in East Berlin as members of the four
occupying powers. It was to be the first of a series that were
soon to bring the simmering crisis to a boil.

It was a good two weeks before General Clay could cross the
Atlantic. In the interim another incident made it clear how
vital it was that the person in charge of operations in Berlin
have a sharp sense of what was politically, as well as militarily,
opportune.

During the first week of September, Jack Paar, the host of

NBC's "The Tonight Show," flew into Berlin with his blond assistant, Peggy Cass. To give their American television viewers a vivid idea of what it meant to be cooped up behind police- and dog-patrolled stretches of barbed wire and slowly rising walls of concrete, they went down to the Wannsee Golf Club, near the southwestern limits of the U.S. sector, and managed (after a first, unsuccessful shot) to hook a golf ball off the fairway and into the Soviet zone so that East German Grepos could be filmed refusing to toss back the "lost" ball.

The talk show host then persuaded the Information Officer of the U.S. Berlin Command, Lt. Col. Dallas Hoadley, to lend him a few GIs and officers for a close-up of the intersector border. While four television cameras ground away, a number of officers and infantrymen from the Second Battle Group moved up the Friedrichstrasse toward Check-point Charlie. Machine guns and a new 106-mm recoilless rifle were mounted along the "front" in battle-ready positions. Reliving his World War II days as a buck sergeant, Paar, microphone in hand, walked around interviewing the supposedly dug-in GIs.

Beyond the East German traffic barrier, Vopo officers and sergeants watched the goings on through field glasses. Recovering from their stupefaction, they alerted their own photographers and television men, who trotted up to the check point shortly afterward with their camera equipment.

The episode touched off an uproar on both sides of the Atlantic. Berliners who had waited vainly to see armed GIs move up to the intersector border on August 13, were disgusted by the phoniness of this belated "spectacular." For once West Germany's *Bild-Zeitung* and East Germany's *Neues Deutschland* were in agreement. "Disappear, Mr. Paar, we don't want to see you around any longer!" the *B-Z* tabloid demanded, declaring that the grotesque farce had sullied the reputation of the American, British, and French troops stationed in Berlin "to protect the freedom of our city." "What would have happened," asked *Neues Deutschland*, "if one of them [the GIs] in the heat of their wargame antics had absentmindedly pressed the trigger?"

The reactions in Washington were almost as violent. Sen. Mike Mansfield declared himself shocked at the idea that a grim tragedy could "be made into some kind of game for the personal profit of personalities in the entertainment world." Hubert Humphrey told the Senate that this was all Khrushchev needed for his propaganda and that he was sure "to beat us over the head with it." Sen. Leverett Saltonstall commented, "I couldn't believe it when I saw it."

From the White House, which was equally upset by the incredible shenanigans, instructions were sent to the Pentagon to have disciplinary action taken against the U.S. Army officers who had shown such poor judgment in cooperating in a tasteless exhibition of military muscle. Lt. Col. Dallas Hoadley was momentarily relieved of his duties as the U.S. Berlin Command's Information Officer, while Lt. Col. John Deane, commanding the Second Battle Group, was treated to a severe dressing-down.

Ten days after this distressing episode, the voters of West Germany went to the polls to elect a new parliament. On September 18, when the ballots were finally in and counted, Konrad Adenauer's coalition had lost its absolute majority, dropping from 50.1 to 45.2 percent of the total vote. Willy Brandt's Social Democrats, although still a minority, had picked up two million votes, increasing their share of the national total from 31.8 to 36.3 percent—the highest they had ever reached since 1919.

No elaborate postmortems were needed to explain this significant shift of opinion. Konrad Adenauer had obviously disappointed his electorate by his partisan and unstatesmanlike reaction to the East German *coup de force* of August 13. Even within his own party there was a growing feeling that der Alte had outlived his time in office. It was weeks before the inhabitants of the Federal Republic were to know what new government would emerge and whether Adenauer would still be heading it.

The resultant political uncertainty did nothing to facilitate General Clay's task when he finally reached Berlin on September 19. But the welcome he received could not have been more heartening. From Tempelhof all the way to the U.S. headquarters in Dahlem the streets and avenues were lined with cheering Berliners hailing the man who had saved them in 1948–1949 and who, they hoped, was returning to save them a second time.

No one was more conscious of the delicacy and difficulty of his mission than General Clay. Although he had been given the title of ambassador and was the president's personal representative in Berlin, the instructions issued from Washington had specified that in diplomatic status he ranked below Ambassador Dowling in Bonn. Instead of occupying the U.S. ambassador's residence on the Spechtstrasse, the general and Mrs. Clay had to be lodged in a hastily refurnished guesthouse on the Wannsee.

The evening of their arrival, the general had himself and Mrs. Clay driven to the Friedrichstrasse check point. Getting out of the sedan, they crossed into the Soviet sector and took a long walk up the Friedrichstrasse. Nobody in East or West Berlin had been given advance notice of this visit, and the general wasn't even sure that the Vopo guards at the check point knew who he was. It was not his intention to create an incident on the day of his arrival, but he wanted to make it clear from the outset that he was not renouncing his right as a member of the occupying powers, to enter the Soviet sector any time he chose.

2

In the four weeks that had passed since Lyndon Johnson's lightning visit, the city-splitting wall had been pursuing its slow, relentless growth. Along the southeastern extremity of the U.S. sector, the wall was still no more than a triple-tiered barbed-wire fence cutting across fields and orchards; but on the eastern side, the fields had been plowed up and stripped of vegetation and the cherry, apple, and pear trees reduced to reddish-brown and yellow-white stumps. A clear field of fire was thus afforded the pairs of Vopos posted at regular intervals, and the hawklike helicopter cruising overhead had a less obstructed field of view.

Along the eastern bank of the Teltow Canal, a low, ground-hugging wall extended as far as the eye could see, with iron stakes and coils of already-rusting wire bristling from its back. Behind it, invariably in pairs, East German guards covered the still waters with their submachine guns and binoculars.

At the Sonnenallee check point, near which Ursula Heinemann had managed to slip across four weeks before, concrete blocks protruded from both sides of the avenue, like intermeshing teeth, to form a closely guarded slalom through which the nonexistent traffic had to pass. A funeral wreath had been propped against a curb on the western side and allowed to remain there by the Schupos. "A last greeting from Klaus, Irmgard and Heinz," read the pathetic inscription on the white memorial ribbon.

The sparsely populated Kiefhollzstrasse, was obstructed by a four-foot wall isolating it from the warehouses and garden plots on its western side. During the last days of August, Emil Goltz could still occasionally come close enough to exchange a few words with his wife, Anna, who would stop here on walks with their daughter, Beate; but these hurried and often interrupted chats had not altered her hostility to the idea of trying to escape to the West. Now he could not even get within speaking distance on those rare occasions when he caught a glimpse of his wife and daughter beyond the police cordons of the Elsenstrasse.

The Heidelberger Strasse, which Schupo Paul Erdmann and patrons of the *Heidelberger Krug* could cross at will five weeks earlier, was now obstructed by two barbed-wire fences. The westernmost, following the curb, left only the sidewalk for people on the U.S.-sector side to come and go. In the middle of the street, East German guards were stationed at twenty-yard intervals ready to open up with their submachine guns on anybody, including one of their own who might make a dash for freedom.

In a children's playground near the intersection of the Heidelberger Strasse and the Bouchéstrasse, groups of West Berliners now gathered daily to wave to friends or relatives massed 150 yards away behind cordons of police and soldiers with fixed bayonets. Some of the West Berliners even turned up with opera glasses in an effort to decipher the distant pantomime of those who were condemned to live, in the most literal sense, beyond the pale.

One block farther on, where police sergeant Joachim Arzleben still walked the beat at night, ornately designed doorbells glistened next to doors that had been condemned on the eastern side of the Harzer Strasse. Bricks could be seen behind their panes of glass. The windows, too, had been walled up from inside. Some of them looked like eyeless sockets in an Edvard Munch painting, for their panes had been tarpapered to hide the bricks behind. In side gardens and cabbage patches trees had been sawed down and ungainly plank fences put up along the demarcation line.

Once a through street leading to the Landwehr Canal, the Harzer Strasse was now a cul-de-sac sealed by a gray wall. Behind it, Grepos armed with fire hoses were ready to squirt water at anyone approaching too close. To reach the canal, pedestrians had to duck into the last house on the left and come out through the back and onto the quay, where mothers still pushed their prams in the warm September sun. On the other side of the water, soldiers and an occasional jeep patrolled the eastern bank behind a fencework of barbed wire. High up on a fifth-floor iron balcony, Vopos armed with field glasses surveyed the waterway and its approaches, occasionally pausing to take another swig from the beer bottles at their feet.

The elevated railway bridge spanning the canal was now doubly guarded—to the left by a solitary Schupo, to the right by a team of Vopos, dark-uniformed transport policemen, and Free German Youth members sporting a yellow and blue FDJ flag. Farther east, in the direction of the Spree, a concrete wall blocked the Schlesische Strasse, which Emil Goltz and other inhabitants of Treptow had so often used to visit the Kreuzberg district. Above the grim python blocks, now throttling this artery, two signboards loomed. One, featuring the black silhouette of a man with a Tommy gun, advertised a murder film. The other exhibited the usual exhortations: Peace and the Unity of the Nation with the Peace Treaty! Forward with Socialism Toward Happiness for the People! Vote for Candidates of the National Front!

The Oberbaumbrücke, no longer used by the U-Bahn to cross the Spree, was blocked by a traffic check point at the western end, and there was a fenced-off walk for pedestrians along the bridge's stone foundations. The cranes along the eastern bank were still visible, but for the inhabitants of Kreuzberg, the Spree itself had disappeared, the gaps between warehouses having been walled up with reddish gray slabs of pressed brick rubble.

There was another dead end where the Köpenicker Strasse ran smack into the concrete barring the Bethaniendamm, close to the Costa Rica bar, dear to truck driver Kurt Sedlacek and his hard-drinking pals. Those, like the Sedlaceks and the Protestant pastor Heinz Paul, who lived on the southwestern rim of the crescent, could still reach the front entrances of their apartment houses by walking up the curving sidewalk corridor between the house fronts and a neck-high wall, which was topped by five ugly strands of thorny wire. On the other side, Grepos and Vopos paced up and down along the bulldozed central strip, where trees, bushes, and lovers' benches had been uprooted and removed on August 13. One week later the Catholic sacristan Hans Klar could still cross over to offer Sunday-morning mass to his parishioners of the Saint Michael Community Church, but that was the last time. Now he was completely cut off from the yellow brick church, whose verdigris-covered archangel he could contemplate from the windows of his apartment on the Leuschnerdamm.

At the southeastern end of the Sebastianstrasse a sign had been put up to warn West Berliners that "the sidewalk you are using belongs to the territory of the DDR and the state boundary follows the line of the houses. We expect you in your own interest to avoid any provocation while on this territory; otherwise we will undertake the necessary security measures." The fencework suddenly stopped at the Heinrich-Heine-Strasse intersection, where West Germans were allowed to enter the Soviet sector through a concrete car trap. But beyond it, where Klara Michaelis lived in the sole surviving house on the western side, the obstructions resumed their march up the rest of the Sebastianstrasse, which was now cut by two parallel barbed-wire fences and a low concrete wall. The effect at night was particularly eerie, as Klara and her neighbors found themselves walking with their feet in shadowy darkness while their eyes were blinded by the harsh arc lights on the other side of the street.

The nearby Zimmerstrasse had fared no better, cut down the middle by a five-foot parapet bristling with barbed wire. No respecter of names or persons, it cut brutally across the north –south Markgrafenstrasse, Charlottenstrasse, and Wilhelmstrasse, sparing only the Friedrichstrasse, which was now blocked by an elaborate police trap for zigzagging cars.

The Kreuzberg *Kinderfest* of August 12 was no more than a bittersweet memory. For lack of clients from East Berlin, the City Kino movie theater, where Heinz Schenck had worked as a projection assistant, had been forced to close down, and the stationery shop next door was rapidly going out of business. The tobacconist Hans-Horst Brandt had been less hard hit, although his shop was no longer visited by Party members from the House of Ministries. The jovial sexagenarian Otto Müller had lost half his cheap-watch and gold-chain clientele, but he was trying to make up for the loss by selling souvenirs and trinkets to new tourists from the West, lured to the Friedrichstrasse by the serpentine invasion of concrete and barbed wire.

Equally hard hit was the luckless Hans Dornberg, already on the verge of bankruptcy. The August 13 seal-off had eliminated almost all his shoe-buying clients and separated him from his pregnant mistress. Several weeks later she had given birth to a child, and since then, with an empty cash register, he was digging into his savings to send parcels of baby food and other products over to his sweetheart in East Berlin.

Much the same fate had overtaken the makeshift stalls near the Stresemannstrasse and Niederkirchnerstrasse intersection, where police sergeant Anton Schmidt had once kicked a soccer ball back and forth across the boundary with playful Vopos. At the Potsdamer Platz only one such booth was still in business— one specializing in the sale of underwear. Beneath the gaily striped canopy, bright blue, rose, and yellow petticoats and panties still undulated in the autumn breeze, but not a customer was to be seen.

The Aladin and the Camera movie theaters on the nearby Potsdamer Strasse had closed down forever on August 13. Their owner, Friedrich-Wilhelm Foss, had been vacationing on Sylt

Island in the Baltic when he received an urgent telephone call from his secretary in Berlin. No one, she told him, had turned up for the ten o'clock Sunday-morning showing. Foss, who had already lost two movie houses in East Berlin, understood immediately. Without waiting to hear more, he suspended further operations. After the final Saturday-night showing, one of his box-office girls had returned to her home in East Berlin. He had not seen her since.

3

General Clay's first major action, undertaken just two days after his arrival, was enough to reveal the almost impossible conditions under which he was working. During a tour of the U.S.-sector border, he was informed that the three hundred inhabitants of Steinstücken, a small suburban community which officially belonged to the Zehlendorf borough and was thus a part of the U.S.-occupied sector, had been completely cut off from the rest of West Berlin since August 13. Prior to that date, its inhabitants could travel back and forth to West Berlin by using the S-Bahn Ufastadt station or by driving over a country road through the Potsdam Woods. But since August 13 the little community had been subjected to ceaseless harassment. East German Grepos had been wiring in the farmers' fields, little children had been roughly treated, and a *Schlagbaum* barrier had been placed across the country road linking the isolated village to West Berlin. Nonresidents could no longer drive out to the village, on the grounds that the country road crossed the territory of the DDR, which was off limits to all West Berliners.

Clay decided that something had to be done fast to save this all-but-abandoned community. The best way of doing this, he concluded, was to get into his official U.S. Army car and have himself driven to Steinstücken over the Potsdam Woods road. The matter, which he discussed with General Watson and Allan Lightner, was to have been kept secret. But somehow somebody in Zehlendorf Town Hall—it might have been the mayor himself—got wind of the project. When Clay turned up the next morning at the check point leading into the Soviet zone, he found a flock of West Berlin newspapermen and photographers ready to chronicle the event. The East Germans, thus generously forewarned, were now virtually certain to prevent the general from proceeding along the country road to Steinstücken.

Deciding that this was a test he could not afford to fail if he were to maintain his personal prestige, Clay had himself driven back to U.S. headquarters, and shortly thereafter he was airborne in a U.S. Army helicopter. The helicopter put down on a grass field that was part of the isolated enclave. Recovering from the shock caused by this noisy apparition, a middle-aged lady who had been weeding her small garden nearby hurried over to embrace the general, whose aquiline profile she had immediately recognized.

Soon an excited crowd had gathered to shake the general's hand and escort him to Steinstücken's one and only *Gaststube* for a meeting with the mayor. Tipped off to what was happening, the restaurant's owner, a red-cheeked fellow with the robust name of Johannes Steinweg, came bicycling in from the fields as fast as he could pedal. Several bottles of choice wine were uncorked for the illustrious visitor, who told them, speaking via the interpreter he had brought with him, that he was leaving shortly for a meeting with governing Mayor Willy Brandt in the Schöneberg Rathaus. He was going to inform the governing mayor of this visit, and he wanted them to know that if they had any problems, they should feel free to address themselves directly to the U.S. occupation authorities. Although the East German Border Guards were fencing its people in and generally creating difficulties, Steinstücken was still part of the U.S. sector and thus under American protection.

The following day, a Friday, another helicopter flight was made, this time with a detachment of American MPs, three of whom were billeted in the village. These flights, Clay announced, would continue as long as necessary until the East Germans stopped harassing the inhabitants of Steinstücken. The West Berliners were as delighted as the villagers, while *Neues Deutschland* and other East German papers fulminated against these new "provocations."

Five days later, again acting with Clay's specific authorization, a U.S. Army helicopter flew out seven East Germans who had taken refuge in the enclave. There were new howls of rage in the East German press, as well as threats that the U.S. Army helicopters were going to be fired upon. The flights continued, nonetheless, and just as Clay had anticipated, the Grepos (now officially incorporated into the Nationale Volksarmee) did not open up with their automatic weapons.

This demonstration of firmness, although heartening to the demoralized inhabitants of West Berlin, was not much appreciated by Gen. Bruce Clarke, commanding the U.S. Seventh Army in Heidelberg. Although he had studied under Clay at West Point and even served with him for a while on a civil works' project with the Corps of Engineers, Clarke had mixed feelings about a military colleague who had won his stars doing everything except actually commanding troops on the field of battle. He had been annoyed by the casual way in which Washington had chosen to inform him of Clay's appointment to Berlin (through a copy of the telegram that Dean Rusk had sent to Walter Dowling in Bonn) when he was assigned the duty of providing Clay with the necessary means of transport, office space, clerical help, and quarters. Now, to make matters worse, he was receiving reports from Berlin to the effect that Clay was planning to open direct communications with the isolated Steinstücken enclave by "punching a hole" into the Soviet zone with two U.S. infantry companies, which were already undergoing combat training for this operation in the Grünewald Forest.

The report must have come from some officer on General Watson's staff who wished Clay no good, for there was not a word of truth in it—as Clarke was able to ascertain on September 24, when he flew to Berlin on an official visit. The visit did little, however, to calm the crusty tankman's simmering discontent. Clay's presence in Berlin was a disturbing factor, because it cut across the normal rules of military chain of command. The only troops he could use for his local morale-building measures were those belonging to the U.S. Berlin Command, which was directly subordinated to the headquarters of the U.S. Army in Europe, at Heidelberg, and more distantly to NATO's Supreme Allied headquarters near Paris.

Clarke, being a military man and nothing else, viewed the Berlin problem in a purely military light. Basically, to his mind, the Allied position in Berlin was militarily indefensible, which was why there should be no room for adventurism of any kind. Clay, on the other hand, was a political general who viewed the problem in broader terms of prestige and on-the-spot determination. The barbed wire and the slowly growing wall had not been put up by the Russians; they were being systematically unrolled and developed by military units of Ulbricht's East German republic in flagrant defiance of Berlin's Four-Power agreements, which had specifically banned the presence of both East and West German soldiers from Germany's erstwhile capital. This was not something Uncle Sam could meekly accept without a catastrophic loss of face.

Just what could be done about it at this late date was a major problem. But it was not, in the nature of things, a problem that Clay could first talk over quietly with Bruce Clarke in Heidelberg. There simply wasn't time for this kind of communication, even if a minimum of good will and understanding had existed at the Heidelberg end.

Nor was there anything to be gained by going over Clarke's head to NATO's supreme commander, Gen. Lauris Norstad, who had his headquarters at Roquencourt, near Paris. Although West Berlin was covered by NATO's broad "umbrella," the supreme Allied commander could not initiate any action without consulting the permanent NATO Council, composed of fifteen members, most of whom were solidly committed to the British line of doing nothing that might rock the boat. Clay's ultimate authority, and the only one that he could really accept as his personal representative, was President Kennedy, whom he could call at any time by using the red telephone on his office desk.

The day after Clarke's visit to Berlin, Kennedy traveled to New York to deliver a major address before the UN General Assembly. The speech, a formal statement of U.S. foreign policy, dealt in part with the Berlin crisis. "The elementary fact about this crisis is that it is unnecessary," the U.S. president declared.

The elementary tools for a peaceful settlement are to be found in the Charter. Under its law, agreements are to be kept, unless changed by those who made them. Established rights are to be respected. The political disposition of peoples should rest upon their own wishes, freely expressed in plebiscites and free elections. If there are legal problems, they can be solved by legal means. . . . We are committed to no rigid formula. We seek no perfect solution. We recognize that troops and tanks can, for a time, keep a nation divided against its will, however unwise that policy may seem to us. But we believe a peaceful agreement is possible which protects the freedom of West Berlin and Allied presence and rights, while recognizing the historic and legitimate interests of others in assuring European security.

The superficial toughness of the speech could no longer deceive Kennedy's one-time admirers in Germany. What had been specific in his televised speech of July 25—a demand for a plebiscite on the presence of Allied troops in West Berlin—was now presented in general terms. There was not a word about the reunification of Germany. There was not a word about the Berlin Wall, not a hint that certain fundamental Four-Power guarantees had been violated by its construction. Finally, there was an almost word-for-word repetition of the formula Kennedy had used on July 25 in undertaking to recognize "the historic and legitimate interests of others in assuring European security."

The West German newspaper magnate Axel Springer, who had been impressed by Kennedy's July 25 speech, could no longer conceal his dismay. Just what, demanded the *Bild-Zeitung*, was meant by "the historic and legitimate interests of others?" Did these interests include the right to split Germany forever? Officials in Bonn's Foreign Ministry were equally upset by the deliberate downgrading of points and principles they regarded as vital. As Heinrich von Brentano put it to a Christian Democratic caucus, the Federal Republic was going to have to "brace itself with all its strength against tendencies to reach a Berlin settlement at West Germany's expense."

In East Berlin the president's speech was hailed as a new milestone along the rocky road to peaceful coexistence. Herman Axen's *Neues Deutschland*, which had finally come out strongly against Kennedy's July 25 address, hailed this one as "remarkable because it shows an American willingness to negotiate."

In Moscow the conciliatory tone of the speech was interpreted as a sign of weakness to be exploited. Shortly after his arrival, Clay had announced that the United States was going to patrol the Helmstedt–Berlin autobahn with MP jeeps—a practice that had been abandoned six years earlier under Soviet pressure. The East German press had fulminated against this new "provocation," but the Russians had kept quiet. Now, emboldened by Kennedy's speech and by press reports of Clay's difficulties with Clarke, they decided to act. A stiff note, signed by Marshal Koniev, was delivered to U.S. headquarters in Dahlem demanding the immediate cessation of the "illegal" autobahn patrols. Were this warning to be disregarded, the direst consequences could follow.

Washington's response was a hasty capitulation. Clay received instructions to halt the autobahn patrols forthwith. What he had achieved through his symbolic Steinstücken action was destroyed at one stroke. He was back to square 1. The panicky exodus of West Berliners, now abandoning the city at the rate of seventeen hundred a week, was likely to get worse. Even those who were determined to stay on were now persuaded that Ulbricht and the Russians were winning the battle of Berlin and that it was merely a question of time before the western sectors were taken over by the Communists.

4

At the Plaza Hotel, near the Kurfürstendamm, seventeen-year-old Ursula Heinemann still had not recovered from the shock of being separated from her mother. Although she was certain that she had done the right thing in escaping to the West, she was nagged by a sense of guilt. At night she had troubled dreams in which she relived the same obsessive experience. Helplessly she was trying to clamber up a steep slope, at the top of which helmeted men with guns were waiting with rifle

butts to push her back into the ditch below. While she lay
panting on the ground, she could feel the bullets of their
strangely silent submachine guns ripping the wool on the back of
her sweater.

On the Boyenstrasse, separating the French from the Soviet
sector, not far from the cemetery where Hegel, Fichte, and
Bertolt Brecht lay buried, Charlotte Hansen had finally recovered from the nervous breakdown she had suffered in the
immediate wake of August 13. But she had difficulty reconciling
herself to the disaster that had overtaken their short street. A
five-foot wall had replaced the chicken-wire fence which the
Vopos had erected that fateful Sunday morning. Her twin sister,
Irma, was now trapped on the other side, and they could no
longer spend their weekends together.

Irma's husband, Otto, seemed to have taken the sudden
change in his usual submissive style. He had made no attempt to
escape with his wife, and now, when passing on the opposite
sidewalk, he never once raised his eyes to the Hansens' third-
floor windows to wave or smile a greeting. It was as though his
sister-in-law and her husband had ceased to exist.

During the first few days, it had been fairly easy to lob chocolate bars or even a whole carton of Ernte cigarettes over the wire
fence and onto the opposite sidewalk, where Irma could hurriedly retrieve them. But with the building of the wall, all signs
of leniency had vanished. Border Guards who had once begged
for Western cigarettes through the chicken-wire mesh now de-
monstratively stamped on any that might be thrown over and
ground them to shreds under their bootheels. Great care had to
be taken in lobbing over cigarettes or doubly wrapped bags of
coffee, lest Irma be caught red-handed picking up this contraband from the sidewalk. But there was nothing to keep the
twin sisters from standing well back from their windows so that
the guards below could not see them signaling to each other
every day from the middle of their respective rooms.

More fortunate than the Boyenstrasse, since it was not divided by a wall, the kilometer-long Bernauer Strasse looked
dismal nonetheless. The entrance to the red brick Reconciliation
Church had been cemented up and the feet of its buttresses now
protruded through the wall like the paws of a trapped animal.

Wir sind doch alle Brüder, ("We Are Brothers All the Same") read the sign on one of the buttresses, as though in anticipation of this martyrdom. Not far away, the ominous black letters *KZ,* for *Konzentrationslager* ("concentration camp"), were smeared over the gray expanse.

Although some houses on the eastern side of the Bernauer Strasse had been blinded right up to the roof level, in others there were still rows of unclogged windows on the second- and third-floor levels—peepholes for the Vopos to spy from. Throngs of West Berliners now gathered daily on the cobbled street below to watch the lugubrious spectacle of masons in white overalls slowly walling themselves in. One could tell from the speed with which they worked whether there were any guards behind them. When there were not, the trowels would come up at an extraordinarily slow pace to lay the thin coating of cement, after which a minute or two would pass before the next brick would make its slow-motion appearance, as though ponderously raised all the way from the basement.

Sometimes the kids watching from below would call up and encourage the bricklayers to jump to freedom while they could; at other times the onlookers would gape upward in awed silence. Eventually the mason's face would disappear behind the rising fence of bricks, and all that could be seen was a hand and a cement-smudged sleeve going through its gruesome motions. *"Sozialistischer Aufbau!"* ("Socialist construction!"), an old man would shout, waving his fist at the slowly closing aperture, before climbing onto his bicycle and pedaling sadly away.

Occasionally one of the windows would open, and almost immediately a sizable crowd would collect to watch what was going to happen. A young man and his girl friend had chosen this moment to sit on the window ledge and enjoy the afternoon sun. The couple kept talking quietly, only occasionally glancing at the people below who were watching in silent fascination for the telltale signal—the downward flutter of a piece of paper, the casual flick of a cigarette, the merest nod of the head—which would send someone running for a police van or fire truck with a sheet or ladder that could be used if they wished to jump or clamber down to freedom. But after a fifteen-to-twenty-minute wait, the two got up from the sill, and the young man closed the window with an enigmatic smile which was sad rather than un-friendly.

Like so many other East Berliners, they were resigned to their fate.

5

In early October the horizon darkened even more. Invited to receive the Freedom House Award for 1961, Willy Brandt flew to New York to deliver a speech in which, among other things, he said that "the Wall in Berlin must come down." During his short visit he had hoped to see Kennedy. But the U.S. pres-ident, whose schedule included an important meeting with Andrei Gromyko, could not find the time to receive the govern-ing mayor, although he did talk to him at some length on the telephone.

While Brandt was in New York, Clay's policy of firmness in Berlin received yet another setback. Alarmed by reports of shooting incidents along the intersector border, Washington issued instructions that the U.S. military units that had been brought up to the border on August 23 were to be pulled back. The slump in West Berlin morale now spread to the soldiers of the U.S. garrison, who, in asserting their armed presence near the border, had begun to feel that there was some purpose to their being stationed in Berlin.

Clay reacted as vigorously as possible, recommending that West Berlin's underarmed Schupos be issued submachine guns to put them on an equal footing with the Grepos and Vopos of the East. But this recommendation could not halt the downward drift in local morale, given new impetus by Walter Lippmann's tranquil affirmation, in his New York *Herald Tribune* "Today and Tomorrow" column, that West Berlin, thanks to the build-ing of Ulbricht's wall, was no longer a "show-window for the West" and destined to "wither on the vine."

Growing more cocky with each passing day, the East Germans

now decided to humiliate the Western Allies even further by forcing them to show their identity papers when entering the Soviet sector of Berlin—something the Allies had never had to do before. The wily Saxon was going to show the world who was truly sovereign in East Berlin.

On October 16 Ulbricht left for Moscow to attend the long-awaited Communist Party Congress of the Soviet Union. The next day, Khrushchev—who had decided to initiate a highly personal and secret correspondence with Kennedy through his son-in-law, Alexei Adjubei, and Mikhail Kharlamov, an official employed by the Soviet embassy in Washington—delivered an important speech during which, after uttering the usual boasts and threats, he made no mention of the December deadline he had earlier set for the signing of a German peace treaty.

Although Ulbricht could not openly challenge this significant omission, the speech he delivered three days later sounded as intransigent as ever. It was almost as though Khrushchev had said nothing on the subject. The rapid conclusion of a German peace treaty, Ulbricht declared, was a "task of the utmost urgency."

Exactly two days later, on the evening of Sunday, October 22, the head of the U.S. mission, Allan Lightner, and his wife left their Dahlem home to see a play in an East Berlin theater. At the Friedrichstrasse check point, their Volkswagen was stopped by Vopos who demanded to see their papers, even though vehicles with the license plates of the occupying powers had hitherto enjoyed the right to pass freely from one sector to another.

For the past week the Vopos had been resorting to spot checks, asking the occupants of certain Allied vehicles to show their papers while letting others through with a casual wave of the arm. The British had made no fuss and had immediately complied. But the Americans were under orders not to show their papers to any but Soviet officers or officials. Allan Lightner's own secretary had thus been held up a few days before, and finding herself unable to talk her way past the Vopo guards, she had turned her car around and driven home.

The chief of the State Department mission in Berlin accordingly refused to show his identification papers to the Vopos. He insisted on seeing a Soviet officer. But this being a quiet Sunday evening, there was no Russian officer present or, apparently, within hailing distance. The Vopos kept insisting on seeing Lightner's papers, and he no less stubbornly refused.

The argument had been going on in this deadlocked fashion for about forty-five minutes—enough time, Lightner figured, for them to have got a Russian officer over from Karlshorst—when he announced, "Look, I'm sorry, but I'm going to assert my Allied right for us to enter any sector of Berlin, and we're coming through. *Get out of the way!*"

He then gunned the engine, forcing the Vopos who were standing in front of the Volkswagen to jump aside. The police trap at the Friedrichstrasse intersection consisted of three protruding barriers—two jutting out from the right-hand sidewalk, the third from the left—through which vehicles could only "slalom" at low speeds. The angry Vopos thus had no trouble catching up with Lightner's Volkswagen before it could clear the final barrier. Now really worked up over this act of defiance, the Vopos told Lightner that he was not going any farther. "You are not entering. You can wait here until morning for a Russian officer to show up—if he shows up even then."

In the midst of this altercation, the U.S. provost marshal, Lt. Col. Robert Sabolyk, drove up in a military staff car. The Vopos automatically waved him through the first barrier. He wound his way to the second, placing his car directly ahead of the Lightners' Volkswagen. In the process he almost squeezed several of the booted Vopos in between the bumpers of the two cars, which made the East Germans angrier than ever.

News that the chief of the State Department mission to Berlin had been stopped at the Friedrichstrasse check point had meanwhile been transmitted by telephone to U.S. headquarters in Dahlem and from there to General Watson and General Clay, who immediately repaired to the headquarters' Emergency Operations Center. Both agreed that this Volkspolizei action was an intolerable challenge to the little that remained of U.S. occupation rights. The affront could not be swallowed in silence or ignored once again. It had to be met head on. An alert platoon from the Second Battle Group was accordingly dispatched to the scene in two armored troop carriers, closely followed by four M-48 tanks.

At the Friedrichstrasse check point, the U.S. provost marshal had been no more successful than Lightner in persuading the Vopos to relent. The argument was still raging when a U.S. MP lieutenant came up and suggested that Mrs. Lightner get out of the immobilized Volkswagen, since sitting there must be a hardship for her. But Lightner refused. So did his wife, Dorothy, a strong-willed New Englander. They were in this fix and they were going to see it through together.

The MP lieutenant soon returned from his control shack to say, "I'm sorry, but General Clay *orders* Mrs. Lightner to get out." He added, in a low voice, "We have a project in which we don't want Mrs. Lightner to be involved."

The wife of the U.S. chief of mission was accordingly escorted back to the MP control shed on the U.S. side of the border. Shortly thereafter, two infantry squads, each carrying four GIs armed with bayoneted rifles, took up their positions on the two sides of the Friedrichstrasse. Behind them, with their gun barrels pointed directly up the street, were the four medium tanks that the U.S. commandant and General Clay had ordered to the scene.

Before this unexpected show of force, the Vopos drew back in some confusion. Putting his car into low gear, Lightner drove forward, flanked by the two U.S. Army squads to the right and left. Having passed the last barrier, the platoon leader asked if they should stop there. "No," said Lightner firmly, "we'll go on up the street a ways." The Volkswagen continued up the street at the same slow pace until they had reached an intersection, at which point the U.S. mission chief turned his car around and started back. Everyone was aware of the gravity of the situation. This was virtually the first time in the postwar history of Berlin that a fully armed infantry unit from the U.S. occupying forces had marched into the Soviet sector.

Back on the American side of the border, Lightner turned his Volkswagen around once more. Albert Hemsing, the U.S. public information officer, who meanwhile had reached the scene, jumped in next to him. Maybe the Vopos, having been taught a lesson, would now let them drive into East Berlin without further trouble. But no, at the first barrier a Vopo officer stopped them, saying he was not at all amused by these military antics. Through his rolled-down window, Lightner signaled with his arm to the U.S. detachment behind him. The bayonet-wielding GIs moved up and again escorted the Volkswagen through the zigzag obstructions and up the Friedrichstrasse.

Howard Trivers, the U.S. mission's political adviser, meanwhile had telephoned to Karlshorst to say that a Russian officer should immediately be sent to the Friedrichstrasse check point. By the time Lightner's Volkswagen returned, still flanked by the U.S. infantrymen, Major Lazarev, the acting Soviet political adviser, had reached the scene and was conferring with the U.S. provost marshal inside the Volkspolizei shack.

Still accompanied by Albert Hemsing, Lightner, followed by another U.S. mission car carrying two American civilians, drove up to the first East German barrier. The Vopos, acting under Major Lazarev's orders, made no attempt to stop them. The two American vehicles drove all the way up the Friedrichstrasse to Unter den Linden, then turned and made for the Brandenburg Gate before deciding to head back toward the check point. Thus, by 11:00 P.M. on this Sunday night, the U.S. commandant, inspired and directed by General Clay, had made it clear to the East Germans that the Americans were not going to be deprived of one additional right as one of the occupying powers simply to suit Walter Ulbricht's whim.

The next day the government of the DDR published an official decree declaring that all foreigners—except Allied military officers in uniform—would henceforth be required to show their identification papers to Volkspolizei officials before being allowed to enter Democratic Berlin.

Describing the Sunday evening incident as a very serious "border provocation," an ADN news dispatch declared that an unknown civilian [Allan Lightner] had been stopped at the border in the company of an unknown woman, and had later been joined by a drunken civilian [Albert Hemsing]. This latter individual who had also refused to show his papers, was suspected of being, in reality, a colonel and the head of the U.S. Military Police! When the identities of the "unknown civilians" was finally established, an East German radio announcer, in an English-language broadcast beamed at U.S. soldiers stationed in Berlin, exulted, "And it will be a long time before Minister Lightner takes his girl friend out and tries to shack up with her in East Berlin over the weekend."

Kennedy's first reaction to news of the Lightner incident was one of annoyance. "We didn't send him to Berlin to go to the opera in East Berlin" was his comment, which revealed a lack of understanding of the fundamental issues and an ignorance of Allied prerogatives almost equal to Macmillan's. But this time, Clay's mind was made up. In a message couched in very strong language, the State Department and the White House were informed that the latest East German attempt to ridicule and humiliate the Western Allies had to be met head on if they were to retain anything of their fast-vanishing credibility as guarantors of West Berlin's threatened freedom.

On the morning of Wednesday, October 25, two U.S. officers in mufti were sent to the Friedrichstrasse check point in a U.S. Army sedan. The car was stopped by the Vopos and papers demanded. The U.S. provost marshal was immediately alerted. But this time he found himself confronted by a stranger who introduced himself as Lieutenant Colonel Alexeiev, newly appointed to the post of Soviet provost marshal and political adviser. General Clay's presence in Berlin and the forceful action of the previous Sunday had obviously jolted the Russians into the realization that a senior KGB officer was needed to handle the tricky situation at the border.

Howard Trivers of the U.S. mission reached the check point shortly thereafter and had himself and Irwin Firestone, the Berlin Command's Russian interpreter, driven over to the first East German barrier in a U.S. Army jeep. Alexeiev was accompanied by his own officer-interpreter and Major Lazarev. For half an hour the Americans and the Russians walked back and forth in the space between the U.S. and the East German barriers while crowds of onlookers collected on both sides of the Friedrichstrasse check point. Trivers undertook a detailed historical review of the various agreements reached, beginning with the first Military Governors' Agreement of 1945, which had authorized the members of the occupying powers to travel freely back and forth in properly licensed vehicles. The U.S. Command could not accept the new ruling of the East German government, since the only authority the

United States recognized in East Berlin was that of the Soviet commandant in Karlshorst. This was countered by the standard Russian reply that East Berlin was the capital of the German Democratic Republic, now a fully sovereign state empowered to take whatever measures it deemed fit on its territory. The Russian colonel did, however, agree to Trivers's suggestion that the Soviet and U.S. commandants meet that afternoon in Karlshorst to discuss the situation.

Clay, masterminding the show from the U.S. headquarters' Emergency Operations Center, had instructed General Watson to move ten M-48 tanks to the Friedrichstrasse check point. Trivers, telephoning through from the MP shed on the U.S. side, recommended that the U.S. sedan be sent through with the two army officers in mufti to test the Vopos' reaction. Again the sedan was held up at the first East German barrier.

Three U.S. MP jeeps, carrying men armed with bayoneted rifles, were brought up to form a convoy. One jeep placed itself ahead of the sedan while the other two took up positions behind. The convoy moved forward through the zigzag barriers and into the Soviet sector without opposition from the Vopos, drove up the Friedrichstrasse, then turned and headed back.

When Trivers returned from the U.S. MP shed, he found Major Lazarev, alone. Alexeiev had climbed into a car and had been driven into the U.S. sector to see how many tanks and other forces the Americans had brought up. Lazarev heatedly protested the impropriety of U.S. Army troops escorting a civilian vehicle through the East German check point, but Trivers reminded him that it was the Vopos, not the Americans, who had started the trouble.

At three that afternoon, General Watson drove over to Karlshorst for a meeting with Colonel Solovyov. The Russian commandant obviously lacked authority to overrule the East Germans and their recent decree, but he could and did resort to the usual subterfuge. He declared the use of a troop escort an "open provocation" that must be terminated forthwith, adding, "We, too, have tanks."

Duly informed of this fruitless encounter, General Clay refused to abandon the military escorts. He was pleased to learn that the Russians were beginning to get worried. This was exactly what he wanted.

6

On Wednesday afternoon, October 25, several other American civilian cars were escorted into East Berlin by MP jeeps and armed GIs. The Vopos now resorted to a dangerous ruse. As one of these civilian cars, with U.S.-occupation license plates, was being escorted back, preceded by an MP jeep and protected on each side by two GIs with rifles and fixed bayonets, it was suddenly rushed by an East German car which came roaring out of a side street. The accompanying foot soldier turned, his finger on the trigger, his bayoneted rifle pointed straight at the windshield of the oncoming car. The intimidated driver slammed on his brakes and brought the vehicle to a screeching halt yards short of the sedan, which he had obviously intended to ram.

The barely averted accident had been contrived to sustain the contention that the Americans were becoming a serious traffic hazard and therefore had to be subjected to new controls and regulations. The quick-wittedness of a GI had spared the U.S. Berlin Command a most embarrassing dilemma.

Yankee ingenuity was also needed to confound the East Germans during the nocturnal hours. Clearly nettled by the challenging proximity of U.S. tanks, the East Germans brought up powerful floodlights, which made it difficult for persons on the U.S. side to see what was going on in the Soviet sector. An American tank was accordingly equipped with a monster searchlight and sent up to Check-point Charlie. At a given signal, the crew turned on the juice. The one-hundred-thousand-candlepower beam sent one Vopo staggering back, virtually blinded, while his companions hastily turned their backs or retreated into their control shack. Shortly thereafter, they extinguished their floodlights, and the U.S. tank and searchlight crew withdrew.

But the lesson had to be repeated the following evening,

when once again the Vopos switched on their floodlights. This time the U.S. searchlight boys completely cleared the area beyond the East German barriers with their blinding beam. Having had their fill, the Vopos switched off their floodlights. They were never lit again.

Wednesday evening, as he was dropping off his secretary at her East Berlin apartment, Adam Kellett-Long was stopped by a Volksarmee soldier standing by a tree. His curiosity aroused— he never had seen a soldier posted there before—the Reuters correspondent returned half an hour later, just in time to see a column of Soviet tanks rumble by. The tankmen's uniforms were recognizably different from those of the Nationale Volksarmee. Going to his office, he filed a dispatch saying that Russian tanks had just entered East Berlin. When the news came off the ticker tape in London, Reuters' foreign editor refused to believe it.

The Russian tanks were no figment of a schnapps-fired imagination. The next morning they were spotted in the bombed-out ruins of the Kronprinzen Palace, just off Unter den Linden. To make sure that they were really Soviet and not East German tanks, a Russian-speaking American was sent to investigate. Stopping his jeep near one of the tanks, he asked the crew in German, "*Wie fährt man nach Karlshorst?*" ("How does one get to Karlshorst?"). All he got was a blank stare. He then repeated the question in Russian: "*Nou, skajitye, do Karlshorsta kak?*"

"*Do Karlshorsta?*" answered one of the crewmen, his face brightening. "*Nou, tyebye pokajou*" ("Well, I'll show you").

When the news was brought to Clay that thirty-three Soviet tanks had been identified, discreetly parked some distance away from the Friedrichstrasse check point in a bombed-out lot, he refused to be rattled. That afternoon the general told members of the Berlin press that "the United States is determined to continue showing force, if necessary, until this issue is resolved with the Soviet Union."

On Friday, October 27, after an American civilian car had again been escorted through the Friedrichstrasse check point by MPs and armed GIs, Marshal Koniev put in a call to the Kremlin. The Americans, he told Khrushchev, now had ten tanks lined up opposite the Friedrichstrasse check point. What was he to do? Khrushchev told him to match the Americans by bringing ten Soviet tanks up to the border. But they were not to start shooting. They must first wait to see what the Americans were going to do.

Ten Russian tanks were now ordered to move out of their bombed-out emplacement and down the Friedrichstrasse. Stopping thirty yards short of the triple-tiered zigzag barrier, five of them took up positions on the right side and four on the left side of Friedrichstrasse, while the tenth tank was parked in front of the U-Bahn entrance in the middle of the street.

The U.S. tanks, which had withdrawn to their usual positions after the escorted car had returned safely through the East German barrier, were immediately ordered back to Check-point Charlie.

It was now shortly after 6:00 P.M. General Clay lost no time calling a press conference at U.S. headquarters in Dahlem. "The fiction that it was the East Germans who were responsible for trying to prevent Allied access to East Berlin is now destroyed," he declared in a carefully worded statement. "The fact that Soviet tanks appeared on the scene proves that the harassments which were taking place on the Friedrichstrasse were not those of the self-styled East German government but ordered by its Soviet masters."

The confrontation, announced the next morning in glaring newspaper headlines, sent tremors through the chancelleries of the West. The British were frankly appalled. The fear, ever strong in Whitehall circles, that "those American generals are about to go off half-cocked" was now being dramatically confirmed. An emergency cabinet meeting was called at Number 10 Downing Street that evening to see what could be done to save the peace of the world.

At 2:15 the following morning, Howard Trivers and his wife were awakened by the insistent ringing of the telephone. It was Keith Matthews, the new British political adviser; he just wanted Howard to know that he was getting his clothes on and coming over right away to see him.

Half an hour later Matthews was at the door. "I had to come now," he explained to Trivers. "I have an *immediate* from the

Cabinet in London." The British government, he explained, was seriously concerned by the confrontation between Russian and American tanks. It wanted to know the reasons for this dangerous situation.

Trivers said there was no cause for alarm. There wasn't going to be any wild shooting. The U.S. officers and men stationed at the Friedrichstrasse check point had precise instructions and were very cool and disciplined fellows. General Clay's primary concern had been to force the Soviets to reassert their overall authority in the eastern sector, and this objective was now achieved.

In Washington, as in most NATO capitals, there was also much anguished hand wringing. But unlike others in the White House, Kennedy himself kept cool. To show how relaxed he was, he even put his feet up on the table as a call was put through to Berlin. It was close to 5:00 P.M. Washington time, almost 10:00 P.M. at the other end. An emergency meeting had just been called with Dean Rusk, Foy Kohler, Robert McNamara, General Lemnitzer, Paul Nitze, and Martin Hillenbrand, head of the State Department's German Affairs Section. The president wanted to find out how the situation looked to the people on the spot.

General Clay was down in the map room with General Watson when he was informed that the White House was on the wire. He first thought that McGeorge Bundy was calling. But it was the president himself who asked, "How are things up there?"

Clay told him things were fine. "We have ten tanks at Check-point Charlie. The Russians have ten tanks there, too. So now we're equal."

At that moment a note was handed to the general. "Mr. President," Clay went on, "I'll have to rectify that statement. The Russians have brought up twenty more tanks. This is proof of the accuracy of their information. That is the number of tanks we have in Berlin. So we'll bring up our remaining twenty tanks as well."

"Tell me," asked Kennedy, "are you nervous?"

"Nervous? No, we're not nervous here," answered Clay. "If anybody's nervous, Mr. President, it will probably be people in Washington" (a pointed reference to those in the White House and on Capitol Hill who he knew had not liked his appointment and were out to clip his hawkish wings).

"Well," said Kennedy, "there may well be a lot of nervous people around here, but I'm not one of them."

The next morning Marshal Koniev called the Kremlin for new instructions. He briefly described the situation, saying that it seemed grotesque to him. After a moment of silence, Khrushchev said, "All right. Pull back your tanks. The Americans can't pull theirs back for reasons of prestige. So it's up to us to begin. It's absurd to start a tank battle in narrow streets when they're only a few meters from each other."

At 10:30 A.M. the Soviet tanks began withdrawing from the Friedrichstrasse check point. Half an hour later the U.S. tanks were pulled back in their turn. The confrontation, which had lasted sixteen hours, was over.

Although it had seemed a scary business to people living hundreds or thousands of miles away, to observers on the spot this muzzle-to-muzzle confrontation had even had its comic moments. Adam Kellett-Long had been watching a gunner on the lead U.S. tank nervously fingering his machine gun when a U.S. helicopter suddenly loomed overhead. A frightened Volkspolizei captain ran hastily up to where the Reuters correspondent was standing. "*Sie schiessen! Sie schiessen! Weg! Weg!*" ("They're shooting! They're shooting! Get out of the way!") he cried, dragging Kellett-Long over to the side.

But not a shot was fired—even though some of the U.S. tankmen later amused themselves and the crowd of West Berliners who had gathered by swivelling their machine guns in simulated bursts of fire. Taking out their sandwiches, they sank their teeth into them with ostentatious relish while the Russians looked on a bit stupidly. Next to the small Russians, the dismounted U.S. tankmen looked like giants. Word spread that they were from Texas, where everything is outsized!

The next day, after attending Sunday mass at St. Stephen's Church, John Kennedy was flown in his presidential jet to Fort Smith, Arkansas, where he was to make an official address. There wasn't going to be a war—of that he was now sure; and he was more than ever persuaded that the Berlin crisis was over.

EPILOGUE

The Berlin crisis was not over. In a sense it had only just begun—as General Clay and his superiors in Washington were soon to discover.

Dramatic though it was, the tank confrontation at Checkpoint Charlie solved none of the basic problems. The U.S. Berlin Command made no further attempt to have American officials in civilian clothes escorted into the Soviet sector by armed GIs. The Ulbricht regime's right to oblige all foreign civilians to show their identity papers in order to gain admission to East Berlin was thus tacitly accepted.

By one of those ironies that so frequently mark the course of human affairs, the Friedrichstrasse confrontation, although tactically a victory, undermined rather than enhanced Clay's overall prestige. In Washington many in influential places felt that the hawkish general had exceeded his authority in acting on his own initiative without first consulting the White House. Whitehall condemned the whole business as "foolish posturing over an essentially minor issue." The British minister and deputy commandant in Berlin, Geoffrey McDermott, even hied himself over to Unter den Linden for an unofficial visit to the Soviet embassy, where, between rounds of vodka, the surprised but delighted Russians were informed that General Clay's days in West Berlin were numbered. Although Her Majesty's minister was several months off in his forecast, the incident did nothing to improve Clay's testy relations with the British commandant, who had come to the conclusion that "he must be stark raving mad."

If Clay had hoped through his bold action to stiffen Washington's shaky resolve, he was destined to be disappointed. In Moscow Nikita Khrushchev candidly admitted to Hans Kroll that he never would have allowed a tank-to-tank confrontation to escalate into a nuclear war. But in Washington there was a renewed clamor for negotiations as the only way to spare the world future clashes of this dangerous kind.

As he prepared for a series of exploratory talks with Andrei Gromyko, U.S. ambassador Llewellyn Thompson was instructed to assume a "flexible" position. There was to be no talk of tearing down the Berlin Wall or of asking for its removal. In three short months this "anti-Fascist bulwark" had come to be accepted by the West as a "fact of international life." It was no longer a negotiable or even mentionable issue.

What *was* negotiable was the continuing Allied presence in Berlin, or, more exactly, the Allied access routes. These were to be given rock-hard guarantees through the establishment of an International Access Authority composed of an equal number of representatives from the NATO and Warsaw Pact blocs, in addition to three neutral countries: Switzerland, Austria, and Sweden. And East Berlin, like Bonn, was to be a member of this authority. The intention may not have been explicit, but the drift was clear. It was one more way of legitimizing the illegitimate, of placing the East German regime on the same footing as the Federal Republic.

Although this hair-brained scheme finally ran aground on the obstructions put up by the French and West German governments, it helped to consolidate the Communists' conviction that Kennedy was basically a diplomatic softie who liked to talk big but who—as in the Bay of Pigs fiasco—developed cold feet when the going got tough. Such was the almost universal sentiment in official Moscow circles in January of 1962, when Kyril Tidmarsh, correspondent for the London *Times*, called on a deputy editor of *Pravda*. When the thorny issue of Berlin was broached, and with it the question of how the Americans would react if new pressure was brought to bear by the East against the West, he replied, "*Amerikantsy?* Do you really believe the Americans will do anything? Look at what they did the last time, when they started building the wall there in Berlin. They sent their vice-president over to West Berlin to distribute fountain pens, and they mobilized half a regiment in a show of force. Half a regiment! You'll see," he went on in the same vein, "the day we decide to cut those access routes, it will be done just like that." He snapped his fingers for emphasis. "There may be a whimper or two, but that will be the extent of the American reaction."

Not long after this conversation, the Kremlin decided to crank up the crisis once again by harassing French, British, and American airplanes flying the three Allied air corridors. Parts of the corridors were "requisitioned" for Soviet air exercises—at moments deliberately chosen to interfere with regular commercial-flight schedules—and commercial airliners were buzzed by Soviet fighters. In March, when the crisis reached its height, tin-foil chaff was scattered through the air lanes to interfere with radar communications. Although BEA, Air France, and Pan American continued to fly their planes in and out on schedule, General Clay was overruled in his recommendation that the airliners be provided with fighter escorts and that U.S. Air Force C-130 cargo planes be flown into Berlin above the meekly accepted ten-thousand-foot ceilings.

On April 12 Clay flew back to Washington to inform President Kennedy of his desire to return to the United States. The Soviets had suddenly terminated their campaign of aerial harassment, and the West Berliners had recovered sufficiently from the traumatic shock of August 13 to make the general feel that his presence was no longer absolutely vital to local morale.

The news of Clay's resignation could not have reached Moscow at a more opportune moment. Nikita Khrushchev was once again under heavy pressure from the Chinese and Albanians, as well as from Walter Ulbricht and his Kremlin supporters, to remove "this bone stuck in our throat" (West Berlin) once and for all. The issue was heatedly debated during meetings of the Presidium that lasted from April 22 to April 25. As a result of these debates, two Soviet marshals lost their jobs. A third Soviet marshal—none other than Ivan Koniev—had already been summoned back to Moscow to resume his previous functions at the Ministry of National Defense.

It was months before the Sovietologists in Washington were able to fathom the real motives for these various shifts and dismissals. Only later did they begin to understand why on April 28 Khrushchev had had a long talk with Osmani Cien-

fuegos, the Cuban Minister of Public Works, prior to another
meeting with the Cuban ambassador, held on May 5. Only
then did they realize that the "good way" of solving the Berlin
crisis—as the Chinese ambassador in Moscow was soon to put
it—involved nothing less than a transfer of the crisis from
Europe to the Caribbean.

The scheme called for a massive increase in military aid to
Cuba, culminating in the installation of nuclear launching
pads on Fidel Castro's island. The Americans—so Khrushchev
and his fellow gamblers reckoned—would be too absorbed by
the autumn election campaign to be able to react effectively
before the nuclear rockets were in place. At that point, the
first secretary of the Party and the chairman of the Council of
Ministers could cross the Atlantic and attend the UN session
with the game all but sewn up in advance.

The extraordinary horse deal that Khrushchev intended to
propose amounted to this: "How about an honest exchange?
We have put nuclear rockets into Cuba to protect a socialist
regime against the attacks of émigrés and other reactionary
elements who have been supported by right-wing circles in
the United States. You Americans have chosen to maintain a
permanent focus of tension and international provocation in
Central Europe by basing troops in West Berlin, sixteen years
after the official end of World War II, even though you are not
a European power. Now why, in the interest of world peace
and in the name of reciprocity, don't we both agree to respect
each others' spheres of influence? Why don't we agree to
withdraw our respective troops and weapons? If you will
withdraw your garrison from West Berlin and accept a demilitarized free city, as we have so often proposed in the past,
then we will remove our rockets from Cuba. But otherwise,
they'll stay."

Although General Clay had no advance knowledge of the proposed scheme that was brewing in the chambers of the Kremlin,
his instinct had told him that something of the sort could be
expected. If Uncle Sam didn't stand up to the Soviet challenge
in Berlin, the Russians sooner or later would move it one step
closer to the United States. America's failure to respond to the
first blockade challenge of 1948 by running an armored train

through to Berlin had later encouraged Stalin to launch the Korean War. In the same way America's mouselike reaction to the challenge of August 13 and the erection of Walter Ulbricht's wall was to lead to the Cuban missile crisis of October 1962.

Khrushchev let the cat out of the bag several weeks before the crisis finally broke in a characteristically frank conversation with visiting American poet Robert Frost. The Western democracies, he intimated, were too old, wobbly-kneed, and spent to be willing to risk a fight with an ardent, young, dynamic, and upcoming nation like the Soviet Union. The Western democracies reminded him of the melancholy avowal of impotence once made by Leo Tolstoy in his bearded old age to a young and robust Maxim Gorky: "I am too weak and infirm to do it anymore, but I still suffer from the desire."

GLOSSARY
OF GERMAN TERMS AND DEFINITIONS

ADN — Allgemeiner Deutscher Nachrichtendienst: General German News Service. East German equivalent of Reuters or AP.

Arbeiter-und-Bauern-Macht — Workers-and-Peasants-State. Used in East Germany to designate the country.

Betriebskampfgruppen — Factory militia.

BfV — Bundesamt für Verfassungsschutz: Federal Office for Protection of the Constitution. West German equivalent of the FBI, with headquarters in Cologne.

BND — Bundesnachrichtendienst: Federal News Service. Appellation of Gen. Reinhard Gehlen's intelligence service, with headquarters at Pullach, near Munich. West German equivalent of the CIA.

Bundeswehr — West German army.

CDU — Christlich Demokratische Union: Konrad Adenauer's Christian Democratic Union.

CSU — Christlich Sozialistische Union: Franz-Josef Strauss's Christian Socialist Union.

DFD — Demokratischer Frauenbund Deutschlands: Democratic Women's League of Germany. East German women's organization.

DDR — Deutsche Demokratische Republik: German Democratic Republic. Official name for East Germany.

DPA — Deutsche Presse Agentur. West German equivalent of Reuters or AP.

Deutschlandsender — One of East Berlin's two broadcasting stations in 1961 (the other being Radio Berlin).

Deutsches Fernsehen — East Germany's one and only television network in 1961.

FDGB — Freier Deutscher Gewerkschaftsbund: Free German Labor Federation. East Germany's state-controlled labor federation.

FDJ — Freie Deutsche Jugend: Free German Youth. East Germany's youth movement, membership starting at fourteen and extending into the twenties.

Frontstadt — East German term for the "front-line" city of Berlin. Used to emphasize its beleaguered and also "aggressive" position.

497

Grenzgänger	Border crosser. Used to designate a Berliner living in the Soviet sector and going to work in West Berlin; or, vice versa, a West Berliner whose place of work is in East Berlin.
Grepo	Contraction of *Grenzpolizist*. Member of the Grenzpolizei (East German Border Police).
GST	Gesellschaft für Sport und Technik: Association for Sport and Technics. East German paramilitary sport movement, with heavy emphasis on such activities as parade-ground drill, rifle practice, and parachute and commando training.
HO	Handelsorganisation: Trade organization. A coverall term used for all nationalized stores, shopping centers, wholesale and retail establishments, restaurants, and hotels in East Germany.
Junge Pioniere	Young Pioneers. The "Boy Scout" branch of the FDJ, with membership (as compulsory as possible) from ages of six to fourteen.
KVP	Kasernierte Volkspolizei: Garrisoned Police. The forerunner of the NVA, whose function fell between the regular police and the East German army.
LPG	Landesproduktionsgenossenschaft: Land-Production-Cooperative. East German barbarism for a collective farm.
Menschenhandel	Literally "man-trade." Often combined in East German propaganda with *Kopfjäger* ("headhunter") to designate the traffic in human beings (that is, refugees) in which the West German authorities were supposedly indulging at Marienfelde and other reception centers.
Neues Deutschland	*New Germany*. Official daily newspaper and mouthpiece for the SED (Communist) party in East Germany.
NKVD	*Narodny Kommissariat Vnutrennykh Dyel*: People's Commissariat for Internal Affairs. Successor of the CHEKA and forerunner of the KGB (Soviet secret police).
NVA	Nationale Volksarmee: National People's Army (East Germany).
PGH	Produktionsgenossenschaft des Handels: Trade Production Cooperative. East German term for the state-controlled guilds that virtually all hitherto independent artisans and shopkeepers were forced to join.
RIAS	Rundfunk im amerikanischen Sektor: Broadcasting station in the American sector. Radio sta-

	tion in West Berlin, financed by the United States and under State Department control.
SBZ	Contraction for *Sowjetische Besatzungszone*: Soviet zone of occupation. This term and "Zone" are frequently used to designate East Germany, as opposed to East Berlin, which was still in 1961 (and is still today) under the theoretical control of all four occupying powers.
Schupo	Contraction for Schutzpolizist. Member of the West Berlin *Schutzpolizei* ("Protection Police"). Responsible for maintaining law and order and for keeping an eye on the sector boundaries separating West Berlin from the Soviet sector and the Soviet zone.
SED	Sozialistische Einheitspartei Deutschlands: Socialist Unity party of Germany. Euphemism for East Germany's dominant Communist party, being the result of a forced merger with the intimidated Socialists, carried out on Easter Sunday, 1946.
SFB	Sender Freies Berlin: Free Berlin Broadcaster. West Berlin's German-run (although Allied licensed) radio station.
SPD	Sozialdemokratische Partei Deutschlands. Willy Brandt's Social Democratic party (West Germany, West Berlin).
Spitzbart	Goatee. Nickname for Walter Ulbricht.
Spitzel	Spy or informer. Generally used in an East German context.
SSD	Staatssicherheitsdienst: State Security Service. East German equivalent of the Gestapo.
Stasi	Member of the SSD.
S-Bahn	Contraction of *Stadtbahn*, or City Railway. A mostly overhead, partly underground, partly open-air railway connecting East and West Berlin and extending into the surrounding Soviet occupation zone.
Trapo	Contraction of *Transportpolizist*. Member of the East German Transport Police, particularly concerned with checking papers of railway, underground, and Stadtbahn passengers.
U-Bahn	Untergrund-Bahn: Underground or subway. Joined East and West Berlin until August 13, 1961.
VEB	Volkseigener Betrieb: People's Own Enterprise. East German term for a state-run factory or business firm.

VP, Vopo	Contractions for *Volkspolizei, Volkspolizist:* People's Police, People's Policeman (East Germany).
Zone	Contraction for *SBZ* (which see): Soviet zone of occupation.

ACKNOWLEDGMENTS

For his invaluable help in interviewing many of the persons who figure in this book, I am deeply indebted to Horst Froehlich. Without his assistance this narrative would have been different and far less dramatic. I also owe a debt of thanks to Hans Werner Richter for allowing me to use Klemens Krüger's diary notations, first broadcast over the Norddeutscher Rundfunk on October 10, 1961, and later included in the Rowohlt paperback *Die Mauer*.

Among the Berliners to whom I owe special thanks for letting me interview them or for helping me in other ways are Dr. Franz Amrehn, Dietrich Spangenberg, Kurt Mattick, Dr. Walter Klein, Joachim Prill, Peter Boenisch, Guenther Buch, Werner Dassui, and Landespolizeidirektor Erhard Börner and his assistants, Guenter Dittmann, Egon Lesnick, and Heinz Hackbart. With them belong four persons who, although not of German origin, have a right to consider themselves *alte Berliner*, or Berliners by adoption: George Bailey, Robert Lochner, James O'Donnell, and William Walley.

In Bonn I was greatly encouraged and assisted in my research by Drs. Eugen Gerstenmaier, Heinrich Krone, Anneliese Poppinga, Horst Osterheld, Hans Stercken, Klaus Gotto, and my old friend Rüdiger von Pachelbel. I also owe thanks to Dr. Franz-Josef Bach, who kindly received me in Aachen, and to Dr. Wilhelm Grewe, who answered my queries in writing from distant Tokyo, where he was then serving as ambassador of the Federal Republic.

Among those who helped me in France I am much indebted to Gen. Jean Lacomme, Jean Laloy, Col. Michel Barré de Saint-Venant, Ambassadors Claude Lebel, François Seydoux, Jean-Claude Winckler, and Patrick Habans of *Paris-Match*.

For the British point of view I owe special thanks to Gen. Sir Rohan Delacombe, Lord Inchyra, Lord Harlech, Sir Frank Roberts, Sir Philip de Zulueta, Lance Pope, Gen. Sir Thomas

Pearson, Maj. Gen. and Mrs. Goff Hamilton, Brig. L. F. Richards, Sir Bernard Ledwidge, George Turner, Ralph Banfield, Adam Kellett-Long, Anthony Powell, Kyril Tidmarsh, and Terence Prittie.

I owe an even greater debt of thanks to the many Americans who were involved in the August 1961 crisis and who generously filled me in on different aspects of a complex situation. They include former secretary of state Dean Rusk, Paul Nitze, William Tyler, Ambassador and Mrs. Walter Dowling, and Ambassadors Foy Kohler, Allan Lightner, and George McGhee; the late Gen. Lucius Clay, Gens. Maxwell Taylor, Bruce Clarke, Charles Palmer, William Hall, Albert Watson, Frederick Hartel, and Chester Clifton; McGeorge Bundy, Evelyn Lincoln, Walt Rostow, Bromley Smith, Pierre Salinger, Tom Sorensen, and the late Kenneth O'Donnell; John Ausland, Henry Cox, Eleanor Dulles, Jay Gildner, Albert Hemsing, James Hoofnagle, David Klein, Stephen Koczak, George Muller, Yoichi Okamoto, George Reedy, Richard Smyser, Frank Trinka, and Howard Trivers; Cols. Thomas Foote, Thomas Ayres, Louis Waple, and Lawrence Vogel. I also owe special thanks to Cols. Ernest von Pawel and Glover Johns, both of whom provided me with written accounts of their personal experiences during the critical August of 1961.

I would like to thank Benjamin Cate, Marc Catudal, David Chavchavadze, Col. Thomas Cunningham, Edward English, William Griffith, Robert Haeger, Peter Lisagor, Dmitri Panitza, Robert Pfaltzgraff, Peter Prifti, and Warren Rogers for their assistance, information, or advice, and David Powers, William Moss, Ann Travis, and Joan Hoopes for kindly allowing me to tap the resources of the John F. Kennedy Memorial Library, then located at Waltham, Massachusetts.

Last but by no means least, I wish to thank George de Kay for having made it financially possible for me to undertake a job of extensive research, and Diane Gedymin for having been so helpful in tracking people down and in arranging appointments for me.

C. C.

BIBLIOGRAPHY

Acheson, Dean. Oral History Interview with Lucius D. Battle, 27 April 1964. John F. Kennedy Library, Waltham, Mass.

Adenauer, Konrad. *Erinnerungen*, 4 vols. Stuttgart: Deutsche Verlags-Anstalt, 1965–68.

Alphand, Hervé. *L'étonnement d'être, Journal 1939–1973*. Paris: Arthème Fayard, 1977.

Ausland, John C. "Kennedy, Khrushchev and Berlin." Mimeographed. Washington, D.C., n.d.

Bader, W. *Civil War in the Making: The Combat Groups of the Working Class in East Germany*. Translated from the original German (Cologne: Markus Verlag). London: Independent Information Centre, n.d.

Bailey, George. *Germans: The Biography of an Obsession*. New York: Thomas Y. Crowell, 1972.

Bark, Dennis. *Agreement on Berlin: Study of the 1970–72 Quadripartite Negotiations*. Hoover Institution Series, no. 45. Washington, D.C.: American Enterprise, 1974.

Barron, John. *KGB: The Secret Work of Soviet Secret Agents*. New York: Reader's Digest Press, Bantam, 1974.

Binder, David. *The Other German: Willy Brandt's Life and Times*. Washington, D.C.: New Republic, 1975.

Bohlen, Charles. *Witness to History*. New York: W. W. Norton, 1973.

Bradlee, Benjamin C. *Conversations with Kennedy*. New York: W. W. Norton, 1975.

Brandt, Willy. *Begegnungen und Einsichten: Die Jahre 1960–1975*. Hamburg: Hoffmann & Campe, 1976.

———. *In Exile: Essays, Reflections and Letters, 1933–1947*. Philadelphia: University of Pennsylvania Press, 1971.

———. *My Road to Berlin*. New York: Doubleday, 1960.

Buber-Neumann, Margarete. *Als Gefangene bei Stalin und Hitler*. Stuttgart: Deutsche Verlagsanstalt, 1958.

———. *Von Potsdam nach Moskau: Stationen eines Irrweges*. Stuttgart: DVA, 1957.

Buch, Günther, *Namen und Daten: Biographien wichtiger Personen der DDR*. Berlin and Bonn: Dietz, 1973.

Bundesministerium für Gesamtdeutsche Fragen. *Die Flucht aus der Soujetzone und die Sperrmassnahmen des kommunistischen Regimes vom 13 August 1961 in Berlin*. Bonn and Berlin: 1961.

Cate, Curtis. *Antoine de Saint-Exupéry*. New York: Putnam, 1970.

Catudal, Honoré Marc, Jr. *Steinstücken: A Study in Cold War Politics*. New York: Vantage Press, 1971.

Chayes, Abram. Oral History Interview with Eugene Gordon, 18 May 1964. John F. Kennedy Library, Waltham, Mass.

Childs, Marquis. *Witness to Power.* New York: McGraw-Hill, 1975.

Clay, Lucius D. *Decision in Germany.* New York: Doubleday, 1950.

———. Oral History Interview with Richard Scammon, 1 July 1964. John F. Kennedy Library, Waltham, Mass.

Corcelle, Charles. *Les Alliés occidentaux à Berlin depuis 1945.* Paris: Albatros, 1976.

De Gaulle, Charles. *Mémoires de Guerre,* 3 vols. Paris: Plon, 1954, 1956, 1959.

———. *Mémoires d'Espoir: Le Renouveau, 1958–1962.* Paris: Plon, 1970.

Dodd, Thomas J. *Freedom and Foreign Policy.* New York: Bookmailer, 1962.

Drath, Viola Herms. *Willy Brandt: Prisoner of His Past.* Radnor, Pa.: Chilton, 1975.

Dulles, Eleanor Lansing. *American Foreign Policy in the Making.* New York: Harper & Row, 1968.

———. *The Wall: A Tragedy in Three Acts.* Columbia, S.C.: University of South Carolina Press, 1972.

———. *The Wall is Not Forever.* Chapel Hill, N.C.: University of North Carolina Press, 1967.

Ellis, William Donohue, and Cunningham, Thomas J., Jr. *Clarke of St. Vith: The Sergeants' General.* Cleveland: Dillon/Liederbach, 1974.

Forster, Thomas M. *NVA: Die Armee der Sowjetzone.* Cologne: Markus, 1966–67.

Galante, Pierre. *The Berlin Wall.* London: A. Barker, 1965.

Gniffke, Ernst W. *Jahre mit Ulbricht.* Cologne: Verlag Wissenschaft & Politik, 1966.

Gotto, Klaus. *Konrad Adenauer und seine Zeit.* Stuttgart: Deutsch Verlags-Anstalt, 1976.

Gradl, Johann Baptist. *Für deutsche Einheit.* Stuttgart: Seewald, 1975.

Heidelmeyer, Wolfgang, and Hindrichs, Guenter, eds. *Documents on Berlin, 1943–1963.* Munich: R. Oldenbourg, 1963.

Heller, Deane and David. *The Berlin Wall.* New York: Walker, 1962.

Hornstein, Erika von. *Die deutsche Not: Flüchtlinge berichten.* Cologne: Kiepenheuer & Witsch, 1960. (English translation: *Beyond the Berlin Wall.* London: Oswald Wolff, 1962.)

———. *Staatsfeinde: Sieben Prozesse in der "DDR."* Cologne: Kiepenheuer & Witsch, 1963.

Hoxha, Enver. *Vepra [Works].* Vol. 21. Tirana: 1976.

John F. Kennedy Presidential Papers, Appointments Book, 1961. Kept by Kenneth O'Donnell. John F. Kennedy Library, Waltham, Mass.

Kantorowicz, Alfred. *Deutsches Tagebuch.* Vols. 1 and 2. Munich: Kindler, 1959, 1961.

Kennan, George. Oral History Interview with Louis Fischer, 23 March 1965. John F. Kennedy Library, Waltham, Mass.

Khrushchev, Nikita S. *Khrushchev Remembers*. Boston: Little, Brown, 1970.

———. *Khrushchev Remembers: The Last Testament*. Boston: Little, Brown, 1974.

Kohler, Foy D. *Understanding the Russians: A Citizen's Primer*. New York: Harper & Row, 1970.

Kroll, Hans. *Lebenserinnerungen eines Botschafters*. Cologne: Kiepenheuer & Witsch, 1967. (French translation: *Mémoires d'un ambassadeur*. Paris: Fayard, 1968.)

Legien, Rudolf. *The Four Power Agreements on Berlin: Alternative Solutions to the Status Quo?* (Translated from the German) Berlin: Carl Heymanns, 1961.

Lemmer, Ernst. Preface to *Es Geschah an der Mauer*. Photo album published by the Arbeitsgemeinschaft des 13. August, Berlin, n.d.

Leonhard, Wolfgang. *Kreml ohne Stalin*. Cologne,: Verlag für Politik & Wissenchaft, 1959.

———. *Die Revolution entlässt ihre Kinder*. Cologne: Kiepenheuer & Witsch, 1955. (English translation: *Child of the Revolution*. London: Collins, 1957.)

Lincoln, Evelyn. *My Twelve Years with John F. Kennedy*. New York: David McKay, 1965.

Lippmann, Heinz. *Honecker and the New Politics of Europe*. London: Angus & Robertson, 1973.

McDermott, Geoffrey. *Berlin: Success of a Mission?* London: André Deutsch, 1963.

Macmillan, Harold. *Riding the Storm 1956–1959*. New York: Harper & Row, 1971.

———. *Pointing the Way 1959–1961*. New York: Harper & Row, 1972.

Malraux, André. *Les chênes qu'on abat . . .* Paris: Gallimard Folio, 1971.

Mander, John. *Berlin: Hostage for the West*. London: Penguin, 1962.

Morsey, Rudolf, and Repgen, Konrad. *Adenauer Studien III: Untersuchungen zur Ostpolitik und Biographie*. Mainz: Grünewald, 1974.

Murphy, Robert. *Diplomat among Warriors*. New York: Doubleday, 1964.

O'Donnell, Kenneth, and Powers, David. *Johnny, We Hardly Knew Ye: Memories of John Fitzgerald Kennedy*. Boston: Little, Brown, 1972.

Opotowsky, Stan. *The Kennedy Government*. New York: E. P. Dutton, 1961.

Osterheld, Horst. *Konrad Adenauer: Ein Charakterbild*. Bonn: Eichholz, 1973.

Paul, Wolfgang. *Kampf um Berlin*. Munich: Langen-Müller, 1962.

Poppinga, Anneliese. *Meine Erinnerungen an Konrad Adenauer*. Stuttgart: Deutsche Verlags-Anstalt, 1970.

———. *Konrad Adenauer: Geschichtsverständnis, Weltanschauung und politische Praxis*. Stuttgart: DVA, 1975.

Prittie, Terence. *Germany Divided: The Legacy of the Nazi Era*. Boston: Little, Brown, 1960.

————. *Willy Brandt: Portrait of a Statesman*. London: Weidenfeld & Nicolson, 1974.

Richter, Hans Werner, ed. *Die Mauer, oder der 13. August*. Hamburg: Rowohlt, 1961.

Rostow, Walt Whitman. *The Diffusion of Power: 1957–1972*. New York: Macmillan, 1972.

Rühmland, Ullrich. *NVA: Nationale Volksarmee der DDR in Stichworten*, 4th ed. Bonn: Bonner Druck- und Verlagsgesellschaft, 1974.

Salinger, Pierre. *With Kennedy*. New York: Doubleday, 1966.

Schenck, Fritz. *Im Vorzimmer der Diktatur: 12 Jahre Pankow*. Cologne: Kiepenheuer & Witsch, 1962.

Schick, Jack M. *The Berlin Crisis: 1958–1962*. Philadelphia: University of Pennsylvania Press, 1971.

Schlesinger, Arthur M., Jr. *A Thousand Days*. Boston: Houghton Mifflin, 1965.

Schub, Anatole. *An Empire Loses Hope: The Return of Stalin's Ghost*. New York: W. W. Norton, 1970.

Seydoux, Francois. *Mémoires d'outre-Rhin*. Paris: Grasset, 1975.

Shell, Kurt L. *Bedrohung und Bewährung*. Cologne: Westdeutscher Verlag, 1965.

Slusser, Robert M. *The Berlin Crisis of 1961*. Baltimore, Md.: Johns Hopkins Press, 1973.

Smith, Jean Edward. *The Defense of Berlin*. Baltimore, Md.: Johns Hopkins Press, 1963.

Sorensen, Theodore. *Kennedy*. New York: Harper & Row, 1965.

Stern, Carola. *Ulbricht: Eine politische Biographie*. Cologne: Kiepenheuer & Witsch, 1963.

————. *Willy Brandt*. Hamburg: Rowohlt, 1975.

Stützle, Walter. *Kennedy und Adenauer in der Berlin-Krise, 1961–1962*. Bonn: Neue Gesellschaft, 1973.

Tatu, Michel. *Le Pouvoir en URSS: Du déclin de Khrouchtchev à la direction collective*. Paris: Grasset, 1967.

Taylor, Maxwell. *Swords and Plowshares*. New York: W. W. Norton, 1972.

The Papers of the Presidents: John F. Kennedy, 1961. Washington, D.C., 1962.

Thomas, Helen. *Dateline: White House*. New York: Macmillan, 1975.

Thompson, Llewellyn. Oral History Interview with Elizabeth Donohue, 25 March 1964. John F. Kennedy Library, Waltham, Mass.

Trivers, Howard. *Three Crises in American Foreign Affairs and a Continuing Revolution*. Carbondale, Ill.: Southern Illinois University Press, 1972.

Truman, Harry S. *Years of Decision* Vol. 2. New York: Doubleday, 1956.

U.S. Senate, Committee on Foreign Relations. *Documents on Germany, 1944–1961*. Washington, D.C.: Government Printing Office, 1961.

Weintal, Edward, and Bartlett, Charles. *Facing the Brink: An Intimate Study of Crisis Diplomacy*. New York: Charles Scribner's Sons, 1967.

Weymar, Paul. *Adenauer, His Authorized Biography*. New York: Doubleday, 1957.

Zolling, Hermann, and Bahnsen, Uwe. *Kalter Winter im August: Die Berlin-Krise 1961/63, Ihre Hintergründe und Folgen*. Oldenburg and Hamburg: Gerhard Stalling, 1967.

NOTES

Where the information obtained has come from interviews undertaken by the author or his assistant, Horst Froehlich, no precise reference generally has been given. Many individual names have been changed at the request of the informants, most of whom have relatives in East Germany who could be exposed to reprisals on the part of the DDR regime.

The notes indicate sources for information obtained from books, newspapers, or other written material. For purposes of brevity the following abbreviations have been used:

DM	*Daily Mirror* (London)
DT	*Daily Telegraph* (London)
EB	East Berlin
F.a.d.S.	*Flucht aus der Sowjetzone, Flüchtlingsaussagen*
FAZ	*Frankfurter Allgemeine Zeitung*
FR	*Frankfurter Rundschau*
ND	*Neues Deutschland*
NYHT	*New York Herald Tribune*
NYT	*New York Times*
NZZ	*Neue Zürcher Zeitung*
OHI	Oral History Interview (John F. Kennedy Library)
PISFR	Press & Information Service of the Federal Republic, Bonn
Sp. Vb.	*Spandauer Volksblatt*
WB	West Berlin

PART ONE

Pp. 3-4	Barbara Groneweg, *FR*, 5 August 1961.
Pp. 4-6	For Klemens Krüger's diary notations, see Hans Werner Richter, ed., *Die Mauer, oder der 13. August*, pp. 7–17.
Pp. 6-17	On freedom of movement within Berlin, notwithstanding the stresses of the Berlin blockade, see, for example, Howard Trivers, *Three Crises in American Foreign Affairs and a Continuing Revolution*, pp. 24–25, where he writes:

> This freedom of movement within the city was grounded in explicit agreements with the Soviets. On July 7, 1945, in a meeting in Berlin

508

between General Clay and Marshal Zhukov, it was agreed that transportation and movement within Berlin were to be unrestricted between the sectors. The right of free movement had been confirmed by practice, and was likewise supported by interpretation of the May 4, 1949 quadripartite agreement which terminated the Berlin blockade, and by the June 1949 agreement of the Four Power Council of Foreign Ministers.

See also Lucius D. Clay, *Decision in Germany*, pp. 27–30.

Pp. 17-18   Khrushchev's trip to Vienna as described in TASS dispatches and by N. Novikov in *Pravda*, 31 May–2 June 1961.

Pp. 18-20   For varying accounts of Kennedy's trip to Paris and Vienna, see Theodore Sorensen, *Kennedy*, pp. 541–50; Arthur M. Schlesinger, Jr., *A Thousand Days*, chap. 14; Evelyn Lincoln, *My Twelve Years with John F. Kennedy*, pp. 262–71; Kenneth O'Donnell and David Powers, *Johnny, We Hardly Knew Ye*, pp. 284–98; Charles Bohlen, *Witness to History*, pp. 479–83; and Pierre Salinger, *With Kennedy*, chap. 11.

Pp. 21-23   Harold Macmillan, *Pointing the Way 1959–1961*, pp. 329–59. Macmillan's trip to the USSR (February 1959) is described in *Riding the Storm 1956–1959*, pp. 557–634.

P. 23   Lincoln, *My Twelve Years*, p. 274.

P. 24   Regarding the East German Defense Ministry banquets, see *ND*, 8 June 1961.

P. 25   On JFK being "weak and irresolute" at Vienna, see information transmitted to Otto Frei of *NZZ* in David Binder, *The Other German: Willy Brandt's Life and Times*, pp. 180, 361, fn. 46.

P. 25   Jean Edward Smith, *The Defense of Berlin*, pp. 235–36; Robert Slusser, *The Berlin Crisis of 1961*, pp. 4–6.

Pp. 25-33   This account of Ulbricht's uneasy relations with Khrushchev is for the most part derived from Carola Stern, *Ulbricht, eine politische Biographie*.

P. 26   See Otto Frei, "Berlin: The Broken City," *The Atlantic Monthly*, December 1963, p. 120.

P. 26   Smith, *The Defense of Berlin*, p. 223; Michel Tatu, *Le Pouvoir en URSS: du déclin de Khrouchtchev à la direction collective*, pp. 41–42.

Pp. 33-36   For descriptions of Wandlitz compound, see Stern, *Ulbricht*, pp. 240–42; Fritz Schenck, *Im Vorzimmer der Diktatur: 12 Jahre Pankow*, p. 235; an article by H. G. West in *Tagesspiegel* (WB), 28 January 1960; and *Die Welt*, 29 August 1960.

Pp. 35-40   On Erich Mielke, see the European news magazine *Kontinent*, 9 August 1961; and an article by Karl Wilhelm Fricke in *FAZ*, 28 November 1975.

P. 37   On Mielke's activities in Spain, see Alfred Kantorowicz, *Deutsches Tagebuch*, Vol. 1, p. 51.

Pp. 38-39   Schenck, *Im Vorzimmer der Diktatur*, pp. 306 ff.

Pp. 40-41   For description of Adenauer's office, see Anneliese Poppinga, ence Prittie, *Germany Divided: The Legacy of the Nazi Era*, pp. 341–43:

> 1950. Creation of Ministry of State Security, take-over of police powers from Russians. Single-list elections for Volkskammer: 99.7% vote. Fled to the West: 197,788.
>
> 1951. Workers lose right to negotiate wage agreements. SSD-rigged trials of 19 young people (Werdau) sentenced to total of 130 years of imprisonment. Fled to West: 165,640.
>
> 1952. Establishment of *Totenstreife* [death-strip]. Law authorizes seizure of property of persons indulging in *Republikflucht*. Fled to the West: 182,393.
>
> 1953. Regime raises work norms by 10%, touching off Stalinallee riots, June 17 uprising. Eighteen young persons condemned to death, 1,200 sentenced to over 4,000 years in jail. Fled to West: 331,390.
>
> 1954. 99.4% vote for second Volkskammer. Youth initiation drive launched, along with campaign against religious instruction in schools. Fled to West: 181,198.
>
> 1955. Drive to nationalize private industry and to continue collectivization of farms. Fled to West: 252,870.
>
> 1956. First public trials of those encouraging *Republikflucht*. Regime presses drive to destroy private enterprise. Fled to West: 279,189.
>
> 1957. Ulbricht denounces those leaving as "traitors to the working class." New passport law imposes 3-year jail sentence on anyone making unauthorized trip outside DDR. Fled to West: 261,622.
>
> 1958. New law introduced condemning "calumny of the state" (*Staatsverleumdung*). School children forced to work for certain periods in industry and agriculture. Fled to West: 204,092.
>
> 1959. Ministry of Cultural Affairs orders purge of universities and technical colleges. Volkskammer deputies are told it is not their duty to "represent" wishes of their constituents. Fled to the West: 143,917.
>
> 1960. Ulbricht relaunches farm collectivization drive. New travel restrictions imposed. Autobahn and goods-trains traffic harassment. Fled to West: 186,600.*

Pp. 42-49   For description of Adenauer's office, see Anneliese Poppinga, *Meine Erinnerungen an Konrad Adenauer*, pp. 11–14, 20–22. The rest of this section is based on Hans Kroll's Memoirs (cited hereafter in the French edition—*Memoires d'un Ambassadeur*).

Pp. 58-65   For the text of Ulbricht's press conference and Khrushchev's television speech, see *ND*, 16 June 1961.

P. 65   *Tagesspiegel* (WB), 16 June 1961.

Pp. 66-67   On Globke issuing orders to "Massenmörder" Eichmann,

---

*The last two figures and the 1960 résumé have been added by the author, since Prittie's book was written in 1959.

see, for example, *ND*, 1,2,3,6,22,23 June 1961. On "Spionage-Lemmer" as "V-Mann des Gestapo," see *ND*, 21 June 1961, where he is described as "the worst of the Bonn Ultras."

P. 70 *ND*, 22 June 1961, carried the full text of Khrushchev's speech and a photograph of him wearing *shapka* and standing beside Gens. Rodintsev, Chuikov, and other World War II generals.

P. 71 *ND*, 23 June 1961.

P. 72 *ND*, 25 June 1961.

P. 73 *ND, NYT*, 29 June 1961; Slusser, *The Berlin Crisis of 1961*, p. 43.

P. 73 *Tagesspiegel*, 7 July 1961.

Pp. 75-78 Hans Zielinski in *Die Welt*, and *Berliner Morgenpost*, 14 July 1961.

P. 76 For a description of the Marienfelde entrance, see also Erika von Hornstein, *Die deutsche Not: Flüchtlinge berichten*, p. 9.

P. 79 *Newsweek*, July 3, and as quoted in a UPI dispatch in *NZZ*, 1 July 1961.

P. 79 *NYT*, 3 July 1961.

P. 79 *NYT*, 4 July 1961.

P. 79 *NYT*, 6 July 1961.

P. 79 *ND, NYT*, 2 July 1961.

Pp. 79-80 West German Defense Ministry press release, 2 July 1961; *NYT*, 3 July 1961.

P. 80 *ND*, 22, 24 July 1961; *NYT*, 5 July 1961.

P. 80 *NYT*, 1 July 1961.

P. 80 *Tagesspiegel* (WB), 1 July 1961.

P. 80 *NYT*, 2 July 1961.

Pp. 80-81 *NYT*, 2 July 1961.

P. 81 *NYT*, 1 July 1961.

P. 81 *NYT*, 2 July 1961.

Pp. 81-82 Dean Acheson, OHI with Lucius D. Battle, pp. 19–20; Sorensen, *Kennedy*, pp. 588–89; Schlesinger, *A Thousand Days*, pp. 380–83; Reston, *NYT*, 7 July 1961. In an interview granted to the author in December 1961, Acheson said it was "absurd" to have to threaten a nuclear war each time our interests in Berlin were threatened, and that the proper answer to this problem was to have an armored U.S. corps ready "to barrel up the Helmstedt–Berlin autobahn" in case of need and as a permanent warning to the Russians to be on their best behavior in Berlin.

P. 82 On Kennedy's desire to get away from the Dulles policy, see Jack M. Schick, *The Berlin Crisis: 1958–1962*, pp. 141–45. See also JFK's University of Rochester speech, October 1959, in V. Lasky, *JFK: The Man and the Myth*, New Rochelle, N.Y.: Arlington House, 1963. p. 570.

P. 83   On Kennedy's reasons for choosing Dean Rusk as secretary of
             state, see Acheson, OHI, pp. 5–7.
Pp. 83-84   Acheson, OHI, pp. 13–14.
P. 84   Macmillan, *Riding the Storm*, pp. 587–88.
P. 84   Macmillan, *Pointing the Way*, pp. 389–90.
P. 84   Abram Chayes, OHI with Eugene Gordon, pp. 244–45.
Pp. 84-85   From the author's own interviews with State Department and
             other officials.
P. 85   Chayes, OHI, pp. 246–47.
Pp. 85-86   Schlesinger, *A Thousand Days*, pp. 383–90.
P. 86   *NYT*, 9 July 1961; Slusser, *The Berlin Crisis of 1961*, pp.
             51–57.
P. 86   Schlesinger, *A Thousand Days*, p. 386.
Pp. 87-88   *Sp. Vb.*, 15 July 1961.

PART TWO: The Panic

P. 93   *ND*, 13 July 1961.
P. 93   On Adenauer's attitude to Bismarck, trips to Berlin, etc., see
             Johann Baptist Gradl's essay in *Konrad Adenauer und seine
             Zeit, Vol. 1*, Klaus Gotto.
P. 94   Terence Prittie, *Willy Brandt: Portrait of a Statesman*, pp.
             110–18, 128–31; David Binder, *The Other German: Willy
             Brandt's Life and Times*, pp. 170–76.
Pp. 94-95   Prittie, *Willy Brandt*, p. 111.
P. 95   Willy Brandt, *Begegnungen und Einsichten: Die Jahre
             1960–1975*, p. 50.
Pp. 95-96   Brandt, *Begegnungen und Einsichten*, p. 49.
P. 96   Kroll, pp. 312, 324–32.
P. 96   PISFR Bulletin, 14 July 1961.
P. 96   *Sp. Vb., ND, NYT*, 11 July 1961.
P. 97   This information was supplied by a city hall official inter-
             viewed by Horst Froehlich.
Pp. 97-98   *NYT*, 9, 12 July 1961.
P. 98   PISFR Bulletin, 13 July 1961.
P. 98   For border-crosser figures, see *Sp. Vb.*, 5 August 1961, and
             Der Abend (WB), 11 August 1961. Otto Frei, in *NZZ*, 2 July
             1961, estimated the number of West Berliners working in
             East Berlin at seven thousand.
Pp. 98-99   *ND*, 11 July 1961; *Spiegel*, 19 July 1961.
P. 99   *Berliner Morgenpost, Tagesspiegel* (WB), 14 July 1961.

P. 99	PISFR Bulletin, 13 July 1961; *NYT*, 14 July 1961.
P. 99	*Sp. Vb.* (WB), 14 July 1961.
P. 99	*ND*, 14 July 1961.
P. 99	*Berliner Morgenpost*, 18 July 1961. There were 2,931 refugees registered.
P. 100	Kroll, p. 330; *NYT*, 13, 15 July 1961.
P. 100	François, Seydoux, *Mémoires d'outre-Rhin*, pp. 249, 278.
Pp. 100-01	Kroll, pp. 330–32.
P. 101	Letter to the author from Wilhelm Grewe.
Pp. 101-2	Kroll, pp. 332–34.
P. 102	Kroll, p. 335; *NYT*, 26 July 1961.
P. 102	*NYT*, 23 July 1961.
P. 103	Sorensen, *Kennedy*, p. 590.
P. 103	Schlesinger, *A Thousand Days*, p. 384; Chayes, OHI, pp. 257–63; declassified unsigned White House memorandum, 17 July 1961, John F. Kennedy Library.
Pp. 103-4	Chayes, OHI, pp. 245–46, 264–315.
Pp. 103-4	Chayes, OHI, p. 270; O'Donnell and Powers, *Johnny, We Hardly Knew Ye*, p. 299. This position was also taken by Walter Lippmann and explains why he was advocating de facto recognition of the DDR.
P. 104	Reston, *NYT*, 12 July 1961.
Pp. 104-5	Warren Rogers, *NYHT*, 16 July 1961; Slusser, *The Berlin Crisis of 1961*, pp. 64–65; Walt Whitman Rostow, *Diffusion of Power: 1957–1972*, p. 230.
Pp. 105-6	Sorensen, *Kennedy*, p. 587; Slusser, *The Berlin Crisis of 1961*, p. 79.
P. 106	Still classified memorandum in the John F. Kennedy Library from Rostow dated 20 July 1961, beginning: "The Attorney General asked me yesterday to consider our Berlin problem as if it were a political campaign."
P. 106	Rostow, *Diffusion of Power*, p. 230. McGeorge Bundy followed up on July 22 with a two-page memorandum entitled "A High Noon Stance on Berlin." (Still classified, John F. Kennedy Library.)
Pp. 106-7	Reports by Paul Samuelson and Seymour Harris, John F. Kennedy Library; Sorenson, *Kennedy*, pp. 587–90.
P. 107	John F. Kennedy Presidential Papers, Appointments Book, 20 July 1961, John F. Kennedy Library.
P. 107	Declassified six-page telegram to Adenauer, cabled by M. J. Hillenbrand of the State Department to Walter Dowling, in Bonn, on 20 July 1961, John F. Kennedy Library. See also Macmillan, *Pointing the Way*, p. 390.
Pp. 107-8	*NYT*, 16 July 1961.
P. 108	Sorensen, *Kennedy*, p. 591.
Pp. 108-111	As told to the author by James O'Donnell.

Pp. 109-111 For the text of Kennedy's speech, see *The Papers of the Presidents: John F. Kennedy*, 1961, pp. 533–40.
Pp. 111-12   Macmillan, *Pointing the Way*, p. 390.
P. 112   As told to W. Manchester by Fay in April 1962 issue of *Holiday*, quoted by Smith, *The Defense of Berlin*, p. 241.
P. 112   John F. Kennedy Presidential Papers, Appointments Book, 25 July 1961.
Pp. 112-13   Lincoln, *My Twelve Years*, pp. 278–80; Sorensen, *Kennedy*, pp. 591–92.
Pp. 113-14   T. Wicker article and p. 10, *NYT*, 27 July 1961.
P. 114   *NYT*, 28 July 1961.
P. 114   *NYT*, 26 July 1961.
P. 114   *NYT*, 28 July 1961.
P. 114   Reston, *NYT*, 26 July 1961.
P. 114   *NYT*, 25 July 1961.
P. 114   *NYT*, 26 July 1961.
P. 115   *NYT*, 27 July 1961.
P. 115   *Tagesspiegel, Der Tag, Morgenpost, NYT* (WB), 27 July 1961; *Kurier*, 29 July 1961.
P. 115   *ND*, 27 July 1961.
Pp. 115-16   *ND*, 28 July 1961.
P. 116   *NYT*, 27 July 1961.
Pp. 116-17   *NYT*, 28, 29 July, 1 August 1961; Schlesinger, *A Thousand Days*, pp. 392, 454; Sorensen, *Kennedy*, p. 552; Slusser, *The Berlin Crisis of 1961*, pp. 88–92.
Pp. 117-18   Memorandum from Walter W. Heller to President Kennedy, 2 August 1961, in JFK Library. Background information on CDU was supplied by James O'Donnell.
P. 118   *NYT*, 28 July 1961.
P. 119   See, for example, *Sp. Vb.*, 29 July 1961.
Pp. 119-21   *F.a.d.S.*, no. 63, pp. 69–70.
P. 121   Figures for registered refugees, 1961: July 25 (previous twenty-four hours until 4:00 P.M.)—1,046; July 26—973; July 27—1,078; July 28—1,030; July 29—1,200; July 30 (twenty-seven hours)—1,900. Total for July: 30,444. (*Tagesspiegel*, 25 July–1 August 1961.) July total given by *Die Welt*, 4 August 1961, was 30,415, and the figure supplied to the author by Col. Ernest von Pawel was 31,079. Since not all refugees were registered at Marienfelde, this last figure is probably the closest to the truth.
Pp. 121-122 *NYT*, 28 July 1961.
P. 122   *F.a.d.S.*, nos. 45–55, pp. 64–66.
P. 122   Groneweg, *FR*, 5 August 1961.
P. 123   L. Müller-Marein, *Die Zeit*, 11 August 1961.
P. 123   The full greeting was, and is, *Freundschaft mit der Sowjetunion!*

Pp. 123-124   *F.a.d.S.*, no. 48, pp. 64–65.

P. 124   *F.a.d.S.*, no. 51, p. 65.

P. 124   *F.a.d.S.*, no. 50, p. 65.

Pp. 124-25   *F.a.d.S.*, no. 47, p. 64.

Pp. 125-26   *F.a.d.S.*, no. 60, p. 68.

P. 126   Groneweg, *FR*, 5 August 1961.

Pp. 126-27   Müller-Marein, *Die Zeit*, 11 August 1961.

P. 127   Müller-Marein, *Die Zeit*, 11 August 1961.

Pp. 127-28   *ND*, 23 July 1961.

P. 128   Exact figures for East German refugees are not available for the years 1945–49, since it was only in 1949 that a formal registration process was started. The annual average for the years 1946–49 was probably around 250,000. Ernst Lemmer, at a press conference held on August 1, 1961, claimed that four million East Germans had fled since 1945, a figure that is close to George Bailey's estimate in "The Disappearing Satellite," *The Reporter*, 16 March 1961, p. 20, and to Evelyn Anderson's in *Survey*, no. 42 (June 1962), p. 103.

P. 128   For figures on East German factory employment, *see Tagesspiegel* (WB), 9 August 1961, and Anatole Schub, *An Empire Loses Hope: The Return of Stalin's Ghost*, pp. 232–33.

Pp. 128-29   Heinz Lippmann, *Honecker and the New Politics of Europe*. pp. 182, 263.

P. 129   On the nonfulfillment of successive five- and seven-year plans, see Anderson, *Survey*, no. 42, pp. 102–6, and Stephen Thomas, *Survey*, nos. 44–45 (October 1962), pp. 54-65.

P. 129   Schub, *An Empire Loses Hope*, p. 233.

P. 129   Anderson, *Survey*, no. 42, p. 103.

Pp. 129-30   Prittie (*Germany Divided*, pp. 139–40) estimated the amount of reparations exacted from 1945 to 1953 at $17.6 billion. Schub cites Ulbricht's own estimate—$22.5 billion—up to 1955, adding: "Western estimates were often higher." (*An Empire Loses Hope*, p. 232).

P. 130   Prittie, *Germany Divided*, pp. 150–52.

P. 130   October 1957 (information supplied by Horst Froehlich).

Pp. 130-31   *Time*, 31 March 1961, and article by Werner Clausen, *FAZ*, 29 July 1961.

P. 131   Trivers, *Three Crises*, pp. 21–22.

Pp. 131-32   Thomas Forster, *NVA: Die Armee der Sowjetzone*, pp. 26–28.

P. 132   Schub, *An Empire Loses Hope*, p. 236.

P. 132   On the "polio epidemic" in West Germany, see *ND*, *NYT*, 31 July, 1 August 1961.

P. 132   East German soldiers had even been ordered to help man Vopo control points, causing kilometer-long traffic jams. (*Tagesspiegel*, *Telegraf*, 27 July 1961.)

P. 132   A. Doherr (*FR*, 4 August 1961) claimed that not more than one thousand border crossers had agreed to give up their jobs in West Berlin after the first week of intense anti-Grenzgänger pressure.

Pp. 133-38   From *Der Abend* (WB), 5 August 1961.

P. 139   T. Shabad, *NYT*, 1 August 1961.

Pp. 139-40   On Khrushchev's leisurely return to Moscow, see *Pravda*, *Izvestia*, 29, 30 July 1961.

P. 140   On Ulbricht's experiences at Hotel Lux, see Stern, *Ulbricht*, pp. 97–102.

P. 140   *NYT*, *FR*, 1 August 1961.

P. 140   *NYT*, 2 August 1961; Slusser, *The Berlin Crisis of 1961*, p. 100.

P. 140   On Smirnov's recall from Bonn, see *DT*, 2 August 1961.

P. 140   Fulbright's televised statement was made on 30 July 1961 (*NYT*, 3 August 1961), given a big play in *ND* (1 August 1961 and later issues), and violently attacked in the West German press.

Pp. 140-41   Even Franz-Josef Strauss, generally regarded as the coldest of cold warriors, was urging caution on the question of economic sanctions. See, for example, his televised interview in the United States, 29 July 1961 (*FR*, 1 August 1961).

P. 141   East German decree of 28 June 1961 (*NYT*, 29, 30 June, 1 August 1961).

P. 141   On Khrushchev's refusal to close western air lanes, see Kroll, p. 339; see also Gen. Jan Šejna, Czechoslovak deputy minister of defense and chief liaison officer with the Warsaw Pact forces (who later fled to the West), as quoted in *Spiegel*, 16 August 1976, p. 16:

When we arrived in Moscow in July 1961, Khrushchev greeted Ulbricht, and Ulbricht said: "Thank you, Comrade Khrushchev, without your help we cannot solve this terrible problem." Khrushchev answered: "Yes, I agree—but not one millimeter further!" Ulbricht turned pale, for that meant: closing of the border with West Berlin, and not what he had hoped—the take-over of all Berlin and the air corridors.

Although fancifully worded and tremendously abridged, this account basically accords with Kroll's, obtained directly from Khrushchev. Ulbricht was apparently convinced that once the air corridors were cut, West Berlin would fall into his hands like a piece of ripe fruit.

P. 141   On Sarajevo precedent, see Kroll, p. 326, and Khrushchev's later televised speech, 7 August 1961 (*Pravda*, *NYT*, 8 August 1961), in which he stated: "We must not let West Berlin become a kind of Sarajevo—the Serbian town where the shots rang out announcing the outbreak of the First World War."

Pp. 141-42   The new Party program was issued on 30 July 1961 (*Pravda, NYT*, 30 July 1961.

P. 142   Astronaut Virgil Grissom's mishap occurred in the Atlantic on 21 July 1961 (*NYT*, 22 July 1961).

P. 143   On Mikoyan's support of Ulbricht, see Franz-Josef Bach, "Gegen die Mauer-Version von Willy Brandt," *Die politische Meinung*, no. 138 (September-October 1971), p. 17.

Pp. 143-44   Information obtained by Horst Froehlich from a former legal adviser to the East German Volkspolizei, now living in the West. The 1952 contingency plan was known as *Geheime Verschlusssache* ("secret seal-off matter").

P. 145   On Ulbricht's proposal for a meeting of the Warsaw Treaty powers, see Enver Hoxha, *Vepra* [Works], 21 (May-September 1961): 461. I am indebted to Professor Peter R. Prifti of the University of California at San Diego, for kindly providing me with a translation of the passages dealing with the events of early August 1961.

P. 145   For a blow-by-blow description of the violent Hoxha-Shehu altercation with Khrushchev and Mikoyan, see *Le Monde*, 28 February 1976, p. 4 (version provided by the Albanian ATA news agency); see also Andreas Razumowsky, *FAZ*, 7 February 1976, "Der Abfall Albaniens von Moskau," and Khrushchev's less detailed but very revealing account in *Khrushchev Remembers: The Last Testament*, pp. 266–68.

P. 150   I am indebted to Terence Prittie for the full text of this letter, most of which was published in his *Willy Brandt*, p. 139.

Pp. 150-54   *F.a.d.S.*, no. 78, pp. 74–75.

Pp. 154-60   This account is based on a Western intelligence report which was not taken seriously at the time.

P. 154   Hoxha, *Vepra*, pp. 416–25.

P. 155   For havoc in economic planning caused by the autumn 1960 interruptions in interzonal trade, see PISFR Bulletin, 7 June 1961 (on Leuschner's visit to Moscow); *NZZ*, 6 June 1961; Kroll, p. 291; and a first-rate résumé in Schick, *The Berlin Crisis: 1958–1962*, pp. 130–33.

Pp. 155-56   On Bruno Leuschner receiving 'Nkrumah in East Berlin see *NYT*, 2 August 1961. On Ulbricht's absence, see *FAZ, NYHT*, 4 August 1961.

P. 156   *Berliner Zeitung* (EB), *Die Welt*, 2 August 1961.

Pp. 156-57   *Tagesspiegel* (WB), *NYT*, 4 August 1961.

P. 157   *ND*, 28 July, 1, 2 August 1961.

P. 157   *ND*, 11, 14 July 1961, Doherr, *FR*, 4, 5 August 1961; Gilroy, *NYT*, 4 August 1961.

P. 157   *ND*, 1–4 August 1961. For a report on the first anti-Grenz-gänger letters, see *Morgenpost*, 4 July 1961.

Pp. 157-58   On Vopo controls, see *Tagesspiegel* (WB), 4 August 1961; *NYT*, 2–4 August 1961; *Die Welt*, 3 August 1961; *NYHT*, 2 August 1961.

P. 158   Registered refugees for August 1: 1,322; for August 2: 1,110 (including a number of defecting Vopos); for August 3: 1,155. (*Tagesspiegel, Morgenpost, NYT*, 1–3 August 1961.)

P. 158   *Morgenpost*, 4 August 1961.

P. 160   See Hoxha, *Vepra*, pp. 464–65, for the Albanians' fury at not being informed of the secret meeting of the Warsaw Pact's Consultative Political Committee, held in addition to the three-day plenary session.

Pp. 160-61   T. Shabad, S. Topping, *NYT*, 6 August 1961.

P. 161   B. Kirsch, *FR*, 6 August 1961.

P. 161   Kroll, p. 288. The belief that the Allies would do nothing was particularly strong in official East German circles. See, for example, Politburo member Hermann Matern's trenchant statement during a speech made at a machine-tools factory at Plauen on 2 August 1961: "When West Berlin radio stations say that war will come because of West Berlin, I say that no Englishman, no Frenchman, and no American will go to war because of West Berlin or because of the signing of a peace treaty." (*ND*, 3 August 1961.)

P. 161   The KGB was receiving precise information about general Allied policy and contingency planning from Georges Paques, a high French official in NATO headquarters. (See John Barron, *KGB: The Secret Work of Soviet Secret Agents*, p. 31.) General Lacomme told the author that it had been made clear to the three Berlin commandants that the "three essentials" spelled out at Oslo constituted the essence of Allied policy. Hermann Zolling and Uwe Bahnsen (in *Kalter Winter im August: Die Berlin-Krise 1961/63*, p. 78) claim that after reading the Oslo communiqué, a highly upset Egon Bahr (West Berlin City Hall press chief) rushed to Willy Brandt, saying: "This is practically an invitation to the Soviets to do what they want in the Eastern sector."

P. 161   Alexander Shelepin, then head of the KGB, probably made a secret trip to East Berlin while the Warsaw Pact leaders were meeting in Moscow. See "Periscope" report in *Newsweek*, 14 August 1961 and Khrushchev's strange account of his own incognito trip to Berlin (*Last Testament*, p. 506).

P. 161   *Pravda, NYT*, 6 August 1961; *NYHT, FAZ*, 7 August 1961.

P. 162   *DT, NYT*, 5 August 1961.

P. 162   Chayes, *OHI*, pp. 264–78.

Pp. 162-63   Macmillan, *Pointing the Way*, pp. 391–92.
Pp. 164-66   As told to the author by General Lacomme. Willy Brandt was similarly greeted by De Gaulle in June 1959: "And how is the situation in Prussia [Ulbricht's DDR]?" (Brandt, *Begegnungen und Einsichten* pp. 131–32.)
Pp. 167-68   *NYT*, 7, 8 August 1961.
P. 168   B. Kirsch, *FR*, 8 August 1961.
P. 168   *NYT*, 8 August 1961.
P. 168   *NYT, DT*, 7 August 1961.
P. 169   *FR*, 8 August 1961. Kirsch was expelled from the Soviet Union the very next day. (*FR*, 9 August 1961.)
P. 169   *NYT, DT*, 9 August 1961. Information provided Horst Froehlich by a Grepo who later defected.
Pp. 169-70   I am indebted to Werner Dassui for these details about passes, etc.
Pp. 170-72   *Pravda, NYT*, 8 August 1961; and Slusser, *The Berlin Crisis of 1961*, pp. 107–14.
P. 172   *ND*, 8 August 1961.
P. 172   *France-Soir*, 9 August 1961.
Pp. 172-73   *DT*, 9 August 1961, p. 1.
P. 173   T. Szulc, *NYT*, 8 August 1961.
P. 173   *Tagesspiegel*, 6 August 1961; *NYT*, 8 August 1961.
P. 173   *NYT*, 9 August 1961.
Pp. 173-74   PISFR Bulletin, 6 August 1961.
P. 174   *NYT, FR, ND*, 9 August 1961. See also *ND, Nationale Zeitung, Neue Zeit* (EB), 5 August 1961.
P. 174   *Morgenpost, NYT*, 10 August 1961.
P. 174   *FAZ*, 7 August 1961; *DT*, 8 August 1961.
Pp. 174-75   *Montagsecho*, 7 August 1961.
P. 175   Nato Source: Paul Nitze.
P. 175   *DM*, 9 August 1961; *DT, NYT*, 10 August 1961.
Pp. 176-77   *DM, NYT*, 10 August 1961.
P. 177   *Tagesspiegel, Morgenpost*, 10 August 1961.
P. 177   *Sp. Vb., Der Abend, NYT*, 10 August 1961.
P. 177   *Morgenpost, NYT*, 11 August 1961.
Pp. 177-78   *Tagesspiegel*, 9 August 1961.
Pp. 178-83   Sources: Col. Ernest von Pawel's written account, corroborated and amplified by Gen. Sir Thomas Pearson and Col. Michel Barré de Saint-Venant.
Pp. 183-91   *ND, Berliner Zeitung* (EB), 11 August 1961; Kurt Wismach, "What Ulbricht Doesn't Know," *The Atlantic Monthly*, December 1963, and *F.a.d.S.*, no. 95, pp. 81–82.
P. 191   *ND, Die Welt, NZZ*, 12 August 1961.
Pp. 191-92   *DM*, 12 August 1961.
P. 192   Source: City hall official to Horst Froehlich.

P. 193   On Brandt's absences from Berlin, see *Morgenpost, Tages-spiegel*, 5 August 1961, and A. Doherr, *FR*, 9 August 1961.
P. 193   *NYT*, 8 August 1961.
P. 193   Brandt, *Begegnungen und Einsichten*, p. 14.
Pp. 193-94 U.S. Army Garrison Daily Bulletin, 11 August 1961.
Pp. 195-97 *Pravda, DT, NYT*, 12 August 1961; Slusser, *The Berlin Crisis of 1961*, pp. 124–29.
P. 196   As told to the author by Sir Frank Roberts.

PART 3: August 13

P. 207   *Telegraf* (WB), 12 August 1961. Doherr, *FR*, 14 August 1961.
Pp. 207-208 By 4:00 P.M. on Friday, there were 1,537 registered refugees; by 6:00 P.M. on Saturday, August 12, 2,662 (*NYT*, 12, 13 August 1961.)
P. 210   Pierre Galante, *The Berlin Wall*, p. 21.
P. 211   Galante, p. 25.
Pp. 212-13 *FR*, 8 August 1961, p. 2; G. Ziegler, *FR*, 14 August 1961, pp. 3, 11; *FAZ*, 14 August 1961, p. 3.
Pp. 221-24 This account of Heinz Hoffmann's send-off "party" is based on Lt. Col. Martin Herbert Loeffler's description, made in Bonn on 21 September 1962. (See *NYT*, *Morgenpost* [WB], 22 September 1961; *Rheinische Merkur, Christ und Welt*, 28 September 1961; and the English version of a DPA dispatch published by the Foreign Broadcast Information Service, 24 September 1961.
P. 225   As later learned by Robert Lochner from an East German fugitive.
Pp. 255-57 Based on a precise, written account kindly made available to the author by Brigadier L. F. Richards.
P. 261   From a report later published in *Der Kämpfer* [The Fighter], official organ of the Betriebskampfgruppen, and included in Bader, *Civil War in the Making*, pp. 83–89.
P. 262   *The Reporter*, George Bailey, *Germans: The Biography of an Obsession*, pp. 291–92.
Pp. 287-90 From Globke's written account in Eleanor Lansing Dulles, *The Wall: A Tragedy in Three Acts*, pp. 92–93.
P. 292   AP dispatch, filed 0956 hours, Berlin, 13 August 1961.
Pp. 295-96 As related to Horst Froehlich by Joachim Lipschitz's widow.
Pp. 297-98 Information later given to Horst Froehlich by an East Berlin refugee.
Pp. 298-304 This account of the Allied commandants' two meetings is based on what they themselves told the author, supplemented by what was added by Dr. Walter Klein, Allan Lightner,

and George Muller. See also Brandt, *Begegnungen und Ein-sichten*, pp. 11–13; Geoffrey McDermott, *Berlin: Success of a Mission?*, pp. 32–33.

P. 304   Hervé Alphand, *L'étonnement d'être, Journal 1939–1973*, pp. 360–61.

P. 304   John F. Kennedy Presidential Papers, Appointments Book, 11, 12 August 1961.

Pp. 305-306 From a five-page memorandum entitled "The Wall," kindly made available to the author by John Ausland.

Pp. 317-18 Foy Kohler, *Understanding the Russians*, pp. 320–21.

P. 318   Official record of Pierre Salinger's press releases, 11 August 1961 (morning), kindly made available to the author.

P. 319   Source: Howard Trivers.

Pp. 319-21 Trivers, *Three Crises*, pp. 26–29.

P. 322   Quoted by Schick, *The Berlin Crisis: 1958–1962*, p. ix.

P. 322   Stan Opotowsky, *The Kennedy Government*, pp. 56–57; Weintal & Bartlett, *Facing the Brink*, pp. 146-53.

P. 329   On the Kennedy administration's informality and openness to the press, see Salinger, *With Kennedy*, pp. 77, 111–18; O'Donnell and Powers, *Johnny, We Hardly Knew Ye*, pp. 251–57; Lincoln, *My Twelve Years*, pp. 229–32, 240–43; and Helen Thomas, *Dateline: White House*, pp. 12–14, 19–21.

P. 329   Maxwell Taylor, *Swords and Plowshares*, pp. 198–99.

Pp. 330-31 Source: Gen. Chester Clifton.

P. 332   Dean Rusk's personal records indicate that this call to Hyannis Port was made around 11:00 A.M.

P. 332   The expression "talk the fever out of this thing" was used several times during the interview that Dean Rusk was kind enough to grant the author.

Pp. 332-33 For Dean Rusk's official statement, see *NYT*, 14 August 1961, p. 7.

P. 334   The first Foreign Office statement was issued late Sunday evening. See T. Ronan, *NYT*, 14 August 1961, p. 6.

P. 334   Macmillan, *Pointing the Way*, pp. 392–93.

P. 334   Source: Lord Inchyra, then serving as permanent under secretary at the Foreign Office. He had previously served as British ambassador in Bonn under the name of Sir Frederick Hoyer-Millar. He, too, was vacationing in Scotland on August 13, although he recalls having discussed the Berlin situation on the telephone with Lord Home.

P. 334   *NYT*, 14 August 1961.

P. 334   Seydoux, *Mémoires d'Outre-Rhin*, p. 279.

P. 334   See Franz Thedieck's letter to *Bonner Rundschau*, 22 October 1976, regarding the attitudes, information, and activities of Lemmer's Ministry of All-German Affairs before, during, and after 13 August 1961.

P. 335   *FR*, 14 August 1961, and stenographic report, Abgeortneten-
haus von Berlin, Sitzung 66, Sunday, August 13, pp. 251–54.

Pp. 335-36   As described to Horst Froehlich by Rudi Rindt, who escaped
to West Berlin a few hours later.

Pp. 337-38   Chayes, OHI, pp. 267, 279–85.

P. 338   The DDR was officially established, with East Berlin as its
capital, on 7 October 1949, four and a half months after the
promulgation of the *Grundgesetz* ("Constitution") establishing the Federal Republic, with its temporary capital in Bonn.

P. 346   From a written account of the scene, kindly sent to the author
by Gen. Goff Hamilton.

PART FOUR: THE AFTERMATH

P. 355   The two other parliamentary leaders were Heinrich Krone,
of Adenauer's CDU, and Erich Mende, leader of the Free
Democratic party. See Krone's diary in Rudolf Morsey and
Konrad Repgen, *Adenauer Studien III: Untersuchungen zur
Ostpolitik und Biographie*, p. 162.

Pp. 355-56   As told to the author by Eugen Gerstenmaier. See also
Brandt, *Begegnungen und Einsichten*, p. 24.

P. 356   *DM*, 15 August 1961.

Pp. 359-360   As told to Horst Froehlich by Lothar Böhm.

P. 360   *F.a.d.S.*, no. 88, pp. 77–78. *Pflaumig* ("plum-like") and *Was-
chlappen* ("washrags") were just two of many critical terms
used by Berliners about the inert Allies.

P. 361   *Morgenpost, NYT*, 15 August 1961.

P. 362   Krone diary in Morsey and Repgen, *Adenauer Studien III*, p.
162.

P. 363   *Morgenpost*, 15 August 1961.

P. 363   See Paul, *Kampf um Berlin*, and Smith, *The Defense of
Berlin*, pp. 121–23.

P. 366   Globke memorandum in Dulles, *The Wall*, p. 93.

P. 366   Kroll, p. 335.

P. 366   Even if Laloy's suggestion had been transmitted to Couve de
Murville, it would have made no difference. When Hervé
Alphand telephoned from Italy to ask if he should shorten his
vacation and return posthaste to Washington, the French foreign minister replied, *"Pourquoi? On fait une note et voilà
tout."* (Alphand, *L'etonnement d'être*, p. 361.

P. 370   *Morgenpost, NYT, DT*, 15 August 1961.)

Pp. 372-73   D. Martin, *DM*, 15 August 1961.

P. 373   *ND*, 15 August 1961.

Pp. 376-77   Kroll, pp. 335–36.

Pp. 377-78   Based on the full text of Adenauer's speech, kindly made available to the author by Dr. Anneliese Poppinga, along with texts of speeches delivered at Kiel and Essen on 11 August 1961. Brandt's mother was a Lübeck salesgirl named Martha Frahm, who later married a Mecklenburg stonemason. He was given the name of Herbert Ernst Karl Frahm, which he later changed to Willy Brandt. (See Prittie, *Willy Brandt*, pp. 1–2; Viola Herms Drath, *Willy Brandt: Prisoner of His Past*, pp. 102, 176; Binder, *The Other German*, pp. 14, 356; and Willy Brandt, *My Road to Berlin*, pp. 34 ff.

P. 379   *ND, NYT* (Gruson), 15 August 1961.

P. 380   *Documents on Germany*, p. 726; *NYT, DT*, 16 August 1961.

P. 381   *NYT, DT*, 16 August 1961.

P. 383   Bader, *Civil War*, p. 95.

P. 385   According to West Berlin Schutzpolizei records, the nearby Ackerstrasse and the Moltke Bridge, spanning the Spree, were similarly obstructed on this same Tuesday with concrete or pressed rubble slabs.

P. 385   About 3,300 East German refugees were registered between 4:00 P.M. on Saturday and 1:00 A.M. on Sunday, when the seal-off operation began. Up to 5:00 P.M. on Sunday 800 more were registered, bringing the total to 4,130 over a span of twenty-five hours. (*NYT*, 14 August 1961, p. 1.)

P. 386   *Die Welt*, 16 August 1961.

P. 387   *Morgenpost*, 17 August 1961 (with a special eight-page photo spread).

P. 388   Binder, *The Other German*, p. 164.

Pp. 388-89   *Morgenpost*, 17 August 1961, and Clarke's own account in William Donohue Ellis and Thomas J. Cunningham, Jr., *Clarke of St. Vith: The Sergeants' General*, p. 259.

P. 389   Source: George Muller.

P. 389   Source: Member of a Western intelligence agency.

Pp. 389-90   *Tagesspiegel, Morgenpost, Bild Zeitung, NYT, DT*, and Horst Froehlich's eyewitness account. On Howley, see Smith, *The Defense of Berlin*, p. 87.

Pp. 390-91   Brandt, *Begegnungen und Einsichten*, pp. 29–30.

Pp. 391-92   Dulles, *The Wall*, p. 96.

P. 392   According to Pierre Salinger, in his Thursday morning, 17 August 1961, press conference, the letter reached the White House "about midnight last night."

P. 392   As told to the author by Kenneth O'Donnell.

Pp. 392-93   John F. Kennedy Presidential Papers, Appointments Book, 14 August 1961.

P. 393   John F. Kennedy Presidential Papers, Appointments Book, 15 August 1961. Kennan, so the author was informed by several State Department diplomats, followed up with a dispatch written in Belgrade in which he claimed that the Soviets were ready to use atomic weapons if the United States or the Allies did anything to hinder the seal off and construction of the Berlin Wall. West Berlin, he argued, just wasn't worth a world war. Allan Lightner, head of the U.S. mission in Berlin, was so upset by the tone of the dispatch that he wrote Kennan a letter of remonstrance.

P. 394 For a description of the "grim Yorkshire mansion" (Lord Swinton's private home) where Macmillan was vacationing, see *DT*, 16 August 1961.

Pp. 394-95 Clay, OHI, p. 2.

P. 395 *DT*, 17 August 1961.

P. 395 *Le Monde* (Paris), *DT*, 18 August 1961.

P. 395 *DT*, *NYT*, 17 August 1961.

P. 396 P. Salinger, official transcript of press conference.

P. 396 See, for example, photograph and article, "Mac the Gun," in *DM*, 16 August 1961.

P. 397 As described in letter to author by General Goff Hamilton. See also *DT*, *Morgenpost*, 18 August 1961.

Pp. 397-98 R. Peck, *DT*, 18 August 1961.

P. 398 *Documents on Berlin*, pp. 279-280.

Pp. 398-99 *Morgenpost*, *Welt*, 18 August 1961.

Pp. 400-401 Full text of these letters by Günter Grass, Ludwig Marcuse, Wolfdietrich Schnurre, etc. can be found in Richter, *Die Mauer*, pp. 62–68.

P. 402 *ND*, 17 August 1961. For questionnaire, see Michael Mara, "Why the Border Guards Defect," in *Atlantic Monthly*, December 1963, pp. 101–102. On desertions, see *Morgenpost*, 18 August 1961.

Pp. 402-03 John F. Kennedy Presidential Papers, Appointments Book, 18 August 1961.

P. 403 Source: General Clay.

P. 403 Ellis and Cunningham, *Clark of St. Vith*, p. 260.

P. 403 Rostow, *The Diffusion of Power*, p. 232; John F. Kennedy Presidential Papers, Appointments Book, 18 August 1961.

Pp. 403-404 Clay, OHI, pp. 2–5, supplemented by additional information given to the author.

P. 404 The three members of the State Department's Office of German Affairs were Frank Cash, Henry Cox, and Karl Mautner.

P. 405 Source: James O'Donnell.

Pp. 405-406 Source: George Reedy, interviewed by the author's brother.

Pp. 406-407 Poppinga, *Meine Erinnerungen an Konrad Adenauer*, pp. 69–71.

P. 407   Bohlen, *Witness to History*, pp. 386–87.

Pp. 407-408   The idea of a collective Western embargo on trade with the
              Soviet bloc had been unanimously approved by the Bundes-
              tag's Foreign Affairs Committee. (See Globke memorandum
              in Dulles, *The Wall*, p. 96.)

P. 408   Franz-Josef Bach. The U.S. embassy's first secretary at the
              time was LeRoy Percival, and the person he spoke to at the
              chancellery was Henry Cox.

P. 408   Bohlen, *Witness to History*, p. 484.

P. 410   Johnson's two Secret Service bodyguards were Stewart
              Knight and Rufus Youngblood. The latter made the headlines
              later by shielding Jacqueline Kennedy from gunfire during
              her husband's assassination on 22 November 1963 in Dallas,
              Texas.

P. 412   Abgeordnethaus von Berlin, Stenographischer Bericht (67
              Sitzung), 19 August 1961, pp. 255–60.

P. 417 ff.   Ellis and Cunningham, *Clarke of St. Vith*, pp. 260–62, and
              chaps. 22–23.

Pp. 417-23   From Col. Glover Johns's written account of this "excursion"
              to Berlin.

Pp. 423-24   On Kennedy's letter, see Brandt, *Begegnungen und Ein-
              sichten*, pp. 30–31.

Pp. 424-25   Brandt, *Begegnungen und Einsichten*, p. 31.

Pp. 426-27   Brandt, *Begegnungen und Einsichten*, p. 32, confirmed by
              Robert Lochner.

P. 430   The two sculptors were Detlev Timm and Horst Weidemann.
              (Copy of presidential thank you letter in the John F. Kennedy
              Library.)

P. 431   Brandt, in *Begegnungen und Einsichten*, p. 32, mentions this
              shoe episode as occurring on Saturday evening, but this
              seems to be an error of memory.

P. 436   *ND*, 21 August 1961.

P. 437   *DT, DM*, 21 August 1961.

P. 437   *Sunday Telegraph*, 20 August 1961.

P. 437   *DT*, 21 August 1961.

Pp. 438-39   *Tagesspiegel, Morgenpost, DT, DM*, 23 August 1961.

Pp. 439-40   *ND*, 23 August 1961.

P. 441   *Morgenpost, NYT, DT, DM*, 24, 25 August 1961.

P. 441   For General Lacomme's statement, Source: Anthony Powell.

P. 442   *ND, DT*, 24 August 1961, and Bader, *Civil War*, pp. 96–97.
              The attack on Brandt was repeated two days later in another
              major speech made to four thousand Party members in a
              Stalinallee sports arena. (*ND, DT*, 26 August 1961; and O.
              Frei in *NZZ*, 27 August 1961, where Ulbricht was compared
              to Hitler.)

P. 448   *NYT, DT, DM, Morgenpost,* 25 August 1961.

Pp. 448-49 In a letter to the author, Albert Hemsing wrote:

> Many of us on the Allied staffs and not a few editors and politicos saw this as (in some ways) an even more craven reaction, given that the Soviet/ GDR main purpose had been achieved and that on *this* issue the Soviets would probably not have been prepared to stick to their guns.

In *Swords and Plowshares,* pp. 211–12, Gen. Maxwell Taylor tells how he reached much the same conclusion when he was asked by Kennedy to research the question of the wall (should it have been or be torn down?). His recommendation that the Allies should assert their right to enter the Soviet sector through crossing points other than Check-point Charlie met with a cool response from all the President's advisers and also, he claims, from the U.S. mission in Berlin. He gives no date for this job of research beyond the vague indication that it was "several months after the event." If so, it must have been undertaken in October—at least six weeks too late. It would be interesting to know what the general's recommendations were on or around August 25.

P. 449   Macmillan, *Pointing the Way,* pp. 393–94.

Pp. 449-50 On the devious, rude, or obdurate behavior of the French, and particularly of De Gaulle, see Macmillan, *Pointing the Way,* pp. 326–28, 384, 394, 396, and the fascinating account of De Gaulle's later visit to Birch Grove, where Macmillan's suspicions were confirmed (pp. 415–28).

P. 450   Hervé Alphand was told by De Gaulle on August 23 that he had not sent any troops to reinforce the French garrison in Berlin "at the same time as the Americans, for our gesture would have gone unnoticed." The British had sent up "a few old tanks," but for his part he was not prepared to send more than three hundred French soldiers to Berlin. (See Alphand, *L'etonnement d'être,* pp. 362–66.) Even this token gesture does not seem to have been made.

P. 451   Charles De Gaulle, *Mémoires de Guerre,* 3 vols., 1: 193–98, 207–9; 3: 46–48, 68–69, 209–12; and André Malraux, *Les chênes qu'on abat,* p. 34. See also Curtis Cate, "The Road to Moscow: De Gaulle and the Kremlin," *The Atlantic Monthly,* August 1963, and Antoine de Saint-Exupéry's prophetic critique of this continental prejudice in his July 1943 letter to Robert Murphy, as quoted in Georges Pélissier, *Les -Cinq visages de Saint-Exupéry* (p. 43), and in the author's biography *Antoine de Saint-Exupéry,* p. 496.

P. 451   Notably in *Conversations with James Burnham,* which dates from 1950.

Pp. 451-52   Charles De Gaulle, *Mémoires d'Espoir: Le Renouveau,*
             1958–1962, Vol. I, pp. 238–44. Khrushchev's version of their
             talks can be found in his *Last Testament,* pp. 439–42.

Pp. 452-53   *DT, DM,* 28 August 1961, and Macmillan, *Pointing the Way,*
             pp. 394–96.

PART FIVE: THE CONFRONTATION

P. 457   Informationbüro West, in *Tagesspiegel, NYT, DT,* 29
             August 1961.

P. 457   *Documents on Berlin,* pp. 296–98; *NYT,* 24 August 1961.

P. 457   *Pravda, NYT,* 30, 31 August 1961; Slusser, *The Berlin Crisis*
             of 1961, pp. 157–66.

P. 458   The two MPs were Sir Leslie Plummer and Koni Zilliacus.
             NYT, 2 September 1961; Slusser, *The Berlin Crisis of 1961,*
             pp. 166–67.

P. 458   The text of this letter, declassified, is in the John F. Kennedy
             Library.

P. 458   John F. Kennedy Presidential Papers, Appointments Book,
             30 August 1961.

P. 458   *NYT, DT,* 31 August 1961; *Documents on Germany,* p. 763.

Pp. 458-59   *NYT, DT,* 31 August 1961.

Pp. 460-61   *NYT,* 9 September 1961. For Gen. Bruce Clarke's reaction to
             this affair, see Ellis and Cunningham, *Clarke of St. Vith,* pp.
             265–67.

P. 461   *Die Welt, FAZ, NYT,* 18 September 1961; Brandt, *Begeg-*
             nungen und Einsichten, p. 42. In a speech made at Hagan, in
             the Ruhr, on 28 August 1961, Adenauer had resumed his
             attacks on Willy Brandt. Booed by many of his listeners, he
             was severely taken to task in the West German press. See, for
             example, Otto Zehrer in *Die Welt,* 30 August 1961.

Pp. 461-62   *Tagesspiegel, Morgenpost, NYT,* 20 September 1961.

P. 462   As related to the author by General Clay.

Pp. 462-66   This description of the Berlin Wall in mid-September is
             partly based on Eckhart Kroneberg's "Beschreibung einer
             Mauer," in Richter, ed., *Die Mauer,* pp. 90–101.

Pp. 467-69   This account is based on Honoré Marc Catudal, Jr., *Stein-*
             stücken: A Study in Cold War Politics.

Pp. 469-70   Over a luncheon table at his home in Virginia, Gen. Bruce
             Clarke insisted that the author quote him verbatim as expos-
             tulating to General Clay: "Lucius, you keep your cotton-pick-
             ing fingers off my men!" General Clay had no recollection of
             any such heated exchange. Although he has no doubt that

these words reflected how General Clark felt, he claimed that Clarke never actually uttered them in his presence; otherwise, "there would have been an immediate showdown." James O'Donnell, who had returned to Berlin to act as General Clay's press officer, has assured the author that there were many U.S. officers in Heidelberg and one or two in Berlin who were "out to get Clay." For Clarke's own account of this altercation, obviously toned down by the authors, see Ellis and Cunningham, *Clarke of St. Vith*, pp. 267–69.

Pp. 470-71   *The Papers of the Presidents: John F. Kennedy, 1961*, pp. 619–26; NYT, 26 August 1961.

P. 471   *Bild Zeitung*, 27 August 1961; Smith, *The Defense of Berlin*, pp. 313–14.

Pp. 471-72   ND, 27 August 1961.

P. 472   Smith, *The Defense of Berlin*, pp. 315, 318–19.

P. 475   Smith, *The Defense of Berlin*, p. 318; NYT, 7, 8 October 1961; Brandt, *Begegnungen und Einsichten*, p. 35.

P. 475   Smith, *The Defense of Berlin*, pp. 318–19.

P. 476   On the Twenty-second Party Congress, see Slusser, *The Berlin Crisis of 1961*, pp. 303–58.

Pp. 476-79   Smith, *The Defense of Berlin*, pp. 319–24; Trivers, *Three Crises in American Foreign Affairs*, pp. 41–43.

Pp. 479-80   As told to the author by Allan Lightner.

Pp. 480-81   Trivers, *Three Crises in American Foreign Affairs*, pp. 44–50.

P. 482   As told to the author by General Watson.

P. 482   On Searchlights, Source: Richard Smyser.

P. 483   Smith, *The Defense of Berlin*, p. 322.

Pp. 483-84   On Koniev's call to Khrushchev, see Kroll, pp. 338, 340–41. See also Khrushchev, *Last Testament*, pp. 504–8, where he claims that Koniev was attending the Twenty-second Party Congress as a delegate when surprised by the crisis in Berlin. But Khrushchev's memory was playing tricks on him in leading him to think that General Clay's arrival in Berlin preceded Koniev's.

P. 484   Smith, *The Defense of Berlin*, p. 323.

Pp. 484-85   Trivers, *Three Crises in American Foreign Affairs*, pp. 49–50.

P. 485   As told to the author by Evelyn Lincoln. For the rest of this account, the author is indebted to General Clay.

P. 486   Kroll, p. 340, and Khrushchev, *Last Testament*, p. 507.

Pp. 486-87   John F. Kennedy Presidential Papers, Appointments Book, 29 October 1961.

Epilogue

P. 491   Smith, *The Berlin Crisis of 1961*, p. 324, and G. Bailey, "The
              Gentle Erosion of Berlin," in *The Reporter*, 26 April 1962.
              McDermott's own account of these drinking sessions with the
              Soviets is distinctly vague. (See McDermott, *Berlin*, pp.
              48–50.)

P. 491   Gen. Sir Rohan Delacombe's own words to the author.

P. 491   Kroll, pp. 338, 341.

Pp. 492-93   Smith, *The Berlin Crisis of 1961*, pp. 325–28; Schick, *The
              Berlin Crisis: 1958–1962*, pp. 179–93; Ausland, *Kennedy,
              Khrushchev, and Berlin*, pp. 4/6–4/15.

Pp. 493-94   Tatu, *Le Pouvoir en URSS*, pp. 243–60. The two marshals
              were Fyodor Golikov, head of the Political Directorate of the
              Soviet armed forces, and Konstantin Moskalenko, head of the
              USSR's strategic missile forces.

P. 494   Rostow, *The Diffusion of Power*, p. 254:

              Khrushchev's objectives were, then, quite clear: to present Kennedy
              with the installation of the missiles as a fait accompli under the cover
              of an enlarged flow of conventional arms; and to come to New York
              after the congressional elections in November and bargain on Berlin,
              bases, and other matters from a position of strength cheaply
              achieved.

              This is also Howard Trivers' opinion (*Three Crises in Amer-
              ican Foreign Affairs*, pp. 61–62):

              My point is that the erection of the Berlin Wall and the Soviet intro-
              duction of missiles into Cuba were direct consequences of Khru-
              shchev's appraisal of President Kennedy. . . . I can think of no Amer-
              ican leader of the past thirty years who has impressed the Russians in
              quite the same way as George Marshall. This is a long, roundabout
              way of making the simple statement that if General Marshall had
              been President of the United States and met with Khrushchev in
              Vienna in June of 1961, neither the Wall would have been built in
              Berlin nor would the Cuba missile crisis have taken place.

P. 495   Trivers, *Three Crises in American Foreign Affairs*, p. 59; and
              Schlesinger, *A Thousand Days*, p. 821.

INDEX